1994 PGA TOUR

Official Media Guide of the PGA TOUR

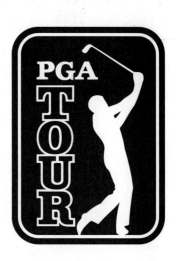

Triumph Books
CHICAGO

TABLE OF CONTENTS

INDEX

A BRIEF HISTORY OF THE PGA TOUR

It is not always easy to discover the exact beginning of something. So it is with the PGA TOUR. Certainly there were professionals who competed against each other from the earliest days of the game.

In 1895, ten professional golfers and one amateur played in the first U.S. Open in Newport, RI. Shortly thereafter, tournaments began to pop up across the country. There was the Western Open in 1899. But this was not "tour" golf. The events lacked continuity.

Interest in the game, however, continued to grow. American professionals were rapidly improving. And when John McDermott became the first American-born player to win the U.S. Open, enthusiasm for the game blossomed.

Adding to this growth was a commercially backed exhibition by Englishmen Harry Vardon and Ted Ray. The duo travelled across the country and attracted good crowds wherever they stopped during the warmer months of 1913. A 20-year-old, Francis Ouimet, defeated the pair in a playoff for the United States Open Championship at Brookline, MA. Suddenly golf became front page news and a game for everyone.

In the early twenties, the PGA TOUR saw its first development. Tournaments were held on the West Coast, Texas and Florida. These events were held in the winter, and the golfers played their way east and up to Pinehurst in the spring. By the middle of the decade, the TOUR was doing relatively well--offering $77,000 in total prize money.

The TOUR became more structured following World War II and exploded in the late 1950s and early '60s. Flip through the **Facts and Figures** section of this book and look at such areas as leading money winners and growth of tournament purses to witness the continuing growth.

When television became a player in the game, the eyes of the world were on golf. This exposure inspired millions to try the game and, at the same time, TV rights fees sent purses soaring. The bulk of these rights fees, which are distributed by the PGA TOUR to all co-sponsors, have gone back into the purses, accounting for the tripling of prize money in the last decade.

The touring professionals began to gain control of the TOUR in late 1968. Joseph C. Dey was the first Commissioner of what was then called the Tournament Players Division. He served from early 1969 through February 28, 1974, and was succeeded by Deane R. Beman, who took office March 1, 1974.

During Beman's administration, the value of tournament purses has escalated at an unprecedented rate: PGA TOUR assets have grown from $730,000 in 1974 to over $200 million today, and total revenues have increased from $3.9 million to $229 million in 1993.

Since 1938, PGA TOUR events have donated more than $230 million dollars to charity. Of that total, $84.7 million has been raised in the 1990s.

The competitive scope of the PGA TOUR also is much broader today. The Senior PGA TOUR is considered by many the sports success story of the 1980s. In 1994, the NIKE TOUR will enjoy its fifth season as a proving ground for professionals, taking golf to 30 additional markets.

Also continuing to grow is the Tournament Players Club Network. When the PGA TOUR opened the Tournament Players Club at Sawgrass in 1980, it introduced the era of Stadium Golf and record-breaking attendance. Owned and operated by the TOUR, the concept means these courses are the only major league sports arenas owned by the players themselves.

CHRONOLOGY OF PGA TOUR

1895 --   First U.S. Open (won by Horace Rawlins) played at Newport (RI) Golf Club

1899 --   Inaugural Western Open (won by Willie Smith) played at Glenview (IL) Golf Club

1900 --   Harry Vardon tour of United States generates widespread interest in game

1913 --   Francis Ouimet captures U.S. Open playoff with Vardon and Ted Ray

1914 --   Walter Hagen wins first of 11 major titles in U.S. Open at Midlothian Country Club outside Chicago

1916 --   PGA of America formed

         Jim Barnes wins first PGA Championship over Jock Hutchison at Siwanoy CC in Bronxville, NY

1922 --   Gene Sarazen (20) becomes youngest ever to win U.S. Open (Skokie Country Club in Glencoe, IL); also wins PGA Championship (Oakmont CC), becoming first to hold both titles at once

1926 --   Los Angeles Open offers $10,000 purse

1927 --   First Ryder Cup matches played, won by United States (Worcester (MA) Country Club)

1930 --   Bob Harlow named manager of PGA Tournament Bureau and broaches idea of year-round tournament circuit; raises annual purse money on the Tour from $77,000 to $130,000 in first year on job; instrumental in creating volunteer system by which TOUR functions to this day; Code of Conduct drawn up

1931 --   Golf Ball and Golf Club Manufacturers Association puts up $5,000 to support sponsors during 1931-32 winter swing

A Brief History of the PGA TOUR, continued

1932 -- "Playing Pros" organization formed, pre-dating by 36 years formation of current PGA TOUR organization

1933 -- Hershey Chocolate Company, at least unofficially, first corporate sponsor on PGA TOUR with Hershey Open

1934 -- Group of players meets to discuss possibilities of year-round tournament circuit
Horton Smith wins first Masters at Augusta National Golf Club
Leading money winner for year Paul Runyan earns $6,767

1937 -- First Bing Crosby Pro-Am/"Clambake" played at San Diego's Rancho Santa Fe CC
Sam Snead becomes nationally recognized figure in golf by winning Oakland Open

1938 -- Palm Beach Invitational makes first TOUR contribution to charity, $10,000

1945 -- Byron Nelson captures 11 consecutive tournaments, seven other official events and one unofficial, a total of 19 wins in one year; voted 1945 Athlete of Year
Tam O'Shanter All-American offers $60,000 purse

1947 -- U.S. Open televised live in St. Louis area

1949 -- Ben Hogan critically injured in head-on collision with Greyhound bus

1950 -- Hogan returns to competitive golf in Los Angeles Open, starting with two-under-par 34 and eventual 280 total tied by Sam Snead; loses playoff ten days later

1953 -- Hogan wins only British Open he ever played
Lew Worsham wins first PGA TOUR event to appear live on national television, Tam O'Shanter World Championship
Golf's "color barrier" broken with PGA constitutional amendment allowing for "Approved Entries," non-members who could play in tournaments if invited by sponsors

1954 -- USGA begins to televise U.S. Open for national audience
"All-Star Golf," first series of matches between pros filmed for television, debuts

1955 -- World Championship of Golf offers first $100,000 purse in PGA TOUR history

1961 -- Caucasians-only clause stricken from PGA constitution; PGA TOUR officially integrated
"Shell's Wonderful World of Golf" begins nine-year run

1965 -- Inaugural Qualifying School held at PGA National Golf Club in Palm Beach Gardens, FL; John Schlee first medalist

1968 -- Association of Professional Golfers (APG), an autonomous tournament players' organization, forms in breakaway from PGA
As compromise, Tournament Players Division of PGA formed under aegis of 10-man policy board late in year

1969 -- Joe Dey becomes first Commissioner of Tournament Players Division

1974 -- Deane Beman succeeds Dey as Commissioner on March 1
Jack Nicklaus captures inaugural Tournament Players Championship (now THE PLAYERS Championship) at Atlanta CC

1977 -- Al Geiberger records first sub-60 round in PGA TOUR history on June 10, a 59 in Danny Thomas Memphis Classic at Colonial CC

1978 -- First "Legends of Golf" played at Onion Creek CC in Austin, TX, precursor of Senior PGA TOUR

1979 -- PGA TOUR Headquarters relocated from Washington, D.C. to Ponte Vedra Beach, FL

1980 -- Senior PGA TOUR organized with four tournaments
First Tournament Players Club opens, the TPC at Sawgrass in Ponte Vedra, FL

1983 -- All-Exempt TOUR put in place, virtually eliminating Monday qualifying; top 125 players exempt
Tournament Players Series (TPS) begins three-year run
PGA TOUR Pension Program begins

1985 -- PGA TOUR Productions created

1986 -- Panasonic Las Vegas Invitational offers first $1 million purse in PGA TOUR history

1987 -- PGA TOUR surpasses $100 million in charitable contributions

1988 -- 30 players compete at Pebble Beach for $2 million in Nabisco Championships, predecessor of THE TOUR Championship

1990 -- Ben Hogan Tour comes into existence as developmental circuit, succeeded by NIKE beginning in 1993

1991 -- Chip Beck matches Geiberger's 1977 feat on October 11, carding a 59 at Sunrise Golf Club during Las Vegas Invitational

1992 -- PGA TOUR surpasses $200 million in charitable contributions

1993 -- The PGA TOUR boasts a record five $1 million winners

1994 PGA TOUR TOURNAMENT SCHEDULE

Date	Tournament Dir./Media Contact	Location	Official/Total Money	Pro-Am	TV	1993 Winner
Jan. 6-9	**Mercedes Championships** *Mike Crosthwaite/Stan Wood* (619) 438-9111 ext. 4612	La Costa Resort & Spa Costa del Mar Road Carlsbad, CA 92008	$1,000,000/$1,010,000	$10,000	ABC ESPN	Davis Love III
Jan. 13-16	**United Airlines Hawaiian Open** *Chester Kahapea/Bill Bachran* (808) 526-1232	Waialae CC 4997 Kahala Ave. Honolulu, HI 96816	$1,200,000/$1,210,000	$10,000	TBS	Howard Twitty
Jan. 20-23	**Northern Telecom Open** *Boyd Drachman/Tim Stilb* (602) 792-4501	Tucson National Starr Pass GC Tucson, AZ 85741	$1,100,000/$1,115,000	$15,000	ESPN	Larry Mize
Jan. 27-30	**Phoenix Open** *Mike Kennedy/Drew Wathey* (602) 870-0163	TPC of Scottsdale 17020 N. Hayden Rd. Phoenix, AZ 85260	$1,200,000/$1,207,500	$10,000	ESPN	Lee Janzen
Feb. 3-6	**AT&T Pebble Beach National Pro-Am** *Louis Russo/Cathy Scherzer* (408) 649-1533	Pebble Beach GL Spyglass Hill GC Poppy Hills GC Pebble Beach, CA 93953	$1,250,000/$1,320,000	$70,000	CBS USA	Brett Ogle
Feb. 10-13	**Nissan Los Angeles Open** *Tom Pulchinski* (213) 482-1311	Riviera CC 1250 Capri Drive Pacific Palisades, CA 90272	$1,000,000/$1,010,000	$ 7,500	NBC USA	Tom Kite
Feb. 16-20	**Bob Hope Chrysler Classic** *Ed Heorodt/Connie Whelchel* (619) 346-8184	Indian Wells CC (host) PGA West (Palmer Course) Bermuda Dunes CC LaQuinta CC LaQuinta, CA 92253	$1,100,000/$1,121,000	$21,000	NBC ESPN	Tom Kite
Feb. 24-27	**Buick Invitational of Calif.** *Tom Wilson/Rick Schloss* (619) 281-4653	Torrey Pines GC 11480 Torrey Pines Rd. San Diego, CA 92037	($1,000,000/$1,015,000)	$15,000	NBC	Phil Mickelson

1994 PGA TOUR TOURNAMENT SCHEDULE *cont.*

Date	Tournament Dir./Media Contact	Location	Official/Total Money	Pro-Am	TV	1993 Winner
Mar. 3-6	**Doral-Ryder Open** *Scott Montgomery/ Judy Janofsky* (305) 477-4653	Doral CC (Blue Course) 4400 NW 87th Ave. Miami, FL 33166	$1,400,000/$1,407,500	$7,500	CBS USA	Greg Norman
Mar. 10-13	**Honda Classic** *Cliff Danley/Charlie Nobles* (305) 384-6000	Weston Hills CC 2608 Country Club Way Ft. Lauderdale, FL 33332	$1,100,000/$1,107,500	$7,500	NBC	Fred Couples
Mar. 17-20	**Nestle Invitational** *Jim Bell/Bob Fowler* (407) 876-2888	Bay Hill Club & Lodge 9000 Bay Hill Blvd. Orlando, FL 32819	$1,200,000/$1,207,500	$7,500	NBC	Ben Crenshaw
Mar. 24-27	**THE PLAYERS Championship** *Henry Hughes/Denise Taylor* (904) 285-7888	TPC at Sawgrass (Stadium) 103 TPC Blvd. Ponte Vedra, FL 32082	$2,500,000	------	NBC USA	Nick Price
Mar. 31- Apr. 3	**Freeport-McMoRan Classic** *Tom Wulff/Maury MaGill* (504) 831-4653	English Turn G&CC One Clubhouse Drive New Orleans, LA 70131	$1,200,000/$1,207,500	$7,500	NBC	Mike Standly
Apr. 7-10	***Masters** (706) 738-7761	Augusta National GC Augusta, GA 30913	($1,500,000)		CBS	Bernhard Langer
Apr. 14-17	**MCI Heritage Classic** *Michael Stevens/Arnie Burdick* (803) 671-2448	Harbour Town GL Hilton Head Island, SC 29928	$1,250,000/$1,257,500	$7,500	CBS USA	David Edwards
Apr. 21-24	**Kmart Greater Greensboro Open** *C. Louis Moore/Lisa Talauera* (919) 379-1570	Forest Oaks CC 4600 Forest Oaks Dr. Greensboro, NC 27406	$1,500,000/$1,507,500	$7,500	CBS USA	Rocco Mediate

1994 PGA TOUR TOURNAMENT SCHEDULE *cont.*

( )—1993 Purses

Date	Tournament Dir./Media Contact	Location	Official/Total Money	Pro-Am	TV	1993 Winner
Apr. 28- May 1	**Shell Houston Open** *Eric Fredricksen/Burt Darden* (713) 367-7999	TPC at The Woodlands 1730 S. Millbend Dr. The Woodlands, TX 77380	$1,300,000/$1,307,500	$7,500	ABC	Jim McGovern
May 5-8	**BellSouth Classic** *Dave Kaplan/John Marshall* (404) 951-8777	Atlanta CC 500 Atlanta CC Dr. Marietta, GA 30067	$1,200,000/$1,207,500	$7,500	CBS	Nolan Henke
May 12-15	**GTE Byron Nelson Classic** *Janie Hebert/Ron Case* (214) 742-3896	TPC at Las Colinas 4200 N. MacArthur Blvd. Irving, TX 75038	$1,200,000/$1,207,500	$7,500	ABC	Scott Simpson
May 19-22	**Memorial Tournament** *John Hines/Bill Jones* (614) 889-6700	Muirfield Village GC 5750 Memorial Drive Dublin, OH 43017	$1,500,000	-----	ABC ESPN	Paul Azinger
May 26-29	**Southwestern Bell Colonial** *Dennis Roberson/Jerre Todd* (817) 927-4277	Colonial CC 3735 Country Club Cir. Ft. Worth, TX 76109	$1,400,000	$7,500	CBS USA	Fulton Allem
June 2-5	**Kemper Open** *Ben Brundred/Don Ruhter* (301) 469-3737	TPC at Avenel 10000 Oaklyn Drive Potomac,MD 20854	$1,300,000/$1,307,500	$7,500	CBS	Grant Waite
June 9-12	**Buick Classic** *Annabelle Marvin/John Hewig* 800/765-4742	Westchester CC Rye, NY 10580	$1,200,000/$1,207,500	$7,500	CBS	Vijay Singh
June 16-19	***United States Open** (908) 719-9494	Oakmont CC Oakmont, PA	($1,500,000)		ABC ESPN	Lee Janzen
June 23-26	**Canon Greater Hartford Open** *C. Allyson Cormier/Jim Schleckser* (203) 522-4171	TPC at River Highlands Golf Club Road Cromwell, CT 06416	$1,200,000/$1,207,500	$7,500	CBS	Nick Price

8

1994 PGA TOUR TOURNAMENT SCHEDULE cont.

Date	Tournament Dir./Media Contact	Location	Official/Total Money	Pro-Am	TV	1993 Winner
June 30- July 3	**Motorola Western Open** *Greg McLaughlin/Gary Hollaway* 708/724-4600	Cog Hill CC 12294 Archer Ave. Lemont, IL 60439	$1,200,000/$1,207,500	$7,500	CBS USA	Nick Price
July 7-10	**Anheuser-Busch Golf Classic** *Johnnie Bender* (804) 253-3985	Kingsmill GC 100 Golf Club. Rd. Williamsburg, VA 23185	$1,100,000/$1,120,000	$20,000	ESPN	Jim Gallagher, Jr.
July 14-17	**Deposit Guaranty Golf Classic** *Robert Morgan/Ace Cleveland* (601) 264-8113	Annandale GC 837 Mannsdale Road Madison, MS 39110	$700,000/$707,500	$7,500	---	Greg Kraft
July 14-17	***British Open*** 011-44-334-72112	Turnberry GL Scotland	------	------	ABC ESPN	Greg Norman
July 21-24	**New England Classic** *Ted Mingolla/Jim Warters* (508) 865-1491	Pleasant Valley CC Armsby Rd. Sutton, MA 01527	$1,000,000/$1,007,500	$7,500	---	Paul Azinger
July 28-31	**Federal Express St. Jude Classic** *Dwight Drinkard/Phil Cannon* (901) 748-0534	TPC at Southwind 3325 Club at Southwind Memphis, TN 38138	$1,250,000/$1,257,500	$7,500	CBS	Nick Price
Aug. 4-7	**Buick Open** *Rich Brochu/Corby Casler* (313) 236-4635	Warwick Hills G&CC G-9057 S. Saginaw Rd. Grand Blanc, MI 48439	($1,000,000/$1,007,500)	$7,500	CBS	Larry Mize
Aug. 11-14	***PGA Championship*** *Jamie Roggero* (407) 624-8400	Southern Hills CC Tulsa, OK 74105	($1,700,000)	------	CBS TBS	Paul Azinger
Aug. 18-21	**The International** *Larry Thiel/Buddy Martin* (303) 688-6000	Castle Pines GC 1000 Hummingbird Dr. Castle Rock, CO 80104	$1,400,000/$1,410,000	$10,000	CBS ESPN	Phil Mickelson

1994 PGA TOUR TOURNAMENT SCHEDULE *cont.*

Date	Tournament Dir./Media Contact	Location	Official/Total Money	Pro-Am	TV	1993 Winner
Aug. 25-28	**NEC World Series of Golf** *Jim Cook/Dean English* (216) 644-2299	Firestone CC 452 E. Warner Rd. Akron, OH 44319	$2,000,000/$2,010,000	$10,000	CBS USA	Fulton Allem
Sept. 1-4	**Greater Milwaukee Open** *Tom Strong/John Counsell* (414) 423-2500	Brown Deer GC 7835 N. Green Bay Ave. Milwaukee, WI 53209	$1,000,000/$1,007,500	$7,500	ABC	Billy Mayfair
Sept. 8-11	**Bell Canadian Open** *Bill Paul/John Gordon* (905) 844-1800	Glen Abbey GC Rural Route #2 Oakville, Ontario Canada, L6J 4Z3	($1,000,000/$1,007,500)	$7,500	ESPN	David Frost
Sept. 15-18	**Hardee's Golf Classic** *Tony Piazzi/Jerry Bretag* (309) 762-4653	Oakwood CC Route 6 Coal Valley, IL 61240	$1,000,000/$1,007,500	$7,500	ESPN	David Frost
Sept. 22-25	**B.C. Open** *Alex Alexander/Pat Vavra* (607) 754-2482	En-Joie GC 722 W. Main Street Endicott, NY 13760	$900,000/$907,500	$7,500	---	Blaine McCallister
Sept. 29- Oct. 2	**Buick Southern Open** *Robert Berry/Walter Mauldin* (706) 324-0411	Callaway Gardens Resort Highway 27 Pine Mtn., GA 31822	$700,000/$707,500	$7,500	---	John Inman
Oct. 6-9	**Walt Disney World/Oldsmobile Classic** *Michael McPhillips/John Story* (407) 824-2285	Magnolia, Palm & Buena Vista Golf Courses Lake Buena Vista, FL 32830	$1,100,000/$1,225,000	$25,000	---	Jeff Maggert
Oct. 13-16	**Texas Open** *Nick Milanovich/Jerry Grotz* (210) 341-0823	Oak Hills CC 5403 Fredericksburg Rd. San Antonio, TX 78229	$1,000,000/1,007,500	$7,500	---	Jay Haas

( )—1993 Purses

Date	Tournament Dir./Media Contact	Location	Official/Total Money	Pro-Am	TV	1993 Winner
Oct. 19-23	**Las Vegas Invitational** *Jim Cook/Rick Dale* (702) 382-6616	TPC at Summerlin Desert Inn & CC Las Vegas CC Las Vegas, NV 89134	$1,400,000/$1,418,000	$18,000	ESPN	Davis Love III
Oct. 27-30	**TOUR Championship** *Ron Cross/Denise Taylor* (904) 285-7888	Olympic Club San Francisco, CA 94102	$3,000,000	$10,000	ABC ESPN	Jim Gallagher, Jr.
Nov. 3-6	**+Lincoln-Mercury Kapalua International** *Gary Planos/Linn Nishikawa* (808)669-0244	Kapalua Resort Kapalua, Maui, HI 96761	$1,000,000	-----	ABC ESPN	Fred Couples
Nov. 10-13	**+World Cup of Golf** *Burch Riber/Tom Place* (513) 624-2100	Dorado Beach Resort Dorado Beach Puerto Rico 00646	TBA	-----	-----	United States
Nov. 17-20	**+Franklin Funds Shark Shoot-Out** *Eric Jonke/Steve Brener* (805) 379-2664	Sherwood CC 2215 Stafford Road Thousand Oaks, CA 91361	$1,100,000	-----	CBS ESPN	Steve Elkington/ Ray Floyd
Nov. 26-27	**+Skins Game** *Steve Brener* (818) 344-6195	BIGHORN GC 215 Kiva Drive Palm Desert, CA 92260	$540,000	-----	ABC	Payne Stewart
Dec. 1-4	**+JCPenney Classic** *Tom Jewell/Dick Dailey* (813) 942-5566	Innisbrook Resort Copperhead Course US Highway 19 South Tarpon Springs, FL 34689	$1,200,000/$1,210,000	$10,000	ABC ESPN	Mike Springer/ Melissa McNamara
Dec. 8-11	**+Diners Club Matches** (310) 393-1115	Site TBA	$1,800,000	-----	ABC ESPN	First-year event

11

TOURNAMENT POLICY BOARD

Richard J. Ferris of Northbrook, IL, was elected Chairman of the PGA TOUR's Tournament Policy Board in December 1993, succeeding E.M. (Del) de Windt, who had served in that position for 11 years.

Currently Chairman and Partner of Guest Quarters Hotels, L.P., Ferris previously served as Chairman and Chief Executive Officer of UAL Corporation, Hilton International Hotels, Westin Hotels, Hertz and Covia.

Ferris, 57, had served two terms on the Senior PGA TOUR Division Advisory Board, including a stint as Chairman, prior to becoming an Independent Director of the PGA TOUR's Tournament Policy Board in 1992.

Richard J. Ferris
Northbrook, IL
Chairman

Roger E. Birk
Washington, DC
Independent Director

Hugh F. Culverhouse
Tampa, FL
Independent Director

Victor J. Ganzi
New York, NY
Independent Director

Brad Faxon
Orlando, FL
Player Director

Rick Fehr
Redmond, WA
Player Director

Jay Haas
Greenville, SC
Player Director

Jeff Sluman
Naples, FL
Player Director

Tom Addis III
El Cajon, CA
PGA Director

Gary Schaal
Surfside Beach, SC
PGA Director

TOURNAMENT POLICY BOARD

The Tournament Policy Board establishes goals and policies for the operation of the PGA TOUR. The 10-member Board is composed of the following:

Four Player Directors elected by the PGA TOUR membership. A Player Director also serves as Vice President of the PGA of America.

Four Independent Directors, representing the public interest. One serves as Chairman of the Board.

Two PGA of America Directors, who are national officers of the PGA of America. A Players Advisory Council consults with the Policy Board.

The Policy Board appoints the Commissioner as chief executive and administrative officer of the PGA TOUR. The tournament staff, serving under the Commissioner, conducts tournament play.

PGA TOUR GOLF COURSE PROPERTIES BOARD

Robert E. Kirby
Chairman,
PGA TOUR Golf Course Properties Board
Retired Chairman of the Board
Westinghouse Electric Corporation

H. James Griggs
Chairman
Pacific Investors

James Clark
President
Clark Construction Group

John L. Steffens
President-Consumer
Markets
Merrill Lynch Pierce,
Fenner & Smith, Inc.

Deane R. Beman

Born: April 22, 1938
Birthplace: Washington, DC
Family: Wife, Judy; five children

Entering his 21st year as Commissioner of the PGA TOUR, since succeeding Joseph C. Dey, Jr., on March 1, 1974, Deane R. Beman has overseen the most explosive period of growth in the TOUR's history.

During the Beman administration, the "business side" of the PGA TOUR has shown dramatic growth and now includes many heretofore uncharted paths, each designed to help encourage continued prosperity and to ensure the future of the game.

PGA TOUR Golf Course Properties has grown to include 14 Tournament Players Clubs nationally with more clubs in the planning stage across the United States. TPC International was started in 1989 with a Players Club in Japan. The Golf Club of Jacksonville, a municipal course operated by the PGA TOUR for the city of Jacksonville, opened in 1989, followed by the Golf Club of Miami the next year. In addition to providing tournament state-of-the-art facilities, Tournament Players Clubs have been instrumental in the growth of the PGA TOUR assets, which have climbed from $730,000 to more than $200 million during the Beman era.

The marketing arm of the PGA TOUR continues to open new opportunities in golf for commercial sponsors and the TOUR's members. Long-term programs with Coca-Cola and IBM that were initiated in 1992 and NIKE replaced the Ben Hogan Company to form the NIKE TOUR in 1993. A new agreement with Anheuser-Busch this year is the latest in a long line of marketing efforts designed for the combined benefit of players, sponsors and charities.

PGA TOUR Partners was started in 1991 to enhance the golf experience for serious fans by giving them a unique, inside look at the PGA TOUR, and providing charitable support to worthy non-profit organizations. Just three years old, the Partners program now includes more than 80,000 members.

PGA TOUR Productions, created in 1985, is the TOUR's in-house TV/audio-visual production entity. Created to produce tournament highlight video films, vignettes, commercials, specialty pieces and the acclaimed "Inside the PGA TOUR," a weekly half-hour show airing on ESPN, Productions added "Inside the Senior PGA TOUR" in 1991.

Other important innovations introduced during the Beman administration include a professional agronomy department, PGA TOUR Statistics Program, electronic scoreboards, "Official Golf Destinations" and establishment of mobile fitness training centers, sponsored by Centinela. Competitively, the Beman era has witnessed the birth of the Senior PGA TOUR, which started with two events in 1980 and has grown to its present 43 events. The NIKE Tour, born in 1990, has been a success by all measures and has provided aspiring professionals with TOUR-like competition as a stepping stone to the PGA TOUR. In all there are 118 tournaments on the combined Tours, and total prize money has increased from $8.2 million in 1974 to nearly $100 million for the 1994 season.

The Player Retirement Plan was instituted in 1983 to help provide PGA TOUR members with a stable source of income upon retirement from tournament competition. At the time, establishment of the plan was viewed as a significant step towards bringing the TOUR closer to the ranks of other "major" sports with respect to player benefits.

Charity easily has been the TOUR's leading money winner during the Beman era. Reaching the $22.8 million mark in 1993,the American Golf Sponsors and the PGA TOUR have donated more than $84.7 million in the 1990s alone. In the fall of 1992, the TOUR and the American Golf Sponsors surpassed the $200 million mark in donations since 1938.

During his active years as a player, Beman established an enviable record, including an outstanding amateur career. He won the U.S. Amateur title in 1960 and 1963 and the British Amateur Championship in 1959. Beman was a member of four Walker Cup teams, four World Amateur Cup teams and three U.S. America's Cup squads.

In 1967, at the age of 29, he left a prosperous insurance brokerage firm in Bethesda, MD, to join the PGA TOUR as a full-time player. During his six-year professional career, he won the 1969 Texas Open, 1970 Greater Milwaukee Open, 1971 Quad Cities Open (unofficial),1972 Quad Cities Open and the 1973 Shrine-Robinson Classic before hanging up his spikes to become Commissioner in 1974.

DEPUTY COMMISSIONER

Timothy W. Finchem
Deputy Commissioner
Chief Operating Officer
PGA TOUR

Timothy W. Finchem has served as Deputy Commissioner of the PGA TOUR since 1990.

He has management responsibility for all TOUR operations as the organization's Chief Operating Officer.

Finchem joined the PGA TOUR staff in 1988 as Vice President for Business Affairs, exercising oversight responsibility for the TOUR's diverse relationship with corporate sponsors, marketing, promotion and television matters.

He came to the TOUR from National Stategies and Marketing Group, a Washington, D.C., firm of which he was co-founder. At NS&MG, he represented the TOUR's legislative interests and was a marketing consultant for the Tournament Players Club network.

Finchem had served at the White House as Deputy Advisor to the president for economic affairs in the early 1980s prior to helping found NS&MG.

A native of Virginia Beach, VA, Finchem is a graduate of the University of Richmond and holds a law degree from the University of Virginia.

SENIOR STAFF MEMBERS

Helen Atter
Vice President of
Human Resources

Gary Becka
Special Assistant to
the Commissioner

Ruffin Beckwith
Vice President of
Corporate Affairs

Mike Bodney
Director of
International Affairs

Bill Calfee
Director of
Player Services

Vernon Kelly
President, PGA TOUR
Golf Course Properties

Ed Moorhouse
Executive Vice President/
General Counsel

Gary Stevenson
Executive Vice President of
Business Affairs

Joe Walser
Chief Operating Officer,
PGA TOUR Golf Course
Properties

Charlie Zink
Executive Vice President/
Chief Financial Officer

TOURNAMENT ADMINISTRATION

Steve Rankin
Executive Vice President-
Tournament Affairs/
Sponsor Relations

Duke Butler
Tournament Director

Arvin Ginn
Assistant Tournament
Director

Allan MacCurrach
Senior Agronomist

Ben Nelson
Assistant Tournament
Director

Mike Shea
Senior Director
of Rules

George Boutell
Tournament Official
Scottsdale, AZ

Jon Brendle
Tournament Official
Orlando, FL

Wade Cagle
Tournament Supervisor
Alpharetta, GA

Jeff Haley
Associate Agronomist
Jacksonville, FL

Frank Kavanaugh
Tournament Official
Pattenburg, NJ

Dennis Leger
Associate Agronomist
Jacksonville, FL

Vaughn Moise
Tournament Official
Kingwood, TX

Mark Russell
Tournament Official
Orlando, FL

Glenn Tait
Tournament Official
LaMesa, CA

Carlton White
Tournament Official
Ormond Beach, FL

COMMUNICATIONS

John Morris
Vice President of
Communications

Sid Wilson
Director of
Public Relations

Dave Lancer
Director
of Information

Denise Taylor
Media Relations
Coordinator

James Cramer
Publications
Editor/NIKE TOUR
Media Official

Chuck Adams
PGA TOUR
Media Official

Marty Caffey
PGA TOUR
Media Official

Bob Hyde
NIKE TOUR
Media Official

Mark Mitchell
PGA TOUR
Media Official

Lee Patterson
Senior PGA
TOUR Media Official

Wes Seeley
PGA TOUR
Media Official

Phil Stambaugh
Senior PGA
TOUR Media Official

Vicki Page
Administrative
Assistant

Jodi Herb
Media Relations
Secretary

Dianne Reed
NIKE TOUR
Communications
Assistant

Leslie Sinadinos
Senior PGA TOUR
Communication
Assistant

BROADCASTING

John Evenson
Vice President, Broadcasting

Teri Montville
Broadcasting Manager

Abbe Moody
Administrative Assistant

PHOTOGRAPHY

Stan Badz
Staff Photographer

Michelle Falcone
Administrative Assistant

Pete Fontaine
Staff Photographer

Sam Greenwood
Staff Photographer

MARKETING

Leo McCullagh
Vice President of Marketing

Jack White
Director of Promotions

Gerald Goodman
Field Manager of Promotions

Rich Pierson
Promotions

Larry Strong
Promotions

Don Wallace
Promotions

PGA TOUR PRODUCTIONS

Donna Geils
Vice President/Executive Producer

Roger Stevenson
Vice President/Operations

Tom Alter
Senior Producer

Laurie White
Senior Producer

Michael O'Connell
Coordinating Producer

Scott Rinehart
Production Manager

Scott Goodall
Manager, Field
Operations

Lowell Thaler
Producer

Seth Giambalvo
Feature Producer

Rick Persons
Feature Producer

Ed Waud
Feature Producer

Glenn Rocha
Associate Producer

Marion Stratford
Associate Producer

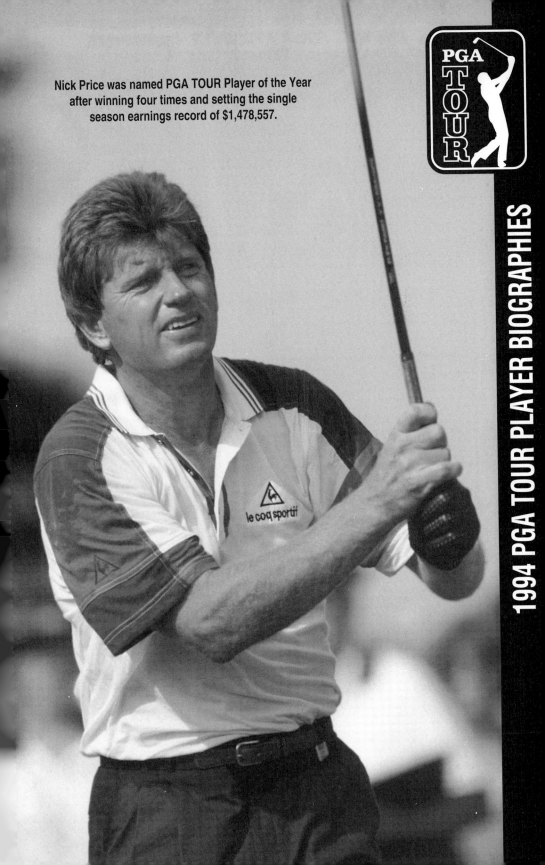

Nick Price was named PGA TOUR Player of the Year after winning four times and setting the single season earnings record of $1,478,557.

ALL EXEMPT TOUR PRIORITY RANKINGS

Each PGA TOUR player has earned a position on the priority ranking system that will be used selecting tournament fields. The complete ranking system, in order of priority, is as follows:

I. SPECIAL EXEMPTIONS

1. Winners of PGA Championship or U.S. Open prior to 1970 or in the last 10 calendar years.

Paul Azinger	Ray Floyd	Don January	Jack Nicklaus	Sam Snead
Jerry Barber	Ed Furgol	Lee Janzen	Andy North	Payne Stewart
Julius Boros	Al Geiberger	Tom Kite	Arnold Palmer	Curtis Strange
Jack Burke	Wayne Grady	Gene Littler	Gary Player	Lee Trevino
Billy Casper	Hubert Green	Dave Marr	Nick Price	Bob Tway
John Daly	Jay Hebert	Orville Moody	Bob Rosburg	Ken Venturi
Dow Finsterwald	Lionel Hebert	Larry Nelson	Scott Simpson	Fuzzy Zoeller
Jack Fleck	Hale Irwin	Bobby Nichols	Jeff Sluman	

2. Winners of the THE PLAYERS Championship in the last 10 calendar years.

Fred Couples	Davis Love III	Mark McCumber	Jodie Mudd	Calvin Peete
Steve Elkington	John Mahaffey			

3. Winners of the NEC WORLD SERIES OF GOLF in the last 10 calendar years.

Fulton Allem	Roger Maltbie	Tom Purtzer	Craig Stadler	Denis Watson
David Frost	Dan Pohl	Mike Reid		

4. Winners of The Masters in the last 10 calendar years.

Ben Crenshaw	Larry Mize

5. Winners of the British Open in the last 10 calendar years. (1990-present)

Ian Baker-Finch	Greg Norman

6. The leader in PGA TOUR official earnings in each of the last five calendar years.

Corey Pavin

7. Winners of PGA TOUR co-sponsored or approved events (except Team events) within the last two calendar years, or during the current year.

Chip Beck	Brad Faxon	Gary Hallberg	Blaine McCallister	David Peoples
Billy Ray Brown	Dan Forsman	Nolan Henke	Jim McGovern	Vijay Singh
Mark Calcavecchia	Fred Funk	John Huston	Rocco Mediate	Mike Standly
Mark Carnevale	Jim Gallagher, Jr.	John Inman	Phil Mickelson	Howard Twitty
John Cook	Bill Glasson	Bruce Lietzke	Brett Ogle	Lanny Wadkins
David Edwards	Jay Haas	Jeff Maggert	Mark O'Meara	Grant Waite
		Billy Mayfair	Steve Pate	Richard Zokol

8. Members of the last-named U.S. Ryder Cup team.

9. Leaders in official PGA TOUR career earnings, as follows:

   a. Players among the Top 50 in career earnings as of the end of the preceding calendar year may elect to use a one-time, one-year exemption for the next year.

   Andy Bean   Hal Sutton

   b. Players among the Top 25 in career earnings as of the end of the preceding calendar year may elect to use this special exemption for a second year, provided that the player remains among the Top 25 on the career money list.

10. Sponsor exemptions (a maximum of eight, which may include amateurs with handicaps of two or less), on the following basis:

   a. Not less than two sponsor invitees shall be PGA TOUR Regular, Life or Past Champion members not otherwise exempt.

   b. Not less than two of the top 50 finishers from the last Qualifying Tournament, if not all of them can otherwise be accommodated (Note: PGA TOUR members may receive unlimited number of sponsor invitations. Non-TOUR members may receive maximum of five per year)

11. Two foreign players designated by the Commissioner.

12. The current PGA Club Professional Champion for a maximum of three open events, in addition to any sponsor selections.

   Jeff Roth

13. PGA Section Champion of the Section in which the tournament is played.

14. Four members of the PGA Section in which the tournament is played, who qualify through Sectional qualifying competitions.

15. Four low scorers at Open Qualifying, which shall normally be held on Monday of tournament week.

16. Past champions of the particular event being contested that week, if co-sponsored by the PGA TOUR and the same tournament sponsor (except for Team events), as follows:

Winners prior to July 28, 1970--unlimited exemptions for such events.
Winners after July 28, 1970—ten years of exemptions for such events.

II. TOP 125, PREVIOUS YEAR'S OFFICIAL MONEY LIST—If not exempt under "Special Exemptions" the top 125 PGA TOUR members on the previous year's Official Money List, in order of their positions on the list.

Gil Morgan	Craig Parry	Jay Delsing	Duffy Waldorf	Ed Dougherty	Ted Tryba
Rick Fehr	Dudley Hart	Greg Twiggs	Brian Claar	Ted Schulz	Doug Tewell
Bob Estes	Loren Roberts	Michael Allen	Jay Don Blake	John Flannery	Larry Rinker
Tom Lehman	Bob Lohr	Brad Bryant	Tom Sieckmann	David Ogrin	Brandel Chamblee
Scott Hoch	D.A. Weibring	Ken Green	Kenny Perry	Ed Humenik	Michael Bradley
Joey Sindelar	Russ Cochran	Peter Jacobsen	Mike Hulbert	Joel Edwards	Don Pooley
Billy Andrade	Greg Kraft	John Adams	Kirk Triplett	Neal Lancaster	David Toms
Mark Wiebe	Andrew Magee	Mike Springer	Steve Lowery	Bob Gilder	Marco Dawson
Keith Clearwater	Mark Brooks	Bruce Fleisher	Brian Kamm	Kelly Gibson	Ronnie Black
Tom Watson	Dave Rummells	Dick Mast	Wayne Levi	Willie Wood	Trevor Dodds
Donnie Hammond	Robert Gamez	Phil Blackmar	Dave Barr	Lennie Clements	Ed Fiori
			Dillard Pruitt	Joe Ozaki	Gene Sauers

III. SPECIAL MEDICAL EXTENSION—If granted by the Commissioner, if not otherwise eligible, and if needed to fill the field, Special Medical Extension.

Tim Simpson	Scott Verplank	Brad Fabel	Mike Sullivan	Jim Woodward

IV. TOP 10 FINISHERS—The top 10 professionals and those tied for 10th in an open tournament whose victory has official status is exempt into the next open tournament whose victory has official status.

V. TOP FIVE MONEY WINNERS ON 1993 NIKE TOUR

Sean Murphy	Doug Martin	Stan Utley	Bob May	John Morse

VI. QUALIFYING TOURNAMENT—The low 40 scorers and ties from the previous year's PGA TOUR Qualifying Tournament , in order of their finish in the tournament, and players 6-10 on the 1993 NIKE TOUR money list.

Ty Armstrong	Larry Silveira*	David Feherty	Mike Heinen	Shaun Micheel
Dave Stockton, Jr.	Clark Dennis	Bob Burns	Rocky Walcher	Jim Furyk
Robin Freeman	Chris DiMarco*	Thomas Levet	Paul Stankowski	Rob Boldt
Jeff Woodland	Dennis Paulson	Steve Stricker	Esteban Toledo	Charles Raulerson
Pete Jordan	Curt Byrum*	John Wilson	D.A. Russell	Chris Kite
Jesper Parnevik	Glen Day	Guy Boros	Steve Lamontagne	Tom Garner
Tommy Moore*	Yoshi Mizumaki	Paul Goydos	Bill Kratzert	Mike Brisky
Joey Rassett	Todd Barranger	Mark Wurtz	Bill Britton	Phil Tataurangi
Olin Browne*	Steve Rintoul	Dicky Pride	Don Reese	Brad Lardon
Morris Hatalsky	Steve Gotsche	Steve Brodie	Ed Kirby	Brad King

(* 6-10 1993 NIKE TOUR money list)

VII. NEXT 25 MEMBERS AFTER TOP 125 MEMBERS FROM PREVIOUS YEAR'S OFFICIAL MONEY LIST—If needed to fill the field, the next 25 PGA TOUR members after the top 125 PGA TOUR members from the previous year's Official Money List, in order of their positions on the list.

Skip Kendall	Russell Beiersdorf	Harry Taylor .	Patrick Burke	Lance Ten Broeck
Brian Henninger	Mike Smith	P.H. Horgan III	Scott Gump	Tom Byrum
Bobby Clampett	Mark Lye	Robert Wrenn	JC Anderson	

VIII. SPECIAL MEMBER/MEDICAL

IX. PAST CHAMPION MEMBERS—If not otherwise eligible and if needed to fill the field, Past Champion Members, in order of the total number of co-sponsored or approved events won, excluding Team events. If two or more players are tied, the player who is higher on the PGA TOUR Career Money List shall be eligible.

X. SPECIAL TEMPORARY—If during the course of a PGA TOUR season, a non-member of the PGA TOUR wins an amount of official money (e.g., by playing in PGA TOUR events through sponsor exemptions, Open Qualifying, etc.) equal to the amount won in the preceding year by the 154th finisher on the official money winning list will be eligible for the remainder of the year.

XI. TEAM CHAMPIONSHIP WINNERS—If not otherwise eligible and if needed to fill the field, winners of co-sponsored team championships, in order of the total number of team championship tournaments won. If two or more players are tied based on the number of such tournaments won, the player who is higher on the official PGA TOUR career money list shall be eligible.

XII. VETERAN MEMBERS—If not otherwise eligible and if needed to fill the field, Veteran Members (players who have made a minimum of 150 cuts during their career), in order of their standing on the PGA TOUR career money list.

PRONUNCIATION GUIDE

BILLY ANDRADE .... AHN-drade

PAUL AZINGER .... AY-zin-ger

RUSSELL BEIERSDORF .... BIRES-dorf

JIM BENEPE .... BEN-a-pee

MARK CALCAVECCHIA .... CAL-kuh-VECK-ee-ah

MARK CARNEVALE .... CAR-neh-vale

BRANDEL CHAMBLEE .... SHAM-blee

BRIAN CLAAR .... CLARE

ED DOUGHERTY .... DOCK-er-ty

DAVID FEHERTY .... FAY-er-tee

RICK FEHR .... FAIR

JIM FURYK .... FEWR-ick

ROBERT GAMEZ .... GAH-mez

STEVE GOTSCHE .... GOT-che

DAN HALLDORSON .... HALL-dur-sun

MORRIS HATALSKY .... huh-TALL-skee

NOLAN HENKE .... HEN-kee

SCOTT HOCH .... HOKE

ED HUMENIK .... HUGH-men-ick

BARRY JAECKEL .... JAY-kull

GARY KOCH .... COKE

STEVE LAMONTAGNE .... LA-mon-tain

WAYNE LEVI .... LEV-ee

BRUCE LIETZKE .... LIT-ski

JEFF MAGGERT .... MAG-ert

ROCCO MEDIATE .... MEE-dee-ate

SHAUN MICHEEL .... muh-KEEL

BRETT OGLE .... O-gul

DAVID OGRIN .... O-Grin

JESPER PARNEVIK .... YES-per PAR-nuh-vik

COREY PAVIN .... PAY-vin

MARK PFEIL .... FILE

DAN POHL .... POLE

TOM SIECKMANN .... SEEK-man

PHIL TATAURANGI .... TAT-uh-RAN-gee

LANCE TEN BROECK .... TEN-brook

DOUG TEWELL .... TOOL

TED TRYBA .... TREE-ba

STAN UTLEY .... UT-lee

D.A. WEIBRING .... WY-bring

MARK WIEBE .... WEE-bee

FUZZY ZOELLER .... ZELL-er

JOHN ADAMS

EXEMPT STATUS: 78th on 1993 money list

FULL NAME: John Greg Adams

HEIGHT: 6' 3"   **WEIGHT:** 220

BIRTH DATE: May 5, 1954   **BIRTHPLACE:** Altus, OK

RESIDENCE: Scottsdale, AZ

FAMILY: Wife, Jane; Benjamin Craig (6/20/83), Kimberly Jill (10/23/85)

COLLEGE: Arizona State University

SPECIAL INTERESTS: Hunting, fishing

TURNED PROFESSIONAL: 1976

Q SCHOOL: Spring 1978; Fall 1979; Fall 1985

PLAYER PROFILE

CAREER EARNINGS: $1,166,235   **PLAYOFF RECORD:** 0-1

BEST-EVER FINISH: 2-1982 Hall of Fame Classic (lost playoff to Jay Haas)

MONEY & POSITION:			
1978--$ 2,025--196	1984--$ 73,567-- 80	1989--$104,824--120
1979--$ 1,785--224	1985--$ 9,613--181	1990--$126,733--122
1980--$ 19,895--123	1986--$ 64,906--124	1991--$117,549--125
1981--$ 17,898--138	1987--$ 51,976--149	1992--$173,069-- 89
1982--$ 54,014-- 85	1988--$ 64,341--140	1993--$221,753-- 78
1983--$ 59,287-- 87		

BEST 1993 FINISHES: T4--Sprint Western Open; T10--Doral-Ryder Open

1993 SUMMARY: Tournaments entered--29; in money--18; top ten finishes--2.

1994 PGA TOUR CHARITY TEAM COMPETITION: THE PLAYERS Championship

1993 SEASON: Enjoyed the finest season of his professional career, surpassing the $200,000 mark in earnings for the first time... Collected two top-10 finishes during the year, including a tie for fourth at the Sprint Western Open... He fired a course-record-tying 9-under-par 63 during the third round at the Dubsdread course at Cog Hill CC... That round propelled him to within three strokes of the lead and ultimately gave him a $49,600 payday... Was one stroke out of the lead the next week at the Anheuser-Busch Golf Classic, before faltering with a 4-over 75 on the last day... Also finished tied for 10th at the Doral-Ryder Open... Another highlight came at the United States Open at Baltusrol, where he finished tied for 11th, and earned invitations to The Masters and to the 1994 United States Open.

CAREER HIGHLIGHTS: Best chance for a win came at the 1982 Hall of Fame Classic on the famed Pinehurst No. 2 course... Adams lost in a playoff there to Jay Haas... He made bogey on the second extra hole...Best finish in recent years came at the 1992 Las Vegas Invitational, where he finished in a tie for third... He fired five rounds in the 60s and finished four strokes behind John Cook...Led the PGA TOUR in Greens in Regulation in 1988, and was third in Driving Distance in 1992 with a 275.8 yards per drive average... Winner of the 1975 Arizona State Amateur.

PERSONAL: Started playing golf as soon as he could hold a club...Held the club and the putter in a crosshanded fashion, "but I gave that up when I was about three years old." Father was a golf professional.

1993 PGA TOUR STATISTICS

Scoring Average	71.30	(99T)
Driving Distance	277.6	(5)
Driving Accuracy	61.9	(174)
Greens in Regulation	65.9	(79T)
Putting	1.808	(119T)
All-Around	818	(94)
Sand Saves	45.6	(166)
Total Driving	179	(78T)
Eagles	7	(37T)
Birdies	297	(61T)

MISCELLANEOUS STATISTICS

Scoring Avg. (before cut)	71.59	(88T)
Scoring Avg. (3rd round)	70.63	(49)
Scoring Avg. (4th round)	72.47	(162)
Birdie Conversion	27.2	(106T)
Par Breakers	18.4	(85T)

1993 Low Round: **63:** Sprint Western Open/3
Career Low Round: **63:** 1993 Sprint Western Open/3
Career Largest Paycheck: **$62,400/**'92 Las Vegas Invitational/T3

FULTON ALLEM

EXEMPT STATUS: Winner, 1993 NEC World Series of Golf

FULL NAME: Fulton Peter Allem

HEIGHT: 5'11"   **WEIGHT:** 215

BIRTH DATE: September 15, 1957

BIRTHPLACE: Kroonstad, South Africa

RESIDENCE: Heathrow, FL

FAMILY: Wife, Colleen; Nadia (7/7/86), Nicholas (1/1/91)

SPECIAL INTERESTS: Riding horses, breeding horses, fishing & hunting

TURNED PROFESSIONAL: 1976

JOINED TOUR: Fall 1987

PLAYER PROFILE

CAREER EARNINGS: $1,810,873

TOUR VICTORIES: **1991** Independent Insurance Agent Open. **1993** Southwestern Bell Colonial,
(TOTAL: 3)   NEC World Series of Golf

MONEY & POSITION:

1987--$ 88,734--105	1990--$ 134,493--116	1993--$851,345--9
1988--$163,911-- 73	1991--$ 229,702-- 71	
1989--$134,706--104	1992--$ 209,982-- 74	

BEST 1993 FINISHES: 1-Southwestern Bell Colonial; 1-NEC World Series of Golf; 5--BellSouth Classic; T7--Shell Houston Open

1993 SUMMARY: Tournaments entered--28; in money--18; top ten finishes--4.

1994 PGA TOUR CHARITY TEAM COMPETITION: Doral-Ryder Open

1993 SEASON: Allem's 1993 season was one that TOUR professionals dream about... He won tournaments on two of the most storied courses in TOUR history--Colonial CC and Firestone CC...Outdueled a red-hot Greg Norman to win the Southwestern Bell Colonial... A second-round 7-under-par 63 propelled him into contention, and a closing 3-under-par 67 was enough to give Allem the plaid jacket...That victory earned him a spot in the NEC World Series of Golf... Was a stroke out of the lead going into the last day at Firestone, and shot a blistering 8-under-par 62...Victory gave him a 10-year exemption, and his largest payday to date on the PGA TOUR, $360,000...Finished five strokes ahead of his nearest competitors.

CAREER HIGHLIGHTS: After struggling through much of the season, broke into the winner's circle for the first time at the 1991 Independent Insurance Agent Open...Played the final two rounds in 11-under-par to defeat Billy Ray Brown, Mike Hulbert and Tom Kite by a single stroke...Was 143rd on the money list going into the last week of the season, but the win in Houston earned him a two-year exemption...Finished second at the 1987 NEC World Series of Golf to earn his PGA TOUR card without going through the Qualifying School...Winner of the 1988 Sun City Million Dollar Challenge...Winner of 11 South African events and 15 total worldwide.

PERSONAL: Started the game at the age of 7 with encouragement from his father... Admits that Gary Player had a large influence in his life... Had 18 second-place finishes before breaking through with a win on the South African Tour.

1993 PGA TOUR STATISTICS

Scoring Average	70.80	(51)
Driving Distance	257.1	(116T)
Driving Accuracy	77.6	(7)
Greens in Regulation	67.7	(47T)
Putting	1.777	(39T)
All-Around	439	(14)
Sand Saves	54.2	(61T)
Total Driving	123	(21)
Eagles	5	(67T)
Birdies	322	(30)

MISCELLANEOUS STATISTICS

Scoring Avg. (before cut)	71.20	(54T)
Scoring Avg. (3rd round)	71.93	(138)
Scoring Avg. (4th round)	70.84	(36T)
Birdie Conversion	29.4	(35T)
Par Breakers	20.2	(28T)

1993 Low Round: **62:** NEC World Series of Golf/4
Career Low Round: **62:** 1993 NEC World Series of Golf/4
Career Largest Paycheck:**$360,000**/1993 NEC WSOG/1

MICHAEL ALLEN

EXEMPT STATUS: 73rd on 1993 money list

FULL NAME: Michael Louis Allen

HEIGHT: 6'1" **WEIGHT:** 185

BIRTH DATE: January 31, 1959

BIRTHPLACE: San Mateo, CA

RESIDENCE: Scottsdale, AZ

FAMILY: Wife, Cynthia; Christy Anna (12/8/93)

COLLEGE: University of Nevada-Reno

SPECIAL INTERESTS: 49ers football, wine tasting, skiing

TURNED PROFESSIONAL: 1984

Q-SCHOOL: 1989, 1990, 1991, 1992

PLAYER PROFILE

CAREER EARNINGS: $385,472

BEST EVER FINISH: T3-- 1993 Northern Telecom Open; T3--1993 Phoenix Open.

MONEY & POSITION: 1990--$95,319--140 1992--$11,455--233 1993--$231,072--73
1991--$47,626--177

BEST 1993 FINISHES: T3--Northern Telecom Open; T3--Phoenix Open; T7--Canon Greater Hartford Open

1993 SUMMARY: Tournaments entered--27; in money--15; top ten finishes--3.

1994 PGA TOUR CHARITY TEAM COMPETITION: THE TOUR Championship

1993 SEASON: Earned full exempt status for the first time in his career...Finished tied for third in both the Northern Telecom Open and the Phoenix Open... Finished up with consecutive 4-under-par 68s on the weekend to secure his best ever finish on the TOUR... Wound up three strokes behind winner Larry Mize and earned $52,800 his largest check to date... Duplicated that finish the very next week at the TPC at Scottsdale... Opened with a 5-under-par 66 and was tied for the lead with five other players.. Closed with three consecutive 70s, and again finished three strokes behind Lee Janzen... The $48,000 payday gave him $100,800 in his first two tournaments, and allowed him the luxury of planning the rest of his schedule... Finished tied for seventh at the Sprint Western Open... Was tied for the lead after the first round of the Nestle Invitational and was one stroke back at the halfway point before finishing tied for 23rd.

OTHER ACHIEVEMENTS: Biggest victory to date came on the European Tour in 1989... Fired a final round 9-under-par 63 to win the Bell's Scottish Open by two strokes over Ian Woosnam and Jose Maria Olazabal... Made seven birdies and an eagle during the last 13 holes... He holed two chips and a bunker shot enroute to a 30 on the back side at Gleneagles... Only had 22 putts during the final round... Later that same year finished second in the Scandanavian Open... Finished the year 15th on the European Order of Merit... Also went on to finish 10th in the Qualifying Tournament in the U.S. in 1989... In 1990, opened with a 9-under-par 63 to claim the first round lead the Nissan Los Angeles Open... Added a 68 for a one stroke lead after two... Finished tied for 12th, for his best PGA TOUR finish before 1993.

PERSONAL: Enjoys wine tasting and skiing... Was planning to be a stockbroker before turning to golf as a profession.

1993 PGA TOUR STATISTICS

Scoring Average	71.10	(76T)
Driving Distance	264.2	(58)
Driving Accuracy	65.3	(141T)
Greens in Regulation	62.8	(154T)
Putting	1.791	(74T)
All-Around	907	(120T)
Sand Saves	45.0	(169)
Total Driving	199	(111T)
Eagles	8	(25T)
Birdies	267	(99T)

MISCELLANEOUS STATISTICS

Scoring Avg. (before cut)	72.07	(126)
Scoring Avg. (3rd round)	70.92	(69)
Scoring Avg. (4th round)	71.47	(93T)
Birdie Conversion	28.1	(74T)
Par Breakers	18.2	(98T)

1993 Low Round: 64: Las Vegas Invitational/2
Career Low Round: 63: 1990 Nissan Los Angeles Open/1
Career Largest Paycheck: $52,800/1993 Northern Telecom Open/T3

BILLY ANDRADE

EXEMPT STATUS: 40th on 1993 money list

FULL NAME: William Thomas Andrade

HEIGHT: 5' 8" **WEIGHT:** 155

BIRTH DATE: January 25, 1964

BIRTHPLACE: Fall River, MA

RESIDENCE: Bristol, RI and Atlanta, GA

FAMILY: Wife, Jody

COLLEGE: Wake Forest University (1987, Sociology)

SPECIAL INTERESTS: All sports

TURNED PROFESSIONAL: 1987

Q SCHOOL: Fall 1987, 1988

PLAYER PROFILE

CAREER EARNINGS: $1,692,588 **PLAYOFF RECORD:** 1-1

TOUR VICTORIES: 1991 Kemper Open, Buick Classic
(TOTAL: 2)

MONEY AND POSITION:	1988--$ 74,950--134	1990--$231,362-- 64	1992--$ 202,509--76
	1989--$202,242-- 69	1991--$615,765 --14	1993--$ 365,759--40

BEST 1993 FINISHES: T2--Buick Southern Open; 3--H-E-B Texas Open; 7--Northern Telecom Open; T7--BellSouth Classic; T9--AT&T Pebble Beach National Pro-Am; T9--Kmart Greater Greensboro Open; T10--Nestle Invitational

1993 SUMMARY: Tournaments entered--29; in money--18, top ten finishes--7.

1994 PGA TOUR CHARITY TEAM COMPETITION: BellSouth Classic

NATIONAL TEAMS: Junior World Cup, 1981 (won team title with Sam Randolph at Portmarnock, Ireland); World Amateur Cup, 1986; Walker Cup, 1987.

1993 SEASON: A very streaky year for the personable Wake Forest graduate... Made the cut in 14 of the first 16 tournaments he entered in 1993... Missed seven consecutive cuts in the latter part of the year, before rebounding at the Buick Southern Open... Finished tied for second at the Callaway Gardens Mountain View Course, losing in a five-way playoff to John Inman... Fired a final-round 5-under-par 67 to get into a playoff for the second time in his career... Made par on the first extra hole, but it wasn't enough to advance... Had his five other top-10s in his first 12 tournaments.

CAREER HIGHLIGHTS: Enjoyed a torrid two-week stretch in 1991 that saw him win on consecutive weeks...Fired rounds of 68-64-64-67 for a 21-under-par 263 total, and a playoff victory over close friend Jeff Sluman at the Kemper Open... Followed that up with an 68-68-69-68, 11-under-par 273 total and a one-stroke victory over Brad Bryant at the Buick Classic in Rye, NY... A three-time All-America selection at Wake Forest...Member of the 1986 National Championship team there...Won the 1986 Sunnehanna and the North and South Amateur tournaments...Ranked as the number one junior player in the nation in 1981.

PERSONAL: Started the game at the age of five... Tagged along with his grandmother... Played in his first tournament at age 11 in Rhode Island... Followed fellow Rhode Island native Brad Faxon, who is three years older than he is... Was the recipient of the Arnold Palmer Scholarship to Wake Forest, where he won four collegiate events…Was named to the All-State team in basketball while in high school.

1993 PGA TOUR STATISTICS

Scoring Average	70.97	(66)
Driving Distance	258.8	(97)
Driving Accuracy	67.9	(98T)
Greens in Regulation	63.6	(137T)
Putting	1.777	(39T)
All-Around	776	(84)
Sand Saves	48.9	(133T)
Total Driving	195	(106T)
Eagles	5	(67T)
Birdies	316	(33T)

MISCELLANEOUS STATISTICS

Scoring Avg. (before cut)	71.53	(84)
Scoring Avg. (3rd round)	71.65	(121)
Scoring Avg. (4th round)	71.50	(95T)
Birdie Conversion	30.0	(21T)
Par Breakers	19.4	(52T)

1993 Low Round: 63:	Northern Telecom Open/1
Career Low Round: 63:	1993 Northern Telecom
Career Largest	Open/1
Paycheck:	**$180,000**/1991 Kemper Open/1
	1991 Buick Classic/1

PAUL AZINGER

EXEMPT STATUS: Winner, 1993 PGA Championship

FULL NAME: Paul William Azinger

HEIGHT: 6' 2"   **WEIGHT:** 175

BIRTH DATE: January 6, 1960

BIRTHPLACE: Holyoke, MA

RESIDENCE: Bradenton, FL

FAMILY: Wife,Toni; Sarah Jean(12/28/85), Josie Lynn(4/21/89)

COLLEGE: Brevard JC and Florida State University

SPECIAL INTERESTS: Fishing, boating

TURNED PROFESSIONAL: 1981

Q SCHOOL: Fall 1981, 1983, 1984

PLAYER PROFILE

CAREER EARNINGS: $6,761,307   **PLAYOFF RECORD:** 1-2

TOUR VICTORIES: (TOTAL: 11) **1987** Phoenix Open, Panasonic-Las Vegas Invitational, Canon-Sammy Davis Jr.-Greater Hartford Open. **1988** Hertz Bay Hill Classic. **1989** Canon Greater Hartford Open. **1990** MONY Tournament of Champions.**1991** AT&T Pebble Beach National Pro-Am. **1992** TOUR Championship.**1993** Memorial Tournament, New England Classic, PGA Championship.

MONEY & POSITION:

1982--$ 10,655--171	1987--$822,481-- 2	1991--$ 685,603-- 9
1984--$ 27,821--144	1988--$594,850-- 11	1992--$ 929,863-- 7
1985--$ 81,179-- 93	1989--$951,649-- 3	1993--$1,458,456-- 2
1986--$254,019-- 29	1990--$944,731-- 4	

BEST 1993 FINISHES: 1--Memorial Tournament; 1--New England Classic; 1--PGA Championship; T2--Doral-Ryder Open; 3--United Airlines Hawaiian Open; T3--Infiniti Tournament of Champions; T3--MCI Heritage Classic; T3--Kmart Greater Greensboro Open; T3--U.S. Open; T3--Las Vegas Invitational; T6--Nissan Los Angeles Open; T6--THE PLAYERS Championship

1993 SUMMARY: Tournaments entered--24; in money--17; top ten finishes--12.

1994 PGA TOUR CHARITY TEAM COMPETITION: Bob Hope Chrysler Classic

NATIONAL TEAMS: Ryder Cup (3), 1989, 1991, 1993; World Cup, 1989

1993 SEASON: Had the best season of his professional career... Kept the longest active winning streak on TOUR, seven years, going with three victories... His last victory may have been his most important, as he defeated Greg Norman in a two-hole playoff at the PGA Championship at Inverness... He won with a par on the second extra hole, after closing with a 3-under-par 68, and a 12-under 272 total... He was one stroke behind Norman going into the final round... Also won The Memorial Tournament in most dramatic fashion... On the 72nd hole, his blast out of a greenside bunker rolled in for a birdie to edge Corey Pavin by one stroke... His third round 7-under-par 64 propelled him to his second victory at the New England Classic... His 10 finishes in the top-3 were the most since Tom Watson in 1980.

CAREER HIGHLIGHTS: Won three times in 1987, finished second on the money list and won the PGA Player of the Year award...Had a superb 1991 season, when he won the AT&T Pebble Beach National Pro-Am... Now has had three consecutive outstanding Ryder Cup campaigns... He managed to halve his singles match with Nick Faldo this year... Previously he had defeated Seve Ballesteros and Jose Maria Olazabal in singles play in 1989 and 1991, respectively... Suffered with pain in his shoulder for years before getting it operated on in 1991... Medalist at the 1984 Qualifying Tournament...led the TOUR in sand saves in 1986, 1987 and 1990, all-around in 1989 and 1990 and eagles in 1990...Winner, 1990 and 1992 BMW Open (Germany)...Winner, 1988 Fred Meyer Challenge (with Bob Tway) and 1991 (with Ben Crenshaw)...Runnerup in 1987 British Open.

PERSONAL: Discovery of lymphoma in right shoulder blade expected to cause him to miss 6-7 months at start of season... Credits much of his success the last couple of years to seeing his teacher John Redman on a regular basis... Started playing at the age of five... Couldn't break 40 for nine holes as a senior in high school, while working at his father's marina in Sarasota.

1993 PGA TOUR STATISTICS

Scoring Average	69.75	(5)
Driving Distance	273.3	(12T)
Driving Accuracy	70.9	(66T)
Greens in Regulation	70.6	(12)
Putting	1.770	(26T)
All-Around	286	(3)
Sand Saves	56.8	(34T)
Total Driving	78	(9)
Eagles	5	(67T)
Birdies	301	(55T)

MISCELLANEOUS STATISTICS

Scoring Avg. (before cut)	70.65	(26)
Scoring Avg. (3rd round)	69.07	(2)
Scoring Avg. (4th round)	70.65	(27)
Birdie Conversion	29.3	(37T)
Par Breakers	21.0	(12)

1993 Low Round: 64: New England Classic /3
Career Low Round: 62: 2 times, most recent 1989 Texas Open/2
Career Largest Paycheck: $360,000/1992 TOUR Championship/1

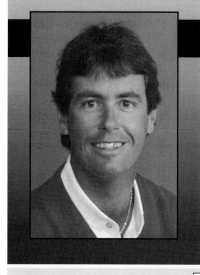

IAN BAKER-FINCH

EXEMPT STATUS: Winner, 1991 British Open

FULL NAME: Ian Baker-Finch

HEIGHT: 6'4"   **WEIGHT:** 190

BIRTH DATE: October 24, 1960

BIRTHPLACE: Nambour, Australia

RESIDENCE: Sanctuary Cove, Queensland, Australia

FAMILY: Wife, Jennie; Hayley (2/7/89), Laura (10/7/91)

SPECIAL INTERESTS: Water sports, wine, tennis, sports

TURNED PROFESSIONAL: 1979

JOINED TOUR: Fall 1988

PLAYER PROFILE

CAREER EARNINGS: $1,916,752   **PLAYOFF RECORD:** 0-1

TOUR VICTORIES: 1989 Southwestern Bell Colonial
(TOTAL: 1)

MONEY & POSITION:	1988--$ 75,840--133	1990--$611,492--16	1992--$261,817-- 58
	1989--$253,309-- 53	1991--$649,513--13	1993--$140,621--114

BEST 1993 FINISH: T3--MCI Heritage Classic

1993 SUMMARY: Tournaments entered--20; in money--12; top ten finishes--1.

1994 PGA TOUR CHARITY TEAM COMPETITION: Federal Express St. Jude Classic

NATIONAL TOUR TEAMS: Four Tours World Championship of Golf (3), 1989, 1990, 1991. Australian World Cup, 1985; Australia/New Zealand Kirin Cup (4), 1985, 1986, 1987, 1988.

1993 SEASON: Solid season for the angular Aussie... Had his best finish of the year at the MCI Heritage Classic... Finished with all four rounds under par, including a final round of 1-under 70 to finish tied for third... Wound up four strokes behind David Edwards for his only top-10 of the year... No surprise that he played well at Harbour Town, as he finished as the runner-up to Davis Love III in 1991... Troubled by shoulder problems for part of the year, nevertheless rebounded with three other top-25 finishes.

CAREER HIGHLIGHTS: Won one of golf's most significant tournaments in July of 1991, capturing the 120th British Open title at Royal Birkdale...Closed with rounds of 64-66, to defeat fellow countryman Mike Harwood by two strokes...Birdied five of the first seven holes on Sunday to claim the victory...Victory was sweet, due to his having led the 1984 British at St. Andrews after three rounds before faltering...Lone PGA TOUR victory came at the Southwestern Bell Colonial in 1989...65s in the first and third rounds gave him a four-stroke victory over David Edwards... Played superbly in the 1990 and 1991 seasons, amassing 15 top-10s during that span...Earned enough in the 1988 NEC World Series of Golf to qualify for his PGA TOUR card...He finished third in Akron that year, and avoided having to go through the Qualifying Tournament.

PERSONAL: Winner of numerous tournaments in Australia, Japan, and Europe...Most notable was the 1988 Australian Masters...Comes from the same "neighborhood" as Greg Norman and Wayne Grady in Queensland, Australia.

1993 PGA TOUR STATISTICS

Statistic	Value	
Scoring Average	71.19	(88)
Driving Distance	252.3	(159T)
Driving Accuracy	73.1	(43T)
Greens in Regulation	63.1	(148T)
Putting	1.820	(148T)
All-Around	1105	(148)
Sand Saves	53.0	(75T)
Total Driving	202	(117T)
Eagles	1	(164T)
Birdies	182	(163)

MISCELLANEOUS STATISTICS

Statistic	Value	
Scoring Avg. (before cut)	72.22	(137)
Scoring Avg. (3rd round)	71.50	(110T)
Scoring Avg. (4th round)	72.25	(151)
Birdie Conversion	26.3	(133T)
Par Breakers	16.7	(151T)

1993 Low Round: 67: Southwestern Bell Colonial/2
Career Low Round: 62: 1991 Anheuser-Busch Golf Classic/1
Career Largest Paycheck: $180,000/1989 Southwestern Bell Colonial/1

DAVE BARR

EXEMPT STATUS: 96th on 1993 money list

FULL NAME: David Allen Barr

HEIGHT: 6' 1"   **WEIGHT:** 200

BIRTH DATE: March 1, 1952

BIRTHPLACE: Kelowna, British Columbia

RESIDENCE: Richmond, B.C.

FAMILY: Wife, Lu Ann; Brent Jason (10/11/80), Teryn Amber (4/13/83)

COLLEGE: Oral Roberts University

SPECIAL INTERESTS: All sports

TURNED PROFESSIONAL: 1974

Q SCHOOL: Fall 1977

PLAYER PROFILE

CAREER EARNINGS: $1,837,220   **PLAYOFF RECORD:** 1-2

TOUR VICTORIES: 1981 Quad Cities Open. **1987** Georgia-Pacific Atlanta Golf Classic. (TOTAL: 2)

MONEY & POSITION:

1978--$11,897--133	1984--$113,336--62	1990--$197,979-- 80
1979--$13,022--142	1985--$126,177--65	1991--$144,389--108
1980--$14,664--141	1986--$122,181--70	1992--$118,859--119
1981--$46,214-- 90	1987--$202,241--54	1993--$179,264-- 96
1982--$12,474--166	1988--$291,244--33	
1983--$52,800-- 96	1989--$190,480--75	

BEST 1993 FINISH: T2--Nissan Los Angeles Open

1993 SUMMARY: Tournaments entered--28; in money--19; top ten finishes--1.

1994 PGA TOUR CHARITY TEAM COMPETITION: BellSouth Classic

NATIONAL TEAMS: World Cup (12), 1977, 1978, 1982, 1983, 1984, 1985, 1987, 1988, 1989, 1990, 1991, 1993 (won individual title in 1983 and team title with Dan Halldorson in 1985). Canadian World Amateur Cup, 1972. Dunhill Cup (6), 1986, 1987, 1988, 1989, 1990, 1993.

1993 SEASON: Another steady season for one of the finest golfers that Canada has ever produced... Only scored one top-10, but added five other finishes in the top-25... Best finish of the year came early at the Nissan Los Angeles Open... Due to heavy rains, the tournament was shortened to 54 holes... On Sunday, Barr went off on the back-side at Riviera Country Club, and promptly fired the days best round, a 5-under-par 66... That score was good enough to vault him into a tie for second, three strokes behind Tom Kite... Barr finished with a 4-under-par 209 total...Next best finish was a tie for 12th at the Federal Express St. Jude Classic.

CAREER HIGHLIGHTS: Collected both of his PGA TOUR victories in spectacular fashion... Barr won the 1987 Georgia-Pacific Atlanta Golf Classic with a torrid 23-under-par total of 265...Outlasted Dan Halldorson, Victor Regalado, Frank Conner and Woody Blackburn to win the 1981 Quad Cities Open... He came from five strokes back on the last day at Moline... The playoff lasted eight holes, and only one on TOUR has ever been longer...Winner of 12 tournaments on the Canadian Tour..:Has won the Canadian Order of Merit four different times, including 1977, 1985, 1986, and 1988...A member of the Canadian World Cup team 12 times, and their Dunhill Cup team six different times...Won the World Cup Individual Title in 1983, and teamed with Dan Halldorson to win the team title in 1985...Winner of seven consecutive SCORE Awards as Canada's top player.

PERSONAL: Uses a baseball grip as opposed to the overlap or interlocking kind.

1993 PGA TOUR STATISTICS

Scoring Average	71.17	(83T)
Driving Distance	258.5	(98T)
Driving Accuracy	70.9	(66T)
Greens in Regulation	70.7	(11)
Putting	1.832	(168T)
All-Around	735	(75)
Sand Saves	49.3	(129T)
Total Driving	164	(60T)
Eagles	7	(37T)
Birdies	280	(83T)

MISCELLANEOUS STATISTICS

Scoring Avg. (before cut)	71.44	(74T)
Scoring Avg. (3rd round)	71.59	(116)
Scoring Avg. (4th round)	71.30	(73)
Birdie Conversion	23.4	(178)
Par Breakers	17.0	(139T)

1993 Low Round: 65:Hardee's Golf Classic/1

Career Low Round: 63:1988 Canon Sammy Davis Jr. Greater Hartford Open/4

Career Largest Paycheck: **$108,000**/1987 Georgia-Pacific Atlanta Golf Classic/1

ANDY BEAN

EXEMPT STATUS: Top 50 Career Earnings

FULL NAME: Thomas Andrew Bean

HEIGHT: 6' 4"   **WEIGHT:** 225

BIRTH DATE: March 13, 1953

BIRTHPLACE: Lafayette, GA

RESIDENCE: Lakeland, FL

FAMILY: Wife, Debbie; Lauren Ashley (4/17/82), Lindsey Ann (8/10/84), Jordan Alise (11/19/85)

COLLEGE: University of Florida (1976, Marketing, Business)

SPECIAL INTERESTS: Hunting, fishing

TURNED PROFESSIONAL: 1975

Q SCHOOL: Fall 1975

PLAYER PROFILE

CAREER EARNINGS: $3,234,265   **PLAYOFF RECORD:** 3-3

TOUR VICTORIES: **1977** Doral-Eastern Open. **1978** Kemper Open, Danny Thomas Memphis Classic,
(TOTAL: 11) Western Open. **1979** Atlanta Classic. **1980** Hawaiian Open. **1981** Bay Hill Classic. **1982** Doral Eastern Open. **1984** Greater Greensboro Open. **1986** Doral Eastern Open, Byron Nelson Golf Classic.

MONEY & POSITION:		
1976--$ 10,761--139	1982--$208,627-- 15	1988--$ 48,961-- 149
1977--$127,312-- 12	1983--$181,246-- 24	1989--$236,097-- 58
1978--$268,241-- 3	1984--$422,995-- 3	1990--$129,669-- 119
1979--$208,253-- 7	1985--$190,871-- 33	1991--$193,609-- 88
1980--$269,033-- 4	1986--$491,938-- 4	1992--$ 30,798-- 195
1981--$105,755-- 35	1987--$ 73,808--120	1993--$ 37,292-- 191

BEST 1993 FINISH: T18--Northern Telecom Open

1993 SUMMARY: Tournaments entered--21; in money--10; top ten finishes--0.

1994 PGA TOUR CHARITY TEAM COMPETITION: Lincoln-Mercury Kapalua International

NATIONAL TEAMS: Ryder Cup, 1987; U.S. vs. Japan, 1984

ANDY BEAN: Has battled a number of injuries for the last several seasons...Suffered another down season in 1993... Made only 10 cuts in 21 starts...Had only one finish in the top-25... Best finish came in his very first start of the year at the Northern Telecom Open... Fired three rounds in the 60s in Tucson to finish tied for 18th... He opened with a 3-under-par 69 and followed that up with a 68, before shooting a 72 on Saturday... Added a 69 on Sunday to finish with a 10-under-par 278 total... He collected $12,466 for his efforts... Later in the year at the unofficial Lincoln-Mercury Kapalua International he finished tied for 25th... His next best official finish was a tie for 35th at the Canadian Open.

CAREER HIGHLIGHTS: An 11-time winner between 1977 and 1986... Was one of the more dominant players during that time... Won the Doral Eastern Open three times in 1977, 1982 and 1986... Again proving that there are horses for courses, he won the Isuzu Kapalua International in 1986 and 1987... Injuries have hampered him since that time... Was a member of the 1987 Ryder Cup team... He defeated Ian Woosnam in singles play that year... Was a member of the 1984 USA vs. Japan matches... Winner of the 1978 Dunlop Phoenix in Japan... Medalist at the ABC Cup matches in Japan... Had an outstanding amateur career winning many times before turning professional in 1975... Won the 1974 Eastern and Falstaff Amateur... Winner of the 1975 Dixie Amateur and Western Amateur... Was a semifinalist that same year in the U.S. Amateur... Was an All-America selection at the University of Florida and captain of the golf team.

PERSONAL: An avid fishing enthusiast... Has been known to take a bite out of his golf balls on occasion.

1993 PGA TOUR STATISTICS

Scoring Average	72.77	(184)
Driving Distance	265.2	(47T)
Driving Accuracy	58.0	(184)
Greens in Regulation	58.3	(186)
Putting	1.823	(154T)
All-Around	1383	(186)
Sand Saves	45.9	(163)
Total Driving	231	(153)
Eagles	2	(144T)
Birdies	173	(168)

MISCELLANEOUS STATISTICS

Scoring Avg. (before cut)	73.32	(184)
Scoring Avg. (3rd round)	72.60	(173T)
Scoring Avg. (4th round)	74.30	(186)
Birdie Conversion	27.0	(110T)
Par Breakers	15.9	(166)

1993 Low Round: 68: 2 Times
Career Low Round: 61: 1979 Atlanta Classic/3
Career Largest
Paycheck: $108,000/1986 Byron Nelson Classic/1

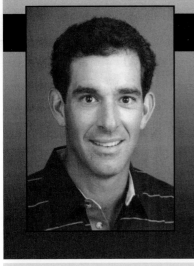

CHIP BECK

EXEMPT STATUS: 1992 tournament winner

FULL NAME: Charles Henry Beck

HEIGHT: 5' 10"   **WEIGHT:** 170

BIRTH DATE: September 12, 1956

BIRTHPLACE: Fayetteville, NC

RESIDENCE: Highland Park, IL

FAMILY: Wife, Karen Marie; Charles (11/12/83), Elizabeth Tuttle (3/16/87), Mary Catherine (7/7/90), Anne Marie (5/28/92)

COLLEGE: University of Georgia (1978, Journalism)

SPECIAL INTERESTS: Tennis, landscaping, water skiing

TURNED PROFESSIONAL: 1978

Q SCHOOL: Fall 1978

PLAYER PROFILE

CAREER EARNINGS: $5,304,632   **PLAYOFF RECORD:** 0-2

TOUR VICTORIES: **1988** Los Angeles Open, USF&G Classic. **1990** Buick Open.
(TOTAL: 4)   **1992** Freeport-McMoRan Classic.

MONEY & POSITION:

1979--$ 4,166--194	1984--$177,289--34	1989--$694,087-- 9
1980--$ 17,109--131	1985--$ 76,038--97	1990--$571,816--17
1981--$ 30,034--110	1986--$215,140--39	1991--$578,535--16
1982--$ 57,608-- 76	1987--$523,003-- 9	1992--$689,704--17
1983--$149,909-- 33	1988--$916,818-- 2	1993--$603,376--25

BEST 1993 FINISHES: 2--Masters Tournament; 2--Anheuser-Busch Golf Classic; T7--AT&T Pebble Beach National Pro-Am; T7--Buick Classic; T10--Doral-Ryder Open.

1993 SUMMARY: Tournaments entered--26; in money--18; top ten finishes--5.

1994 PGA TOUR CHARITY TEAM COMPETITION: Buick Invitational of California

NATIONAL TEAMS: Ryder Cup (3), 1989, 1991, 1993; Kirin Cup, 1988; Asahi Glass Four Tours World Championship of Golf, 1989.

1993 SEASON: Another solid season for one of the nicest players on TOUR... Respected by his peers for his dogged determination and his positive attitude... Collected a pair of runnerup finishes in 1993... Finished alone in second place at The Masters, where he closed with a 2-under-par 70... Wound up four strokes behind Bernhard Langer... Later in the year, finished two strokes behind Jim Gallagher, Jr., at the Anheuser-Busch Golf Classic... He fired three 68s and a 67 at Kingsmill to finish alone in second place... That finish enabled him to accumulate enough points to make the Ryder Cup team for the third time in his career... After being down three holes with five to go, Beck charged back to defeat Barry Lane, 1-up, and give the U.S. its second consecutive victory in the event.

CAREER HIGHLIGHTS: On October 11, 1991, in the third round of the Las Vegas Invitational, Beck joined Al Geiberger as the only players to shoot 59 in a PGA TOUR event...Beck made 13 birdies and no bogeys on the Sunrise Golf Club course...He started on No. 10 and had seven birdies for a 29...Moved to No. 1 and birdied three out of the first four holes, and finished with three consecutive birdies...On the 18th, he fired an 8-iron to three feet and calmly made the putt...He received $500,000 from Hilton Hotels, with another $500,000 going to charities...With his money, he set up the Chip Beck Scholarship Fund...Best year on TOUR was in 1988, when he won the L.A. Open and the USF&G Classic and finished second on the money list... A member of the Kirin Cup team in 1988...A member of the Asahi Glass Four Tours World Championship of Golf team in 1989...Three time All-American while at Georgia...Winner of the 1988 Vardon Trophy...Winner of the 1989 and 1992 Merrill Lynch Shoot-Out Championships.

PERSONAL: Started the game in the summer of his 10th year... By the end of the summer, he won the Pee Wee division at the club... Was a journalism major at the University of Georgia, and was named the Athlete of the Year as a senior.

1993 PGA TOUR STATISTICS

Scoring Average	70.77	(50)
Driving Distance	258.2	(101T)
Driving Accuracy	67.9	(98T)
Greens in Regulation	64.7	(117T)
Putting	1.797	(92T)
All-Around	677	(58T)
Sand Saves	62.6	(7)
Total Driving	199	(111T)
Eagles	8	(25T)
Birdies	284	(76T)

MISCELLANEOUS STATISTICS

Scoring Avg. (before cut)	71.79	(103T)
Scoring Avg. (3rd round)	71.29	(92T)
Scoring Avg. (4th round)	70.00	(9T)
Birdie Conversion	27.7	(89T)
Par Breakers	18.4	(85T)

1993 Low Round: 63: Doral-Ryder Open/4
Career Low Round: 59: 1991 Las Vegas Invitational/3
Career Largest Paycheck: **$216,000**/1987 Nabisco Championships of Golf/2

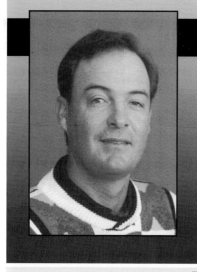

RONNIE BLACK

EXEMPT STATUS: 125th on 1993 money list

FULL NAME: Ronald Jay Black

HEIGHT: 6' 2"   **WEIGHT:** 180

BIRTHDATE: May 26.,1958

BIRTHPLACE: Hobbs, NM

RESIDENCE: Scottsdale, AZ

FAMILY: Wife, Sandra; Justin (12/14/86), Alex (5/11/88)

COLLEGE: Lamar University

SPECIAL INTERESTS: Hunting, basketball, movies

TURNED PROFESSIONAL: 1981

Q SCHOOL: 1981, 1982, 1990

PLAYER PROFILE

CAREER EARNINGS: $1,423,976   **PLAYOFF RECORD:** 1-1

TOUR VICTORIES: **1983** Southern Open. **1984** Anheuser-Busch Classic.
(TOTAL: 2)

MONEY & POSITION:

1982--$ 6,329-- 91	1986-- $166,761-- 56	1990--$ 34,001--190
1983--$ 87,524-- 63	1987-- $144,158-- 77	1991--$ 135,865--113
1984--$172,636-- 35	1988-- $100,603--112	1992--$ 129,386--111
1985--$ 61,684--109	1989-- $264,988-- 51	1993--$ 120,041--125

BEST 1993 FINISH: T12--Greater Milwaukee Open

1993 SUMMARY: Tournaments entered--28; in money--17; top ten finishes--0.

1994 PGA TOUR CHARITY TEAM COMPETITION: Northern Telecom Open

1993 SEASON: Secured his playing privileges for 1994 by finishing tied for 34th at the Las Vegas Invitational... He fired a 5-under-par 67 on the final day and earned $6,626 to finish 125th on the money list... During the year, earned four finishes in the top-25, including a tie for 12th at the Greater Milwaukee Open, his best finish of the year... Was two strokes behind, after three rounds of competition at Tuckaway CC, before shooting a final round 71 and finishing five strokes out of the lead... Finished 68-67 to wind up tied for 19th at the Federal Express St. Jude Classic.

CAREER HIGHLIGHTS: Won the 1983 Southern Open in a four- hole playoff over Scotsman Sam Torrance, who was warming up for the Ryder Cup matches... Black birdied the fourth extra hole... Trailed by seven strokes going into the last day, but fired an 8-under-par 63 to edge Willie Wood and win the Anheuser-Busch Classic in 1984...Lost to Wayne Grady in a playoff at the 1989 Manufacturers Hanover Westchester Classic... Grady made birdie on the first extra hole to win at Westchester CC... Also finished runner up to Bill Britton that same year in the rain-shortened Centel Classic... Went on to enjoy his most lucrative year in 1989... Winner of the 1976 and 1977 New Mexico State High School Championship and the 1981 Southland Collegiate Conference Championship.

PERSONAL: Was nine years old when he first picked up a golf club, however, it was not until he went off to school at Lamar University that he saw a golf course that had bunkers... Grew up in an athletic household, as his father was the local high school basketball coach and his brother was a PGA professional.

1993 PGA TOUR STATISTICS

Scoring Average	71.26	(97)
Driving Distance	263.5	(61)
Driving Accuracy	64.7	(151T)
Greens in Regulation	65.4	(92T)
Putting	1.800	(100T)
All-Around	863	(107)
Sand Saves	50.6	(111)
Total Driving	212	(134T)
Eagles	6	(50T)
Birdies	291	(67T)

MISCELLANEOUS STATISTICS

Scoring Avg. (before cut)	71.29	(64)
Scoring Avg. (3rd round)	71.00	(73T)
Scoring Avg. (4th round)	72.12	(143)
Birdie Conversion	28.1	(74T)
Par Breakers	18.8	(75T)

1993 Low Round: 66: PLAYERS Championship/1
Career Low Round: 63: 1984 Anheuser-Busch Golf Classic/4
Career Largest Paycheck: $108,000/1989 Manufacturers Hanover Westchester Classic/2

PHIL BLACKMAR

EXEMPT STATUS: 83rd on 1993 money list

FULL NAME: Philip Arnold Blackmar

HEIGHT: 6' 7"   **WEIGHT:** 240

BIRTH DATE: September 22, 1957

BIRTHPLACE: San Diego, CA

RESIDENCE: Corpus Christi, TX; plays out of
Kings Crossing C.C.

FAMILY: Wife, Carol; Kristin Ashley (3/21/84);
Kelli Michelle (9/20/85); Philip James (5/9/88);
Mark Fredrik (4/28/92)

COLLEGE: University of Texas (1979, Finance)

SPECIAL INTERESTS: Fishing

TURNED PROFESSIONAL: 1980   **Q SCHOOL:** Fall 1984

PLAYER PROFILE

CAREER EARNINGS: $1,608,425   **PLAYOFF RECORD:** 2-0

TOUR VICTORIES: 1985 Canon Sammy Davis, Jr.-Greater Hartford Open. **1988** Provident Classic.
(TOTAL: 2)

MONEY & POSITION:

	1984--$ 3,374--209	1988--$108,403--105	1992--$242,783--63
	1985--$198,537-- 28	1989--$140,949--100	1993--$207,310--83
	1986--$191,228-- 43	1990--$200,796-- 78	
	1987--$ 99,580-- 97	1991--$218,838-- 77	

BEST 1993 FINISHES: 3--The International; T8--Canadian Open

1993 SUMMARY: Tournaments entered--30; in money--17; top ten finishes--2.

1994 PGA TOUR CHARITY TEAM COMPETITION: Freeport-McMoRan Classic

1993 SEASON: Marked the fourth consecutive year that he surpassed the $200,000 mark in earnings... His year was highlighted by his outstanding play at The International... Finished with a very respectable 33 points, alone in third place, four points out of second place... Collected 15 points during the second round to vault into contention...Trailed Mark O'Meara by one point at the halfway mark...Other top-10 came at the Canadian Open, where he finished tied for eighth...After an opening 69, hovered around the lead for the next three days.

CAREER HIGHLIGHTS: Collected two victories in his career... Defeated Dan Pohl and Jodie Mudd with a birdie on the first extra hole to win the 1985 Canon Sammy Davis, Jr.-Greater Hartford Open...Added his second victory, when he defeated Payne Stewart in a playoff at the Provident Classic in 1988...Rolled in a long birdie putt on the first extra hole for the victory... Was the Rookie of the Year in 1985...Finished as the runner-up in the 1984 PGA TOUR Qualifying Tournament one stroke behind Paul Azinger...Second at the 1985 National Long Drive championship...Winner of the 1983 Missouri State Open... All-Southwest Conference for three years.

PERSONAL: Father won the National Left-Handers title in 1965 and introduced Phil to the game at a young age...Graduated with a degree in Finance from the University of Texas, and put that to work in a bank for several months before trying his hand at the mini-tours.

1993 PGA TOUR STATISTICS

Scoring Average	71.62	(126)
Driving Distance	271.4	(16)
Driving Accuracy	60.9	(178)
Greens in Regulation	63.5	(139T)
Putting	1.781	(52T)
All-Around	829	(97)
Sand Saves	50.0	(116T)
Total Driving	194	(105)
Eagles	8	(25T)
Birdies	287	(72T)

MISCELLANEOUS STATISTICS

Scoring Avg. (before cut)	72.33	(144)
Scoring Avg. (3rd round)	70.87	(64)
Scoring Avg. (4th round)	71.94	(129T)
Birdie Conversion	28.4	(63T)
Par Breakers	18.6	(79T)

1993 Low Round: 65: 2 times

Career Low Round: 63: 1992 GTE Byron Nelson Classic /1

Career Largest Paycheck: $118,800/1992 THE PLAYERS Championship/T2

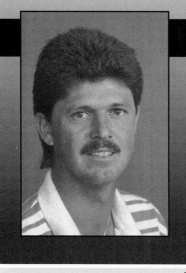

JAY DON BLAKE

EXEMPT STATUS: 86th on 1993 money list

FULL NAME: Jay Don Blake

HEIGHT: 6' 2"   **WEIGHT:** 180

BIRTH DATE: October 28, 1958

BIRTHPLACE: St. George, UT

RESIDENCE: St. George, UT

FAMILY: Jamie Dawn (10/1/79), Bridgette (4/11/83)

COLLEGE: Utah State

SPECIAL INTERESTS: Fishing, hunting, all sports

TURNED PROFESSIONAL: 1981

Q SCHOOL: Fall 1986

PLAYER PROFILE

CAREER EARNINGS: $1,634,087

TOUR VICTORIES: 1991 Shearson Lehman Brothers Open.
(TOTAL: 1)

MONEY & POSITION:

1987--$ 87,634--106	1990--$148,384--106	1992--$ 299,298--51
1988--$131,937-- 90	1991--$563,854-- 21	1993--$ 202,482--86
1989--$200,499-- 71		

BEST 1993 FINISHES: T4--Buick Invitational of California; T4--Buick Open; T6--Nissan Los Angeles Open

1993 SUMMARY: Tournaments entered--26; in money--15, top ten finishes--3.

1994 PGA TOUR CHARITY TEAM COMPETITION: The International

1993 SEASON: Must have been wanting a new car after his performances in three of the four Buick-sponsored events... Finished tied for fourth at the Buick Invitational of California, and also at the Buick Open... Added a T16 at the Buick Southern Open, and didn't play the Buick Classic... Followed the Buick Invitational up with his other top-10 finish, a tie for sixth at the Nissan Los Angeles Open... After missing the cut in his first four starts, rebounded with consecutive top-10s in San Diego and L.A... Led the first round at Riviera, before finishing four strokes behind Tom Kite.

CAREER HIGHLIGHTS: Enjoyed an outstanding 1991 campaign, collecting his first victory at the Shearson Lehman Brothers Open... Closed with consecutive 5-under-par 67s, to edge Bill Sander by two at Torrey Pines... Had five other top-10s during the 1991 campaign, for his most lucrative year to date...Won the PGA TOUR Putting Statistical title in 1991, averaging 1.733 putts per green in regulation...Also finished the 1992 season in the top-10 as well... Winner of the 1980 NCAA Championship as a junior, and was the runnerup a year later while at Utah State... Was named the College Player-of-the-Year in 1981... Won the 1988 Utah State Open.

PERSONAL: Despite little formal instruction, knew by the age of 12, that he wanted to be a professional golfer.

1993 PGA TOUR STATISTICS

Scoring Average	71.24	(93T)
Driving Distance	257.8	(111T)
Driving Accuracy	66.9	(121T)
Greens in Regulation	67.0	(60T)
Putting	1.787	(61T)
All-Around	964	(129)
Sand Saves	46.2	(159T)
Total Driving	232	(154T)
Eagles	3	(116T)
Birdies	275	(89T)

MISCELLANEOUS STATISTICS

Scoring Avg. (before cut)	71.80	(105)
Scoring Avg. (3rd round)	69.93	(14)
Scoring Avg. (4th round)	71.07	(50)
Birdie Conversion	29.1	(41T)
Par Breakers	19.7	(43T)

1993 Low Round: 66: 3 times

Career Low Round: 64: 2 times, most recent 1992 Kemper Open/1

Career Largest Paycheck: $180,000/1991 Shearson Lehman Brothers Open/1

MICHAEL BRADLEY

EXEMPT STATUS: 121st on 1993 money list

FULL NAME: Michael John Bradley

HEIGHT: 6'   **WEIGHT:** 180

BIRTH DATE: July 16, 1966

BIRTHPLACE: Largo, FL

RESIDENCE: Valrico, FL

FAMILY: Wife, Jennifer

COLLEGE: Oklahoma State

SPECIAL INTERESTS: Sports

TURNED PROFESSIONAL: 1988

Q SCHOOL: 1992

PLAYER PROFILE

CAREER EARNINGS: $120,160

BEST-EVER FINISH: T3--1993 Kemper Open

MONEY & POSITION: 1993--$120,160--121

BEST 1993 FINISH: T3--Kemper Open

1993 SUMMARY: Tournaments entered--26; in money--14; top ten finishes--1.

1994 PGA TOUR CHARITY TEAM COMPETITION: BellSouth Classic

1993 SEASON: Made the most of his opportunity to play the PGA TOUR, holding onto his exempt status in his first year on TOUR... Finished the year with one finish in the top-10 and three in the top-25... Made 14 cuts out of the 26 events that he started... Plays well on Tournament Players Club courses... Best-ever finish came at the TPC at Avenel, home of the Kemper Open... He finished tied for third there... Finished up the tournament with rounds of 69 and 68... That 5-under-par total was enough to move him into a tie with Scott Hoch for third place... Left him just two strokes behind the winner, Grant Waite... Earned $75,400 for his efforts... That check was easily the largest of his career... His next best finish was a tie for 18th at the Freeport McMoRan Classic... His 3-over-par 291 total was only 10 strokes behind winner Mike Standly... Earned another $14,500 for his performance at English Turn... Opened with a sterling 7-under-par 64 at the TPC at Southwind, during the first round of the Federal Express St. Jude Classic... He led by a stroke over defending champion Jay Haas and Davis Love III.

CAREER HIGHLIGHTS: Winner of two Canadian PGA Tour events... Was a member of the Australian Tour for the past several years... Finished 52nd in the Australian Tour Order of Merit in 1992... Was a two-time All-American selection while attending Oklahoma State in 1987 and 1988.

PERSONAL: Interested in all sports... Also has an interest in agronomy.

1993 PGA TOUR STATISTICS

Scoring Average	71.67	(131)
Driving Distance	268.8	(29)
Driving Accuracy	55.2	(188)
Greens in Regulation	63.4	(142T)
Putting	1.780	(47T)
All-Around	843	(101T)
Sand Saves	61.7	(10T)
Total Driving	217	(139T)
Eagles	6	(50T)
Birdies	263	(107T)

MISCELLANEOUS STATISTICS

Scoring Avg. (before cut)	71.96	(117T)
Scoring Avg. (3rd round)	72.42	(166)
Scoring Avg. (4th round)	72.14	(145)
Birdie Conversion	29.2	(39T)
Par Breakers	18.9	(73T)

1993 Low Round: 64: FedEx St. Jude Classic/1
Career Low Round: 64: 1993 FedEx St. Jude Classic/1
Career Largest Paycheck: $74,500/FedEx St. Jude Classic/T3

MARK BROOKS

EXEMPT STATUS: 66th on 1993 money list

FULL NAME: Mark David Brooks

HEIGHT: 5' 9"　　　**WEIGHT:** 150

BIRTH DATE: March 25, 1961

BIRTHPLACE: Fort Worth, TX

RESIDENCE: Fort Worth, TX

FAMILY: Wife, Cynthia; Lyndsay (1/24/86), Hollie (9/21/89)

COLLEGE: University of Texas

SPECIAL INTERESTS: All sports, cooking

TURNED PROFESSIONAL: 1983

Q SCHOOL: Fall 1983, 1984, 1985, 1987

PLAYER PROFILE

CAREER EARNINGS: $2,410,031　　　**PLAYOFF RECORD:** 2-2

TOUR VICTORIES: **1988** Canon Sammy Davis, Jr-Greater Hartford Open. **1991** Kmart Greater
(TOTAL: 3)　　Greensboro Open, Greater Milwaukee Open

MONEY & POSITION:	1984--$ 40,438--122	1988--$280,636-- 36	1991--$667,263--11
	1985--$ 32,094--141	1989--$112,834--115	1992--$629,754--21
	1986--$ 47,264--140	1990--$307,948-- 45	1993--$249,696--66
	1987--$ 42,100--165		

BEST 1993 FINISHES: T2--Buick Southern Open; T10--Freeport-McMoRan Classic; T10--Federal Express St. Jude Classic

1993 SUMMARY: Tournaments entered--31; in money--19; top ten finishes--3.

1994 PGA TOUR CHARITY TEAM COMPETITION: Shell Houston Open

1993 SEASON: Something of an off year for Brooks as he failed to surpass the $300,000 mark in earnings for the first time since 1989... Nevertheless collected three top-10 finishes including a playoff loss to John Inman at the Buick Southern Open... He was at 2-under-par for the tournament going into Sunday, when he tied the course record with a blistering 8-under-par 64 to enter the five-way playoff... Had two other finishes in the top-10, both ties for 10th, at the Freeport McMoRan Classic and the Federal Express St. Jude Classic.

CAREER HIGHLIGHTS: 1992 was an excellent season for Brooks, as he recorded 11 finishes in the top-10... Finished tied for third at the Honda Classic, the Nestle Invitational, and the Greater Milwaukee Open... Enjoyed his best year on TOUR in 1991, when he surpassed the $600,000 mark in earnings for the first time...Collected two victories that year...Fired an 8-under-par 64 on the final day to catch Gene Sauers at the Kmart Greater Greensboro Open, and defeat him in a playoff with a par on the third extra hole...Later won the Greater Milwaukee Open by a stroke over Robert Gamez...Opened with a 9-under-par 63...Defeated Joey Sindelar and Dave Barr in a playoff at the 1988 Greater Hartford Open for his first PGA TOUR victory... He made a 10-foot birdie putt on the second extra hole for the win... Attended the Qualifying Tournament four times before finally making it for good in 1987...Went to the University of Texas and was a two-time All-American selection.

PERSONAL: His grandfather introduced him to the game at the age of eight.

1993 PGA TOUR STATISTICS

Scoring Average	70.58	(35)
Driving Distance	257.2	(115)
Driving Accuracy	73.0	(46T)
Greens in Regulation	67.0	(60T)
Putting	1.815	(135T)
All-Around	690	(61)
Sand Saves	51.0	(104T)
Total Driving	161	(53T)
Eagles	4	(89T)
Birdies	305	(53T)

MISCELLANEOUS STATISTICS

Scoring Avg. (before cut)	71.25	(62)
Scoring Avg. (3rd round)	70.53	(42)
Scoring Avg. (4th round)	71.22	(62T)
Birdie Conversion	26.6	(122T)
Par Breakers	18.1	(109T)

1993 Low Round: 64: 2 times	
Career Low Round: 61: 1990 Shearson Lehman Hutton Open/2	
Career Largest Paycheck: $225,000/1991 Kmart Greater Greensboro Open/1	

BILLY RAY BROWN

EXEMPT STATUS: 1992 tournament winner.

FULL NAME: Billy Ray Brown

HEIGHT: 6' 3"   **WEIGHT:** 205

BIRTH DATE: April 5, 1963

BIRTHPLACE: Houston, TX

RESIDENCE: Missouri City, TX

FAMILY: Wife, Cindy

COLLEGE: University of Houston

SPECIAL INTERESTS: Hunting, fishing

TURNED PROFESSIONAL: 1986

Q SCHOOL: Fall 1987

PLAYER PROFILE

CAREER EARNINGS: $1,565,916   **PLAYOFF RECORD:** 2-0

TOUR VICTORIES: 1991 Canon Greater Hartford Open. **1992** GTE Byron Nelson Classic. (TOTAL: 2)

MONEY & POSITION:
1988--$ 83,590--125	1990--$312,466--44	1992--$485,151--29
1989--$162,964-- 85	1991--$348,082--46	1993--$173,662--97

BEST 1993 FINISH: 2--AT&T Pebble Beach National Pro-Am

1993 SUMMARY: Tournaments entered--15; in money--7; top ten finishes--1.

1994 PGA TOUR CHARITY TEAM COMPETITION: Nissan Los Angeles Open

1993 SEASON: A wrist injury at the end of 1992 season hampered his performance in 1993... Was forced to take 16 weeks off in the middle of the year in order to rehabilitate his wrist... Nevertheless finished as the runner-up at the AT&T Pebble Beach National Pro-Am... Closed with an even-par 72 on Sunday to finish three strokes behind the winner Brett Ogle... Started Sunday's round two strokes back after firing a 68 and a 69 in the middle rounds... His next best finish was a tie for 26th at the Shell Houston Open.

CAREER HIGHLIGHTS: Has two victories in his career... Won the rain-shortened GTE Byron Nelson Classic in May of 1992... Rolled in a birdie putt on the first extra hole to defeat Bruce Lietzke, Ray Floyd, and Ben Crenshaw... Closed with rounds of 6-under-par 64 and 66 on the TPC at Las Colinas course... Other TOUR victory also came in a playoff...Won the 1991 Canon Greater Hartford Open in sudden death over Rick Fehr and Corey Pavin...Also won that tournament with a birdie on the first extra hole...Rolled in a 25-foot curler in the playoff...Missed a 15-foot putt on the 72nd hole of the 1990 U.S. Open to miss the Hale Irwin, Mike Donald playoff by a stroke...Was tied for the lead after three rounds at Medinah...Was a four-time All-American selection while at the University of Houston...Winner of the NCAA Championship in 1982 as a freshman...Brown, along with teammate Steve Elkington, led the Cougars to three NCAA team championships.

PERSONAL: Comes from an athletic background, his father played tackle for the Oakland Raiders of the NFL...Brother Chuck played center for the St. Louis Cardinals.

1993 PGA TOUR STATISTICS

Scoring Average	73.29
Driving Distance	254.1
Driving Accuracy	56.6
Greens in Regulation	58.8
Putting	1.781
All-Around	N/A
Sand Saves	47.0
Total Driving	N/A
Eagles	2
Birdies	131

MISCELLANEOUS STATISTICS

Scoring Avg. (before cut)	73.16
Scoring Avg. (3rd round)	73.17
Scoring Avg. (4th round)	72.57
Birdie Conversion	28.1
Par Breakers	16.8

1993 Low Round: 65: Doral-Ryder Open/4

Career Low Round: 64: 4 times, most recent 1992 GTE Byron Nelson Classic/2

Career Largest Paycheck: $198,000/1992 GTE Byron Nelson Classic/1

BRAD BRYANT

EXEMPT STATUS: 74th on 1993 money list

FULL NAME: Bradley Dub Bryant

HEIGHT: 5' 10" **WEIGHT:** 170

BIRTH DATE: December 11, 1954

BIRTHPLACE: Amarillo, TX

RESIDENCE: Winter Garden, FL

FAMILY: Wife, Sue; William Jamieson (1/27/91), Jonathan David (4/26/93)

COLLEGE: University of New Mexico

SPECIAL INTERESTS: Bass fishing, hunting

TURNED PROFESSIONAL: 1976

Q SCHOOL: Fall 1978, 1987, 1988

PLAYER PROFILE

CAREER EARNINGS: $1,454,596   **PLAYOFF RECORD:** 0-1

BEST-EVER FINISHES: 2--1991 Buick Classic; T2--1982 Tournament Players Championship; T2--1982 Quad Cities Open;T2--1983 Byron Nelson Golf Classic. T2-1993 Buick Southern Open (lost playoff to John Inman)

MONEY & POSITION:

1978--$ 4,350--173	1984--$ 36,805--127	1989--$174,393-- 84
1979--$ 63,013-- 67	1985--$ 1,683--232	1990--$189,795-- 86
1980--$ 56,115-- 68	1986--$ 11,290--202	1991--$152,202-- 99
1981--$ 52,070-- 80	1987--$ 17,090--191	1992--$227,529-- 69
1982--$ 99,576-- 37	1988--$ 62,614--141	1993--$230,139-- 74
1983--$ 93,021-- 61		

BEST 1993 FINISHES: T2--Buick Southern Open; 3--Canadian Open; T6--New England Classic.

1993 SUMMARY: Tournaments entered--31; in money--20; top ten finishes--3.

1994 PGA TOUR CHARITY TEAM COMPETITION: Walt Disney World/Oldsmobile Classic

1993 SEASON: For the first time in his career, Bradley Dub Bryant was tied for the lead after 72 holes of a golf tournament...Buick Southern Open at Callaway Gardens Mountain View Course was the site of his first-ever playoff... Closed with a splendid 5-under-par 67 to finish tied with Bob Estes, Mark Brooks, John Inman, and Billy Andrade... Inman won the playoff with a birdie on the second extra hole... Marked the fifth time in his career that he finished in the runner-up position... Two weeks earlier wound up alone in third place at the Canadian Open... He held the lead going into the back-nine before a sizzling David Frost caught him... Most productive year on TOUR from an earnings standpoint.

CAREER HIGHLIGHTS: Former best-ever finish came at the 1991 Buick Classic at the Westchester CC... Bryant finished alone in second place, a mere stroke behind winner Billy Andrade...Has finished tied for second on three other occasions early in his career, including the 1982 Tournament Players Championship... Finished just behind Jerry Pate, and tied with Scott Simpson at inaugural tournament held at the TPC at Sawgrass... Was tied for the lead going into the last day at the '82 TPC.

PERSONAL: An extreme fishing enthusiast... Needs no excuse to wet a hook... Overcame shoulder surgery in 1985 and has been a solid performer since he fully recovered in 1988…Played hurt from 1983 through the operation... Started the game at the age of 10 and began to get serious about it at the age of 15.

1993 PGA TOUR STATISTICS

Scoring Average	71.12	(79)
Driving Distance	268.1	(34)
Driving Accuracy	65.0	(147T)
Greens in Regulation	66.3	(71)
Putting	1.786	(60)
All-Around	613	(47)
Sand Saves	52.1	(89)
Total Driving	181	(84T)
Eagles	7	(37T)
Birdies	353	(12)

MISCELLANEOUS STATISTICS

Scoring Avg. (before cut)	71.20	(54T)
Scoring Avg. (3rd round)	71.10	(84)
Scoring Avg. (4th round)	72.36	(157)
Birdie Conversion	29.4	(35T)
Par Breakers	19.9	(37T)

1993 Low Round: 65: New England Classic/2
Career Low Round: 64: 8 times, most recent 1992 GTE Byron Nelson Classic/1
Career Largest Paycheck: $108,000/1991 Buick Classic/2

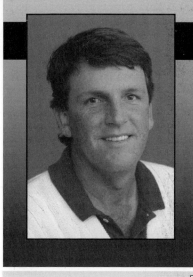

MARK CALCAVECCHIA

EXEMPT STATUS: 1992 tournament winner

FULL NAME: Mark John Calcavecchia

HEIGHT: 6'   **WEIGHT:** 200

BIRTH DATE: June 12, 1960   **BIRTHPLACE:** Laurel, NE

RESIDENCE: West Palm Beach, FL; plays out of Bear Lakes CC, West Palm Beach, FL

FAMILY: Wife, Sheryl; Brittney Jo (8/8/89)

COLLEGE: University of Florida

SPECIAL INTERESTS: Bowling, music

TURNED PROFESSIONAL: 1981

Q SCHOOL: Spring 1981; Fall 1982, 1983

PLAYER PROFILE

CAREER EARNINGS: $4,489,962   **PLAYOFF RECORD:** 0-3

TOUR VICTORIES: 1986 Southwest Golf Classic. **1987** Honda Classic. **1988** Bank of Boston Classic.
(TOTAL: 6)   **1989** Phoenix Open, Nissan Los Angeles Open. **1992** Phoenix Open.

MONEY & POSITION:

1981--$ 404--253	1986--$155,012-- 58	1990--$834,281-- 7
1982--$25,064--134	1987--$522,423-- 10	1991--$323,621--50
1983--$16,313--161	1988--$751,912-- 6	1992--$377,234--39
1984--$29,660--140	1989--$807,741-- 5	1993--$630,366--21
1985--$15,957--162		

BEST 1993 FINISHES: 2--The International; T2--BellSouth Classic; T2--Greater Milwaukee Open; T7--THE TOUR Championship; T8--GTE Byron Nelson Classic; T10--Infiniti Tournament of Champions

1993 SUMMARY: Tournaments entered--30; in money--20; top ten finishes--6.

1994 PGA TOUR CHARITY TEAM COMPETITION: Greater Milwaukee Open

NATIONAL TEAMS: Ryder Cup (3), 1987, 1989, 1991; Kirin Cup 1987; Asahi Glass Four Tours World Championship of Golf (2), 1989, 1990; Dunhill Cup (2), 1989, 1990.

1993 SEASON: Collected three second-place finishes in 1993... First one came at the BellSouth Classic, where he opened with three consecutive 5-under-par 67s, before closing with a 72, and finishing two strokes behind Nolan Henke... Later in the year, had runner-up finishes at The International and the Greater Milwaukee Open... At The International he finished eight points behind Phil Mickelson, after closing with 18 points on Sunday... At Milwaukee, a closing 5-under-par 67 moved him into a playoff with Billy Mayfair and Ted Schulz, subsequently won by Mayfair.

CAREER HIGHLIGHTS: Enjoyed his finest year on the PGA TOUR in 1989, when he won twice on the West Coast swing...Won the Phoenix Open by seven strokes and outdueled Sandy Lyle down the stretch to take the Nissan Los Angeles Open...Perhaps his finest victory was at the 1989 British Open at Troon, where he defeated Wayne Grady and Greg Norman in the Royal and Ancient's multi-hole playoff system... Birdied the fourth and final hole to finish with a flourish... He hit a 5-iron to seven feet from 190 yards on that hole... A member of several national teams, including the Ryder Cup team in 1987, 1989, and 1991... Was a member of the Dunhill Cup team in 1989 and 1990... Winner of the Florida State Junior Championship and the Orange Bowl Championship in 1976... Named first team All-SEC in 1979... Winner of the 1988 Australian Open.

PERSONAL: After his family moved from Nebraska to Florida when he was 13, he was ecstatic because he could play golf every day... Qualified for the TOUR, after just barely turning 21.

1993 PGA TOUR STATISTICS

Scoring Average	70.66	(41)
Driving Distance	265.2	(47T)
Driving Accuracy	62.7	(167T)
Greens in Regulation	65.3	(97T)
Putting	1.780	(47T)
All-Around	610	(45)
Sand Saves	56.0	(42)
Total Driving	214	(136T)
Eagles	10	(9T)
Birdies	333	(24)

MISCELLANEOUS STATISTICS

Scoring Avg. (before cut)	71.19	(52T)
Scoring Avg. (3rd round)	71.61	(117T)
Scoring Avg. (4th round)	70.84	(36T)
Birdie Conversion	29.6	(29T)
Par Breakers	19.9	(37T)

1993 Low Round: 64: 2 times

Career Low Round: 63: 5 times, most recent '92 NEC World Series of Golf/3

Career Largest Paycheck: $180,000 /1989 Nissan Los Angeles Open/1 1991 Phoenix Open/1

MARK CARNEVALE

EXEMPT STATUS: 1992 tournament winner

FULL NAME: Mark Kevin Carnevale

HEIGHT: 6'2"   **WEIGHT:** 238

BIRTH DATE: May 21, 1960

BIRTHPLACE: Annapolis, MD

RESIDENCE: Williamsburg, VA

FAMILY: Single

COLLEGE: James Madison University

SPECIAL INTERESTS: Jazz, travel, sailing, skiing

TURNED PROFESSIONAL: 1983

Q SCHOOL: 1991

PLAYER PROFILE

CAREER EARNINGS: $320,968

TOUR VICTORIES: 1992 Chattanooga Classic.
(TOTAL: 1)

MONEY & POSITION: 1992--$220,921--70   1993--$100,046--145

BEST 1993 FINISH: T13--Buick Southern Open

1993 SUMMARY: Tournaments entered--32; in money--15; top ten finishes--0.

1994 PGA TOUR CHARITY TEAM COMPETITION: Anheuser-Busch Golf Classic

1993 SEASON: A productive follow-up to his outstanding rookie season on TOUR... Carnevale played steady if unspectacular golf... Finished in the top-25 three times, including a tie for 13th at the Buick Southern Open... Largest check of the year came at the Kemper Open, where he finished with a 2-under-par 282 total, and earned $24,050 for the second largest payday of his career... Wound up tied for 14th on the tough TPC at Avenel track... Other high finish was a tie for 17th at the AT&T Pebble Beach National Pro-Am.

CAREER HIGHLIGHTS: Was selected as the **PGA TOUR Rookie of the Year** by his peers for his outstanding season of 1992... Had only one top-10 finish, but made it count, when he won the Chattanooga Classic by two strokes over Ed Dougherty and Dan Forsman... He closed with a final round 8-under-par 64 to win... Was five strokes back after three rounds, which tied him with David Edwards and Lanny Wadkins for best come from behind for victory in 1992...Winner of the 1990 Utah Open and the 1984 Virginia Open...Earned his PGA TOUR card by finishing 19th at the 1991 Qualifying Tournament.

PERSONAL: Quit the game for several months in the late 1980s to go to work for a brokerage firm... Obviously made the correct decision to come back at the 1991 Qualifying Tournament...Father coached the University of North Carolina to its first national championship title game in basketball in 1945.

1993 PGA TOUR STATISTICS

Scoring Average	72.28	(172)
Driving Distance	257.1	(116T)
Driving Accuracy	74.6	(29)
Greens in Regulation	65.3	(97T)
Putting	1.863	(184T)
All-Around	907	(120T)
Sand Saves	52.5	(83T)
Total Driving	145	(36)
Eagles	5	(67T)
Birdies	249	(123T)

MISCELLANEOUS STATISTICS

Scoring Avg. (before cut)	72.19	(136)
Scoring Avg. (3rd round)	73.38	(184)
Scoring Avg. (4th round)	72.00	(133T)
Birdie Conversion	22.4	(187)
Par Breakers	14.9	(180T)

1993 Low Round: 66: 3 times
Career Low Round: 64: 1992 Chattanooga
Career Largest   Classic/4
Paycheck: $144,000/1992 Chattanooga Classic/1

BRANDEL CHAMBLEE

EXEMPT STATUS: 119th on 1993 money list

FULL NAME: Brandel Eugene Chamblee

HEIGHT: 5' 10"   **WEIGHT:** 155

BIRTH DATE: July 2, 1993

BIRTHPLACE: St. Louis, MO

RESIDENCE: Scottsdale, AZ

FAMILY: Wife, Karen

COLLEGE: University of Texas

SPECIAL INTERESTS: Tennis, horses

TURNED PROFESSIONAL: 1985

Q SCHOOL: 1987, 1990, 1991, 1992

PLAYER PROFILE

CAREER EARNINGS: $322,620

BEST-EVER FINISH: T5--1991 Deposit Guaranty Golf Classic

MONEY & POSITION: 1988--$33,618--166   1992--$97,921--133   1993--$126,940--119
1991--$64,141--161

BEST 1993 FINISHES: T9--AT&T Pebble Beach National Pro-Am; T10--Canadian Open

1993 SUMMARY: Tournaments entered--29; in money--13; top ten finishes--2.

1994 PGA TOUR CHARITY TEAM COMPETITION: Nissan Los Angeles Open

1993 SEASON: Proved that diligence does pay off, as he retained his playing privileges for the first time in four tries... Had his best season ever from an earnings standpoint... His best finish of the year was at the AT&T Pebble Beach National Pro-Am where he finished in a tie for ninth... His 2-under-par 70 on Sunday was the third best score shot that day... The $27,969 payday was his largest of the year...Second top-10 came at the Canadian Open, where a 1-under-par 71 on Sunday gave him a 1-under 287 total and a tie for 10th... Finish was worth another $22,167... A second round 6-under-par 64 propelled him to a $16,500 payday... Secured his card in the next to last tournament, the H-E-B. Texas Open, where he finished in a tie for 27th and earned $7,100.

CAREER HIGHLIGHTS: Was a charter member of the Ben Hogan Tour in 1990... During that inaugural campaign, he managed to collect one victory and finished seventh on the money list with $73,251 in official earnings... His victory came at the tough Woodlands CC in Falmouth, ME... At the end of 54 holes, he was the only golfer under par, as he finished with a 1-under-par 215 total.Winner in the 1982 Bluebonnet Bowl Tournament, and the 1983 Rice Planters Championship... Also won the 1983 Southwest Conference Championship and the 1984 Morris Williams Tournament... Won the 1986 TPA Sun City Classic... Was selected as a First Team All-American in 1983...Was second team in 1982 and 1984... Best ever career finish on TOUR was a tie for fifth at the 1991 Deposit Guaranty Golf Classic.

1993 PGA TOUR STATISTICS

Scoring Average	71.09	(74T)
Driving Distance	256.6	(122)
Driving Accuracy	70.1	(76)
Greens in Regulation	66.8	(66)
Putting	1.799	(97T)
All-Around	896	(117)
Sand Saves	46.2	(159T)
Total Driving	198	(110)
Eagles	4	(89T)
Birdies	266	(103)

MISCELLANEOUS STATISTICS

Scoring Avg. (before cut)	71.96	(117T)
Scoring Avg. (3rd round)	70.54	(43)
Scoring Avg. (4th round)	70.31	(13T)
Birdie Conversion	26.8	(116T)
Par Breakers	18.2	(98T)

1993 Low Round: 64: Hardee's Golf Classic/2
Career Low Round: 64: 2 times most recent '93
Career Largest Hardee's Golf Classic/2
Paycheck: $27,969/AT&T Pebble Beach/T9

BRIAN CLAAR

EXEMPT STATUS: 85th on 1993 money list

FULL NAME: Brian James Claar

HEIGHT: 5' 8"   **WEIGHT:** 145

BIRTH DATE: July 29, 1959

BIRTHPLACE: Santa Monica, CA

RESIDENCE: Palm Harbor, FL; plays out of East Lake Woodlands, FL

FAMILY: Wife, Tracy; Zackary (7/15/90)

COLLEGE: University of Tampa (1981)

SPECIAL INTERESTS: Fishing, Tampa Bay Bucs

TURNED PROFESSIONAL: 1981

JOINED TOUR: Fall 1985, 1989.

PLAYER PROFILE

CAREER EARNINGS: $1,056,019

BEST-EVER FINISH: T2--1991 AT&T Pebble Beach National Pro-Am

MONEY & POSITION:
1986--$117,355-- 7	1989--$ 88,010--133	1992--$192,255--78
1987--$ 43,111--162	1990--$161,356-- 98	1993--$202,624--85
1988--$ 30,276--172	1991--$251,309-- 67	

BEST 1993 FINISH: T7--BellSouth Classic

1993 SUMMARY: Tournaments entered--32; in money--24; top ten finishes--1

1994 PGA TOUR CHARITY TEAM COMPETITION: Western Open

1993 SEASON: Very steady season for the 1986 Rookie of the Year... Had missed four cuts in 13 starts coming into the BellSouth Classic... Wound up tied for seventh there when he closed with a final round 1-under-par 71... He finished five strokes behind Nolan Henke... It was his best finish since a tie for eighth at the 1992 Bob Hope Chrysler Classic... Had four other finishes in the top-25 including a tie for 11th at the International, where he finished with 22 points.

CAREER HIGHLIGHTS: After collecting top rookie honors in 1986, his level of play dropped over the next two years, but a tie for fifth at the 1989 United States Open, showed that he was back...Finished with rounds of 68 and 69 at Oak Hill, the two lowest of the weekend...Went on to earn his playing privileges again at the 1989 Qualifying Tournament, and has been a regular on TOUR since...Enjoyed his best-ever finish at the 1991 AT&T Pebble Beach National Pro-Am, where he finished tied for second with Corey Pavin, four strokes behind Paul Azinger... Led the Asian Tour Order of Merit in 1989, when he won the Hong Kong and Thailand Opens.

PERSONAL: Comes from a non-golfing family, but found some balls at home, and took them out and was hitting them with a baseball bat...Neighbor saw this and introduced him to the game... Knew that he wanted to play the TOUR by his junior year in college.

1993 PGA TOUR STATISTICS

Scoring Average	71.05	(71T)
Driving Distance	255.1	(137T)
Driving Accuracy	73.6	(40)
Greens in Regulation	67.0	(60T)
Putting	1.777	(39T)
All-Around	638	(52)
Sand Saves	55.9	(43)
Total Driving	177	(75T)
Eagles	1	(164T)
Birdies	364	(9)

MISCELLANEOUS STATISTICS

Scoring Avg. (before cut)	71.05	(43)
Scoring Avg. (3rd round)	71.43	(104)
Scoring Avg. (4th round)	71.35	(80T)
Birdie Conversion	27.9	(78T)
Par Breakers	18.8	(75T)

1993 Low Round: 65: H-E-B Texas Open/4
Career Low Round: 62: 1991 Anheuser-Busch Golf Classic/3
Career Largest Paycheck: $96,800/1991 AT&T Pebble Beach National Pro-Am/T2

KEITH CLEARWATER

EXEMPT STATUS: 44th on 1993 money list

FULL NAME: Keith Allen Clearwater

HEIGHT: 6' **WEIGHT:** 180

BIRTH DATE: September 1, 1959

BIRTHPLACE: Long Beach, CA

RESIDENCE: Orem, Utah

FAMILY: Wife, Sue; Jennifer (3/9/85); Melissa (6/30/88)

COLLEGE: Brigham Young University

SPECIAL INTERESTS: Family and church activities, home building, all sports, water sports

TURNED PROFESSIONAL: 1982

Q SCHOOL: Fall 1986

PLAYER PROFILE

CAREER EARNINGS: $1,818,238

TOUR VICTORIES: 1987 Colonial National Invitation, Centel Classic. (TOTAL: 2)

MONEY & POSITION:

1987--$320,007-- 31	1990--$130,103--118	1992--$609,273--22
1988--$ 82,876--127	1991--$239,727-- 69	1993--$348,763--44
1989--$ 87,490--136		

BEST 1993 FINISHES: T4--United Airlines Hawaiian Open; T4--Bob Hope Chrysler Classic; T7--Phoenix Open; T7--Buick Invitational of California; T9--Southwestern Bell Colonial; T10--Walt Disney World/Oldsmobile Classic

1993 SUMMARY: Tournaments entered--31; in money--23; top ten finishes--6.

1994 PGA TOUR CHARITY TEAM COMPETITION: BellSouth Classic

1993 SEASON: Had his second most productive year from an earnings standpoint in 1993, thanks in large part to six finishes in the top-10...Collected two ties for fourth place by the fifth week of the season... Thanks to middle rounds of 66 and 68, he finished T4 at the United Airlines Hawaiian Open... Several weeks later closed with an 8-under-par 64 at the Bob Hope Chrysler Classic to once again finish tied for fourth... Played his best golf of the year at the storied Colonial Country Club, home of the Southwestern Bell Colonial and a course that he won on in 1987... Fired a course-record 9-under-par 61 in the second round to vault to within three strokes of the lead... He wound up tied for ninth after consecutive 69s on the weekend.

CAREER HIGHLIGHTS: Has earned two victories in his PGA TOUR career, both in his rookie season of 1987...Fired back-to-back 6-under-par 64s on the final day of Colonial to equal the tournament record...Finished wth a 14-under 266 total after playing 36 holes on the final day...Gained more national attention in 1987 by equalling U.S. Open record with 6-under-par 64 in the the third round at The Olympic Club...Centel Classic victory closed out the official season... 1987 MasterCard Rookie of the Year...Winner of the 1982 North and South Amateur...member of the 1981 National Championship team at Brigham Young...All-American selection in 1981...Winner of the 1985 Alaska State Open.

PERSONAL: Due to intensive weightlifting is regarded as one of the strongest players on the PGA TOUR... Started playing golf at the age of 12...College teammate of Rick Fehr, Richard Zokol, and Bobby Clampett.

1993 PGA TOUR STATISTICS

Scoring Average	70.53	(33)
Driving Distance	257.9	(108T)
Driving Accuracy	70.2	(73T)
Greens in Regulation	67.5	(51T)
Putting	1.788	(65T)
All-Around	440	(15)
Sand Saves	59.9	(16)
Total Driving	181	(84T)
Eagles	11	(6T)
Birdies	384	(4)

MISCELLANEOUS STATISTICS

Scoring Avg. (before cut)	70.38	(14)
Scoring Avg. (3rd round)	71.40	(103)
Scoring Avg. (4th round)	71.17	(57)
Birdie Conversion	30.4	(17)
Par Breakers	21.1	(11)

1993 Low Round: **61**: Southwestern Bell Colonial/2
Career Low Round: **61**: 1993 Southwestern Bell Colonial/2
Career Largest Paycheck: **$123,200**/1992 Doral Ryder Open/T2

LENNIE CLEMENTS

EXEMPT STATUS: 113th on 1993 money list

FULL NAME: Leonard Clyde Clements

HEIGHT: 5' 8"   **WEIGHT:** 160

BIRTH DATE: January 20, 1957

BIRTHPLACE: Cherry Point, NC

RESIDENCE: San Diego, CA

FAMILY: Wife, Jan; Elizabeth (11/19/83);
Christopher (7/16/86)

COLLEGE: San Diego State University

SPECIAL INTERESTS: Family activities, all sports

TURNED PROFESSIONAL: 1980

JOINED TOUR: 1981   **Q SCHOOL:** 1992

PLAYER PROFILE

CAREER EARNINGS: $880,045

BEST-EVER FINISH: T3--1983 Miller High Life Quad Cities Open

MONEY & POSITION:
1981--$ 7,766-- 178	1986--$112,642-- 79	1991--$ 62,827--163
1982--$44,796-- 97	1987--$124,989-- 83	1992--$ 30,121--198
1983--$44,455-- 110	1988--$ 86,332--120	1993--$141,526--113
1984--$25,712-- 146	1989--$ 69,399--147	
1985--$49,383-- 120	1990--$ 80,095--146	

BEST 1993 FINISHES: T8--Northern Telecom Open; T8--Anheuser-Busch Golf Classic

1993 SUMMARY: Tournaments entered--26; in money--16; top ten finishes--2.

1994 PGA TOUR CHARITY TEAM COMPETITION: Walt Disney World/Oldsmobile Classic

1993 SEASON: Returned to playing the game the way that he did when he played in the mid-1980s...During that span, he retained his playing privileges for four consecutive years from 1985 through 1988... His best finish of 1993 came in his very first tournament... He finished up with two consecutive 2-under-par 70s on the Tucson National GC course to wind up in a tie for eighth place at the Northern Telecom Open...That earned him his largest paycheck of the year, a $29,700 pay day...Other top-10 finish came at the Anheuser-Busch Golf Classic... Shot a smooth 5-under-par 66 on the Kingsmill GC course, and was three strokes out after two rounds... Closed with back to back 69s and also finished tied for eighth...Easily his best year from an earnings standpoint.

CAREER HIGHLIGHTS: His best-ever finish came in 1983 at the Miller High Life Quad Cities Open... He finished tied for third at Oakwood CC in Moline, IL... Clements fired all four rounds in the 60s, including a solid 5-under-par 65 during the third round to vault into contention... He added a 67 on Sunday to finish one stroke out of a Danny Edwards/Morris Hatalsky playoff... Winner of the 1975 California State High School Championship, and was the medalist in the 1979 California State Amateur... Also won the Southwestern Amateur that same year... Won five times while in college at San Diego State, and was a two-time All-America selection...Winner of the 1982 Timex Open in France and the 1983 Sahara Nevada Open...Winner of the 1988 Spalding Invitational on the Monterey Peninsula.

PERSONAL: Driving, short irons and putting are the strong points to his game... Very big family man... Enjoys all sports.

1993 PGA TOUR STATISTICS

Scoring Average	70.73 (45)
Driving Distance	254.4 (146)
Driving Accuracy	73.9 (32T)
Greens in Regulation	68.8 (27)
Putting	1.781 (52T)
All-Around	579 (39)
Sand Saves	58.1 (26)
Total Driving	178 (77)
Eagles	4 (89T)
Birdies	279 (85T)

MISCELLANEOUS STATISTICS

Scoring Avg. (before cut)	71.02 (41)
Scoring Avg. (3rd round)	70.21 (24)
Scoring Avg. (4th round)	71.06 (48T)
Birdie Conversion	28.2 (69T)
Par Breakers	19.7 (43T)

1993 Low Round: 66: 2 times

Career Low Round: 63: 2 times, most recent

Career Largest 1985 Bank of Boston/2

Paycheck: $31,500/1987 Beatrice Western Open/T4

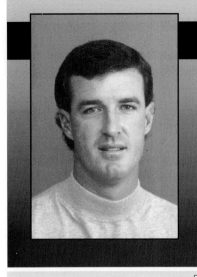

RUSS COCHRAN

EXEMPT STATUS: 59th on 1993 money list

FULL NAME: Russell Earl Cochran

HEIGHT: 6' **WEIGHT:** 160

BIRTH DATE: October 31, 1958

BIRTHPLACE: Paducah, KY

RESIDENCE: Paducah, KY

FAMILY: Wife, Jackie; Ryan (9/4/83); Reed (9/28/85); Case (4/5/89), Kelly Marie(2/21/92)

COLLEGE: University of Kentucky

SPECIAL INTERESTS: Basketball

TURNED PROFESSIONAL: 1979

Q SCHOOL: Falll 1982

PLAYER PROFILE

CAREER EARNINGS: $2,283,493   **PLAYOFF RECORD:** 0-1

TOUR VICTORIES: 1991 Centel Western Open.
(TOTAL: 1)

MONEY & POSITION:

1983--$ 7,968--188	1987--$148,110-- 74	1991--$684,851 --10
1984--$133,342-- 51	1988--$148,960-- 80	1992--$326,290 --46
1985--$ 87,331-- 87	1989--$132,678--107	1993--$293,868 --59
1986--$ 89,817-- 92	1990--$230,278-- 65	

BEST 1993 FINISHES: T2--Freeport-McMoRan Classic; T6--Buick Southern Open

1993 SUMMARY: Tournaments entered--27; in money--19; top ten finishes--2.

1994 PGA TOUR CHARITY TEAM COMPETITION: Bob Hope Chrysler Classic

1993 SEASON: Another steady season for the southpaw as he surpassed the $250,000 mark in earnings for the third consecutive season... Typically was in the hunt for his second TOUR title a number of times... Best chance for that came at the Freeport-McMoRan Classic, where he finished in a tie for second with Payne Stewart, and one stroke behind Mike Standly...Opened with a 3-over 75 on a very windy English Turn GC course, but closed with a 3-under-par 69 on Sunday... Next best finish of the year came at the Buick Southern Open where a third-round 7-under-par 65 propelled him into a tie for sixth.

CAREER HIGHLIGHTS: Broke through into the winner's circle at the 1991 Centel Western Open... Trailed Greg Norman by five strokes with eight holes to play... While Norman struggled down the stretch, Cochran played steady golf and finished with a 4-under-par 68, and won by two strokes...Finest season on TOUR was in 1991, where in addition to the victory, also lost in playoffs to Craig Stadler in THE TOUR Championship, and to Larry Silveira in the Deposit Guaranty Golf Classic... Certainly one of the finest left-handers to play the game since Bob Charles in the 60s... Winner of two Tournament Players Series events in 1983, Magnolia Classic and the Greater Baltimore Open... Finished as the leading money winner through eight events, and was exempted onto the PGA TOUR in 1984... Has kept his playing privileges since then... Winner of the 1975 Kentucky State High School Championships.

PERSONAL: Started playing golf at 10 years old, when his older brother picked up the game... Started playing with a ladies set, because he couldn't find any other left-handed clubs... Kentucky basketball fan.

1993 PGA TOUR STATISTICS

Scoring Average	70.76	(48T)
Driving Distance	260.7	(80T)
Driving Accuracy	70.2	(73T)
Greens in Regulation	68.1	(40)
Putting	1.760	(11T)
All-Around	405	(12)
Sand Saves	54.5	(59)
Total Driving	153	(42T)
Eagles	7	(37T)
Birdies	344	(15)

MISCELLANEOUS STATISTICS

Scoring Avg. (before cut)	71.11	(45)
Scoring Avg. (3rd round)	70.42	(34T)
Scoring Avg. (4th round)	70.70	(29)
Birdie Conversion	29.9	(25)
Par Breakers	20.8	(15T)

1993 Low Round: 64: Southwestern Bell Colonial/4
Career Low Round: 63: 1991 Deposit Guaranty Golf Classic/4
Career Largest Paycheck: $216,000/1991 THE TOUR Championship/2

JOHN COOK

EXEMPT STATUS: 1992 tournament winner

FULL NAME: John Neuman Cook

HEIGHT: 6'   **WEIGHT:** 175

BIRTH DATE: October 2, 1957

BIRTHPLACE: Toledo, OH

RESIDENCE: Rancho Mirage, CA

FAMILY: Wife, Jan; Kristin (7/20/81); Courtney (4/11/84); Jason (1/10/86)

COLLEGE: Ohio State University

SPECIAL INTERESTS: Auto racing, skiing, all sports

TURNED PROFESSIONAL: 1979

Q SCHOOL: Fall 1979

PLAYER PROFILE

CAREER EARNINGS: $3,845,252   **PLAYOFF RECORD:** 3-3

TOUR VICTORIES: **1981** Bing Crosby National Pro-Am. **1983** Canadian Open. **1987** The International.
(TOTAL: 6)   **1992** Bob Hope Chrysler Classic, United Airlines Hawaiian Open, Las Vegas Invitational

MONEY & POSITION:

1980--$ 43,316-- 78	1985--$ 63,573--106	1990--$ 448,112-- 28
1981--$127,608-- 25	1986--$255,126-- 27	1991--$ 546,984-- 26
1982--$ 57,483-- 77	1987--$333,184-- 29	1992--$1,165,606-- 3
1983--$216,868-- 16	1988--$139,916-- 84	1993--$ 342,321-- 45
1984--$ 65,710-- 89	1989--$ 39,445--172	

BEST 1993 FINISHES: T5--Infiniti Tournament of Champions; T6--PGA Championship; 7--Walt Disney/Oldsmobile Classic; T7--Canon Greater Hartford Open; T8--MCI Heritage Classic

1993 SUMMARY: Tournaments entered--23; in money--18; top ten finishes--5.

1994 PGA TOUR CHARITY TEAM COMPETITION: Canon Greater Hartford Open

NATIONAL TEAMS: World Cup, 1983; World Amateur Cup, 1979; Ryder Cup, 1993.

1993 SEASON: Another solid season for the 14-year TOUR veteran... He earned five finishes in the top-10, including a tie for fifth at the Infiniti Tournament of Champions... From mid-April through mid-August he was at his most consistent, as he didn't miss a cut in 11 tournaments... Finished tied for eighth at the MCI Heritage Classic and tied for sixth at the PGA Championship...Second-round 5-under-par 66 propelled him into contention at Inverness... A member of the victorious U.S. Ryder Cup team.

CAREER HIGHLIGHTS: He earned three victories in 1992 and surpassed the $1 million mark in single season earnings...Won the Bob Hope Chrysler Classic in a five-way playoff... In the four extra holes that he played to outlast Gene Sauers he went birdie-birdie-birdie-eagle... Won the United Airlines Hawaiian Open by two strokes over Paul Azinger... Shot a course record 10-under-par 62 enroute to a two-stroke victory in the Las Vegas Invitational...First victory of his career came at Pebble Beach in 1981...He prevailed on the third extra hole, defeating four other players...Two years later he defeated Johnny Miller in a six-hole playoff at the Canadian Open...Eagled the 17th hole, which was good for five points, to win the 1987 International...Winner of the 1978 U.S. Amateur...Winner of the 1974 World Junior and the 1977 and 1979 Sunnehanna Amateur...Winner of the 1978 and 1979 Northeast Amateur...selected as an All-American in 1977, 1978, and 1979...Member of the 1979 Ohio State NCAA Championship team...Winner of the 1982 Sao Paulo-Brazilian Open... Combined with Rex Caldwell to win the 1983 World Cup Team title.

PERSONAL: Overcame physical problems in the late 1980s to contend on TOUR again... Even though he grew up in southern California, Jack Nicklaus and Tom Weiskopf convinced him to attend Ohio State.

1993 PGA TOUR STATISTICS

Scoring Average	70.45	(29)
Driving Distance	256.2	(124T)
Driving Accuracy	73.7	(38T)
Greens in Regulation	71.7	(4)
Putting	1.790	(73)
All-Around	723	(71)
Sand Saves	42.7	(181)
Total Driving	162	(55T)
Eagles	2	(144T)
Birdies	286	(75)

MISCELLANEOUS STATISTICS

Scoring Avg. (before cut)	71.15	(49T)
Scoring Avg. (3rd round)	69.67	(5)
Scoring Avg. (4th round)	71.21	(60T)
Birdie Conversion	26.4	(128T)
Par Breakers	19.0	(67T)

1993 Low Round: 65: 3 times
Career Low Round: 62: 1992 Las Vegas Invitational/3
Career Largest Paycheck: $234,000/1992 Las Vegas Invitational/1

FRED COUPLES

EXEMPT STATUS: Winner, 1992 Masters Tournament

FULL NAME: Frederick Stephen Couples

HEIGHT: 5' 11"   **WEIGHT:** 185

BIRTH DATE: October 3, 1959

BIRTHPLACE: Seattle, WA

RESIDENCE: Dallas, TX

COLLEGE: University of Houston

SPECIAL INTERESTS: Following all sports, tennis, antiques, bicycling, vintage cars

TURNED PROFESSIONAL: 1980

Q SCHOOL: Fall 1980

PLAYER PROFILE

CAREER EARNINGS: $6,263,495   **PLAYOFF RECORD:** 4-3

TOUR VICTORIES: **1983** Kemper Open. **1984** Tournament Players Championship. **1987** Byron
(TOTAL: 10)   Nelson Golf Classic. **1990** Nissan Los Angeles Open. **1991** Federal Express St. Jude Classic, B.C. Open. **1992** Nissan Los Angeles Open, Nestle Invitational, Masters. **1993** Honda Classic

MONEY & POSITION:

1981--$ 78,939--53	1986--$116,065--76	1990--$ 757,999-- 9
1982--$ 77,606--53	1987--$441,025--19	1991--$ 791,749-- 3
1983--$209,733--19	1988--$489,822--21	1992--$1,344,188-- 1
1984--$334,573-- 7	1989--$693,944--11	1993--$ 796,579--10
1985--$171,272--38		

BEST 1993 FINISHES: 1--Honda Classic; 2--Canadian Open; T2--Nissan Los Angeles Open; T4--Memorial Tournament; T5--GTE Byron Nelson Classic; T6--Doral-Ryder Open; T9--Bob Hope Chrysler Classic; T10--Infiniti Tournament of Champions; T10--THE TOUR Championship

1993 SUMMARY: Tournaments entered--19; in money--17; top ten finishes--9.

1994 PGA TOUR CHARITY TEAM COMPETITION: Mercedes Championships

NATIONAL TEAMS: U.S.A. vs. Japan, 1984; Ryder Cup (3), 1989, 1991, 1993; Asahi Glass Four Tours World Championship of Golf (2), 1990, 1991; Dunhill Cup (2), 1992,1993; World Cup (2), 1992,1993.

1993 SEASON: Over the last several seasons has left an indelible mark upon the game...1993 was no different, as he earned the 10th official victory of his PGA TOUR career at the wind-shortened Honda Classic... Couples opened with an 8-under-par 64, and closed with a 2-under-par 70 to finish tied with Robert Gamez... In scrambling for his 70, Couples holed a bunker shot for birdie on the 17th hole to force the playoff... He won the playoff with a par on the second extra hole... Also finished as runner up in the Nissan Los Angeles Open and the Canadian Open... Later in the year won the unofficial Lincoln-Mercury Kapalua International.

CAREER HIGHLIGHTS: Won his second consecutive **PGA TOUR Player of the Year** award in 1992, as he collected three victories, including the Nissan Los Angeles Open, Nestle Invitational and The Masters... First TOUR win came in the 1983 Kemper Open in a five-man playoff...Next win came at the prestigious Tournament Players Championship in 1984...Set the course record at the TPC at Sawgrass that year with an 8-under-par 64, a record he would break by a stroke in 1992...Won for the first time in three years at the 1990 Nissan Los Angeles Open...Had a multiple win season for the first time in 1991 collecting titles at the Federal Express St. Jude Classic and the B.C.Open...Has represented the United States on the last three Ryder Cup teams...Won the 1991 Johnnie Walker World Championship of Golf in Jamaic...Paired with Ray Floyd to win the 1990 RMCC Invitational hosted by Greg Norman...Three weeks later teamed with Mike Donald to win the Sazale Classic...Joined Davis Love III to win the 1992 and 1993 World Cups.

PERSONAL: Attended the University of Houston and was a teammate of Blaine McCallister... CBS Broadcaster Jim Nantz was a part of that team, and he and Fred remain close to this day... Introduced to the game by his father, who worked in the Seattle Parks and Recreation Department... Was quite a soccer player as a youth.

1993 PGA TOUR STATISTICS

Scoring Average	69.85	(7)
Driving Distance	275.0	(7)
Driving Accuracy	60.4	(179)
Greens in Regulation	68.3	(37T)
Putting	1.774	(31T)
All-Around	495	(24)
Sand Saves	58.6	(23)
Total Driving	186	(94T)
Eagles	8	(25T)
Birdies	273	(92T)

MISCELLANEOUS STATISTICS

Scoring Avg. (before cut)	70.41	(16T)
Scoring Avg. (3rd round)	70.47	(38T)
Scoring Avg. (4th round)	70.41	(19T)
Birdie Conversion	31.3	(7)
Par Breakers	22.0	(2T)

1993 Low Round: 63: GTE Byron Nelson Classic/2
Career Low Round: 62: 1990 Nissan Los Angeles Open/3
Career Largest Paycheck: $270,000/1992 Masters/1

BEN CRENSHAW

EXEMPT STATUS: Winner, 1984 Masters Tournament

FULL NAME: Ben Daniel Crenshaw

HEIGHT: 5' 9"   **WEIGHT:** 170

BIRTH DATE: January 11, 1952

BIRTHPLACE: Austin, TX

RESIDENCE: Austin, TX; plays out of Barton Creek
Club in Austin

FAMILY: Wife, Julie; Katherine Vail (10/6/87);
Claire Susan (4/23/92)

COLLEGE: University of Texas

SPECIAL INTERESTS: Fishing, bird watching, golf artifacts,
golf course architecture, country music

TURNED PROFESSIONAL: 1973

JOINED TOUR: Fall 1973

PLAYER PROFILE

CAREER EARNINGS: $5,448,507   **PLAYOFF RECORD:** 0-8

TOUR VICTORIES: 1973 San Antonio-Texas Open. **1976** Bing Crosby National Pro-Am, Hawaiian
(TOTAL: 17)   Open, Ohio Kings Island Open. **1977** Colonial National Invitation. **1979** Phoenix
Open, Walt Disney World Team Championship (with George Burns). **1980**
Anheuser-Busch Classic. **1983** Byron Nelson Classic. **1984** Masters Tournament. **1986** Buick Open,
Vantage Championship. **1987** USF&G Classic. **1988** Doral Ryder Open. **1990** Southwestern Bell
Colonial. **1992** Centel Western Open. **1993** Nestle Invitational.

MONEY & POSITION:

1973--$ 76,749-- 34	1980--$237,727-- 5	1987--$638,194-- 3
1974--$ 71,065-- 31	1981--$151,038-- 20	1988--$696,895-- 8
1975--$ 63,528-- 32	1982--$ 54,277-- 83	1989--$433,095-- 21
1976--$257,759-- 2	1983--$275,474-- 7	1990--$351,193-- 33
1977--$123,841-- 16	1984--$270,989-- 16	1991--$224,563-- 75
1978--$108,305-- 21	1985--$ 25,814-149	1992--$439,071-- 31
1979--$236,769-- 5	1986--$388,169-- 8	1993--$318,605-- 51

BEST 1993 FINISH: 1--Nestle Invitational

1993 SUMMARY: Tournaments entered--22; in money--15; top ten finishes--1.

1994 PGA TOUR CHARITY TEAM COMPETITION: Buick Open

NATIONAL TEAMS: Ryder Cup (3), 1981, 1983, 1987; World Cup (2), 1987, 1988 (won individual title
in 1988); U.S. vs. Japan, 1983; Kirin Cup, 1988.

1993 PGA TOUR STATISTICS

Scoring Average	71.15	(80)
Driving Distance	259.0	(95T)
Driving Accuracy	63.0	(164T)
Greens in Regulation	61.0	(170T)
Putting	1.755	(8)
All-Around	902	(118)
Sand Saves	58.0	(27)
Total Driving	259	(168)
Eagles	6	(50T)
Birdies	222	(140)

MISCELLANEOUS STATISTICS

Scoring Avg. (before cut)	71.63	(92)
Scoring Avg. (3rd round)	71.85	(134)
Scoring Avg. (4th round)	71.33	(75T)
Birdie Conversion	28.5	(60T)
Par Breakers	17.8	(119T)

1993 Low Round: 65: GTE Byron Nelson Classic/4
Career Low Round: 61: 1979 Phoenix Open/2
Career Largest
Paycheck: $198,000/1992 Centel Western Open/1

1993 SEASON: Continued his winning ways by earning the 17th victory of his PGA TOUR career, this year at the Nestle Invitational... Was under par for all four days, but a third round 3-under-par 69 propelled him into contention... Shot a final round 2-under-par 70 on the final day to outlast Davis Love III... It was his second victory in less than 12 months... Had seven other finishes in the top-25, including a tie for 11th at the Shell Houston Open... He was three strokes back after the first round with a 5-under-par 67.

CAREER HIGHLIGHTS: Biggest victory to date came in 1984, when the extremely popular Crenshaw won The Masters...Finished with a 4-under-par 68, giving him an 11-under-par 277 total...Ended up two strokes ahead of Tom Watson...First victory came in the 1973 San Antonio-Texas Open, the event marked his first start as an official member of the PGA TOUR...Winless from 1988 through May in 1990, where he broke through and won the Southwestern Bell Colonial for the second time... Now is tied for 39th in All-Time Career victories with 17... Winner of the NCAA Championship in 1971, 1972 and 1973...tied with Tom Kite in 1972...Winner of the Fred Haskins Award, as the nation's best collegiate player during those same years...Winner of the 1976 Irish Open...Winner of the 1980 Texas State Open... Won the 1973 Qualifying Tournament by a then record 12 strokes.

PERSONAL: One of the more noted golf historians in the game... Also enjoys golf course architecture.

JOHN DALY

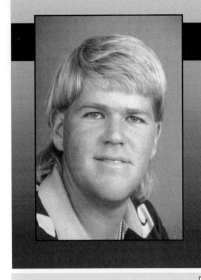

EXEMPT STATUS: Winner, 1991 PGA Championship

HEIGHT: 5' 11" **WEIGHT:** 175

BIRTH DATE: April 28,1966

BIRTHPLACE: Sacramento, CA

RESIDENCE: Orlando, FL

COLLEGE: University of Arkansas

FAMILY: Shynah Hale (6/10/92)

SPECIAL INTERESTS: Most sports

TURNED PROFESSIONAL: 1987

Q SCHOOL: Fall 1990

PLAYER PROFILE

CAREER EARNINGS: $1,187,829

TOUR VICTORIES: 1991 PGA Championship. **1992** B.C. Open.
(TOTAL: 2)

MONEY & POSITION: 1991--$ 574,783--17   1992--$387,455--37   1993--$225,591--76

BEST 1993 FINISH: 3--Masters Tournament

1993 SUMMARY: Tournaments entered--24; in money--15; top ten finishes--1

1994 PGA TOUR CHARITY TEAM COMPETITION: NEC World Series of Golf

1993 SEASON: Something of a disappointing year for the big hitter out of Arkansas... Recorded only one top-10 finish during the year... That came in April at The Masters, where he finished tied for third... Closed with a 3-under-par 69 on Sunday, and finished six strokes behind Bernhard Langer... He earned $81,600 there... Had four other finishes in the top 25, including a tie for 11th at the NEC World Series of Golf.

CAREER HIGHLIGHTS: Delighted the golf world, when he raced to his stirring victory at the 1991 PGA Championship... Informed Wednesday night that he was in the field, his first look at Crooked Stick was during the first round... Shot a 69 and was two strokes out of the lead... Added rounds of 67-69-71 and finished with a three-stroke victory over Bruce Lietzke...Finished rookie season with a third-place finish at THE TOUR Championship at Pinehurst No. 2... Voted the 1991 **PGA TOUR Rookie of the Year**... A member of the Ben Hogan Tour in 1990, Daly won the only Ben Hogan Tour Qualifying Tournament... Later that year won the Ben Hogan Utah Classic... Went on to finish ninth on the money list with over $64,000 in earnings... Has won several events on the South African Tour...Winner of the 1987 Missouri Open.

PERSONAL: Picked up the game at an early age, when his father gave him a full size set of clubs... Played a nearby nine-hole golf course for much of his youth.

1993 PGA TOUR STATISTICS

Scoring Average	71.70	(133T)
Driving Distance	288.9	(1)
Driving Accuracy	59.1	(182)
Greens in Regulation	61.7	(164)
Putting	1.837	(171)
All-Around	942	(126)
Sand Saves	55.2	(49T)
Total Driving	183	(89T)
Eagles	12	(3T)
Birdies	205	(150T)

MISCELLANEOUS STATISTICS

Scoring Avg. (before cut)	72.83	(168)
Scoring Avg. (3rd round)	72.45	(167T)
Scoring Avg. (4th round)	72.29	(152T)
Birdie Conversion	26.2	(135)
Par Breakers	17.1	(137T)

1993 Low Round: **66:** 3 times
Career Low Round: **63:** 1991 Las Vegas Invitational/2
Career Largest Paycheck: **$230,000**/1991 PGA Championship/1

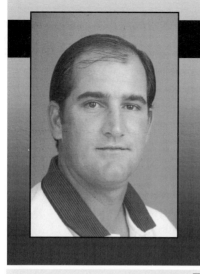

MARCO DAWSON

EXEMPT STATUS: 124th on 1993 money list

FULL NAME: Marco Thomas Dawson

HEIGHT: 6' **WEIGHT:** 180

BIRTH DATE: November 17, 1963

BIRTHPLACE: Freising, Germany

RESIDENCE: Lakeland, FL

FAMILY: Single

COLLEGE: Florida Southern University

SPECIAL INTERESTS: Jazz, all sports

TURNED PROFESSIONAL: 1986

Q SCHOOL: 1990, 1991

PLAYER PROFILE

CAREER EARNINGS: $330,682

BEST-EVER FINISH: T5--1992 GTE Byron Nelson Classic; T5--1993 H-E-B Texas Open.

MONEY & POSITION: 1991--$96,756--137 1992--$113,464--123 1993--$120,462--124

BEST 1993 FINISH: T5--H-E-B Texas Open

1993 SUMMARY: Tournaments entered--32; in money--21; top ten finishes--1

1994 PGA TOUR CHARITY TEAM COMPETITION: Shell Houston Open

1993 SEASON: Despite making 21 cuts, Dawson had to finish tied for fifth at the H-E-B Texas Open in order to retain his playing privileges for the 1994 season... A third-round 6-under-par 65 propelled him into contention at Oak Hills... He closed with a 68, and finished six strokes out of a Jay Haas/ Bob Lohr playoff, subsequently won by Haas... Finished with all four rounds in the 60s, and tied his career best finish... Had three other finishes in the top 25, including a tie for 18th at the Northern Telecom Open.

CAREER HIGHLIGHTS: Best previous performance before 1993, was a tie for fifth at the 1992 GTE Byron Nelson Classic... He finished one stroke out of a playoff with Billy Ray Brown, Ray Floyd, Ben Crenshaw and Bruce Lietzke... He fired a 7-under-par 63 in the second round of that tournament... First year on TOUR was in 1991, when he finished 137th on the money list... Best finish that year was a tie for ninth at the Kmart Greater Greensboro Open... A member of the Ben Hogan Tour in its inaugural year of 1990, Dawson finished with $29,972 in earnings, good for 31st on the money list... A winner of 12 mini-tour events.

PERSONAL: Was a college teammate of Lee Janzen and Rocco Mediate while attending Florida Southern.

1993 PGA TOUR STATISTICS

Scoring Average	71.70	(133T)
Driving Distance	267.8	(36)
Driving Accuracy	59.6	(181)
Greens in Regulation	65.3	(97T)
Putting	1.825	(161)
All-Around	954	(127)
Sand Saves	46.7	(153)
Total Driving	217	(139T)
Eagles	9	(16T)
Birdies	311	(38T)

MISCELLANEOUS STATISTICS

Scoring Avg. (before cut)	71.66	(93T)
Scoring Avg. (3rd round)	71.70	(124)
Scoring Avg. (4th round)	73.76	(182)
Birdie Conversion	25.2	(155T)
Par Breakers	16.9	(143T)

1993 Low Round: 65: 2 times
Career Low Round: 63: 1992 GTE Byron Nelson Classic/2
Career Largest Paycheck: $40,150/1992 Byron Nelson Classic/T5

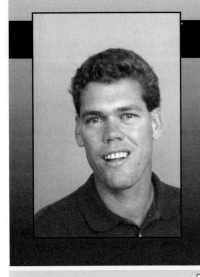

JAY DELSING

EXEMPT STATUS: 71st on 1993 money list

FULL NAME: James Patrick Delsing

HEIGHT: 6' 5 1/2"   **WEIGHT:** 185

BIRTH DATE: October 17, 1960

BIRTHPLACE: St. Louis, MO

RESIDENCE: St. Louis, MO

FAMILY: Wife, Kathy; Mackenzie (5/31/89); Gemma (12/9/91)

COLLEGE: UCLA (1983, Economics)

SPECIAL INTERESTS: Fishing, all sports

TURNED PROFESSIONAL: 1984

Q SCHOOL: Fall 1984, 1988, 1989

PLAYER PROFILE

CAREER EARNINGS: $1,130,795

BEST-EVER FINISH: T2--1993 New England Classic

MONEY & POSITION:

1985--$ 46,480--125	1988--$ 45,504--152	1991--$149,775--100
1986--$ 65,407--123	1989--$ 26,565--187	1992--$296,740-- 52
1987--$ 58,657--136	1990--$207,740-- 74	1993--$233,484-- 71

BEST 1993 FINISHES: T2--New England Classic; T8--Federal Express St. Jude Classic; T10--Walt Disney World/Oldsmobile Classic.

1993 SUMMARY: Tournaments entered--29; in money--20; top ten finishes--3.

1994 PGA TOUR CHARITY TEAM COMPETITION: Kmart Greater Greensboro Open

1993 SEASON: Another solid year for the lanky Delsing, as he finished in the top-10 on three different occasions... Enjoyed his career-best finish on the PGA TOUR when he finished tied for second at the New England Classic, four strokes behind the winner, Paul Azinger... Improved his position every day at Pleasant Valley, after finishing Thursday's round 10 strokes behind the leader... Closing 4-under-par 67 on the final day, gave him a $88,000 pay day, the richest of his career to date... Followed that up with another strong finish the next week at the Federal Express St. Jude Classic... Fired a course record 10-under-par 61 to vault into a tie for eighth at the TPC at Southwind... Picked up $121,000 during those two weeks... Other top 10 came at Walt Disney World/Oldsmobile Classic where a closing 6-under 66 gave him a tie for tenth... Year started slowly, as he missed the cut in four of his first nine starts, but only missed five cuts the remainder of the year.

CAREER HIGHLIGHTS: One of the course-record holders at En Joie Golf Club, site of the B.C. Open... He shot a 9-under 62 there in 1985…Was a two-time All-America selection at UCLA....As a youth, was the medalist in the Missouri Amateur.

PERSONAL: Was a teammate of TOUR professionals Corey Pavin, Steve Pate and Duffy Waldorf at UCLA...His father, Jim, played professional baseball for the New York Yankees, the Chicago White Sox, the St. Louis Browns and the Kansas City A's... Father was the pinch runner for Eddie Gaedel, the dwarf who went to bat for the Browns.

1993 PGA TOUR STATISTICS

Scoring Average	71.10	(76T)
Driving Distance	274.8	(8)
Driving Accuracy	62.0	(173)
Greens in Regulation	64.9	(112T)
Putting	1.803	(107T)
All-Around	698	(66)
Sand Saves	51.3	(100T)
Total Driving	181	(84T)
Eagles	13	(2)
Birdies	314	(36)

MISCELLANEOUS STATISTICS

Scoring Avg. (before cut)	71.33	(65T)
Scoring Avg. (3rd round)	72.15	(155T)
Scoring Avg. (4th round)	71.25	(67T)
Birdie Conversion	26.9	(112T)
Par Breakers	18.2	(98T)

1993 Low Round: **61:** FedEx St. Jude/4

Career Low Round: **61:** 1993 FedEx St. Jude/4

Career Largest

Paycheck: **$88,000**/1993 New England Classic/T2

TREVOR DODDS

EXEMPT STATUS: 126th on 1993 money list

FULL NAME: Trevor George Dodds

HEIGHT: 6' 1"   **WEIGHT:** 195

BIRTH DATE: September 26, 1959

BIRTHPLACE: Windhoek, Southwest Africa-(Namibia)

RESIDENCE: St. Louis, MO

FAMILY: Wife, Kristin

SPECIAL INTERESTS: Books, sports

TURNED PROFESSIONAL: 1985

Q SCHOOL: 1985, 1986, 1988, 1992

PLAYER PROFILE

CAREER EARNINGS: $287,749

BEST EVER FINISH: T3--1993 AT&T Pebble Beach National Pro-Am

MONEY & POSITION:
1986--$15,738--190	1989--$47,086--166	1991--$ 57,786--167
1987--$48,933--155	1990--$74,544--153	1993--$119,436--126
1988--$17,404--202		

BEST 1993 FINISH: T3--AT&T Pebble Beach National Pro-Am

1993 SUMMARY: Tournaments entered--30; in money--13; top ten finishes--1.

1994 PGA TOUR CHARITY TEAM COMPETITION: GTE Byron Nelson Classic

1993 SEASON: Gained fully exempt status on TOUR for the first time in seven tries...Surpassed the $100,000 mark in earnings for the first time in his career... Had one finish in the top-10 and another in the top-25... Finished tied for third at the AT&T Pebble Beach National Pro-Am... Was three strokes back after three rounds, and wound up four behind Brett Ogle... It was his best career finish on TOUR, and the $65,000 payday was the largest of his career... Only made 13 cuts during the year, but made nine of 11 at one point.

CAREER HIGHLIGHTS: Played the PGA TOUR from 1986 through 1991, without ever retaining his playing privileges... Attended the final stage of Qualifying on four different occasions...His best ever finish prior to the 1993 season was a tie for eighth at the 1987 Buick Open in Flint, MI... Had a third-round 9-under-par 63 in the third round at Warwick Hills, but still finished well back of Robert Wrenn's near record-setting performance...Matched that T8 finish in 1990, when he finished with a 2-over-par 282 total at the NEC World Series of Golf... Got to play the NEC World Series of Golf by virtue of his victory at the 1990 South African Open... Also won the South African Tournament of Champions the same season... Winner of the 1988 Goodyear Classic... Was a first team All-America selection in 1985.

PERSONAL: Was born in Southwest Africa, now the country of Namibia, a small country in southern Africa... Very few golf courses, but still developed a healthy interest in the game early.

1993 PGA TOUR STATISTICS

Scoring Average	71.87	(146T)
Driving Distance	257.9	(108T)
Driving Accuracy	63.1	(161T)
Greens in Regulation	61.8	(162T)
Putting	1.832	(168T)
All-Around	1322	(180)
Sand Saves	39.2	(187)
Total Driving	269	(172)
Eagles	4	(89T)
Birdies	243	(129T)

MISCELLANEOUS STATISTICS

Scoring Avg. (before cut)	72.67	(160)
Scoring Avg. (3rd round)	70.55	(44)
Scoring Avg. (4th round)	73.23	(178)
Birdie Conversion	26.0	(139T)
Par Breakers	16.3	(161)

1993 Low Round: **64**: GTE Byron Nelson Classic/3
Career Low Round: **63**: 1987 Buick Open/3
Career Largest
Paycheck: **$65,000**/1993 AT&T Pebble Beach/T3

ED DOUGHERTY

EXEMPT STATUS: 99th on 1993 money list

FULL NAME: Edward Matthew Dougherty

HEIGHT: 6' 1"   **WEIGHT:** 215

BIRTH DATE: November 4, 1947

BIRTHPLACE: Chester, PA

RESIDENCE: Linwood, PA

FAMILY: Wife, Carolyn

SPECIAL INTERESTS: Lionel toy trains, all sports

TURNED PROFESSIONAL: 1969

Q-SCHOOL: Fall, 1975, 1986, 1989

PLAYER PROFILE

CAREER EARNINGS: $978,430   **PLAYOFF RECORD:** 0-1

BEST-EVER FINISH: T2--1990 Greater Milwaukee Open (lost playoff to Jim Gallagher); 2--1992 Anheuser Busch Golf Classic; 2--1992 Chattanooga Classic.

MONEY & POSITION:

1975--$ 9,374--129	1980--$ 9,113--168	1990--$124,505--123
1976--$ 17,333--113	1982--$ 27,948--128	1991--$201,958-- 82
1977--$ 17,606--113	1987--$ 76,705--115	1992--$237,525-- 66
1978--$ 9,936--141	1988--$ 22,455--195	1993--$167,651-- 99
1979--$ 24,802--115	1989--$ 1,800--267	

BEST 1993 FINISHES:.T6--Honda Classic; T10--Canadian Open; T10--B.C. Open

1993 SUMMARY: Tournaments entered--34; in money--22; top ten finishes--3

1994 PGA TOUR CHARITY TEAM COMPETITION: Nestle Invitational

1993 SEASON: Another successful year for one of the ironmen on the PGA TOUR...Has led the TOUR or tied for the lead in tournaments played in each of the last three years...1993 season was highlighted by his final round 5-under-par 67 at the Honda Classic, which vaulted him to a tie for sixth...Was inconsistent for much of the first half of the year, but wound up making nine consecutive cuts starting with the New England Classic.

CAREER HIGHLIGHTS: Winner of the 1985 PGA Club Pro Player of the Year...Also won the PGA Club Pro Championship that same year...Was a TOUR regular from 1975 until 1982, when he decided to work as a club professional at Edgemont CC in Pennsylvania...Won several section events during his tenure there...Returned to the Qualifying School in 1989 and earned his card...Finished 123rd on the money list in 1990 to keep his playing privileges, and has done it with ease for the last three seasons.

PERSONAL: A very serious model train enthusiast...Visits train stores in most of the cities the PGA TOUR visits...Married his high school sweetheart after not seeing her for a number of years.

1993 PGA TOUR STATISTICS

Scoring Average	71.42	(113)
Driving Distance	256.8	(120T)
Driving Accuracy	69.9	(79)
Greens in Regulation	65.9	(79T)
Putting	1.827	(164T)
All-Around	906	(119)
Sand Saves	46.5	(155)
Total Driving	199	(111T)
Eagles	5	(67T)
Birdies	341	(18)

MISCELLANEOUS STATISTICS

Scoring Avg. (before cut)	71.39	(71)
Scoring Avg. (3rd round)	72.60	(173T)
Scoring Avg. (4th round)	71.76	(117T)
Birdie Conversion	25.9	(143T)
Par Breakers	17.3	(133T)

1993 Low Round: **65:** 3 times
Career Low Round: **62:** 1992 Chattanooga Classic/3
Career Largest Paycheck: **$82,133**/1992 Anheuser-Busch Golf Classic/T2

DAVID EDWARDS

EXEMPT STATUS: 1993 tournament winner

FULL NAME: David Wayne Edwards

HEIGHT: 5' 8" **WEIGHT:** 155

BIRTH DATE: April 18, 1956

BIRTHPLACE: Neosho, MO

RESIDENCE: Edmond, OK; plays out of Oak Tree Country Club.

FAMILY: Wife, Jonnie; Rachel Leigh (12/21/85)

COLLEGE: Oklahoma State University

SPECIAL INTERESTS: Automobiles, motorcycles, radio controlled miniature cars, flying own plane

TURNED PROFESSIONAL: 1978

Q SCHOOL: Fall 1978

PLAYER PROFILE

CAREER EARNINGS: $2,961,573   **PLAYOFF RECORD:** 1-0

TOUR VICTORIES: **1980** Walt Disney World National Team Championship (with Danny Edwards).
(TOTAL: 4)   **1984** Los Angeles Open.**1992** Memorial Tournament.**1993** MCI Heritage Classic.

MONEY & POSITION:

1979--$ 44,456-- 88	1984--$236,061-- 23	1989--$239,908-- 57
1980--$ 35,810-- 93	1985--$ 21,506--157	1990--$166,028-- 95
1981--$ 68,211-- 65	1986--$122,079-- 71	1991--$396,695-- 38
1982--$ 49,896-- 91	1987--$148,217-- 73	1992--$515,070-- 27
1983--$114,037-- 48	1988--$151,513-- 76	1993--$653,086-- 20

BEST 1993 FINISHES:1--MCI Heritage Classic; T3--Las Vegas Invitational; T5--H-E-B Texas Open; 6--NEC World Series of Golf; T6--Kmart Greater Greensboro Open; T6--Southwestern Bell Colonial.

1993 SUMMARY: Tournaments entered--21; in money--17; top ten finishes--6.

1994 PGA TOUR CHARITY TEAM COMPETITION: GTE Byron Nelson Classic

1993 SEASON: After not winning for eight years, he collected two victories on TOUR in less than one year... His victory at the 1993 MCI Heritage Classic was highlighted by second-round 5-under-par 66, which moved him into a tie for the lead... He was again tied for the lead after three rounds, but his closing 2-under-par 69 was enough for a two-stroke victory over David Frost... It was his second win in 11 months...Went out the next week and finished tied for sixth at the Kmart Greater Greensboro Open... Was forced to take some time off due to a rib injury, but returned with another T6 finish at the Southwestern Bell Colonial... Ended the year in strong fashion, concluding with a T5 at the H-E-B Texas Open and a T3 at the Las Vegas Invitational.

CAREER HIGHLIGHTS: Earned two PGA TOUR victories before the 1992 campaign...First came at the 1980 Walt Disney World National Team Championship with brother Danny... Next victory came at the 1984 Los Angeles Open at Riviera Country Club... Fired a magnificent 7-under-par 64 during the final round to win by three strokes over Jack Renner... Winner of the 1978 NCAA Championship... Was selected as a Collegiate All-American in 1977 and 1978... Winner of the 1973 Oklahoma State Junior title.

PERSONAL: Started tagging along to the golf course with older brother Danny, when he was about 12 years old... Danny is the founder of the Royal Grip golf grip company... David enjoys flying his own plane to tournaments.

1993 PGA TOUR STATISTICS

Scoring Average	70.32	(22T)
Driving Distance	252.0	(163T)
Driving Accuracy	78.3	(5)
Greens in Regulation	72.1	(3)
Putting	1.787	(61T)
All-Around	603	(43)
Sand Saves	57.0	(31T)
Total Driving	168	(65T)
Eagles	N/A	
Birdies	288	(70T)

MISCELLANEOUS STATISTICS

Scoring Avg. (before cut)	70.24	(9)
Scoring Avg. (3rd round)	69.88	(11)
Scoring Avg. (4th round)	71.41	(87T)
Birdie Conversion	28.5	(60T)
Par Breakers	20.5	(24T)

1993 Low Round: 63: Southwestern Bell Colonial/3
Career Low Round: 61: 1987 Bob Hope Chrysler Classic/1
Career Largest Paycheck:$234,000/1992 Memorial Tournament/1

JOEL EDWARDS

EXEMPT STATUS: 106th on 1993 money list

FULL NAME: Joel Ashley Edwards

HEIGHT: 6'   **WEIGHT:** 165

BIRTH DATE: November 22, 1961

BIRTHPLACE: Dallas, TX

RESIDENCE: Irving, TX

FAMILY: Wife, Rhonda

COLLEGE: North Texas State

SPECIAL INTERESTS: Music, movies

TURNED PROFESSIONAL: 1984

Q SCHOOL: 1988, 1989, 1990

PLAYER PROFILE

CAREER EARNINGS: $521,367

BEST EVER FINISH: T2--1992 B.C. Open

MONEY & POSITION: 1989--$ 46,851-- 167   1991--$106,820-- 131   1993--$150,623--106
1990--$109,808-- 132   1992--$107,264-- 126

BEST 1993 FINISH: T11--THE PLAYERS Championship

1993 SUMMARY: Tournaments entered--30; in money--15; top ten finishes--0.

1994 PGA TOUR CHARITY TEAM COMPETITION: Nissan Los Angeles Open

1993 SEASON: Playing as a fully exempt player for the first time in his career, Edwards made the most of his opportunity... Played a full schedule of 30 events, and finished in the top-25 on five different occasions... His best finish of the year came at THE PLAYERS Championship, where he finished tied for 11th... He opened with a 6-under-par 66, and followed that up with a 69... Was three strokes back at the halfway point... Shot 1-over-par on the weekend, but picked up $53,000... That was the largest payday of his career... His next best finish was a tie for 16th at the Buick Invitational of California.

CAREER HIGHLIGHTS: Put together four rounds in the 60s to finish runner-up at the 1992 B.C. Open... That finish enabled him to retain his playing privileges for the first time in his career... He closed with a 3-under-par 68, and finished six strokes behind John Daly... Winner of the 1988 North Dakota Open... Was named to the All Southland Conference team, while attending North Texas State...Was an American Junior Golf Association All-American...Best-ever finish before the B.C. Open was a tie for fifth at the 1991 USF&G Classic.

PERSONAL: Had this comment after his runner-up finish at the 1992 B.C. Open -- "Andy Warhol promised me this (15 minutes of fame), so I'm just going to enjoy it."

1993 PGA TOUR STATISTICS

Scoring Average	71.61	(125)
Driving Distance	253.2	(153T)
Driving Accuracy	71.6	(61)
Greens in Regulation	65.7	(86)
Putting	1.820	(148T)
All-Around	1064	(141)
Sand Saves	50.3	(113T)
Total Driving	214	(136T)
Eagles	2	(144T)
Birdies	270	(98)

MISCELLANEOUS STATISTICS

Scoring Avg. (before cut)	72.02	(121T)
Scoring Avg. (3rd round)	71.29	(92T)
Scoring Avg. (4th round)	71.87	(126)
Birdie Conversion	25.4	(150T)
Par Breakers	16.8	(149T)

1993 Low Round:	66: 2 times
Career Low Round:	64: 3 times, most recent
Career Largest Paycheck:	1991 Chattanooga Classic/3
	$53,000/1993 PLAYERS Championship/T11

STEVE ELKINGTON

EXEMPT STATUS: Winner, 1991 THE PLAYERS Championship

FULL NAME: Stephen John Elkington

HEIGHT: 6' 2" **WEIGHT:** 190

BIRTH DATE: December 8, 1962

BIRTHPLACE: Inverell, Australia

RESIDENCE: Sydney, Australia

FAMILY: Wife, Lisa

COLLEGE: University of Houston (1985, Recreation)

SPECIAL INTERESTS: Character drawing, fishing, hunting

TURNED PROFESSIONAL: 1985

Q SCHOOL: Fall 1986

PLAYER PROFILE

CAREER EARNINGS: $2,976,192 **PLAYOFF RECORD:** 1-3

TOUR VICTORIES: **1990** Kmart Greater Greensboro Open. **1991** THE PLAYERS Championship.
(TOTAL: 3) **1992** Infiniti Tournament of Champions.

MONEY & POSITION:
1987--$ 75,738--118 1990--$548,564--18 1992--$746,352--12
1988--$149,972-- 79 1991--$549,120--25 1993--$675,383--17
1989--$231,062-- 61

BEST 1993 FINISHES: 2--Kmart Greater Greensboro Open; 3--Masters Tournament; T6--Buick Open; T7--Shell Houston Open; T7--NEC World Series of Golf; T9--AT&T Pebble Beach National Pro-Am; T9--Bob Hope Chrysler Classic; T10--Doral-Ryder Open.

1993 SUMMARY: Tournaments entered--23; in money--23; top ten finishes--8.

1994 PGA TOUR CHARITY TEAM COMPETITION: Bell Canadian Open

1993 SEASON: Consistency is one Elkington's best qualities, as he finished with eight finishes in the top-10... Since 1990, he has 25 finishes of 10th or better on TOUR... His best performance in 1993, was a playoff loss to Rocco Mediate at the Kmart Greater Greensboro Open, a tournament that Elkington won in 1990...The runnerup finish was special because his parents were over from Australia to see it... Two weeks before at the Masters he finished tied for third... The week following Greensboro he finished tied for seventh at the Shell Houston Open... Didn't miss a cut during the 1993 season, making it in all 23 starts.

CAREER HIGHLIGHTS: Won the 1992 Infiniti Tournament of Champions in a playoff over Brad Faxon... After closing with an even par 72 at La Costa, he edged Faxon with a birdie on the first extra hole... Later in 1992, lost a playoff to Nick Price at the H-E-B Texas Open... Scored his biggest victory to date by outdueling Fuzzy Zoeller down the stretch to win by a stroke at THE PLAYERS Championship in 1991...Collected the $288,000 first place check, his largest to date on TOUR...started on TOUR in 1987, and his first victory came at the 1990 Kmart Greater Greensboro Open...Was seven strokes behind on the last day, but shot a 6-under-par 66 ...Winner, 1980 Australia-New Zealand Amateur...1981 Australian Amateur and Doug Sanders Junior World Championship...Two-time All-American while at Houston..Two-time Southwest Conference Champion...Member of the 1984 and 1985 NCAA Championship teams...runnerup at the 1986 Qualifying Tournament... Winner of the 1992 Australian Open.

PERSONAL: Grew up idolizing fellow Aussie Bruce Devlin... Grew up in the Outback, and has been playing the game since he was 10... Teammate of Billy Ray Brown, while at Houston... Spotted at the 1981 Doug Sanders Junior World Championships by Houston coach Dave Williams who gave him a scholarship.

1993 PGA TOUR STATISTICS

Statistic	Value	
Scoring Average	69.97	(8)
Driving Distance	267.5	(37)
Driving Accuracy	68.6	(92)
Greens in Regulation	69.0	(24T)
Putting	1.780	(47T)
All-Around	384	(9)
Sand Saves	53.4	(69)
Total Driving	129	(26T)
Eagles	6	(50T)
Birdies	317	(31T)

MISCELLANEOUS STATISTICS

Statistic	Value	
Scoring Avg. (before cut)	69.73	(3)
Scoring Avg. (3rd round)	70.29	(29)
Scoring Avg. (4th round)	71.50	(95T)
Birdie Conversion	29.0	(46T)
Par Breakers	20.4	(26T)

1993 Low Round: 63: Bob Hope Chrysler Classic/2
Career Low Round: 62: 3 times, most recent '91
Career Largest Paycheck: $288,000/1991 THE PLAYERS Championship/1 — Southwestern Bell Colonial/3

BOB ESTES

EXEMPT STATUS: 32nd on 1993 money list

FULL NAME: Bob Alan Estes

HEIGHT: 6' 1"　　　　　　**WEIGHT:** 175

BIRTH DATE: February 2, 1966

BIRTHPLACE: Graham, TX

RESIDENCE: Austin, TX; plays out of The Hills of Lakeway, near Austin

COLLEGE: University of Texas

SPECIAL INTERESTS: Music, hunting

TURNED PROFESSIONAL: 1988

Q SCHOOL: Fall 1988

PLAYER PROFILE

CAREER EARNINGS: $1,133,048　　　**PLAYOFF RECORD:** 0-2

BEST-EVER FINISH: 2--1989 B.C. Open (lost playoff to Mike Hulbert); T2--1993 Buick Southern Open (lost playoff to John Inman)

MONEY & POSITION:　　1988--$ 5,968--237　　1990--$212,090-- 69　　1992--$190,778--80
　　　　　　　　　　　　　　1989--$135,628--102　　1991--$147,364--105　　1993--$447,187--32

BEST 1993 FINISHES: T2--Buick Southern Open; T3--Las Vegas Invitational; 4--H-E-B Texas Open; 5--Kemper Open; T6--PGA Championship

1993 SUMMARY: Tournaments entered--28; in money--23; top ten finishes--5.

1994 PGA TOUR CHARITY TEAM COMPETITION: Nissan Los Angeles Open

1993 SEASON: Enjoyed the most lucrative year of his TOUR career, just missing a spot in the season-ending TOUR Championship by one place on the money list... A playoff loss to John Inman was his best finish of the year... He along with Inman, Billy Andrade, Brad Bryant and Mark Brooks all finished at 10-under-par 278 totals... Estes and Inman advanced to the second hole with birdies...Inman won with another birdie there...That outstanding play carried over the H-E-B. Texas Open where a third round 6-under 64 propelled him to a fourth place finish... The next week he finished tied for third at the Las Vegas Invitational... All five of his rounds were in the 60s at Las Vegas.

CAREER HIGHLIGHTS: Was named the Rookie of the Year in 1989...Best career finish came that year, when he lost in a playoff to local favorite Mike Hulbert at the B.C. Open...Didn't make a bogey on the final day, until the first playoff hole...Nevertheless made enough to secure his playing privileges...Went through the Qualifying Tournament in the Fall of 1988, after being named the Jack Nicklaus and Fred Haskins awards as the college player of the year... Won numerous events as an amateur, including the 1983 Texas High School Championship, 1988 Texas State Amateur, 1985 Trans-Mississippi Amateur, and six collegiate events... Won the Bogey Hills Invitational in St. Charles, MO in his first event as a professional.

PERSONAL: Gained All-District Honors around Abilene, TX in his junior and senior years of high school... First played golf at the age of four... Set his sites on the TOUR at the age of 12.

1993 PGA TOUR STATISTICS

Scoring Average	70.25	(18)
Driving Distance	262.3	(67)
Driving Accuracy	71.8	(60)
Greens in Regulation	67.9	(41T)
Putting	1.783	(57T)
All-Around	463	(18)
Sand Saves	46.4	(156)
Total Driving	127	(23T)
Eagles	8	(25T)
Birdies	343	(16T)

MISCELLANEOUS STATISTICS

Scoring Avg. (before cut)	70.55	(22)
Scoring Avg. (3rd round)	70.30	(30)
Scoring Avg. (4th round)	71.27	(70)
Birdie Conversion	28.7	(56T)
Par Breakers	19.9	(37T)

1993 Low Round: 64: H-E-B Texas Open
Career Low Round: 61: 1991 Chattanooga Classic/2
Career Largest Paycheck: $72,800/1993 Las Vegas Invitational/T3

BRAD FAXON

EXEMPT STATUS: 1992 tournament winner.

FULL NAME: Bradford John Faxon Jr.

HEIGHT: 6' 1"   **WEIGHT:** 170

BIRTH DATE: August 1, 1961

BIRTHPLACE: Oceanport, NJ

RESIDENCE: Barrington, RI

FAMILY: Wife, Bonnie; Melanie (1/3/89), Emily (5/13/91)

COLLEGE: Furman University (1983, Economics)

SPECIAL INTERESTS: Racquet sports, sports psychology

TURNED PROFESSIONAL: 1983

Q SCHOOL: Fall 1983

PLAYER PROFILE

CAREER EARNINGS: $2,452,805   **PLAYOFF RECORD:** 1-2

TOUR VICTORIES: 1986 Provident Classic. **1991** Buick Open. **1992** New England Classic,
(TOTAL: 4)   The International.

MONEY & POSITION:

1984--$ 71,688-- 82	1988--$162,656-- 74	1991--$422,088-- 34
1985--$ 46,813--124	1989--$222,076-- 63	1992--$812,093-- 8
1986--$ 92,716-- 90	1990--$197,118-- 81	1993--$312,023-- 55
1987--$113,534-- 90		

BEST 1993 FINISHES: T4--Memorial Tournament; T5--Infiniti Tournament of Champions; T6--The
International; 9--Masters Tournament

1993 SUMMARY: Tournaments entered--25; in money--19; top ten finishes--4.

1994 PGA TOUR CHARITY TEAM COMPETITION: New England Classic

NATIONAL TEAMS: Walker Cup, 1983

1993 SEASON: Injured his rib cage in a skiing accident and didn't really return to form until the middle of the season... After finishing tied for fifth at the Infiniti Tournament of Champions didn't play again until the Doral-Ryder Open... Despite the rustiness, still missed only five cuts... Best finish of the year came at The Memorial Tournament, where he finished tied for fourth... Played well at The International as the defending champion finishing tied for sixth... He was two points out of the lead at the halfway point in Castle Pines.

CAREER HIGHLIGHTS: Had the first multiple-win season in his career in 1992, winning at home at the New England Classic and at The International... Fired four rounds in the 60s at Pleasant Valley to win by two strokes... Had a 14-point performance on Sunday to win the International...Also had two playoff losses in 1992...Powered by a final round 7-under-par 63, Faxon won his first TOUR event in 1986 at the Provident Classic...Next victory came in 1991, when he finished in a tie with Chip Beck at 17-under-par 271 at the end of regulation at the Buick Open...Won playoff with a par on the first extra hole of sudden death... Winner of the 1983 Fred Haskins, Golf Magazine, and NCAA Coaches awards as the nation's outstanding collegiate player...Member of the 1983 Walker Cup team...Winner of the 1979 and 1980 Rhode Island Amateur...Winner of the 1980 and 1981 New England Amateur...Winner of 11 collegiate events...Selected as an All-American in 1982 and 1983.

PERSONAL: Grandmother owned a golf course in Cape Cod, and Brad and his father would go play there...Started at the age of six...Works on a consistent basis with sports psychologist Dr. Bob Rotella.

1993 PGA TOUR STATISTICS

Scoring Average	70.68	(42)
Driving Distance	254.5	(145)
Driving Accuracy	64.9	(149)
Greens in Regulation	61.9	(161)
Putting	1.741	(2)
All-Around	810	(89T)
Sand Saves	58.3	(25)
Total Driving	294	(179T)
Eagles	5	(67T)
Birdies	310	(40T)

MISCELLANEOUS STATISTICS

Scoring Avg. (before cut)	70.82	(30)
Scoring Avg. (3rd round)	70.94	(71)
Scoring Avg. (4th round)	72.21	(149)
Birdie Conversion	32.7	(3T)
Par Breakers	20.6	(23)

1993 Low Round: 65: 2 times
Career Low Round: 62: 1986 Provident Classic/2
**Career Largest
Paycheck:** $216,000/1992 The International/1

RICK FEHR

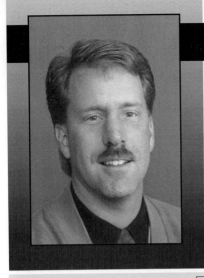

EXEMPT STATUS: 28th on 1993 money list

FULL NAME: Richard Elliott Fehr

HEIGHT: 5' 11"   **WEIGHT:** 160

BIRTH DATE: August 28, 1962

BIRTHPLACE: Seattle, WA

RESIDENCE: Redmond, WA

FAMILY: Wife, Terri; Jeremy Douglas (1/26/91)

COLLEGE: Brigham Young University (1984, Finance)

INTERESTS: Bicycling, basketball, fishing, Christianity

TURNED PROFESSIONAL: 1984

Q SCHOOL: Fall 1985.

PLAYER PROFILE

CAREER EARNINGS: $1,898,467   **PLAYOFF RECORD:** 0-3

TOUR VICTORIES: 1986 B.C. Open.
(TOTAL: 1)

MONEY & POSITION:

1985--$ 40,101--133	1988--$ 79,080--130	1991--$288,983-- 55
1986--$151,162-- 61	1989--$ 93,142--131	1992--$433,003-- 33
1987--$106,808-- 94	1990--$149,867--105	1993--$556,322-- 28

BEST 1993 FINISHES: 2--Bob Hope Chrysler Classic; T2--Federal Express St.Jude Classic; 5--THE TOUR Championship; T6--Nissan Los Angeles Open; T7--Sprint Western Open; T8--B.C. Open

1993 SUMMARY: Tournaments entered--26; in money--23; top ten finishes--6.

1994 PGA TOUR CHARITY TEAM COMPETITION: Freeport-McMoRan Classic

NATIONAL TEAMS: Walker Cup, 1983

1993 SEASON: Has now increased his earnings each year for five consecutive years... Finished as the runnerup in the Bob Hope Chrysler Classic for the second year in a row... A fourth-round 10-under-par 62 at Indian Wells, moved him to within a stroke of the lead... Wound up six strokes behind Tom Kite after tying him the previous year at the Hope, when he shot a 5-under-par 67... Had five other finishes in the top-10, including a tie for second at the Federal Express St. Jude Classic... He was also the runnerup at the TPC at Southwind in 1991... Wound up in the top-30 on the money list for the first time in his career.

CAREER HIGHLIGHTS: First and only PGA TOUR victory came at the 1986 B.C. Open...Entered trying to retain his playing privileges and eventually wound up with a two-stroke victory over Larry Mize...He earned his exemption and $72,000 as well...In 1991, finished in the runnerup position twice, including a playoff loss to Billy Ray Brown at the Canon Greater Hartford Open... In 1992, he finished in second twice... Lost in a five-way playoff to John Cook at the Bob Hope Chrysler Classic, and later to David Edwards at The Memorial... Has six runner-up finishes since 1991... Two-time All-America selection while at BYU...Low amateur in the 1984 Masters and the 1984 U.S. Open...Winner of the 1979 Washington State Junior and the PGA National Junior Championships at Callaway Gardens resort, now home of the Buick Southern Open...Winner of the 1982 Western Amateur...Won seven collegiate events.

PERSONAL: Started the game at the age of 11, playing with his father... A member of the PGA TOUR Policy Board from 1992-1994.

1993 PGA TOUR STATISTICS

Scoring Average	70.09	(10)
Driving Distance	260.4	(86)
Driving Accuracy	72.6	(49T)
Greens in Regulation	68.5	(31T)
Putting	1.775	(33T)
All-Around	491	(21)
Sand Saves	44.9	(170T)
Total Driving	135	(29T)
Eagles	5	(67T)
Birdies	343	(16T)

MISCELLANEOUS STATISTICS

Scoring Avg. (before cut)	70.13	(6)
Scoring Avg. (3rd round)	70.33	(31T)
Scoring Avg. (4th round)	71.00	(45T)
Birdie Conversion	28.4	(63T)
Par Breakers	19.7	(43T)

1993 Low Round: 62: Bob Hope Chrysler Classic/4
Career Low Round: 62: 1993 Bob Hope Chrysler Classic/4
Career Largest
Paycheck: $140,400/1992 Memorial Tournament/2

ED FIORI

EXEMPT STATUS: 127th on 1993 money list

FULL NAME: Edward Ray Fiori

HEIGHT: 5' 7" **WEIGHT:** 190

BIRTH DATE: April 21, 1953

BIRTHPLACE: Lynwood, CA

RESIDENCE: Stafford, TX

FAMILY: Wife, Debbie; Kelly Ann (1/29/82); Michael Ray (10/21/84)

COLLEGE: University of Houston

SPECIAL INTERESTS: Fishing, bird hunting

TURNED PROFESSIONAL: 1977

Q SCHOOL: Fall 1977

PLAYER PROFILE

CAREER EARNINGS: $1,723,565   **PLAYOFF RECORD:** 2-0

TOUR VICTORIES: 1979 Southern Open. **1981** Western Open. **1982** Bob Hope Desert Classic. (TOTAL: 3)

MONEY & POSITION:

1978--$ 19,846-- 109	1984--$ 41,582--119	1990--$108,816--133
1979--$ 64,428-- 65	1985--$116,002-- 71	1991--$120,722--123
1980--$ 79,488-- 52	1986--$ 70,828--119	1992--$124,537--115
1981--$105,510-- 48	1987--$104,570-- 95	1993--$117,617--127
1982--$ 91,599-- 45	1988--$193,765-- 58	
1983--$175,619-- 26	1989--$188,637-- 77	

BEST 1993 FINISHES: T10--Freeport-McMoRan Classic; T10--Kemper Open

1993 SUMMARY: Tournaments entered--31; in money--16; top ten finishes--2.

1994 PGA TOUR CHARITY TEAM COMPETITION: Texas Open

1993 SEASON: Started year off poorly, missing the cut in the first six tournaments that he entered...However, rebounded to make 16 cuts out of his next 25 starts...Had two top-10s during the year... Finished tied for 10th at the Freeport McMoRan Classic...He fired consecutive 1-under-par 71s on the weekend to finish at even-par 288, and seven strokes behind Mike Standly...Also finished tied for 10th at the Kemper Open...Opened with a 4-under-par 67 and was one stroke out of the lead at the TPC at Avenel...Had two other finishes in the top-25, including a T20 at the Hardee's Classic and two weeks later he finished with a T19 at the Buick Southern Open.

CAREER HIGHLIGHTS: Collected three victories in a four-year span near the start of his career...First victory came at the 1979 Southern Open, where he defeated Tom Weiskopf in a playoff...Later went on to win the 1981 Western Open by four strokes...Finishing rounds of 67-69-67 paved the way...In 1982 outdueled Tom Kite in a playoff to win the Bob Hope Desert Classic...Was the medalist at the 1977 PGA TOUR Fall Qualifying Tournament at Pinehurst Country Club... Attended the University of Houston, after attending Wharton Junior College for a semester...Was an important cog in the Cougars' 1977 National Championship Team... Collected All-American honors in 1977.

PERSONAL: Nicknamed "The Grip" for the unusual way in which he holds the club...Used to sneak onto a nine-hole course near his home growing up...Graduated from high school, and worked odd jobs for approximately four years before going off to college.

1993 PGA TOUR STATISTICS

Scoring Average	71.41	(110T)
Driving Distance	244.7	(187)
Driving Accuracy	77.3	(8)
Greens in Regulation	65.4	(92T)
Putting	1.833	(170)
All-Around	924	(124)
Sand Saves	59.2	(18)
Total Driving	195	(106T)
Eagles	3	(116T)
Birdies	253	(117T)

MISCELLANEOUS STATISTICS

Scoring Avg. (before cut)	71.52	(82T)
Scoring Avg. (3rd round)	71.88	(136)
Scoring Avg. (4th round)	71.76	(117T)
Birdie Conversion	22.7	(185T)
Par Breakers	15.0	(176T)

1993 Low Round: 66: 2 times
Career Low Round: 63: 2 times, most recent 1992 Phoenix Open/2
Career Largest Paycheck: $68,000/1989 Kmart Greater Greensboro Open/3

JOHN FLANNERY

EXEMPT STATUS: 102nd on 1993 money list

FULL NAME: John Conrad Flannery

HEIGHT: 6'1"   **WEIGHT:** 170

BIRTH DATE: April 11, 1962

BIRTHPLACE: Salinas, CA

RESIDENCE: La Quinta, CA

FAMILY: Wife, Laura

COLLEGE: University of Southern California

SPECIAL INTEREST: Basketball and gardening

TURNED PROFESSIONAL: 1985

JOINED TOUR: 1993

PLAYER PROFILE

CAREER EARNINGS: $161,234

BEST-EVER FINISH: T9--1993 AT&T Pebble Beach National Pro-Am

MONEY & POSITION: 1993--$161,234--102

BEST 1993 FINISH: T9--AT&T Pebble Beach National Pro-Am

1993 SUMMARY: Tournaments entered--31; in money--23; top ten finishes--1.

1994 PGA TOUR CHARITY TEAM COMPETITION: THE TOUR Championship

1993 SEASON: Overall had an outstanding rookie season on the PGA TOUR... Wound up with four finishes in the top-25, including one in the top-10... Very consistent performer who only missed eight cuts in 31 starts...Best streak was in the summer, when he made seven straight and picked up a solo 12th at the Buick Open... His best tournament of the year came early at the AT&T Pebble Beach National Pro-Am... Was four strokes behind Brett Ogle going into the last day, and wound up tied for ninth... His next best performance was a tie for 13th at the Northern Telecom Open.

CAREER HIGHLIGHTS: Was selected by his peers as the **1992 Ben Hogan Tour Player of the Year**... Was the leading money winner that year, with over $160,000 in earnings... Won three times on that circuit, including the South Carolina Classic, the Quicksilver Open, and the Sonoma County Open... Led the Tour in birdies, scoring, and par breakers... Posted 11 top-10 finishes in 28 events... Played the Hogan Tour in 1990, finishing 38th on the money list... Finished first on the Golden State Tour Order of Merit in 1991, after not gaining any playing privileges on TOUR... Became one of a handful of Monday Qualifiers to ever win an event, when he won the Ben Hogan Reno Open in a playoff in 1991... Finished 48th on the money list that year...Winner of the California State Open in 1987.

PERSONAL: A native of California, he attended USC with Sam Randolph and Brian Henninger.

1993 PGA TOUR STATISTICS

Scoring Average	71.38	(108)
Driving Distance	256.2	(124T)
Driving Accuracy	63.5	(158)
Greens in Regulation	64.0	(132)
Putting	1.753	(6)
All-Around	879	(110)
Sand Saves	51.3	(100T)
Total Driving	282	(177)
Eagles	5	(67T)
Birdies	370	(7)

MISCELLANEOUS STATISTICS

Scoring Avg. (before cut)	71.22	(58)
Scoring Avg. (3rd round)	72.53	(170)
Scoring Avg. (4th round)	72.18	(146T)
Birdie Conversion	30.9	(11T)
Par Breakers	20.0	(33T)

1993 Low Round: 64: 2 times

Career Low Round: 64: 2 times, most recent 1993 H-E-B Texas Open/4

Career Largest Paycheck: $27,969/1993 AT&T Pebble Beach National Pro-Am/9

BRUCE FLEISHER

EXEMPT STATUS: 81st on 1993 money list

FULL NAME: Bruce Fleisher

HEIGHT: 6' 3" **WEIGHT:** 198

BIRTH DATE: October 16, 1948

BIRTHPLACE: Union City, IN

RESIDENCE: Ballen Isles, FL

FAMILY: Wife, Wendy; Jessica (3/23/80)

COLLEGE: Miami Dade JC

SPECIAL INTERESTS: reading, helping others

TURNED PROFESSIONAL: 1970

Q SCHOOL: Fall 1971

PLAYER PROFILE

CAREER EARNINGS: $1,004,376   **PLAYOFF RECORD:** 1-0

TOUR VICTORIES: 1991 New England Classic
(TOTAL: 1)

MONEY & POSITION:

1972--$ 9,019--	1980--$ 13,649--149	1988--$ 2,198--268
1973--$ 14,610--	1981--$ 69,221-- 64	1989--$ --
1974--$ 33,975-- 77	1982--$ 36,659--110	1990--$ 10,626--227
1975--$ 7,773--141	1983--$ 50,285--102	1991--$219,335-- 76
1976--$ 11,295--137	1984--$ 30,186--138	1992--$236,516-- 68
1977--$ 9,101--155	1985--$ --	1993--$214,279-- 81
1978--$ 8,347--154	1986--$ 7,866--213	
1979--$ 11,420--149	1987--$ 2,405--254	

BEST 1993 FINISH: T2--New England Classic

1993 SUMMARY: Tournaments entered--28; in money--16; top ten finishes--1.

1994 PGA TOUR CHARITY TEAM COMPETITION: Doral-Ryder Open

1993 SEASON: Proved that there really are "horses for courses" in 1993, when he finished as the runnerup at the New England Classic... Fired a solid 2-under-par 69 on the last day at Pleasant Valley, to wind up four strokes behind Paul Azinger... Finished second or better for the second time in three years there... Was three stokes back going into the last day... Eight of his last 10 rounds at Pleasant Valley have been at par or better... Finished tied for 11th at the Canon Greater Hartford Open, after a second-round 5-under-par 65 moved him to within four strokes of the lead.

CAREER HIGHLIGHTS: Electrified the golf world in 1991 by defeating Ian Baker-Finch in a seven-hole playoff to win the New England Classic...Rolled in a 50-foot birdie putt on the seventh extra hole to best Baker-Finch, who would go on to win the British Open the very next week...Joined the PGA TOUR in 1972, after a much heralded amateur career...Winner of the 1968 U.S. Amateur, and was the low amateur in the 1969 Masters... Won the 1989 PGA Club Pro Championship and a member of the 1990 PGA Cup team... Won the 1971 Brazilian Open before owning a PGA TOUR card... Co-winner 1991 Hilton Bounceback Award... Winner, 1990 Jamaica, Bahamas and Brazilian Opens.

PERSONAL: Won his Amateur Championship at Scioto CC in Columbus, OH...That honor paired him with Arnold Palmer during the first round of the 1969 Masters, where he bested the King 69-73... Is the fourth youngest competitor to ever win the U.S. Amateur at 19 years and 11 months.

1993 PGA TOUR STATISTICS

Scoring Average	71.01	(69T)
Driving Distance	249.8	(175T)
Driving Accuracy	75.6	(18)
Greens in Regulation	66.1	(72T)
Putting	1.789	(69T)
All-Around	886	(113)
Sand Saves	48.4	(137)
Total Driving	193	(103T)
Eagles	0	N/A
Birdies	298	(60)

MISCELLANEOUS STATISTICS

Scoring Avg. (before cut)	71.42	(73)
Scoring Avg. (3rd round)	70.60	(46T)
Scoring Avg. (4th round)	71.38	(83T)
Birdie Conversion	27.8	(84T)
Par Breakers	18.4	(85T)

1993 Low Round: 65: Canon Greater Hartford Open/2
Career Low Round: 63: 1974 Quad Cities Open/2
Career Largest
Paycheck: $180,000/1991 New England Classic/1

RAYMOND FLOYD

EXEMPT STATUS: Winner 1969 PGA Championship

FULL NAME: Raymond Loran Floyd

HEIGHT: 6' 1"   **WEIGHT:** 200

BIRTH DATE: Sept. 4, 1942

BIRTHPLACE: Fort Bragg, NC

RESIDENCE: Miami, FL (Plays out of The Bahama Club, Great Exuma, Bahamas)

FAMILY: Wife, Maria; Raymond Jr. (9/20/74), Robert Loran (1/23/76), Christina Loran (8/29/79)

COLLEGE: University of North Carolina

TURNED PROFESSIONAL: 1961

JOINED TOUR: 1963

PLAYER PROFILE

CAREER EARNINGS: $5,033,997   **PLAYOFF RECORD:** 5-10

TOUR VICTORIES: **1963** St. Petersburg Open. **1965** St. Paul Open. **1969** Jacksonville Open, American **(TOTAL: 22)** Golf Classic, PGA Championship. **1975** Kemper Open. **1976** Masters, World Open. **1977** Byron Nelson Classic, Pleasant Valley Classic. **1979** Greensboro Open. **1980** Doral-Eastern Open. **1981** Doral-Eastern Open, Tournament Players Championship, Manufacturers Hanover-Westchester Classic. **1982** Memorial Tournament, Danny Thomas-Memphis Classic, PGA Championship. **1985** Houston Open. **1986** U.S. Open, Walt Disney/Oldsmobile Classic. **1992** Doral Ryder Open

MONEY & POSITION:

1963--$ 10,529-- 58	1974--$119,385-- 18	1984--$102,813-- 68
1964--$ 21,407-- 30	1975--$103,627-- 13	1985--$378,989-- 5
1965--$ 36,692-- 25	1976--$178,318-- 7	1986--$380,508-- 9
1966--$ 29,712-- 32	1977--$163,261-- 7	1987--$122,880-- 86
1967--$ 25,254-- 47	1978--$ 77,595-- 30	1988--$169,549-- 69
1968--$ 63,002- -24	1979--$122,872-- 26	1989--$ 74,699-- 145
1969--$109,957-- 8	1980--$192,993-- 10	1990--$264,078-- 55
1970--$ 47,632-- 24	1981--$359,360-- 2	1991--$284,897-- 56
1971--$ 70,607-- 32	1982--$386,809-- 2	1992--$741,918-- 13
1972--$ 35,624-- 70	1983--$208,353-- 20	1993--$126,516-- 120
1973--$ 39,646-- 77		

BEST 1993 FINISHES: T7--U.S. Open; T8--GTE Byron Nelson Classic

1993 SUMMARY: Tournaments entered--6; in money--5; top ten finishes--2.

1994 PGA TOUR CHARITY TEAM COMPETITION: The International

NATIONAL TEAMS: Ryder Cup (8), 1969, 1975, 1977, 1981, 1983, 1985, 1991, 1993. Captain of 1989 Ryder Cup team. U.S. vs. Japan, 1982. Nissan Cup, 1985.

1993 SEASON: Divided his time between the PGA TOUR and the Senior PGA TOUR... As a result only played in six tournaments... Nevertheless still managed to collect two top-10 finishes... His best finish of the year was at the U. S. Open at Baltusrol, where a final round 2-under-par 68 moved him into a tie for seventh...Played in the Ryder Cup for the eighth time in his career... Teamed with Steve Elkington to win Franklin Funds Shark Shoot-Out.

CAREER HIGHLIGHTS: Won the 1992 Doral Ryder Open at the age of 49... Later in the same year, after turning 50, he won the GTE North Classic, making him the first player to win a tournament on both the PGA TOUR and the Senior PGA TOUR... He joins Sam Snead as the only player to win in four different decades...Before Hale Irwin's victory in 1990, Floyd had the distinction of being the oldest player to win the U.S. Open...Downed Lanny Wadkins and Chip Beck down the stretch to win at Shinnecock Hills in 1986...Served as the Ryder Cup captain in 1989... In his career has won The Masters, the Tournament Players Championship, the PGA Championship and the U.S.Open...Winner of the 1983 Vardon Trophy...Winner of the 1985 Chrysler Team Championship with Hal Sutton...Winner of the 1988 Skins Game...Winner of the 1990 RMCC Invitational with Fred Couples.

PERSONAL: Grew up in Fort Bragg, North Carolina, the son of an Army man...Had the option of playing professional baseball, but chose golf instead... Still a devoted fan of the Chicago Cubs... Victory at the Doral-Ryder Open, came after his home in Miami burned just a couple of weeks earlier. Has two golfing sons: Raymond, Jr. attends Wake Forest, Robert will attend University of Florida in the Fall.

1993 PGA TOUR STATISTICS

Scoring Average	70.07	N/A
Driving Distance	266.2	N/A
Driving Accuracy	69.4	N/A
Greens in Regulation	69.9	N/A
Putting	1.827	N/A
All-Around	N/A	
Sand Saves	53.8	N/A
Total Driving	N/A	
Eagles	N/A	
Birdies	64	N/A

MISCELLANEOUS STATISTICS

Scoring Avg. (before cut)	70.33	N/A
Scoring Avg. (3rd round)	71.00	N/A
Scoring Avg. (4th round)	70.60	N/A
Birdie Conversion	23.1	N/A
Par Breakers	16.2	N/A

1993 Low Round: 66: GTE Byron Nelson Classic/1
Career Low Round: 63: 2 times, most recent 1992 MCI Heritage Classic/2
Career Largest Paycheck: $252,000/1992 Doral Ryder Open/1

DAN FORSMAN

EXEMPT STATUS: 1992 tournament winner

FULL NAME: Daniel Bruce Forsman

HEIGHT: 6' 4"   **WEIGHT:** 195

BIRTH DATE: July 15, 1958

BIRTHPLACE: Rhinelander, WI

RESIDENCE: Provo, UT

FAMILY: Wife, Trudy; Ricky (1/18/85), Thomas (12/15/89)

COLLEGE: Arizona State University

SPECIAL INTERESTS: Snow skiing, reading

TURNED PROFESSIONAL: 1982

Q SCHOOL: Fall 1982

PLAYER PROFILE

CAREER EARNINGS: $2,684,807   **PLAYOFF RECORD:** 1-0

TOUR VICTORIES: **1985** Lite Quad Cities Open. **1986** Hertz Bay Hill Classic. **1990** Shearson Lehman
(TOTAL: 4)   Hutton Open. **1992** Buick Open.

MONEY & POSITION:

1983--$ 37,859--118	1987--$157,727-- 63	1991--$214,175-- 78
1984--$ 52,152--105	1988--$269,440-- 40	1992--$763,190-- 10
1985--$150,334-- 53	1989--$141,174-- 99	1993--$410,150-- 36
1986--$169,445-- 54	1990--$319,160-- 43	

BEST 1993 FINISHES: T2--Canon Greater Hartford Open; T5--H-E-B Texas Open; T7--Infiniti Tournament of Champions; T7--Masters Tournament; T7--Sprint Western Open; T9--AT&T Pebble Beach National Pro-Am.

1993 SUMMARY: Tournaments entered--25; in money--19; top ten finishes--6.

1994 PGA TOUR TEAM CHARITY COMPETITION: Walt Disney World/Oldsmobile Classic

1993 SEASON: Another steady season for Forsman, as he surpassed the $400,000 mark in earnings for the second consecutive year...Finished in the top-10 six time...Best opportunity for victory came at the Canon Greater Hartford Open... A final-round 5-under-par 65 at the TPC at River Highlands gave him a tie for second just one stroke behind Nick Price... Was tied for second place with Chip Beck after three rounds at The Masters before finishing in seventh place... Finished tied for fifth at the H-E-B Texas Open, after an opening 7-under-par 64.

CAREER HIGHLIGHTS: 1992 was Forsman's best year with over $440,000 in earnings over his previous best season... In 1992, he won the Buick Open, and finished runner-up three other times...The victory at Warwick Hills came after a final round 5-under-par 67 left him tied with Brad Faxon and Steve Elkington... He made par on the second extra hole for his fourth TOUR victory... He won for the third time at the Shearson Lehman Hutton Open in 1990...Followed that up in 1991 with a third-place finish as defending champion...Other victories came at the 1985 Lite Quad Cities Open and the rain-shortened 1986 Hertz Bay Hill Classic...Was a two-time All-American while attending Arizona State...winner of the 1987 MCI Long Distance Driving Competition...led the PGA TOUR in birdies in 1987 and again in 1988.

PERSONAL: Was introduced to the game at 13 by his father, who was an avid golfer... Grew up in the San Francisco Bay area, where he competed against the likes of Bobby Clampett as an amateur.

1993 PGA TOUR STATISTICS

Scoring Average	70.38	(27T)
Driving Distance	260.5	(84T)
Driving Accuracy	69.5	(85)
Greens in Regulation	67.8	(45T)
Putting	1.769	(24T)
All-Around	537	(29)
Sand Saves	51.5	(95T)
Total Driving	169	(68)
Eagles	5	(67T)
Birdies	309	(42T)

MISCELLANEOUS STATISTICS

Scoring Avg. (before cut)	70.46	(20)
Scoring Avg. (3rd round)	70.67	(51T)
Scoring Avg. (4th round)	71.21	(60T)
Birdie Conversion	29.1	(41T)
Par Breakers	20.1	(32)

1993 Low Round:	64: 3 times
Career Low Round:	62: 1988 Bob Hope Chrysler Classic/2
Career Largest Paycheck:	$180,000/1992 Buick Open/1

DAVID FROST

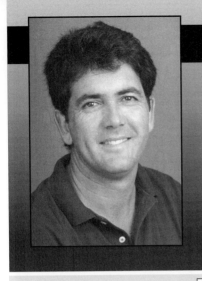

EXEMPT STATUS: Winner, 1989 NEC World Series of Golf

FULL NAME: David Laurence Frost

HEIGHT: 5' 11" **WEIGHT:** 172

BIRTH DATE: Sept. 11, 1959

BIRTHPLACE: Cape Town, South Africa

RESIDENCE: Dallas, TX

FAMILY: Sean (2/24/88), Noelle (1/15/90)

SPECIAL INTERESTS: All sports, rugby

TURNED PROFESSIONAL: 1981

Q SCHOOL: Fall 1984

PLAYER PROFILE

CAREER EARNINGS: $4,428,831   **PLAYOFF RECORD:** 2-2

TOUR VICTORIES: **1988** Southern Open, Northern Telecom Tucson Open. **1989** NEC World Series
(TOTAL: 8)   of Golf. **1990** USF&G Classic. **1992** Buick Classic, Hardee's Golf Classic. **1993**
Canadian Open, Hardee's Golf Classic.

MONEY & POSITION:			
	1985--$118,537--70	1988--$691,500-- 9	1991--$ 171,262-- 93
	1986--$187,944--46	1989--$620,430-- 11	1992--$ 717,883-- 15
	1987--$518,072--11	1990--$372,485-- 32	1993--$1,030,717-- 5

BEST 1993 FINISHES: 1--Canadian Open; 1--Hardee's Golf Classic; 2--MCI Heritage Classic; T2--
THE TOUR Championship; T3--Buick Classic; 4--Doral-Ryder Open; T5--GTE Byron Nelson Classic;
T6--Honda Classic; T7--NEC World Series of Golf.

1993 SUMMARY: Tournaments entered--22; in money--15; top ten finishes--9.

1994 PGA TOUR CHARITY TEAM COMPETITION: NEC World Series of Golf

1993 SEASON: Enjoyed the finest year of his career in 1993... He collected two victories, two runner-up finishes, and one third-place finish... Surpassed the $1 million mark in earnings for the first time... Earned back-to-back victories at the Canadian Open and the Hardee's Classic... He closed with a 4-under-par 68 to edge Fred Couples by a stroke in Canada... He was the defending champion at the Hardee's Classic...His 259 total was two strokes off the TOUR record for 72 holes... He won by seven strokes... In 1994, he will attempt to become the first player since Tom Watson in 1978-80 to win the same event three consecutive years.

CAREER HIGHLIGHTS: Won twice in 1992, capturing titles at the Buick Classic and the Hardee's Classic... Won in Westchester by a whopping eight strokes... Captured the biggest win of his career at the 1989 NEC World Series of Golf...Defeated Ben Crenshaw with a par on the second extra hole at Firestone...The win gave him a 10-year exemption into all PGA TOUR co-sponsored events...Holed a bunker shot for birdie on the 72nd hole at the 1990 USF&G Classic to beat Greg Norman by a stroke...Won 1988 Southern Open and Northern Telecom Tucson Open..Beat Bob Tway in a playoff at the Southern, and won in Tucson by five strokes...Winner of the 1983 Gordon's Gin Classic and the 1984 Cannes Open...Winner of the 1987 South African Masters and the Merrill Lynch Shoot-Out Finals...Winner of the Sun City Million Dollar Challenge in both 1989 and 1990.

PERSONAL: Got started in the game by caddying for his father at the age of 14... Came to the U.S. in 1981 with little success... Returned to South Africa and in 1983 finished second in the Order of Merit on that Tour... Went from there to Europe, and finally back to the States in 1985.

1993 PGA TOUR STATISTICS

Scoring Average	69.48	(3)
Driving Distance	260.8	(77T)
Driving Accuracy	67.7	(102T)
Greens in Regulation	66.7	(67T)
Putting	1.739	(1)
All-Around	573	(38)
Sand Saves	57.4	(29)
Total Driving	179	(78T)
Eagles	2	(144T)
Birdies	287	(72T)

MISCELLANEOUS STATISTICS

Scoring Avg. (before cut)	70.18	(7)
Scoring Avg. (3rd round)	69.86	(10)
Scoring Avg. (4th round)	70.20	(12)
Birdie Conversion	32.7	(3T)
Par Breakers	22.0	(2T)

1993 Low Round: 63: Hardee's Golf Classic/2
Career Low Round: 60: 1990 Tucson Open/2
Career Largest
Paycheck: $198,750/ 1993 TOUR Championship/T2

FRED FUNK

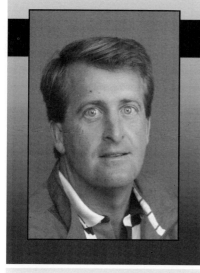

EXEMPT STATUS: 1992 tournament winner

FULL NAME: Frederick Funk

HEIGHT: 5'8"   **WEIGHT:** 165

BIRTH DATE: June 14, 1956

BIRTHPLACE: Takoma Park, MD

RESIDENCE: Ponte Vedra Beach, FL

FAMILY: Eric (8/2/91)

COLLEGE: University of Maryland (1980, Law Enforcement)

SPECIAL INTERESTS: Water, snow skiing

Q SCHOOL: Fall 1988, 1989.

PLAYER PROFILE

CAREER EARNINGS: $1,192,322

TOUR VICTORIES: 1992 Shell Houston Open. (TOTAL:1)

MONEY & POSITION:
1989--$ 59,695--157	1991--$226,915--73	1993--$309,435--56
1990--$179,346-- 91	1992--$416,930--34	

BEST 1993 FINISHES: T6--Federal Express St. Jude Classic; T6--Buick Open; T7--U.S. Open; T8--Anheuser-Busch Golf Classic; T10--Buick Classic.

1993 SUMMARY: Tournaments entered--34; in money--24; top ten finishes--5.

1994 PGA TOUR CHARITY TEAM COMPETITION: Kemper Open

1993 SEASON: Was extremely hot during the middle part of the season, as he collected all five of his top-10 finishes between the middle of June and the first of August... In the span of seven tournaments, five of his finishes were in the top-10... Finished tied for sixth on consecutive weeks at the Federal Express St. Jude Classic and the Buick Open... Was two strokes out of the lead going into the final day in Memphis after a 6-under-par 65 on Saturday... At the Buick Open, a third-round 5-under 67 moved him into the top-10 as well... His next best finish was a tie for seventh at the United States Open at Baltusrol... One of five golfers to compete in 34 events, the most on TOUR in 1993.

CAREER HIGHLIGHTS: A course record 10-under-par 62, followed by a solid 2-under 70 on the final day, gave him his first PGA TOUR victory at the Shell Houston Open... Went on to win by two strokes over Kirk Triplett at the TPC at The Woodlands... His best previous finishes were T3s in the 1990 Chattanooga Classic and 1989 Deposit Guaranty Golf Classic...earned exempt status for the first time after fine 1990 season that saw him post three top-10 finishes and earn $179,346...improved in 1991 to $226,915 and posted five top-10s...won the 1984 Foot-Joy National Assistant Pro Championship and numerous Mid-Atlantic Section PGA events...shot 59 on the 5,908-yard Desert Course at the TPC of Scottsdale during a separate pro-am at the 1992 Phoenix Open…Won the 1993 Mexican Open.

PERSONAL: Golf coach at the University of Maryland for eight years before joining the TOUR... Had it not been for golf, he probably would have been in the law enforcement field... Picked up the game at 10 years of age.

1993 PGA TOUR STATISTICS

Scoring Average	70.86	(57)
Driving Distance	251.2	(170T)
Driving Accuracy	80.6	(3)
Greens in Regulation	68.2	(39)
Putting	1.793	(77T)
All-Around	593	(41)
Sand Saves	54.6	(58)
Total Driving	173	(70)
Eagles	3	(116T)
Birdies	394	(3)

MISCELLANEOUS STATISTICS

Scoring Avg. (before cut)	71.03	(42)
Scoring Avg. (3rd round)	71.04	(79)
Scoring Avg. (4th round)	71.25	(67T)
Birdie Conversion	27.9	(78T)
Par Breakers	19.2	(62T)

1993 Low Round:	**64:** 2 times
Career Low Round:	**62:** 2 times, most recent
Career Largest	1992 Shell Houston Open/3
Paycheck:	**$216,000**/1992 Shell Houston Open/1

JIM GALLAGHER, JR.

EXEMPT STATUS: 1993 tournament winner
FULL NAME: James Thomas Gallagher, Jr.
HEIGHT: 6'   **WEIGHT:** 180
BIRTH DATE: March 24, 1961
BIRTHPLACE: Johnstown, PA

RESIDENCE: Greenwood, MS; plays out of Brickyard
                 Crossing, Indianapolis, IN
FAMILY: Wife, Cissye; Mary Langdon (1/13/92),
                 James Thomas III(12/1/93)
COLLEGE: University of Tennessee (1983, Marketing)

SPECIAL INTERESTS: Music, duck hunting, following
                         family golf careers
TURNED PROFESSIONAL: 1983
Q SCHOOL: Fall 1983, 1984

PLAYER PROFILE

CAREER EARNINGS: $3,200,723   **PLAYOFF RECORD:** 1-1
TOUR VICTORIES: 1990 Greater Milwaukee Open. **1993** Anheuser-Busch Golf Classic, THE TOUR
(TOTAL: 3)   Championship

MONEY & POSITION: | 1984--$ 22,249--148 | 1988--$ 83,766--124 | 1992--$ 638,314--19 |
|---|---|---|
| 1985--$ 19,061--159 | 1989--$265,809-- 50 | 1993--$1,078,870-- 4 |
| 1986--$ 79,967--107 | 1990--$476,706-- 25 | |
| 1987--$ 39,402--166 | 1991--$570,627-- 18 | |

BEST 1993 FINISHES: 1--Anheuser-Busch Golf Classic; 1--THE TOUR Championship: T2--NEC World
Series of Golf; T3--Northern Telecom Open; T4--Bob Hope Chrysler Classic; T10--Canadian Open.

1993 SUMMARY: Tournaments entered--27; in money--18; top ten finishes--6.

1994 PGA TOUR TEAM CHARITY COMPETITION: Deposit Guaranty Golf Classic

NATIONAL TEAMS: 1991 Four Tours World Championship of Golf; Ryder Cup, 1993

1993 SEASON: The 1993 season is one that Jim Gallagher, Jr. will never forget...Not only did he break through and win his second tournament, he won his third as well... Top that off with a splendid performance in the Ryder Cup Matches, and note that he broke the $1 million mark for single season earnings... After nursing a pinched nerve during the middle part of the season, came back strong with his second career victory at the Anheuser-Busch Classic...Closed with a superb 7-under-par 65 on the last day to edge Ryder Cup teammate Chip Beck by two strokes...That victory gave him enough points to make his first Ryder Cup team... Finished off the Ryder Cup matches with a solid 3-and-2 defeat of Seve Ballesteros in singles play... More than doubled his yearly earnings by winning THE TOUR Championship by a stroke over Greg Norman and David Frost...He opened with a course record 8-under-par 63, and closed with a 2-under-par 69 on Sunday for his third career victory...That victory earned $540,000, the largest first-place check ever on TOUR.

CAREER HIGHLIGHTS: Milwaukee will always have a special place in Gallagher's heart...after losing his playing privileges in 1987, relied on sponsor's exemptions in 1988...received one to the GMO and responded with second-place finish...came back in 1990 to win at Tuckaway...finished tied at 17-under-par 271 with Billy Mayfair and Ed Dougherty...defeated both of them with a par on the first extra hole... Winner of two TPS events in 1985, Magnolia Classic and the Charley Pride Golf Fiesta...leading money winner on the circuit that year...1982 (as amateur) and 1983 Indiana State Open Champion...Winner of the 1982 Indiana State Amateur...Honorable Mention All-American at Tennessee...AJGA Junior All-American in 1979.

PERSONAL: Comes from a golf background... Married to former LSU Tiger golfer Cissye, who was a member of the LPGA...Sister Jackie is a member of the LPGA... Brother Jeff has been a member of the Nike Tour since 1990...Father Jim is a PGA Professional in Marion, IN, at Meshingomesia CC... Started the game at the age of two.

1993 PGA TOUR STATISTICS

Scoring Average	71.05	(71T)
Driving Distance	268.7	(30T)
Driving Accuracy	64.5	(154T)
Greens in Regulation	67.7	(47T)
Putting	1.794	(82T)
All-Around	771	(81)
Sand Saves	44.9	(170T)
Total Driving	184	(91T)
Eagles	4	(89T)
Birdies	312	(37)

MISCELLANEOUS STATISTICS

Scoring Avg. (before cut)	71.87	(108)
Scoring Avg. (3rd round)	70.56	(45)
Scoring Avg. (4th round)	70.33	(15T)
Birdie Conversion	28.8	(53T)
Par Breakers	19.7	(43T)

1993 Low Round:	63: 2 times
Career Low Round:	61: 1991 Las Vegas Invitational/4
Career Largest Paycheck:	$540,000/1993 TOUR Championship/1

ROBERT GAMEZ

EXEMPT STATUS: 70th on 1993 money list

FULL NAME: Robert Anthony Gamez

HEIGHT: 5'9"   **WEIGHT:** 170

BIRTH DATE: July 21, 1968

BIRTHPLACE: Las Vegas, NV

RESIDENCE: Las Vegas, NV; plays out of Ko Olina GC at Ewa Beach, Oahu, HI

COLLEGE: University of Arizona

SPECIAL INTERESTS: Music and movies

TURNED PROFESSIONAL: 1989

Q SCHOOL: Fall 1989

PLAYER PROFILE

CAREER EARNINGS: $1,193,862   **PLAYOFF RECORD:** 0-1

TOUR VICTORIES: 1990 Northern Telecom Tucson Open, Nestle Invitational. (TOTAL: 2)

MONEY & POSITION: 1989 -- $ 4,827 -- 237   1991 -- $280,349--59   1993 -- $236,458--70
                          1990 -- $461,407 -- 27   1992 -- $215,648--72

BEST 1993 FINISHES: 2--Honda Classic; T8--Northern Telecom Open; T10--Las Vegas Invitational.

1993 SUMMARY: Tournaments entered--25; in money--15; top ten finishes--3.

1994 PGA TOUR CHARITY TEAM COMPETITION: JCPenney Classic

NATIONAL TEAMS: 1989 Walker Cup

1993 SEASON: Started his year strongly with a playoff loss to Fred Couples at the wind-shortened Honda Classic... Couples won with a par on the second extra hole... Opened and closed with 4-under-par 68s at Weston Hills CC... Finished tied for eighth at the Northern Telecom Open... Was four strokes back at the halfway point in Tucson... Other top-10 came at home, at the Las Vegas Invitational, where he finished tied for 10th.

CAREER HIGHLIGHTS: As a rookie, won in his first official start on the PGA TOUR...Captured the Northern Telecom Open by four strokes over Mark Calcavecchia in his debut in 1990...Turned in rounds of 65-66-69-70 to win with relative ease...Electrified the golf world, when he holed a 7-iron from 176 yards for an eagle, and an eventual one-stroke victory over Greg Norman at the Nestle Invitational...Was selected as the **1990 PGA TOUR Rookie of the Year**...In 1989 was named the winner of the Fred Haskins and Jack Nicklaus Awards as the outstanding collegiate player of the year...Winner of six collegiate titles while attending the University of Arizona...Also won the 1989 Porter Cup...Was a member of the 1989 Walker Cup team.

PERSONAL: First time he swung a cut down golf club was when he was two years old... His father would take him to the range when he had to babysit... His brother Randy was his caddie in both TOUR victories, and still carries the bag from time to time... Prefers Robert over Bob or Bobby.

1993 PGA TOUR STATISTICS

Scoring Average	71.66	(129T)
Driving Distance	259.1	(93T)
Driving Accuracy	72.7	(48)
Greens in Regulation	65.9	(79T)
Putting	1.810	(125T)
All-Around	825	(96)
Sand Saves	48.1	(142)
Total Driving	141	(34)
Eagles	3	(116T)
Birdies	299	(59)

MISCELLANEOUS STATISTICS

Scoring Avg. (before cut)	71.90	(111T)
Scoring Avg. (3rd round)	72.00	(139T)
Scoring Avg. (4th round)	71.80	(119T)
Birdie Conversion	31.1	(10)
Par Breakers	20.7	(19T)

1993 Low Round:	**65:** Hope Chrysler Classic/4
Career Low Round:	**61:** 1991 Greater Milwaukee Open/1
Career Largest Paycheck:	**$162,000**/1990 Tucson Open/1 1990 Nestle Invitational/1

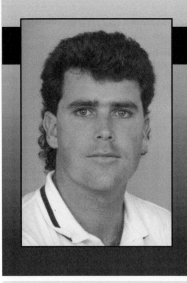

KELLY GIBSON

EXEMPT STATUS: 110th on 1993 money list

FULL NAME: Kelly Michael Gibson

BIRTH DATE: May 2, 1964

BIRTHPLACE: New Orleans, LA

RESIDENCE: New Orleans, LA; plays out of English Turn GC

FAMILY: Single

COLLEGE: Lamar University

SPECIAL INTERESTS: Saints football

TURNED PROFESSIONAL: 1986

Q SCHOOL: 1991

PLAYER PROFILE

CAREER EARNINGS: $285,987

BEST-EVER FINISH: T4-1992 Buick Southern Open

MONEY & POSITION: 1992 - $137,984-- 105   1993 - $ 148,003--110

BEST 1993 FINISH: T12--Bob Hope Chrysler Classic

1993 SUMMARY: Tournaments entered--33; in money--20; top ten finishes--0.

1994 PGA TOUR CHARITY TEAM COMPETITION: Freeport-McMoRan Classic

1993 SEASON: Very steady sophomore season for the Louisiana native... Gibson recorded six finishes in the top-25 to retain his playing priviliges for the second consecutive season...His best finish of the year was a tie for 12th at the Bob Hope Chrysler Classic...Opened with consecutive 5-under-par 67s and then added a 6-under 66 to move within two strokes of the lead, before closing with a 69 and a 70... Finished alone in 14th at his windswept home course of English Turn GC at the Freeport-McMoRan Classic... Finished tied for ninth in eagles with 10.

CAREER HIGHLIGHTS: Best ever finish came at the 1992 Buick Southern Open, where he finished tied for fourth... Was tied for the lead after the first round at Callaway, and wound up four strokes back... One of the top players on the 1991 Ben Hogan Tour...finished 14th on the money list with $50,097...earned $33,550 (26th) in 1990...final-round 9-under-par 63 earned him the victory in the 1991 Ben Hogan Tri-Cities Open by two strokes over Jerry Anderson...played the Canadian Tour for four years...placed third in the Canadian Tour Order Of Merit in 1991...Led the Canadian Tour in scoring average in 1991 with an average of 69.75.

PERSONAL: An avid New Orleans Saints football and Louisiana State University athletics fan.

1993 PGA TOUR STATISTICS

Scoring Average	71.56	(121)
Driving Distance	270.9	(17)
Driving Accuracy	67.0	(119T)
Greens in Regulation	64.9	(112T)
Putting	1.813	(129T)
All-Around	585	(40)
Sand Saves	58.8	(21)
Total Driving	136	(31T)
Eagles	10	(9T)
Birdies	325	(26)

MISCELLANEOUS STATISTICS

Scoring Avg. (before cut)	71.90	(111T)
Scoring Avg. (3rd round)	72.19	(159)
Scoring Avg. (4th round)	71.89	(127)
Birdie Conversion	27.3	(99T)
Par Breakers	18.2	(98T)

1993 Low Round: **64:** MCI Heritage Classic/2
Career Low Round: **63:** 1992 Chattanooga Classic/4
Career Largest Paycheck: **$30,125**/1992 New England Classic/T7

71

BOB GILDER

EXEMPT STATUS: 108th on 1993 money list

FULL NAME: Robert Bryan Gilder

HEIGHT: 5' 9"   **WEIGHT:** 165

BIRTH DATE: Dec. 31, 1950   **BIRTHPLACE:** Corvallis, OR

RESIDENCE: Corvallis, OR

FAMILY: Wife, Peggy; Bryan (3/24/75); Cammy Lynn
(6/10/77); Brent (3/3/81)

COLLEGE: Arizona State (1973, Business Administration)

SPECIAL INTERESTS: All sports, car racing

TURNED PROFESSIONAL: 1973

Q SCHOOL: Fall 1975

PLAYER PROFILE

CAREER EARNINGS: $2,342,243   **PLAYOFF RECORD:** 1-0

TOUR VICTORIES: **1976** Phoenix Open. **1980** Canadian Open. **1982** Byron Nelson Classic, Manufacturers
(TOTAL: 6)   Hanover Westchester Classic, Bank of Boston Classic. **1983** Phoenix Open.

MONEY & POSITION:

1976--$101,262-- 24	1982--$308,648-- 6	1988--$144,523-- 82
1977--$ 36,844-- 72	1983--$139,125-- 39	1989--$187,910-- 78
1978--$ 72,515-- 36	1984--$ 23,313--147	1990--$154,934--102
1979--$134,428-- 22	1985--$ 47,152--123	1991--$251,683-- 66
1980--$152,597-- 19	1986--$ 98,181-- 85	1992--$170,761-- 91
1981--$ 74,756-- 59	1987--$ 94,310--100	1993--$148,496--108

BEST 1993 FINISHES: T7--Buick Classic; T8--Anheuser-Busch Golf Classic

1993 SUMMARY: Tournaments entered--27; in money--13; top ten finishes--2.

1994 PGA TOUR CHARITY TEAM COMPETITION: United Airlines Hawaiian Open

NATIONAL TEAMS: Ryder Cup, 1983; World Cup, 1982; U.S. vs. Japan, 1982.

1993 SEASON: Typically got hot in the middle of the year collecting both top-10 finishes in the span of five tournaments... Finished tied for seventh at the Buick Classic, (a tournament that he won in 1982) three strokes out of the Vijay Singh/ Mark Wiebe playoff... Other top-10 came at the Anheuser-Busch Golf Classic where a 5-under 66, followed by a 3-under 68 on the weekend propelled him into contention.

CAREER HIGHLIGHTS: First PGA TOUR victory came at the 1976 Phoenix Open...Best year on TOUR came in 1982, when he collected victories at the Byron Nelson Classic, Manufacturers Hanover Westchester Classic and the Bank of Boston Classic...19-under-par 261 total at Westchester was highlighted by a double-eagle on the 509-yard 18th hole during the third round (driver-3-wood)...His 14-under-par 266 total at the Byron Nelson was the lowest score in the 16 years that the tournament was played at Preston Trail...Won the Phoenix Open again in 1983, this time in a playoff over Johnny Miller, Rex Caldwell and Mark O'Meara... Winner of several international tournaments, including the 1974 New Zealand Open, where he defeated Jack Newton and Bob Charles in a playoff...Defeated John Mahaffey by two strokes in 1988 to win the Isuzu Kapalua International...Later that same year teamed with Doug Tewell to win the Acom Team title in Japan...Also won the 1982 Bridgestone International and the 1990 Acom P.T., both of which were contested in Japan.

PERSONAL: Was a college teammate of Howard Twitty and Tom Purtzer, while at Arizona State... Earned his card at the 1975 Fall Qualifying Tournament... In his first start as a TOUR member in 1976, he missed the cut at Tucson... However, the very next week, he overtook Roger Maltbie on the last day to win the Phoenix Open.

1993 PGA TOUR STATISTICS

Scoring Average	71.21	(91)
Driving Distance	257.8	(111T)
Driving Accuracy	71.0	(64T)
Greens in Regulation	65.2	(101T)
Putting	1.805	(110T)
All-Around	819	(95)
Sand Saves	60.6	(13T)
Total Driving	175	(72T)
Eagles	2	(144T)
Birdies	256	(113T)

MISCELLANEOUS STATISTICS

Scoring Avg. (before cut)	72.02	(121T)
Scoring Avg. (3rd round)	70.73	(54T)
Scoring Avg. (4th round)	71.23	(65)
Birdie Conversion	27.9	(78T)
Par Breakers	18.4	(85T)

1993 Low Round: **66:** 3 times
Career Low Round: 62: 1979 New Orleans Open/3
Career Largest
Paycheck: $72,000/1982 Westchester Classic/1

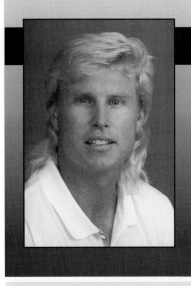

BILL GLASSON

EXEMPT STATUS: 1992 tournament winner

FULL NAME: William Lee Glasson, Jr.

HEIGHT: 5' 11"   **WEIGHT:** 165

BIRTH DATE: April 29, 1960   **BIRTHPLACE:** Fresno, CA

RESIDENCE: Stillwater, OK

FAMILY: Wife, Courtney; Maxwell Alexander (9/30/88), Dakota Jade (2/26/92)

COLLEGE: Oral Roberts University (1982, Business)

SPECIAL INTERESTS: Flying own plane

TURNED PROFESSIONAL: 1983

Q SCHOOL: Fall 1983, 1984

PLAYER PROFILE

CAREER EARNINGS: $ 2,129,023

TOUR VICTORIES: 1985 Kemper Open. **1988** B.C. Open, Centel Classic. **1989** Doral-Ryder Open.
(TOTAL: 5)   **1992** Kemper Open.

MONEY & POSITION:

1984--$ 17,845--162	1988--$380,651-- 30	1992--$283,765-- 54
1985--$195,449-- 29	1989--$474,511-- 19	1993--$299,799--57
1986--$121,516-- 72	1990--$156,791--100	
1987--$151,701-- 69	1991--$ 46,995--178	

BEST 1993 FINISHES: 3--B.C. Open; 7--Canadian Open; 8--Bob Hope Chrysler Classic; T8--Buick Southern Open; T9--United Airlines Hawaiian Open; T10--Memorial Tournament.

1993 SUMMARY: Tournaments entered--22; in money--16; top ten finishes--6.

1994 PGA TOUR CHARITY TEAM COMPETITION: AT&T Pebble Beach National Pro-Am

1993 SEASON: Very solid year for Glasson...Collected six different top-10 finishes during the year...Only three times did Glasson go more than three tournaments without a top-10 finish...Wound up the year in strong fashion, as he reeled off high finishes in three consecutive starts...Rallied for a final-round 4-under-par 67, for his best finish of the year, a solo third at the B.C. Open...Best round of the year came at the Bob Hope Chrysler Classic when he fired an 8-under-par 64 in the second round.

CAREER HIGHLIGHTS: Played the 1992 season on a special medical exemption...Sat out most of the 1991 season due to problems in his lower back...Also has had problems with his knees...First victory of his career came at the 1985 Kemper Open, where he rolled in a 40-foot birdie putt on the final hole and held on to win...Was a two-time winner in 1988, collecting titles at the B.C. Open and the Centel Classic...Started off hot in 1989, with a victory at the Doral Ryder Open, where he collected a check for $234,000, the largest of his career... Ended a 38-month winless skein in 1992, when he won the Kemper Open for the second time... His teacher is Ken Cayce, who is the head pro at Congressional, site of his first Kemper Open victory.

PERSONAL: Was a two-time All-America selection at Oral Roberts...Led the PGA TOUR in Driving Distance in 1984 (his rookie season), averaging 276.5 yards per drive... Flies own plane to many TOUR stops.

1993 PGA TOUR STATISTICS

Scoring Average	70.49	(30)
Driving Distance	267.9	(35)
Driving Accuracy	73.7	(38T)
Greens in Regulation	72.3	(2)
Putting	1.791	(74T)
All-Around	434	(13)
Sand Saves	51.9	(92T)
Total Driving	73	(7)
Eagles	4	(89T)
Birdies	291	(67T)

MISCELLANEOUS STATISTICS

Scoring Avg. (before cut)	70.41	(16T)
Scoring Avg. (3rd round)	70.27	(27T)
Scoring Avg. (4th round)	70.81	(33)
Birdie Conversion	29.0	(46T)
Par Breakers	21.3	(9)

1993 Low Round: **65**: 2 times
Career Low Round: **62**: 1985 Panasonic Las
Career Largest   Vegas Invitational/1
Paycheck: **$234,000**/1989 Doral Ryder Open/1

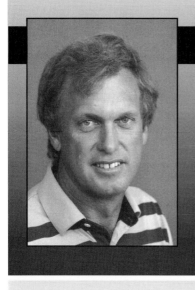

WAYNE GRADY

EXEMPT STATUS: Winner, 1990 PGA Championship

FULL NAME: Wayne Desmond Grady

HEIGHT: 5' 9"   **WEIGHT:** 160

BIRTH DATE: July 26, 1957

BIRTHPLACE: Brisbane, Australia

RESIDENCE: Queensland, Australia

FAMILY: Wife, Lyn; Samantha (11/23/86)

SPECIAL INTERESTS: Cricket, fishing, all sports

TURNED PROFESSIONAL: 1978

Q SCHOOL: Fall 1984

PLAYER PROFILE

CAREER EARNINGS: $1,687,521   **PLAYOFF RECORD:** 1-0

TOUR VICTORIES: 1989 Manufacturers Hanover Westchester Classic. **1990** PGA Championship.
(TOTAL: 2)

MONEY & POSITION:

1985--$167,497-- 41	1988--$111,536--102	1991--$126,650--118
1986--$ 49,417--137	1989--$402,364-- 27	1992--$183,361-- 83
1987--$ 73,552--122	1990--$527,185-- 21	1993--$ 45,959--187

BEST 1993 FINISH: T16--Doral-Ryder Open

1993 SUMMARY: Tournaments entered--20; in money--8; top ten finishes--0.

NATIONAL TEAMS: Australian World Cup (3) 1978, 1983, 1989; Australian Nissan Cup, 1985; Australian Four Tours World Championship of Golf (2), 1989, 1990. Dunhill Cup (2), 1989,1990.

1993 SEASON: Had his share of troubles during the 1993 campaign... During the 20 tournaments that he entered, only made consecutive cuts twice during the year... His best finish of the year came in his first start ... Wound up tied for 16th at the Doral-Ryder Open.

CAREER HIGHLIGHTS: Biggest victory to date came in the 1990 PGA Championship at Shoal Creek...Was never headed after a second round 5-under-par 67...Closed with a 72 and a 71 for a 6-under-par 282, and a three-stroke victory over Fred Couples...First PGA TOUR victory came at the 1989 Manufacturers Hanover Westchester Classic...He finished with a 7-under-par 277 total, and defeated Ronnie Black in a playoff with a birdie on the first extra hole...Later that same year lost in a playoff to Mark Calcavecchia at the British Open... Greg Norman was also involved in that playoff... Has played on a number of national teams for Australia, including their World Cup team in 1978, 1983, and 1989...A member of their Dunhill, and Four Tours World Championship of Golf teams in 1989 and 1990...Has won a number of tournaments both at home in Australia and in Europe, including the 1984 German Open and the 1988 Australian PGA.

PERSONAL: Wanted to be a pilot for the Australian Air Force as a youngster... Picked up golf at the age of 14... Turned professional two years later, but soon applied to get his amateur status back... Turned professional for good at the age of 21.

1993 PGA TOUR STATISTICS

Scoring Average	72.17	(168T)
Driving Distance	251.1	(172)
Driving Accuracy	67.8	(100T)
Greens in Regulation	62.9	(151T)
Putting	1.815	(135T)
All-Around	1372	(184)
Sand Saves	49.4	(127T)
Total Driving	272	(173)
Eagles	1	(164T)
Birdies	147	(182)

MISCELLANEOUS STATISTICS

Scoring Avg. (before cut)	72.97	(175)
Scoring Avg. (3rd round)	70.86	(63)
Scoring Avg. (4th round)	74.71	(189)
Birdie Conversion	25.0	(159T)
Par Breakers	15.8	(167)

1993 Low Round: 68: 3 times

Career Low Round: 63: 1991 Hardee's Golf Classic/2

Career Largest Paycheck: $225,000/1990 PGA Championship/1

HUBERT GREEN

EXEMPT STATUS: Winner, 1985 PGA Championship

FULL NAME: Hubert Myatt Green

HEIGHT: 6' 1"   **WEIGHT:** 175

BIRTH DATE: Dec. 28, 1946

BIRTHPLACE: Birmingham, AL

RESIDENCE: Birmingham, AL

FAMILY: Wife, Karen; Hubert Myatt, Jr. (8/18/75); Patrick (10/17/78); J.T. (2/11/84)

COLLEGE: Florida State University (1968)

SPECIAL INTERESTS: Fishing, gardening

TURNED PROFESSIONAL: 1970

Q SCHOOL: Fall 1970

PLAYER PROFILE

CAREER EARNINGS: $2,575,610   **PLAYOFF RECORD:** 2-3

TOUR VICTORIES: **1971** Houston Champions International. **1973** Tallahassee Open, B.C. Open. **1974** Bob Hope Classic, Greater Jacksonville Open, Philadelphia Classic, Walt Disney World National Team Play (with Mac McLendon). **1975** Southern Open. **1976** Doral-Eastern Open, Jacksonville Open, Sea Pines Heritage Classic. **1977** U.S. Open. **1978** Hawaiian Open, Sea Pines Heritage Classic. **1979** Hawaiian Open, New Orleans Open. **1981** Sammy Davis, Jr.-Greater Hartford Open. **1984** Southern Open. **1985** PGA Championship.
(TOTAL: 19)

MONEY & POSITION:

1970--$ 1,690--218	1978--$247,406-- 5	1986--$120,051-- 73
1971--$ 73,439-- 29	1979--$183,111-- 13	1987--$ 63,349--129
1972--$ 44,113-- 58	1980--$ 83,307-- 50	1988--$ 52,268--147
1973--$114,397-- 11	1981--$110,133-- 32	1989--$161,190-- 86
1974--$211,709-- 3	1982--$ 77,448-- 54	1990--$ 65,948--165
1975--$113,569-- 12	1983--$ 29,171--135	1991--$ 18,031--212
1976--$228,031-- 4	1984--$181,585-- 33	1992--$ 23,602--204
1977--$140,255-- 9	1985--$233,527-- 16	1993--$ 29,786--199

BEST 1993 FINISH: T20--Canon Greater Hartford Open

1993 SUMMARY: Tournaments entered--19; in money--7; top ten finishes--0.

NATIONAL TEAMS: Ryder Cup (3), 1977, 1979, 1985.

1993 SEASON: Showed some flashes of the old brilliance, making the cut in seven of the 19 events that he entered... His best finish of the year was a tie for 20th at the Canon Greater Hartford Open... He closed with a 2-under-par 68 to finish just nine strokes behind Nick Price... That started a stretch where he made the cut in five out of the next six events that he entered... His next best finish was a tie for 29th at the Anheuser-Busch Golf Classic... An opening round 6-under-par 66 had him two strokes out of the lead at the Walt Disney World/Oldsmobile Classic.

CAREER HIGHLIGHTS: Has won 19 times in his 24 years on TOUR, including the 1977 U.S. Open at Southern Hills in Tulsa, and the 1985 PGA Championship at Cherry Hills in Denver...Outdueled Lee Trevino down the stretch for the stirring victory in Denver...One of the truly outstanding players in the world in the 1970's...In fact 16 of his victories came during that decade...First victory came at the 1971 Houston Champions International...Has won four different events twice -- Greater Jacksonville Open, Southern Open, Heritage Classic, and the Hawaiian Open...During one three-week period in 1976, Green won three consecutive tournaments...Dominated at the Doral Eastern Open, the Greater Jacksonville Open and the Sea Pines Heritage Classic...Was the 1971 Rookie of the Year on TOUR...Winner of the 1975 Dunlop Phoenix in Japan...Winner of the 1977 Irish Open...Winner of two Southern Amateurs as a youth...Former Player Director on the PGA TOUR Policy Board...Was the co-winner in the 1980 Jerry Ford Invitational...Also been a member of three Ryder Cup teams in 1977, 1979 and 1985.

PERSONAL: Started golf at the age of five, but played all sports as a kid... Swing is considered a little unorthodox, but effective... Worked for a summer as an assistant at Merion GC in Ardmore, PA, before trying his hand at the TOUR... Now spends a considerable amount of time designing golf courses... Worked with Fuzzy Zoeller on the TPC at Southwind.

1993 PGA TOUR STATISTICS

Scoring Average	72.87	(186)
Driving Distance	245.8	(185)
Driving Accuracy	74.7	(27T)
Greens in Regulation	58.6	(183T)
Putting	1.809	(123T)
All-Around	1247	(170)
Sand Saves	54.2	(61T)
Total Driving	212	(134T)
Eagles	1	(164T)
Birdies	145	(184T)

MISCELLANEOUS STATISTICS

Scoring Avg. (before cut)	72.76	(165)
Scoring Avg. (3rd round)	71.75	(130)
Scoring Avg. (4th round)	72.88	(171)
Birdie Conversion	25.4	(150T)
Par Breakers	15.0	(176T)

1993 Low Round:	**66:** Walt Dis./Olds. Classic/1
Career Low Round:	**62:** 1978 San Antonio Texas Open/1
Career Largest Paycheck:	**$125,000:** 1985 PGA Championship/1

KEN GREEN

EXEMPT STATUS: 75th on 1993 money list

FULL NAME: Kenneth J. Green

HEIGHT: 5' 10"   **WEIGHT:** 175

BIRTH DATE: July 23, 1958   **BIRTHPLACE:** Danbury, CT

RESIDENCE: West Palm Beach, FL; plays out of the Highlands at Molokai, Hawaii

FAMILY: Kenny (12/19/81), Brad (6/26/83), Brooke (7/17/85), Hunter (9/30/88)

COLLEGE: Palm Beach JC

SPECIAL INTERESTS: Bowling, platform tennis

TURNED PROFESSIONAL: 1979

Q SCHOOL: Fall 1981, 1982, 1984

PLAYER PROFILE

CAREER EARNINGS: $3,019,069   **PLAYOFF RECORD:** 0-2

TOUR VICTORIES: **1985** Buick Open. **1986** The International. **1988** Canadian Open, Greater Milwaukee
(TOTAL: 5)   Open. **1989** Kmart Greater Greensboro Open.

MONEY & POSITION:		
1982--$ 11,899--167	1986--$317,835-- 16	1990--$267,172-- 54
1983--$ 40,263--114	1987--$237,271-- 36	1991--$263,034-- 65
1984--$ 20,160--156	1988--$779,181-- 4	1992--$360,397-- 41
1985--$151,355-- 52	1989--$304,754-- 37	1993--$229,750--75

BEST 1993 FINISHES: T3--Walt Disney World/Oldsmobile Classic; 6--Greater Milwaukee Open; T6--THE PLAYERS Championship.

1993 SUMMARY: Tournaments entered--22; in money--10; top ten finishes--3.

1994 PGA TOUR CHARITY TEAM COMPETITION: NEC World Series of Golf

NATIONAL TEAMS: Ryder Cup, 1989; Four Tours World Championship of Golf, 1989

1993 SEASON: Something of an inconsistent year for the five-time winner on TOUR... Only cashed a check in 10 of the events that he entered... His best finish of the year came at the Walt Disney World/Oldsmobile Classic... A third-round 8-under-par 63 propelled him into a tie for third... Shot four rounds in the 60s in Milwaukee to finish alone in sixth place... Largest check of the year came at THE PLAYERS Championship where he finished tied for sixth and earned $80,937.50.

CAREER HIGHLIGHTS: Was having something of a disappointing season during 1988, before winning on consecutive weeks at the Canadian Open and the Greater Milwaukee Open... Had a sterling 11-under-par 61 at Tuckaway to give him a decisive victory... After losing the Kmart Greater Greensboro Open in 1988 in a playoff to Sandy Lyle, rebounded to take the title the next year... Winner of the Connecticut Open in 1985 and 1992...Also has collected titles in four other mini-tour events... Has won twice in the Orient, taking titles in the 1988 Dunlop Phoenix in Japan, and later winning the 1990 Hong Kong Open...Was a member of the Ryder Cup team that tied the Europeans in 1989.

PERSONAL: Picked up the game at the age of 12, when his family moved to Honduras, where his father became the principal of the American School.

1993 PGA TOUR STATISTICS

Scoring Average	71.90	(148T)
Driving Distance	257.7	(113)
Driving Accuracy	66.0	(132T)
Greens in Regulation	64.7	(117T)
Putting	1.750	(3)
All-Around	961	(128)
Sand Saves	64.4	(1)
Total Driving	245	(159T)
Eagles	2	(144T)
Birdies	216	(144)

MISCELLANEOUS STATISTICS

Scoring Avg. (before cut)	73.02	(176)
Scoring Avg. (3rd round)	69.60	(4)
Scoring Avg. (4th round)	71.60	(104)
Birdie Conversion	31.2	(8T)
Par Breakers	20.4	(26T)

1993 Low Round: **66**: 2 times
Career Low Round: **61**: 1988 Greater Milwaukee
Career Largest   Open/3
Paycheck: **$180,000**/1989 Kmart GGO/1

JAY HAAS

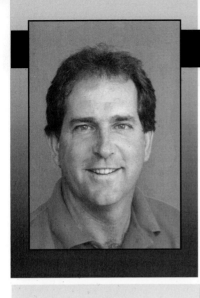

EXEMPT STATUS: 1993 tournament winner

FULL NAME: Jay Dean Haas

HEIGHT: 5' 10''   **WEIGHT:** 170

BIRTH DATE: December 2, 1953

BIRTHPLACE: St. Louis, MO

RESIDENCE: Greenville, SC

CLUB AFFILIATION: Thornblade GC in Greenville.

FAMILY: Wife, Janice; Jay, Jr. (3/8/81); William Harlan (5/24/82); Haley (1/18/84); Emily Frances (9/25/87); Georgia Ann (3/12/92).

COLLEGE: Wake Forest

SPECIAL INTERESTS: All sports

TURNED PROFESSIONAL: 1976   **Q SCHOOL:** Fall 1976

PLAYER PROFILE

CAREER EARNINGS: $4,011,176   **PLAYOFF RECORD:** 3-0

TOUR VICTORIES: **1978** Andy Williams-San Diego Open. **1981** Greater Milwaukee Open, B.C. Open.
(TOTAL: 9)   **1982** Hall of Fame Classic, Texas Open. **1987** Big "I" Houston Open. **1988** Bob Hope Chrysler Classic. **1992** Federal Express St. Jude Classic. **1993** H-E-B Texas Open.

MONEY & POSITION:

1977--$ 32,326--77	1983--$191,735--23	1989--$248,830--54
1978--$ 77,176--31	1984--$146,514--45	1991--$200,637--84
1979--$102,515--34	1985--$121,488--69	1990--$180,023--89
1980--$114,102--35	1986--$189,204--45	1992--$632,628--20
1981--$181,894--15	1987--$270,347--37	1993--$601,603--26
1982--$229,746--13	1988--$490,409--20	

BEST 1993 FINISHES: 1--H-E-B Texas Open; T4--Bob Hope Chrysler Classic; T4--Buick Invitational of California; T4--Memorial Tournament; T10--Nestle Invitational; T10--THE TOUR Championship.

1993 SUMMARY: Tournaments entered--29; in money--27; top ten finishes--6.

1994 PGA TOUR CHARITY TEAM COMPETITION: THE PLAYERS Championship

NATIONAL TEAMS: Ryder Cup, 1983; Walker Cup, 1975.

1993 SEASON: Surpassed the $600,000 mark in earnings for the second time in his career and picked up his ninth PGA TOUR victory along the way... Closed with a final round 7-under-par 64 and wound up tied with Bob Lohr at the end of regulation at the H.E.B. Texas Open... He won the subsequent playoff with a birdie on the second extra hole... Made 24 consecutive cuts to start the season... Had five other finishes in the top-10 including a tie for fourth at the Bob Hope Chrysler Classic... Was one stroke out of the lead after consecutive 6-under-par 66s to start the tournament.

CAREER HIGHLIGHTS: Closed with consecutive 7-under-par 64s on the weekend to win the 1992 Federal Express St. Jude Classic... Edged Robert Gamez and Dan Forsman by one stroke at the TPC at Southwind... The $198,000 winner's check was the largest of his career... Opened with a 9-under-par 63 at the Bob Hope Chrysler Classic in 1988 enroute to victory ...Rolled in a miraculous 70-foot putt on the 72nd hole to tie Buddy Gardner in the 1987 Big "I" Houston...Went on to defeat Gardner with a par on the first extra hole...Was a multiple winner in both 1981 and 1982... Winner of the 1975 NCAA Championship, while attending Wake Forest...Was selected as an All-American in 1975 and 1976...Awarded the Fred Haskins Award as the nation's outstanding collegiate player in 1975...Winner of the 1976 Southwestern and Missouri Opens...Winner of the 1991 Mexican Open.

PERSONAL: Teammate of Curtis Strange while attending Wake Forest... His uncle is former Masters Champion Bob Goalby, who got him started in the game at a very young age... Haas was seven when he played in and won his first trophy at the National Pee Wee Championship in Orlando, FL...The tournament consisted of two five-hole rounds and Haas, always a model of consistency, shot 26-26--52 to finish in third place.

1993 PGA TOUR STATISTICS

Scoring Average	70.32	(22T)
Driving Distance	260.3	(87)
Driving Accuracy	69.3	(88)
Greens in Regulation	69.7	(19)
Putting	1.806	(112T)
All-Around	478	(19)
Sand Saves	55.3	(48)
Total Driving	175	(72T)
Eagles	8	(25T)
Birdies	374	(5)

MISCELLANEOUS STATISTICS

Scoring Avg. (before cut)	70.37	(13)
Scoring Avg. (3rd round)	70.80	(59)
Scoring Avg. (4th round)	71.22	(62T)
Birdie Conversion	26.6	(122T)
Par Breakers	18.9	(73T)

1993 Low Round: 64: H-E-B Texas Open/4

Career Low Round: 63: 3 times, most recent 1990 Nissan Los Angeles Open/3

Career Largest Paycheck: $198,000/1992 Federal Express St. Jude Classic/1

GARY HALLBERG

EXEMPT STATUS: 1992 tournament winner

FULL NAME: Gary George Hallberg

HEIGHT: 5' 10"   **WEIGHT:** 155

BIRTH DATE: May 31, 1958

BIRTHPLACE: Berwyn, IL

RESIDENCE: Castle Rock, CO

FAMILY: Wife, Shirley; Christina (8/19/92)

COLLEGE: Wake Forest University

SPECIAL INTERESTS: Family, sports, TOUR Bible study

TURNED PROFESSIONAL: July 2, 1980

JOINED TOUR: July, 1980

PLAYER PROFILE

CAREER EARNINGS: $1,804,014   **PLAYOFF RECORD:** 0-2

TOUR VICTORIES: **1983** Isuzu-Andy Williams San Diego Open. **1987** Greater Milwaukee Open. **1992**
(TOTAL: 3)   Buick Southern Open.

MONEY & POSITION:

1980--$ 64,244-- 63	1985--$108,872-- 75	1990--$128,954--121
1981--$ 45,793-- 91	1986--$ 68,479--121	1991--$273,546-- 62
1982--$ 36,192--111	1987--$210,786-- 48	1992--$236,629-- 67
1983--$120,140-- 45	1988--$ 28,551--179	1993--$147,706--111
1984--$187,260-- 30	1989--$146,833-- 95	

BEST 1993 FINISH: T11--Phoenix Open.

1993 SUMMARY: Tournaments entered--27; in money--19; top ten finishes--0.

1994 PGA TOUR CHARITY TEAM COMPETITION: Honda Classic

1993 SEASON: Played his best golf early in the year, as he collected two of his four top-25 finishes by the end of January... Started year off with a tie for 15th at the Infiniti Tournament of Champions... A third-round 3-under-par 69 moved him into contention... Followed that up three weeks later, with his best finish of the year... Wound up tied for 11th at the Phoenix Open... A third-round 4-under-par 67 moved him to within four strokes of the lead... Faltered with a final round 2-over 73.

CAREER HIGHLIGHTS: Has surpassed the $200,000 barrier in earnings three times, including 1991 and 1992...Shot all three rounds in the 60s to earn his third career victory at the rain-shortened 1992 Buick Southern Open... His final-round 3-under 69 was good enough to hold off Jim Gallagher, Jr....Victory at the 1987 Greater Milwaukee Open was keyed by a birdie chip-in of 50-feet on the 17th hole...Edged Robert Wrenn and Wayne Levi by two strokes at Tuckaway CC...Shot a final round 66 and held on to defeat Tom Kite at the 1983 Isuzu-Andy Williams San Diego Open...Became the first four-time first-team All-American selection in history...Winner of the 1979 NCAA Championship...Winner of the 1982 Chunichi Crowns in Japan...Teamed with Scott Hoch to win the 1986 Chrysler Team Championship...Winner of the 1988 Jerry Ford Invitational.

PERSONAL: Became the first player to earn his PGA TOUR card by winning the $8,000 needed at that time (1980) to obtain his playing privileges without going through the Qualifying Tournament... Started to play at the age of nine, and ironically played in a Father/Son tournament at Callaway Gardens, site of his 1992 Buick Southern Open title.

1993 PGA TOUR STATISTICS

Scoring Average	71.60	(123T)
Driving Distance	265.0	(51T)
Driving Accuracy	62.3	(171T)
Greens in Regulation	59.9	(176T)
Putting	1.771	(29T)
All-Around	765	(79)
Sand Saves	63.3	(5)
Total Driving	222	(141T)
Eagles	8	(25T)
Birdies	308	(44T)

MISCELLANEOUS STATISTICS

Scoring Avg. (before cut)	71.58	(87)
Scoring Avg. (3rd round)	72.05	(147T)
Scoring Avg. (4th round)	73.16	(176)
Birdie Conversion	31.4	(5T)
Par Breakers	19.3	(55T)

1993 Low Round: 67: 4 times
Career Low Round: 63: 4 times, most recent '91
Career Largest Fed. Ex. St. Jude Classic/2
Paycheck: $126,000/1992 Buick Southern Open/1

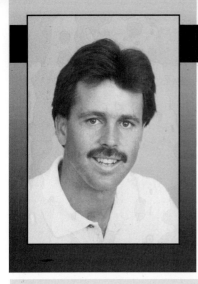

DONNIE HAMMOND

EXEMPT STATUS: 47th on 1993 money list

FULL NAME: Donald William Hammond

HEIGHT: 5'10"   **WEIGHT:** 170

BIRTH DATE: April 1, 1957

BIRTHPLACE: Frederick, MD

RESIDENCE: Winter Park, FL

FAMILY: Wife, Kathy; Matthew William (10/22/86); Brittany Marie (3/8/89)

COLLEGE: Jacksonville University (1979, Psychology)

SPECIAL INTERESTS: Sports, cars, gardening, tennis, flying

TURNED PROFESSIONAL: 1979

Q SCHOOL: Fall 1982, 1991

PLAYER PROFILE

CAREER EARNINGS: $2,131,143   **PLAYOFF RECORD:** 1-0

TOUR VICTORIES: 1986 Bob Hope Chrysler Classic. **1989** Texas Open presented by Nabisco. (TOTAL: 2)

MONEY & POSITION:			
	1983--$ 41,336--112	1987--$157,480-- 64	1991--$102,668--135
	1984--$ 67,874-- 86	1988--$256,010-- 44	1992--$197,085-- 77
	1985--$102,719-- 77	1989--$458,741-- 20	1993--$340,432-- 47
	1986--$254,987-- 28	1990--$151,811--104	

BEST 1993 FINISHES: T2--Nissan Los Angeles Open; T3--Shell Houston Open; 7--Greater Milwaukee Open.

1993 SUMMARY: Tournaments entered--23; in money--20; top ten finishes--3.

1994 PGA TOUR CHARITY TEAM COMPETITION: Canon Greater Hartford Open.

1993 SEASON: Very steady season for Hammond, as he earned over $130,000 before leaving the West Coast... Collected three finishes in the top 10 including a second and a third... Finished tied for second at the Nissan Los Angeles Open, after firing an even-par 71 on the final day... Ended up three strokes behind Tom Kite... A final-round 4-under-par 68 left him one stroke out of the Jim McGovern/John Huston playoff at the Shell Houston Open... Was a stroke out of the lead at the halfway point of the Greater Milwaukee Open before finishing alone in seventh.

CAREER HIGHLIGHTS: Winner of two PGA TOUR events in his career, the last coming at the 1989 Texas Open presented by Nabisco...Had a four-day total of 258 (22-under-par), after rounds of 65-64-65-64...That was the second lowest cumulative score in PGA TOUR history, and missed tying the record by a single stroke...Won the 1986 Bob Hope Chrysler Classic...Defeated John Cook in a playoff with a birdie on the first extra hole... Was the medalist at the 1982 PGA TOUR Qualifying Tournament...Won that event by a record 14 strokes...Set a then-course record of 65 on the TPC at Sawgrass course...Winner of the 1982 Florida Open...Was the co-winner in the Jerry Ford Invitational in 1989 and 1990... Won five events in college, including the Sun Belt Conference title in 1979.

PERSONAL: Picked up the game at 13, when he and his father would go watch the Baltimore Colts training camp, then play a nine-hole golf course close by... A charter member of the Jacksonville University Sports Hall of Fame.

1993 PGA TOUR STATISTICS

Scoring Average	70.51	(31T)
Driving Distance	259.5	(92)
Driving Accuracy	74.9	(25)
Greens in Regulation	68.4	(35T)
Putting	1.758	(9T)
All-Around	544	(31T)
Sand Saves	47.3	(149)
Total Driving	117	(17)
Eagles	2	(144T)
Birdies	309	(42T)

MISCELLANEOUS STATISTICS

Scoring Avg. (before cut)	70.72	(27)
Scoring Avg. (3rd round)	70.47	(38T)
Scoring Avg. (4th round)	71.47	(93T)
Birdie Conversion	30.2	(19)
Par Breakers	20.8	(15T)

1993 Low Round: 64: 2 times
Career Low Round: 63: 2 times, most recent
Career Largest 1992 H-E-B Texas Open/2
Paycheck: $108,000/1986 Bob Hope Chrysler Classic/1; 1989 Texas Open/1

DUDLEY HART

EXEMPT STATUS: 52nd on 1993 money list

FULL NAME: Howard Dudley Hart

HEIGHT: 5' 10"   **WEIGHT:** 170

BIRTH DATE: August 4, 1968

BIRTHPLACE: Rochester, NY

RESIDENCE: West Palm Beach, FL

COLLEGE: University of Florida

SPECIAL INTERESTS: Sports

TURNED PROFESSIONAL: 1990

Q SCHOOL: Fall 1990

PLAYER PROFILE

CAREER EARNINGS: $697,870

BEST-EVER FINISH: T3--1992 Greater Milwaukee Open; T3--1993 Northern Telecom Open; T3-- 1993 Kmart Greater Greensboro Open.

MONEY & POSITION: 1991--$ 126,217--120   1992--$254,903--61   1993--$316,750--52

BEST 1993 FINISHES: T3--Northern Telecom Open; T3--Kmart Greater Greensboro Open; T6--PGA Championship; T8--Canadian Open.

1993 SUMMARY: Tournaments entered--30; in money--16; top ten finishes--4.

1994 PGA TOUR CHARITY TEAM COMPETITION: Shell Houston Open

1993 SEASON: Continues to show tremendous improvement every year on TOUR... Had locked up his card by April, with a couple of top-three finishes at the Northern Telecom Open (where he finished T4 in 1992), and at the Kmart Greater Greensboro Open... Was tied for the lead after the second and third rounds in Tucson, before finishing three strokes behind Larry Mize... Second-round 7-under-par 65 at Forest Oaks CC in Greensboro moved him to within two strokes of the pace... Wound up a stroke out of the Rocco Mediate/Steve Elkington playoff won by Mediate... Finished off the year with a tie for sixth at the PGA Championship... Was two strokes out going into the final day, but a 1-over-par 72 hurt his chances.

CAREER HIGHLIGHTS: Was a four-time All-America selection in college...After three seasons on the PGA TOUR, is still one of the youngest players on the circuit...A solid tie for fifth at the Buick Southern Open, earned him his PGA TOUR card in 1991...It was his best finish, prior to the 1992 season...Turned professional in 1990 and won both the Florida Open and the Louisiana Open...Joined the TOUR in 1990, when he finished tied for 21st at the Qualifying Tournament.

PERSONAL: Grew up in Buffalo, NY, and was an avid hockey player as a youth... Introduced to golf at a young age by his father.

1993 PGA TOUR STATISTICS

Scoring Average	70.93	(62)
Driving Distance	265.2	(47T)
Driving Accuracy	65.5	(136T)
Greens in Regulation	66.6	(69)
Putting	1.815	(135T)
All-Around	702	(67T)
Sand Saves	60.4	(15)
Total Driving	183	(89T)
Eagles	6	(50T)
Birdies	267	(99T)

MISCELLANEOUS STATISTICS

Scoring Avg. (before cut)	71.70	(96T)
Scoring Avg. (3rd round)	70.93	(70)
Scoring Avg. (4th round)	71.81	(122)
Birdie Conversion	24.6	(166)
Par Breakers	16.8	(149T)

1993 Low Round:	65: Kmart Gr. Grbro. Open/2
Career Low Round:	64: 2 times, most recent '92
Career Largest Paycheck:	Las Vegas Invitational/5 $78,000/1993 Kmart GGO/T3

NOLAN HENKE

EXEMPT STATUS: 1993 tournament winner

FULL NAME: Nolan Jay Henke

HEIGHT: 6'   **WEIGHT:** 165

BIRTH DATE: November 25, 1964

BIRTHPLACE: Battle Creek, MI

RESIDENCE: Fort Myers, FL; plays out of Vines Country Club

FAMILY: Wife, Marcy

COLLEGE: Florida State University

SPECIAL INTERESTS: Jet ski, tennis

TURNED PROFESSIONAL: 1987

Q SCHOOL: Fall 1988, 1989.

PLAYER PROFILE

CAREER EARNINGS: $1,699,629

TOUR VICTORIES: 1990 B.C. Open. **1991** Phoenix Open. **1993** BellSouth Classic. (TOTAL: 3)

MONEY & POSITION:

1989--$ 59,465--159	1991--$518,811--28	1993--$502,375--31
1990--$294,592-- 48	1992--$326,387--45	

BEST 1993 FINISHES: 1--BellSouth Classic; T6--PGA Championship; T7--United Airlines Hawaiian Open; T7--U.S. Open.

1993 SUMMARY: Tournaments entered--26; in money--20; top ten finishes--4.

1994 PGA TOUR CHARITY TEAM COMPETITION: Nestle Invitational

1993 SEASON: Flawless play at the BellSouth Classic earned him third PGA TOUR victory this past year... Four strokes behind Nick Price at the start of Sunday, he fired a smooth 5-under-par bogeyless 67 to win by two strokes over Price, Tom Sieckmann and Mark Calcavecchia... The $216,000 payday was the largest of his career... Had three other top-10s, including a T6 at the PGA Championship and a T7 at the U.S. Open... Shot 7-under for the weekend to contend at Inverness, finishing five strokes out of the Paul Azinger/Greg Norman playoff.

CAREER HIGHLIGHTS: A three-time winner on the PGA TOUR, his last previous victory came at the 1991 Phoenix Open...Led by four strokes at the start of Sunday's round, but was forced to roll in an 18-foot birdie putt on the 18th green to clinch the victory over Tom Watson, Curtis Strange and Gil Morgan at the TPC of Scottsdale...A second-round 64 propelled him to his first victory at the B.C. Open... He downed Mark Wiebe by three strokes there.

PERSONAL: Outstanding collegiate golfer, winning seven tournaments... Also won the 1986 Porter Cup, the 1987 American Amateur, and the 1987 Monroe Invitational...Was runnerup in the 1987 NCAA Championship...First team All-American selection in 1987...Began hitting balls "as soon as I could stand up," and became really serious about the game in his early teens.

1993 PGA TOUR STATISTICS

Scoring Average	71.01	(69T)
Driving Distance	265.5	(45)
Driving Accuracy	67.7	(102T)
Greens in Regulation	65.2	(101T)
Putting	1.774	(31T)
All-Around	604	(44)
Sand Saves	52.5	(83T)
Total Driving	147	(37)
Eagles	3	(116T)
Birdies	339	(20)

MISCELLANEOUS STATISTICS

Scoring Avg. (before cut)	71.00	(37T)
Scoring Avg. (3rd round)	72.35	(162)
Scoring Avg. (4th round)	71.40	(86)
Birdie Conversion	30.7	(13T)
Par Breakers	20.2	(28T)

1993 Low Round: 65: 2 times
Career Low Round: 63: 1992 Las Vegas Invitational/4
Career Largest Paycheck: $216,000/1993 BellSouth Classic/1

SCOTT HOCH

EXEMPT STATUS: 37th on 1993 money list

FULL NAME: Scott Mabon Hoch

HEIGHT: 5' 11"   **WEIGHT:** 160

BIRTH DATE: November 24, 1955

BIRTHPLACE: Raleigh, NC

RESIDENCE: Orlando, FL

FAMILY: Wife, Sally; Cameron (5/1/84), Katie (5/16/86)

COLLEGE: Wake Forest University
(1978, BA in Communications)

SPECIAL INTERESTS: All sports

TURNED PROFESSIONAL: 1979

Q SCHOOL: Fall 1979

PLAYER PROFILE

CAREER EARNINGS: $3,868,696   **PLAYOFF RECORD:** 0-1

TOUR VICTORIES: **1980** Quad Cities Open. **1982** USF&G Classic. **1984** Lite Quad Cities Open. **1989** (TOTAL: 4)   Las Vegas Invitational.

MONEY & POSITION:

1980--$ 45,600--75	1985--$186,020--35	1990--$333,978-- 40
1981--$ 49,606--85	1986--$222,077--36	1991--$520,038-- 27
1982--$193,862--16	1987--$391,747--20	1992--$ 84,798--146
1983--$144,605--37	1988--$397,599--26	1993--$403,742-- 37
1984--$224,345--27	1989--$670,680--10	

BEST 1993 FINISHES: T3--Kemper Open; T5--U.S. Open; T6--Freeport-McMoRan Classic; T6--PGA Championship; 9--Doral-Ryder Open; T10--Walt Disney World/Oldsmobile Classic.

1993 SUMMARY: Tournaments entered--28; in money--18; top ten finishes--6.

1994 PGA TOUR CHARITY TEAM COMPETITION: United Airlines Hawaiian Open

NATIONAL TEAMS: World Amateur Cup, 1978; Walker Cup, 1979.

1993 SEASON: Remarkable year for Hoch, as he overcame shoulder surgery in 1992 to finish over the $400,000 mark in earnings for only the third time in his career... Wound up the year with six finishes in the top-10 including a tie for third at the Kemper Open... Closed with a smooth 3-under-par 68 at the TPC at Avenel and ended up two strokes behind Grant Waite... Finished tied for fifth at the U.S. Open...Also finished tied for sixth at the PGA Championship.

CAREER HIGHLIGHTS: Enjoyed finest campaign in 1989 with earnings of $670,680 and a 10th place finish on the money list... Won 1989 Las Vegas Invitational... Donated $100,000 of $225,000 paycheck to the Arnold Palmer Children's Hospital in Orlando, FL, where son Cameron had successfully treated for a rare bone infection in right leg... Las Vegas triumph came in a playoff with Robert Wrenn...First triumph came in initial season on TOUR... 1980 Quad Cities Open, where he set the tournament record of 14-under-par 266... Wake Forest teammates Curtis Strange and Gary Hallberg finished second and third respectively... Won the same tournament four years later... Won Vardon Trophy for low stroke average in 1986, nearly repeated in 1987... Winner 1982 Pacific Masters, 1982 and 1986 Casio World Open (both Japan), 1990-91 Korean Opens... Winner 1986 Chrysler Team Championship with Gary Hallberg... Runnerup in 1978 U.S. Amateur... All-American selection in 1977 and 1978... A member of the 1975 NCAA Championship team at Wake Forest... Winner of the 1977 and 1978 ACC tournament... Winner, 1977 Northeast Amateur and the 1976, 1979 North Carolina Amateur.

PERSONAL: Comes from an athletic family... Father preceded him at Wake Forest, where he won All-ACC honors in baseball... Brother Buddy is a professional golfer... At one time or another was teammates with Curtis Strange, Jay Haas, Bob Byman, Robert Wrenn, Gary Hallberg.

1993 PGA TOUR STATISTICS

Scoring Average	70.36	(26)
Driving Distance	258.0	(105T)
Driving Accuracy	72.1	(57T)
Greens in Regulation	71.2	(7)
Putting	1.780	(47T)
All-Around	521	(26)
Sand Saves	51.7	(94)
Total Driving	162	(55T)
Eagles	3	(116T)
Birdies	347	(14)

MISCELLANEOUS STATISTICS

Scoring Avg. (before cut)	70.91	(31T)
Scoring Avg. (3rd round)	70.06	(17)
Scoring Avg. (4th round)	69.39	(3)
Birdie Conversion	29.1	(41T)
Par Breakers	20.9	(13T)

1993 Low Round:	**65:** Hope Chrysler Classic/4
Career Low Round:	**63:** 7 times, most recent 1991
Career Largest	Buick Open/1
Paycheck: $225,000/1989 Las Vegas Invitational/1	

MIKE HULBERT

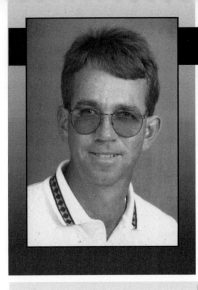

EXEMPT STATUS: 89th on 1993 money list

FULL NAME: Michael Patrick Hulbert

HEIGHT: 6'   **WEIGHT:** 175

BIRTH DATE: April 14, 1958 **BIRTHPLACE:** Elmira, NY

RESIDENCE: Orlando, FL

FAMILY: Wife, Teresa; Justin Michael (7/25/93)

COLLEGE: East Tennessee State
(1980, Business Management).

SPECIAL INTERESTS: Fishing, running

TURNED PROFESSIONAL: 1981

Q SCHOOL: Fall 1984; 1985

PLAYER PROFILE

CAREER EARNINGS: $2,345,966   **PLAYOFF RECORD:** 2-0

TOUR VICTORIES: **1986** Federal Express-St. Jude Classic. **1989** B.C. Open. **1991** Anheuser Busch
(TOTAL: 3)   Golf Classic.

MONEY & POSITION:

1985--$ 18,368--161	1988--$127,752-- 94	1991--$551,750-- 24
1986--$276,687-- 21	1989--$477,621-- 16	1992--$279,577-- 55
1987--$204,375-- 49	1990--$216,002-- 67	1993--$193,833-- 89

BEST 1993 FINISH: T11--THE PLAYERS Championship.

1993 SUMMARY: Tournaments entered--31; in money--21; top ten finishes--0.

1994 PGA TOUR CHARITY TEAM COMPETITION: Mercedes Championship

1993 SEASON: Another consistent season for one of the ironmen on the PGA TOUR... Has played in at least 31 tournaments every year, since the 1987 campaign... Best finish of the year came at THE PLAYERS Championship... He was six strokes behind winner Nick Price, finishing tied for 11th... Made 13 consecutive cuts during the middle part of the year, and earned $116,785 during that span.

CAREER HIGHLIGHTS: A three-time winner on the TOUR, his last victory came at the 1991 Anheuser-Busch Golf Classic...Hulbert two-putted for par from 40-feet on the first playoff hole to defeat Kenny Knox in near darkness...His 1989 victory in the B.C. Open was special because he grew up less than an hour away from Endicott, NY, in Horseheads...He defeated Bob Estes in a playoff there... Edged childhood friend Joey Sindelar by a stroke for his first victory at the Federal Express St. Jude Classic... During the years that he has won a tournament, he has finished no worse than 24th on the money list.

PERSONAL: 1993 was highlighted by the birth of his son, Justin... An avid fisherman, he claimed that, at 8 lbs., 3 oz., he was "just perfect for mounting."...Selected as an All-American in 1980...Won the 1987 Chrysler Team Championship with Bob Tway.

1993 PGA TOUR STATISTICS

Scoring Average	71.20	(89T)
Driving Distance	253.0	(155T)
Driving Accuracy	66.6	(124)
Greens in Regulation	65.2	(101T)
Putting	1.787	(61T)
All-Around	810	(89T)
Sand Saves	54.8	(54T)
Total Driving	279	(175T)
Eagles	9	(16T)
Birdies	315	(35)

MISCELLANEOUS STATISTICS

Scoring Avg. (before cut)	71.71	(98)
Scoring Avg. (3rd round)	71.61	(117T)
Scoring Avg. (4th round)	71.95	(132)
Birdie Conversion	26.8	(116T)
Par Breakers	18.0	(111T)

1993 Low Round: 63: SW Bell Colonial/4

Career Low Round: 63: 2 times, most recent

Career Largest   1993 SW Bell Colonial/4

Paycheck: $180,000/1991 Anheuser-Busch Golf Classic/1

ED HUMENIK

EXEMPT STATUS: 105th on 1993 money list

FULL NAME: Edward Francis Humenik

HEIGHT: 5'11"   **WEIGHT:** 210

BIRTH DATE: June 29, 1959

BIRTHPLACE: Detroit, MI

RESIDENCE: Hobe Sound, FL

FAMILY: Wife, Lori; Nancy (9/24/84), Ed, Jr. (5/12/89)

COLLEGE: Michigan (1983)

SPECIAL INTERESTS: Basketball, fishing

TURNED PROFESSIONAL: 1984

Q SCHOOL: Fall 1988

PLAYER PROFILE

CAREER EARNINGS: $ 472,780

BEST EVER FINISH: T4--1992 Buick Southern Open.

MONEY & POSITION: 1989--$ 46,384--168   1992--$149,337--100   1993--$152,562--105
1991--$124,497--121

BEST 1993 FINISHES: 5--Nestle Invitational; T10--Doral-Ryder Open; T10--B.C. Open.

1993 SUMMARY: Tournaments entered--31; in money--18; top ten finishes--3.

1994 PGA TOUR CHARITY TEAM COMPETITION: Buick Classic

1993 SEASON: Another solid season for the fourth-year TOUR veteran... His season was basically made by the middle of March, where he collected two of the three top-10s that he earned during the year... A tie for 10th at the Doral Ryder Open gave him a solid foundation for the year... After finishing tied for 20th at the Honda Classic, Humenik closed with a 2-under-par 70 to finish alone in fifth place at the Nestle Invitational... He was two strokes back at the halfway point, and wound up four behind Ben Crenshaw... Other top-10 came at the B.C. Open, where he opened with a 5-under-par 66.

CAREER HIGHLIGHTS: Played the PGA TOUR in 1989, and led the TOUR in Driving Distance with an average of 280.9 per drive that season...Lost his exempt status, but found a home on the Ben Hogan Tour the following season...After not attending TOUR School due to an illness in the family, wound up winning the Ben Hogan Macon Open (after Monday Qualifying the week before and finishing in the top-10) and the Ben Hogan Santa Rosa Open, and finished fifth on the money list...That finish on the Hogan Tour money list earned him his exempt status for 1991... Has not had any problem keeping his card since... Winner of the 1988 Michigan Open, Michigan Match Play, and was selected as the Player of the Year in Michigan in 1988.

PERSONAL: Known for his length with the driver, however, is generally a club shorter on iron shots.

1993 PGA TOUR STATISTICS

Scoring Average	71.24	(93T)
Driving Distance	272.7	(15)
Driving Accuracy	66.4	(125T)
Greens in Regulation	67.8	(45T)
Putting	1.820	(148T)
All-Around	649	(53)
Sand Saves	49.3	(129T)
Total Driving	140	(33)
Eagles	12	(3T)
Birdies	300	(58)

MISCELLANEOUS STATISTICS

Scoring Avg. (before cut)	71.66	(93T)
Scoring Avg. (3rd round)	72.00	(139T)
Scoring Avg. (4th round)	71.24	(66)
Birdie Conversion	26.4	(128T)
Par Breakers	18.6	(79T)

1993 Low Round: 64: Disney/Olds Classic2
Career Low Round: 63: 1991 United Airlines Hawaiian Open/1
Career Largest Paycheck: $48,375/1991 Las Vegas Invitational/T7

JOHN HUSTON

EXEMPT STATUS: 1992 tournament winner

FULL NAME: Johnny Ray Huston

HEIGHT: 5' 10" **WEIGHT:** 155

BIRTH DATE: June 1, 1961

BIRTHPLACE: Mt. Vernon, IL

RESIDENCE: Palm Harbor, FL; plays out of Innisbrook Golf Resort

FAMILY: Wife, Suzanne; Jessica (11/9/87)

COLLEGE: Auburn University

SPECIAL INTERESTS: All sports

TURNED PROFESSIONAL: 1983

Q SCHOOL: Fall 1987

PLAYER PROFILE

CAREER EARNINGS: $2,381,944 **PLAYOFF:** 0-1

TOUR VICTORIES: 1990 Honda Classic.**1992** Walt Disney World/Oldsmobile Classic. (TOTAL: 2)

MONEY & POSITION:

1988--$150,301--78	1990--$435,690--30	1992--$515,453--26
1989--$203,207--68	1991--$395,853--40	1993--$681,441--15

BEST 1993 FINISHES: 2--Shell Houston Open; T2--THE TOUR Championahip; T5--Hardee's Golf Classic; T6--Southwestern Bell Colonial; T6--Las Vegas Invitational; 9--Infiniti Tournament of Champions.

1993 SUMMARY: Tournaments entered--30; in money--26; top ten finishes--6.

1994 PGA TOUR CHARITY TEAM COMPETITION: Buick Classic

1993 SEASON: One of the most consistent players on TOUR, Huston had his fourth consecutive season of earning at least $395,000... Best finishes of the year came at the TPC at the Woodlands and The Olympic Club... Lost in a playoff to Jim McGovern at the Shell Houston Open... At THE TOUR Championship, he finished tied for second with Greg Norman, Scott Simpson and David Frost, one stroke behind Jim Gallagher, Jr... Steady throughout the year, finished in the top-25 in 15 out of the 30 tournaments that he entered.

CAREER HIGHLIGHTS: Collected his first TOUR victory at the wind-swept Honda Classic in 1990...Held off a strong challenge from Mark Calcavecchia to win by two strokes at the TPC at Eagle Trace... Earned his second victory in 1992 by outdueling Mark O'Meara to win the Walt Disney World/Oldsmobile Classic... Fired a closing 10-under-par 62 for the win... His winning 26-under 262 total was one stroke off of the All-Time TOUR mark for most strokes under par... Took only six years to surpass the $2 million mark in career earnings...Regarded as one of the finest putters on the TOUR, he finished in a tie for third in the putting statistic in 1991 and 11th in 1992...Medalist at the 1987 PGA TOUR Qualifying Tournament...Won 1988 JCPenney Classic with Amy Benz as his partner...Won 1985 Florida Open, and 10 mini-tour events before joining the TOUR in 1988.. Father first put a golf club in his hands at the age of seven.

PERSONAL: Says that if he wasn't a PGA TOUR professional, he would be a mini-tour professional.

1993 PGA TOUR STATISTICS

Scoring Average	70.60	(37T)
Driving Distance	270.6	(18T)
Driving Accuracy	63.1	(161T)
Greens in Regulation	68.4	(35T)
Putting	1.768	(21T)
All-Around	539	(30)
Sand Saves	48.3	(138T)
Total Driving	179	(78T)
Eagles	6	(50T)
Birdies	426	(1)

MISCELLANEOUS STATISTICS

Scoring Avg. (before cut)	70.28	(11)
Scoring Avg. (3rd round)	71.12	(85)
Scoring Avg. (4th round)	71.31	(74)
Birdie Conversion	30.9	(11T)
Par Breakers	21.4	(7T)

1993 Low Round:	**65:** 3 times
Career Low Round:	**62:** 1992 Walt Disney World/Oldsmobile Classic/4
Career Largest Paycheck:	**$198,750/** 1993 TOUR Championship/T2

JOHN INMAN

EXEMPT STATUS: 1993 tournament winner

FULL NAME: John Samuel Inman

HEIGHT: 5' 10"   **WEIGHT:** 155

BIRTH DATE: November 26, 1962

BIRTHPLACE: Greensboro, NC

RESIDENCE: Roswell, GA

FAMILY: Wife, Patti

COLLEGE: University of North Carolina

SPECIAL INTERESTS: Fishing, music

TURNED PROFESSIONAL: 1985

Q SCHOOL: Fall 1986, 1990

PLAYER PROFILE

CAREER EARNINGS: $899,826   **PLAYOFF RECORD:** 1-0

TOUR VICTORIES: 1987 Provident Classic. **1993** Buick Southern Open.
(TOTAL: 2)

MONEY & POSITION:

1987--$148,386-- 72	1990--$ 85,289--143	1992--$ 173,828--87
1988--$ 66,305--137	1991--$ 84,501--167	1993--$ 242,140--69
1989--$ 99,378--178		

BEST 1993 FINISHES: 1--Buick Southern Open; T10--Kemper Open.

1993 SUMMARY: Tournaments entered--32; in money--18; top ten finishes--2.

1994 PGA TOUR CHARITY TEAM COMPETITION: Buick Southern Open

1993 SEASON: Enjoyed the most lucrative year of his career and collected the second victory of his TOUR career... Was hovering around the 125 mark on the money list before winning the Buick Southern Open in a five-way playoff... He defeated Bob Estes, Billy Andrade, Mark Brooks, and Brad Bryant with a birdie on the second extra hole... The tournament was highlighted by his course-record 8-under-par 64 on Callaway Gardens Mountain View Course during the third round... He started the final round two strokes behind Estes, and a 2-under-par 70 was all that it took to propel him into his first TOUR playoff... Other top-10 came at the Kemper Open, where middle rounds of 68 and 69 moved him into contention.

CAREER HIGHLIGHTS: His previous biggest moment on the PGA TOUR came in 1987, when he won the Provident Classic...Put together rounds of 65-67-67-66, good for a 15-under-par 265 total and a one stroke victory over Rocco Mediate and Bill Glasson...Finished 23rd in the 1991 Qualifying Tournament...Winnner of the 1984 Fred Haskins Award as the nation's top collegiate golfer...Winner of the 1982 NCAA Championship...Broke Ben Crenshaw's tournament record by two strokes at the NCAAs finishing at 17-under...Winner of 10 collegiate events.

PERSONAL: Older brother Joe was a former member of the TOUR, and won the 1976 Kemper Open... Has relied on Joe's teachings to prepare him for TOUR life.

1993 PGA TOUR STATISTICS

Scoring Average	71.41	(110T)
Driving Distance	245.0	(186)
Driving Accuracy	75.1	(22)
Greens in Regulation	62.2	(158T)
Putting	1.775	(33T)
All-Around	817	(92T)
Sand Saves	56.5	(36T)
Total Driving	208	(131)
Eagles	4	(89T)
Birdies	306	(52)

MISCELLANEOUS STATISTICS

Scoring Avg. (before cut)	71.91	(114)
Scoring Avg. (3rd round)	70.75	(56T)
Scoring Avg. (4th round)	71.56	(100T)
Birdie Conversion	27.9	(78T)
Par Breakers	17.6	(126T)

1993 Low Round:	64: Buick Southern Open/3
Career Low Round:	64: 1993 Buick Southern Open/3
Career Largest Paycheck:	$126,000/1993 Buick Southern Open/1

HALE IRWIN

EXEMPT STATUS: Winner, 1990 United States Open

FULL NAME: Hale S. Irwin

HEIGHT: 6'   **WEIGHT:** 175

BIRTH DATE: June 3, 1945

BIRTHPLACE: Joplin, MO

RESIDENCE: Frontenac, MO; plays out of Kapalua, Maui, HI

FAMILY: Wife, Sally Stahlhuth; Becky (12/15/71), Steven (8/6/74)

COLLEGE: University of Colorado (1968, Marketing)

SPECIAL INTERESTS: Fishing, hunting, photography

TURNED PROFESSIONAL: 1968

Q SCHOOL: Spring 1968

PLAYER PROFILE

CAREER EARNINGS: $4,839,627   **PLAYOFF RECORD:** 4-5

TOUR VICTORIES: **1971** Heritage Classic. **1973** Heritage Classic. **1974** U. S. Open. **1975** Western
(TOTAL: 19)   Open, Atlanta Classic. **1976** Glen Campbell Los Angeles Open, Florida Citrus Open.
1977 Atlanta Classic, Hall of Fame Classic, San Antonio-Texas Open. **1979** U. S.
Open. **1981** Hawaiian Open, Buick Open. **1982** Honda-Inverrary Classic. **1983** Memorial Tournament.
1984 Bing Crosby Pro-Am. **1985** Memorial Tournament. **1990** U.S. Open, Buick Classic.

MONEY & POSITION:			
1968--$ 9,093--117	1977--$221,456-- 4	1986--$ 59,983--128
1969--$ 18,571-- 88	1978--$191,666-- 7	1987--$100,825-- 96
1970--$ 46,870-- 49	1979--$154,168-- 19	1988--$164,996-- 72
1971--$ 99,473-- 13	1980--$109,810-- 38	1989--$150,977-- 93
1972--$111,539-- 13	1981--$276,499-- 7	1990--$838,249-- 6
1973--$130,388-- 7	1982--$173,719-- 19	1991--$422,652-- 33
1974--$152,529-- 7	1983--$232,567-- 13	1992--$ 98,208--131
1975--$205,380-- 4	1984--$183,384-- 31	1993--$252,686-- 65
1976--$252,718-- 3	1985--$195,007-- 31	

BEST 1993 FINISHES: T6--PGA Championship; T8--Greater Milwaukee Open.
1993 SUMMARY: Tournaments entered--21; in money--14; top ten finishes--2.
1994 PGA TOUR CHARITY TEAM COMPETITION: Lincoln-Mercury Kapalua International
NATIONAL TEAMS: World Cup (2), 1974, 1979 (won individual title in 1979); Ryder Cup (5), 1975, 1977,
1979, 1981, 1991; U.S. vs. Japan, 1983.

1993 SEASON: Rebounded after a something of a down year in 1992 to have his fifth most productive year from an earnings standpoint... Finished the year with two top-10 finishes which he collected at the end of the year... Best finish of the year came at the PGA Championship where he finished in a tie for sixth... Was one stroke out of the lead after three rounds, but a final round 2-over 73 left him tied with seven other players... Still cashed a check of $47,812.50, his largest of the year... Wound up tied for eighth at the Greater Milwaukee Open.

CAREER HIGHLIGHTS: Owner of three U.S. Open titles, most recent of which came in a grueling 19-hole playoff with Mike Donald at Medinah... Made a 60-foot putt on the 72nd hole to force playoff... Ended playoff with a 10-foot birdie putt in sudden death, and became -- at age 45 -- oldest to ever win a Open... Rode U.S. Open victory wave to Buick Classic triumph the very next week... Carded four rounds in the 60s at Westchester CC and posted a two stroke victory over Paul Azinger...Finished the 1990 campaign with a career best $838,249... Other two Open victories came at Winged Foot in 1974 and Inverness in 1979... Early 1975 through 1978 played 86 tournaments without missing a cut, third best streak in TOUR history...1974-75 Picadilly World Match Play Champion... Winner 1978 Australian PGA, 1979 South African PGA , 1981 Bridestone Classic (Japan), 1982 Brazilian Open, 1986 Bahamas Classic, 1987 Fila Classic... Was the 1967 NCAA Champion, while attending the University of Colorado.

PERSONAL: Was a two-time All Big-Eight selection as a defensive back in football, while at Colorado.

1993 PGA TOUR STATISTICS

Scoring Average	70.30	(21)
Driving Distance	253.7	(149T)
Driving Accuracy	79.8	(4)
Greens in Regulation	68.3	(37T)
Putting	1.782	(55T)
All-Around	751	(78)
Sand Saves	47.8	(144T)
Total Driving	153	(42T)
Eagles	1	(164T)
Birdies	232	(135)

MISCELLANEOUS STATISTICS

Scoring Avg. (before cut)	70.63	(24)
Scoring Avg. (3rd round)	70.42	(34T)
Scoring Avg. (4th round)	70.93	(42T)
Birdie Conversion	28.2	(69T)
Par Breakers	19.3	(55T)

1993 Low Round: **66**: 4 times
Career Low Round: **61**: 1982 Southern Open/4
Career Largest
Paycheck: **$220,000**/1990 U.S. Open/1

PETER JACOBSEN

EXEMPT STATUS: 77th on 1993 money list

FULL NAME: Peter Erling Jacobsen

HEIGHT: 6'-3"   **WEIGHT:** 200

BIRTH DATE: March 4, 1954

BIRTHPLACE: Portland, OR

RESIDENCE: Portland, OR

FAMILY: Wife, Jan; Amy (7/19/80), Kristen (2/23/82), Mickey (10/12/84)

COLLEGE: University of Oregon

SPECIAL INTEREST: Music, antique car collection

TURNED PROFESSIONAL: 1976

Q-SCHOOL: Fall 1976

PLAYER PROFILE

CAREER EARNINGS: $3,260,745   **PLAYOFF RECORD**: 1-3

TOUR VICTORIES: 1980 Buick-Goodwrench Open. **1984** Colonial National Invitation, Sammy Davis, (Total: 4)   Jr.-Greater Hartford Open. **!990** Bob Hope Chrysler Classic.

MONEY & POSITION:

1977--$ 12,608--129	1983--$158,765-- 29	1989--$267,241-- 48
1978--$ 34,188-- 82	1984--$295,025-- 10	1990--$547,279-- 19
1979--$ 49,439-- 44	1985--$214,959-- 23	1991--$263,180-- 64
1980--$138,562-- 8	1986--$112,964-- 78	1992--$106,100--127
1981--$ 85,624-- 44	1987--$ 79,924--111	1993--$222,291-- 77
1982--$145,832-- 25	1988--$526,765-- 16	

BEST 1993 FINISHES: T6--Nissan Los Angeles Open; T6--New England Classic; T10--B.C. Open.

1993 SUMMARY: Tournaments entered--23; in money--17; top ten finishes--3.

1994 PGA TOUR CHARITY TEAM COMPETITION: New England Classic

1993 SEASON: Collected three top-10 finishes, regaining his fully exempt status... Only missed six cuts in 23 starts, and more than doubled his earnings from the previous year... Finished tied for sixth at Nissan Los Angeles Open and New England Classic...At New England he earned his largest paycheck of the year at $32,375... Later in the year, added a tie for 10th at the B.C. Open, after opening 69-68... He was one stroke out of the lead at that point.

CAREER HIGHLIGHTS: Returned after back surgery in 1987 to collect his last victory at the 1990 Bob Hope Chrysler Classic, one stroke victory over Scott Simpson and Brian Tennyson... Best year on TOUR was in 1984 as he finished 10th on the money list... Won in a playoff over Payne Stewart at the Colonial NIT, and dedicated the win to his father, who had just undergone a very serious operation... Later that same year, won the Sammy Davis, Jr. Greater Hartford Open... Came from six strokes back on the last day to earn his first victory at the Buick-Goodwrench Open... Winner of the 1974 PAC-Eight Conference title... Was a collegiate All-American from 1974 through 1976... Turned pro in 1976 and won the Oregon Open and the Northern California Open... Winner of the 1979 Western Australia Open, and the 1981 and 1982 Johnny Walker Cup (Madrid, Spain)... Player Director on TOUR from 1983-85 and again from 1990-92...Winner of the 1986 Fred Meyer Challenge with Curtis Strange.

PERSONAL: Started playing golf at the age of 12... Mostly taught by his late father and brother David...Noted for his mimicry of other players swings... Founder of Jake Trout and the Flounders, a musical group that has performed at PGA TOUR events.

1993 PGA TOUR STATISTICS

Scoring Average	70.38	(27T)
Driving Distance	262.1	(68T)
Driving Accuracy	73.9	(32T)
Greens in Regulation	68.5	(31T)
Putting	1.796	(90T)
All-Around	480	(20)
Sand Saves	51.9	(92T)
Total Driving	100	(11)
Eagles	9	(16T)
Birdies	256	(113T)

MISCELLANEOUS STATISTICS

Scoring Avg. (before cut)	70.96	(34T)
Scoring Avg. (3rd round)	70.81	(60)
Scoring Avg. (4th round)	70.82	(34)
Birdie Conversion	26.0	(139T)
Par Breakers	18.4	(85T)

1993 Low Round:	66: Hope Chrysler Classic
Career Low Round:	62: 1982 Manufacturers Hanover Westchester Classic/2
Career Largest Paycheck:	$180,000/1990 Bob Hope Chrysler Classic/1

LEE JANZEN

EXEMPT STATUS: Winner, 1993 U.S. Open

FULL NAME: Lee MacLeod Janzen

HEIGHT: 6'   **WEIGHT:** 175

BIRTH DATE: August 28, 1964

BIRTHPLACE: Austin, MN

RESIDENCE: Kissimmee, FL

CLUB AFFILIATION: Bloomingdale Golfers' Club, Brandon, FL

FAMILY: Wife, Beverly,Connor Macleod (10/20/93)

SPECIAL INTERESTS: Music, movies, snow skiing, all sports

COLLEGE: Florida Southern (1986, Marketing)

TURNED PROFESSIONAL: 1986

JOINED TOUR: Fall 1989.

PLAYER PROFILE

CAREER EARNINGS: $2,088,843

TOUR VICTORIES: 1992 Northern Telecom Open. **1993** Phoenix Open, U.S. Open. (TOTAL: 3)

MONEY & POSITION: 1990--$ 132,986--115   1992--$795,279--9   1993--$932,335--7
1991--$ 228,242-- 72

BEST 1993 FINISHES:1--Phoenix Open; 1--U.S. Open; T3--Buick Classic; 6--AT&T Pebble Beach National Pro-Am; T6--Kmart Greater Greensboro Open; T7--Kemper Open; T10--Doral-Ryder Open.

1993 SUMMARY: Tournaments entered--26; in money--23; top ten finishes--7.

1994 PGA TOUR CHARITY TEAM COMPETITION: The International

NATIONAL TEAMS: Ryder Cup, 1993

1993 SEASON: Earned the biggest victory of career to date, when he won the United States Open at Baltusrol... Finished with four rounds in the 60s, and scored a two-stroke victory over Payne Stewart... The victory earned him a $290,000 payday, and a 10-year exemption on TOUR... His 272 total tied Jack Nicklaus for the lowest cumulitive score in the history of the U.S. Open... Earlier in the year won the Phoenix Open, for his second PGA TOUR victory... A second round 6-under-par 65 moved him into a tie for the lead, and a final round 68 gave him a two stroke victory over Andrew Magee.

CAREER HIGHLIGHTS: 1992 was an excellent season for Janzen as he earned his first victory at the Northern Telecom Open... He was 17-under-par during the last three rounds, including a final round 7-under-par 65... Also was the runner-up at The International behind Brad Faxon and THE TOUR Championship behind Paul Azinger... Has improved in each of his four years on TOUR...earned exempt status in his rookie season by finishing 115th on the money list... Winner of the 1986 Division II National Championship...won six events while attending Florida Southern...Selected as a first team All-American in 1985 and 1986...Was the leading money winner on the U.S. Golf (mini) Tour in 1989.

PERSONAL: Was a college teammate of fellow TOUR professionals Rocco Mediate and Marco Dawson... Started to take the game seriously at the age of 14... Won his first tournament at the age of 15 as a member of the Greater Tampa Junior Golf Association.

1993 PGA TOUR STATISTICS

Scoring Average	70.21	(16)
Driving Distance	257.1	(116T)
Driving Accuracy	71.0	(64T)
Greens in Regulation	66.1	(72T)
Putting	1.766	(18T)
All-Around	494	(23)
Sand Saves	53.3	(70T)
Total Driving	180	(82T)
Eagles	7	(37T)
Birdies	340	(19)

MISCELLANEOUS STATISTICS

Scoring Avg. (before cut)	70.44	(19)
Scoring Avg. (3rd round)	72.05	(147T)
Scoring Avg. (4th round)	70.91	(41)
Birdie Conversion	30.7	(13T)
Par Breakers	20.7	(19T)

1993 Low Round:	65: 4 times
Career Low Round:	61: 1993 Southwestern
Career Largest	Bell Colonial/4
Paycheck:	$290,000/1993 U.S. Open/1

BRIAN KAMM

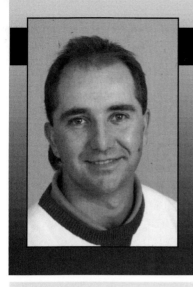

EXEMPT STATUS: 94th on 1993 money list

FULL NAME: Brian Thomas Kamm

HEIGHT: 5'6"   **WEIGHT:** 160

BIRTH DATE: September 3, 1961

BIRTHPLACE: Rochester, NY

RESIDENCE: Tampa, FL

FAMILY: Wife, Yvette; Brandy, Michael

COLLEGE: Florida State University

SPECIAL INTEREST: All sports

TURNED PROFESSIONAL: 1985

Q-SCHOOL: Fall 1989, 1990, 1992

PLAYER PROFILE

CAREER EARNINGS: $293,913

BEST EVER FINISH: T7--1993 Canon Greater Hartford Open

MONEY & POSITION: 1990--$ 8,775--237   1992--$20,020--211   1993--$183,185--94
1991--$ 81,932--146

BEST 1992 FINISHES: T7--Canon Greater Hartford Open; T8--Greater Milwaukee Open; T10--Las Vegas Invitational.

1992 SUMMARY: Tournaments entered--27; in money--17; top ten finishes--3.

1993 PGA TOUR CHARITY TEAM COMPETITION: Buick Open

1993 SEASON: Had a very solid season, in this his fourth crack at the PGA TOUR... Surpassed his combined previous earnings total by over $70,000... Finished up the season with over $183,185, and collected three finishes in the top-10, and four more in the top-25... Recorded his best ever finish at the Canon Greater Hartford Open... Closed with an excellent 6-under-par 64 on the final day at the TPC at River Highlands... Wound up six strokes behind the winner, Nick Price... Also grabbed a tie for eighth at the Greater Milwaukee Open... Fired three consecutive 3-under-par 69s, before closing with a 67 and finishing four strokes out of a Billy Mayfair/Ted Schulz/Mark Calcavecchia playoff, subsequently won by Mayfair... Earned the largest pay check of his career, at the last full-field event of the year... A closing 4-under-par 68 gave him a tie for 10th at the Las Vegas Invitational and a $35,000 pay day.

CAREER HIGHLIGHTS: Burst into prominence at the 1991 United State Open at Hazeltine... Fired an opening round 3-under-par 69, and was just two strokes back after the first round of play... Shot consecutive 1-over 73s before finishing with a 79, and a tie for 31st... Earned his exempt status for the 1993 season by finishing seventh on the money list on the Ben Hogan Tour in 1992... Finished up the season with a total of $88,607... Earned his lone Hogan Tour victory in his fifth start ever on Tour... Closed with a steady 3-under-par 69 on the final day and won by a stroke over Jeff Gallagher to win the Ben Hogan Panama City Classic... Decided to play the Tour full-time after that... Went on to finish with nine top-10s in 1992 on the Hogan Tour... Winner of the 1987 North Dakota Open.

1993 PGA TOUR STATISTICS

Scoring Average	70.88	(58)
Driving Distance	264.8	(56)
Driving Accuracy	66.4	(125T)
Greens in Regulation	66.1	(72T)
Putting	1.775	(33T)
All-Around	563	(34)
Sand Saves	58.7	(22)
Total Driving	181	(84T)
Eagles	5	(67T)
Birdies	307	(46T)

MISCELLANEOUS STATISTICS

Scoring Avg. (before cut)	71.54	(85)
Scoring Avg. (3rd round)	72.07	(150)
Scoring Avg. (4th round)	69.06	(1)
Birdie Conversion	30.0	(21T)
Par Breakers	20.2	(28T)

1993 Low Round: 64: 3 times

Career Low Round: 64: 4 times, most recent 1993 Canon Greater Hartford Open/4

Career Largest Paycheck: $35,000/1993 Las Vegas Invitational/T10

TOM KITE

EXEMPT STATUS: Winner, 1992 U.S. Open

FULL NAME: Thomas O. Kite, Jr.

HEIGHT: 5' 8"   **WEIGHT:** 155

BIRTH DATE: December 9, 1949

BIRTHPLACE: Austin, TX

RESIDENCE: Austin, TX

FAMILY: Wife, Christy; Stephanie Lee (10/7/81); David Thomas and Paul Christopher (twins) (9/1/84)

COLLEGE: University of Texas

SPECIAL INTERESTS: Landscaping

TURNED PROFESSIONAL: 1972

Q SCHOOL: Fall 1972

PLAYER PROFILE

CAREER EARNINGS: $8,500,730   **PLAYOFF RECORD:**6-4

TOUR VICTORIES: 1976 IVB-Bicentennial Golf Classic. 1978 B.C. Open. 1981 American Motors-
(TOTAL: 19) Inverrary Classic. 1982 Bay Hill Classic. 1983 Bing Crosby National Pro-Am. 1984 Doral-Eastern Open, Georgia-Pacific Atlanta Classic. 1985 MONY Tournament of Champions. 1986 Western Open. 1987 Kemper Open. 1989 Nestle Invitational, THE PLAYERS Championship, Nabisco Championships. 1990 Federal Express St. Jude Classic. 1991 Infiniti Tournament of Champions. 1992 BellSouth Classic, U.S. Open. 1993 Bob Hope Chrysler Classic, Nissan Los Angeles Open

MONEY & POSITION:							
1972--$	2,582--233	1980--$	152,490-- 20	1987--$	525,516-- 8
1973--$	54,270-- 56	1981--$	375,699-- 1	1988--$	760,405-- 5
1974--$	82,055-- 26	1982--$	341,081-- 3	1989--$1,395,278-- 1
1975--$	87,045-- 18	1983--$	257,066-- 9	1990--$	658,202-- 15
1976--$	116,180-- 21	1984--$	348,640-- 5	1991--$	396,580-- 39
1977--$	125,204-- 14	1985--$	258,793-- 14	1992--$	957,445-- 6
1978--$	161,370-- 11	1986--$	394,164-- 7	1993--$	887,811-- 8
1979--$	166,878-- 17				

BEST 1993 FINISHES: 1--Bob Hope Chrysler Classic; 1--Nissan Los Angeles Open; 2--Infiniti Tournament of Champions; 2--Kemper Open; T6--Federal Express St. Jude Classic; T7--THE TOUR Championship; 8--Doral-Ryder Open; T10--Buick Classic.

1993 SUMMARY: Tournaments entered--20; in money--14 top ten finishes--8.

1994 PGA TOUR CHARITY TEAM COMPETITION: Kmart Greater Greensboro Open

1993 SEASON: Collected two victories, a second, and an eighth in the first five events that he entered...Was absolutely untouchable at the Bob Hope Chrysler Classic...Closed with rounds of 64-65-62 to set an All-Time PGA TOUR mark for most strokes under par in a 90 hole event... He finished with a 35-under 325 total and a six stroke victory over Rick Fehr... In his next tournament, the Nissan Los Angeles Open, he was again untouchable ... Fired a sterling 4-under-par 67 on the final day of the rain-shortened event to collect his 19th career victory.

CAREER HIGHLIGHTS: Kite will always remember 1992, for his very special victory at the United States Open at Pebble Beach... Fired an even-par 72 on Sunday in tough conditions to win by two over Jeff Sluman... Earlier in the year won the BellSouth Classic to break a 16 month victory drought...In 1989 he set the mark, subsequently broken by Nick Price and Paul Azinger, for the most money won in a single season with $1,395,278..Earned the Arnold Palmer Award for the second time in his career...Also the leading money winner in 1981...Is PGA TOUR's All-Time leading money winner with over $8.5 million...Voted the 1981 GWAA Player of the Year...Won the 1979 Bob Jones Award...Was the 1973 Rookie of the Year...Co-winner of the 1972 NCAA Championship with Ben Crenshaw...Player Director on TOUR's Policy Board in 1980-81...winner of the 1981-82 Vardon Trophy...Wonof 1980 European Open..Led the TOUR in scoring average in 1981 and 1982...Led par-breakers in 1982.

PERSONAL: Began the game at the age of six, and at 11 won his first tournament.

1993 PGA TOUR STATISTICS

Scoring Average	69.74	(4)
Driving Distance	263.3	(62T)
Driving Accuracy	72.0	(59)
Greens in Regulation	69.4	(21T)
Putting	1.768	(21T)
All-Around	596	(42)
Sand Saves	45.3	(167)
Total Driving	121	(19)
Eagles	2	(144T)
Birdies	267	(99T)

MISCELLANEOUS STATISTICS

Scoring Avg. (before cut)	70.56	(23)
Scoring Avg. (3rd round)	69.77	(6)
Scoring Avg. (4th round)	69.21	(2)
Birdie Conversion	31.4	(5T)
Par Breakers	22.0	(2T)

1993 Low Round: 62: Bob Hope/5
Career Low Round: 62: 3 times, most recent 1993
Career Largest Bob Hope Chrysler Classic/5
Paycheck: $450,000/1989 Nabisco Championships/1

GREG KRAFT

EXEMPT STATUS: 60th on 1993 money list

FULL NAME: Gregory Thomas Kraft

HEIGHT: 5'11"   **WEIGHT:** 170

BIRTH DATE: April 4, 1964

BIRTHPLACE: Detroit, MI

RESIDENCE: Clearwater, FL

FAMILY: Single

COLLEGE: University of Tampa

SPECIAL INTEREST: Sports

TURNED PROFESSIONAL: 1986

Q-SCHOOL: 1991, 1992

PLAYER PROFILE

CAREER EARNINGS: $379,405

BEST EVER FINISH: 1--1993 Deposit Guaranty Golf Classic (unofficial); 2--1993 Walt Disney World/ Oldsmobile Classic

MONEY & POSITION: 1992--$88,824--140   1993--$290,581--60

BEST 1993 FINISHES: 1--Deposit Guaranty Classic (unofficial); 2--Walt Disney World/Oldsmobile Classic; T4--B.C. Open; T6--Freeport-McMoRan Classic.

1993 SUMMARY: Tournaments entered--24; in money--13; top ten finishes--4.

1994 PGA TOUR CHARITY TEAM COMPETITION: Buick Invitational of California

1993 SEASON: Finished as the third leading money winner out of the 1992 Qualifying Tournament... His season was highlighted by his unofficial victory in the Deposit Guaranty Golf Classic... Opened with a 5-under-par 65 and was a stroke out of the lead... After a third round 64 he found himself tied with Barry Jaeckel with a one stroke lead over Tad Rhyan... Finished with a 2-under-par 68 and won by a stroke over Morris Hatalsky and Rhyan... The $54,000 payday was his largest ever at the time... Prepped for the event by finishing tied for sixth at the Freeport-McMoRan Classic... He was 4-under-par after three rounds at English Turn and held a one stroke lead over Payne Stewart and Russ Cochran... Unfortunately, closed with a 3-over 75... Perhaps his best tounaments came at the end of the year... After finishing tied for fourth at the B.C. Open, he carded four sub-70 rounds to finish alone in second at the Walt Disney World/Oldsmobile Classic... His closing 8-under-par 64, followed by a smooth 66 was the weekend's best performance... The runner-up finish netted him $118,800 for his largest TOUR check ever.

CAREER HIGHLIGHTS: Was successful in the qualfiying tournament in 1991 and 1992... At the 1992 Q-School he birdied the last two holes to make the cut... Then fired a sterling 5-under-par 31 on the back side of the TPC at The Woodlands to qualify for his TOUR card... Prior to 1993 his best-ever finish was a tie for sixth at the Kemper Open... After a second round 3-under-par 68, he was one stroke out of the lead at the TPC at Avenel... Finished just two strokes behind the winner, Bill Glasson.

PERSONAL: Family is involved in Kraft Foods, Inc.

1993 PGA TOUR STATISTICS

Scoring Average	71.17	(83T)
Driving Distance	257.0	(119)
Driving Accuracy	65.2	(143T)
Greens in Regulation	63.1	(148T)
Putting	1.760	(11T)
All-Around	1024	(135)
Sand Saves	47.0	(151)
Total Driving	262	(170)
Eagles	5	(67T)
Birdies	241	(132)

MISCELLANEOUS STATISTICS

Scoring Avg. (before cut)	72.02	(121T)
Scoring Avg. (3rd round)	69.92	(13)
Scoring Avg. (4th round)	71.58	(103)
Birdie Conversion	29.5	(31T)
Par Breakers	19.0	(67T)

1993 Low Round: 64: 2 times
Career Low Round: 64: 3 times, most recent 1993
Career Largest   Walt Disney/Olds Classic/3
Paycheck:$118,000/1993 Disney/Olds Classic/2

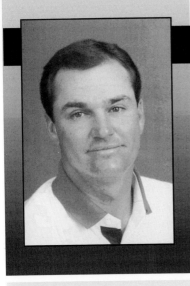

NEAL LANCASTER

EXEMPT STATUS: 107th on 1993 money list

FULL NAME: Grady Neal Lancaster

HEIGHT: 6'   **WEIGHT:** 170

BIRTH DATE: September 13,1960

BIRTHPLACE: Smithfield, NC

RESIDENCE: Smithfield, NC

FAMILY: Wife, Lou Ann

SPECIAL INTERESTS: Fishing, Movies

TURNED PROFESSIONAL: 1985

Q SCHOOL: 1989, 1990

PLAYER PROFILE

CAREER EARNINGS: $562,054

BEST EVER FINISH: T5--1991 Greater Milwaukee Open..

MONEY & POSITION: 1990--$ 85,769--142   1992--$146,967--103   1993--$149,381--107
1991--$180,037-- 90

BEST 1993 FINISHES: T6--Freeport-McMoRan Classic; T9--Buick Open.

1993 SUMMARY: Tournaments entered--32; in money--19; top ten finishes--2.

1994 PGA TOUR CHARITY TEAM COMPETITION: United Airlines Hawaiian Open.

1993 SEASON: Very consistent performer who only missed 13 cuts in 32 starts...Nearly matched his career best finish when he finished in a tie for sixth at the Freeport-McMoRan Classic... Wound up with a 1-under-par 287 total including a 1-under 71 on the final day at the wind swept English Turn GC course... Other top-10 came at the Buick Open, where he closed with a 5-under-par 67...Led the Buick Southern Open for the second time in three years after one round... Finished tied for 11th there... Finished with two other top-25 finishes... Only Ted Tryba, Kelly Gibson, Ed Dougherty, Fred Funk and Jim McGovern made more starts than Lancaster.

CAREER HIGHLIGHTS: Had his best career finish at the Greater Milwaukee Open in 1991 when he finished tied for fifth...Started with rounds of 67 and 66... Followed that up with a tie for eighth at the Canadian Open, which was good enough to secure his playing privileges for the first time in his career... Has averaged playing almost 32 events a year since joining the TOUR in 1990... Winner of the PineTree Open in Birmingham, AL, and the Utah State Open in 1989... Was the leading money winner on one of the mini-tours that year.

PERSONAL: Never took a golf lesson until 1992, looked at pictures in golf magazines before then... Got his first lesson from L.B. Floyd, the father of Raymond Floyd, and fellow North Carolina resident.

1993 PGA TOUR STATISTICS

Scoring Average	71.25	(96)
Driving Distance	266.2	(42)
Driving Accuracy	62.7	(167T)
Greens in Regulation	67.0	(60T)
Putting	1.793	(77T)
All-Around	702	(67T)
Sand Saves	51.2	(102T)
Total Driving	209	(132T)
Eagles	12	(3T)
Birdies	335	(23)

MISCELLANEOUS STATISTICS

Scoring Avg. (before cut)	71.59	(88T)
Scoring Avg. (3rd round)	71.31	(95)
Scoring Avg. (4th round)	71.33	(75T)
Birdie Conversion	27.8	(84T)
Par Breakers	19.3	(55T)

1993 Low Round: 66: 3 times
Career Low Round: 64: 1992 Southwestern Bell
Career Largest Colonial/2.4
Paycheck: $38,000/1991 Greater Milwaukee Open/T5

TOM LEHMAN

EXEMPT STATUS: 33rd on 1993 money list

FULL NAME: Thomas Edward Lehman

HEIGHT: 6' 2"   **WEIGHT:** 190

BIRTH DATE: March 7,1959

BIRTHPLACE: Austin, MN

RESIDENCE: Scottsdale, AZ

FAMILY: Wife, Melisa; Rachael (5/30/90); Holly (8/13/92)

COLLEGE: University of Minnesota

SPECIAL INTERESTS: Hunting, Church activities.

TURNED PROFESSIONAL: 1982

PLAYER PROFILE

CAREER EARNINGS: $1,040,882

BEST EVER FINISH: T2-1992 Hardee's Golf Classic

MONEY & POSITION:
1983--$9,413--183	1985--$ 20,232--158	1993--$422,761--33
1984--$9,382--184	1992--$579,093-- 24	

BEST 1993 FINISHES: 3--The Masters; T5--Buick Classic; T5--H-E-B Texas Open; T6--Buick Southern Open; T8--MCI Heritage Classic; T9--Phoenix Open.

1993 SUMMARY: Tournaments entered--28; in money--20; top ten finishes--6.

1994 PGA TOUR CHARITY TEAM COMPETITION: Buick Open

1993 SEASON: Since re-emerging on TOUR in 1992, Lehman has played extremely well...1993 saw him collect six top-10 finishes, including a tie for third at The Masters... Opened with a 5-under-par 67 at Augusta National, and was tied for the lead with Lee Janzen, Jack Nicklaus, Corey Pavin and Larry Mize in his first competitive round there... Closed with a 68 and earned $81,600 for his efforts... Followed that up the next week with a tie for eighth at the MCI Heritage Classic... His next best finish was a tie for fifth at the Buick Classic.

CAREER HIGHLIGHTS: Played the TOUR briefly in the early 1980s with little success, but returned in 1992 with a flourish... Had nine finishes in the top-10 that year including a tie for second at the Hardee's Classic... Opened with a 6-under-par 64 and finished three strokes behind the winner, David Frost... Collected $88,000 for the largest check of his career... Was named the **Ben Hogan Tour Player of the Year** in 1991...Posted 11 top-10 finishes of which six were either first or second...Won three times in 1991...Two of the victories came in playoffs as he defeated two other players over eight grueling holes in the Ben Hogan Mississippi Classic...Won the Ben Hogan South Carolina Classic on the first extra hole...Led the Hogan circuit in scoring and in eagles in 1991.

PERSONAL: Earned Just under $40,000 on TOUR in 1983-85... Bounced around on several of the mini-tours before joining the Ben Hogan Tour in 1990... Credits his marriage to Melissa for giving him the focus to do well on TOUR.

1993 PGA TOUR STATISTICS

Scoring Average	70.18	(13T)
Driving Distance	269.5	(23)
Driving Accuracy	67.3	(111T)
Greens in Regulation	68.6	(29T)
Putting	1.794	(82T)
All-Around	448	(16)
Sand Saves	49.3	(129T)
Total Driving	134	(28)
Eagles	11	(6T)
Birdies	324	(27T)

MISCELLANEOUS STATISTICS

Scoring Avg. (before cut)	70.96	(34T)
Scoring Avg. (3rd round)	69.90	(12)
Scoring Avg. (4th round)	70.35	(17)
Birdie Conversion	27.6	(94)
Par Breakers	19.6	(48T)

1993 Low Round: **63**: H-E-B Texas Open/2
Career Low Round:**63**: 1993 H-E-B Texas Open/2
Career Largest
Paycheck: **$88,000**/1992 Hardee's Golf Classic

WAYNE LEVI

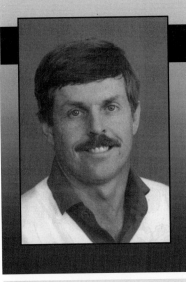

EXEMPT STATUS: 95th on 1993 money list

FULL NAME: Wayne John Levi

HEIGHT: 5' 9"   **WEIGHT:** 165

BIRTH DATE: February 22, 1952

BIRTHPLACE: Little Falls, NY

RESIDENCE: New Hartford, NY

FAMILY: Wife, Judy; Michelle (7/29/79), Lauren (1/20/83), Christine (12/30/84); Brian (5/1/88)

COLLEGE: Oswego State (NY.

SPECIAL INTERESTS: Financial and stock markets, reading

TURNED PROFESSIONAL: 1973

Q SCHOOL: Spring, 1977

PLAYER PROFILE

CAREER EARNINGS: $3,990,816   **PLAYOFF RECORD:** 2-1

TOUR VICTORIES: **1978** Walt Disney World National Team Play (with Bob Mann). **1979** Houston Open. **1980** Pleasant Valley-Jimmy Fund Classic. **1982** Hawaiian Open; LaJet Classic. **1983** (TOTAL: 12) Buick Open. **1984** B. C. Open. **1985** Georgia-Pacific Atlanta Classic. **1990** BellSouth Atlanta Classic, Centel Western Open, Canon Greater Hartford Open, Canadian Open.

MONEY & POSITION:

1977--$ 8,136--159	1983--$ 193,252-- 22	1989--$ 499,292-- 16
1978--$ 25,039-- 99	1984--$ 252,921-- 20	1990--$1,024,647-- 2
1979--$ 141,612-- 20	1985--$ 221,425-- 22	1991--$ 195,861-- 87
1980--$ 120,145-- 32	1986--$ 154,777-- 59	1992--$ 237,935-- 65
1981--$ 62,177-- 69	1987--$ 203,322-- 53	1993--$ 179,521-- 95
1982--$ 280,681-- 8	1988--$ 190,073-- 61	

BEST 1993 FINISHES: T9--United Airlines Hawaiian Open; T9--Bob Hope Chrysler Classic.

1993 SUMMARY: Tournaments entered--25; in money--14; top ten finishes--2.

1994 PGA TOUR CHARITY TEAM COMPETITION: Deposit Guaranty Golf Classic

NATIONAL TEAMS: Four Tours World Championship, 1990; Ryder Cup, 1991.

1993 SEASON: Earned both of his top-10 finishes in the span of three starts early in the season... A second-round 7-under-par 65 propelled him into contention at the United Airlines Hawaiian Open... He wound up tied for ninth... Fired five consecutive rounds in the 60s to finish tied for ninth at the Bob Hope Chrysler Classic... Had four other finishes in the top-25.

CAREER HIGHLIGHTS: Had a career year in 1990... Collected four victories from May to September and for that accomplishment was selected by his peers as the first **PGA TOUR Player of the Year**... Became the fifth player to surpass the $1 million mark in single season earnings...Finished second on the money list to Greg Norman that year...Won the BellSouth Atlanta Classic after a six-hour rain delay in near darkness...1990 marked the first time that a player had won five times in a year since Curtis Strange did it in 1988... Became the first player to win using a colored golf ball (orange) when he won the 1982 Hawaiian Open...A member of the victorious Ryder Cup team in 1991...Played the Four Tours World Championship for the PGA TOUR in 1990...Won the 1988 Chrysler Team Championship with George Burns.

PERSONAL: An avid family man, Levi prefers to spend much of his time at home... Once took off five of the preceding six weeks to watch his daughter learn to crawl, and then came back and won the next tournament that he played (1983 Buick Open)... Consistently follows the stock and financial markets.

1993 PGA TOUR STATISTICS

Scoring Average	70.83	.(54)
Driving Distance	260.8	(77T)
Driving Accuracy	73.1	(43T)
Greens in Regulation	67.4	(54)
Putting	1.758	(9T)
All-Around	534	(28)
Sand Saves	46.6	(154)
Total Driving	120	(18)
Eagles	7	(37T)
Birdies	276	(88)

MISCELLANEOUS STATISTICS

Scoring Avg. (before cut)	71.19	(52T)
Scoring Avg. (3rd round)	70.50	(41)
Scoring Avg. (4th round)	71.80	(119T)
Birdie Conversion	30.0	(21T)
Par Breakers	20.7	(19T)

1993 Low Round: 63: SW Bell Colonial/4
Career Low Round: 62: 1989 Byron Nelson Golf Classic/1
Career Largest Paycheck: $180,000/4 times, most recent: 1990 Canadian Open/1

BRUCE LIETZKE

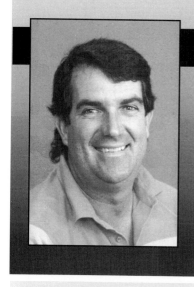

EXEMPT STATUS: 1992 tournament winner

FULL NAME: Bruce Alan Lietzke

HEIGHT: 6' 2"   **WEIGHT:** 185

BIRTH DATE: July 18, 1951

BIRTHPLACE: Kansas City, KS

RESIDENCE: Dallas, TX

FAMILY: Wife, Rosemarie; Stephen Taylor (10/5/83); Christine (10/11/86)

COLLEGE: University of Houston

SPECIAL INTERESTS: Serious fishing, racing cars

TURNED PROFESSIONAL: 1974

Q SCHOOL: Spring 1975

PLAYER PROFILE

CAREER EARNINGS: $4,875,942   **PLAYOFF RECORD:** 6-4

TOUR VICTORIES: **1977** Joe Garagiola-Tucson Open, Hawaiian Open. **1978** Canadian Open. **1979** Joe
(TOTAL: 12) Garagiola-Tucson Open. **1980** Colonial National Invitation. **1981** Bob Hope Desert
Classic, Wickes-Andy Williams San Diego Open, Byron Nelson Classic. **1982**
Canadian Open. **1984** Honda Classic. **1988** GTE Byron Nelson Classic. **1992** Southwestern Bell Colonial.

MONEY & POSITION:

1975--$ 30,780--74	1982--$217,447--14	1988--$500,815-- 19
1976--$ 69,229--39	1983--$153,255--32	1989--$307,987-- 36
1977--$202,156-- 5	1984--$342,853-- 6	1990--$329,294-- 41
1978--$113,905--18	1985--$136,992--59	1991--$566,272-- 19
1979--$198,439-- 8	1986--$183,761--47	1992--$703,805-- 16
1980--$163,884--16	1987--$154,383--68	1993--$163,241--101
1981--$343,446-- 4		

BEST 1993 FINISHES: T4--Greater Milwaukee Open; T4--Canadian Open.

1993 SUMMARY: Tournaments entered--16; in money--10; in money--2.

1994 PGA TOUR CHARITY TEAM COMPETITION: Bell Canadian Open

NATIONAL TEAMS: Ryder Cup, 1981; U.S. vs. Japan, 1984.

1993 SEASON: Something of a down year for Lietzke, as he didn't finish in the top-75 on the money list for the first time in his career... Only made 16 starts and his best stretch came late in the year when he collected consecutive ties for fourth at the Greater Milwaukee Open and the Canadian Open... A year earlier he lost in a playoff to Greg Norman at the Canadian... Closed with a 5-under-par 67 to miss the Billy Mayfair/Ted Schulz/Mark Calcavecchia playoff by one stroke in Milwaukee.

CAREER HIGHLIGHTS: The 1992 season was a fine one for the affable Lietzke... He collected the 12th victory of his career and won the Southwestern Bell Colonial for the second time.. Shot 64-66 on the weekend and finished tied with Corey Pavin at 13-under-par 267... Made a birdie putt on the first extra hole to give him his first victory since 1988... First victory came at the 1977 Joe Garagiola-Tucson Open...captured the tournament in a four hole playoff over Gene Littler... Winner of the 1971 Texas State Amateur...was a member of the victorious Ryder Cup team in 1981...played in the U.S. versus Japan matches in 1984.

PERSONAL: Plays an extremely limited schedule in order to spend as much time as possible with his family... After leaving the University of Houston in the spring of 1973, he actually quit the game for six months... He returned, became a professional in 1974, and made it through the Qualifying Tournament in 1975... Started the game at the age of five... Has the distinction of being the only player who was in the field when both Al Geiberger and Chip Beck shot their 59s.

1993 PGA TOUR STATISTICS

Scoring Average	70.95	(63T)
Driving Distance	259.9	(89)
Driving Accuracy	76.6	(12T)
Greens in Regulation	69.9	(17)
Putting	1.817	(142T)
All-Around	568	(35)
Sand Saves	60.6	(13T)
Total Driving	101	(12)
Eagles	6	(50T)
Birdies	169	(170T)

MISCELLANEOUS STATISTICS

Scoring Avg. (before cut)	71.00	(37T)
Scoring Avg. (3rd round)	71.00	(73T)
Scoring Avg. (4th round)	70.33	(15T)
Birdie Conversion	26.9	(112T)
Par Breakers	19.4	(52T)

1993 Low Round: 66: 3 times
Career Low Round: 63: 4 times, most recent 1992
Career Largest Paycheck: $234,000/'92 Southwestern Bell Colonial/1

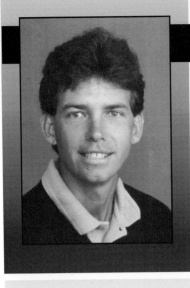

ROBERT LOHR

EXEMPT STATUS: 54th on 1993 money list

FULL NAME: Robert Harold Lohr

HEIGHT: 6' 1"   **WEIGHT:** 185

BIRTH DATE: November 2, 1960

BIRTHPLACE: Cincinnati, OH

RESIDENCE: Orlando, FL

FAMILY: Wife, Marie; Matthew Robert (7/15/91)

COLLEGE: Miami University of Ohio (1983 Marketing)

SPECIAL INTERESTS: Hunting, fishing, snow skiing

TURNED PROFESSIONAL: 1983

Q SCHOOL: Fall, 1984

PLAYER PROFILE

CAREER EARNINGS: $1,747,794   **PLAYOFF RECORD:** 1-1

TOUR VICTORIES: 1988 Walt Disney World Oldsmobile Classic.
(TOTAL: 1)

MONEY & POSITION:

1985--$ 93,651-- 81	1988--$315,536-- 32	1991--$386,759-- 41
1986--$ 85,949-- 99	1989--$144,242-- 98	1992--$128,307--112
1987--$137,108-- 80	1990--$141,260--109	1993--$314,982-- 54

BEST 1993 FINISHES: 2--H-E-B Texas Open; 3--Sprint Western Open; T4--Bob Hope Chrysler Classic.

1993 SUMMARY: Tournaments entered--26; in money--17; top ten finishes--3.

1994 PGA TOUR CHARITY TEAM COMPETITION: Greater Milwaukee Open

1993 SEASON: Had his third most lucrative year ever from an earnings standpoint... Surpassed the $300,000 mark for the third time... Got his year started in good fashion with a tie for fourth at the Bob Hope Chrysler Classic... Shot three consecutive 6-under-par 66s during the middle rounds to vault into contention... Finished alone in third place at the Sprint Western Open, when he fired a closing 3-under-par 69... Saved his best performance of the year for the H-E-B Texas Open, where he lost in a playoff to Jay Haas... Fired 7-under-par 64s in the second and fourth rounds to finish with a 21-under-par 263 total... Haas won with a birdie on second extra hole... Opened with another 64 the next week at Las Vegas.

CAREER HIGHLIGHTS: Was wire-to-wire winner in his only PGA TOUR victory, the 1988 Walt Disney World/Oldsmobile Classic...Finished regulation play tied with Chip Beck at 25-under-par 263...Won the playoff on the fifth extra hole with a birdie while Beck bogeyed in near darkness...Opened with a 10-under-par 62 on the Palm Course... Birdied the final hole to force the playoff ...Winner of the 1990 Mexican Open...Named All Mid-America Conference three years... Was an Honoroble Mention All-America selection in 1983.

PERSONAL: Started golf at a relatively young age, but also was an outstanding baseball pitcher as a youngster... Had to choose between golf and baseball at the Miami University of Ohio because both sports were played in the spring.

1993 PGA TOUR STATISTICS

Scoring Average	70.76	(48T)
Driving Distance	249.8	(175T)
Driving Accuracy	76.8	(11)
Greens in Regulation	65.9	(79T)
Putting	1.765	(16T)
All-Around	694	(63)
Sand Saves	57.0	(31T)
Total Driving	186	(94T)
Eagles	1	(164T)
Birdies	284	(76T)

MISCELLANEOUS STATISTICS

Scoring Avg. (before cut)	70.81	(29)
Scoring Avg. (3rd round)	71.44	(105)
Scoring Avg. (4th round)	71.29	(71T)
Birdie Conversion	28.2	(69T)
Par Breakers	18.6	(79T)

1993 Low Round:	**64:** 2 times
Career Low Round:	**62:** 2 times, most recent '88
Career Largest	Walt Disney/1
Paycheck: $126,000	'88 Walt Disney /1

DAVIS LOVE III

EXEMPT STATUS: Winner, 1992 PLAYERS Championship

FULL NAME: Davis Milton Love III

HEIGHT: 6' 3"   **WEIGHT:** 175

BIRTH DATE: April 13, 1964

BIRTHPLACE: Charlotte, NC

RESIDENCE: Sea Island, GA

FAMILY: Wife, Robin; Alexia (6/5/88), Davis IV(12/4/93)

COLLEGE: University of North Carolina

SPECIAL INTERESTS: Fishing, reading novels, hunting

TURNED PROFESSIONAL: 1985

Q SCHOOL: Fall, 1985

PLAYER PROFILE

CAREER EARNINGS: $4,037,673   **PLAYOFF RECORD:** 0-3

TOUR VICTORIES: **1987** MCI Heritage Classic. **1990** The International. **1991** MCI Heritage Classic. **1992** (TOTAL: 8) THE PLAYERS Championship, MCI Heritage Classic, Kmart Greater Greensboro Open. **1993** Infiniti Tournament of Champions, Las Vegas Invitational.

MONEY & POSITION:

1986--$113,245-- 77	1989--$278,760-- 44	1992--$1,191,630-- 2
1987--$297,378-- 33	1990--$537,172-- 20	1993--$ 777,059--12
1988--$156,068-- 75	1991--$686,361-- 8	

BEST 1993 FINISHES: 1--Infiniti Tournament of Champions; 1--Las Vegas Invitational; T2--Nestle Invitational; T7--United Airlines Hawaiian Open; T10--Memorial Tournament.

1993 SUMMARY: Tournaments entered--26; in money--23; top ten finishes--5.

1994 PGA TOUR CHARITY TEAM COMPETITION: Buick Southern Open

NATIONAL TEAMS: Walker Cup, 1985; Dunhill Cup, 1992; World Cup, (2) 1992,1993; Ryder Cup, 1993.

1993 SEASON: Started and ended his year in fine fashion as he collected the seventh and eighth victories of his career... Opened season with win in Infiniti Tournament of Champions by one shot over close friend Tom Kite... Was one stroke behind Ben Crenshaw after three rounds of the Nestle Invitational and wound up tied for second ... Absolutely blistered the field at the Las Vegas Invitational... His highest round of the tournament was a 5-under-par 67, which he fired in the first and third rounds... Added two 66s and a 65 which was good for an eight stroke victory over Craig Stadler... Only missed three cuts during the year and surpassed $750,000 in earnings for the second consecutive year...Teamed with Fred Couples to defend their title in World Cup.

CAREER HIGHLIGHTS: Won't soon forget his 1992 season in which he earned $1 million quicker than anyone in the history of the TOUR except for Fred Couples... Love won three times in 1992 including the prestigious PLAYERS Championship, finishing with a superb 5-under 67... Earned another four-stroke victory at the MCI Heritage Classic, when he was the defending champion... Final official victory of the year came at the Kmart Greater Greensboro Open, where he fired a 10-under-par 62 on the final day... Love broke through in his sophomore season to win at the MCI Heritage Classic...Won it again in 1991 and 1992...Won the 1990 International by three points... Closed 1992 by teaming with Fred Couples to win the World Cup...Next week, Love eagled the 18th hole to outduel Mike Hulbert and win the Lincoln Mercury Kapalua International by two...Winner of the 1984 North and South Amateur and the ACC Championship...Led the PGA TOUR in Driving Distance in 1986.

PERSONAL: Enjoys hunting and fishing as much as any player on TOUR... Is also a big follower of North Carolina basketball and Atlanta Braves baseball... Enjoys stock car racing as well... Father was an excellent teacher...Davis was born shortly after his father competed and was in contention in the 1964 Masters.

1993 PGA TOUR STATISTICS

Scoring Average	70.28	(20)
Driving Distance	280.2	(2)
Driving Accuracy	63.2	(160)
Greens in Regulation	67.7	(47T)
Putting	1.778	(45)
All-Around	381	(8)
Sand Saves	56.1	(41)
Total Driving	162	(55T)
Eagles	15	(1)
Birdies	361	(10)

MISCELLANEOUS STATISTICS

Scoring Avg. (before cut)	70.50	(21)
Scoring Avg. (3rd round)	70.61	(48)
Scoring Avg. (4th round)	70.52	(22)
Birdie Conversion	29.6	(29T)
Par Breakers	20.9	(13T)

1993 Low Round: **65:** 3 times
Career Low Round: **62:** 1992 Kmart Greater Greensboro Open/4
Career Largest Paycheck: **$324,000/**'92 PLAYERS Championship/1

STEVE LOWERY

EXEMPT STATUS: 92nd on 1993 money list

FULL NAME: Stephen Brent Lowery

HEIGHT: 6'2" **WEIGHT:** 210

BIRTH DATE: October 12, 1960

BIRTHPLACE: Birmingham, AL

RESIDENCE: Orlando, FL

FAMILY: Wife, Kathryn

COLLEGE: University of Alabama

SPECIAL INTEREST: Sports

TURNED PROFESSIONAL: 1983

Q SCHOOL: Fall 1987

PLAYER PROFILE

CAREER EARNINGS: $411,343

BEST EVER FINISH: T3--1991 Chattanooga Classic

MONEY & POSITION:

1988--$44,327-- 157	1990--$68,524-- 159	1992--$22,608--207
1989--$38,699-- 174	1991--$87,597-- 143	1993--$188,287--92

BEST 1993 FINISH: T10--New England Classic.

1993 SUMMARY: Tournaments entered--32; in money--25; top ten finishes--1.

1994 PGA TOUR CHARITY TEAM COMPETITION: Buick Southern Open

1993 SEASON: Made the most of his first fully exempt year on TOUR... Cashed a check in 25 of the 32 events that he entered and claimed eight finishes in the top-25... His best finish of the year was a tie for 10th at the New England Classic... Opened with a 5-under-par 66, and followed that up with consecutive 69s before winding up with a 72 on Sunday...... Next best finish came at the Phoenix Open... After opening with a 2-under-par 69, added a 6-under-par 65 after the second round... Was two strokes out of the lead at the halfway point before winding up tied for 11th... Closed with a 3-under-par 68 at Riviera CC to finish tied for 14th at the Nissan Los Angeles Open... Earned over $60,000 by the time that the TOUR left the West Coast.

CAREER HIGHLIGHTS: Has played the PGA TOUR every year since 1988 after finishing 12th at the 1987 Qualifying Tournament... Managed to secure Special Temporary Membership on TOUR in 1990 and 1991 when he earned as much as the 150th earner on the previous year's money list...His best ever finish came at the 1991 Chattanooga Classic... Was two strokes out of the lead after opening with a 7-under-par 63... Finished up with a 67 and wound up four strokes behind the winner, Dillard Pruitt...That earned him the largest paycheck of his career at $33,600... Went on to play the Ben Hogan Tour in 1992... Finished up the year third on the money list with $114,553 in earnings... Won the Ben Hogan Tulsa Open in a two-hole playoff over Jeff Coston... He made birdie to collect his only title on that Tour... Also ended up third in stroke average in 1992 with a 70.37 average.

PERSONAL: Alabama Crimson Tide football fan...Teammate of Tom Garner while attending Alabama.

1993 PGA TOUR STATISTICS

Scoring Average	70.99	(68)
Driving Distance	267.0	(40)
Driving Accuracy	66.3	(128)
Greens in Regulation	67.3	(55T)
Putting	1.776	(37T)
All-Around	544	(31T)
Sand Saves	48.5	(136)
Total Driving	168	(65T)
Eagles	10	(9T)
Birdies	372	(6)

MISCELLANEOUS STATISTICS

Scoring Avg. (before cut)	70.98	(36)
Scoring Avg. (3rd round)	72.05	(147T)
Scoring Avg. (4th round)	71.33	(75T)
Birdie Conversion	27.9	(78T)
Par Breakers	19.3	(55T)

1993 Low Round: 65: 2 times

Career Low Round: 62: '90 Chattanooga Classic/1

Career Largest Paycheck: $33,600/1991 Chattanooga Classic/T3

ANDREW MAGEE

EXEMPT STATUS: 62nd on 1993 money list

FULL NAME: Andrew Donald Magee

HEIGHT: 6'   **WEIGHT:** 180

BIRTH DATE: May 22, 1962

BIRTHPLACE: Paris, France

RESIDENCE: Paradise Valley, AZ

FAMILY: Wife, Susan; Lindsey Ellenberg (6/23/81), Campbell Joseph (11/27/88); Oliver Andrew (9/5/91)

COLLEGE: University of Oklahoma (1984)

SPECIAL INTERESTS: Travel, swimming, fishing, whistling

TURNED PROFESSIONAL: 1984

Q SCHOOL: Fall 1984

PLAYER PROFILE

CAREER EARNINGS: $2,144,915   **PLAYOFF RECORD:** 1-0

TOUR VICTORIES: 1988 Pensacola Open. **1991** Nestle Invitational, Las Vegas Invitational. (TOTAL: 3)

MONEY & POSITION:

1985--$75,593-- 99	1988--$261,954-- 43	1991--$750,082-- 5
1986--$69,478--120	1989--$126,770--109	1992--$285,946-- 53
1987--$94,598-- 99	1990--$210,507-- 71	1993--$269,986-- 62

BEST 1993 FINISHES: 2--Phoenix Open; T8--Hardee's Golf Classic.

1993 SUMMARY: Tournaments entered--25; in money--14; top ten finishes--2.

1994 PGA TOUR CHARITY TEAM COMPETITION: Northern Telecom Open

1993 SEASON: Best round and finish of campaign came in his second event of year, when he holed out wedge on par-5 15th at TPC of Scottsdale (after putting previous shot in water) enroute to third-round 64 and eventual runnerup placing behind Lee Janzen...7-under-par effort left him one shot off Robert Wrenn lead after 54 holes...Ultimately finished two shots back of Janzen...Had two top-10 finishes on year, one fewer than 1992...Other top-10 (tie for 8th) came in Hardee's Golf Classic...'92 money total third best in nine TOUR campaigns, trailing just 1992 and career-year earnings of $750,082 in 1991.

CAREER HIGHLIGHTS: First TOUR win came in 1988 Pensacola Open, where he rallied from four strokes back to claim title...climaxed strong early-season run in '91 with second career victory in Nestle Invitational...Severe weather ended Bay Hill event after 54 holes...Made eagle-3 with 30-foot putt on 16th hole to gain ultimate two-stroke win...Later in year shot 69-65-67-62-66 for 31-under-par 329 total at Las Vegas Invitational...31-under (matched by D.A. Weibring) set TOUR record for lowest score in 90-hole event, mark since surpassed by Tom Kite's 35-under at 1993 Bob Hope Chrysler Classic...62 came at Las Vegas CC...Defeated Weibring with par on second extra hole to earn $270,000 first prize...Two '91 wins helped produce best season to date...Three top-10 finishes in 1992 led to second-best year.

PERSONAL: Only current member of PGA TOUR born in Paris, while father-- in the oil business--served stint in France...Won 1979 Doug Sanders Junior Invitational...Three-time All-America at University of Oklahoma.

1993 PGA TOUR STATISTICS

Scoring Average	71.31	(101)
Driving Distance	262.6	(65)
Driving Accuracy	70.3	(70T)
Greens in Regulation	67.9	(41T)
Putting	1.797	(92T)
All-Around	616	(48)
Sand Saves	52.7	(80)
Total Driving	135	(29T)
Eagles	10	(9T)
Birdies	243	(129T)

MISCELLANEOUS STATISTICS

Scoring Avg. (before cut)	71.75	(99T)
Scoring Avg. (3rd round)	70.25	(25T)
Scoring Avg. (4th round)	70.93	(42T)
Birdie Conversion	26.9	(112T)
Par Breakers	19.0	(67T)

1993 Low Round:	64: Phoenix Open/3
Career Low Round:	62: 1991 Las Vegas /4
Career Largest	
Paycheck:	$270,000/1991 Las Vegas Invitational/1

JEFF MAGGERT

EXEMPT STATUS: 1993 tournament winner

FULL NAME: Jeffrey Allan Maggert

HEIGHT: 5' 9"

WEIGHT: 165

BIRTH DATE: Feb. 20, 1964

BIRTHPLACE: Columbia, MO

RESIDENCE: The Woodlands, TX

FAMILY: Wife, Kelli; Matt (12/10/88), Macy (10/26/90)

COLLEGE: Texas A&M

SPECIAL INTERESTS: Fishing, hunting, camping, sporting events

TURNED PROFESSIONAL: 1986

JOINED TOUR: 1991

PLAYER PROFILE

CAREER MONEY: $1,411,371

TOUR VICTORIES: 1993 Walt Disney World/Oldsmobile Classic. (TOTAL: 1)

MONEY & POSITION:
1990--$ 2,060--277   1992--$377,408--38   1993--$793,023--11
1991--$240,940-- 68

BEST 1993 FINISHES: 1--Walt Disney World/Oldsmobile Classic; 2--Northern Telecom Open; T2--Federal Express St. Jude Classic; 3--Southwestern Bell Colonial; T4--United Airlines Hawaiian Open; T6--Nissan Los Angeles Open.

1993 SUMMARY: Tournaments entered--28; in money--17; top ten finishes--6.

1994 PGA TOUR CHARITY TEAM COMPETITION: Texas Open

1993 SEASON: Finally broke through in October with first win of PGA TOUR career, a floodlight-aided triumph in Walt Disney World/Oldsmobile Classic…With darkness firmly in place on final Sunday (day in which he was forced to play 36 holes because of earlier weather delays), wrapped up three-shot victory over Greg Kraft in true Disney fashion--with lights used to illuminate driving range in early morning enabling completion of play… Triumph worth much more than $180,000 first-place check, since had held 54-hole leads on previous occasions, only to let victory slip away…Prior to Disney win, earned his first career runner-up finishes: solo second at Northern Telecom Open (worth $118,800), tied for second in Federal Express St. Jude Classic.

CAREER HIGHLIGHTS: Briefly held final-round lead in 1992 PGA Championship…Course-record 65 in Round 3 of PGA at Bellerive CC moved him into second-place tie before eventual final-round 74 produced sixth-place finish…Third-round leader in 1992 Freeport-McMoRan Classic…Also in close contention earlier that year in United Airlines Hawaiian Open…Led 1991 Independent Insurance Agent Open through three rounds on home course at The Woodlands before faltering in fourth…**1990 Ben Hogan Tour Player of Year** with top earnings of $108,644 and victories in Hogan Knoxville and Buffalo Opens…Led Hogan Tour with 70.02 scoring average…As PGA TOUR rookie in '91 ranked behind only John Daly in first-year earnings with $240,940 …T5 in first TOUR start in Northern Telecom Open.

PERSONAL: Won 1989 Malaysian Open on Asian Tour and 1990 Vines Classic on Australasian Tour…All-America at Texas A&M in 1986, year in which also was Morris Williams Intercollegiate Champion…1982 American Junior Golf Association All-American and Texas State High School (5-A) Champion…Winner 1980 Texas State Junior, 1988 and 1990 Texas State Open, 1989 Louisiana Open.

1993 PGA TOUR STATISTICS

Scoring Average	70.24	(17)
Driving Distance	264.5	(57)
Driving Accuracy	76.3	(14)
Greens in Regulation	69.0	(24T)
Putting	1.800	(100T)
All-Around	328	(5)
Sand Saves	55.1	(52)
Total Driving	71	(6)
Eagles	7	(37T)
Birdies	337	(21T)

MISCELLANEOUS STATISTICS

Scoring Avg. (before cut)	70.91	(31T)
Scoring Avg. (3rd round)	70.73	(54T)
Scoring Avg. (4th round)	69.82	(8)
Birdie Conversion	30.1	(20)
Par Breakers	21.2	(10)

1993 Low Round:	**65:** 4 times
Career Low Round:	**64:** 2 times, most recent 1992 GTE Byron Nelson/1
Career Largest Paycheck:	**$180,000**/1993 Walt Disney World/ Oldsmobile Classic/1

JOHN MAHAFFEY

EXEMPT STATUS: Winner, 1986 Tournament Players Championship

FULL NAME: John Drayton Mahaffey

HEIGHT: 5' 9"   **WEIGHT:** 160

BIRTH DATE: May 9, 1948

BIRTHPLACE: Kerrville, TX

RESIDENCE: Houston, TX; plays out of The Woodlands, TX

FAMILY: Wife, Denise; John D. Mahaffey III (8/8/88); Meagan (6/12/92)

COLLEGE: University of Houston (1970, Psychology)

SPECIAL INTERESTS: Fishing

TURNED PROFESSIONAL: 1971   **Q SCHOOL:** 1971

PLAYER PROFILE

CAREER EARNINGS: $3,606,020

PLAYOFF RECORD: 3-2

TOUR VICTORIES: (TOTAL: 10) **1973** Sahara Invitational. **1978** PGA Championship, American Optical Classic. **1979** Bob Hope Desert Classic. **1980** Kemper Open. **1981** Anheuser-Busch Classic. **1984** Bob Hope Classic. **1985** Texas Open. **1986** Tournament Players Championship. **1989** Federal Express St. Jude Classic.

MONEY & POSITION:

1971--$ 2,010--230	1979--$ 81,993--45	1987--$193,938-- 57
1972--$ 57,779-- 39	1980--$165,827--15	1988--$266,416-- 41
1973--$112,536-- 12	1981--$128,795--24	1989--$400,467-- 29
1974--$122,189-- 16	1982--$ 77,047--56	1990--$325,115-- 42
1975--$141,471-- 8	1983--$126,915--44	1991--$ 64,403- 159
1976--$ 77,843-- 33	1984--$252,548--21	1992--$101,512--130
1977--$ 9,847--150	1985--$341,595-- 9	1993--$ 36,913--192
1978--$153,520-- 12	1986--$378,172--11	

BEST 1993 FINISH: T27--Kmart Greater Greensboro Open.

1993 SUMMARY: Tournaments entered--28; in money--11; top ten finishes--0.

1994 PGA TOUR CHARITY TEAM COMPETITION: Nestle Invitational

NATIONAL TEAMS: Ryder Cup, 1979; World Cup (2) 1978, 1979 (medalist in 1978).

1993 SEASON: Failed to achieve top-10 finish for second time in past three years...Also was shut out in 1991 for first time since 1971-72, first two PGA TOUR campaigns...Last top-10 was a tie for seventh in 1992 Chattanooga Classic...Made cut in three of last four starts...Opened year by placing in four of first five appearances...Carded best round of year in final event, second-round 66 in Las Vegas Invitational...Money list placing (No. 192) lowest of career, with exception of 1971...Top finish (tie for 27th at Kmart Greater Greensboro Open) worth $10,425.

CAREER HIGHLIGHTS: High point came in 1978 PGA Championship at Oakmont CC...Won in playoff with Tom Watson and Jerry Pate... Followed next week with triumph in American Optical Classic at Sutton, MA...Earned 10-year exemption with one-stroke victory over Larry Mize in 1986 Tournament Players Championship...Fired third-round 7-under-par 65 on Stadium Course at Sawgrass to move into position to win...Last victory came in '89 Federal Express St. Jude Classic, where he closed with rounds of 66-65 on new TPC at Southwind course to win by three strokes...Splendid amateur career included 1970 NCAA Championship for University of Houston...Member 1979 Ryder Cup team, 1978-79 World Cup squads (medalist in '78)...Captured 1990 Merrill Lynch Shoot-Out Championship and $90,000 at Troon North in Scottsdale, AZ... Led TOUR in Greens in Regulation 1985-86.

PERSONAL: Career has been injury-plagued, starting with hyperextended tendon in left elbow suffered in 1976 PGA Championship at Congressional...Injury made it virtually impossible for him to play in 1977...Past player director on Tournament Policy Board.

1993 PGA TOUR STATISTICS

Scoring Average	72.42	(176T)
Driving Distance	251.7	(166)
Driving Accuracy	74.8	(26)
Greens in Regulation	67.9	(41T)
Putting	1.863	(184T)
All-Around	1200	(162)
Sand Saves	39.3	(186)
Total Driving	192	(101T)
Eagles	1	(164T)
Birdies	196	(156T)

MISCELLANEOUS STATISTICS

Scoring Avg. (before cut)	72.50	(154)
Scoring Avg. (3rd round)	72.00	(139T)
Scoring Avg. (4th round)	74.08	(185)
Birdie Conversion	22.0	(189)
Par Breakers	15.0	(176T)

1993 Low Round:	66: Las Vegas Invitational/2
Career Low Round:	63: 2 times, most recent
Career Largest	1985 USF&G Classic/1
Paycheck:	$180,000 '89 Fed. Ex. St. Jude Classic/1

ROGER MALTBIE

EXEMPT STATUS: Winner, 1985 NEC World Series of Golf

FULL NAME: Roger Lin Maltbie

HEIGHT: 5' 10"   **WEIGHT:** 200

BIRTH DATE: June 30, 1951

BIRTHPLACE: Modesto, CA

RESIDENCE: Los Gatos, CA

FAMILY: Wife, Donna; Spencer Davis (3/3/87); Parker Travis (3/12/90)

COLLEGE: San Jose State University

SPECIAL INTERESTS: Music, 49er Football

TURNED PROFESSIONAL: 1973

Q SCHOOL: 1974

PLAYER PROFILE

CAREER EARNINGS: $2,034,730   **PLAYOFF RECORD:** 2-1

TOUR VICTORIES: **1975** Ed McMahon-Quad Cities Open, Pleasant Valley Classic. **1976** Memorial
(TOTAL: 5)   Tournament. **1985** Manufacturers Hanover Westchester Classic, NEC World
Series of Golf.

MONEY & POSITION:

1975--$ 81,035-- 23	1982--$ 77,067-- 55	1988--$150,602-- 77
1976--$117,736-- 18	1983--$ 75,751-- 70	1989--$134,333--105
1977--$ 51,727-- 59	1984--$118,128-- 56	1990--$ 58,536--169
1978--$ 12,440--129	1985--$360,554-- 8	1991--$ 37,962--188
1979--$ 9,796--155	1986--$213,206-- 40	1992--$109,742--125
1980--$ 38,626-- 84	1987--$157,023-- 65	1993--$155,454--103
1981--$ 75,009-- 58		

BEST 1993 FINISHES: T2--Canon Greater Hartford Open; T8--Northern Telecom Open.

1993 SUMMARY: Tournaments entered--20; in money--10; top ten finishes--2.

1994 PGA TOUR CHARITY TEAM COMPETITION: Anheuser-Busch Golf Classic

1993 SEASON: Continued love affair with New England tournaments by finishing tied for 2nd at Canon Greater Hartford Open...Was first-round co-leader after opening 65...Fired closing 65 to finish one stroke behind Nick Price and tie Dan Forsman, who also shot final round 65s...Canon GHO finish his best tournament placing since solo second in 1986 GHO...Other top-10 finish came in his first start of year, at Northern Telecom Open (T8)...Continued to play somewhat limited schedule because of full-time broadcasting commitment, but still found time to compete in 20 events.

CAREER HIGHLIGHTS: Had back-to-back wins first year on TOUR (1975), in Quad Cities Open and Pleasant Valley Classic (first New England success)...After latter triumph, left $40,000 winner's check in restaurant near course (new check subsequently issued)...Made it three titles in two years on TOUR in '76 with four-hole playoff triumph over Hale Irwin in Memorial Tournament... Captured 1985 NEC World Series of Golf and, along with it, 10-year TOUR exemption...Closing 4-under-par 66 gave him four-stroke win over Denis Watson on demanding Firestone Country Club South Course...Earlier that year won Westchester Classic with birdie on fourth extra hole of playoff with Raymond Floyd and George Burns...New England success history included 36-hole lead and tie for first after 54 holes of 1992 New England Classic (eventual T7 finish)...Also among early leaders at following week's Canon GHO...Winner 1972 and 1973 Northern California Amateur, 1974 California State Open, 1980 Magnolia Classic.

PERSONAL: Member of NBC-TV golf coverage team...During career has undergone two shoulder surgeries...Member PGA TOUR Policy Board 1985-87...Big San Francisco 49er fan...Owns Super Bowl ring given to him by 49er owner Ed Debartolo, Jr.

1993 PGA TOUR STATISTICS

Scoring Average	71.09	(74T)
Driving Distance	255.1	(137T)
Driving Accuracy	68.5	(93)
Greens in Regulation	65.6	(87T)
Putting	1.801	(104T)
All-Around	1034	(136)
Sand Saves	46.2	(159T)
Total Driving	230	(152)
Eagles	5	(67T)
Birdies	185	(161)

MISCELLANEOUS STATISTICS

Scoring Avg. (before cut)	71.45	(76)
Scoring Avg. (3rd round)	72.11	(153)
Scoring Avg. (4th round)	69.50	(5)
Birdie Conversion	26.5	(125T)
Par Breakers	17.9	(117T)

1993 Low Round: 65: 2 times
Career Low Round: 63: 4 times, most recent 1991 Walt Disney World/ 2
Career Largest Paycheck: $126,000/'85 NEC World Series of Golf/1

DOUG MARTIN

EXEMPT STATUS: 2nd on 1993 NIKE TOUR money list

FULL NAME: Douglas Allan Martin

HEIGHT: 6'   **WEIGHT:** 190

BIRTH DATE: December 8, 1966

BIRTHPLACE: Bluffton, OH

RESIDENCE: Florence, KY

FAMILY: Wife, Gaylyn; Cody Alan (12/24/90)

COLLEGE: University of Oklahoma

SPECIAL INTERESTS: Family, sports, Notre Dame football

TURNED PROFESSIONAL: 1989

Q SCHOOL: Fall 1991

PLAYER PROFILE

NIKE TOUR PLAYER RECORD

CAREER NIKE TOUR EARNINGS: $199,901   **PLAYOFF RECORD:** 1-1

NIKE TOUR VICTORIES: **1993** South Texas Open

MONEY & POSITION: 1991--$51,782--12   1992--$1,116--T-220   1993--$147,003--2

BEST 1993 FINISH: 1--South Texas Open

1993 NIKE TOUR SUMMARY: Tournaments entered--20; in money--19; top ten finishes--13

1994 PGA TOUR CHARITY TEAM COMPETITION: AT&T Pebble Beach National Pro-Am

1993 NIKE TOUR SEASON: Began final round of South Texas Open in 11th place five strokes behind leaders (Guy Boros and Rick Pearson) and defeated Boros on first playoff hole...That effort tied for best come from behind win of '93 NIKE TOUR season...Also involved in playoff at Permian Basin Open, losing to Franklin Langham on second playoff hole...Finished $19,290 behind leading money-winner Sean Murphy despite playing in six fewer events than Murphy...Five total top-three finishes last year...Along with two playoffs, finished second in Greenville, T2 in New Mexico and T3 in Central Georgia...Following early season win at South Texas, elected to concentrate on balance of 1993 on NIKE TOUR despite having PGA TOUR membership by virtue of his 150th finish on 1992 money list.

CAREER HIGHLIGHTS: Member of PGA TOUR in 1992 and 1993...Earned $77,204 in 1992 to finish 150th on money list and $21,381 in 1993 to finish 212th...Best 1993 (and best-ever) PGA TOUR finish was T4 at Deposit Guaranty Classic...Official PGA TOUR career earnings prior to 1994--$98,585...Played NIKE TOUR in 1991, finishing 12th on money list with $51,782...Best 1991 finishes were T2 at South Texas and T2 at Cleveland Open...Three-time All-American at Oklahoma, member of 1989 Walker Cup Team...Also winner of Oklahoma Open and 1984 USGA Junior Champion.

PERSONAL: Tremendous fan of Notre Dame football...Has spent several Saturday afternoons pacing sidelines as guest of good friend Lou Holtz...Says he's not just a Saturday fan, "I've gone to some of their games on Monday, meaning I get there Monday, go to practice all week and then go to the game on Saturday."...Father gave him his first golf club before he could walk and entered first competition at seven...Was an All-State basketball selection.

1993 PGA TOUR STATISTICS

Scoring Average	N/A
Driving Distance	N/A
Driving Accuracy	N/A
Greens in Regulation	N/A
Putting	N/A
All-Around	N/A
Sand Saves	N/A
Total Driving	N/A
Eagles	N/A
Birdies	N/A

MISCELLANEOUS STATISTICS

Scoring Avg. (before cut)	N/A
Scoring Avg. (3rd round)	N/A
Scoring Avg. (4th round)	N/A
Birdie Conversion	N/A
Par Breakers	N/A

1993 Low Round: 65: Dep. Guaranty/4
Career Low Round: 65: 1993 Deposit
Career Largest Guaranty Golf Classic/4
Paycheck: $33,500/1992 Nissan L.A. Open/7

DICK MAST

EXEMPT STATUS: 82nd on 1993 money list

FULL NAME: Richard Lyle Mast

HEIGHT: 5'11" **WEIGHT:** 180

BIRTH DATE: March 23, 1951

BIRTHPLACE: Bluffton, OH

RESIDENCE: Winter Garden, FL

FAMILY: Wife, Roberta; Richard (4/9/79), Joshua(4/1/83), Caleb (6/11/86), Jonathan (3/14/89), Jacob (12/5/91)

COLLEGE: St. Petersburg Junior College

SPECIAL INTERESTS: TOUR Bible study group, fishing, water skiing

TURNED PROFESSIONAL: 1972

Q SCHOOL: Fall 1973, 1977, 1978, 1985, 1991

PLAYER PROFILE

CAREER EARNINGS: $736,303

BEST EVER FINISH: 2--1992 Greater Milwaukee Open

MONEY & POSITION:

1974--$ 7,108--156	1986--$ 79,389--109	1990--$ 4,200-- 252
1975--$ 280--276	1987--$ 90,768--103	1991--$ 17,274-- 216
1977--$ 4,387--182	1988--$128,568-- 56	1992--$150,847-- 98
1979--$ 5,715--180	1989--$ 38,955--173	1993--$210,125-- 82
1985--$ 2,887--219		

BEST 1993 FINISHES: 4--Honda Classic; T6--Freeport-McMoRan Classic; 7--B.C. Open; T10--Las Vegas Invitational.

1993 SUMMARY: Tournaments entered--28; in money--16; top ten finishes--4.

1994 PGA TOUR CHARITY TEAM COMPETITION: MCI Heritage Classic

1993 SEASON: Enjoyed 1992 success so much went himself one better in '93...Bettered $200,000 plateau by earning $35,000 for T10 finish in Walt Disney World/Oldsmobile Classic, his final event of year...Disney placing one of four top-10 finishes on year, best performance ever...Had two top-10s in three starts early in season, solo fourth Honda Classic followed by T4 Freeport-McMoRan Classic three weeks later...Also had solo seventh at B.C Open in September, fashioned by closing 65...Opened Southwestern Bell Colonial with low round of year (and tied career low), 64 for one-shot lead...Stood just two strokes off lead after 54 holes...Finished in money his final seven events.

CAREER HIGHLIGHTS: Best career finish, solo second in 1992 Greater Milwaukee Open, provided largest payday to date: $108,000...1992 also his best year prior to 1993...GMO finish, two strokes behind Richard Zokol's winning 269 total, occurred when he posted season-low 64 and defending champion Mark Brooks stumbled on 72nd hole...Also had T7 in 1992 Chattanooga Classic...Earned TOUR card for 1991 by finishing third on 1990 Ben Hogan Tour money list with $92,521...Won three Hogan Tour events in 1990: Mississippi Gulf Coast Classic (his third start), Pensacola Open, Fort Wayne Open...Had begun 1990 thinking about making fields through Monday Qualifying and sponsor's exemptions...After playing first Hogan event decided to play entire season...Prior to Milwaukee best finish T4 1987 USF&G Classic.

PERSONAL: Noted after 1992 GMO, "I've played virtually ever tour—except the ladies"...Had particular success on mini-tours, with more than 25 victories...Set record score of 32-under-par 25G during 1985 Regional Qualifying Tournament on par-72 Palmaire Course in Sarasota, FL (had final round 60).

1993 PGA TOUR STATISTICS

Scoring Average	71.16	(81T)
Driving Distance	252.1	(162)
Driving Accuracy	66.7	(123)
Greens in Regulation	60.6	(173T)
Putting	1.754	(7)
All-Around	916	(122T)
Sand Saves	61.7	(10T)
Total Driving	285	(178)
Eagles	2	(144T)
Birdies	311	(38T)

MISCELLANEOUS STATISTICS

Scoring Avg. (before cut)	71.61	(90T)
Scoring Avg. (3rd round)	71.33	(96T)
Scoring Avg. (4th round)	71.94	(129T)
Birdie Conversion	32.8	(2)
Par Breakers	20.0	(33T)

1993 Low Round: 64: SW Bell Colonial/1
Career Low Round: 64: 5 times, most recent 1993 SW Bell Colonial/1
Career Largest
Paycheck: $108,000/1992 Greater Milwaukee Open/2

BOB MAY

EXEMPT STATUS: 4th on 1993 NIKE TOUR money list

FULL NAME: Robert Anthony May

HEIGHT: 5' 7" **WEIGHT:** 155

BIRTH DATE: October 6, 1968

BIRTHPLACE: Lynwood, CA

RESIDENCE: Las Vegas, NV

FAMILY: Wife, Brenda

COLLEGE: Oklahoma State

SPECIAL INTERESTS: Jet skiing, snow skiing, motorcyles

TURNED PROFESSIONAL: 1991

JOINED TOUR: 1994

PLAYER PROFILE

NIKE TOUR PLAYER RECORD

CAREER NIKE TOUR EARNINGS: $132,656   **PLAYOFF RECORD:** 0-1

MONEY & POSITION: 1992--$28,594--53   1993--$132,656--4

BEST 1993 FINISHES: 2--Shreveport Open; T2--Greater Ozarks Open

1993 NIKE TOUR SUMMARY: Tournaments entered--28; in money--24; top ten finishes--11

1994 PGA TOUR CHARITY TEAM COMPETITION: Las Vegas Invitational

1993 NIKE TOUR SEASON: Set NIKE TOUR record for consecutive cuts made at 21 (old mark 19)...His $132,656 earned also record for highest earnings without victory...Consistent play throughout year saw him with five top-three and eight top-five finishes...In addition to his second place finishes, finished T3 at Connecticut and Boise, third at NIKE TOUR Championship, fourth at South Carolina, T5 at Yuma and Central Georgia..Led NIKE TOUR with 376 birdies...Additional statistical notes: finished ninth in par breakers with 22.5%; T10 among eagle leaders with 8; third in scoring with a 70.05 stroke average.

CAREER HIGHLIGHTS: Played seven NIKE TOUR events in 1992 as non-member, earned $28,594, good for 53rd on money list...Finished in money each time, with three top-ten finishes...Best '92 effort was second at Wichita Charity Classic...Lost that tournament to Jeff Woodland on sixth playoff hole, which is second longest playoff in NIKE TOUR history (longest was Tom Lehman's eight playoff-hole win over John Wilson and Tim Straub in 1991 Mississippi Gulf Coast Classic)...Lists one of biggest thrills in golf as being member of 1991 Walker Cup Team...College team won 1991 NCAA championship...Enjoyed outstanding amateur career in Southern California before turning pro...Also played soccer and baseball before turning full concentration to golf.

PERSONAL: Received financial backing early in golf career from actor Joe Pesci and syndicated radio host Rick Dees.

1993 PGA TOUR STATISTICS

Scoring Average	N/A
Driving Distance	N/A
Driving Accuracy	N/A
Greens in Regulation	N/A
Putting	N/A
All-Around	N/A
Sand Saves	N/A
Total Driving	N/A
Eagles	N/A
Birdies	N/A

MISCELLANEOUS STATISTICS

Scoring Avg. (before cut)	N/A
Scoring Avg. (3rd round)	N/A
Scoring Avg. (4th round)	N/A
Birdie Conversion	N/A
Par Breakers	N/A

1993 Low Round:	N/A
Career Low Round:	N/A
Career Largest Paycheck:	N/A

BILLY MAYFAIR

EXEMPT STATUS: 1993 tournament winner

FULL NAME: William Fred Mayfair

HEIGHT: 5' 8"   **WEIGHT:** 175

BIRTH DATE: August 6, 1966

BIRTHPLACE: Phoenix, AZ

RESIDENCE: Phoenix, AZ; Plays out of Troon &Troon North GC

FAMILY: Single

COLLEGE: Arizona State

SPECIAL INTERESTS: All sports

TURNED PROFESSIONAL: 1988

Q SCHOOL: Fall 1988

PLAYER PROFILE

CAREER EARNINGS: $1,696,275   **PLAYOFF RECORD:** 1-2

TOUR VICTORIES: 1993 Greater Milwaukee Open
(TOTAL: 1)

MONEY & POSITION:	1989--$111,998--116	1991--$ 185,668--89	1993--$513,072--30
	1990--$693,658-- 12	1992--$ 191,878--79	

BEST 1993 FINISH: 1--Greater Milwaukee Open; T2--GTE Byron Nelson Classic; T7--Kemper Open; T8--Walt Disney World/Oldsmobile Classic; T10--B.C. Open.

1993 SUMMARY: Tournaments entered--32; in money--22; top ten finishes--5.

1994 PGA TOUR CHARITY TEAM COMPETITION: JCPenney Classic

NATIONAL TEAMS: Walker Cup, 1987; Four Tours World Championship of Golf,1991.

1993 SEASON: In first four years on TOUR came closest to tasting victory in two 1990 playoff losses, first of which was in Greater Milwaukee Open...In what might be called poetic justice, finally broke through with first PGA TOUR win in GMO last September...Defeated Mark Calcavecchia on fourth hole of yet another playoff in final tournament at Tuckaway CC...Winning shot a 20-foot chip-in with Calcavecchia facing a six-foot putt for birdie (which he missed)...Win capped a on year that saw him struggle at outset...Missed four of first five cuts and five of eight...Posted back-to-back top-10 finishes in GTE Byron Nelson Classic (T2) and Kemper Open (T7)...Fired career-low 61 in second round of Nelson, establishing TPC at Las Colinas course record...Had best earnings year since sophomore campaign in 1990.

CAREER HIGHLIGHTS: Had most financially rewarding second year in PGA TOUR history in 1990, with earnings of $693,658...Established first-two-years' earnings standard of $805,656 for 1989-90, since surpassed by John Daly in 1991-92...At 1990 GMO tied for second with Ed Dougherty after losing to Jim Gallagher, Jr., on first playoff hole...Also lost to Jodie Mudd in season-ending Nabisco Championships when Mudd birdied first extra hole...Had five other top-10 finishes in '90 season...Best finish in rookie year of '89 was tie for 12th in Doral-Ryder Open.

PERSONAL: Celebrated amateur player won 1987 U.S. Amateur and 1986 U.S. Public Links...1987 Fred Haskins Award recipient as outstanding college player of year...Also named Arizona player of year in '87...Captured seven collegiate events...1985-87 Arizona Stroke Play champion...Four-time winner Arizona State Juniors...Member 1987 Walker Cup, 1991 Four Tours World Championship of Golf teams.

1993 PGA TOUR STATISTICS

Scoring Average	70.95	(63T)
Driving Distance	253.0	(155T)
Driving Accuracy	76.2	(15)
Greens in Regulation	70.1	(15)
Putting	1.807	(117T)
All-Around	691	(62)
Sand Saves	46.3	(157T)
Total Driving	170	(69)
Eagles	4	(89T)
Birdies	356	(11)

MISCELLANEOUS STATISTICS

Scoring Avg. (before cut)	71.52	(82T)
Scoring Avg. (3rd round)	70.27	(27T)
Scoring Avg. (4th round)	71.04	(47)
Birdie Conversion	25.7	(148T)
Par Breakers	18.2	(98T)

1993 Low Round:	**61:** GTE B. Nelson Classic/2
Career Low Round:	**61:** 1993 GTE Byron Nelson Classic/2
Career Largest	
Paycheck:$270,000/1990 Nabisco Championships/2	

BLAINE McCALLISTER

EXEMPT STATUS: 1993 tournament winner

FULL NAME: Blaine McCallister

HEIGHT: 5' 9"   **WEIGHT:** 175

BIRTH DATE: October 17, 1958

BIRTHPLACE: Ft. Stockton, TX

RESIDENCE: Ponte Vedra, FL; plays out of Ft. Stockton GC

FAMILY: Wife, Claudia

COLLEGE: University of Houston

SPECIAL INTERESTS: Hunting, fishing, tennis, baseball

TURNED PROFESSIONAL: 1981

Q SCHOOL: Fall 1981; 1982; 1985

PLAYER PROFILE

CAREER EARNINGS: $2,088,043   **PLAYOFF RECORD:** 1-1

TOUR VICTORIES: 1988 Hardee's Golf Classic. **1989** Honda Classic, Bank of Boston Classic.
(TOTAL: 5)   **1991** H-E-B. Texas Open. **1993** B.C. Open.

MONEY & POSITION:			
	1982--$ 7,894--180	1988--$225,660-- 49	1991--$ 412,974--36
	1983--$ 5,218--201	1989--$593,891-- 15	1992--$ 261,187--59
	1986--$ 88,732-- 94	1990--$152,048--103	1993--$ 290,434--61
	1987--$120,005-- 87		

BEST 1993 FINISHES: 1--B.C. Open; T3--Shell Houston Open.

1993 SUMMARY: Tournaments entered--27; in money--16; top ten finishes--2.

1994 PGA TOUR CHARITY TEAM COMPETITION: Hardee's Golf Classic

1993 SEASON: Finished with third-best campaign of 10-year PGA TOUR career...Earnings total of $290,434 surpassed only by 1989 and 1991 money-won figures...Highlight of year fifth career victory, a one-stroke win over Denis Watson in the B.C. Open in late September...Also finished one shot out of Jim McGovern-John Huston playoff (won by McGovern) at Shell Houston Open...Missed month of August due to surgery for removal of infected tonsils...Closed 1993 with runnerup finish to Fred Couples in Lincoln Mercury Kapalua International.

CAREER HIGHLIGHTS: Fashioned pair of victories in best season to date, 1989...With 65-64 finish, captured Honda Classic by four strokes over Payne Stewart...Later in '89 fired closing-round 66 to win Bank of Boston Classic by one shot over Brad Faxon; lost 1986 Boston event in playoff with Gene Sauers...Became part of TOUR history in winning Hardee's Golf Classic in 1988...Middle two rounds of 62-63--125 matched TOUR record for back-to-back rounds...15-under total for those two rounds over par-70 Oakwood CC layout helped produce Hardee's-winning 19-under-par 261...Weakened by mononucleosis in early weeks of 1990, rebounded in '91 with victory in H.E.B. Texas Open after T3 week before in B.C. Open.

PERSONAL: Wife Claudia, who suffers from rare degenerative eye disease pseudoxanthoma elasticum (PXE)...Has become actively involved with eyesight organizations because of Claudia's affliction..."Three-footers are not as meaningful to me as they used to be," he has said...Three-time All-America at University of Houston, where roomed with Fred Couples one year and CBS-TV sportscaster Jim Nantz for three...runnerup 1981 Canadian Amateur...Natural lefthander who plays game righthanded, but putts southpaw.

1993 PGA TOUR STATISTICS

Scoring Average	70.90	(59T)
Driving Distance	265.0	(51T)
Driving Accuracy	75.5	(19T)
Greens in Regulation	70.3	(13)
Putting	1.793	(77T)
All-Around	526	(27)
Sand Saves	48.9	(133T)
Total Driving	70	(5)
Eagles	2	(144T)
Birdies	328	(25)

MISCELLANEOUS STATISTICS

Scoring Avg. (before cut)	71.12	(46)
Scoring Avg. (3rd round)	71.13	(86T)
Scoring Avg. (4th round)	70.31	(13T)
Birdie Conversion	29.5	(31T)
Par Breakers	20.8	(15T)

1993 Low Round:	64: 2 times
Career Low Round:	62: 1988 Hardee's Golf
Career Largest	Classic/2
Paycheck: $162,000/1991 H-E-B Texas Open/1	

MARK McCUMBER

EXEMPT STATUS: Winner, 1988 THE PLAYERS Championship

FULL NAME: Mark Randall McCumber

HEIGHT: 5' 8"   **WEIGHT:** 170

BIRTH DATE: September 7, 1951

BIRTHPLACE: Jacksonville, FL

RESIDENCE: Jacksonville, FL

FAMILY: Wife, Paddy; Addison (1/28/76); Megan (6/14/80); Mark Tyler (4/4/91)

SPECIAL INTERESTS: Family activities, golf course architecture

TURNED PROFESSIONAL: 1974

Q SCHOOL: Spring 1978

PLAYER PROFILE

CAREER EARNINGS: $3,215,570   **PLAYOFF RECORD:** 1-0

TOUR VICTORIES: **1979** Doral-Eastern Open. **1983** Western Open, Pensacola Open **1985** Doral-
(TOTAL: 7)   Eastern Open. **1987** Anheuser-Busch Classic. **1988** THE PLAYERS Championship. **1989** Beatrice Western Open.

MONEY & POSITION:

1978--$ 6,948--160	1984--$133,445--50	1989--$546,587-- 14
1979--$ 67,886-- 60	1985--$192,752--32	1990--$163,413-- 97
1980--$ 36,985-- 88	1986--$110,442--80	1991--$173,852-- 92
1981--$ 33,363--103	1987--$390,885--22	1992--$136,653--106
1982--$ 31,684--119	1988--$559,111--13	1993--$363,269-- 41
1983--$268,294-- 8		

BEST 1993 FINISHES: T2--Doral-Ryder Open; T3--MCI Heritage Classic; T6--Nestle Invitational.

1993 SUMMARY: Tournaments entered--21; in money--18; top ten finishes--3.

1994 PGA TOUR CHARITY TEAM COMPETITION: Walt Disney World/Oldsmobile Classic

NATIONAL TEAMS: World Cup (2), 1988, 1989; Ryder Cup 1989.

1993 SEASON: With increasing involvement in course design activities impacting his game, chose last year to put full focus on golf when playing tournaments…Revised approach produced positive results…Money-won total his best since 1989, when finished No. 14…Had early pair of top-10 finishes in consecutive March starts, T2 Doral-Ryder Open and T6 Nestle Invitational…Had third and final top-10 placing of season in April, T3 at MCI Heritage Classic…Second-place tie at Doral best finish since winning 1989 Western Open…Three top-10s in same year best since recorded trio in 1990…Registered low round of season (65) twice, last time in opening round of Walt Disney World/Oldsmobile Classic.

CAREER HIGHLIGHTS: Jacksonville, FL, native and resident achieved extremely popular hometown victory in March 1989 by winning THE PLAYERS Championship…Thousands in gallery, many loyal local followers, roared salute to champion-to-be as he walked onto 18th green at Stadium Course at Sawgrass…Captured first tournament win, 1979 Doral-Eastern Open, in second year on TOUR…Hit stride in 1983 with pair of victories in Western and Pensacola Opens…Repeat victor in Doral-Eastern Open (1985) and Beatrice Western Open (1989), latter in playoff with Peter Jacobsen…Member 1989 Ryder Cup team, 1988-89 World Cup squads (victors in '88)…Also winner of 1987 Anheuser-Busch Classic.

PERSONAL: On-course commentator for NBC-TV at 1993 Ryder Cup…Making big impact in golf course design with Mark McCumber and Associates, design arm of McCumber Golf, company he operates with his brothers…Three McCumber courses used in first stage of 1993 PGA TOUR Qualifying Tournament…Member American Society of Golf Course Architects.

1993 PGA TOUR STATISTICS

Scoring Average	70.27	(19)
Driving Distance	264.9	(55)
Driving Accuracy	72.4	(52T)
Greens in Regulation	69.5	(20)
Putting	1.795	(86T)
All-Around	515	(25)
Sand Saves	49.6	(123T)
Total Driving	107	(13)
Eagles	5	(67T)
Birdies	283	(80)

MISCELLANEOUS STATISTICS

Scoring Avg. (before cut)	70.35	(12)
Scoring Avg. (3rd round)	70.65	(50)
Scoring Avg. (4th round)	71.22	(62T)
Birdie Conversion	29.0	(46T)
Par Breakers	20.5	(24T)

1993 Low Round: **65:** 2 times
Career Low Round: **63:** 1980 Texas Open/2
Career Largest
Paycheck: **$225,000**/1988 THE PLAYERS/1

JIM McGOVERN

EXEMPT STATUS: 1993 tournament winner

FULL NAME: James David McGovern

HEIGHT: 6'2"   **WEIGHT:** 195

BIRTH DATE: February 5, 1965

BIRTHPLACE: Teaneck, NJ

RESIDENCE: River Edge, NJ

FAMILY: Wife, Lauren

COLLEGE: Old Dominion

SPECIAL INTERESTS: All sports

TURNED PROFESSIONAL: 1988

Q SCHOOL: 1991

PLAYER PROFILE

CAREER EARNINGS: $846,252   **PLAYOFF RECORD:** 1-0

TOUR VICTORIES: 1993 Shell Houston Open.
(TOTAL: 1)

MONEY & POSITION: 1991--$88,869--141   1992--$169,889--92   1993--$587,495--27

BEST 1993 FINISHES: 1--Shell Houston Open; T4--Memorial Tournament; T6--Honda Classic.

1993 SUMMARY: Tournaments entered--34; in money--27; top ten finishes--3.

1994 PGA TOUR CHARITY TEAM COMPETITION: Northern Telecom Open

1993 SEASON: "Jersey Kid" captured initial PGA TOUR victory in May, defeating John Huston with birdie on second playoff hole to win weather-shortened Shell Houston Open… After back-to-back bogeys in final round, hit fairway driver to within three feet for eagle on No. 15, then sank eight-footer for par on final hole to tie Huston…Said of win: "Now I don't have to worry about making my house payments anymore"…Houston victory was worth $234,000…Had two other top-10s during season, T6 at Honda Classic in March and T4 at Memorial in June.

CAREER HIGHLIGHTS: Hard-working youngster quickly acquired "iron man" label for number of tournaments played during brief three-year PGA TOUR career…Prior to '93 top TOUR finish had been solo fourth in 1992 Federal Express St. Jude Classic…Memphis appearance featured TPC at Southwind record-tying 62 in second round…Qualified for TOUR in '91 by finishing second on 1990 Ben Hogan Tour money list…Road to Hogan Tour not easy, since failed to earn card at PGA TOUR Qualifying Tournament and gained only alternate spot in Hogan Tour Q-Tournament… Victory in Hogan Lake City Classic provided not only first-place check of $20,000 but also exemption into remaining tournaments…Later won Texarkana and New Haven Opens…Led Hogan Tour in birdies with 292…Winner 1988 Metropolitan Open, '87 Metropolitan Amateur… 1987 Virginia State Intercollegiate Champion.

PERSONAL: First exposed to game when parents bought house adjacent to Hackensack (NJ) Golf Club…Because of minimum age restriction couldn't gain admittance to club until tree knocked down connecting fence during storm, then with brothers hit balls on course until late at night…Brother Rob played linebacker in NFL.

1993 PGA TOUR STATISTICS

Scoring Average	70.71	(44)
Driving Distance	267.1	(38T)
Driving Accuracy	73.2	(42)
Greens in Regulation	65.8	(83T)
Putting	1.777	(39T)
All-Around	389	(10)
Sand Saves	49.7	(122)
Total Driving	80	(10)
Eagles	10	(9T)
Birdies	412	(2)

MISCELLANEOUS STATISTICS

Scoring Avg. (before cut)	70.79	(28)
Scoring Avg. (3rd round)	71.50	(110T)
Scoring Avg. (4th round)	71.70	(113)
Birdie Conversion	29.5	(31T)
Par Breakers	19.9	(37T)

1993 Low Round: 64: Shell Houston Open/2
Career Low Round: 62: 1992 Fed. Ex. St. Jude Classic/2
Career Largest Paycheck: $234,000/1993 Shell Houston Open/1

ROCCO MEDIATE

EXEMPT STATUS: 1993 tournament winner

FULL NAME: Rocco Anthony Mediate

HEIGHT: 6' 1"   **WEIGHT:** 200

BIRTH DATE: December 17, 1962

BIRTHPLACE: Greensburg, PA

RESIDENCE: Ponte Vedra, FL

FAMILY: Wife, Linda; Rocco Vincent (9/19/90); Nicco Anthony (1/29/93)

COLLEGE: Florida Southern

SPECIAL INTERESTS: Photography, music, collecting trading cards

TURNED PROFESSIONAL: 1985

Q SCHOOL: Fall 1985, 1986

PLAYER PROFILE

CAREER EARNINGS: $2,215,680   **PLAYOFF RECORD:** 2-0

TOUR VICTORIES: 1991 Doral-Ryder Open. **1993** Kmart Greater Greensboro Open. (TOTAL: 2)

MONEY & POSITION:	1986--$ 20,670--174	1989--$132,501--108	1992--$301,896--49
	1987--$112,099-- 91	1990--$240,625-- 62	1993--$680,623--16
	1988--$129,829-- 92	1991--$597,438-- 15	

BEST 1993 FINISHES: 1--Kmart Greater Greensboro Open; T2--Nestle Invitational; T6--Honda Classic; T6--THE PLAYERS Championship; T7--Canon Greater Hartford Open; 9--The International.

1993 SUMMARY: Tournaments entered--24; in money--21; top ten finishes--6.

1994 PGA TOUR CHARITY TEAM COMPETITION: Las Vegas Invitational

---

1993 SEASON: Captured second PGA TOUR title in April, birdieing fourth playoff hole to defeat Steve Elkington and win Kmart Greater Greensboro Open...Both career victories earned via playoff route...GGO triumph climaxed five-tournament string that featured four top-10 finishes...First three events in that skein: T6 Honda Classic, T2 Nestle Invitational, T6 THE PLAYERS Championship...Three weeks later finished T47 in MCI Heritage Classic, then rebounded with Greensboro win...Other top-10s came at Canon GHO and The International...Forced to withdraw from Las Vegas Invitational with back problem, ailment that carried over to TOUR Championship.

CAREER HIGHLIGHTS: Earned first TOUR title in sixth season...1991 Doral-Ryder Open victory on Blue Monster course came in playoff with Curtis Strange...Caught Strange, who carded final-round 5-under-par 67 for 12-under 276, with birdies on 17th and 18th holes...Sank 10-footers on each green...Captured playoff and $252,000 winner's check by making five-foot birdie putt on first extra hole...Got out of blocks in spectacular fashion in '91, posting six top-10 finishes in first seven starts, 13th in other...Began 1992 with top-5 finishes in three of his first six events...Winner 1992 Perrier French Open...Winner 1984 South Florida Invitational.

PERSONAL: Successful employer of 49-inch putter...Finalist 1984 Western Amateur...Grew up in Greensburg, PA, nearby Latrobe home of Arnold Palmer...Played golf with Palmer for first time at 19...Got delayed start in game because baseball his sport as youngster...Attended California (PA) State College before transferring to Florida Southern...Wife Linda stood in as birth coach for fellow PGA TOUR pro Jim Hallet when his wife delivered their first child in January 1993 and Hallet arrived late; Linda gave birth to second son Nicco five days later.

1993 PGA TOUR STATISTICS

Scoring Average	70.59	(36)
Driving Distance	261.3	(73)
Driving Accuracy	73.8	(36T)
Greens in Regulation	68.5	(31T)
Putting	1.824	(156T)
All-Around	611	(46)
Sand Saves	53.1	(72T)
Total Driving	109	(15T)
Eagles	3	(116T)
Birdies	284	(76T)

MISCELLANEOUS STATISTICS

Scoring Avg. (before cut)	71.00	(37T)
Scoring Avg. (3rd round)	71.05	(80)
Scoring Avg. (4th round)	71.41	(87T)
Birdie Conversion	26.5	(125T)
Par Breakers	18.3	(94T)

1993 Low Round:	64: Disney/Olds Classic/2
Career Low Round:	63: 2 times, most recent 1991 Bob Hope Chrysler Classic/2
Career Largest Paycheck:	$270,000/1993 Kmart GG Open/1

PHIL MICKELSON

EXEMPT STATUS: 1993 tournament winner

FULL NAME: Phil A. Mickelson

HEIGHT: 6' 2"　　**WEIGHT:** 190

BIRTH DATE: June 16, 1970

BIRTHPLACE: San Diego, CA

RESIDENCE: Scottsdale, AZ

FAMILY: Single

COLLEGE: Arizona State University

SPECIAL INTERESTS: Snow and water skiing

JOINED TOUR: June 1992

PLAYER PROFILE

CAREER MONEY: $800,449

TOUR VICTORIES: 1991 Northern Telecom Open. **1993** Buick Invitational of California,
(TOTAL: 3)　　　　The International.

MONEY & POSITION:　　1992--$171,713 --90　　1993--$628,735--22

BEST 1993 FINISHES: 1--Buick Invitational of California; 1--The International; T6--PGA Championship;
T8--Northern Telecom Open.

1993 SUMMARY: Tournaments entered--24; in money--14; top ten finishes--4.

1994 PGA TOUR CHARITY TEAM COMPETITION: Phoenix Open

NATIONAL TEAMS: Walker Cup, 1989,1991.

1993 SEASON: Picked up second and third PGA TOUR titles in just second year of TOUR membership…His initial two as professional …Playing before home crowd at Torrey Pines, captured Buick Invitational of California after opening with 75 (highest first round for winner in '93)…Closed with 65, good for four-shot win over Dave Rummells…Followed T6 in PGA Championship at Inverness with his second victory of campaign, an eight-point win over Mark Calcavecchia worth $234,000 at the International…Also had top-10 finish in first start of season, T8 in Northern Telecom Open, event he won as amateur in '91.

CAREER HIGHLIGHTS: Turned professional at 1992 U.S. Open, where he missed cut…Opened impressively with 68 before skying to 81 in Round 2…Proceeded to cash in next two events, including second at New England Classic worth $108,000…While still playing for Arizona State captured 1991 Northern Telecom Open by one stroke over Bob Tway and Tom Purtzer…Birdies on two of last three holes to win…Winner 1989-90-92 NCAA Championships for Arizona State…Won 1990 U.S. Amateur, only lefthander ever to do so…Joined Jack Nicklaus as only players to win NCAA and U.S. Amateur titles in same year…One of four collegians (Ben Crenshaw, Curtis Strange, Billy Ray Brown) to win NCAA title in freshman year.

PERSONAL: Four-time first-team All-America 1989-92 (only Gary Hallberg and David Duval have achieved same status)…Winner 1990-92 Fred Haskins and Jack Nicklaus Awards as collegiate player of year…1991 Golf World Amateur Player of Year…1989, '91 Walker Cupper…1990-92 PAC-10 Player of Year…Low amateur 1990-91 U.S. Opens, 1991 Masters…Golf Magazine Junior Player of Year 1986-88…Righthanded in everything but golf (when father started him in game, became mirror image process).

1993 PGA TOUR STATISTICS

Scoring Average	71.20	(89T)
Driving Distance	269.2	(25)
Driving Accuracy	65.4	(138T)
Greens in Regulation	66.1	(72T)
Putting	1.800	(100T)
All-Around	772	(82)
Sand Saves	50.4	(112)
Total Driving	163	(59)
Eagles	6	(50T)
Birdies	246	(127T)

MISCELLANEOUS STATISTICS

Scoring Avg. (before cut)	71.50	(79T)
Scoring Avg. (3rd round)	72.15	(155T)
Scoring Avg. (4th round)	71.64	(107T)
Birdie Conversion	28.3	(66T)
Par Breakers	19.2	(62T)

1993 Low Round:	**65:** 3 times
Career Low Round:	**63:** 1992 B.C. Open/2
Career Largest	
Paycheck: $234,000/1993 International/1	

LARRY MIZE

EXEMPT STATUS: Winner 1987 Masters Tournament

FULL NAME: Larry Hogan Mize

HEIGHT: 6'   **WEIGHT:** 165

BIRTH DATE: Sept. 23, 1958

BIRTHPLACE: Augusta, GA

RESIDENCE: Columbus, GA

FAMILY: Wife, Bonnie; David (4/17/86), Patrick (2/12/89), Robert (4/2/93)

COLLEGE: Georgia Tech

SPECIAL INTERESTS: Fishing, all sports

TURNED PROFESSIONAL: 1980

Q SCHOOL: Fall 1981

PLAYER PROFILE

CAREER EARNINGS: $3,908,682   **PLAYOFF RECORD:** 1-2

TOUR VICTORIES: 1983 Danny Thomas-Memphis Classic. **1987** Masters. **1993** Northern Telecom Open, (TOTAL: 4)   Buick Open

MONEY & POSITION:

1982--$ 28,787--124	1986--$314,051--17	1990--$668,198--14
1983--$146,325-- 35	1987--$561,407-- 6	1991--$279,061--60
1984--$172,513-- 36	1988--$187,823--62	1992--$316,428--47
1985--$231,041-- 17	1989--$278,388--45	1993--$724,660--13

BEST 1993 FINISHES: 1--Northern Telecom Open; 1--Buick Open; 3--Honda Classic; 6--Shell Houston Open; T7--BellSouth Classic; ; T10--Nestle Invitational; T10--Walt Disney World/Oldsmobile Classic.

1993 SUMMARY: Tournaments entered--22; in money--17; top ten finishes--7.

1994 PGA TOUR CHARITY TEAM COMPETITION: AT&T Pebble Beach National Pro-Am

NATIONAL TEAMS: Ryder Cup, 1987.

1993 SEASON: Captured Northern Telecom Open, then added Buick Open triumph, his first two wins since the 1987 Masters...Those two victories helped produce finest earnings season of 12-year career...Tucson payday ($198,000) his largest ever...Gained final-round lead at Tucson National when 54-hole co-leaders Dudley Hart and Phil Mickelson faltered, then held off Jeff Maggert for his third TOUR win... After holding solo lead after first two rounds at Warwick Hills, came from four strokes off Fuzzy Zoeller's third-round advantage to make Buick Open win his fourth career title.

CAREER HIGHLIGHTS: Probably best known for "impossible" shot that captured 1987 Masters...Finished regulation tied with Greg Norman and Seve Ballesteros (3-under-par 285) after birdieing final hole...After Ballesteros went out on first playoff hole, used sand wedge to sink 140-foot chip from right of green on second extra hole...Norman's long birdie putt miss from right fringe gave him second career victory...First win was in 1983 Danny Thomas-Memphis Classic, where sank 25-foot birdie putt to edge Fuzzy Zoeller, John Mahaffey and Chip Beck...Lost playoff to Norman in 1986 Kemper Open...Best previous money-won season (1990/$668,198) featured playoff loss to Payne Stewart in MCI Heritage Classic, along with seconds in BellSouth Atlanta and Anheuser-Busch Golf Classics...'87 Masters title propelled to top-10 money list finish with $561,407.

PERSONAL: Member 1987 Ryder Cup team...Player Director, PGA TOUR Policy Board 1988-90...Winner 1988 Casio World Open, 1989-90 Dunlop Phoenix (both Japan)...Winner Atlanta Amateur Championship...Played No. 1 three years at Georgia Tech, captain for two.

1993 PGA TOUR STATISTICS

Scoring Average	70.18	(13T)
Driving Distance	259.0	(95T)
Driving Accuracy	74.7	(27T)
Greens in Regulation	67.3	(55T)
Putting	1.768	(21T)
All-Around	397	(11)
Sand Saves	62.7	(6)
Total Driving	122	(20)
Eagles	6	(50T)
Birdies	261	(110)

MISCELLANEOUS STATISTICS

Scoring Avg. (before cut)	70.41	(16T)
Scoring Avg. (3rd round)	70.07	(18T)
Scoring Avg. (4th round)	71.35	(80T)
Birdie Conversion	28.4	(63T)
Par Breakers	19.5	(50T)

1993 Low Round: 64: 2 times

Career Low Round: 62: 1985 Los Angeles Open/2

Career Largest

Paycheck: $198,000/1993 Northern Telecom Open/1

GIL MORGAN

EXEMPT STATUS: 24th on 1993 money list

FULL NAME: Gilmer Bryan Morgan

HEIGHT: 5' 9" **WEIGHT:** 175

BIRTH DATE: Sept. 25, 1946

BIRTHPLACE: Wewoka, OK

RESIDENCE: Oak Tree Golf Club, Edmond, OK

FAMILY: Wife, Jeanine; Molly (5/18/81), Maggie (8/10/82), Melanie (9/24/84)

COLLEGE: East Central State College (1968, B.S.), Southern College of Optometry (1972, Doctor of Optometry)

SPECIAL INTERESTS: Cars

TURNED PROFESSIONAL: 1972

Q SCHOOL: Fall 1973

PLAYER PROFILE

CAREER EARNINGS: $4,426,179   **PLAYOFF RECORD:** 3-4

TOUR VICTORIES: **1977** B.C. Open. **1978** Glen Campbell-Los Angeles Open, World Series of Golf.
(TOTAL: 7)   **1979** Danny Thomas-Memphis Classic. **1983** Joe Garagiola-Tucson Open, Glen Campbell-Los Angeles Open. **1990** Kemper Open.

MONEY & POSITION:

1973--$ 3,800--204	1980--$135,308--28	1987--$133,980--81
1974--$ 23,880-- 94	1981--$171,184--18	1988--$288,002--34
1975--$ 42,772-- 60	1982--$139,652--26	1989--$300,395--39
1976--$ 61,372-- 42	1983--$306,133-- 5	1990--$702,629--11
1977--$104,817-- 24	1984--$281,948--13	1991--$232,913--70
1978--$267,459-- 2	1985--$133,941--62	1992--$272,959--56
1979--$115,857-- 29	1986--$ 98,770--84	1993--$610,312--24

BEST 1993 FINISHES: T3--THE PLAYERS Championship; T3--Kmart Greater Greensboro Open; 5--Federal Express St. Jude Classic; T5-- H-E-B Texas Open; T8--MCI Heritage Classic; T8--Greater Milwaukee Open; 9--Las Vegas Invitational; T9--Phoenix Open; T9--AT&T Pebble Beach National Pro-Am.

1993 SUMMARY: Tournaments entered--24; in money--20; top ten finishes--9.

1994 PGA TOUR CHARITY TEAM COMPETITION: Honda Classic

NATIONAL TEAMS: Ryder Cup (2), 1979, 1983.

1993 SEASON: Had back-to-back top-10s in consecutive weeks three times, beginning with pair of T9s in Phoenix Open and AT&T Pebble Beach National Pro-Am (starts 2-3 of year)…Included in that stretch were consecutive top-10s in MCI Heritage Classic (T8) and Kmart Greater Greensboro Open (T3)… Closing 65 at TPC at Sawgrass final-round low in '93 PLAYERS… Near end of season shared 36-hole lead in back-to-back events, H-E-B Texas Open (T5) and Las Vegas Invitational (9)…Money-won total second only to 1990 earnings of $702,629.

CAREER HIGHLIGHTS: Had leg up on one of great U.S. Opens of all time in 1992…Became first ever to reach 10-under-par in Open early in Round 3, then climbed to 12-under through 43 holes…Ultimately tumbled back to 5-over-par T13…Handled tournament adversity and post-Open followup like class act he is, head-on and with dignity…Biggest victory came in 1978 World Series of Golf…Defeated Hubert Green in playoff to emerge year's No. 2 money winner behind Tom Watson…Had left shoulder rotator cuff surgery in September 1986…After nine-month layoff returned to TOUR in early May 1987 and was near top of game by midsummer…Any lingering questions about completeness of comeback were answered by most successful year in '90…Captured Kemper Open, first win since 1983 and seventh career…Began 1983 season by finishing in top eight in seven straight tournaments…Won first two events of '83, Joe Garagiola-Tucson Open in playoff with Lanny Wadkins and Glen Campbell-Los Angeles Open…1967 Oklahoma collegiate champion, 1968 collegiate All-America…Winner 1978 Pacific Masters…Named to NAIA Hall of Fame 1982.

PERSONAL: Holds Doctor of Optometry Degree (1972) from Southern College of Optometry, but has never practiced…Junior year at East Central State (OK) decided to pursue career in golf, but waited until he earned doctor's degree.

1993 PGA TOUR STATISTICS

Scoring Average	70.12	(11)
Driving Distance	265.4	(46)
Driving Accuracy	76.1	(16)
Greens in Regulation	71.1	(8T)
Putting	1.781	(52T)
All-Around	252	(1)
Sand Saves	56.5	(36T)
Total Driving	62	(3)
Eagles	9	(16T)
Birdies	295	(64)

MISCELLANEOUS STATISTICS

Scoring Avg. (before cut)	69.75	(4)
Scoring Avg. (3rd round)	69.83	(8T)
Scoring Avg. (4th round)	70.90	(39T)
Birdie Conversion	26.8	(116T)
Par Breakers	19.6	(48T)

1993 Low Round: 64; 2 times
Career Low Round: 62; 1988 Shearson Lehman
Career Largest Paycheck: $180,000/1990 Kemper Open/1   Hutton Andy Williams Open/2

JOHN MORSE

EXEMPT STATUS: 5th on 1993 NIKE TOUR money list

FULL NAME: John Paul Morse

HEIGHT: 5' 10"   **WEIGHT:** 180

BIRTH DATE: February 16, 1958

BIRTHPLACE: Marshall, MI

RESIDENCE: Casselberry, FL

FAMILY: Wife, Kelly; Christina (7/31/92)

COLLEGE: University of Michigan

SPECIAL INTERESTS: Fishing

TURNED PROFESSIONAL: 1981

JOINED TOUR: 1994

PLAYER PROFILE

NIKE TOUR PLAYER RECORD

CAREER NIKE TOUR EARNINGS: $122,627   **PLAYOFF RECORD:** 0-0

NIKE TOUR VICTORIES: 1993 New England Classic

MONEY & POSITION: 1993--$122,627--5

BEST 1993 FINISH: 1--New England Classic

1993 NIKE TOUR SUMMARY: Tournaments entered--26; in money--19; top ten finishes--9

1994 PGA TOUR CHARITY TEAM COMPETITION: Federal Express St. Jude Classic

1993 NIKE TOUR SEASON: Win at New England highlighted five top-three performances...During final three weeks of August, had consecutive T2 performances (New Mexico and Wichita) followed by a T3 in Texarkana...In that stretch, averaged 67.58 for 12 rounds with no round over par...Low round was 64 in third round of Texarkana...Also finished T3 at Hawkeye Open.

CAREER HIGHLIGHTS: Played Australasian Tour from 1989-92...Returned to Australia following conclusion of '93 NIKE TOUR for select events, his 277 was two behind Ian Baker-Finch at 1993 Australian PGA (Baker-Finch won in playoff)...Overseas tour highlight was winning 1990 Australian Open...Trailed Craig Parry by four shots heading into final round, shot 4-under while Parry shot par to force playoff, which Morse won...Other professional career victories include 1989 Quebec Open, 1990 Monro Interiors Nedlands Masters, 1991 Air New Zealand Shell Open...Australian Open win earned Morse spot in 1991 NEC World Series of Golf, where he earned $9,116 for a T27 finish, his only PGA TOUR paycheck prior to 1994...Played U.S. Open in 1984 and 1987, missing both cuts...Played in four other PGA TOUR events during career, missing those cuts as well.

PERSONAL: Morse attempted to gain PGA TOUR card at six Q-schools without success but says he very much enjoys playing in Australia...His decision to play the '93 NIKE TOUR rather than return to Australia based on fact he did not want to be away from new daughter, Christina...Success last year earned him exempt status on PGA TOUR but plans to continue to play select events in Australia when possible...In addition to his golf success, was also all-conference selection in basketball during high school.

1993 PGA TOUR STATISTICS

Scoring Average	N/A
Driving Distance	N/A
Driving Accuracy	N/A
Greens in Regulation	N/A
Putting	N/A
All-Around	N/A
Sand Saves	N/A
Total Driving	N/A
Eagles	N/A
Birdies	N/A

MISCELLANEOUS STATISTICS

Scoring Avg. (before cut)	N/A
Scoring Avg. (3rd round)	N/A
Scoring Avg. (4th round)	N/A
Birdie Conversion	N/A
Par Breakers	N/A

1993 Low Round: N/A

Career Low Round: 69: 1991 NEC World

Career Largest Series of Golf/3

Paycheck:$9,116/1991 NEC W S of Golf/T27

JODIE MUDD

EXEMPT STATUS: Winner, 1990 THE PLAYERS Championship

FULL NAME: Joseph Martin Mudd

HEIGHT: 5' 11"   **WEIGHT:** 150

BIRTH DATE: April 23, 1960

BIRTHPLACE: Louisville, KY

RESIDENCE: Louisville, KY

COLLEGE: Georgia Southern University

SPECIAL INTERESTS: Thoroughbred racing, outdoors

TURNED PROFESSIONAL: 1982

JOINED TOUR: April 1982

PLAYER PROFILE

CAREER EARNINGS: $2,735,887   **PLAYOFF RECORD:** 2-2

TOUR VICTORIES: **1988** Federal Express St. Jude Classic. **1989** GTE Byron Nelson Golf Classic. **1990**
(TOTAL: 4)   THE PLAYERS Championship, Nabisco Championships.

MONEY & POSITION:			
	1982--$ 34,216--114	1986--$182,812--48	1990--$911,746-- 5
	1983--$ 21,515--145	1987--$203,923--51	1991--$148,453--102
	1984--$ 42,244--114	1988--$422,022--23	1992--$ 88,081--141
	1985--$186,648-- 34	1989--$404,860--26	1993--$ 89,366--150

BEST 1993 FINISH: T6--Nissan Los Angeles Open.

1993 SUMMARY: Tournaments entered--20; in money--9; top ten finishes--1.

1994 PGA TOUR CHARITY TEAM COMPETITION: B.C. Open

NATIONAL TEAMS: World Cup, 1990; Four Tours World Championship of Golf, 1990;Walker Cup, 1981.

1993 SEASON: Money-list ranking lowest of 12-year career, even though earnings showed slight increase over 1992...Continued to play limited schedule (just 20 events for second year in row, 18 in 1991)... Also for second consecutive campaign posted best finish early in year in weather-shortened event in California...T6 in Nissan Los Angeles Open matched 1992 T6 in Buick Invitational of California...Los Angeles placing capped best stretch of year, preceded by top-25s in Bob Hope Chrysler Classic (T19) and Buick Invitational (T25)...Back-to-back 66s in Bob Hope his lowest rounds of season.

CAREER HIGHLIGHTS: Enjoyed finest season of PGA TOUR career in 1990, when won twice and finished fifth on money list with earnings over $900,000...'90 victories came in THE PLAYERS and Nabisco Championships, TOUR's two richest events...Earned 10-year exemption in THE PLAYERS, battling Mark Calcavecchia to wire and making clutch birdie on treacherous 17th at TPC at Sawgrass...In Nabisco Championships birdied last two holes, then birdied first playoff hole to defeat Billy Mayfair and earn $450,000 first-place check...Tailed off in '91, collecting three top-10 finishes, including T7 at Masters and T8 in next start at BellSouth Atlanta Classic...Joined TOUR week after finishing low amateur in '82 Masters...Two weeks later tied for fifth at USF&G Classic, earning over $10,000.

PERSONAL: Raises thoroughbreds in Kentucky...Three-time All-America at Georgia Southern...U.S. Public Links champion 1980-81...Winner 1981 Sunnehanna Amateur, plus eight collegiate events...Low amateur 1982 Masters (T20)...Member 1981 Walker Cup, 1990 World Cup, 1990 Four Tours World Championship of Golf teams.

1993 PGA TOUR STATISTICS

Scoring Average	71.75	(138T)
Driving Distance	273.3	(12T)
Driving Accuracy	65.4	(138T)
Greens in Regulation	63.3	(144)
Putting	1.788	(65T)
All-Around	817	(92T)
Sand Saves	61.4	(12)
Total Driving	150	(38T)
Eagles	3	(116T)
Birdies	197	(154T)

MISCELLANEOUS STATISTICS

Scoring Avg. (before cut)	72.17	(134T)
Scoring Avg. (3rd round)	70.75	(56T)
Scoring Avg. (4th round)	71.56	(100T)
Birdie Conversion	29.8	(26T)
Par Breakers	19.2	(62T)

1993 Low Round: 66: 2 times
Career Low Round: 63: 1986 Bob Hope Chrysler Classic/3
Career Largest Paycheck: $450,000/1990 Nabisco Championships/1

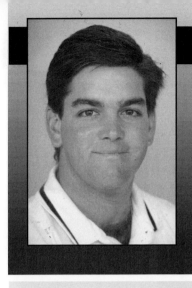

SEAN MURPHY

EXEMPT STATUS: 1st on 1993 NIKE TOUR money list

FULL NAME: Sean Patrick Murphy

HEIGHT: 5' 8"   **WEIGHT:** 150

BIRTH DATE: August 17, 1965

BIRTHPLACE: Des Moines, IA

RESIDENCE: Lovington, NM

FAMILY: Single

COLLEGE: University of New Mexico

SPECIAL INTERESTS: Music, theatre, handicapped children, sports

TURNED PROFESSIONAL: 1988

Q SCHOOL: Fall 1989, 1990

PLAYER PROFILE

NIKE TOUR PLAYER RECORD

CAREER NIKE TOUR EARNINGS: $231,768   **PLAYOFF RECORD:** 1-0

NIKE TOUR VICTORIES: **1992** Louisiana Open. **1993** Central Georgia Open, Greater Greenville
(TOTAL: 5)   Classic, Utah Classic, Sonoma County Open

MONEY & POSITION: 1992--$54,283--22   1993--$166,293--1

BEST 1993 FINISHES: 1--Central Georgia Open, Greater Greenville Classic, Utah Classic, Sonoma County Open

1993 NIKE TOUR SUMMARY: Tournaments entered--26; in money--21; top ten finishes--8

1994 PGA TOUR CHARITY TEAM COMPETITION: Memorial Tournament

1993 NIKE TOUR SEASON: Selected NIKE TOUR Player of the Year...Set NIKE TOUR record for most wins in a season (4)...Coupled with victory at 1992 Louisiana Open, his five career wins are also NIKE TOUR record...Also set mark for most money won in single season ($166,293)...His 11-under 61 at NIKE Central Georgia was low round on NIKE TOUR for '93 and a course record at River North CC...Five consecutive birdies during Greater Greenville Classic equalled Tour best for '93...Won only NIKE TOUR playoff appearance in battle with Curt Byrum, Jim Carter and Tommy Moore at Utah Classic...Four-way playoff tied for most players in playoff in NIKE TOUR history...Won Greater Greenville Classic with eagle on 72nd hole on 51-foot putt from the fringe to defeat Doug Martin by one stroke.

CAREER HIGHLIGHTS: Member PGA TOUR during 1990 and 1991...Finished 211th on money list with $19,705 in 1990 and 203rd on money list with $24,203 in 1991...Best-ever PGA TOUR finish is T24 at 1990 B.C. Open, where he picked up check for $5,968...No PGA TOUR events in '92, missed cut at U.S. Open in only 1993 PGA TOUR outing...Outstanding amateur career, New Mexico High School State Champion in 1982 and American Junior Golf Association Southwest Champion in 1983...1988 Western Athletic Conference (WAC) Player-of-the-Year with eight fop-5 finishes in 11 tournaments...1986 Honorable Mention All-American.

PERSONAL: Donated a portion of his winner's check in 1993 Utah Classic to Special Olympics (tournament charity). "My sister is a special education teacher in Lovington (NM), those kids are very special to me. Some kids are dealt bad cards and I like to do all that I can for them."...Was All-State punter on Lovington High's football team...Father started him in golf when he four years old, entered first tournament at age 8 and finished third.

1993 PGA TOUR STATISTICS	
Scoring Average	N/A
Driving Distance	N/A
Driving Accuracy	N/A
Greens in Regulation	N/A
Putting	N/A
All-Around	N/A
Sand Saves	N/A
Total Driving	N/A
Eagles	N/A
Birdies	N/A

MISCELLANEOUS STATISTICS	
Scoring Avg. (before cut)	N/A
Scoring Avg. (3rd round)	N/A
Scoring Avg. (4th round)	N/A
Birdie Conversion	N/A
Par Breakers	N/A

1993 Low Round: N/A
Career Low Round: 66: 3 times, most recent
Career Largest   1991 Phoenix Open/2
Paycheck: $5,990/1990 Gr Milwaukee Open/T27

LARRY NELSON

EXEMPT STATUS: Winner, 1987 PGA Championship

FULL NAME: Larry Gene Nelson

HEIGHT: 5' 9"   **WEIGHT:** 150

BIRTH DATE: Sept. 10, 1947

BIRTHPLACE: Ft. Payne, AL

RESIDENCE: Marietta, GA

FAMILY: Wife, Gayle; Drew (10/7/76); Josh (9/28/78)

COLLEGE: Kennesaw Junior College (1970)

SPECIAL INTERESTS: Golf course architecture, snow skiing

TURNED PROFESSIONAL: 1971

Q SCHOOL: Fall 1973

PLAYER PROFILE

CAREER EARNINGS:$3,206,418   **PLAYOFF RECORD:** 2-2

TOUR VICTORIES: 1979 Jackie Gleason-Inverrary Classic, Western Open. **1980** Atlanta Classic. **1981** (TOTAL: 10)   Greater Greensboro Open, PGA Championship. **1983** U.S. Open. **1984** Walt Disney World Golf Classic. **1987** PGA Championship, Walt Disney World/Oldsmobile Classic. **1988** Georgia-Pacific Atlanta Classic.

MONEY & POSITION:

1974--$ 24,022--93	1981--$193,342--10	1988--$411,284-- 25
1975--$ 39,810--66	1982--$159,134--21	1989--$186,869-- 79
1976--$ 66,482--41	1983--$138,368--40	1990--$124,260--124
1977--$ 99,876--26	1984--$154,689--42	1991--$160,543-- 96
1978--$ 65,686--45	1985--$143,993--54	1992--$ 94,930--135
1979--$281,022-- 2	1986--$124,338--69	1993--$ 54,870--177
1980--$182,715--11	1987--$501,292--14	

BEST 1993 FINISH: T13--Sprint Western Open.

1993 SUMMARY: Tournaments entered--18; in money--9; top ten finishes--0.

1994 PGA TOUR CHARITY TEAM COMPETITION: Mercedes Championships

NATIONAL TEAM: Ryder Cup (3) 1979, 1981, 1987.

1993 SEASON: Continued to play limited schedule, although did enter three more tournaments than 1992…Money-won total lowest since second year on PGA TOUR (1975), when earned just $39,810…Also experienced first season without top-10 finish since joining TOUR fulltime in 1974 (had no top-10s in three 1973 starts after earning card that fall)…Best placing T13 in Sprint Western Open, where carded 67 (matching best round of year) in Round 3…Only other top-25 came in MCI Heritage Classic (T25)…Had just eight rounds in 60s all season, five of which were 67s…As has become his practice, primarily plays tournaments in Southeastern U.S.

CAREER HIGHLIGHTS: With exception of 1979 Western Open and 1983 U.S. Open, all career victories have been achieved in Southeastern U.S.: four in Florida (including 1987 PGA Championship at PGA National), three Georgia (including 1981 PGA at Atlanta Athletic Club) and one North Carolina…Finest year on TOUR was '87, when won PGA Championship in playoff with Lanny Wadkins at Palm Beach Gardens…Later in year captured second Walt Disney World/ Oldsmobile Classic en route to earnings of over $500,000 for only time in career…Had three top-10 finishes in just 16 tournaments in 1991…Fired final-round 68 at Hazeltine National to finish T3, just three strokes out of Payne Stewart-Scott Simpson U.S. Open playoff…Tied with Robert Gamez for third-round lead at Buick Southern Open, only to record final-round even-par 72 and finish T3 at Callaway Gardens as David Peoples won by three strokes.

PERSONAL: Member 1979-81-87 Ryder Cup teams…Winner 1980 Tokai Classic, 1983 Dunlop International, 1989 Suntory Open, all Japan…Former Player Director, PGA TOUR Policy Board.

1993 PGA TOUR STATISTICS

Scoring Average	71.87	(146T)
Driving Distance	256.2	(124T)
Driving Accuracy	69.8	(80T)
Greens in Regulation	65.6	(87T)
Putting	1.795	(86T)
All-Around	985	(130)
Sand Saves	52.3	(86T)
Total Driving	204	(122T)
Eagles	4	(89T)
Birdies	178	(165)

MISCELLANEOUS STATISTICS

Scoring Avg. (before cut)	71.95	(116)
Scoring Avg. (3rd round)	70.89	(66T)
Scoring Avg. (4th round)	73.44	(179)
Birdie Conversion	27.4	(97T)
Par Breakers	18.4	(85T)

1993 Low Round: 67: 5 times

Career Low Round: 63: 5 times, most recent '89

Career Largest GTE Byron Nelson Classic/1

Paycheck: $150,000/1987 PGA Championship/1

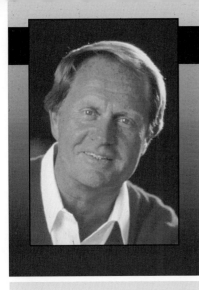

JACK NICKLAUS

EXEMPT STATUS: Winner, 1962 United States Open

FULL NAME: Jack William Nicklaus

HEIGHT: 5' 11"   **WEIGHT:** 190

BIRTH DATE: Jan. 21, 1940

BIRTHPLACE: Columbus, OH

RESIDENCE: North Palm Beach, FL, and Muirfield Village, OH

FAMILY: Wife, Barbara Bash; Jack II(9/23/61); Steven(4/11/63); Nancy Jean(5/5/65); Gary(1/15/69); Michael(7/24/73)

COLLEGE: Ohio State University

SPECIAL INTERESTS: Fishing, hunting, tennis and skiing

TURNED PROFESSIONAL: 1961

JOINED TOUR: 1962

PLAYER PROFILE

CAREER EARNINGS: $5,360,662   **PLAYOFF RECORD:** 13-10

TOUR VICTORIES:
(TOTAL: 70)
1962 U.S. Open, Seattle World's Fair, Portland. **1963** Palm Springs, Masters, Tournament of Champions, PGA Championship, Sahara. **1964** Portland, Tournament of Champions, Phoenix, Whitemarsh. **1965** Portland, Masters, Memphis Thunderbird Classic, Philadelphia. **1966** Masters, Sahara. **1967** U.S. Open, Sahara, Bing Crosby, Western, Westchester. **1968** Western, American Golf Classic. **1969** Sahara, Kaiser, San Diego. **1970** Byron Nelson, Four-Ball (with Arnold Palmer). **1971** PGA Championship, Tournament of Champions, Byron Nelson, National Team (with Arnold Palmer), Disney World. **1972** Bing Crosby, Doral-Eastern, Masters, U.S. Open, Westchester, Match Play, Disney. **1973** Bing Crosby, New Orleans, Tournament of Champions, Atlanta, PGA Championship, Ohio Kings Island, Walt Disney. **1974** Hawaii, Tournament Players Championship. **1975** Doral-Eastern Open, Heritage Classic, Masters, PGA Championship, World Open. **1976** Tournament Players Championship, World Series of Golf. **1977** Gleason Inverrary, Tournament of Champions, Memorial. **1978** Gleason Inverrary, Tournament Players Championship, IVB-Philadelphia Classic. **1980** U.S. Open, PGA Championship. **1982** Colonial National Invitation. **1984** Memorial. **1986** Masters.

MONEY & POSITION:

1962--$ 61,869-- 3	1972--$320,542-- 1	1983--$256,158-- 10
1963--$100,040-- 2	1973--$308,362-- 1	1984--$272,595-- 15
1964--$113,285-- 1	1974--$238,178-- 2	1985--$165,456-- 43
1965--$140,752-- 1	1975--$298,149-- 1	1986--$226,014-- 34
1966--$111,419-- 2	1976--$266,438-- 1	1987--$ 64,685--127
1967--$188,998-- 1	1977--$284,509-- 2	1988--$ 28,845--177
1968--$155,286-- 2	1978--$256,672-- 4	1989--$ 96,595--129
1969--$140,167-- 3	1979--$ 59,434-- 71	1990--$ 68,054--160
1970--$142,149-- 4	1980--$172,386-- 13	1991--$123,797--122
1971--$244,490-- 1	1981--$178,213-- 16	1992--$ 14,868--223
	1982--$232,645-- 12	1993--$ 51,532--182

BEST 1993 FINISH: T10--Doral-Ryder Open.

1993 SUMMARY: Tournaments entered--10; in money--4; top ten finishes--1.

OTHER ACHIEVEMENTS: PGA Player of the Year five times (1967, 1972, 1973, 1975 and 1976). U.S. Amateur champion in 1959 and 1961. NCAA champion in 1961. Winner of British Open in 1966, 1970 and 1978. Six-time winner Australian Open (1964, 1968, 1971, 1975, 1976 and 1978). Winner 1970 World Match Play. Winner of World Series of Golf (old format) four times (1962, 1963, 1967 and 1970). Named Athlete-of-Decade, 1970-79. Has total of 18 international titles. Member World Golf Hall of Fame. Winner, 1982 Card Walker Award for outstanding contributions to junior golf. Winner 1983 Chrysler Team Invitational (with Johnny Miller). 1988 named "Player-of-the-Century".

NATIONAL TEAMS: Walker Cup (2), 1959, 1961; World Cup (6), 1963, 1964, 1966, 1967, 1971, 1973 (medalist three times); Ryder Cup (6), 1969, 1971, 1973, 1975, 1977, 1981; Ryder Cup Captain (2), 1983, 1987.

SENIOR PGA TOUR SUMMARY

SENIOR PGA TOUR VICTORIES:1990 Tradition at Desert Mountain,
(TOTAL: 6)   Mazda Senior Tournament Players Championship. **1991** Tradition at Desert Mountain; PGA Seniors Championship, U.S. Senior Open. **1993** U.S. Senior Open

1993 SENIOR PGA TOUR SUMMARY:
Tournaments entered--6; in money--6; top ten finishes--3.

COMBINED CAREER EARNINGS: $ 6,364,972

1993 PGA TOUR STATISTICS

Scoring Average	71.99
Driving Distance	253.6
Driving Accuracy	70.7
Greens in Regulation	63.6
Putting	1.832
All-Around	N/A
Sand Saves	39.6
Total Driving	N/A
Eagles	1
Birdies	76

MISCELLANEOUS STATISTICS

Scoring Avg. (before cut)	72.79
Scoring Avg. (3rd round)	75.00
Scoring Avg. (4th round)	71.75
Birdie Conversion	24.6
Par Breakers	15.8

1993 Low Round: 67: 2 times
Career Low Round: 62: 2 times, most recent '73 Ohio Kings Island Open
Career Largest Paycheck: $144,000/1986 Masters/1

GREG NORMAN

EXEMPT STATUS: Winner, 1993 British Open

FULL NAME: Gregory John Norman

HEIGHT: 6' 1"   **WEIGHT:** 185

BIRTH DATE: February 10, 1955

BIRTHPLACE: Queensland, Australia

RESIDENCE: Hobe Sound, FL

FAMILY: Wife, Laura; Morgan-Leigh (10/5/82); Gregory (9/19/85)

SPECIAL INTERESTS: Fishing, hunting, scuba diving

TURNED PROFESSIONAL: 1976

JOINED TOUR: 1983

PLAYER PROFILE

CAREER EARNINGS: $6,607,562

PLAYOFF RECORD: 3-7

TOUR VICTORIES: (TOTAL: 11) 1984 Kemper Open, Canadian Open. 1986 Panasonic-Las Vegas Invitational, Kemper Open. 1988 MCI Heritage Classic. 1989 The International, Greater Milwaukee Open, 1990 Doral-Ryder Open, The Memorial Tournament. 1992 Canadian Open.1993 Doral-Ryder Open

MONEY & POSITION:

1983--$ 71,411--74	1987--$ 535,450-- 7	1991--$ 320,196--53
1984--$310,230-- 9	1988--$ 514,854--17	1992--$ 676,443--18
1985--$165,458--42	1989--$ 835,096-- 4	1993--$1,359,653-- 3
1986--$653,296-- 1	1990--$1,165,477-- 1	

BEST 1993 FINISHES: 1--Doral-Ryder Open; 2--Southwestern Bell Colonial; 2--Sprint Western Open; 2--PGA Championship; T2--TOUR Championship; 3--Buick Open; T3--THE PLAYERS Championship; 4--Freeport-McMoRan Classic; T4--Memorial Tournament; T4--The International; T7--NEC World Series of Golf; T10--Nestle Invitational.

1993 SUMMARY: Tournaments entered--15; in money--14; top ten finishes--12.

1994 PGA TOUR CHARITY TEAM COMPETITION: Western Open

NATIONAL TEAMS: Australian Nissan Cup (2) 1985, 1986; Australian Kirin Cup, 1987; Australian Dunhill Cup (7) 1985, 1986, 1987, 1988, 1989, 1990, 1992; Australian Four Tours, 1989.

1993 SEASON: Captured second major championship/second British Open title at Royal St. George's in down-to-wire shootout with Nick Faldo, Nick Price, Bernhard Langer and Corey Pavin... Campaign featured just one missed cut (U.S. Open) and 12 top-10 finishes in 15 starts...Had one victory, four seconds and three thirds...After missing Open cut concluded year with six straight top-10s, including T2 in TOUR Championship...11th PGA TOUR title in Doral-Ryder Open came in record-setting (23-under-par 265) fashion, four shots better than Paul Azinger and Mark McCumber...Doral performance also included course-record-tying 62 (his own record) in Round 3...PGA Championship loss to Azinger gave him distinction of losing playoffs in all four majors...Unable to defend Canadian Open title due to strained ligament in left shoulder.

CAREER HIGHLIGHTS: Winner of 63 tournaments around world, including 1986 British Open at Royal Troon...Ended 27-month winless drought with playoff victory over Bruce Lietzke in 1992 Canadian Open...In '86 won twice on PGA TOUR and seven times overseas: British and European Opens, Suntory World Match Play and four consecutive events in native Australia...Also held lead going into final round of all four majors that year...Suffered back-to-back heartbreaks in 1986-87 Masters, finishing T2 in '86 and losing '87 playoff to Larry Mize's unbelievable 140-foot chip for birdie...First victory was at West Lakes Classic in Australia in October 1976...Had 15-year stretch during which won at least one tournament.

PERSONAL: Well known for charitable involvements, including annual hosting of Franklin Funds "Shark Shootout"...Recipient 1986 and 1990 Arnold Palmer Awards for leading money winner...Winner 1989-90 Vardon Trophies...Owns two Dunhill Cup team victories.

1993 PGA TOUR STATISTICS

Scoring Average	68.90	(1)
Driving Distance	274.4	(9)
Driving Accuracy	73.9	(32T)
Greens in Regulation	70.0	(16)
Putting	1.751	(4)
All-Around	374	(7)
Sand Saves	62.4	(8)
Total Driving	41	(1)
Eagles	1	(164T)
Birdies	224	(139)

MISCELLANEOUS STATISTICS

Scoring Avg. (before cut)	69.54	(1)
Scoring Avg. (3rd round)	68.31	(1)
Scoring Avg. (4th round)	70.54	(24)
Birdie Conversion	32.9	(1)
Par Breakers	23.1	(1)

1993 Low Round: 62: Doral-Ryder Open/3
Career Low Round: 62: 4 times, most recent 1993 Doral-Ryder Open/3
Career Largest Paycheck: $252,000/ 1990 and 1993 Doral/1

ANDY NORTH

EXEMPT STATUS: Winner, 1985 United States Open

FULL NAME: Andrew Stewart North

HEIGHT: 6' 4"   **WEIGHT:** 200

BIRTH DATE: March 9, 1950

BIRTHPLACE: Thorpe, WI

RESIDENCE: Madison, WI; plays out of Beaver Creek, Vail, CO

FAMILY: Wife, Susan; Nichole (11/30/74), Andrea (8/22/78)

COLLEGE: University of Florida (1972)

SPECIAL INTERESTS: All sports

TURNED PROFESSIONAL: 1972

Q SCHOOL: Fall 1972

PLAYER PROFILE

CAREER EARNINGS: $1,360,849

TOUR VICTORIES: **1977** American Express-Westchester Classic. **1978** U.S. Open. **1985** U.S. Open. (TOTAL: 3)

MONEY & POSITION:

1973--$ 48,672--64	1980--$ 55,212-- 69	1987--$ 42,876--163
1974--$ 58,409--64	1981--$111,401-- 30	1988--$ 10,759--212
1975--$ 44,729--53	1982--$ 82,698-- 49	1989--$ 13,620--204
1976--$ 71,267--37	1983--$ 52,416-- 98	1990--$ 99,651--137
1977--$116,794--18	1984--$ 22,131--149	1991--$ 24,653--201
1978--$150,398--14	1985--$212,268-- 24	1992--$ 16,360--218
1979--$ 73,873--54	1986--$ 41,651--146	1993--$ 14,500--230

BEST 1993 FINISH: T16--Buick Classic.

1993 SUMMARY: Tournaments entered--4; in money--1; top ten finishes--0.

NATIONAL TEAMS: Ryder Cup, 1985; World Cup, 1978.

1993 SEASON: Added to already impressive medical history but made fewest starts ever of 21-year PGA TOUR career…Because of off-season knee surgery made first appearance of year in June at Buick Classic, where finished T16…After that made just three more starts, missing cut in each: U.S., Western and Greater Milwaukee Opens…Focused primarily on growing career as on-course reporter for ESPN, role into which he stepped at 1992 Hardee's Golf Classic after Gary Koch suffered broken ankle.

CAREER HIGHLIGHTS: Winner of two U.S. Open Championships, one of few players ever to do so…First came at Cherry Hills in Denver in 1978, second at Oakland Hills in Birmingham, MI in 1985…At Cherry Hills had four-stroke lead with five holes to play…By time reached 18 needed bogey to win, and that's what he got for victory over Dave Stockton and J.C. Snead…At Oakland Hills 279 total was one shot better than international runnerup trio of T.C. Chen of Taiwan, Dave Barr of Canada and Denis Watson of Zimbabwe…Only other victory in injury-plagued career was 1977 Westchester Classic…Winner 1969 Wisconsin State Amateur, 1971 Western Amateur…Three-time All-America University of Florida …Member 1978 World Cup and 1985 Ryder Cup teams.

PERSONAL: Along with latest knee surgery, medical history includes the following: 1983 bone spurs right elbow, 1987-1989 knee surgery, 1989 bone spurs/neck, 1991 four operations to remove skin cancers on nose and left cheek, 1989 also injured shoulder and was through for year…Turned to golf in seventh grade because bone in knee stopped growing and was disintegrating, causing him to give up other sports…Later returned to basketball, earning all-state honors…Tasked with preparing Brown Deer GC, new home of Greater Milwaukee Open.

1993 PGA TOUR STATISTICS

Scoring Average	71.10	(76T)
Driving Distance	262.1	(68T)
Driving Accuracy	68.9	(89)
Greens in Regulation	67.5	(51T)
Putting	1.799	(97T)
All-Around	625	(51)
Sand Saves	54.8	(54T)
Total Driving	157	(48T)
Eagles	4	(89T)
Birdies	305	(53T)

MISCELLANEOUS STATISTICS

Scoring Avg. (before cut)	71.15	(49T)
Scoring Avg. (3rd round)	71.53	(112)
Scoring Avg. (4th round)	71.29	(71T)
Birdie Conversion	29.2	(39T)
Par Breakers	20.0	(33T)

1993 Low Round: **70:** 3 times
Career Low Round: 63: 1975 B.C. Open/1
Career Largest
Paycheck: $103,000/1985 U.S. Open/1

BRETT OGLE

EXEMPT STATUS: 1993 tournament winner

FULL NAME: Brett James Ogle

HEIGHT: 6' 2"　　**WEIGHT:** 165

BIRTH DATE: July 14, 1964

BIRTHPLACE: Paddington, Australia

RESIDENCE: Melbourne, Australia

FAMILY: Wife, Maggie; Christopher (10/1/90)
　　　　　　Rachel Louise (11/5/93)

SPECIAL INTERESTS: Snooker, tennis, all sports

TURNED PROFESSIONAL: 1985

Q SCHOOL: Fall 1992

PLAYER PROFILE

CAREER EARNINGS: $337,374

TOUR VICTORIES: 1993 AT&T Pebble Beach National Pro-Am.
(TOTAL: 1)

MONEY & POSITION:　　1993--$337,374--48

BEST 1993 FINISHES: 1--AT&T Pebble Beach National Pro-Am; T4--United Airlines Hawaiian Open.

1993 SUMMARY: Tournaments entered--18; in money--12; top ten finishes--2.

1994 PGA TOUR CHARITY TEAM COMPETITION: Honda Classic

NATIONAL TEAMS: World Cup, 1992

1993 SEASON: Gregarious Aussie, whose long-stated goal had been to play PGA TOUR, took TOUR by storm...As co-medalist at 1992 Qualifying Tournament, had top-10 finishes in two of his first four starts, including three-stroke victory in AT&T Pebble Beach National Pro-Am...That win, worth $225,000 assured him two-year TOUR exemption...Began year with T4 in United Airlines Hawaiian Open...Three weeks later had first TOUR win...Back-to-back 68s, the first at Pebble Beach and the second at Poppy Hills, gave him one-stroke lead ...Widened margin to two and then three over Billy Ray Brown next two rounds, going 69-71 for win...With wife expecting second child (born in November), became commuter between U.S. and ranch in Australia...Practitioner of unorthodox cross-handed putting style (a la Bernhard Langer), back trouble late in golf year caused change to long putter...Strong contender for Rookie of Year honors won by Vijay Singh.

CAREER HIGHLIGHTS: Finished six-round PGA TOUR Qualifying Tournament tied with Massy Kuramoto, Skip Kendall, Perry Moss and fellow Aussie Neale Smith for medalist honors...Of that group, only one to retain playing privileges for 1994...Qualified for 1991 NEC World Series of Golf by winning 1990 Australian PGA Championship...Finished T25 at Firestone CC, closing 71-71-69 after opening 76...Earned $10,175 for that placing...Other career victories came in 1989 Mirage Queensland Open, 1985 New South Wales Amateur Championship, 1985 Australian Junior Championship

PERSONAL: With his "gift for gab," an instant favorite among TOUR galleries...Finished eighth in 1993 Merrill Lynch Shoot-Out Championship, earning $32,000 at The Experience at Koele on Lanai, Hiawaii.

1993 PGA TOUR STATISTICS

Scoring Average	71.95	(152)
Driving Distance	276.9	(6)
Driving Accuracy	63.3	(159)
Greens in Regulation	66.0	(77T)
Putting	1.824	(156T)
All-Around	891	(114)
Sand Saves	52.0	(90T)
Total Driving	165	(64)
Eagles	8	(25T)
Birdies	184	(162)

MISCELLANEOUS STATISTICS

Scoring Avg. (before cut)	72.40	(146)
Scoring Avg. (3rd round)	71.45	(106T)
Scoring Avg. (4th round)	73.45	(180)
Birdie Conversion	27.3	(99T)
Par Breakers	18.8	(75T)

1993 Low Round: 67: UA Hawaiian Open/1
Career Low Round: 67: 1993 United Airlines
Career Largest Hawaiian Open/1
Paycheck: $225,000/1993 AT&T Pebble
Beach National Pro-Am/1

DAVID OGRIN

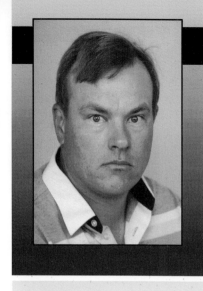

EXEMPT STATUS: 104th on 1993 money

FULL NAME: David Allen Ogrin

HEIGHT: 6'   **WEIGHT:** 220

BIRTH DATE: December 31, 1957

BIRTHPLACE: Waukegan, IL

RESIDENCE: Garden Ridge, TX

FAMILY: Wife, Sharon; Amy (6/20/88) Jessica (9/6/89) Dana (3/6/92) Clark Addison (10/18/93)

COLLEGE: Texas A&M (1980, Economics)

SPECIAL INTERESTS: Christianity, Chicago Cubs, children

TURNED PROFESSIONAL: 1980

Q SCHOOL: Fall 1982, 1992

PLAYER PROFILE

CAREER EARNINGS: $947,355   **PLAYOFF RECORD:** 0-1

BEST EVER FINISH: 2--1985 St. Jude Classic (lost playoff to Hal Sutton); 2--1989 Hawaiian Open

MONEY & POSITION:

1983--$ 36,003--121	1987--$ 80,149--110	1991--$ 8,024--235
1984--$ 45,461--113	1988--$138,807-- 86	1992--$ 33,971--193
1985--$ 76,294-- 95	1989--$234,196-- 59	1993--$155,016--104
1986--$ 75,245--113	1990--$ 64,190--167	

BEST 1993 FINISHES: T4--B.C. Open; T5--Hardee's Golf Classic; T10--Walt Disney World/Oldsmobile Classic.

1993 SUMMARY: Tournaments entered--28; in money--18; top ten finishes--3.

1994 PGA TOUR CHARITY TEAM COMPETITION: Texas Open

1993 SEASON: With three top-10 finishes, had best campaign both in terms of earnings and money list ranking since 1989…Also regained playing privileges for first time since 1990 season…More than two-thirds of season's earnings ($104,257) came during last five tournaments, including all three top-10s…Began run with T5 in Hardee's Golf Classic followed very next week by T4 at B.C. Open…T10 at Walt Disney World/Oldsmobile Classic in next-to-last start of campaign fashioned by back-to-back 65s final two rounds.

CAREER HIGHLIGHTS: Finest season came in 1989, when earned $234,196 and finished second in rain-shortened Hawaiian Open...Career seemingly on upswing at that juncture after earnings of previous year… However, failed to keep card after No. 167 rnoney list placing in 1990… Reached low ebb with just $8,024 in 1991…Rebounded ever so slightly in 1992 en route to solid finish in '93…Lost 1985 St. Jude Classic playoff to Hal Sutton birdie on first extra hole…Did score unofficial victory in 1987 Deposit Guaranty Golf Classic…Final-round 64 provided one-stroke win over Nick Faldo at Hattiesburg CC worth $36,000 (official) …Made it through Qualifying Tournament on fourth attempt…Winner 1975 Illinois State lligh School championship…Winner three collegiate events, including 1979 Harvey Penick Invitational… Winner 1980 Illinois State Open, 1988 Peru Open…Winner 1989 Chrysler Team Championlship (with Ted Schulz).

PERSONAL: The ultimate Chicago Cubs fan so much so that named fourth child/first son "Clark Addison" for two streets adjoining Wrigley Field…Had dream of becoming switch-hitting catcher, but golf won out …Father first put sawed off golf club in his hands when two years old.

1993 PGA TOUR STATISTICS

Scoring Average	71.16	(81T)
Driving Distance	249.6	(177)
Driving Accuracy	75.0	(23T)
Greens in Regulation	68.5	(31T)
Putting	1.807	(117T)
All-Around	869	(109)
Sand Saves	50.0	(116T)
Total Driving	200	(114T)
Eagles	1	(164T)
Birdies	307	(46T)

MISCELLANEOUS STATISTICS

Scoring Avg. (before cut)	71.77	(102)
Scoring Avg. (3rd round)	70.12	(20T)
Scoring Avg. (4th round)	71.63	(105T)
Birdie Conversion	27.0	(110T)
Par Breakers	18.6	(79T)

1993 Low Round: 64: B.C. Open/3
Career Low Round: 64: 2 times, most recent
Career Largest   1993 B.C. Open/3
Paycheck: $81,000/1989 Hawaiian Open/2

MARK O'MEARA

EXEMPT STATUS: 1992 tournament winner

FULL NAME: Mark Francis O'Meara

HEIGHT: 6' **WEIGHT:** 180

BIRTH DATE: January 13, 1957

BIRTHPLACE: Goldsboro, NC

RESIDENCE: Windermere, FL

FAMILY: Wife, Alicia; Michelle (3/14/87), Shaun Robert (8/29/89)

COLLEGE: Long Beach State (1980, Marketing)

SPECIAL INTERESTS: Golf course consulting, hunting, fishing

TURNED PROFESSIONAL: 1980

Q SCHOOL: Fall 1980

PLAYER PROFILE

CAREER EARNINGS: $4,998,267   **PLAYOFF RECORD:** 1-4

TOUR VICTORIES: **1984** Greater Milwaukee Open. **1985** Bing Crosby Pro-Am, Hawaiian Open. **1989** AT&T
(TOTAL: 8) Pebble Beach National Pro-Am. **1990** AT&T Pebble Beach National Pro-Am, H-E-B Texas Open. **1991** Walt Disney World/Oldsmobile Classic. **1992** AT&T Pebble Beach National Pro-Am

MONEY & POSITION:

1981--$ 76,063-- 55	1986--$252,827--30	1990--$707,175--10
1982--$ 31,711--118	1987--$327,250--30	1991--$563,896--20
1983--$ 69,354-- 76	1988--$438,311--22	1992--$759,648--11
1984--$465,873-- 2	1989--$615,804--13	1993--$349,516--43
1985--$340,840-- 10		

BEST 1993 FINISHES: T3--Infiniti Tournament of Champions; 5--THE PLAYERS Championship; T6--Nestle Invitational; T9--United Airlines Hawaiian Open.

1993 SUMMARY: Tournaments entered--26; in money--18; top ten finishes--4.

1994 PGA TOUR CHARITY TEAM COMPETITION: B.C. Open

NATIONAL TEAMS: Ryder Cup (3), 1985, 1989, 1991; U.S. vs. Japan, 1984; Nissan Cup, 1985.

1993 SEASON: After four top-10 finishes in first four months, best placing rest of way was T12 in Kmart Greater Greensboro Open...As direct result missed finishing Top-30 for first time since 1983...Had streak of TOUR Championship appearances broken at seven...Began year with back-to-back top-10s, T3 Tournament of Champions and T9 United Airlines Hawaiian Open...Had consecutive top-10s in Nestle Invitational (T6) and THE PLAYERS Championship, where earned biggest paycheck of year ($100,000) for solo fifth...Saw his consecutive-years TOUR victory string snapped at four.

CAREER HIGHLIGHTS: Of eight TOUR victories, five have come in pro-am events, including four at Pebble Beach...Other pro-am win was 1991 Walt Disney World/Oldsmobile Classic...Also lost playoffs at 1990 and '92 pro-am Bob Hope Chrysler Classics...Shot final-round 64 to defeat David Peoples by a stroke in Disney Classic...Part of five-man playoff in 1992 Hope won by John Cook...In '90 Hope matched Corey Pavin at then-TOUR record 29-under-par for 90 holes...Pavin chipped in for birdie on first extra hole to win... Came from four shots off pace with final-round 63 to win 1990 H-E-B Texas Open.

PERSONAL: Member three Ryder Cup teams (1985, 1989, 1991)...Also member 1984 U.S. vs. Japan and 1985 Nissan Cup squads...Winner 1979 U.S. Amateur, defeating John Cook...Also winner '79 California State and Mexican Amateurs...All-America at Long Beach State...1981 TOUR Rookie of Year...Winner 1985 Kapalua International, Fuji Sankei Classic (Japan), 1986 Australian Masters, 1987 Lawrence Batley International (England), 1992 Tokai Classic (Japan)...Numbers among his neighbors Orlando Magic center Shaquille O'Neal.

1993 PGA TOUR STATISTICS

Scoring Average	71.10	(76T)
Driving Distance	262.1	(68T)
Driving Accuracy	68.9	(89)
Greens in Regulation	67.5	(51T)
Putting	1.799	(97T)
All-Around	625	(51)
Sand Saves	54.8	(54T)
Total Driving	157	(48T)
Eagles	4	(89T)
Birdies	305	(53T)

MISCELLANEOUS STATISTICS

Scoring Avg. (before cut)	71.15	(49T)
Scoring Avg. (3rd round)	71.53	(112)
Scoring Avg. (4th round)	71.29	(71T)
Birdie Conversion	29.2	(39T)
Par Breakers	20.0	(33T)

1993 Low Round: 64: Hope Chrysler Classic/3
Career Low Round: 62: 1981 Sammy Davis Jr. Greater Hartford Open/2
Career Largest Paycheck: $198,000/'92 AT&T Pebble Beach/1

JOE OZAKI

EXEMPT STATUS: 115th on 1993 money list

FULL NAME: Naomichi Ozaki

HEIGHT: 5' 8"   **WEIGHT:** 155

BIRTH DATE: May 18, 1956

BIRTHPLACE: Tekushima, Japan

RESIDENCE: Chiba, Japan

FAMILY: Wife, Yoshie, Takamasa

SPECIAL INTERESTS: Singing, aerobics

TURNED PROFESSIONAL: 1977

JOINED TOUR: Spring 1993

PLAYER PROFILE

CAREER EARNINGS: $139,784

BEST EVER FINISH: T6--1991 NEC World Series of Golf; T6--1992 Federal Express St. Jude Classic; T6--1993 THE PLAYERS Championship

MONEY & POSITION:	1985--$ 880--259	1990--$ 37,330--185	1992--$ 75,946--151
	1989--$1,605--274	1991--$ 38,850--185	1993--$139,784--115

BEST 1993 FINISH: T6--THE PLAYERS Championship.

1993 SUMMARY: Tournaments entered--12; in money--8; top ten finishes--1.

1994 PGA TOUR CHARITY TEAM COMPETITION: Greater Milwaukee Open

1993 SEASON: Achieved special temporary membership with T6 finish in THE PLAYERS Championship, where 278 total was worth $80,938…Carded middle rounds of 68-68 on Stadium Course at TPC of Sawgrass…Achieved exempt status for 1994 by finishing No. 115 on TOUR money list with earnings of $139,784…Next-best finish 21st in NEC World Series of Golf worth $26,550…Other top-25 finish was T25 at U.S. Open, where closed with 69…Low round of TOUR season third-round 66 at Inverness Club during PGA Championsilip.

CAREER HIGHLIGHTS: Winner of 24 events in Japan...Victories in Japan include 1988 Japanese Series, 1989 JPGA Match Play Championship, 1990 Gene Sarazen Jun Classic…Did not win in Japan in 1993, but had three victories in 1992…1992 earnings total of $1,120,862 ranked him 14th on world list …Has earned more than $6 million during professional career…T6 in 1993 PLAYERS Championship matched his best-ever TOUR finish...Also had T6s in 1991 NEC World Series of Golf and 1992 Federal Express St. Jude Classic.

PERSONAL: Youngest of three golfing Ozaki brothers...Masashi (Jumbo) is 47, Tateo (Jet) is 40...1988 "Year of the Ozakis" in Japan, when three combined for 12 victories in 35 events (Jumbo six, Joe four, Jet two)...Brothers also had nine seconds and four thirds...Jumbo and Joe finished 1-2 on the money list, with Jet No. 7...Earnings total for trio that year $2,292,246.

1993 PGA TOUR STATISTICS

Scoring Average	71.38
Driving Distance	261.3
Driving Accuracy	64.2
Greens in Regulation	58.1
Putting	1.825
All-Around	N/A
Sand Saves	54.5
Total Driving	N/A
Eagles	0
Birdies	117

MISCELLANEOUS STATISTICS

Scoring Avg. (before cut)	72.54
Scoring Avg. (3rd round)	72.25
Scoring Avg. (4th round)	73.38
Birdie Conversion	28.0
Par Breakers	16.3

1993 Low Round: **66:** PGA Championship/3
Career Low Round: **65:** 1992 Fed Ex St. Jude Classic/1
Career Largest Paycheck: **$80,938**/1993 Players Championship/T6

ARNOLD PALMER

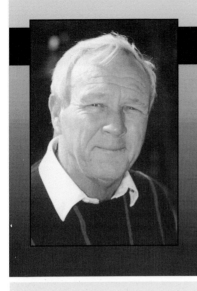

EXEMPT STATUS: Winner, 1960 United States Open

FULL NAME: Arnold Daniel Palmer

HEIGHT: 5' 10"   **WEIGHT:** 185

BIRTH DATE: September 10, 1929

BIRTHPLACE: Latrobe, PA

RESIDENCE: Latrobe, PA and Bay Hill, FL

FAMILY: Wife, Winifred Walzer; Peggy (2/26/56), Amy (8/4/58), four grandchildren

COLLEGE: Wake Forest University

SPECIAL INTERESTS: Flying, business, club-making

TURNED PROFESSIONAL: 1954

JOINED TOUR: 1955

PLAYER PROFILE

CAREER EARNINGS: $1,904,668   **PLAYOFF RECORD:** 14-10

TOUR VICTORIES: **1955** Canadian. **1956** Insurance City, Eastern. **1957** Houston, Azalea, Rubber City, San Diego. **1958** St. Petersburg, Masters, Pepsi Golf. **1959** Thunderbird (Calif.) Invitation, Oklahoma City, (TOTAL: 60) West Palm Beach. **1960** Insurance City, Masters, Palm Springs Classic, Baton Rouge, Pensacola, U.S. Open, Mobile Sertoma, Texas Open. **1961** San Diego, Texas, Baton Rouge, Phoenix, Western. **1962** Masters, Palm Springs Classic, Texas, Phoenix, Tournament of Champions, Colonial National, American Golf Classic. **1963** Thunderbird, Pensacola, Phoenix, Western, Los Angeles, Cleveland, Philadelphia. **1964** Oklahoma City, Masters. **1965** Tournament of Champions. **1966** Los Angeles, Tournament of Champions, Houston Champions International, **1967** Los Angeles, Tucson, American Golf Classic, Thunderbird Classic. **1968** Hope Desert Classic, Kemper. **1969** Heritage, Danny Thomas--Diplomat. **1970** Four-Ball (with Jack Nicklaus). **1971** Hope Desert Classic, Citrus, Westchester, National Team (with Jack Nicklaus). **1973** Bob Hope Desert Classic.

MONEY & POSITION:

Year	Money	Pos	Year	Money	Pos	Year	Money	Pos
1955	$7,958	32	1968	$114,602	7	1981	$4,164	197
1956	$16,145	19	1969	$105,128	9	1982	$6,621	198
1957	$27,803	5	1970	$128,853	5	1983	$16,904	159
1958	$42,608	1	1971	$209,603	3	1984	$2,452	217
1959	$32,462	5	1972	$84,181	25	1985	$3,327	214
1960	$75,263	1	1973	$89,457	27	1986	$	--
1961	$61,091	2	1974	$36,293	72	1987	$1,650	269
1962	$81,448	1	1975	$59,017	36	1988	$	--
1963	$128,230	1	1976	$17,017	115	1989	$2,290	253
1964	$113,203	2	1977	$21,950	101	1990	$	--
1965	$57,770	10	1978	$27,073	94	1991	$7,738	237
1966	$110,467	3	1979	$9,276	159	1992	$	--
1967	$184,065	2	1980	$16,589	133	1993	$1,970	316

BEST 1993 FINISH: T71 Nestle Invitational

1993 SUMMARY: Tournaments entered--5; in money--1; top ten finishes--0.

COMBINED CAREER EARNINGS: $3,222,227

NATIONAL TEAMS: Ryder Cup (6), 1961, 1963, 1965, 1967, 1971, 1973; Ryder Cup Captain (2), 1963, 1975; World Cup (7), 1960, 1962, 1963, 1964, 1965, 1966, 1967; Captain and member of Chrysler Cup team (5), 1986, 1987, 1988, 1989, 1990.

OTHER ACHIEVEMENTS: 1954 U. S. Amateur champion. Winner of 19 foreign titles, including 1961 and 1962 British Open, 1966 Australian Open, 1975 Spanish Open, and 1975 British PGA. 1961, 1963, 1965, 1967, 1971, and 1973 Ryder Cup team. 1960, 1962, 1963, 1964, 1965, 1966, and 1967 World Cup team. Captain, 1986, 1987, 1988 Chrysler Cup Team.

SENIOR PGA TOUR SUMMARY

SENIOR PGA TOUR VICTORIES: **1980** PGA Seniors. **1981** U.S. (Total: 10)   Senior Open. **1982** Marlboro Classic, Denver Post Champions of Golf. **1983** Boca Grove Senior Classic. **1984** PGA Seniors, Senior Tournament Players Championship, Quadel Senior Classic. **1985** Senior Tournament Players Championship. **1988** Crestar Classic.

1993 SENIOR PGA TOUR SUMMARY:
Tournaments entered--18; in money--18; top ten finishes--0.

COMBINED CAREER EARNINGS: $ 3,296,462

1993 PGA TOUR STATISTICS

Scoring Average	N/A
Driving Distance	N/A
Driving Accuracy	N/A
Greens in Regulation	N/A
Putting	N/A
All-Around	N/A
Sand Saves	N/A
Total Driving	N/A
Eagles	N/A
Birdies	N/A

MISCELLANEOUS STATISTICS

Scoring Avg. (before cut)	N/A
Scoring Avg. (3rd round)	N/A
Scoring Avg. (4th round)	N/A
Birdie Conversion	N/A
Par Breakers	N/A

1993 Low Round: **68:** Hope Chrysler Classic/3

Career Low Round: 62: 2 times, most recent 1966 Los Angeles Open/3

Career Largest Paycheck: $50,000/ 1971 Westchester Classic/1

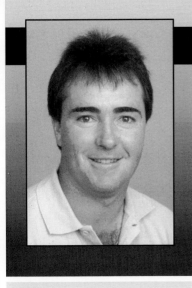

CRAIG PARRY

EXEMPT STATUS: 50th on 1993 money list

FULL NAME: Craig David Parry

HEIGHT: 5'6" **WEIGHT:** 170

BIRTH DATE: December 1, 1966

BIRTHPLACE: Sunshine, Victoria, Australia

RESIDENCE: Kardinya, W. Australia

FAMILY: Wife, Jenny; April (8/22/92)

SPECIAL INTERESTS: Sailing, water sports, cricket, rugby

TURNED PROFESSIONAL: 1985

JOINED TOUR: April 1992

PLAYER PROFILE

CAREER EARNINGS: $564,969

BEST EVER FINISH: T3--1992 Kmart Greater Greensboro Open; T3--1993 U.S. Open

MONEY & POSITION:
1989--$ 1,650--282	1991--$ 63,767--218	1993--$323,068--50
1990--$43,351--181	1992--$241,901--64	

BEST 1993 FINISHES: T3--U.S. Open; 5--Honda Classic; T7--Kemper Open; T8--Northern Telecom Open; T8--Greater Milwaukee Open; 10--The International.

1993 SUMMARY: Tournaments entered--23; in money--16; top ten finishes--6.

1994 PGA TOUR CHARITY TEAM COMPETITION: Federal Express St. Jude Classic

NATIONAL TEAMS: Kirin Cup, 1988; Four Tours World Championship of Golf (3), 1989, 1990, 1991.

1993 SEASON: Matched his best career finish with T3 in U.S. Open...Shared first-round lead after an opening 66, closed 69-68 to finish knotted with Paul Azinger, five shots behind Lee Janzen...Gained first top-10 in second start of season with strong final-round 65 at Northern Telecom Open...Second-best tournament of campaign came in his first Florida start, solo fifth in Honda Classic...Other top-10s came in May (T7 Kemper Open), August (10th The International) and September (T8 Greater Milwaukee Open).

CAREER HIGHLIGHTS: Became Special Temporary Member of PGA TOUR in April 1992...Final money-won total of $241,901 provided exemption for '93 season...Best '92 finish T3 at Kmart Greater Greensboro Open...Was one shot off lead at midpoint of '92 PLAYERS Championship...Tied with Ian Woosnam for 36-hole lead in Masters, then held third-round lead outright at 12-under-par 204 before skying to final-round 78 and T13...Winner of nine events worldwide, including four on PGA European Tour...Pair of European victories came in 1989 playoffs: Wang Four Stars National Pro-Celebrity and German Open...Other two European Tour wins registered in '91: Lancia Martini Italian Open and Bell's Scottish Open...In native Australia won 1992 Australian Masters, 1987-92 New South Wales Opens wins...Also captured Canadian Tournament Players Championship in '87, Bridgestone ASO in Japan in 1989 (his third title that year).

PERSONAL: 1984-85 State Junior and State Amateur Champion, 1985 State Foursomes Champion in Australia...Low amateur 1985 Australian Masters, Tasmanian and SA Opens...1988 co-recipient Epson Shooting Star Award...Member 1988-91 Asahi Glass Four Tours, 1988 Kirin Cup, 1991 Dunhill Cup teams.

1993 PGA TOUR STATISTICS

Scoring Average	70.82	(52T)
Driving Distance	260.2	(88)
Driving Accuracy	69.4	(86T)
Greens in Regulation	63.8	(134)
Putting	1.770	(26T)
All-Around	851	(104)
Sand Saves	48.8	(135)
Total Driving	174	(71)
Eagles	2	(144T)
Birdies	254	(115T)

MISCELLANEOUS STATISTICS

Scoring Avg. (before cut)	71.23	(59T)
Scoring Avg. (3rd round)	72.00	(139T)
Scoring Avg. (4th round)	71.53	(97T)
Birdie Conversion	30.3	(18)
Par Breakers	19.5	(50T)

1993 Low Round:	65: Northern Telecom Open/4
Career Low Round:	65: 1993 Northern Telecom
Career Largest	Open/4
Paycheck:	$78,557/1993 U.S. Open/T3

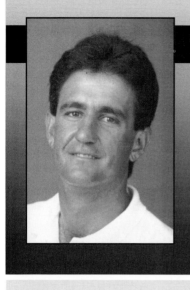

STEVE PATE

EXEMPT STATUS: 1992 tournament winner.

FULL NAME: Stephen Robert Pate

HEIGHT: 6'   **WEIGHT:** 175

BIRTH DATE: May 26, 1961

BIRTHPLACE: Ventura, CA

RESIDENCE: Orlando, FL

FAMILY: Wife, Sheri; Nicole (3/12/88); Sarah (10/8/90)

COLLEGE: UCLA (1984, Psychology)

SPECIAL INTERESTS: Fishing

TURNED PROFESSIONAL: 1983

Q SCHOOL: Fall 1984

PLAYER PROFILE

CAREER EARNINGS: $3,280,182   **PLAYOFF RECORD:** 0-2

TOUR VICTORIES: **1987** Southwest Classic. **1988** MONY Tournament of Champions, Shearson Lehman
(TOTAL: 5)   Hutton-Andy Williams Open.**1991** Honda Classic. **1992** Buick Invitational of California.

MONEY & POSITION:

1985--$ 89,358--86	1988--$582,473--12	1991--$727,997-- 6
1986--$176,100--51	1989--$306,554--35	1992--$472,626--30
1987--$335,728--26	1990--$334,505--39	1993--$254,841--64

BEST 1993 FINISHES: T6--Honda Classic; T6--The International; T7--Infiniti Tournament of Champions; T8--MCI Heritage Classic.

1993 SUMMARY: Tournaments entered--28; in money--19; top ten finishes--4.

1994 PGA TOUR CHARITY TEAM COMPETITION: MCI Heritage Classic

NATIONAL TEAMS: Ryder Cup, 1991, Kirin Cup, 1988.

1993 SEASON: Had four top-10 finishes and earnings of $254,841… Opened year with T7 in Tournament of Champions…Top finishes for season T6s in Honda Classic and at The International, an event he traditionally does well in…Best round of year, 65, came in opening round of Greater Milwaukee Open…One shot off lead at that juncture, ultimately finished T19…Other top-10 a T8 in MCI Heritage Classic.

CAREER HIGHLIGHTS: Fifth career victory came in 1992 Buick Invitational of California…Tournament shortened to 54 holes by Saturday fog…Two-time winner of San Diego event (also 1988)…Enjoyed finest season of career in 1991, posting earnings of $727,997…Scored three-stroke Honda Classic win over Paul Azinger and Dan Halldorson…High final-day winds at Eagle Trace allowed him to parlay closing 75 into relatively easy victory…Later that season lost BellSouth Atlanta Classic playoff to good friend Corey Pavin…First TOUR victory came in 1987 Southwest Classic, then won twice on West Coast to start 1988: MONY Tournament of Champions and Shearson Lehman Hutton-Andy Williams Open…Was second at '90 International after making double-eagle two, using driver/2-iron on 535-yard hole to earn eight points.

PERSONAL: Has earned nickname "Volcano" for his sometimes volatile on-course temper…Consistency has been key to his game…Member 1991 Ryder Cup team, but deep hip bruise suffered when three limos collided en route to opening banquet limited play to one team match…Member 1988 Kirin Cup squad…Made Santa Barbara, CA, high school team as freshman, won California Interscholastic Federation title as senior…Teammate of Pavin and Jay Delsing at UCLA…Won 1983 PAC-10 Championship, along with four collegiate events…1983 All-American.

1993 PGA TOUR STATISTICS

Scoring Average	71.07	(73)
Driving Distance	258.3	(100)
Driving Accuracy	66.1	(129T)
Greens in Regulation	66.1	(72T)
Putting	1.797	(92T)
All-Around	784	(85)
Sand Saves	61.9	(9)
Total Driving	229	(150T)
Eagles	4	(89T)
Birdies	288	(70T)

MISCELLANEOUS STATISTICS

Scoring Avg. (before cut)	71.23	(59T)
Scoring Avg. (3rd round)	71.07	(81)
Scoring Avg. (4th round)	71.44	(91)
Birdie Conversion	27.2	(106T)
Par Breakers	18.2	(98T)

1993 Low Round:	65: 2 times
Career Low Round:	62: 1989 Bob Hope Chrysler Classic/3
Career Largest Paycheck:	$180,000/1991 Honda Classic/1; 1992 Buick Invitational of California/1

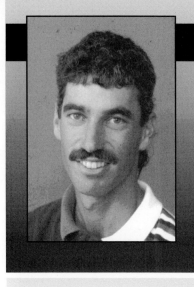

COREY PAVIN

EXEMPT STATUS: 1992 tournament winner

FULL NAME: Corey Pavin

HEIGHT: 5' 9"   **WEIGHT:** 150

BIRTH DATE: November 16, 1959

BIRTHPLACE: Oxnard, CA

RESIDENCE: Orlando, FL

FAMILY: Wife, Shannon; Ryan (5/29/86) Austin
James (3/5/93)

COLLEGE: UCLA

TURNED PROFESSIONAL: 1982

Q SCHOOL: Fall 1983

PLAYER PROFILE

CAREER EARNINGS: $4,929,138   **PLAYOFF RECORD:** 5-2

TOUR VICTORIES: **1984** Houston Coca-Cola Open **1985** Colonial National Invitation **1986** Hawaiian Open,
(TOTAL: 10)   Greater Milwaukee Open. **1987** Bob Hope Chrysler Classic, Hawaiian Open. **1988**
Texas Open presented by Nabisco. **1991** Bob Hope Chrysler Classic, BellSouth Atlanta
Classic **1992** Honda Classic.

MONEY & POSITION:

1984--$260,536--18	1988--$216,768--50	1991--$979,430-- 1
1985--$367,506-- 6	1989--$177,084--82	1992--$980,934-- 5
1986--$304,558--19	1990--$468,830--26	1993--$675,087--18
1987--$498,406--15		

BEST 1993 FINISHES: 2--Memorial Tournament; T2--GTE Byron Nelson Classic; 4--Canon Greater
Hartford Open; T4--Buick Open; T7--TOUR Championship; T9--Southwestern Bell Colonial.

1993 SUMMARY: Tournaments entered--24; in money--21; top ten finishes--6.

1994 PGA TOUR CHARITY TEAM COMPETITION: Southwestern Bell Colonial

NATIONAL TEAMS: Ryder Cup (2),1991, 1993; Walker Cup, 1981; Nissan Cup, 1985.

1993 SEASON: Had third-highest money won total of career...Continued U.S. successes for year by winning World Match Play Championship over Nick Faldo in the finals...Had pair of runnerup finishes in '93, to Scott Simpson at the GTE Byron Nelson Classic in May and to Paul Azinger's bunker hole-out at the Memorial in June...In between was a T9 in the Southwestern Bell Colonial...Later ran off three straight "fours": solo Canon Greater Hartford Open, T4s British Open and Buick Open...Ended year with T7 in THE TOUR Championship, event in which shared runnerup honors with Lee Janzen in 1992.

CAREER HIGHLIGHTS: Holed dramatic 136-yard 8-iron for eagle on final hole of 1992 Honda Classic to force playoff with Fred Couples, then won with birdie on second extra hole...Lost playoff to Bruce Lietzke in '92 Colonial...Won Arnold Palmer Award as PGA TOUR's Money Leader in 1991.. Named 1991 PGA of America Player of Year...'91 season featured pair of playoff victories: over Mark O'Meara in Bob Hope Chrysler Classic and Steve Pate in BellSouth Atlanta Classic...Also lost Canon Greater Hartford Open playoff to Billy Ray Brown...Hope finish was 29-under-par 331, then-TOUR record for 90-holes...Scored victories first five years on TOUR, beginning with Houston Open in 1984...Captured 1988 Texas Open with 21-under-par 259, becoming just fifth player in TOUR history to better 260.

PERSONAL: Played in first Ryder Cup in 1991...Also member of 1981 Walker Cup and 1985 Nissan Cup teams...At 17, won Junior World title and became youngest winner of Los Angeles City Men's crown...1981 winner North-South Amateur, Southwest Amateur, Maccabiah Games...Won 11 college tournaments at UCLA, including 1982 PAC-10 title...Winner 1983 South African PGA, German Open, Calberson Classic (France).

1993 PGA TOUR STATISTICS

Scoring Average	71.07	(73)
Driving Distance	258.3	(100)
Driving Accuracy	66.1	(129T)
Greens in Regulation	66.1	(72T)
Putting	1.797	(92T)
All-Around	784	(85)
Sand Saves	61.9	(9)
Total Driving	229	(150T)
Eagles	4	(89T)
Birdies	288	(70T)

MISCELLANEOUS STATISTICS

Scoring Avg. (before cut)	71.23	(59T)
Scoring Avg. (3rd round)	71.07	(81)
Scoring Avg. (4th round)	71.44	(91)
Birdie Conversion	27.2	(106T)
Par Breakers	18.2	(98T)

1993 Low Round:	**65:** 3 times
Career Low Round:	**62:** 1990 H-E-B Texas Open/3
Career Largest Paycheck:	**$198,000/**'91 Bob Hope /1
	'92 Honda Classic/1

CALVIN PEETE

EXEMPT STATUS: Winner, 1985 Tournament Players Championship

FULL NAME: Calvin Peete

HEIGHT: 5' 10"   **WEIGHT:** 165

BIRTH DATE: July 18, 1943

BIRTHPLACE: Detroit, MI

RESIDENCE: Ponte Vedra Beach, FL

FAMILY: Wife, Pepper; Calvin (8/9/68); Dennis (12/4/69); Rickie (12/13/69); Kalvanetta Kristina (5/3/75); Elaine Alsha(11/30/93)

TURNED PROFESSIONAL: 1971

Q SCHOOL: Spring 1975

PLAYER PROFILE

CAREER EARNINGS: $2,302,363   **PLAYOFF RECORD:** 0-1

TOUR VICTORIES: **1979** Greater Milwaukee Open. **1982** Greater Milwaukee Open, Anheuser-Busch Clas-
(TOTAL: 12)   sic, B.C. Open, Pensacola Open. **1983** Georgia-Pacific Atlanta Classic, Anheuser-Busch Classic. **1984** Texas Open. **1985** Phoenix Open, Tournament Players Championship. **1986** MONY Tournament of Champions, USF&G Classic.

MONEY & POSITION:

1976--$ 22,966-- 94	1982--$318,470-- 4	1988--$138,310-- 87
1977--$ 20,525--105	1983--$313,845-- 4	1989--$ 38,584--175
1978--$ 20,459--108	1984--$232,124-- 25	1990--$ 54,379--173
1979--$122,481-- 27	1985--$384,489-- 3	1991--$ 4,978--256
1980--$105,716-- 42	1986--$374,953-- 12	1992--$ --
1981--$ 93,243-- 43	1987--$ 56,841--140	1993--$ --

1993 SUMMARY: Tournaments entered--5; in money--0; top ten finishes--0.

NATIONAL TEAMS: Ryder Cup (2) 1983, 1985; U.S. vs. Japan (2) 1982, 1983; Nissan Cup, 1985

1993 SEASON: Turned 50 on July 18th and joined Senior PGA TOUR, making debut in First of America Classic where he finished T42...Made four other starts in Senior TOUR events, finishing with earnings of $6,976...Did enter 5 PGA TOUR events but failed to make cut in any as physical ailments that have plagued him past few years continued.

CAREER HIGHLIGHTS: Won 11 tournaments during five-year span in mid-1980s...Most prestigious victory came in 1985 Tournament Players Championship, when final-round 66 provided three-stroke edge over D.A. Weibring and 10-year PGA TOUR exemption...First TOUR win came in 1979 Greater Milwaukee Open...Repeated GMO success in 1982, when won four times...Last triumphs were in 1986: MONY-Tournament of Champions and USF&G Classic...Won driving accuracy title 10 straight years (1981-1990)...Led TOUR three times in hitting greens in regulation...Won Vardon Trophy for low stroke average in 1984...Named recipient of Ben Hogan Award, given by Golf Writers Association of America, in 1983...Hogan Award goes to person who overcame physical handicap or illness to play golf...As youngster suffered broken left elbow, and to this day cannot extend arm...Member 1983 and '85 Ryder Cup teams...Member 1982-83 USA vs. Japan, 1985 Nissan Cup squads.

PERSONAL: Physical problems have included left shoulder rotator cuff tear and back trouble...Took up golf at 23 in 1966 at urging of friends in Rochester, NY... Spent most of early life on Florida farm with 18 brothers and sisters--through two marriages by father...Dropped out of school at early age, got into business of selling goods to migrant farm workers...Travels took him from Florida to upstate New York, which is where start in golf occurred.

1993 PGA TOUR STATISTICS

Scoring Average	N/A
Driving Distance	N/A
Driving Accuracy	N/A
Greens in Regulation	N/A
Putting	N/A
All-Around	N/A
Sand Saves	N/A
Total Driving	N/A
Eagles	N/A
Birdies	N/A

MISCELLANEOUS STATISTICS

Scoring Avg. (before cut)	N/A
Scoring Avg. (3rd round)	N/A
Scoring Avg. (4th round)	N/A
Birdie Conversion	N/A
Par Breakers	N/A

1993 Low Round: 71: PLAYERS Chp./2

Career Low Round: 63: 3 times, most recent
Career Largest   "83 GA-Pacific Atlanta/3

Paycheck: $162,000 '85 PLAYERS Championship/1

DAVID PEOPLES

EXEMPT STATUS: 1992 tournament winner

FULL NAME: David Roy Peoples

HEIGHT: 5' 9"   **WEIGHT:** 170

BIRTH DATE: January 9, 1960

BIRTHPLACE: Augusta, ME

RESIDENCE: Orlando, FL

FAMILY: Wife, Melissa; Andrew David (10/20/89)
                Benjamin Thomas (6/4/92)

COLLEGE: University of Florida

SPECIAL INTERESTS: Fishing, Bible study, hunting

TURNED PROFESSIONAL: 1981

Q-SCHOOL: Fall 1982, 1983, 1985, 1986, 1987, 1989.

PLAYER PROFILE

CAREER EARNINGS: $1,582,185

TOUR VICTORIES: 1991 Buick Southern Open. **1992** Anheuser Busch Golf Classic (TOTAL: 2)

MONEY & POSITION:			
	1983--$28,446--137	1988--$ 65,537--139	1991--$414,346-- 35
	1984--$18,124--160	1989--$ 82,624--140	1992--$539,531-- 25
	1986--$37,668--154	1990--$259,367-- 57	1993--$105,309--142
	1987--$31,234--180		

BEST 1993 FINISHES: T9--Buick Invitational of California; T10--New England Classic.

1993 SUMMARY: Tournaments entered--29; in money--15; top ten finishes--2.

1994 PGA TOUR CHARITY TEAM COMPETITION: Kemper Open

1993 SEASON: Disappointing season had somewhat successful aftermath when finished T5 in Lincoln Mercury Kapalua International, earning $34,000...That showing, albeit in an unofficial event, provided positive conclusion to an otherwise "down" year...Began season with T15 in Tournament of Champions, then had only two top-10 finishes rest of way... After T9 in Buick Invitational of California in February, season turned flat...Only bright spot from that point forward T10 in New England Classic in July...$25,000 paycheck for Pleasant Valley showing his official money high point...Tied course record with third-round 62.

CAREER HIGHLIGHTS: Earned second career victory in 1992 Anheuser-Busch Golf Classic...Had one-stroke win over Jim Gallagher, Jr., Bill Britton and Ed Dougherty...1992, far-and-away best financial season of career, included first appearance in TOUR Championship...Year featured five top-10 finishes, including four in nine-tournament stretch, beginning with fifth at BellSouth Classic in May and concluding with T5 at NEC World Series in August...1990 brought first taste of victory with (unofficial) title in Isuzu Kapalua International...First official win came in 1991 Buick Southern Open...Recorded first TOUR 62 in Round 2 of 1990 Buick Southern Open at Green Island Country Club...Winner 1979 Florida State Amateur.

PERSONAL: Classic example of how persistence pays...Entered Qualifying Tournament each year from 1981-89, earning card six times...Annual appearances in what he jokingly called his "favorite tournament of the year" ended in 1990...Noted that Q-Tournament is "survival" school: Your life's on the line. It's a whole year of your life in six rounds and six days".

1993 PGA TOUR STATISTICS

Scoring Average	71.81	(143T)
Driving Distance	265.1	(50)
Driving Accuracy	70.0	(77T)
Greens in Regulation	70.2	(14)
Putting	1.852	(181T)
All-Around	843	(101T)
Sand Saves	50.0	(116T)
Total Driving	127	(23T)
Eagles	3	(116T)
Birdies	249	(123T)

MISCELLANEOUS STATISTICS

Scoring Avg. (before cut)	72.04	(124)
Scoring Avg. (3rd round)	71.08	(82T)
Scoring Avg. (4th round)	72.87	(170)
Birdie Conversion	23.6	(177)
Par Breakers	16.7	(151T)

1993 Low Round: **62:** New England Classic/2
Career Low Round: 62: 2 times, most recent
Career Largest   1993 New England Classic/3
Paycheck: $198,000'92 Anheuser-Busch /1

KENNY PERRY

EXEMPT STATUS: 88th on 1993 money list

FULL NAME: James Kenneth Perry

HEIGHT: 6' 1"   **WEIGHT:** 190

BIRTH DATE: August 10, 1960

BIRTHPLACE: Elizabethtown, KY

RESIDENCE: Franklin, KY; plays out of Franklin CC

FAMILY: Wife, Sandy; Lesslye (5/20/84), Justin (11/23/85), Lindsey (4/27/88)

COLLEGE: Western Kentucky

SPECIAL INTERESTS: Restoring old cars, all sports

TURNED PROFESSIONAL: 1982

Q SCHOOL: Fall 1986

PLAYER PROFILE

CAREER EARNINGS: $1,484,744   **PLAYOFF RECORD:** 1-0

TOUR VICTORIES: 1991 Memorial Tournament.
(TOTAL:1)

MONEY & POSITION:

1987--$107,239--93	1990--$279,881--50	1992--$190,455--81
1988--$139,421--85	1991--$368,784--44	1993--$196,863--88
1989--$202,099--70		

BEST 1993 FINISHES: T5--Canon Greater Hartford Open; T8--Hardee's Golf Classic; T10--Canadian Open.

1993 SUMMARY: Tournaments entered--29; in money--18; top ten finishes--3.

1994 PGA TOUR CHARITY TEAM COMPETITION: Honda Classic

1993 SEASON: Rebounded somewhat from 1992 campaign that saw his money total drop for first time in career…Earned better than $6,000 more than '92 earnings, even though money list placing fell by seven positions…Money-won total fourth best of seven-year career…Opened year by missing four of first five cuts, then had to play catch-up to save his card…Back-to-back top-10s in September (T10 Canadian Open, T8 Hardee's Golf Classic) helped put him over top…Only other top-10 came in June, a T5 at Canon Greater Hartford Open…First tournament of year in which he posted three rounds in 60s.. Later matched that output in his next-to-last event of year, Buick Southern Open, where finished T16.

CAREER HIGHLIGHTS: Claimed first TOUR victory at The Memorial in 1991…Muirfield Village course-record nine-under-par 63 in Round 2 pro-pelled to lead…Hale Irwin caught him on final day, forcing playoff…Birdie on first extra hole provided win and $216,000 first-place check…Memorial triumph led to best year with earnings of $386,784…'91 season included two other top-10 finishes: T8 Anheuser-Busch Golf Classic, T10 Canon Greater Hartford Open…Best finishes prior to Memorial were T2s 1989 MCI Heritage Classic and 1990 AT&T Pebble Beach National Pro-Am.

PERSONAL: Encouraged by his "biggest fan," Kenny Perry, Sr., to start playing golf at age seven…Father used to sit for hours teeing golf balls up for him…First competition came at 11… Won 1978 Kentucky State High School Championship…Played collegiately at Western Kentucky…Finished second in Charley Pride Classic on TPS.

1993 PGA TOUR STATISTICS

Scoring Average	70.82	(52T)
Driving Distance	269.1	(26T)
Driving Accuracy	69.7	(82)
Greens in Regulation	67.9	(41T)
Putting	1.806	(112T)
All-Around	672	(56)
Sand Saves	41.8	(183T)
Total Driving	108	(14)
Eagles	3	(116T)
Birdies	307	(46T)

MISCELLANEOUS STATISTICS

Scoring Avg. (before cut)	71.57	(86)
Scoring Avg. (3rd round)	70.12	(20T)
Scoring Avg. (4th round)	71.39	(85)
Birdie Conversion	27.8	(84T)
Par Breakers	19.0	(67T)

1993 Low Round:	**66:** Three times
Career Low Round:	**63:** 1991 Memorial/2
Career Largest Paycheck:	**$216,000**/1991 Memorial/1

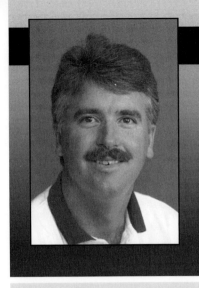

DAN POHL

EXEMPT STATUS: Winner, 1986 NEC World Series of Golf

FULL NAME: Danny Joe Pohl

HEIGHT: 5' 11" **WEIGHT:** 175

BIRTH DATE: April 1, 1955

BIRTHPLACE: Mt. Pleasant, MI

RESIDENCE: Mt. Pleasant, MI

FAMILY: Wife, Mitzi; Michelle (2/2/78), Joshua Daniel (9/10/84), Taylor Whitney (9/10/86)

COLLEGE: University of Arizona

SPECIAL INTERESTS: Fishing, hunting

TURNED PROFESSIONAL: 1977

Q SCHOOL: Spring 1978,1979

PLAYER PROFILE

CAREER EARNINGS: $2,721,118   **PLAYOFF RECORD:** 1-2

TOUR VICTORIES: 1986 Colonial National Invitational, NEC World Series of Golf
(TOTAL: 2)

MONEY & POSITION:		
1978--$ 1,047--224	1984--$182,653-- 32	1989--$195,789-- 74
1979--$ 38,393--100	1985--$198,829-- 27	1990--$ --
1980--$105,008-- 44	1986--$463,630-- 5	1991--$163,438-- 95
1981--$ 94,303-- 42	1987--$465,269-- 17	1992--$131,486--110
1982--$ 97,213-- 39	1988--$396,400-- 27	1993--$ 97,830--146
1983--$ 89,830-- 62		

BEST 1993 FINISHES: T10--Nestle Invitational; T10--Federal Express St. Jude Classic.

1993 SUMMARY: Tournaments entered--20; in money--9; top ten finishes--2.

1994 PGA TOUR CHARITY TEAM COMPETITION: Bob Hope Chrysler Classic

NATIONAL TEAMS: Ryder Cup, 1987

1993 SEASON: After strong early start, chronic back trouble reared its ugly head once again…Either forced to withdraw or missed cut in 10 of final 14 starts…Had to withdraw from Kmart Greater Greensboro Open after player on son's baseball team fouled "soft toss" into his mouth, loosening his front teeth and requiring 24 stitches…Had T10 finish at Nestle Invitational…Only other top-10 finish, also a T10 in Federal Express St. Jude Classic, featured final-round 65, by two strokes his low round of season…Money list placing lowest of career, other than partial year in 1978.

CAREER HIGHLIGHTS: After enduring back pain for years, finally underwent surgery October 2, 1989…Spent entire 1990 season in rehabilitation, returning to TOUR for 1991 campaign… Considering circumstances, produced excellent year in 1991, finishing 95th on money list…Made first four cuts, later finished T8 at Anheuser-Busch Golf Classic and T7 at Canon Greater Hartford Open…At Anheuser-Busch had two-stroke lead after three rounds (64-67-65) before lengthy rain delay made it impossible to stretch out back…Finished with 77…At Hartford was around lead all four rounds, including tie for lead on back nine Sunday…Won twice in 1986 when captured Colonial National Invitation and NEC World Series of Golf, earning 10-year TOUR exemption.

PERSONAL: Nickname "Pohl Cat"…Member 1987 Ryder Cup team…Winner 1987 Vardon Trophy…Winner 1987 All-Around category…Winner 1988 EPSON Stats Match…TOUR driving distance leader 1980-81…Michigan State Amateur champion 1975, '77…One of leading proponents of and possibly most frequent visitor to Centinela Fitness Trailer, working to get loose before every event, then has followup regimen at conclusion of play each day.

1993 PGA TOUR STATISTICS

Scoring Average	71.48	(116)
Driving Distance	270.5	(20)
Driving Accuracy	67.4	(106T)
Greens in Regulation	71.5	(5)
Putting	1.840	(172)
All-Around	882	(111)
Sand Saves	41.9	(182)
Total Driving	126	(22)
Eagles	4	(89T)
Birdies	169	(170T)

MISCELLANEOUS STATISTICS

Scoring Avg. (before cut)	71.76	(101)
Scoring Avg. (3rd round)	70.67	(51T)
Scoring Avg. (4th round)	72.00	(133T)
Birdie Conversion	25.0	(159T)
Par Breakers	18.3	(94T)

1993 Low Round: 65: Phoenix Open/1
Career Low Round: 62: 1989 Honda Classic/2
Career Largest Paycheck: $126,000/'86 NEC World Series of Golf/1

DON POOLEY

EXEMPT STATUS: 122nd on 1993 money list

FULL NAME: Sheldon George Pooley, Jr.

HEIGHT: 6' 3"   **WEIGHT:** 185

BIRTH DATE: August 27, 1951

BIRTHPLACE: Phoenix, AZ

RESIDENCE: Tucson, AZ; plays out of LaPaloma CC, Tucson, AZ

FAMILY: Wife, Margaret; Lynn (1/19/80); Kerri (5/19/82)

COLLEGE: University of Arizona (1973, Business Administration)

SPECIAL INTERESTS: Tennis, basketball

TURNED PROFESSIONAL: 1973

Q SCHOOL: Fall 1975, 1976

PLAYER PROFILE

CAREER EARNINGS: $ 2,507,342

TOUR VICTORIES: 1980 B.C. Open. **1987** Memorial Tournament. (TOTAL: 2)

MONEY & POSITION:

1976--$ 2,139--208	1982--$ 87,962--48	1988--$239,534-- 46
1977--$ 24,507-- 94	1983--$145,979--36	1989--$214,662-- 66
1978--$ 31,945-- 84	1984--$120,699--54	1990--$192,570-- 83
1979--$ 6,932--170	1985--$162,094--46	1991--$ 67,549--156
1980--$157,973-- 18	1986--$268,274--22	1992--$135,683--107
1981--$ 75,730-- 57	1987--$450,005--18	1993--$123,105--122

BEST 1993 FINISHES: T3--MCI Heritage Classic; T7--Canon Greater Hartford Open.

1993 SUMMARY: Tournaments entered--15; in money--8; top ten finishes--2.

1994 PGA TOUR CHARITY TEAM COMPETITION: New England Classic

1993 SEASON: A bad back caused him to miss four months (January-February and July-August) of season…Still managed to put together enough playing time to finish 122nd on money list and retain playing privileges…Had two top-10 finishes on year, T3 in MCI Heritage Classic in April after opening 67, and T7 at Canon Greater Hartford Open in June…Third-round 66 in Hartford left him one shot behind Corey Pavin's 54-hole lead at five-under-par 205…Lower back problems caused him to miss cut in first start of year, Northern Telecom Open, and made it impossible to compete following week in Phoenix…Forced to withdraw from last event of year, Buick Southern Open.

CAREER HIGHLIGHTS: Hampered past three seasons by lower back problems and other ailments…Suffered neck disc injury taking swing while trying to play way back from back problem which hampered him throughout 1991…Received special medical extension for 12 tournaments in 1992…First victory came in 1980 B.C. Open, where closed with 68 for one-stroke win over Peter Jacobsen…Came from four strokes behind final day of 1987 Memorial Tournament to overtake Scott Hoch and win by three…Scored Million Dollar Hole-in-One at 1987 Bay Hill Classic…192-yard 4-iron hit 17th hole flagstick two feet above cup and dropped straight down…Arnold Palmer Children's Hospital got $500,000, with his share being paid in $2,083.33 monthly installments for 20 years.

PERSONAL: Made swing change in 1992 to take pressure off lower back… Won 1985 Vardon Trophy with stroke average of 70.36...Led TOUR in 1988 with 1.729 putting average…Winner 1989 Ebel Match Play, 1992 Amoco Centel Championship…Has regular Centinlela Fitness Trailer regimen designed to strengthen lower back.

1993 PGA TOUR STATISTICS

Scoring Average	71.27
Driving Distance	250.3
Driving Accuracy	76.0
Greens in Regulation	65.7
Putting	1.852
All-Around	N/A
Sand Saves	53.9
Total Driving	N/A
Eagles	0
Birdies	132

MISCELLANEOUS STATISTICS

Scoring Avg. (before cut)	72.28
Scoring Avg. (3rd round)	71.00
Scoring Avg. (4th round)	72.50
Birdie Conversion	25.4
Par Breakers	16.7

1993 Low Round: **65:** H-E-B Texas Open/3
Career Low Round: 61: 1986 Phoenix Open/2
Career Largest
Paycheck: $140,000/1987 Memorial Tournament/1

NICK PRICE

EXEMPT STATUS: Winner, 1993 PLAYERS Championship

FULL NAME: Nicholas Raymond Leige Price

HEIGHT: 6'   **WEIGHT:** 190

BIRTH DATE: January 28, 1957

BIRTHPLACE: Durban, South Africa

RESIDENCE: Orlando, FL

FAMILY: Wife, Sue; Gregory (8/9/91), Robyn Frances (8/5/93)

SPECIAL INTERESTS: Water skiing, tennis, fishing, flying

TURNED PROFESSIONAL: 1977

JOINED TOUR: 1983

PLAYER PROFILE

CAREER EARNINGS: $5,226,491   **PLAYOFF RECORD:** 1-1

TOUR VICTORIES: **1983** World Series of Golf. **1991** GTE Byron Nelson Classic, Canadian Open.
(TOTAL: 9)   **1992** PGA Championship, H-E-B Texas Open. **1993** The PLAYERS Championship, Canon Greater Hartford Open, Sprint Western Open, Federal Express St. Jude Classic.

MONEY & POSITION:

1983--$ 49,435--103	1987--$334,169--28	1991--$ 714,389--7
1984--$109,480-- 66	1988--$266,300--42	1992--$1,135,773--4
1985--$ 96,069-- 80	1989--$296,170--42	1993--$1,478,557--1
1986--$225,373-- 35	1990--$520,777--22	

BEST 1993 FINISHES: 1--THE PLAYERS Championship; 1--Canon Greater Hartford Open; 1--Sprint Western Open; 1--Federal Express St. Jude Classic; T2--BellSouth Classic; T2--NEC World Series of Golf; T10--Nestle Invitational; T10--Canadian Open.

1993 SUMMARY: Tournaments entered--17; in money--16; top ten finishes--8.

1994 PGA TOUR CHARITY TEAM COMPETITION: BellSouth Classic

NATIONAL TEAMS: Zimbabwe Dunhill Cup, 1993; World Cup, 1993

1993 SEASON: Proved he had ability to win consistently in 1993 by capturing THE PLAYERS Championship, then rattling off victories in three consecutive starts: Canon Greater Hartford Open, Western Open, Federal Express St. Jude Classic...Named **PGA TOUR Player of Year** (voted by his peers), PGA Player of the Year, and Vardon Trophy winner (69.11 adjusted scoring average)...Unable to defend H-E-B Texas Open title because of commitment to play for Zimbabwe in Dunhill Cup, first time in 17 years he had been able to represent his home country...Money total of $1,478,557 a TOUR record.

CAREER HIGHLIGHTS: Won first major championship title at 1992 PGA Championship at Bellerive CC... First PGA TOUR victory came in 1983 NEC World Series of Golf, then waited until 1991 season for next win(s)...Captured GTE Byron Nelson Classic and Canadian Open in 1991...Qualified for '83 World Series as leader of South African Order of Merit...Four-stroke victory over Jack Nicklaus provided 10-year TOUR exemption...Two-time runnerup in British Open, in 1982 and 1988.

PERSONAL: Born in South Africa, moved to Rhodesia (now Zimbabwe) at early age...Served two years in Rhodesian Air Force...Since parents were British citizens, carries British passport...At 17 won Junior World at Torrey Pines in LaJolla, CA...In 1975 played South African and European Tours as amateur...Owns 16 tournament victories outside U.S., including 1979 Asseng Invitational (South Africa), 1980 Swiss Open, 1981 South African Masters and Italian Open, 1982 Vaal Reefs Open (South Africa), 1985 ICL International (South Africa) and Lancome Trophy (Paris), 1989 West End South Australian Open, 1992 Air New Zealand Shell Open and PGA Grand Slam...Caddy Jeff (Squeeky) Medlin also has achieved "celebrity" status.

1993 PGA TOUR STATISTICS

Scoring Average	69.11	(2)
Driving Distance	273.9	(11)
Driving Accuracy	73.9	(32T)
Greens in Regulation	71.3	(6)
Putting	1.766	(18T)
All-Around	296	(4)
Sand Saves	63.6	(3T)
Total Driving	43	(2)
Eagles	3	(116T)
Birdies	264	(106)

MISCELLANEOUS STATISTICS

Scoring Avg. (before cut)	69.61	(2)
Scoring Avg. (3rd round)	69.38	(3)
Scoring Avg. (4th round)	70.41	(19T)
Birdie Conversion	29.8	(26T)
Par Breakers	21.5	(5T)

1993 Low Round:	**64:** 3 times
Career Low Round:	**62:** 2 times, most recent '92 H-E-B Texas Open/2
Career Largest Paycheck:	**$450,000**/1993 PLAYERS Championship/1

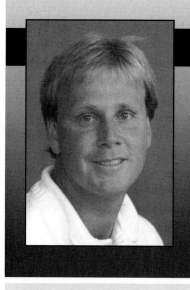

DILLARD PRUITT

EXEMPT STATUS: 98th on 1993 money list

HEIGHT: 5' 11"   **WEIGHT:** 180

BIRTH DATE: September 24, 1961

BIRTHPLACE: Greenville, SC

RESIDENCE: Greenville, SC

FAMILY: Wife, Fran

COLLEGE: Clemson

SPECIAL INTERESTS: Music, Harley-Davidson motorcycles

TURNED PROFESSIONAL: 1985

Q SCHOOL: Fall 1988,1989,1990

PLAYER PROFILE

CAREER EARNINGS: $739,759

TOUR VICTORIES: 1991 Chattanooga Classic
(TOTAL: 1)

MONEY & POSITION: 1988--$33,889--164   1991--$271,861--63   1993--$ 168,053--98
1990--$76,352--150   1992--$189,604--82

BEST 1993 FINISHES: T7--BellSouth Classic; T8--Anheuser-Busch Golf Classic.

1993 SUMMARY: Tournaments entered--26; in money--20; top ten finishes--2.

1994 PGA TOUR CHARITY TEAM COMPETITION: Honda Classic

1993 SEASON: High points of season came in May and July… Finished T7 BellSouth Classic and T20 GTE Byron Nelson Classic consecutive weeks in May, then T13 Western Open/T8 Anheuser-Busch Golf Classic back-to-back in July…Third-round course-record-tying 62 at Kingsmill GC gave him 54-hole lead in A-B Classic where he finished eighth…In addition to Kingsmill 62, also fashioned 64 at venerable Oak Hills CC during Round 2 of H-E-B Texas Open…Model of consistency during year, making 20 of 26 cuts.

CAREER HIGHLIGHTS: Fired 20-under-par 260 for two-stroke win over Lance Ten Broeck in 1991 Chattanooga Classic…$126,000 winner's share keyed '91 money-won total of $271,861, best of career… Other 1991 top-10 finish NEC World Series of Golf…Was third-round leader on 30th birthday, but finished with 77 and T6 at 2-over 282…Prior to Chattanooga best previous finish had been T9 in the 1990 International…Long-stated dream was to play in Masters, opportunity which Chattanooga victory provided… Finished T13 at Augusta National in 1992, allowing return engagement in '93 (missed cut).

PERSONAL: Played European Tour in 1986-87, posting sixth-place finishes in 1987 German Open and Benson & Hedges event in England…Winner Sunnehanna Amateur…Three-time All-ACC, one-time All-American…Winner two collegiate tournaments…Used to skip classes at Clemson to attend Masters, finally had chance to play in 1992-93…Various family connections to golf: Jay Haas is brother-in-law, Scott Verplank is married to his sister-in-law; Jay and brother Jerry Haas' uncle is Bob Goalby…Jay Haas has had strong influence on development of his game and career…Enjoys riding Harley-Davidson motorcycles on roads around Greenville, SC, home.

1993 PGA TOUR STATISTICS

Scoring Average	70.91	(61)
Driving Distance	254.8	(141)
Driving Accuracy	81.7	(2)
Greens in Regulation	71.1	(8T)
Putting	1.818	(144T)
All-Around	730	(73)
Sand Saves	44.7	(173)
Total Driving	143	(35)
Eagles	5	(67T)
Birdies	267	(99T)

MISCELLANEOUS STATISTICS

Scoring Avg. (before cut)	71.14	(48)
Scoring Avg. (3rd round)	70.47	(38T)
Scoring Avg. (4th round)	71.84	(123)
Birdie Conversion	24.3	(171)
Par Breakers	17.6	(126T)

1993 Low Round: 62: Anheuser-Busch/3
Career Low Round: 62: 2 times, most recent
Career Largest 1993 Anheuser-Busch/3
Paycheck: $126,000/1991 Chattanooga Classic/1

TOM PURTZER

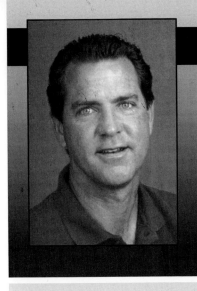

EXEMPT STATUS: Winner, 1991 NEC World Series of Golf

FULL NAME: Thomas Warren Purtzer

HEIGHT: 6'   **WEIGHT:** 180

BIRTH DATE: Dec. 5, 1951

BIRTHPLACE: Des Moines, IA

RESIDENCE: Scottsdale, AZ

FAMILY: Laura (7/3/80), Ashley (12/5/83), Eric (11/5/85)

COLLEGE: Arizona State (1973, Business)

SPECIAL INTERESTS: All sports, music, auto racing

TURNED PROFESSIONAL: 1973

Q SCHOOL: Spring 1975

PLAYER PROFILE

CAREER EARNINGS: $2,942,809   **PLAYOFF RECORD:** 2-0

TOUR VICTORIES: **1977** Glen Campbell-Los Angeles Open. **1984** Phoenix Open. **1988** Gatlin Brothers-
(TOTAL: 5) Southwest Classic. **1991** Southwestern Bell Colonial; NEC World Series of Golf

MONEY & POSITION:	1975--$ 2,093--194	1982--$100,118-- 36	1988--$197,740-- 57
	1976--$ 26,682-- 82	1983--$103,261-- 55	1989--$154,868-- 88
	1977--$ 79,337-- 37	1984--$164,244-- 39	1990--$285,176-- 49
	1978--$ 58,618-- 55	1985--$ 49,979--119	1991--$750,568-- 4
	1979--$113,270-- 30	1986--$218,281-- 37	1992--$166,722-- 93
	1980--$118,185-- 34	1987--$123,287-- 85	1993--$107,570--136
	1981--$122,812-- 27		

BEST 1993 FINISH: T8--Walt Disney World/Oldsmobile Classic.

1993 SUMMARY: Tournaments entered--21; in money--10; top ten finishes--1.

1994 PGA TOUR CHARITY TEAM COMPETITION: Phoenix Open

NATIONAL TEAMS: U.S. vs. Japan, 1979 (medalist).

1993 SEASON: Had second-lowest money list finish of career, topped only by partial-season 194th in first campaign of 19-year career, 1975…Did close year in positive fashion…Had only top-10 in final regular-season start, finishing T8 in Walt Disney World/Oldsmobile Classic after opening 64 gave him share of lead…Stood one shot off pace after 36 holes before closing 71-69…Disney 64 matched another registered in his fourth round of season, Round 2 of Phoenix Open, for his low 18s of year…Week after season ended had another T8, this one in Lincoln Mercury Kapalua International worth unofficial $21,600…Won Fred Meyer Challenge with Steve Elkington in August.

CAREER HIGHLIGHTS: Had finest campaign in 1991, winning twice and finishing fourth on money list…Victories came in Southwestern Bell Colonial and NEC World Series of Golf…World Series victory came in playoff with Jim Gallagher, Jr., and Davis Love III…Win at age 39 gave him 10-year TOUR exemption and prompted comment: "Now I can play right on to the Senior TOUR (age 50) without any worries"…First victory came in 1977 Glen Campbell-Los Angeles Open…Next win came on home turf, 1984 Phoenix Open…Also captured 1984 Southwest Classic in playoff with Mark Brooks.

PERSONAL: Often described as having "sweetest" swing on TOUR…Member (also medalist) 1979 USA vs. Japan team…Member 1991 Four Tours World Championship of Golf squad…1972 Arizona State Amateur and Southwest Open champion…Winner 1986 JCPenney Mixed Team Classic (with Juli Inkster)…Played high school football before started to concentrate on golf…Brother Paul played TOUR for a while…Close friend future baseball Hall of Famer Robin Yount.

1993 PGA TOUR STATISTICS

Scoring Average	71.59	(122)
Driving Distance	268.4	(32)
Driving Accuracy	66.4	(125T)
Greens in Regulation	65.8	(83T)
Putting	1.796	(90T)
All-Around	770	(80)
Sand Saves	52.8	(78T)
Total Driving	157	(48T)
Eagles	8	(25T)
Birdies	175	(167)

MISCELLANEOUS STATISTICS

Scoring Avg. (before cut)	72.15	(131T)
Scoring Avg. (3rd round)	72.00	(139T)
Scoring Avg. (4th round)	71.00	(45T)
Birdie Conversion	26.4	(128T)
Par Breakers	18.2	(98T)

1993 Low Round: **64:** 2 times
Career Low Round: 62: 1988 Northern Telecom open/2
Career Largest Paycheck: $216,000 '91 Southwestern Bell /1 '91 NEC World Series of Golf/1

MIKE REID

EXEMPT STATUS: Winner, 1988 NEC World Series of Golf

FULL NAME: Michael Daniel Reid

HEIGHT: 5' 11"   **WEIGHT:** 160

BIRTH DATE: July 1, 1954

BIRTHPLACE: Bainbridge, MD

RESIDENCE: Provo, UT

FAMILY: Wife, Randolyn; Brendalyn (2/3/81), Lauren Michelle (8/14/83), Michael Daniel (10/2/86), Clarissa Ann (5/27/90), John William (9/29/93)

COLLEGE: Brigham Young University

SPECIAL INTERESTS: Snow skiing, family activities, fishing

TURNED PROFESSIONAL: 1976

Q SCHOOL: Fall 1976

PLAYER PROFILE

CAREER EARNINGS: $ 2,874,570   **PLAYOFF RECORD:** 1-2

TOUR VICTORIES: 1987 Seiko Tucson Open. **1988** NEC World Series of Golf. (TOTAL: 2)

MONEY & POSITION:

1977--$ 26,314--90	1983--$ 99,135--58	1989--$401,665-- 28
1978--$ 37,420--79	1984--$134,672--49	1990--$249,148-- 60
1979--$ 64,046--66	1985--$169,871--40	1991--$152,678-- 98
1980--$206,097-- 9	1986--$135,143--66	1992--$121,376--117
1981--$ 93,037--44	1987--$365,334--24	1993--$ 5,125--270
1982--$ 80,167--51	1988--$533,343--15	

BEST 1993 FINISH: T67--THE PLAYERS Championship

1993 SUMMARY: Tournaments entered--5; in money--1; top ten finishes--0.

1994 PGA TOUR CHARITY TEAM COMPETITION: Kemper Open

NATIONAL TEAMS: World Cup, 1980; Kirin Cup 1988.

1993 SEASON: Missed most of campaign as result of table tennis injury (yes, table tennis!) suffered in Japan fall of 1992…After resting what was first diagnosed as chip fracture to right wrist, made return to action mid-March…After making just five appearances/one cut through early May, further examination determined injury was separated tendon…Underwent surgery to reattach tendon and was expected to be fully recovered for 1994…Only cut made was in THE PLAYERS Championship, where recorded only sub-70 round of abbreviated season (opening 68) and ultimately finished T67…Oh yes, was leading 17-6 when injury occurred.

CAREER HIGHLIGHTS: Two career victories came in back-to-back years, with first setting up second…After ten winless years on TOUR finally broke through in 11th season, winning 1987 Seiko Tucson Open…Tucson triumph provided entry into 1988 NEC World Series of Golf, which won in playoff with Tom Watson…Par on first extra hole was good for title and 10-year TOUR exemption…Another freak injury, this one to his back, curtailed play from late March to early June '91.

PERSONAL: One of TOUR's straightest drivers…Member 1980 World Cup, 1988 Kirin Cup teams…Winner 1983, '85 Utah Opens, 1990 Casio World Open (Japan)…Teamed with Bob Goalby to win 1983 Shootout at Jeremy Ranch in Park City, UT (Senior PGA TOUR event)…Low amateur 1976 U.S. Open…1976 Western Athletic Conference champion…Winner 1976 Pacific Coast Amateur…Collegiate All-America 1974-75…Brother is TPC at Sawgrass General Manager Bill Reid.

1993 PGA TOUR STATISTICS

Scoring Average	N/A
Driving Distance	N/A
Driving Accuracy	N/A
Greens in Regulation	N/A
Putting	N/A
All-Around	N/A
Sand Saves	N/A
Total Driving	N/A
Eagles	N/A
Birdies	N/A

MISCELLANEOUS STATISTICS

Scoring Avg. (before cut)	N/A
Scoring Avg. (3rd round)	N/A
Scoring Avg. (4th round)	N/A
Birdie Conversion	N/A
Par Breakers	N/A

1993 Low Round: **68:** PLAYERS Championship/1

Career Low Round: **64:** 7 times, most recent 1991 Anheuser-Busch/4

Career Largest Paycheck: **$162,000:** '88 NEC World Series of Golf/1

LARRY RINKER

EXEMPT STATUS: 118th on 1993 money list

FULL NAME: Lawrence Ronnie Rinker

HEIGHT: 5' 9" **WEIGHT:** 145

BIRTH DATE: July 20, 1957

BIRTHPLACE: Stuart, FL

RESIDENCE: Winter Park, FL

FAMILY: Wife, Jan; Devon Lyle (11/15/88), Trevor William (2/12/91), Morgan Elizabeth(6/4/92)

COLLEGE: University of Florida (1979, Finance)

SPECIAL INTERESTS: Guitar, jazz, tennis, running, cooking

TURNED PROFESSIONAL: 1979

Q SCHOOL: Spring 1981

PLAYER PROFILE

CAREER EARNINGS: $1,303,100

BEST-EVER FINISH: 2--1984 USF&G Classic; T2--1985 Bing Crosby Pro-Am; 1--JCPenny Mixed Team Classic (unofficial)

MONEY & POSITION:

1981--$ 2,729--211	1986--$ 80,635--106	1990--$132,442--117
1982--$ 26,993--132	1987--$ 72,173--123	1991--$115,956--127
1983--$ 31,394--128	1988--$125,471-- 95	1992--$163,954-- 94
1984--$116,494-- 60	1989--$109,305--117	1993--$130,613--118
1985--$195,390-- 30		

BEST 1993 FINISHES: T8--GTE Byron Nelson Classic; T8--Hardee's Golf Classic.

1993 SUMMARY: Tournaments entered--28; in money--11; top ten finshes--2.

1994 PGA TOUR CHARITY TEAM COMPETITION: Kmart Greater Greensboro Open

1993 SEASON: Despite missing 17 cuts in 28 starts still managed to keep his playing privileges...Two top-10 finishes keys to his cause, with a T8 in the Hardee's Golf Classic putting him over the top in September...Rounds of 69-67-65-69 at Oakwood CC produced $26,000 payday and requisite dollar amount to retain TOUR card...Third-round 65 his best 18 of year...Five weeks earlier earned identical $26,000 for T13 at The International...In May also posted four sub-70 rounds in GTE Byron Nelson Classic...68-69-67-69 performance good for another T8 and $34,800 paycheck, his tops for '93.

CAREER HIGHLIGHTS: Won 1985 JCPenney/Mixed Team Classic with sister Laurie...Has now earned over $100,000 six straight years...Has pair of career second-place finishes: solo 1984 USF&G Classic, T2 1985 Bing Crosby National Pro-Am...Later in '85 finished third in Tournament Players Championship for his biggest payday to date, $61,200...Led TOUR in eagles that year with 14...Best '91 finish T5 in Buick Classic, helped by third-round 65 and hole-in-one in that round...Low rounds of '91 came at Las Vegas Invitational: 9-under-par 63 in second round, 8-under 64 in fifth and final round...Missed just two cuts in first 14 starts in 1992.

PERSONAL: Comes from golfing family...Sister Laurie member of LPGA Tour...Brother Lee played PGA TOUR in 1984...Kellii, wife of brother Laine, played ladies tour...Successful mini-tour player before joining PGA TOUR...Won 10 tournaments, including six in 1980, when was leading money winner on Space Coast mini-tour...For that accomplishment voted "Player of Year" by Florida Golf Week Magazine...Won 1978 Southeastern Conference championship...An accomplished guitar player.

1993 PGA TOUR STATISTICS

Scoring Average	71.33	(104)
Driving Distance	251.3	(168T)
Driving Accuracy	70.0	(77T)
Greens in Regulation	63.7	(135T)
Putting	1.795	(86T)
All-Around	1062	(140)
Sand Saves	49.2	(132)
Total Driving	245	(159T)
Eagles	5	(67T)
Birdies	235	(134)

MISCELLANEOUS STATISTICS

Scoring Avg. (before cut)	72.11	(127)
Scoring Avg. (3rd round)	70.78	(58)
Scoring Avg. (4th round)	70.90	(39T)
Birdie Conversion	27.7	(89T)
Par Breakers	18.0	(111T)

1993 Low Round: 65: two times
Career Low Round: 62: 1982 Tallahasee Open /1
Career Largest Paycheck: $61,200/1985 Tournament Players Championship/3

LOREN ROBERTS

EXEMPT STATUS: 53rd on 1993 money list

FULL NAME: Loren Lloyd Roberts

HEIGHT: 6'2"   **WEIGHT:** 190

BIRTH DATE: June 24, 1955

BIRTHPLACE: San Luis Obispo, CA

RESIDENCE: Memphis, TN

FAMILY: Wife, Kimberly; Alexandria (10/14/86), Addison(10/15/91)

COLLEGE: Cal Poly San Luis Obispo

SPECIAL INTERESTS: Golf

TURNED PROFESSIONAL: 1975

Q SCHOOL: Fall 1980, 1982, 1983, 1986, 1987

PLAYER PROFILE

CAREER EARNINGS: $2,115,727

BEST-EVER FINISH: T2--1992 Hardee's Golf Classic

MONEY & POSITION:

1981--$ 8,935--172	1986--$53,655--133	1990--$478,522--24
1983--$ 7,724--189	1987--$57,489--138	1991--$281,174--58
1984--$67,515-- 87	1988--$136,890--89	1992--$338,673--43
1985--$92,761-- 83	1989--$275,882--46	1993--$316,506--53

BEST 1993 FINISHES: T3--Walt Disney/World Oldsmobile Classic; T4--Southwestern Bell Colonial; T6--Anheuser-Busch Golf Classic; T7--Shell Houston Open.

1993 SUMMARY: Tournaments entered--28; in money--19; top ten finishes--4.

1994 PGA TOUR CHARITY TEAM COMPETITION: Buick Invitational of California

1993 SEASON: With T3 and $52,800 payday at Walt Disney World/ Oldsmobile Classic, supplanted Bobby Wadkins as PGA TOUR money leader without a tournament win…Total at conclusion of 1993: $2,115,727 to $2,073,328 for Wadkins…'93 produced third-best earnings campaign of 12-year career, behind just 1990 ($478,522) and 1992 ($338,673)…Had three other top-10 finishes, including T4 in Southwestern Bell Colonial…Colonial placing, fashioned with three 66s, earned largest check of '93 ($57,200)…Other top-10s came in Shell Houston Open (T7) and Anheuser-Busch Golf Classic (T6), which featured a closing 66.

CAREER HIGHLIGHTS: Had best finish and collected largest check--$88,000--for T2 with Tom Lehman in 1992 Hardee's Golf Classic (behind wire-to-wire winner David Frost)…Was solo third two weeks later at Buick Southern Open, three strokes off Gary Hallberg's lead when final round cancelled due to wet conditions…Also finished three shots behind Frost at Hardee's…Prior to '92, best finishes had been thirds: solo in 1985 Isuzu-Andy Williams San Diego Open and T3 1990 Centel Western Open…At San Diego opened with 65, followed with three more rounds in 60s, and finished one stroke out of Woody Blackburn-Ron Streck playoff… First achieved exempt status in 1984-85, then lost card each of next two seasons…Made changes primarily involving putting for 1988 and has retained playing privileges ever since.

PERSONAL: Regarded by peers as one of hardest workers on TOUR…Said of first six years of limited success: "It was just a matter of making a few changes and having the experience to count on when things were tough"…Winner 1979 Foot-Joy National Assistant Pro Championship…Has tasted victory while TOUR member, winning 1992 Ben Hogan Pebble Beach Invitational.

1993 PGA TOUR STATISTICS

Scoring Average	70.61	(39)
Driving Distance	249.9	(173T)
Driving Accuracy	77.2	(9)
Greens in Regulation	68.9	(26)
Putting	1.789	(69T)
All-Around	570	(36)
Sand Saves	57.0	(31T)
Total Driving	182	(88)
Eagles	4	(89T)
Birdies	307	(46T)

MISCELLANEOUS STATISTICS

Scoring Avg. (before cut)	70.64	(25)
Scoring Avg. (3rd round)	71.16	(89)
Scoring Avg. (4th round)	71.10	(53)
Birdie Conversion	26.0	(139T)
Par Breakers	18.2	(98T)

1993 Low Round: 65: Walt Disney/2
Career Low Round: 63: 1986 Provident Classic/4
Career Largest
Paycheck: $88,000/1992 Hardee's Classic/T2

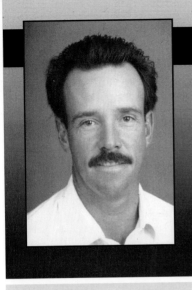

DAVE RUMMELLS

EXEMPT STATUS: 67th on 1993 money list

FULL NAME: David Lawrence Rummells

HEIGHT: 6' **WEIGHT:** 150

BIRTH DATE: January 26, 1958

BIRTHPLACE: Cedar Rapids, IA

RESIDENCE: West Branch, IA

FAMILY: Wife,Ira; Melissa (12/23/89), Eric (7/1/90)

COLLEGE: University of Iowa

SPECIAL INTERESTS: Fishing, bowling, basketball

TURNED PROFESSIONAL: 1981

Q SCHOOL: Fall 1985, 1990, 1992

PLAYER PROFILE

CAREER EARNINGS: $1,601,058

BEST-EVER FINISH: 2--1993 Buick Invitational of California

MONEY & POSITION:
1986--$ 83,227--103	1989--$419,979-- 24	1992--$ 95,203--134
1987--$154,720-- 67	1990--$111,539--131	1992--$247,963-- 67
1988--$274,800-- 38	1991--$213,627-- 79	

BEST 1993 FINISHES: 2--Buick Invitational of California; T3--Anhesuer-Busch Golf Classic.

1993 SUMMARY: Tournaments entered--28; in money--11; top ten finishes--2.

1994 PGA TOUR CHARITY TEAM COMPETITION: Las Vegas Invitational

1993 SEASON: Regained playing privileges and finished No. 67 on money list, largely through play early in season...Made cut in seven of first eight events, including solo second in Buick Invitational of California...Second-round 64 at Torrey Pines brought him to within three strokes of 36 hole lead...With third-round 71 held 54-hole lead by one stroke, ultimately finishing four shots behind Phil Mickelson...$108,000 payday largest of career...After T16 at THE PLAYERS Championship had amassed more than $180,000 in first three months...Next best finish was a T3 at Anheuser-Busch Golf Classic...Fired opening 67 at Kingsmill GC, then closed 66-68 to pick up $57,200 paycheck.

CAREER HIGHLIGHTS: Buick Invitational runnerup finish was the best of his career...T3 in 1993 Anheuser-Busch Classic matched best previous finish, in 1988 Bank of Boston Classic, 1989 Hawaiian Open and Canon Greater Hartford Open (solo in latter), and 1991 Chattanooga Classic...Chattanooga third came on strength of final-round 61 at Valleybrook CC, second consecutive year he recorded closing 61 on that course...Hawaii and Hartford thirds keyed finest season on TOUR, with earnings of $419,979...To that point had increased money won each successive year on TOUR (three times)... Fell back in 1990, when had to return to Qualifying Tournament following No. 131 finish...Rebounded in 1991, only to lose playing privileges again after making $95,203 in 1992...Finished fifth in 1989 PGA Championship, sixth year before.

PERSONAL: Father introduced him to golf at age five...He and childhood friends taught each other how to play...Attended University of Iowa on golf scholarship...Won three mini-tour events.

1993 PGA TOUR STATISTICS

Scoring Average	71.49	(117)
Driving Distance	266.4	(41)
Driving Accuracy	67.1	(115T)
Greens in Regulation	67.1	(58T)
Putting	1.784	(59)
All-Around	695	(64)
Sand Saves	47.8	(144T)
Total Driving	156	(46T)
Eagles	11	(6T)
Birdies	262	(109)

MISCELLANEOUS STATISTICS

Scoring Avg. (before cut)	71.26	(63)
Scoring Avg. (3rd round)	72.09	(151T)
Scoring Avg. (4th round)	72.09	(141T)
Birdie Conversion	27.5	(95T)
Par Breakers	19.2	(62T)

1993 Low Round: 63: Hope Chrysler Classic/1

Career Low Round: 61: 4 times most recent 1991 Chattanooga Classic/4

Career Largest Paycheck: $108,000/1993 Buick Inv. of Calif./2

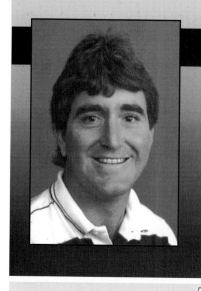

GENE SAUERS

EXEMPT STATUS: 128th on 1993 money list

FULL NAME: Gene Craig Sauers

HEIGHT: 5' 8"　　　　**WEIGHT:** 150

BIRTH DATE: August 22, 1962

BIRTHPLACE: Savannah,GA

RESIDENCE: Savannah, GA

FAMILY: Wife, Tammy; Gene, Jr. (1/23/89); Rhett (7/16/90); Dylan Thomas (8/30/93)

COLLEGE: Georgia Southern

SPECIAL INTERESTS: Snow skiing, hunting, sport fishing

TURNED PROFESSIONAL: 1984

Q SCHOOL: Fall 1983

PLAYER PROFILE

CAREER EARNINGS: $2,440,344　　　**PLAYOFF RECORD:** 1-2

TOUR VICTORIES: 1986 Bank of Boston Classic. **1989** Hawaiian Open. (TOTAL: 2)

MONEY & POSITION:

1984--$ 36,537--128	1988--$280,719--35	1991--$400,535-- 37
1985--$ 48,526--121	1989--$303,669--38	1992--$434,566-- 32
1986--$199,044-- 42	1990--$374,485--31	1993--$117,608--128
1987--$244,655-- 38		

BEST 1993 FINISH: T12--Kmart Greater Greensboro Open.

1993 SUMMARY: Tournaments entered--28; in money--19; top ten finishes--0.

1994 PGA TOUR CHARITY TEAM COMPETITION: Anheuser-Busch Golf Classic

1993 SEASON: For first time, in 10th year on TOUR, failed to increase money-won total over previous seasons…Retained playing privileges by slimmest of margins….Finished 128th on money list--but but kept his card since neither Bernhard Langer (No. 23) nor Nick Faldo (No. 91) was TOUR member, and $26,550 won by Joe Ozaki (officially No. 115) in NEC World Series of Golf did not count toward computation of Top 125…$6,627 earned in final event of season, Las Vegas Invitational, proved to be enough to save his card…Top finish of year, T12, came in Kmart Greater Greensboro Open.

CAREER HIGHLIGHTS: Best year of career, 1992, could have been even better…Birdied all four holes of Bob Hope Chrysler Classic playoff, yet lost to John Cook's chip-in eagle on final hole…Finished in four-way tie for second behind Nick Price in PGA Championship…Posted 10-under-par 278 at Nestle Invitational, yet wound up solo second because of Fred Couples' incredible 269…Finished with career-high $434,566, his eighth successive money-won increase over previous year…Recorded playoff win over Blaine McCallister in 1986 Bank of Boston Classic…Won second event at rain-shortened 1989 Hawaiian Open…In '90 captured unofficial Deposit Guaranty Golf Classic…Had share of lead entering final round of 1987 MCI Heritage Classic, played near hometown of Savannah, GA, but closed with 73 for T3…Lost three-hole playoff to Mark Brooks in 1991 Kmart Greater Greensboro Open.

PERSONAL: Was youngest player on TOUR in 1984 after qualifying in fall of '83…Winner of three Georgia State Opens, one as amateur…Winner Trans America Athletic Conference title at Georgia Southern…An avid sport fisherman who has won tournaments…Only coincidence that youngest son was named "Dylan Thomas" (in other words, was <u>not</u> named for the Irish poet).

1993 PGA TOUR STATISTICS

Scoring Average	71.36 (105T)
Driving Distance	261.0 (75T)
Driving Accuracy	67.8 (100T)
Greens in Regulation	64.1 (130T)
Putting	1.788 (65T)
All-Around	674 (57)
Sand Saves	52.8 (78T)
Total Driving	175 (72T)
Eagles	9 (16T)
Birdies	316 (33T)

MISCELLANEOUS STATISTICS

Scoring Avg. (before cut)	71.46 (77)
Scoring Avg. (3rd round)	72.16 (158)
Scoring Avg. (4th round)	71.75 (116)
Birdie Conversion	29.0 (46T)
Par Breakers	19.1 (66)

1993 Low Round:	66: 2 times
Career Low Round:	62: 2 times, most recent '90
Career Largest Paycheck:	Southwestern Bell Colonial/4 $135,000 '89 Hawaiian Open/1 '91 Kmart/2

TED SCHULZ

EXEMPT STATUS: 100th on 1993 money list

FULL NAME: Theodore James Schulz

HEIGHT: 6'2"   **WEIGHT:** 195

BIRTH DATE: Oct. 29, 1959

BIRTHPLACE: Louisville, KY

RESIDENCE: Louisville, KY

FAMILY: Wife, Diane; Samuel Tucker (11/10/91)

COLLEGE: University of Louisville (1982, Phys. Ed)

SPECIAL INTERESTS: All sports, Bible study

TURNED PROFESSIONAL: 1984

JOINED TOUR: Fall 1986, 1988

PLAYER PROFILE

CAREER EARNINGS: $1,534,341   **PLAYOFF RECORD:** 0-1

TOUR VICTORIES: 1989 Southern Open. **1991** Nissan Los Angeles Open. (TOTAL: 2)

MONEY & POSITION:

1987--$ 17,838--190	1990--$193,126--82	1992--$259,204-- 60
1989--$391,855-- 30	1991--$508,058--29	1993--$164,260--100

BEST 1993 FINISH: T2--Greater Milwaukee Open.

1993 SUMMARY: Tournaments entered--31; in money--17; top ten finishes--1.

1994 PGA TOUR CHARITY TEAM COMPETITION: The International

1993 SEASON: Had all but given up hope of retaining TOUR card going into Greater Milwaukee Open...Had earnings of just $74,340 starting play at Tuckaway CC...Proceeded to fashion rounds of 69-67-68-66, tying eventual winner Billy Mayfair and Mark Calcavecchia at 270...Bogeyed first hole of four-hole playoff, but earned $88,000--and saved his playing privileges--with T2...GMO success only top-10 finish...Only other top-25 finish a T20 in Freeport-McMoRan Classic...Earnings total/money-list placing lowest since first TOUR season.

CAREER HIGHLIGHTS: Had storybook year in 1991...Shot 12-under-par 272 to claim one-stroke win over Jeff Sluman in Nissan Los Angeles Open...Went from 119th on money list going into Los Angeles to final overall finish of 29th...That placing provided berth in TOUR Championship field, where finished T13...Had five top-10 finishes during season, including T3 at Las Vegas Invitational...'91 earnings more than $116,000 better than previous high...Went from 190th on 1987 money list to being off TOUR in 1988...Regained card for '89, finished T14 in Bob Hope Desert Classic and T7 Phoenix Open before going on to win Southern Open and $391,855 for season...'91 L.A. Open victory provided entry into 1992 Masters, where finished T6 (only top-10 finish in '92).

PERSONAL: Has learned meaning of patience throughout career...Turned professional in fall of '83, ran driving range at Bermuda Dunes winter of 1984...Finally made it through Qualifying Tournament in fall of '86...After losing card after '87 season, played Asian Tour in 1988...Won 1983 Kentucky State Amateur, 1984 and '88 Kentucky State Opens...Won 1989 Chrysler Team Championship with David Ogrin.

1993 PGA TOUR STATISTICS

Scoring Average	71.86 (145)
Driving Distance	260.8 (77T)
Driving Accuracy	66.0 (132T)
Greens in Regulation	63.2 (145T)
Putting	1.824 (156T)
All-Around	1131 (154)
Sand Saves	50.8 (108T)
Total Driving	209 (132T)
Eagles	2 (144T)
Birdies	273 (92T)

MISCELLANEOUS STATISTICS

Scoring Avg. (before cut)	72.31 (143)
Scoring Avg. (3rd round)	73.12 (182)
Scoring Avg. (4th round)	72.18 (146T)
Birdie Conversion	25.3 (152T)
Par Breakers	16.1 (164)

1993 Low Round: 66: Greater Milwaukee Open/4

Career Low Round: 63: 3 times, most recent '91 Chattanooga Classic/1

Career Largest Paycheck: $180,000 '91 Nissan Los Angeles Open/1

TOM SIECKMANN

EXEMPT STATUS: 87th on 1993 money list

FULL NAME: Thomas Edward Sieckmann

HEIGHT: 6' 5" **WEIGHT:** 220

BIRTH DATE: January 14, 1955

BIRTHPLACE: York, NE

RESIDENCE: Omaha, NE; Plays out of Shadow Ridge GC in Omaha, NE

FAMILY: Wife, Debbie

COLLEGE: Oklahoma State University

SPECIAL INTERESTS: Tennis, basketball, reading

TURNED PROFESSIONAL: 1977

Q-SCHOOL: Fall 1984, 1985, 1987

PLAYER PROFILE

CAREER EARNINGS: $1,247,353 **PLAYOFF RECORD:** 1-0

TOUR VICTORIES: 1988 Anheuser-Busch Classic (TOTAL: 1)

MONEY & POSITION:

1985--$30,052--143	1988--$209,151-- 54	1991--$278,598--61
1986--$63,395--125	1989--$ 97,465--128	1992--$173,424--88
1987--$52,259--146	1990--$141,241--110	1993--$201,429--87

BEST 1993 FINISHES: T2--BellSouth Classic; T10--Walt Disney World/Oldsmobile Classic.

1993 SUMMARY: Tournaments entered--31; in money--19; top ten finishes--2.

1994 PGA TOUR CHARITY TEAM COMPETITION: JCPenney Classic

1993 SEASON: Hard-working veteran achieved third-best season of nine-year career...Had to overcome rocky start that saw him miss cut in four of opening five events and eight of first eleven...Rebounded to make money in 16 of his next 20 tournaments...Best effort came in May in BellSouth Classic where he finished T2 with Nick Price and Mark Calcavecchia (two strokes behind Nolan Henke)...Had season-low 64 in second round...Put together four sub-70 rounds at Walt Disney World/Oldsmobile Classic (69-66-69-69), good for T10...One of his better finishes, T15 at Buick Invitational of California in February, came during his bad early-season stretch.

CAREER HIGHLIGHTS: Lone TOUR victory came in 1988 Anheuser-Busch Golf Classic...Won playoff with Mark Wiebe by parring from left fringe while Wiebe bogeyed second extra hole...Two had finished 14-under-par 270 at Kingsmill Country Club...Victory turned year around, since had made cut in only three of previous 16 starts...Had three consecutive top-10 finishes in '91--Doral Ryder Open (10), Nestle Invitational (2), USF&G Classic (3...Then proceeded to make cut in nine of final 13 tournaments...Tied for eighth in 1990 U.S. Open at Medinah...Only 1992 top-10 finish, T6 in THE PLAYERS Championship, was worth $62,550...That same year was just one shot off lead entering final round of Nissan Los Angeles Open (finished T12).

PERSONAL: Played basketball as youngster before focusing on golf...Started college at Nebraska before transferring to Oklahoma State, where teammates included Bob Tway and Willie Wood...Winner 1981 Philippines, Thailand and Brazilian Opens, 1982 Rolex Open (Switzerland), 1984 Singapore Open...Medalist 1985 Qualifying Tournament.

1993 PGA TOUR STATISTICS

Scoring Average	71.41 (110T)
Driving Distance	262.5 (66)
Driving Accuracy	65.4 (138T)
Greens in Regulation	64.5 (123)
Putting	1.775 (33T)
All-Around	733 (74)
Sand Saves	51.4 (98T)
Total Driving	204 (122T)
Eagles	9 (16T)
Birdies	324 (27T)

MISCELLANEOUS STATISTICS

Scoring Avg. (before cut)	71.75 (99T)
Scoring Avg. (3rd round)	71.25 (91)
Scoring Avg. (4th round)	71.53 (97T)
Birdie Conversion	29.1 (41T)
Par Breakers	19.3 (55T)

1993 Low Round:	64: BellSouth Classic/4
Career Low Round:	62: '89 Texas Open
Career Largest	Presented by Nabisco/1
Paycheck:	$117,000/1988 Anheuser-Busch /1

SCOTT SIMPSON

EXEMPT STATUS: Winner, 1987 U.S. Open

FULL NAME: Scott William Simpson

HEIGHT: 6' 2"　　　　　**WEIGHT:** 180

BIRTH DATE: Sept. 17, 1955　**BIRTHPLACE:** San Diego, CA

RESIDENCE: Kailua, HI; Plays out of Makaha Valley, Oahu

FAMILY: Wife, Cheryl; Brea Yoshiko (10/10/82);
Sean Tokuzo (10/14/86)

COLLEGE: Univ. of Southern California
(1978, Business Administration)

SPECIAL INTERESTS: Ocean sports, Bible study,
family activities, jogging

TURNED PROFESSIONAL: 1977　　**Q SCHOOL:** Fall 1978

PLAYER PROFILE

CAREER EARNINGS: $3,665,273　　　　**PLAYOFF RECORD:** 1-2

TOUR VICTORIES: **1980** Western Open. **1984** Manufacturers Hanover Westchester Classic. **1987** Greater
(TOTAL: 6)　Greensboro Open, U.S. Open. **1989** BellSouth Atlanta Classic. **1993** GTE Byron
Nelson Classic.

MONEY & POSITION:

1979--$ 53,084--74	1984--$248,581-- 22	1989--$298,920--40
1980--$141,323--24	1985--$171,245-- 39	1990--$235,309--63
1981--$108,793--34	1986--$202,223-- 41	1991--$322,936--51
1982--$146,903--24	1987--$621,032-- 4	1992--$155,284--97
1983--$144,172--38	1988--$108,301--106	1993--$707,166--14

BEST 1993 FINISHES: 1--GTE Byron Nelson Classic; T2--THE TOUR Championship; 3--Bob Hope
Chrysler Classic; T4--The International; T6--PGA Championship.

1993 SUMMARY: Tournaments entered--22; in money--19; top ten finishes--5.

1994 PGA TOUR CHARITY TEAM COMPETITION: Lincoln-Mercury Kapalua International

NATIONAL TEAMS: Ryder Cup, 1987; Walker Cup, 1977.

1993 SEASON: Enjoyed finest year of PGA TOUR career in his 15th campaign...$707,166 in earnings surpassed previous high of $621,032 back in 1987...Captured his sixth TOUR title by winning GTE Byron Nelson Classic in May...Recorded a one-shot victory over Corey Pavin, Billy Mayfair and D.A. Weibring at the TPC at Las Colinas...Nelson triumph was worth $198,750...Also had T2 in season-ending TOUR Championship, good for $198,750...Finished T8 in Lincoln Mercury Kapalua International very next week...Finished third in Bob Hope Chrysler Classic in fourth start of season, then later had back-to-back top-10s in PGA Championship (T6) and The International (T4).

CAREER HIGHLIGHTS: Battled Tom Watson down stretch to win 1987 U.S. Open at San Francisco's Olympic Club...On final nine made three birdies and saved par three times from off green to win by stroke...Has turned Open into own personal showcase since '87 victory...Almost recaptured finest professional moment in 1991, when lost to Payne Stewart 75-to-77 in 18-hole playoff at Hazeltine National...Finished T6 in 1988-89 Opens, T14 in '90...Defeated Bob Tway in playoff to win 1989 BellSouth Atlanta Classic...Claimed first title in second year on TOUR, Western Open in 1980.

PERSONAL: Member 1987 Ryder Cup, 1977 Walker Cup teams...Winner 1976-77 NCAA Championship, 1976 Porter Cup, 1975 and 1977 PAC-8 Championship...Collegiate All-America 1976-77...Winner California and San Diego junior titles...Winner 1979, 1981 Hawaii State Opens...Winner 1984 and 1988 Chunichi Crowns, Dunlop Phoenix (both Japan), 1990 Perrier Invitational (France)...Takes family time away from TOUR late in season.

1993 PGA TOUR STATISTICS

Scoring Average	70.33 (25)
Driving Distance	255.4 (134T)
Driving Accuracy	70.8 (68T)
Greens in Regulation	65.4 (92T)
Putting	1.752 (5)
All-Around	711 (70)
Sand Saves	58.9 (19T)
Total Driving	202 (117T)
Eagles	1 (164T)
Birdies	278 (87)

MISCELLANEOUS STATISTICS

Scoring Avg. (before cut)	70.91 (31T)
Scoring Avg. (3rd round)	70.71 (53)
Scoring Avg. (4th round)	70.72 (30)
Birdie Conversion	30.5 (15T)
Par Breakers	20.0 (33T)

1993 Low Round: 63: Bob Hope Chrysler Classic/4
Career Low Round: 62: 1991 United Airlines Hawaiian Open/1
Career Largest Paycheck: $216,000 '93 GTE Byron Nelson /1

JOEY SINDELAR

EXEMPT STATUS: 38th on 1993 money list

FULL NAME: Joseph Paul Sindelar

HEIGHT: 5' 10" **WEIGHT:** 200

BIRTH DATE: March 30, 1958

BIRTHPLACE: Ft. Knox, KY

RESIDENCE: Horseheads, NY

FAMILY: Wife, Suzanne Lee; Jamison Prescott (2/2/90); Ryan Joseph (5/13/93)

COLLEGE: Ohio State University (1981, Education)

SPECIAL INTERESTS: All sports, fishing, electronics

TURNED PROFESSIONAL: 1981

Q SCHOOL: Fall 1983

PLAYER PROFILE

CAREER EARNINGS: $3,247,940 **PLAYOFF RECORD:** 1-1

TOUR VICTORIES: **1985** Greater Greensboro Open, B. C. Open. **1987** B. C. Open. **1988** Honda Classic,
(TOTAL: 6) The International. **1990** Hardee's Golf Classic.

MONEY & POSITION:

1984--$116,528--59	1988--$813,732-- 3	1991--$168,352--94
1985--$282,762--12	1989--$196,092--72	1992--$396,354--35
1986--$341,231--14	1990--$307,207--46	1993--$391,649--38
1987--$235,033--40		

BEST 1993 FINISHES: 2--United Airlines Hawaiian Open; T3--AT&T Pebble Beach National Pro-Am; T4-
-New England Classic; T7--Buick Invitational of California; 9--Nestle Invitational.

1993 SUMMARY: Tournaments entered--22; in money--14; top ten finishes--5.

1994 PGA TOUR CHARITY TEAM COMPETITION: Hardee's Golf Classic

NATIONAL TEAMS: Kirin Cup, 1988; World Cup, 1990.

1993 SEASON: Was enjoying one of finest seasons of 10-year career until wrist injury forced his withdrawal from second round of PGA Championship at Inverness Club…Diagnosed as fracture of hook of hamate bone, injury forced him to sidelines for remainder of campaign…Was in a cast for 3 1/2 months, expected to return to action in early 1994…Stood 24th on money list going into Inverness, wound up year 38th without playing in last ten regular-season events…Finished T4 in last start before PGA Championship, the New England Classic in July…Opened year with four top-10 finishes in first eight starts: 2nd United Airlines Hawaiian Open, T3 AT&T Pebble Beach National Pro-Am and T7 Buick Invitational of California (back-to-back starts), 9th Nestle Invitational.

CAREER HIGHLIGHTS: Career year was 1988, with victories in Honda Classic and The International, earnings of $813,732 (No. 3)…Has twice won B.C. Open in front of hometown fans (lives in nearby Horseheads, NY)…First B.C. victory came in 1985 and featured hole-in-one on 14th hole (second was in 1987)…First TOUR victory in 1985 Greater Greensboro Open preceded initial B.C. Open win…Exhibited steady nerves in making final-hole par-saving eight-foot putt to win GGO…Defeated Willie Wood in playoff to win 1990 Hardee's Golf Classic.

PERSONAL: Member 1988 Kirin Cup, 1990 World Cup teams…Winner 1972 New York State Junior, 1980 New York State Amateur, 1981 New York State Open…Member 1979 NCAA Championship team at Ohio State…Winner 10 collegiate titles, including 1981 Big Ten Championship (by 12 strokes)…Three-time All-America…Named 1981 Ohio State Athlete-of-Year…Winner 1986 MCI Long Distance driving competition…1992 inductee Ohio State University Athletic Hall of Fame.

1993 PGA TOUR STATISTICS

Scoring Average	70.65	(40)
Driving Distance	267.1	(38T)
Driving Accuracy	67.2	(113T)
Greens in Regulation	67.5	(51T)
Putting	1.798	(95T)
All-Around	746	(77)
Sand Saves	43.8	(177)
Total Driving	151	(40)
Eagles	6	(50T)
Birdies	220	(142T)

MISCELLANEOUS STATISTICS

Scoring Avg. (before cut)	71.20	(54T)
Scoring Avg. (3rd round)	72.31	(161)
Scoring Avg. (4th round)	71.64	(107T)
Birdie Conversion	25.7	(148T)
Par Breakers	17.8	(119T)

1993 Low Round: 65: THE PLAYERS Championship/1
Career Low Round: 62: 3 times, most recent
Career Largest 1987 Provident Classic/1
Paycheck: $180,000/1988 International/1
1990 Hardee's/1

VIJAY SINGH

EXEMPT STATUS: 1993 tournament winner

FULL NAME: Vijay Singh

HEIGHT: 6' 2"   **WEIGHT:** 198

BIRTH DATE: February 22, 1963

BIRTHPLACE: Lautoka, Fiji

RESIDENCE: London, England

FAMILY: Wife, Ardena Seth; Qass Seth (6/19/90)

SPECIAL INTERESTS: Snooker, cricket, rugby, soccer

TURNED PROFESSIONAL: 1982

JOINED TOUR: Spring 1993

PLAYER PROFILE

CAREER EARNINGS: $657,831   **PLAYOFF RECORD:** 1-0

TOUR VICTORIES: 1993 Buick Classic.
(TOTAL: 1)

MONEY & POSITION: 1993--$657,831--19

BEST 1993 FINISHES: 1--Buick Classic; T2--Nestle Invitational; 4--PGA Championship; 5--Freeport-McMoRan Classic; 5--NEC World Series of Golf; T9--Kmart Greater Greensboro Open.

1993 SUMMARY: Tournaments entered--14; in money--12; top ten finishes--6.

1994 PGA TOUR CHARITY TEAM COMPETITION: Kemper Open

1993 SEASON: Earned **PGA TOUR Rookie of the Year** honors for stellar season...Gained special temporary membership by winning $74,667 in first start, T2 at Nestle Invitational...Earned full TOUR membership status and two-year exemption by winning seventh start, playoff victory over Mark Wiebe in Buick Classic...With final-round 66 at Westchester CC came from five strokes off lead, as did Wiebe, to finish deadlocked at 280...Birdied third extra hole to claim first TOUR title and $180,000 winner's check...Held second-round lead in PGA Championship after firing Inverness Club record 63...Tied PGA 36-hole mark of 131 (had opened with 68), equaled lowest 18-hole score in PGA Championship and matched lowest 18-hole total ever posted in major.

CAREER HIGHLIGHTS: Prior to miss in U.S. Open, had made cut in every U.S. start—a string of eleven straight that included Memorial Tournament and Federal Express St. Jude Classic in 1992, and in 1991...Winner of 13 tournaments outside United States...First title came in 1984 Malaysian PGA Championship...Joined PGA European Tour in 1989, winning Volvo Open in rookie season there...Followed with European Tour wins in El Bosque Open (1990), Turespana Masters and Volvo German Open (1992)...Also has captured titles in Nigeria, Sweden, Zimbabwe, the Ivory Coast and Morocco...Won Nigerian Open in 1988-89...Led Order of Merit of Safari Tour in Africa in 1988.

PERSONAL: Only world-class golfer produced by Fiji... Of Indian ancestry...As teenager in Fiji chose Tom Weiskopf as role model...Father taught him basics of game...Has no swing coach, preferring to work by himself...Left Fiji to pursue dream of becoming professional golfer...Tried Australian Tour, later took club job in Malaysia...Wife Ardena one of his students...Brothers Mira and Krishna also golfers; father an airplane technician who taught golf .

1993 PGA TOUR STATISTICS

Scoring Average	69.51
Driving Distance	273.2
Driving Accuracy	67.4
Greens in Regulation	65.8
Putting	1.760
All-Around	N/A
Sand Saves	49.1
Total Driving	N/A
Eagles	5
Birdies	184

MISCELLANEOUS STATISTICS

Scoring Avg. (before cut)	70.48
Scoring Avg. (3rd round)	71.18
Scoring Avg. (4th round)	69.82
Birdie Conversion	31.7
Par Breakers	21.4

1993 Low Round: **63:** PGA Championship/2
Career Low Round: **63:** 1993 PGA
Career Largest   Championship/2
Paycheck: $180,000/1993 Buick Classic/1

JEFF SLUMAN

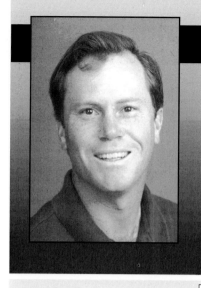

EXEMPT STATUS: Winner, 1988 PGA Championship

FULL NAME: Jeffrey George Sluman

HEIGHT: 5' 7"   **WEIGHT:** 140

BIRTH DATE: Sept. 11, 1957

BIRTHPLACE: Rochester, NY

RESIDENCE: Chicago, IL

FAMILY: Wife, Linda

COLLEGE: Florida State University (1980, Finance)

SPECIAL INTERESTS: Old cars, stock market, TOUR Policy Board, akitas

TURNED PROFESSIONAL: 1980

Q SCHOOL: Fall 1982, 1984

PLAYER PROFILE

CAREER EARNINGS: $2,995,571   **PLAYOFF RECORD:** 0-3

TOUR VICTORIES: 1988 PGA Championship
(TOTAL: 1)

MONEY & POSITION:

1983--$ 13,643--171	1987--$335,590--27	1991--$552,979--23
1984--$ 603--281	1988--$503,321--18	1992--$729,027--14
1985--$100,523-- 78	1989--$154,507--89	1993--$187,841--93
1986--$154,129-- 60	1990--$264,012--56	

BEST 1993 FINISH: T9--Kmart Greater Greensboro Open.

1993 SUMMARY: Tournaments entered--27; in money--21; top ten finishes--1.

1994 PGA TOUR CHARITY TEAM COMPETITION: B.C. Open

1993 SEASON: With just one top-10 finish, fell back to lowest money-list position since first two years on TOUR, 1983-84… Earnings total also lowest since 1989 ($154,507)…Sole top-10 came at end of three-tournament April stretch when finished 17th or better in each: 17th Masters, T12 MCI Heritage Classic, T9 Kmart Greater Greensboro Open…Second-round 65 in GGO matched season low…Two starts after GGO had fourth Top-25 of campaign, T22 in Kemper Open…Final top-25s came back-to-back in June, T11 in U.S. Open at Baltusrol, followed by T20 in Canon Greater Hartford Open…Three of six missed cuts came in last five starts.

CAREER HIGHLIGHTS: 1992 season punctuated by remarkable accomplishments, including final-round 71 in U.S. Open at Pebble Beach (just one of four sub-par rounds that day), where finished second to Tom Kite…Had earlier second in AT&T Pebble Beach National Pro-Am, losing playoff to Mark O'Meara…Also had T4 in '92 Masters, where became first player to ace fourth hole during opening-round 65 that produced tie for lead…Recorded one of great finishing rounds in PGA Championship history to win 1988 title…Started day three strokes behind Paul Azinger, fired 6-under-par 65 at Oak Tree Golf Club to win by three over Azinger…Two birdies and eagle (holed 115-yard sand wedge) on outgoing nine, three birdies on way home…Nearly won twice in 1991, losing playoff to Billy Andrade in Kemper Open and finishing second to Ted Schulz in Nissan Los Angeles Open…Lost three-hole playoff to Sandy Lyle at 1987 Tournament Players Championship …Had unofficial victory in 1985 Tallahassee Open, part of Tournament Players Series.

PERSONAL: Player Director PGA TOUR Policy Board…Winner 1980 Metro Conference Championship.

1993 PGA TOUR STATISTICS

Scoring Average	71.17	(83T)
Driving Distance	260.7	(80T)
Driving Accuracy	66.9	(121T)
Greens in Regulation	64.1	(130T)
Putting	1.800	(100T)
All-Around	831	(99T)
Sand Saves	55.2	(49T)
Total Driving	201	(116)
Eagles	4	(89T)
Birdies	296	(63)

MISCELLANEOUS STATISTICS

Scoring Avg. (before cut)	71.47	(78)
Scoring Avg. (3rd round)	71.21	(90)
Scoring Avg. (4th round)	72.29	(152T)
Birdie Conversion	26.4	(128T)
Par Breakers	17.2	(136)

1993 Low Round: **65:** 4 times
Career Low Round: **62:** 1992 GTE Byron Nelson
Career Largest   Classic/3
Paycheck: **$160,000**/1988 PGA Championship/1

SAM SNEAD

EXEMPT STATUS: Winner, 1942 PGA Championship

FULL NAME: Samuel Jackson Snead

HEIGHT: 5' 11"   **WEIGHT:** 190

BIRTH DATE: May 27, 1912

BIRTHPLACE: Hot Springs, VA

RESIDENCE: Hot Springs, VA

FAMILY: Sam, Jr. (6/30/44); Terrance (5/27/52)

SPECIAL INTERESTS: Hunting, fishing

TURNED PROFESSIONAL: 1934

JOINED TOUR: 1937

PLAYER PROFILE

CAREER EARNINGS: $620,126   **PLAYOFF RECORD:** 8-6

TOUR VICTORIES: **1936** WestVirginia PGA. **1937** St. Paul Open, Nassau Open, Miami Open, Oakland Open,
(TOTAL: 81)   Bing Crosby ProAm. **1938** Greensboro Open, Inverness Four-Ball, Goodall Round Robin,
Chicago Open,Canadian Open, Westchester 108 Hole Open, White Sulphur Springs Open,
Bing Crosby Pro-Am. **1939** Miami Open,St. Petersburg Open, Miami Biltmore Four-Ball. **1940** Inverness Four-Ball,
Canadian Open, Anthracite Open.**1941** Canadian Open, St.Petersburg Open, North and South Open, Rochester
Times Union Open, Henry Hurst Invitational, Bing Crosby Pro-Am. **1942** St. Petersburg Open, PGA Championship.
1944 Richmond Open, Portland Open. **1945** Los Angeles Open, Gulfport Open,Pensacola Open, JacksonvilleOpen,
Dallas Open,Tulsa Open. **1946** Miami Open,Greensboro Open,Jacksonville Open,Virginia Open, World Champi-
onship.**1948** Texas Open. **1949** Greensboro Open, PGA Championship,Masters,Washington Star Open, Dapper
Dan Open, Western Open. **1950** Texas Open, MiamiOpen,GreensboroOpen,InvernessFour-Ball, North and South
Open, Los Angeles Open, Western Open, Miami Beach Open, Colonial National Inv.,Reading Open, Bing Crosby
Pro-Am. **1951** Miami Open, PGA Championship. **1952** Inverness Four-Ball, Masters, All American, Eastern Open,
Palm Beach Round Robin. **1953** Baton Rouge Open. **1954** Masters, Palm Beach Round Robin. **1955** Miami Open,
Greensboro Open, Palm Beach Round Robin, Insurance City Open.**1956** Greensboro Open. **1957** Dallas Open,
Palm Beach Round Robin. **1958** Dallas Open. **1960** Greensboro Open, De Soto Open
1961 Tournament of Champions. **1965** Greensboro Open.

MONEY & POSITION:

1937--$10,243-- 3	1952--$19,908-- 4	1967--$ 7,141--104
1938--$19,534-- 1	1953--$14,115-- 15	1968--$43,106-- 39
1939--$ 9,712-- 2	1954--$ 7,889-- 29	1969--$15,439--100
1940--$ 9,206-- 3	1955--$23,464-- 7	1970--$25,103-- 85
1941--$12,848-- 2	1956--$ 8,253-- 36	1971--$22,258-- 94
1942--$ 8,078-- 3	1957--$28,260-- 4	1972--$35,462-- 71
1943--$ --	1958--$15,905-- 18	1973--$38,685-- 78
1944--$ 5,755-- 7	1959--$ 8,221-- 45	1974--$55,562-- 49
1945--$24,436-- 4	1960--$19,405-- 19	1975--$ 8,285--138
1946--$18,341-- 6	1961--$23,906-- 17	1976--$ 2,694--198
1947--$ 9,703-- 12	1962--$ 9,169-- 59	1977--$ 488--256
1948--$ 6,980-- 18	1963--$28,431-- 16	1978--$ 385--265
1949--$31,593-- 1	1964--$ 8,383-- 74	1979--$ 4,671--190
1950--$35,758-- 1	1965--$36,889-- 24	
1951--$15,072-- 6	1966--$12,109-- 72	

SENIOR PGA TOUR SUMMARY

SENIOR VICTORIES: **1964, 1965, 1967, 1970, 1972, 1973** PGA
(TOTAL: 13)   Seniors. **1964,1965,1970,1972,1973** World
Seniors. **1980** Golf Digest Commemorative
Pro-Am; **1982** Legends of Golf (with Don January)

CAREER EARNINGS:
(Regular/Senior TOURS combined): $726,700.

OTHER ACHIEVEMENTS: Credited with 135 victories by independent record keepers. 1949 Player-of-the-Year. 1938, 1949, 1950,1955
Vardon Trophy winner. 1937, 1939, 1941, 1947, 1949, 1951, 1953
and1955 Ryder Cup team. Member winning World Cup team in1956,
1960 and 1961 (won individual title in 1961). Shot age, then bettered
it at 1979 Quad Cities (67-66). Member PGA Golf Hall of Fame,
World Golf Hall of Fame. Winner, 1946 British Open.

1993 PGA TOUR STATISTICS	
Scoring Average	N/A
Driving Distance	N/A
Driving Accuracy	N/A
Greens in Regulation	N/A
Putting	N/A
All-Around	N/A
Sand Saves	N/A
Total Driving	N/A
Eagles	N/A
Birdies	N/A

MISCELLANEOUS STATISTICS	
Scoring Avg. (before cut)	N/A
Scoring Avg. (3rd round)	N/A
Scoring Avg. (4th round)	N/A
Birdie Conversion	N/A
Par Breakers	N/A

Career Low Round: **60:** 1957 Dallas Open/2
Career Largest
Paycheck: **$11,000**/1965 Greater Greensboro /1

MIKE SPRINGER

EXEMPT STATUS: 79th on 1993 money list

FULL NAME: Michael Paul Springer

HEIGHT: 5'11"   **WEIGHT:** 210

BIRTH DATE: Nov. 3, 1965

BIRTHPLACE: San Francisco, CA

RESIDENCE: Fresno, CA

FAMILY: Wife, Crystol; Haylee Danielle (5/26/93)

COLLEGE: University of Arizona

SPECIAL INTERESTS: Hunting, skiing

TURNED PROFESSIONAL: 1988

JOINED TOUR: 1991

PLAYER PROFILE

CAREER EARNINGS: $537,632

BEST EVER FINISH: T2--1992 Kemper Open

MONEY & POSITION: 1991-- $178,587--91   1992--$144,316--104   1993--$214,729--79

BEST 1993 FINISHES: T3--Phoenix Open; T5--Canon Greater Hartford Open; 6--BellSouth Classic; T7--Shell Houston Open.

1993 SUMMARY: Tournaments entered--30; in money--14; top ten finishes--4.

1994 PGA TOUR CHARITY TEAM COMPETITION: Deposit Guaranty Golf Classic

1993 SEASON: Battled left elbow and wrist problems virtually entire season, missing 16 cuts and failing to either finish or even start 14 of final 19 tournaments entered…Diagnosis given: elbow and wrist out of alignment…Still managed to finish 79th on money list, his best placing in three years on TOUR…After T3 in Phoenix Open, third start of year, and subsequent T33 two weeks later at Bob Hope Chrysler Classic, was forced to withdraw from next three events…April chiropractic treatment just prior to Shell Houston Open helped produce T7 in that event and another top-10 the next week, sixth in BellSouth Classic…Managed just one more top-10 thereafter: T5 at Canon Greater Hartford Open...Teamed with Melissa McNamara to win JCPenny Classic in December.

CAREER HIGHLIGHTS: Finished in four-way T2 in 1992 Kemper Open, one shot behind winner Bill Glasson…Was in three-way tie for lead after 36 holes of fog-shortened '92 Buick Invitational of California, but finished T6…Trailed only John Daly, Jeff Maggert and Scott Gump in 1991 rookie earnings with $178,587…Finished third in BellSouth Atlanta Classic, missing eagle putt on final hole to finish stroke out of Corey Pavin-Steve Pate playoff…Earned TOUR playing privileges by finishing fourth on 1990 Ben Hogan Tour money list with $82,906…Won first-ever Hogan Tour event at Bakersfield, closed inaugural campaign by winning two of final three tournaments--Reno and El Paso Opens--to finish in top five.

PERSONAL: 1986-88 Second-Team All-America selection at University of Arizona…Arizona teammates included Robert Gamez and Larry Silveira…Winner John Burns Invitational, Fresno State Classic, 1986 California State Amateur.

1993 PGA TOUR STATISTICS

Scoring Average	71.36 (105T)
Driving Distance	266.1 (43)
Driving Accuracy	65.3 (141T)
Greens in Regulation	64.8 (114T)
Putting	1.782 (55T)
All-Around	803 (88)
Sand Saves	51.4 (98T)
Total Driving	184 (91T)
Eagles	5 (67T)
Birdies	275 (89T)

MISCELLANEOUS STATISTICS

Scoring Avg. (before cut)	71.50 (79T)
Scoring Avg. (3rd round)	71.46 (108)
Scoring Avg. (4th round)	71.33 (75T)
Birdie Conversion	28.8 (53T)
Par Breakers	19.0 (67T)

1993 Low Round:	64: Shell Houston Open/3
Career Low Round:	63: 2 times, most recent '92 Bob Hope/3
Career Largest Paycheck:	$72,600/1992 Kemper Open/T2

CRAIG STADLER

EXEMPT STATUS: Winner, 1992 NEC World Series of Golf

FULL NAME: Craig Robert Stadler

HEIGHT: 5' 10"   **WEIGHT:** 210

BIRTH DATE: June 2, 1953

BIRTHPLACE: San Diego, CA

RESIDENCE: San Diego, CA

FAMILY: Wife, Sue; Kevin (2/5/80), Christopher (11/23/82)

COLLEGE: University of Southern California

SPECIAL INTERESTS: Snow skiing, hunting

TURNED PROFESSIONAL: 1975

Q SCHOOL: Spring 1976

PLAYER PROFILE

CAREER EARNINGS: $5,131,606   **PLAYOFF RECORD:** 2-2

TOUR VICTORIES: **1980** Bob Hope Desert Classic, Greater Greensboro Open. **1981** Kemper Open.
(TOTAL: 10) **1982** Joe Garagiola-Tucson Open, Masters Tournament, Kemper Open, World Series of Golf. **1984** Byron Nelson Classic.**1991** THE TOUR Championship. **1992** NEC World Series of Golf.

MONEY & POSITION:

1976--$ 2,702--196	1982--$446,462-- 1	1988--$278,313--37
1977--$ 42,949-- 66	1983--$214,496--17	1989--$409,419--25
1978--$ 63,486-- 48	1984--$324,241-- 8	1990--$278,482--52
1979--$ 73,392-- 55	1985--$297,926--11	1991--$827,628-- 2
1980--$206,291-- 8	1986--$170,076--53	1992--$487,460--28
1981--$218,829-- 8	1987--$235,831--39	1993--$553,623--29

BEST 1993 FINISHES: 2--Las Vegas Invitational; T2--NEC World Series of Golf; T3--Walt Disney World/Oldsmobile Classic; T4--Canadian Open; T9--Buick Invitational of California.

1993 SUMMARY: Tournaments entered--24; in money--17; top ten finishes--5.

1994 PGA TOUR CHARITY TEAM COMPETITION: United Airlines Hawaiian Open

NATIONAL TEAMS: Ryder Cup (2) 1983, 1985; Walker Cup, 1975; U.S. vs. Japan, 1982.

1993 SEASON: After almost throwing in towel on chances of making TOUR Championship field, went T2-T4-T3-2 in last four starts of year to earn trip to San Francisco...LVI solo second worth $151,200 put him over top...Closing rounds in those four events: 67-69-67-65...In final five events of year, including TOUR Championship, earned $443,266...Had amassed $110,357 in first 19 starts...Other top-10 came was a T9 at Buick Invitational of California.

CAREER HIGHLIGHTS: Captured NEC World Series of Golf in 1992, ten years after earning same title in 1982...Both victories carried ten-year exemptions, most recent will virtually take him to Senior TOUR...Start of '92 campaign delayed due to off-season skiing collision with young girl (Dec. 1991) made it impossible for him to play in Tournament of Champions, for which had qualified by winning 1991 TOUR Championship...That victory, his first in seven years, propelled him to second place on 1991 money list with $827,628...Led in earnings with $446,462 in 1982, when won four times, including Masters (playoff with Dan Pohl) and World Series (playoff with Raymond Floyd)...Also captured Kemper Open for second time in '82, year that began with victory in Joe Garagiola-Tucson Open...Named 1982 PGA TOUR Arnold Palmer Award recipient as leading money winner...First title came in 1980 Bob Hope Chrysler Classic.

PERSONAL: Nicknamed "Walrus"...Member 1983 and '85 Ryder Cup, 1975 Walker Cup, 1982 U.S. vs. Japan teams...Winner 1971 World Junior Championship, 1973 U.S. Amateur...Two-time All-America at USC (1974-75)...Winner Southern California Interscholastic, 1978 Magnolia Classic, 1985 European Masters, 1987 Dunlop Phoenix (Japan), 1988 Fred Meyer Challenge (with Joey Sindelar), 1990 Scandinavian Open (Sweden), 1992 Argentine open .

1993 PGA TOUR STATISTICS

Scoring Average	70.60 (37T)
Driving Distance	268.2 (33)
Driving Accuracy	68.4 (94T)
Greens in Regulation	68.6 (29T)
Putting	1.813 (129T)
All-Around	624 (49T)
Sand Saves	50.8 (108T)
Total Driving	127 (23T)
Eagles	5 (67T)
Birdies	265 (104T)

MISCELLANEOUS STATISTICS

Scoring Avg. (before cut)	71.35 (67)
Scoring Avg. (3rd round)	70.88 (65)
Scoring Avg. (4th round)	70.63 (26)
Birdie Conversion	26.8 (116T)
Par Breakers	18.8 (75T)

1993 Low Round: **65:** 2 times

Career Low Round: 62: 4 times, most recent '87

Career Largest Paycheck: $360,000/'91 THE TOUR Championship/1

Shearson Lehman/2

151

MIKE STANDLY

EXEMPT STATUS: 1993 tournament winner

FULL NAME: Michael Dean Standly

HEIGHT: 6'   **WEIGHT:** 200

BIRTH DATE: May 19, 1964

BIRTHPLACE: Abilene, TX

RESIDENCE: Houston, TX

FAMILY: Wife, Nicole; Charles Allen(11/16/88); Suzanne Augusta (12/11/92)

COLLEGE: University of Houston

SPECIAL INTERESTS: Fishing, hunting

TURNED PROFESSIONAL: 1986

Q-SCHOOL: Fall 1990

PLAYER PROFILE

CAREER EARNINGS: $593,444

TOUR VICTORIES: 1993 Freeport-McMoRan Classic (TOTAL:1)

MONEY & POSITION: 1991-- $55,846--171   1992--$213,712--73   1993--$323,886--49

BEST 1993 FINISHES: 1--Freeport-McMoRan Classic; T5--H-E-B Texas Open.

1993 SUMMARY: Tournaments entered--30; in money--17; top ten finishes--2.

1994 PGA TOUR CHARITY TEAM COMPETITION: Texas Open

1993 SEASON: After 1992 near-miss, when finished T2 behind Chip Beck at English Turn, broke into PGA TOUR win column for first time with one-stroke victory over Russ Cochran and Payne Stewart in Freeport-McMoRan Classic…Carded final-round 67 in coming from two shots off Greg Kraft's 54-hole lead…Triumph provided berth in following week's Masters field, appropriate for someone whose daughter's middle name is "Augusta"…New Orleans triumph came between missed cuts week before in PLAYERS Championship and at Masters…Best finish in nine events leading to New Orleans was a T24 in Honda Classic…Only other top-10 placing, T5 in H-E-B Texas Open, was preceded by two missed cuts and followed by one to close out year…Third-round 65 in homestate tournament at Oak Hills CC his low for year.

CAREER HIGHLIGHTS: Prior to winning Freeport-McMoRan Classic, best finish had been second-place tie at English Turn in 1992…Closed with rounds of 66-69 to finish one shot behind Beck…Made cut in 22 of 29 tournaments in '92…Best previous finish had been T18 in 1991 Phoenix Open…Medalist in 1991 Qualifying Tournament…Played Ben Hogan Tour in 1990, with earnings of $10,446 in 28 events.

PERSONAL: Runnerup 1986 NCAA Championship…1986 All-America…Winner 1984 Boone Links Invitational.

1993 PGA TOUR STATISTICS

Scoring Average	71.40 (109)
Driving Distance	269.9 (22)
Driving Accuracy	64.1 (157)
Greens in Regulation	65.2 (101T)
Putting	1.803 (107T)
All-Around	773 (83)
Sand Saves	50.3 (113T)
Total Driving	179 (78T)
Eagles	8 (25T)
Birdies	297 (61T)

MISCELLANEOUS STATISTICS

Scoring Avg. (before cut)	72.06 (125)
Scoring Avg. (3rd round)	71.13 (86T)
Scoring Avg. (4th round)	71.69 (112)
Birdie Conversion	27.4 (97T)
Par Breakers	18.4 (85T)

1993 Low Round: **65:** H-E-B Texas Open/3
Career Low Round: **63:** 1991 Las Vegas /3
Career Largest
Paycheck: **$180,000**/'93 Freeport-McMoRan/1

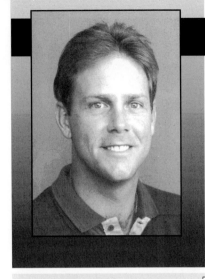

PAYNE STEWART

EXEMPT STATUS: Winner, 1991 U.S. Open

FULL NAME: William Payne Stewart

HEIGHT: 6'1"   **WEIGHT:** 180

BIRTH DATE: Jan. 30, 1957

BIRTHPLACE: Springfield, MO

RESIDENCE: Orlando, FL

FAMILY: Wife, Tracey Ferguson; Chelsea (11/13/85); Aaron (4/2/89)

COLLEGE: Southern Methodist University (1979, Business)

SPECIAL INTERESTS: Hunting, fishing, cooking

TURNED PROFESSIONAL: 1979

Q SCHOOL: Spring 1981

PLAYER PROFILE

CAREER EARNINGS: $6,377,573   **PLAYOFF RECORD:** 1-5

TOUR VICTORIES: **1982** Quad Cities Open. **1983** Walt Disney World Classic. **1987** Hertz Bay Hill Classic. (TOTAL: 8)   **1989** MCI Heritage Classic, PGA Championship. **1990** MCI Heritage Classic, GTE Byron Nelson Classic. **1991** U.S. Open

MONEY & POSITION:

1981--$ 13,400--157	1986--$ 535,389-- 3	1990--$ 976,281-- 3
1982--$ 98,686-- 38	1987--$ 511,026--12	1991--$ 476,971-- 31
1983--$178,809-- 25	1988--$ 553,571--14	1992--$ 334,738-- 44
1984--$288,795-- 11	1989--$1,201,301-- 2	1993--$ 982,875-- 6
1985--$225,729-- 19		

BEST 1993 FINISHES: 2--U.S. Open; T2--Nissan Los Angeles Open; T2--Freeport-McMoRan Classic; T2--Hardee's Golf Classic; 3--Buick Invitational of California; 3--Memorial Tournament; T3--Shell Houston Open; T5--GTE Byron Nelson Classic; T7--Buick Classic; 9--The Masters; T9--AT&T Pebble Beach National Pro-Am; T9--Buick Open.

1993 SUMMARY: Tournaments entered--26; in money--22; top ten finishes--12.

1994 PGA TOUR CHARITY TEAM COMPETITION: Memorial Tournament

NATIONAL TEAMS: Ryder Cup (4), 1987, 1989, 1991, 1993; Kirin Cup, 1987; Asahi Glass Four Tours World Championship of Golf (2), 1989, 1990. World Cup, 1987, 1990. Nissan Cup, 1986.

1993 SEASON: Was $17,125 shy of second million-dollar campaign...Was runnerup finisher four times, including head-to-head battle with Lee Janzen in U.S. Open...Placed third at Memorial, where Paul Azinger holed out from bunker on 72nd hole to supplant him as tournament leader ...Had 12 top-10 finishes for yea...Apart from PGA TOUR, earned three points in Ryder Cup matches, and captained the victorious U.S. Dunhill Cup squad which also included Fred Couples and John Daly...Won third consecutive Skins Game event with $280,000.

CAREER HIGHLIGHTS: Owns victory in two majors, 1989 PGA Championship and 1991 U.S. Open...Won Open in 18-holeplayoff with Scott Simpson 75-77 after both finished 6-under-par 282 at Hazeltine National...Also captured MCI Heritage Classic and lost Nabisco Championship playoff to Tom Kite in '89 to finish second on money list with $1,201,301...Defended Heritage Classic title in 1990, year in which also won GTE Byron Nelson Classic...Donated 1987 Bay Hill Classic winner's check of $108,000 to Florida Hospital Circle of Friends in memory of his father, who died two years before...Missed 10 weeks of 1991 season with nerve problem in neck.

PERSONAL: Member last four Ryder Cup teams (1987-89-91-93)...Member 1987 Kirin Cup, 1989-90 Asahi Glass Four Tours World Championship of Golf, 1987 and '90 World Cup, 1986 Nissan Cup teams...Winner All-Around Category, 1988 Statistics...Winner 1981 Indian and Indonesian Opens on Asian Tour...Winner 1982 Tweed Head Classic (Australia)...Met and married Tracey Ferguson of Australia in Malaysia...Winner 1982 Magnolia Classic...1979 Southwest Conference co-champion...1979 All-America...1979 Missouri Amateur champion...Finished 2-1-1 in 1991-93 Morocco Opens.

1993 PGA TOUR STATISTICS

Scoring Average	69.82 (6)
Driving Distance	269.1 (26T)
Driving Accuracy	69.6 (83T)
Greens in Regulation	69.4 (21T)
Putting	1.765 (16T)
All-Around	266 (2)
Sand Saves	58.4 (24)
Total Driving	109 (15T)
Eagles	5 (67T)
Birdies	365 (8)

MISCELLANEOUS STATISTICS

Scoring Avg. (before cut)	70.02 (5)
Scoring Avg. (3rd round)	70.15 (22)
Scoring Avg. (4th round)	70.55 (25)
Birdie Conversion	30.5 (15T)
Par Breakers	21.4 (7T)

1993 Low Round: 64: Bob Hope Chrysler Classic/3
Career Low Round: 61: 1990 Walt Disney World/Oldsmobile Classic/3
Career Largest Paycheck: $270,000/1989 Nabisco/2

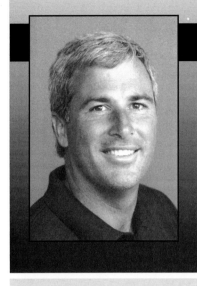

CURTIS STRANGE

EXEMPT STATUS: Winner, 1988 United States Open

FULL NAME: Curtis Northrop Stange

HEIGHT: 5' 11"   **WEIGHT:** 170

BIRTH DATE: January 30, 1955

BIRTHPLACE: Norfolk, VA

RESIDENCE: Kingsmill, VA

FAMILY: Wife Sarah; Thomas Wright III (8/25/82), David Clark (4/3/85)

COLLEGE: Wake Forest University

SPECIAL INTERESTS: Hunting and fishing

TURNED PROFESSIONAL: 1976

Q SCHOOL: Spring 1977

PLAYER PROFILE

CAREER EARNINGS: $6,042,561   **PLAYOFF RECORD:** 6-3

TOUR VICTORIES: **1979** Pensacola Open. **1980** Michelob-Houston Open, Manufacturers Hanover Westch-
(TOTAL: 17)   ester Classic. **1983** Sammy Davis, Jr.-Greater Hartford Open. **1984** LaJet Classic. **1985**
Honda Classic, Panasonic-Las Vegas Invitational, Canadian Open. **1986** Houston
Open. **1987** Canadian Open, Federal Express-St. Jude Classic, NEC World Series of Golf. **1988** Independent
Insurance Agent Open, Memorial Tournament, U.S. Open, Nabisco Championships. **1989** U.S. Open.

MONEY & POSITION:

1977--$ 28,144--87	1983--$ 200,116--21	1989--$ 752,587-- 7
1978--$ 29,346--88	1984--$ 276,773--14	1990--$ 277,172--53
1979--$138,368--21	1985--$ 542,321-- 1	1991--$ 336,333--48
1980--$271,888-- 3	1986--$ 237,700--32	1992--$ 150,639--90
1981--$201,513-- 9	1987--$ 925,941-- 1	1993--$ 262,697--63
1982--$263,378--10	1988--$1,147,644-- 1	

BEST 1993 FINISHES: T3--Anheuser-Busch Golf Classic; T6--New England Classic; T7--Sprint Western
Open; T8--Federal Express St. Jude Classic; T10--Walt Disney World/Oldsmobile Classic.

1993 SUMMARY: Tournaments entered--24; in money--16; top ten finishes--5.

1994 PGA TOUR CHARITY TEAM COMPETITION: Anheuser-Busch Golf Classic

NATIONAL TEAMS: Ryder Cup (4) 1983, 1985, 1987, 1989; Nissan Cup, 1985; Kirin Cup (2) 1987, 1988;
Four Tours Championship, 1989; Dunhill Cup (5), 1987, 1988, 1989, 1990, 1991; World Amateur Team,
1974; Walker Cup, 1975.

1993 SEASON: Rebounded strongly from 1992 season that saw his earnings total fall below $200,000 for first time in 13 years... Seemed to finally have behind him mysterious malady which impacted his play past few years...Posted four consecutive top-10 finishes: Western Open (T7), Anheuser-Busch Golf Classic (T3), New England Classic (T6) and Federal Express St. Jude Classic (T8)...Final top-10 of season came in Walt Disney World/Oldsmobile Classic...T10 was fueled by opening-round 65, matching low round of year.

CAREER HIGHLIGHTS: Won back-to-back U.S. Opens in 1988 and 1989, first to do so since Ben Hogan (1950-51)...1988 Open victory at The Country Club in Brookline, MA, came in playoff with Nick Faldo, 71-75...Captured '89 crown at Oak Hills CC in Rochester, NY...Three-time recipient of Arnold Palmer Award as TOUR's leading money winner (1985, 1987-88)...Became first player to surpass $1 million in yearly earnings in 1988...Biggest payday--$360,000-- came in victory at Nabisco Championships...Had T2 in 1989 PGA Championship...Had seven-year tournament victory streak (1983-89)...Earned first victory since 1989 U.S. Open at Greg Norman Holden Classic in Australia in December.

PERSONAL: Winner 1973 Southeastern Amateur, 1974 NCAA Championship, 1974 Western Amateur, 1975 Eastern Amateur, 1975-76 North and South Amateur, 1975-76 Virginia State Amateur...1974 College Player-of-Year...1985, '87-88 Golf Writers Player-of-Year...1988 PGA Player-of-Year...Winner 1989-90 Skins Games... Winner 1986 ABC Cup (Japan)...Holder of Old Course record (62) at St. Andrews, Scotland, in 1987 Dunhill Cup matches.

1993 PGA TOUR STATISTICS

Scoring Average	70.51	(31T)
Driving Distance	254.7	(142T)
Driving Accuracy	75.5	(19T)
Greens in Regulation	67.2	(57)
Putting	1.769	(24T)
All-Around	663	(55)
Sand Saves	49.5	(125T)
Total Driving	161	(53T)
Eagles	3	(116T)
Birdies	271	(96T)

MISCELLANEOUS STATISTICS

Scoring Avg. (before cut)	71.00	(37T)
Scoring Avg. (3rd round)	70.00	(15T)
Scoring Avg. (4th round)	70.50	(21)
Birdie Conversion	28.6	(58T)
Par Breakers	19.4	(52T)

1993 Low Round: 65: 3 times
Career Low Round: 62: 2 times, most recent '83
Career Largest Sammy Davis Jr./2
Paycheck: $360,000/1988 Nabisco/1

HAL SUTTON

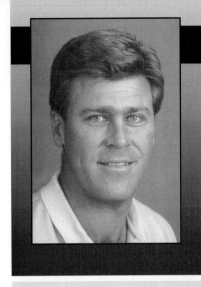

EXEMPT STATUS: Top 50 Career Earnings

FULL NAME: Hal Evan Sutton

HEIGHT: 6' 1"   **WEIGHT:** 185

BIRTH DATE: April 28, 1958

BIRTHPLACE: Shreveport, LA

RESIDENCE: Shreveport, LA

COLLEGE: Centenary College (Business)

SPECIAL INTERESTS: Horses, hunting and fishing

TURNED PROFESSIONAL: 1981

Q SCHOOL: Fall 1981

PLAYER PROFILE

CAREER EARNINGS: $3,391,692   **PLAYOFF RECORD:** 3-1

TOUR VICTORIES: **1982** Walt Disney World Golf Classic. **1983** Tournament Players Championship,
(TOTAL: 7) PGA Championship. **1985** St. Jude Memphis Classic, Southwest Classic. **1986**
Phoenix Open, Memorial Tournament.

MONEY & POSITION:

1982--$237,434--11	1986--$429,434-- 6	1990--$207,084-- 75
1983--$426,668-- 1	1987--$477,996--16	1991--$346,411-- 47
1984--$227,949--26	1988--$137,296--88	1992--$ 39,234--185
1985--$365,340-- 7	1989--$422,703--23	1993--$ 74,144--161

BEST 1993 FINISH: T9--Buick Invitational of California

1993 SUMMARY: Tournaments entered--29; in money--13; top ten finishes--1.

1994 PGA TOUR CHARITY TEAM COMPETITION: Memorial Tournament

NATIONAL TEAMS: USA vs. Japan, 1983; Ryder Cup (2), 1985, 1987.

1993 SEASON: Had encouraging early start, featuring T9 in Buick Invitational of California, his best since T7 in 1991 Greater Milwaukee Open…Final-round 69 at Torrey Pines helped fashion Buick Invitational finish…Earnings of $74,144 almost doubled 1992 total, but 161st place money-list ranking insufficient to renew exempt status after expiration of 10-year exemption for winning 1983 PGA Championship…Instead chose for 1994 to take one-time exemption for being Top-50 on all-time money list (No. 32 entering campaign).

CAREER HIGHLIGHTS: Enjoyed finest year in 1983, his second on TOUR…Finished atop money list with earnings of $426,668 and victories in PGA and Tournament Players Championships…Wire-to-wire PGA effort good for one-shot win over Jack Nicklaus at Riviera CC…Players Championship victory came on TPC at Sawgrass course, just second tournament held at Ponte Vedra layout…Outlasted Bob Eastwood down stretch for win…Defeated Bill Britton in four-hole playoff to win first title in final event of rookie season, 1982 Walt Disney World Classic…Doubled up with wins in last two victory seasons: 1985 St. Jude Memphis and Southwest Classics, 1986 Phoenix Open and Memorial Tournament…Won 1985 Chrysler Team Championship with Raymond Floyd.

PERSONAL: Member 1985, '87 Ryder Cup, 1983 USA vs. Japan teams…1983 PGA and Golf Writers Player-of-Year…Winner 1980 U.S. Amateur…1980 Golf Magazine College Player of Year…Collegiate All-America…runnerup 1981 NCAA Championship…Winner 1974 Louisiana State Juniors.

1993 PGA TOUR STATISTICS

Scoring Average	72.12 (164T)
Driving Distance	256.0 (129)
Driving Accuracy	64.8 (150)
Greens in Regulation	64.2 (129)
Putting	1.798 (95T)
All-Around	1239 (169)
Sand Saves	35.8 (189)
Total Driving	279 (175T)
Eagles	3 (116T)
Birdies	273 (92T)

MISCELLANEOUS STATISTICS

Scoring Avg. (before cut)	72.49 (152T)
Scoring Avg. (3rd round)	72.09 (151T)
Scoring Avg. (4th round)	72.38 (158T)
Birdie Conversion	27.8 (84T)
Par Breakers	18.0 (111T)

1993 Low Round: 66: New England Classic/2
Career Low Round: 62: 1987 Seiko Tucson/2
Career Largest
Paycheck: **$135,000**/1987 Panasonic Las Vegas/2

DOUG TEWELL

EXEMPT STATUS: 117th on1993 money list

FULL NAME: Douglas Fred Tewell

HEIGHT: 5' 10"   **WEIGHT:** 190

BIRTH DATE: August 27, 1949

BIRTHPLACE: Baton Rouge, LA

RESIDENCE: Edmond, OK; plays out of Oak Tree GC

FAMILY: Wife, Pam; Kristi (9/24/69); Jay (3/31/75)

COLLEGE: Oklahoma State University
(1971, Speech-Communications)

SPECIAL INTERESTS: Golf course management & design, family, automobiles

TURNED PROFESSIONAL: 1971

JOINED TOUR: June 1975

PLAYER PROFILE

CAREER EARNINGS: $2,201,210   **PLAYOFF RECORD:** 1-0.

TOUR VICTORIES: **1980** Sea Pines Heritage Classic, IVB-Philadelphia Classic. **1986** Los Angeles Open.
(TOTAL: 4)   **1987** Pensacola Open.

MONEY & POSITION:

1975--$ 1,812--201	1982--$ 78,770--52	1988--$209,196-- 53
1976--$ 3,640--185	1983--$112,367--49	1989--$174,607-- 83
1977--$ 33,162-- 76	1984--$117,988--57	1990--$137,795--112
1978--$ 16,629--113	1985--$137,426--58	1991--$137,360--111
1979--$ 84,500-- 43	1986--$310,285--18	1992--$159,856-- 96
1980--$161,684-- 17	1987--$150,116--71	1993--$132,478--117
1981--$ 41,540-- 94		

BEST 1993 FINISH: T7--Sprint Western Open.

1993 SUMMARY: Tournaments entered--21; in money--11; top ten finishes--1.

1994 PGA TOUR CHARITY TEAM COMPETITION: MCI Heritage Classic

1993 SEASON: Shoulder pain caused premature shutdown to his year after Buick Southern Open, where he finished T36 on Oct. 3...Knew he had retained playing privileges for 1994, so decidedto go home and rest shoulder in order to be ready for fresh start in new year...Enjoyed best tournament of campaign at Cog Hill G&CC in suburban Chicago, where middle rounds of 69-68 over tough Dubsdread Course propelled him to T7 finish in Western Open...Next-best-finish T11 in GTE Byron Nelson Classic, where opened 68-66 before posting back-to-back 70s...Had six top-25 finishes for season, one each month from March to August...Beginning with THE PLAYERS Championship, where finished T20...Opened with consecutive 67s on TPC at Sawgrass Stadium Course and was two shots off Nick Price lead after 36 holes...Closed "streak" by finishing T23 in Federal Express St. Jude Classic, which concluded Aug. 1...Led TOUR in Driving Accuracy for second consecutive year.

CAREER HIGHLIGHTS: Best earnings year 1986, when finished with $310,285 (No. 18)...Season featured third career victory, runaway win over Clarence Rose in Los Angeles Open...Closed with rounds of 66-63 to capture title by seven strokes...Highest money-list placing No. 17 in 1980, with winnings of $161,684...Two-time victor in '80, defeating Jerry Pate in Sea Pines Heritage Classic playoff and scoring come-from-behind win over Tom Kite in IVB-Philadelphia Classic...Most recent TOUR victory three-shot 1987 Pensacola Open triumph over Danny Edwards and Phil Blackmar... Went over $2 million in career earnings with T21 finish at 1992 PLAYERS Championship.

PERSONAL: Winner 1988 Acom Team title (Japan) with Bob Gilder...Winner 1978 South Central PGA, 1971 Tulsa Intercollegiate, 1966 Oklahoma State Junior and Scholastic titles.

1993 PGA TOUR STATISTICS

Scoring Average	70.95 (63T)
Driving Distance	253.4 (151)
Driving Accuracy	82.5 (1)
Greens in Regulation	66.7 (67T)
Putting	1.820 (148T)
All-Around	895 (116)
Sand Saves	52.6 (81T)
Total Driving	152 (41)
Eagles	0
Birdies	189 (160)

MISCELLANEOUS STATISTICS

Scoring Avg. (before cut)	71.85 (107)
Scoring Avg. (3rd round)	71.36 (100T)
Scoring Avg. (4th round)	71.18 (58)
Birdie Conversion	25.0 (159T)
Par Breakers	16.7 (151T)

1993 Low Round: 66: GTE Byron Nelson/2
Career Low Round: 62: 1987 Phoenix Open/3
Career Largest
Paycheck: $81,000/1986 Los Angeles Open/1

DAVID TOMS

EXEMPT STATUS: 123rd on 1993 money list

FULL NAME: David Toms

HEIGHT: 5' 10"   **WEIGHT:** 160

BIRTH DATE: January 4, 1967

BIRTHPLACE: Monroe, LA

RESIDENCE: Bossier City, LA

FAMILY: Wife, Sonya

COLLEGE: Louisiana State University

SPECIAL INTERESTS: Hunting, fishing

TURNED PROFESSIONAL: 1989

Q SCHOOL: Fall 1991

PLAYER PROFILE

CAREER EARNINGS: $ 269,664

BEST-EVER FINISH: 3--1992 Northern Telecom Open.

MONEY & POSITION: 1992--$148,712--101   1993--$120,952--123

BEST 1993 FINISHES: T8--Buick Southern Open; T9--Buick Open; T10--B.C. Open.

1993 SUMMARY: Tournaments entered--32; in money--12; top ten finishes--3.

1994 PGA TOUR CHARITY TEAM COMPETITION: JCPenney Classic

1993 SEASON: Missed 20 of 32 cuts but parlayed top-10 finishes in each of final three months into just over $65,000, salvaging his playing privileges for 1994...Three top-10s were among just four placings in final ten events of season...Had T9 at Buick Open in August...Then, after four straight cuts, in consecutive weeks finished T10 in the B.C. Open last week of September/T8 in the Buick Southern Open first week of October...Keys to back-to-back top-10s were final rounds of 66 at En-Joie GC and 65 over the Callaway Gardens Resort course in Pine Mountain, GA...The 65 his low round of year...Louisiana native finished T15 in Freeport-McMoRan Classic in New Orleans.

CAREER HIGHLIGHTS: Had best finish of two-year career in third start of rookie campaign, solo third in 1992 Northern Telecom Open punctuated by final-round 63...Secured biggest payday of season/career, $74,800...Also had course record-tying 63 to begin '92 Kemper Open...Unique aspect of Kemper round fact that was seeing TPC at Avenel layout for first time...Had been married Saturday before, delaying arrival in D.C. area...The rain and pro-am play precluded any opportunity for practice round...Part of four-way tie for Kemper lead after 36 holes at 8-under 134, but closed 76-73 for T25.

PERSONAL: Qualified for TOUR by placing 24th in 1991 Q-Tournament ...Was third qualifying attempt...1988-89 First-Team All-America at LSU, where teammates included Robert Friend, Emlyn Aubrey, Perry Moss and Greg Lesher...1988 and '89 Southeastern Conference Player of Year...Semifinalist 1988 U.S. Amateur.

1993 PGA TOUR STATISTICS

Statistic	Value	
Scoring Average	72.11	(162T)
Driving Distance	259.1	(93T)
Driving Accuracy	65.5	(136T)
Greens in Regulation	63.6	(137T)
Putting	1.799	(97T)
All-Around	1101	(146)
Sand Saves	40.6	(185)
Total Driving	229	(150T)
Eagles	6	(50T)
Birdies	274	(91)

MISCELLANEOUS STATISTICS

Statistic	Value	
Scoring Avg. (before cut)	72.75	(164)
Scoring Avg. (3rd round)	71.73	(128)
Scoring Avg. (4th round)	72.08	(140)
Birdie Conversion	28.0	(76T)
Par Breakers	18.2	(98T)

1993 Low Round:	**65:** Buick Southern Open/4
Career Low Round:	**63:** 2 times, most recent 1992 Kemper Open/1
Career Largest Paycheck:	**$74,800**/1992 Northern Telecom Open/3

KIRK TRIPLETT

EXEMPT STATUS: 90th on 1993 money list

FULL NAME: Kirk Alan Triplett

HEIGHT: 6' 3"   **WEIGHT:** 200

BIRTH DATE: March 29, 1962

BIRTHPLACE: Moses Lake, WA

RESIDENCE: Nashville, TN

FAMILY: Wife, Cathi

COLLEGE: University of Nevada (1985, Civil Engineering)

SPECIAL INTERESTS: Basketball, reading, computers

TURNED PROFESSIONAL: 1985

Q SCHOOL: Fall 1989

PLAYER PROFILE

CAREER EARNINGS: $ 686,051

BEST-EVER FINISH: 2--1992 Shell Houston Open

MONEY & POSITION: 1990--$183,464-- 88   1992--$175,868--85   1993--$189,418--90
1991--$137,302--112

BEST 1993 FINISH: T3--Phoenix Open; T7--BellSouth Classic.

1993 SUMMARY: Tournaments entered--27; in money--19; top ten finishes--2.

1994 PGA TOUR CHARITY TEAM COMPETITION: Bob Hope Chrysler Classic

1993 SEASON: Had best finish in second start, T3 in Phoenix Open worth $48,000 that provided impetus toward best earnings campaign of four years on TOUR…Shared first-round PLAYERS Championship lead with Nick Price after opening 64, but skyed to 78 in Round 2 on TPC at Sawgrass Stadium Course and eventually finished T39…Recorded another 64, matching career low, in final round of BellSouth Classic…That finish produced T7 in Atlanta event, his only other top-10 of year.

CAREER HIGHLIGHTS: Best finish came in 1992 Shell Houston Open, where final-round 67 brought him to within two strokes of Fred Funk's winning 272 total…Rounds of 68-70-69-67--274 were good for runnerup check of $129,600 in $1.2 million event at TPC at The Woodlands…Placed third in TOUR rookie earnings in 1990 with $183,464, trailing only Robert Gamez ($461,407) and Peter Persons ($218,505)…Had solo third in '90 Buick Classic after holding first-round lead with 6-under-par 65…Fell back with second-round 74 at Westchester CC before closing 67-66…Earlier in 1990 finished fourth in Shearson Lehman Hutton Open…Top 1991 finish T11 in Shearson Lehman Brothers Open…Closed '91 with T12 in Independent Insurance Agent Open.

PERSONAL: Played Australian, Asian and Canadian Tours 1987-89…Winner 1988 Alberta Open, Sierra Nevada Open, Ft. McMurray Classic…says of foreign tours play: "I wouldn't trade the experience for anything…I learned so much, not only about golf but about myself…I'll be telling stories about Asia until the day I die"…Wife Cathi occasionally caddies for him.

1993 PGA TOUR STATISTICS

Scoring Average	70.98 (67)
Driving Distance	255.6 (132T)
Driving Accuracy	72.3 (54T)
Greens in Regulation	67.6 (50)
Putting	1.780 (47T)
All-Around	553 (33)
Sand Saves	54.9 (53)
Total Driving	186 (94T)
Eagles	9 (16T)
Birdies	310 (40T)

MISCELLANEOUS STATISTICS

Scoring Avg. (before cut)	71.36 (68)
Scoring Avg. (3rd round)	70.89 (66T)
Scoring Avg. (4th round)	71.35 (80T)
Birdie Conversion	27.7 (89T)
Par Breakers	19.3 (55T)

1993 Low Round: 64: 2 times
Career Low Round: 64: 3 times, most recent 1993 BellSouth Classic/4
Career Largest Paycheck: $129,600/1992 Shell Houston Open/2

TED TRYBA

EXEMPT STATUS: 116th on 1993 money list

FULL NAME: Ted N. Tryba

HEIGHT: 6' 4" **WEIGHT:** 205

BIRTH DATE: January 15, 1967

BIRTHPLACE: Wilkes-Barre, PA

RESIDENCE: Orlando, FL

COLLEGE: Ohio State University (1989, Marketing)

SPECIAL INTERESTS: Basketball

TURNED PROFESSIONAL: 1989

Q SCHOOL: Fall 1989

PLAYER PROFILE

CAREER EARNINGS: $147,377

BEST-EVER FINISH: T3--1993 Walt Disney World/Oldsmobile Classic

MONEY & POSITION: 1990--$10,708--226   1993--$136,670   116

BEST 1993 FINISHES: T3--Walt Disney World/Oldsmobile Classic; T8--Anheuser-Busch Golf Classic.

1993 SUMMARY: Tournaments entered--33; in money--16; top ten finishes--2.

1994 PGA TOUR CHARITY TEAM COMPETITION: Buick Invitational of California

---

1993 SEASON: A T3 in his third-to-last event, Walt Disney World/Oldsmobile Golf Classic, provided retention of playing privileges for 1994...Opening 64 at Disney propelled to three-way share of lead with Keith Clearwater and Tom Purtzer...Held share of second place after 36 and 54 holes before closing with 71...$52,800 payday secured place in top 125 en route to final finish at No. 116...Disney 64 low round of fledgling PGA TOUR career...Previous best 65 in Round 2 of Anheuser-Busch Golf Classic, where finished T8 for only other top-10 of season...Next-best placing T26 at Nissan Los Angeles Open, where carded three even-par 71s...Had T27 at Buick Open, with back-to-back middle rounds of 69...Made cut in three of final four starts, 16 of 33 overall.

CAREER HIGHLIGHTS: Gained PGA TOUR card in first attempt in 1989...Lost card after finishing 226th on money list in 1990, with earnings of $10,708 ...Also played Ben Hogan Tour in '90...Won 1990 Gateway Open to finish 42nd on Hogan Tour money list...Won 1991 Hogan Utah Classic...Earned $46,490 to finish 16th on Hogan money list...Regained TOUR card by finishing fourth on 1992 Hogan list with earnings of $105,951... Won Shreveport Open to become only player to win three consecutive years on Hogan (now NIKE) Tour...Followed that victory with triumph in Macon Open...Earned Top Five spot (and TOUR card) by shooting 69 on final day of season to finish T3 in Fresno Open...Tied for first on Hogan Tour eagles with 12 in '92.

PERSONAL: Four-time All-Big Ten and three-time NCAA All-America at Ohio State...Pennsylvania State High School Champion.

1993 PGA TOUR STATISTICS

Scoring Average	71.69 (132)
Driving Distance	262.1 (68T)
Driving Accuracy	68.0 (96T)
Greens in Regulation	65.0 (110T)
Putting	1.794 (82T)
All-Around	728 (72)
Sand Saves	54.3 (60)
Total Driving	164 (60T)
Eagles	4 (89T)
Birdies	317 (31T)

MISCELLANEOUS STATISTICS

Scoring Avg. (before cut)	72.23 (138T)
Scoring Avg. (3rd round)	70.85 (62)
Scoring Avg. (4th round)	71.80 (119T)
Birdie Conversion	28.8 (53T)
Par Breakers	19.0 (67T)

1993 Low Round: **64:** WDW/Oldsmobile Classic/1
Career Low Round: **64:** 1993 WDW/Oldsmobile Classic/1
Career Largest Paycheck: **$52,800**/'93 WDW/Oldsmobile Classic/T3

BOB TWAY

EXEMPT STATUS: Winner, 1986 PGA Championship

FULL NAME: Robert Raymond Tway

HEIGHT: 6' 4"   **WEIGHT:** 180

BIRTH DATE: May 4, 1959

BIRTHPLACE: Oklahoma City, OK

RESIDENCE: Edmond, OK; plays out of Oak Tree Golf Club

FAMILY: Wife, Tammie; Kevin (7/23/88),
          Carly Paige (11/8/93)

COLLEGE: Oklahoma State University

SPECIAL INTERESTS: Snow skiing, fishing, all sports

TURNED PROFESSIONAL: 1981

Q SCHOOL: Fall 1984

PLAYER PROFILE

CAREER EARNINGS: $ 2,914,016   **PLAYOFF RECORD:** 2-3

TOUR VICTORIES: **1986** Shearson Lehman Bros.-Andy Williams Open, Manufacturers Hanover
(TOTAL: 6)   Westchester Classic, Georgia Pacific Atlanta Classic, PGA Championship. **1989**
          Memorial Tournament. **1990** Las Vegas Invitational.

MONEY & POSITION:
1985--$164,023--45	1988--$381,966--29	1991--$322,931-- 52
1986--$652,780-- 2	1989--$488,340--17	1992--$ 47,632--179
1987--$212,362--47	1990--$495,862--23	1993--$148,120--109

BEST 1993 FINISHES: 4--Hardee's Golf Classic; T6--Las Vegas Invitational.

1993 SUMMARY: Tournaments entered--25; in money--11; top ten finishes--2.

1994 PGA TOUR CHARITY TEAM COMPETITION: Mercedes Championships

NATIONAL TEAMS: World Amateur Cup, 1980; Nissan Cup, 1986.

1993 SEASON: After struggling through worst season of eight-year career in 1992, continued to flounder first half of campaign… Following T15 at Honda Classic, best finish since 1991, proceeded to miss eight consecutive cuts and 11-of-14…However, two top-10s near year's end may have provided evidence he's back on track …Solo fourth in Hardee's Golf Classic, highest finish since he and Tom Purtzer tied for second behind amateur Phil Mickelson in 1991 Northern Telecom Open, featured four sub-70 rounds, including closing 65…Concluded campaign with T6 in Las Vegas Invitational, carding rounds of 68-68-67-68 after an opening 70…Jumped from 142 to 109 on money list with that performance…Improved money-list finish 70 places over 1992.

CAREER HIGHLIGHTS: Enjoyed dream sophomore season in 1986, collecting four victories, including PGA Championship…Won PGA title by holing out from bunker on 72nd hole at Inverness to defeat Greg Norman…Went on to be named PGA Player of Year and finished No. 2 on money list, just $516 behind Norman…Defeated Fuzzy Zoeller by two strokes in 1989 Memorial Tournament and parred first playoff hole to edge John Cook in 1990 Las Vegas Invitational…Finished in top-10 in four of first five 1991 tournament starts…Included was T2 with Purtzer in Northern Telecom Open.

PERSONAL: Member 1986 Nissan Cup, 1980 World Amateur Cup teams…Three-time All-America selection at Oklahoma State (1979-81)…Winner 1981 Fred Haskins Trophy as outstanding collegiate player…Member 1978, '80 NCAA Championship teams…Winner 1978 Trans-Mississippi Amateur, 1979 Southern Amateur, 1983 Sandpiper-Santa Barbara Open (TPS Series), 1987 Oklahoma State Open…Winner 1987 Chrysler Team Championship (with Mike Hulbert), 1988 Fred Meyer Challenge (with Paul Azinger).

1993 PGA TOUR STATISTICS

Scoring Average	72.05 (157)
Driving Distance	253.3 (152)
Driving Accuracy	56.9 (186)
Greens in Regulation	61.2 (169)
Putting	1.788 (65T)
All-Around	1300 (177)
Sand Saves	53.0 (75T)
Total Driving	338 (187)
Eagles	1 (164T)
Birdies	211 (145T)

MISCELLANEOUS STATISTICS

Scoring Avg. (before cut)	72.94 (171)
Scoring Avg. (3rd round)	72.00 (139T)
Scoring Avg. (4th round)	71.73 (114T)
Birdie Conversion	28.2 (69T)
Par Breakers	17.3 (133T)

1993 Low Round: 65: Hardee's Golf Classic/4
Career Low Round: 61: 1989 Walt Disney /1
Career Largest
Paycheck: $234,000/1990 Las Vegas /1

GREG TWIGGS

EXEMPT STATUS: 72nd on 1993 money list

FULL NAME: Gregory Wofford Twiggs

HEIGHT: 6' 2"   **WEIGHT:** 235

BIRTH DATE: October 31, 1960

BIRTHPLACE: Los Angeles, CA

RESIDENCE: Greensboro, NC

FAMILY: Wife, Teresa; Amber Alexandra (10/16/87); Tianna (7/20/90)

COLLEGE: San Diego State University

SPECIAL INTERESTS: Peace of mind

TURNED PROFESSIONAL: 1984

Q SCHOOL: Fall 1984, 1986, 1988

PLAYER PROFILE

CAREER EARNINGS: $672,083

TOUR VICTORIES: 1989 Shearson Lehman Hutton Open
(TOTAL:1)

MONEY & POSITION:

1985--$33,559--139	1988--$ 2,999--262	1991--$ 65,080--158
1986--$41,418--147	1989--$154,302-- 90	1992--$ 74,761--153
1987--$21,443--186	1990--$ 49,696--178	1993--$231,823-- 72

BEST 1993 FINISHES: T3--AT&T Pebble Beach National Pro-Am; T4--Buick Invitational of California; T6--Nissan Los Angeles Open.

1993 SUMMARY: Tournaments entered--29; in money--16; top ten finishes--3.

1994 PGA TOUR CHARITY TEAM COMPETITION: Kmart Greater Greensboro Open

1993 SEASON: Enjoyed finest campaign of nine-year PGA TOUR career, both in terms of earnings and money-list finish...Ranked 72nd with $231,823, $77,521 more than best previous season (1989)...Lion's share of earnings--$151,167--came in first six events of year...After missed cut in United Airlines Hawaiian Open, had three top-10s in next five starts...Success streak began with T3 AT&T Pebble Beach National Pro-Am...After T42 in Bob Hope Chrysler Classic, went T4 Buick Invitational of California and T6 Nissan Los Angeles Open last two weeks of February.

CAREER HIGHLIGHTS: Lone TOUR victory came in 1989 Shearson Lehman Hutton Open...Lived in San Diego area and had played Torrey Pines on many occasions...Win also after he finished 52nd (final qualifier) at 1988 Qualifying Tournament...Recorded 64 in third round, then closed with 69 for three-stroke victory...Winner's check of $126,000, largest TOUR payday to date, also surpassed earnings total for first four years...Finished in four-way tie for second in 1992 Deposit Guaranty Golf Classic...Shared first-round lead at Hattiesburg CC after opening 65, was two shots off lead after 54 holes...Finished one stroke behind winner Richard Zokol after closing 69...62 in 1984 Provident Classic lowest score in history of old Tournament Players Series.

PERSONAL: As youngster excelled in various sports...Member of 1976 United States Junior World Hockey team...Also played American Legion baseball...1982-83 All-America at San Diego State...Winner 1984 California State Open...Winner several mini-tour events.

1993 PGA TOUR STATISTICS

Scoring Average	71.24 (93T)
Driving Distance	265.0 (51T)
Driving Accuracy	65.1 (145T)
Greens in Regulation	66.9 (64T)
Putting	1.791 (74T)
All-Around	688 (60)
Sand Saves	52.5 (83T)
Total Driving	196 (109)
Eagles	8 (25T)
Birdies	308 (44T)

MISCELLANEOUS STATISTICS

Scoring Avg. (before cut)	71.90 (111T)
Scoring Avg. (3rd round)	70.40 (33)
Scoring Avg. (4th round)	71.56 (100T)
Birdie Conversion	28.7 (56T)
Par Breakers	19.7 (43T)

1993 Low Round: 67: 5 times
Career Low Round: 64: 1989 Shearson Lehman Hutton Open/3
Career Largest Paycheck: $126,000/1989 Shearson Lehman Hutton Open/1

HOWARD TWITTY

EXEMPT STATUS: 1993 tournament winner

FULL NAME: Howard Allen Twitty

HEIGHT: 6' 5" **WEIGHT:** 210

BIRTH DATE: Jan. 15, 1949

BIRTHPLACE: Phoenix, AZ

RESIDENCE: Paradise Valley, AZ

FAMILY: Wife, Sheree; Kevin Scott (10/2/76); Jocelyn Noel (11/20/80); Charles Barnes Barris (6/7/89); Mary Caroline Claire (9/11/90); Alicia Anne Marie (1/22/92)

COLLEGE: Arizona State University (1972, Business Administration)

SPECIAL INTERESTS: All sports

TURNED PROFESSIONAL: 1974 **Q SCHOOL:** Spring 1975

PLAYER PROFILE

CAREER EARNINGS: $2,393,071　　　**PLAYOFF RECORD:** 1-0

TOUR VICTORIES:　**1979** B. C. Open. **1980** Sammy Davis, Jr.-Greater Hartford Open.
(TOTAL: 3)　　　　　**1993** United Airlines Hawaiian Open.

MONEY & POSITION:

1975--$ 8,211--139	1982--$ 57,355-- 78	1988--$ 87,985--119
1976--$ 54,268-- 51	1983--$ 20,000--150	1989--$107,200--119
1977--$ 60,091-- 49	1984--$ 51,971--106	1990--$129,444--120
1978--$ 92,409-- 25	1985--$ 92,958-- 82	1991--$ 226,426-- 74
1979--$179,619-- 15	1986--$156,119-- 57	1992--$ 264,042-- 57
1980--$166,190-- 14	1987--$169,442-- 61	1993--$ 416,833-- 34
1981--$ 52,183-- 79		

BEST 1993 FINISHES: 1--United Airlines Hawaiian Open; T6--Nissan Los Angeles Open.

1993 SUMMARY: Tournaments entered--29; in money--20; top ten finishes--2.

1994 PGA TOUR CHARITY TEAM COMPETITION: Phoenix Open

1993 SEASON: Scored popular victory in first start of year in January, capturing United Airlines Hawaiian Open...Established PGA TOUR record for longest period of time between victories, 12 years and seven months...Last previous win had been in Sammy Davis, Jr.-Greater Hartford Open in 1980...Surpassed previous standard held by Leonard Thompson of 12 years...Hawaii victory third of career...Opened at Waialae CC with 9-under-par 63, low start of year by winner (later matched by Jim Gallagher, Jr., at THE TOUR Championship)...Round 2 65 in Texas Open featured hole-in-one on his final shot of round, enabling him to make cut...Had two top-10 finishes on year...Concluded February with T6 in Nissan Los Angeles Open...Raised money-won figure for fifth consecutive season.

CAREER HIGHLIGHTS: Best money list finish No. 14 in 1980 (sixth year on TOUR), when earned $166,190...Summer of '80 featured run of 13-of-14 rounds in 60s with cumulative total of 57-under-par...Hot streak included Sammy Davis, Jr.-Greater Hartford Open playoff victory over Jim Simons, second-place finish at Greater Milwaukee Open, fifth at Hardee's Golf Classic, and opening rounds of 64-66 at IVB-Philadelphia Classic...Posted first TOUR victory in 1979 B.C. Open, holding off Doug Tewell and Tom Purtzer down stretch...Went over $200,000 in season earnings for first time in 1991, year which featured 11 consecutive cuts made and five straight events in which finished no worse than 20th.

PERSONAL: Collaborated with Roger Maltbie on course redesign of TPC at River Highlands...Player director on PGA TOUR Policy Board 1981-82...Played Asian Tour, winning 1975 Thailand Open...Winner 1970 Sunnehanna and Porter Cup events...1970, '72 All-American at Arizona State.

1993 PGA TOUR STATISTICS

Scoring Average	70.70 (43)
Driving Distance	268.7 (30T)
Driving Accuracy	67.4 (106T)
Greens in Regulation	65.0 (110T)
Putting	1.779 (46)
All-Around	572 (37)
Sand Saves	49.4 (127T)
Total Driving	136 (31T)
Eagles	6 (50T)
Birdies	323 (29)

MISCELLANEOUS STATISTICS

Scoring Avg. (before cut)	71.13 (47)
Scoring Avg. (3rd round)	71.72 (127)
Scoring Avg. (4th round)	70.53 (23)
Birdie Conversion	30.0 (21T)
Par Breakers	19.9 (37T)

1993 Low Round: 63: United Airlines Hawaiian Open/1
Career Low Round: 62: 2 times, most recent 1990 Buick Southern Open/1
Career Largest Paycheck: $216,000/1993 United Airlines Hawaiian Open/1

STAN UTLEY

EXEMPT STATUS: 3rd on 1993 NIKE TOUR money list

FULL NAME: Stanley Frank Utley

HEIGHT: 6"   **WEIGHT:** 170

BIRTH DATE: January 16, 1962

BIRTHPLACE: Thayer, MO

RESIDENCE: Colombia, MO; Plays out of CC of Missouri

FAMILY: Wife, Elayna

COLLEGE: Missouri (1984, Business Administration)

SPECIAL INTERESTS: Church, basketball, hunting, fishing

TURNED PROFESSIONAL: 1984

Q SCHOOL: Fall 1988

PLAYER PROFILE

CAREER EARNINGS: $411,188

TOUR VICTORIES: 1988 Chattanooga Classic
(TOTAL: 1)

MONEY & POSITION:

1989--$107,400--118	1991--$127,849--115	1993--$ 17,371--223
1990--$143,604--108	1992--$ 14,964--222	

BEST 1993 FINISH: T10--Deposit Guaranty Golf Classic.

1993 SUMMARY: Tournaments entered--5; in money--4; top ten finishes--1.

1994 PGA TOUR CHARITY TEAM COMPETITION: GTE Byron Nelson Classic

1993 NIKE TOUR SEASON: Victory in $250,000 Cleveland Open, richest NIKE TOUR event of 1993, earned him $49,500 and moved him to second on money list behind Sean Murphy...Took money list lead away from Murphy following week and held the top spot for much of the remaining season...Never lower than third on money list after Cleveland win...Posted five other top-three finishes during 1993: T2 at Monterrey; 3rd at Shreveport; T3 in Connecticut; 2nd at Dakota Dunes and 2nd at Tri-Cities.

OTHER ACHIEVEMENTS: Victory at 1989 Chattanooga Classic best-ever finish...Played in five PGA TOUR events in 1993 in addition to NIKE TOUR schedule, finishing in money four times with T10 at Deposit Guaranty Classic best outing...Three-time All-Big Eight selection and twice an All-American at Missouri...Winner 1986 Kansas Open, 1988 & '89 Missouri Open and 1980 Missouri Junior Championship.

PERSONAL: Began playing golf at age nine with help of his father...A big supporter of University of Missouri athletics...Served as volunteer in the flood relief efforts in Rocheport, MO (Missouri River)..."One night I was down there bagging sand with only about 30 other people, when we needed a couple of hundred...It was difficult experience working alongside folks who were trying to save their homes and possessions."...His annual "Go For The Gold" Skins Game (featuring fellow PGA TOUR members) in Columbia has been benefitting Rainbow House, a safe house for children in Columbia, since 1991.

1993 PGA TOUR STATISTICS

Scoring Average	N/A
Driving Distance	N/A
Driving Accuracy	N/A
Greens in Regulation	N/A
Putting	N/A
All-Around	N/A
Sand Saves	N/A
Total Driving	N/A
Eagles	N/A
Birdies	N/A

MISCELLANEOUS STATISTICS

Scoring Avg. (before cut)	N/A
Scoring Avg. (3rd round)	N/A
Scoring Avg. (4th round)	N/A
Birdie Conversion	N/A
Par Breakers	N/A

1993 Low Round: **66:** Deposit Guaranty/2
Career Low Round: **64:** 4 times, most recent
Career Largest 1991 Kemper Open/3
Paycheck: $90,000/1989 Chattanooga Classic/1

LANNY WADKINS

EXEMPT STATUS: 1992 tournament winner

FULL NAME: Jerry Lanston Wadkins

HEIGHT: 5' 9" **WEIGHT:** 170

BIRTH DATE: Dec. 5, 1949

BIRTHPLACE: Richmond, VA

RESIDENCE: Dallas, TX; plays out of Mauna Lani, HI

FAMILY: Wife, Penelope; Jessica (10/14/73); Travis (8/25/87); Tucker (8/19/92)

COLLEGE: Wake Forest University

SPECIAL INTERESTS: Fishing, hunting, snow skiing, scuba-diving.

TURNED PROFESSIONAL: 1971

Q SCHOOL: Fall 1971

PLAYER PROFILE

CAREER EARNINGS: $5,877,257　　　**PLAYOFF RECORD:** 3-2

TOUR VICTORIES: **1972** Sahara Invitational. **1973** Byron Nelson Classic, USI Classic. **1977** PGA Championship, World Series of Golf. **1979** Glen Campbell Los Angeles Open, Tournament Players Championship. **1982** Phoenix Open, MONY--Tournament of Champions, Buick Open. **1983** Greater Greensboro Open, MONY--Tournament of Champions. **1985** Bob Hope Classic, Los Angeles Open, Walt Disney World/Oldsmobile Classic. **1987** Doral-Ryder Open. **1988** Hawaiian Open, Colonial National Invitation. **1990** Anheuser-Busch Golf Classic. **1991** United Hawaiian Open. **1992** Canon Greater Hartford Open.
(TOTAL: 21)

MONEY & POSITION:

1971--$ 15,291--111	1979--$195,710--10	1987--$501,727--13
1972--$116,616-- 10	1980--$ 67,778--58	1988--$616,596--10
1973--$200,455-- 5	1981--$ 51,704--81	1989--$233,363--60
1974--$ 51,124-- 54	1982--$306,827-- 7	1990--$673,433--13
1975--$ 23,582-- 88	1983--$319,271-- 3	1991--$651,495--12
1976--$ 42,849-- 64	1984--$198,996--29	1992--$366,837--40
1977--$244,882-- 3	1985--$446,893-- 2	1993--$244,544--68
1978--$ 53,811-- 61	1986--$264,931--23	

BEST 1993 FINISHES: T3--The Masters; T3--Anheuser-Busch Golf Classic.

1993 SUMMARY: Tournaments entered--22; in money--12; top ten finishes--2.

1994 PGA TOUR CHARITY TEAM COMPETITION: Doral-Ryder Open

NATIONAL TEAMS: Ryder Cup (8), 1977, 1979, 1983, 1985, 1987, 1989, 1991; 1993 World Cup (3), 1977, 1984, 1985; Walker Cup (2) 1969, 1971; World Amateur Cup, 1970; U.S. vs. Japan (2), 1982, 1983; Nissan Cup, 1985; Kirin Cup 1987.

1993 SEASON: Battled system infection from Kmart Greater Greensboro Open in April through to early summer...Rebounded with T3 at Anheuser-Busch Golf Classic, featuring third-round 64, low round of season (later matched)...Injured his back after PGA Championship, placing in jeopardy his ability to play Ryder Cup...Captain's choice for team, pairing with Corey Pavin for pair of team wins in opening day of Cup competition...Volunteered to have Tom Watson place his name in envelope as non-playing Sunday participant...Earlier in year had Masters T3 with Tom Lehman, John Daly and Steve Elkington at 283, six strokes behind Bernhard Langer...Followed up Augusta National performance with T12 at MCI Heritage Classic, after opening with a 66.

CAREER HIGHLIGHTS: Captured 21st title in 22nd year on TOUR, winning Canon Greater Hartford Open in August 1992...Birdied five of first seven holes to come from five strokes off lead for win...Named PGA Player of the Year in 1985, when he won three times...Had highest money list finish that year, No. 2...Won 1977 PGA Championship in playoff with Gene Littler, then won World Series of Golf...Claimed 1979 Tournament Players Championship in fierce winds on Sawgrass course, scoring five-stroke victory over Tom Watson.

PERSONAL: One of TOUR's fiercest competitors...Member of eight Ryder Cup teams (1977-79-83-85-87-89-91-93)...Member 1977, '84, '85 World Cup, 1969, '71 Walker Cup, 1970 World Amateur Cup, 1982-83 U.S. vs. Japan, 1985 Nissan Cup, 1987 Kirin Cup teams...Winner 1963-64 National Pee-Wee, 1970 U.S. Amateur, 1970 Western Amateur, 1968 and '70 Southern Amateur, 1969 Eastern Amateur...1970-71 All-America...Won 1978 Canadian PGA and Garden State PGA(Australia), 1979 Bridgestone Open (Japan), 1984 World Nissan Championship (Japan), 1990 Fred Meyer Challenge with (Bobby Wadkins).

1993 PGA TOUR STATISTICS

Scoring Average	71.28 (98)
Driving Distance	251.2 (170T)
Driving Accuracy	72.4 (52T)
Greens in Regulation	67.1 (58T)
Putting	1.764 (14T)
All-Around	885 (112)
Sand Saves	44.2 (176)
Total Driving	222 (141T)
Eagles	6 (50T)
Birdies	248 (126)

MISCELLANEOUS STATISTICS

Scoring Avg. (before cut)	71.24 (61)
Scoring Avg. (3rd round)	69.83 (8T)
Scoring Avg. (4th round)	72.00 (133T)
Birdie Conversion	29.3 (37T)
Par Breakers	20.2 (28T)

1993 Low Round: 64: 2 times

Career Low Round: 62: 1989 Texas Open

Career Largest Presented by Nabisco/1

Paycheck: $198,000/'91 Hawaiian Open/1

GRANT WAITE

EXEMPT STATUS: 1993 tournament winner

FULL NAME: Grant Osten Waite

HEIGHT: 6'   **WEIGHT:** 185

BIRTH DATE: August 11, 1964

BIRTHPLACE: Palmerston, New Zealand

RESIDENCE: Palmerston North, New Zealand

COLLEGE: University of Oklahoma

SPECIAL INTERESTS: Wind surfing, reading, skiing, fitness

TURNED PROFESSIONAL: 1987

Q SCHOOL: Fall 1989, 1992

PLAYER PROFILE

CAREER EARNINGS: $461,481

TOUR VICTORIES: 1993 Kemper Open.
(TOTAL: 1)

MONEY & POSITION: 1990--$50,076--177   1993--$411,405--35

BEST 1993 FINISH: 1--Kemper Open; T4--Deposit Guaranty Golf Classic; T7--AT&T Pebble Beach National Pro-Am; 10--NEC World Series of Golf.

1993 SUMMARY: Tournaments entered--30; in money--16; top ten finishes--4.

1994 PGA TOUR CHARITY TEAM COMPETITION: MCI Heritage Classic

1993 SEASON: After playing TOUR with limited success in 1990, had successful return engagement in '93 after finishing T20 in 1992 Qualifying Tournament ...Captured first TOUR victory in head-to-head battle with Tom Kite...Was first- and second-round leader after rounds of 66-67 before giving way to Kite at 54-hole juncture following third-round 72...Held steady in face of pressure from TOUR's all-time money leader, carding final-round 70 to Kite's 72 for one-shot win...Opened season with pair of missed cuts, then posted T7 at AT&T Pebble Beach National Pro-Am for first of four top-10s on year...Was leader in clubhouse following final-round 63 in Deposit Guaranty Golf Classic, his career low round...Ultimately finished T4, two shots behind winner Greg Kraft...Final top-10 finish came in NEC World Series of Golf, where made ten-stroke improvement over third-round score with closing 65 ...Missed cut in three of final five events of year as he attempted to make TOUR Championship field, ultimately falling four places short (No. 35) ...Finished T19 in final event of year, Las Vegas Invitational, where closed with 72 after going 69-69-69-68 in first four rounds.

CAREER HIGHLIGHTS: Prior to 1993 season his best finish had been T6 in 1990 Hawaiian Open...Finished with 282 total, three strokes behind winner David Ishii...Ranked 25th at 1989 Qualifying Tournament...Winner 1992 New Zealand Open.

PERSONAL: Selected by CBS as "New Breed Player of Year" for 1993...Two-time Australian Junior Champion...Three-time All-American at Oklahoma.

1993 PGA TOUR STATISTICS

Scoring Average	71.18 (86T)
Driving Distance	264.0 (59T)
Driving Accuracy	68.0 (96T)
Greens in Regulation	65.4 (92T)
Putting	1.804 (109)
All-Around	788 (86)
Sand Saves	53.1 (72T)
Total Driving	155 (45)
Eagles	1 (164T)
Birdies	294 (65)

MISCELLANEOUS STATISTICS

Scoring Avg. (before cut)	71.97 (119)
Scoring Avg. (3rd round)	71.67 (122T)
Scoring Avg. (4th round)	71.06 (48T)
Birdie Conversion	27.8 (84T)
Par Breakers	18.2 (98T)

1993 Low Round: 63: Deposit Guaranty/4
Career Low Round: 63: 2 times, most recent
Career Largest 1993 Deposit Guaranty/ 4
Paycheck: $234,000: 1993 Kemper Open/1

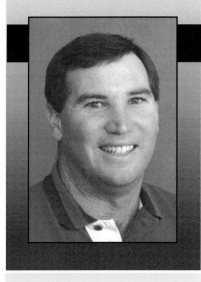

DUFFY WALDORF

EXEMPT STATUS: 84th on 1993 money list

HEIGHT: 5' 11" **WEIGHT:** 225

BIRTH DATE: August 20, 1962

BIRTHPLACE: Los Angeles, CA

RESIDENCE: Valencia, CA

FAMILY: Wife, Vicky; Tyler Lane (7/16/90); Shea Duffy (4/23/92)

COLLEGE: UCLA (1985, Psychology)

SPECIAL INTERESTS: Colorful hats & clothes, wine collecting, football, music.

TURNED PROFESSIONAL: 1985

Q SCHOOL: Fall 1986, 1987, 1988, 1990

PLAYER PROFILE

CAREER EARNINGS: $1,312,854

BEST EVER FINISH: 2--1992 Phoenix Open, 2--1992 Buick Classic

MONEY & POSITION:		
1987--$ 53,175--148	1990--$ 71,673--157	1992--$582,120--23
1988--$ 55,221--143	1991--$196,081-- 86	1993--$202,638--84
1989--$149,945-- 94		

BEST 1993 FINISHES: T4--Southwestern Bell Colonial; T9--United Airlines Hawaiian Open; T10--Freeport-McMoRan Classic; T10--Buick Classic.

1993 SUMMARY: Tournaments entered--25; in money--15; top ten finishes--4.

1994 PGA TOUR CHARITY TEAM COMPETITION: Nestle Invitational

1993 SEASON: Fell off from exceptional 1992 campaign, but still finished with second-best season of his seven-year career…Opened with T9 in United Airlines Hawaiian Open, then had next top-10 finish in April at Freeport-McMoRan Classic (T10)…Carded first-round 65 in Southwestern Bell Colonial, just one shot off Dick Mast's opening pace, then closed with another 65 to finish T4…Best shot at winning in '93 came in Buick Classic…Had share of second- and third-round leads at Westchester CC before final 75 dropped him to T10, four strokes behind Vijay Singh.

CAREER HIGHLIGHTS: Had pair of career-best second-place finishes in 1992, at Phoenix Open and in Buick Classic…Finished five shots behind Phoenix winner Mark Calcavecchia after closing with three 67s…Held or shared second place for last three rounds of Buick Classic, which David Frost won by eight strokes…Held mid-point lead in '92 Western Open, where finished T3…Also had rain-delayed 54-hole lead at Kemper Open that season before falling back to T13…Began 1992 with 19 consecutive rounds of par or better, closed with top-10 finishes in two of final three events, fifth at Walt Disney World/Oldsmobile Classic, seventh in TOUR Championship… Finished two strokes behind Fulton Allem in 1991 Independent Insurance Agent Open…Tied for third-round lead in 1991 Kmart Greater Greensboro Open after course-record tying 63, finished four strokes behind Mark Brooks …Qualifying Tournament medalist his fourth time through in 1990.

PERSONAL: Colorful cap and shirt combinations make him easy to spot on course…Winner 1984 California State Amateur, 1984 Broadmoor Invitational, 1985 Rice Planters (Charleston, SC)…Winner nine college tournaments …1985 College Player of Year at UCLA…1985 All-American.

1993 PGA TOUR STATISTICS

Statistic	Value
Scoring Average	71.46 (114)
Driving Distance	269.3 (24)
Driving Accuracy	66.1 (129T)
Greens in Regulation	66.0 (77T)
Putting	1.815 (135T)
All-Around	862 (106)
Sand Saves	43.2 (179)
Total Driving	153 (42T)
Eagles	6 (50T)
Birdies	259 (112)

MISCELLANEOUS STATISTICS

Statistic	Value
Scoring Avg. (before cut)	72.00 (120)
Scoring Avg. (3rd round)	71.71 (125T)
Scoring Avg. (4th round)	72.07 (137T)
Birdie Conversion	27.3 (99T)
Par Breakers	18.4 (85T)

1993 Low Round:	65: 2 times
Career Low Round:	63: 3 times, most recent '91 Kmart Greater Greensboro /3
Career Largest Paycheck:	$108,000/1992 Phoenix Open/2 1992 Buick Classic/2

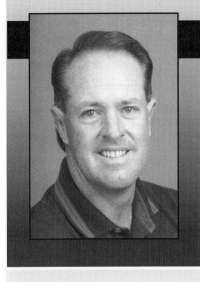

DENIS WATSON

EXEMPT STATUS: Winner, 1984 NEC World Series of Golf

FULL NAME: Denis Leslie Watson

HEIGHT: 6'　　　　　　　　**WEIGHT:** 165

BIRTH DATE: October 18, 1955

BIRTHPLACE: Salisbury, Rhodesia (Zimbabwe)

RESIDENCE: Orlando, FL

FAMILY: Wife, Hilary; Kyle (9/23/86); Paige (4/23/89); Ross (7/31/91)

COLLEGE: Rhodesia (English System)

SPECIAL INTERESTS: Golf course design, fishing, cooking, farming.

TURNED PROFESSIONAL: 1976　**Q SCHOOL:** 1981

PLAYER PROFILE

CAREER EARNINGS: $1,266,503　　　　　　**PLAYOFF RECORD:** 0-1

TOUR VICTORIES: 1984 Buick Open, NEC World Series of Golf, Panasonic Las Vegas Invitational. (TOTAL: 3)

MONEY & POSITION:

1981--$ 49,153--87	1986--$ 59,453--129	1990--$ 43,013--182
1982--$ 59,090--74	1987--$231,074-- 43	1991--$ 17,749--213
1983--$ 59,284--88	1988--$ 51,239--148	1992--$ 16,105--219
1984--$408,562-- 4	1989--$ 3,595--240	1993--$111,977--132
1985--$155,845--48		

BEST 1993 FINISH: 2--B.C. Open.

1993 SUMMARY: Tournaments entered--25; in money--9; top ten finishes--1.

1994 PGA TOUR CHARITY TEAM COMPETITION: Doral-Ryder Open

1993 SEASON: Had best finish in years by placing second to Blaine McCallister in B.C. Open, his best since finishing T2 in 1987 Federal Express St. Jude Classic...Continued to battle back from physical ailments that have hampered him for years...Next-best finish T30 in Canadian Open two weeks prior to B.C. Open...No. 132 money list finish his best since 1987, when ranked 43rd with $231,074...With $111,977 in earnings, first time since '87 he exceeded $100,000...1994 final year of ten-year exemption he earned for winning 1984 NEC World Series of Golf.

CAREER HIGHLIGHTS: After career year of 1984 and solid 1987 campaign, has been plagued by injuries and other physical problems...Had wrist and elbow surgery in 1989, followed by cervical fusion in 1991...Latter procedure corrected neck problem that had existed since 1985...1984 best season of career, with all three TOUR victories, earnings of $408,652 and No. 4 money-list finish...Came close to winning PGA Player of Year honors by joining Tom Watson as only three-time winners that year...Had brilliant seven-week spurt late that summer: 63-68 finish provided Buick Open win; placed 33rd in PGA Championship; shot course-record 8-under-par 62 in Round 2 of NEC World Series of Golf, then stayed in front rest of way to collect $126,000 and ten-year exemption; three events later earned TOUR's richest payday ($162,000) in Las Vegas Invitational...Finished T2 in 1985 U.S. Open, one shot behind Andy North...Finished second to Roger Maltbie in 1985 defense of World Series title.

PERSONAL: Named Rhodesian Sportsman of Year in 1975...Winner 1975 World Amateur Team title with George Harvey...Twice represented South Africa in World Series of Golf (1980 and 1982).

1993 PGA TOUR STATISTICS

Scoring Average	72.62 (180T)
Driving Distance	256.8 (120T)
Driving Accuracy	61.5 (175)
Greens in Regulation	59.7 (178)
Putting	1.764 (14T)
All-Around	1181 (158)
Sand Saves	49.5 (125T)
Total Driving	295 (181T)
Eagles	6 (50T)
Birdies	195 (158T)

MISCELLANEOUS STATISTICS

Scoring Avg. (before cut)	73.15 (180)
Scoring Avg. (3rd round)	72.75 (176)
Scoring Avg. (4th round)	73.88 (183)
Birdie Conversion	29.7 (28)
Par Breakers	18.3 (94T)

1993 Low Round:　**65:** B.C. Open/4
Career Low Round: **62:** 1984 World Series /2
Career Largest
Paycheck: **$162,000**/1984　Las Vegas Invitational/1

TOM WATSON

EXEMPT STATUS: 46th on 1993 money list

FULL NAME: Thomas Sturges Watson

HEIGHT: 5' 9"   **WEIGHT:** 160

BIRTH DATE: Sept. 4, 1949

BIRTHPLACE: Kansas City, MO

RESIDENCE: Mission Hills, KS

FAMILY: Wife, Linda; Meg (9/13/79); Michael Barrett (12/15/82)

COLLEGE: Stanford University (1971, Psychology)

SPECIAL INTERESTS: Hunting, fishing, guitar

TURNED PROFESSIONAL: 1971

Q SCHOOL: Fall 1971

PLAYER PROFILE

CAREER EARNINGS: $6,370,950   **PLAYOFF RECORD:** 8-4

TOUR VICTORIES: **1974** Western Open. **1975** Byron Nelson Golf Classic. **1977** Bing Crosby National Pro-Am, Wickes-Andy Williams San Diego Open, Masters, Western Open. **1978** Joe Garagiola-Tucson Open, Bing Crosby National Pro-Am, Byron Nelson Golf Classic, Colgate Hall of Fame Classic, Anheuser-Busch Classic. **1979** Sea Pines Heritage Classic, Tournament of Champions, Byron Nelson Golf Classic, Memorial Tournament, Colgate Hall of Fame Classic. **1980** Andy Williams-San Diego Open, Glen Campbell-Los Angeles Open, MONY-Tournament of Champions, New Orleans Open, Byron Nelson Classic, World Series of Golf. **1981** Masters, USF&G-New Orleans Open, Atlanta Classic. **1982** Glen Campbell-Los Angeles Open, Sea Pines Heritage Classic, U.S. Open. **1984** Seiko-Tucson Match Play, MONY-Tournament of Champions, Western Open. **1987** Nabisco Championships of Golf.
(TOTAL: 32)

MONEY & POSITION:

1971--$ 2,185--224	1979--$462,636-- 1	1987--$616,351-- 5
1972--$ 31,081-- 79	1980--$530,808-- 1	1988--$273,216--39
1973--$ 74,973-- 35	1981--$347,660-- 3	1989--$185,398--80
1974--$135,474-- 10	1982--$316,483-- 5	1990--$213,988--68
1975--$153,795-- 7	1983--$237,519--12	1991--$354,877--45
1976--$138,202-- 12	1984--$476,260-- 1	1992--$299,818--50
1977--$310,653-- 1	1985--$226,778--18	1993--$342,023--46
1978--$362,429-- 1	1986--$278,338--20	

BEST 1993 FINISHES: 5--PGA Championship; T5--U.S. Open; T6--Southwestern Bell Colonial; 10--THE PLAYERS Championship.

1993 SUMMARY: Tournaments entered--16; in money--14; top ten finishes--4.

1994 PGA TOUR CHARITY TEAM COMPETITION: Canon Greater Hartford Open

NATIONAL TEAMS: Ryder Cup (4), 1977, 1981, 1983, 1989; U.S. vs. Japan (2) 1982, 1984.

1993 SEASON: Captained United States side to 15-13 Ryder Cup victory at The Belfry in Sutton Coldfield, England, in September…While continuing to play limited schedule, had top-10 finishes in two of four majors: U.S. Open (T5) and PGA Championship (5)…Was in second place tie at mid-point of U.S. Open at Baltusrol after second-round 66…Was one stroke back of Greg Norman's pace after 54 holes of PGA Championship at Inverness…In March finished tenth in THE PLAYERS Championship, closing 69-68…Also had T6 at Southwestern Bell Colonial in May…Colonial featured second-round 64 (season low), followed by closing 65…Extended record for consecutive $100,000-plus seasons to 20.

CAREER HIGHLIGHTS: Numbers five British Opens (1975-77-80-82-83), two Masters and 1982 U.S. Open among career titles…Among majors, only PGA Championship has escaped his grasp…Has led TOUR in money won five times, including 1977-80 consecutively…Became first player to earn $500,000 in season in 1980, when won six TOUR events—plus third British Open…Last victory came in 1987 Nabisco Championships…Had two-stroke lead at mid-point of 1991 Masters, trailed eventual winner Ian Woosnam by one shot after 54 holes…Ultimately finished T3.

PERSONAL: Member four Ryder Cup squads (1977-81-83-89)…Member, 1982, '84 USA vs. Japan teams…Winner 1975 World Series of Golf…Winner 1977-79 Vardon Trophies…Winner, 1980 Dunlop Phoenix (Japan), 1992 Hong Kong Open…Six-time PGA Player of the Year (1977-80, '82, '84)…Elected to PGA World Golf Hall of Fame in 1988.

1993 PGA TOUR STATISTICS

Scoring Average	70.19 (15)
Driving Distance	269.1 (26T)
Driving Accuracy	72.6 (49T)
Greens in Regulation	65.2 (101T)
Putting	1.766 (18T)
All-Around	451 (17)
Sand Saves	59.3 (17)
Total Driving	75 (8)
Eagles	5 (67T)
Birdies	205 (150T)

MISCELLANEOUS STATISTICS

Scoring Avg. (before cut)	70.40 (15)
Scoring Avg. (3rd round)	71.54 (113)
Scoring Avg. (4th round)	71.15 (55T)
Birdie Conversion	31.2 (8T)
Par Breakers	20.8 (15T)

1993 Low Round: 64: SW Bell Colonial/2
Career Low Round: 62: 1973 World Open/5
Career Largest Paycheck: $360,000 '87 Nabisco Championships/1

D. A. WEIBRING

EXEMPT STATUS: 58th on 1993 money list

FULL NAME: Donald Albert Weibring, Jr.

HEIGHT: 6' 1"   **WEIGHT:** 190

BIRTH DATE: May 25, 1953

BIRTHPLACE: Quincy, IL

RESIDENCE: Plano, TX

FAMILY: Wife, Kristy; Matt (12/4/79); Katey (12/29/82); Allison Paige (10/3/87)

COLLEGE: Illinois State University

TURNED PROFESSIONAL: 1975

Q SCHOOL: Spring 1977

PLAYER PROFILE

CAREER EARNINGS: $2,839,550   **PLAYOFF RECORD:** 0-2

TOUR VICTORIES: 1979 Quad Cities Open. **1987** Beatrice Western Open. **1991** Hardee's Golf Classic. (TOTAL: 3)

MONEY & POSITION:		
1977--$ 1,681--215	1983--$ 61,631--84	1989--$ 98,686--127
1978--$ 41,052-- 75	1984--$110,325--65	1990--$156,235--101
1979--$ 71,343-- 57	1985--$153,079--50	1991--$ 558,648-- 22
1980--$ 78,611-- 53	1986--$167,602--55	1992--$ 253,018-- 62
1981--$ 92,365-- 45	1987--$391,363--21	1993--$ 299,293-- 58
1982--$117,941-- 31	1988--$186,677- 63	

BEST 1993 FINISHES: T2--GTE Byron Nelson Classic; T2--Hardee's Golf Classic.

1993 SUMMARY: Tournaments entered--22; in money--18; top ten finishes--2.

1994 PGA TOUR CHARITY TEAM COMPETITION: Southwestern Bell Colonial

1993 SEASON: Had head-to-head battle with David Frost in Hardee's Golf Classic, event won twice before, before finishing T2 …Shared second-round lead with Frost and Dave Barr, trailed Frost by two strokes after three… Also had T2, only other top-10 of campaign, at TPC at Las Colinas… 271 total one shot behind Scott Simpson, in three-way tie with Corey Pavin and Billy Mayfair…With almost $300,000 in earnings, year was third best of his career…Bothered periodically by sore left shoulder…Missed cuts or withdrew from first three events of campaign, missed only one cut rest of way—at U.S. Open.

CAREER HIGHLIGHTS: Finest season came in 1991…Campaign featured victory in Hardee's Golf Classic and playoff loss to Andrew Magee at Las Vegas Invitational… Two tied at 31-under-par 329, at that time the TOUR record for lowest 90-hole event total…Finished Hardee's with sizzling 64 to win by stroke over Paul Azinger and Peter Jacobsen…Those two events capped September-October hot streak that saw him fire rounds of par or better 21 of 25 times in six events…Winner of 1987 Western Open by stroke over Larry Nelson and Greg Norman…Also captured 1979 Quad Cities Open, forerunner of Hardee's Classic…Illinois native holds distinction of being only winner of Illinois Slam, with all career wins having come in Land of Lincoln…Finished second in 1985 Tournament Players Championship, fourth 1986 PGA Championship, T3 1987 PGA, T3 1988 U.S. Open.

PERSONAL: Responsible for "fine tuning" of several holes at TPC at Las Colinas…Winner 1985 Polaroid Cup (Japan), '85 Shell-Air New Zealand Open, 1989 Family House Invitational in Pittsburgh…Lost playoff to Payne Stewart in Morocco Open…Co-winner 1991 Hilton Bounceback Award.

1993 PGA TOUR STATISTICS

Scoring Average	70.75	(46T)
Driving Distance	252.5	(158)
Driving Accuracy	77.9	(6)
Greens in Regulation	66.4	(70)
Putting	1.777	(39T)
All-Around	677	(58T)
Sand Saves	58.9	(19T)
Total Driving	164	(60T)
Eagles	1	(164T)
Birdies	254	(115T)

MISCELLANEOUS STATISTICS

Scoring Avg. (before cut)	71.16	(51)
Scoring Avg. (3rd round)	70.44	(36T)
Scoring Avg. (4th round)	71.12	(54)
Birdie Conversion	27.9	(78T)
Par Breakers	18.6	(79T)

1993 Low Round:	65: 2 times
Career Low Round:	64: 8 times, most recent '91
Career Largest	Las Vegas /2&4
Paycheck: $180,000/1991 Hardee's Golf Classic/1	

MARK WIEBE

EXEMPT STATUS: 42nd on 1993 money list

FULL NAME: Mark Charles Wiebe

HEIGHT: 6' 2"   **WEIGHT:** 210

BIRTH DATE: September 13, 1957

BIRTHPLACE: Seaside, OR

RESIDENCE: Denver, CO

FAMILY: Wife, Cathy; Taylor Lynn (9/9/86); Gunner (1/1/89): Collier (4/17/92)

COLLEGE: San Jose State

SPECIAL INTERESTS: Fishing, skiing

TURNED PROFESSIONAL: 1980

Q SCHOOL: Fall 1983, 1984

PLAYER PROFILE

CAREER EARNINGS: $2,120,875   **PLAYOFF RECORD:** 1-1

TOUR VICTORIES: 1985 Anheuser-Busch Classic. **1986** Hardee's Golf Classic. (TOTAL: 2)

MONEY & POSITION:

1984--$ 16,257--166	1988--$392,166--28	1991--$100,046--136
1985--$181,894-- 36	1989--$296,269--41	1992--$174,763-- 86
1986--$260,180-- 25	1990--$210,435--72	1993--$360,213-- 42
1987--$128,651-- 82		

BEST 1993 FINISHES: 2--Buick Classic; T4--Sprint Western Open; T6--Kmart Greater Greensboro Open; T7--Phoenix Open; T9--Buick Invitational of California.

1993 SUMMARY: Tournaments entered--27; in money--19; top ten finishes--5.

1994 PGA TOUR CHARITY TEAM COMPETITION: Buick Classic

1993 SEASON: Continued strong comeback from right shoulder (bicep tendon) problem encountered in 1992 to register second-best season of career...Money-won total of $360,213 topped only by $392,166 amassed in 1988... Had two top-10 finishes in three starts on two occasions: T7 Phoenix Open and T9 Buick Invitational of California, with missed cut at Pebble Beach in between; solo second Buick Classic and T4 Western Open, with T77 U.S. in middle...Other top-10 was T6 at Kmart Greater Greensboro Open...Carded low round of campaign in next-to-last start, 64 in Round 1 of H-E-B Texas Open...Closing rounds of 67-66 at Westchester CC produced Buick Classic tie with Vijay Singh at 280...Singh went on to capture first PGA TOUR title with birdie on third playoff hole...Closed with 67 in Buick Invitational and 69 at Western Open...Final money list ranking (No. 42) best since 1989.

CAREER HIGHLIGHTS: Enjoyed finest earnings season of ten-year career in 1988 with $392,166...Finished 64-68 in 1988 Anheuser-Busch Golf Classic to tie Tom Sieckmann, who won playoff on second extra hole...A-B Classic provided first TOUR win in 1985, this time with his own playoff victory over John Mahaffey...Captured second tournament title next year, winning Hardee's Golf Classic...Also in '86 had second-place finish in Byron Nelson Classic, plus T3 at Pebble Beach...Had best money-list placing, 25th, in '86...Had second-place finishes in 1989 Shearson Lehman Hutton Open and 1990 B.C. Open...Best 1992 finish came in first start of year, T4 in AT&T Pebble Beach National Pro-Am.

PERSONAL: Winner 1986 Colorado Open, 1981 "Texas Dolly" Match Play Championship...Second team All-American at San Jose State ...Winner California junior college title at Palomar J.C.

1993 PGA TOUR STATISTICS

Scoring Average	70.90	(59T)
Driving Distance	261.1	(74)
Driving Accuracy	69.4	(86T)
Greens in Regulation	65.1	(107T)
Putting	1.776	(37T)
All-Around	650	(54)
Sand Saves	46.9	(152)
Total Driving	160	(52)
Eagles	7	(37T)
Birdies	307	(46T)

MISCELLANEOUS STATISTICS

Scoring Avg. (before cut)	71.61	(90T)
Scoring Avg. (3rd round)	70.83	(61)
Scoring Avg. (4th round)	70.89	(38)
Birdie Conversion	29.0	(46T)
Par Breakers	19.3	(55T)

1993 Low Round: 64: H-E-B Texas Open/1
Career Low Round: 61: '88 Northern Telecom/3
Career Largest Paycheck: $108,000 '93 Buick Classic/2

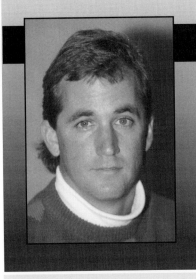

WILLIE WOOD

EXEMPT STATUS: 112th on 1993 money list

FULL NAME: Willie West Wood

HEIGHT: 5' 7"   **WEIGHT:** 145

BIRTH DATE: October 1, 1960

BIRTHPLACE: Kingsville, TX

RESIDENCE: Edmond, OK

FAMILY: William King (12/17/86); Kelby Curtis (6/15/88)

COLLEGE: Oklahoma State

SPECIAL INTERESTS: Fishing, physical fitness

TURNED PROFESSIONAL: 1983

Q SCHOOL: 1983, 1992

PLAYER PROFILE

CAREER EARNINGS: $974,944

PLAYOFF RECORD: 0-1

BEST-EVER FINISHES: 2--1984 Anheuser Busch Classic; 2-- 1986 Manufacturers Hanover Weschester Classic; 2--1990 Hardee's Golf Classic (lost playoff to Joey Sindelar)

MONEY & POSITION:

1984--$115,741- -61	1988--$ 53,064--146	1991--$ 48,033--176
1985--$153,706-- 49	1989--$ 9,677--212	1992--$ 57,748--168
1986--$172,629-- 52	1990--$179,972-- 90	1993--$146,206--112
1987--$ 95,916-- 98		

BEST 1993 FINISHES: T6--New England Classic; T8--Hardee's Golf Classic; T8--Buick Southern Open.

1993 SUMMARY: Tournaments entered--25; in money--16; top ten finishes--3.

1994 PGA TOUR CHARITY TEAM COMPETITION: Hardee's Golf Classic

NATIONAL TEAMS: 1983 Walker Cup Team

1993 SEASON: Regained playing privileges largely on strength of two late season T8 finishes, in Hardee's Golf Classic and at Buick Southern Open...Earned combined $46,300 for those two placings...In July had T6 in New England Classic...Was mid-point leader at Pleasant Valley after rounds of 68-65...133 total good for one-stroke lead over Bobby Clampett...Missed cut just twice over his final 12 events...Only top-25 finish during first half of year T22 at Buick Classic...Earnings total of $146,206 fourth best of ten-year career.

CAREER HIGHLIGHTS: Closest brush with victory came in 1990 Hardee's Golf Classic, where lost playoff to Joey Sindelar...Lost playoff with bogey on first extra hole...Lost 1984 Anheuser-Busch Classic by one shot as Ronnie Black came from seven strokes back with closing 63 to win...1990 also produced best earnings campaign, with $179,972...That total marked first time over $100,000 since first three years on TOUR, 1984-86...Also won non-TOUR event in 1990, the Oklahoma Open...Also had runnerup finish in 1986 Manufacturers Hanover Westchester Classic...Career took back seat when wife, Holly, became seriously ill, eventually dying of cancer in 1989... All-time low score 61 at 49ers Club in Tucson, when high school senior.

PERSONAL: Won five major junior titles, including 1977 USGA Junior, 1978 PGA National Junior and 1979 Western Junior...Winner 1979 Nevada State Open, 1984 Colorado State Open...Two-time All-American at Oklahoma State, where won nine collegiate events... Awarded 1982 Fred Haskins Trophy as outstanding collegiate player... Member 1983 U.S. Walker Cup team...Medalist 1983 TOUR Qualifying Tournament ...Sister Deanie played LPGA Tour...Got start in game at age nine, learning from father, head professional at Shreveport (LA) Country Club at time.

1993 PGA TOUR STATISTICS

Scoring Average	70.85 (55T)
Driving Distance	255.8 (130T)
Driving Accuracy	65.7 (134T)
Greens in Regulation	63.2 (145T)
Putting	1.810 (125T)
All-Around	1040 (138)
Sand Saves	54.8 (54T)
Total Driving	264 (171)
Eagles	4 (89T)
Birdies	229 (137)

MISCELLANEOUS STATISTICS

Scoring Avg. (before cut)	71.40 (72)
Scoring Avg. (3rd round)	71.00 (73T)
Scoring Avg. (4th round)	71.33 (75T)
Birdie Conversion	25.8 (145T)
Par Breakers	16.6 (155T)

1993 Low Round:	**65:** New England Classic/4
Career Low Round:	**63:** 3 times, most recent
Career Largest	1990 Hardee's Classic/2
Paycheck:	**$108,000**/1990 Hardee's Classic/2

FUZZY ZOELLER

EXEMPT STATUS: Winner, 1984 United States Open

FULL NAME: Frank Urban Zoeller

HEIGHT: 5' 10"   **WEIGHT:** 190

BIRTH DATE: Nov. 11, 1951

BIRTHPLACE: New Albany, IN

RESIDENCE: New Albany, IN

FAMILY: Wife, Diane; Sunnye Noel (5/5/79); Heidi Leigh (8/23/81); Gretchen Marie (3/27/84) ; Miles Remington (6/1/89)

COLLEGE: Edison Junior College in Ft. Myers, FL, and University of Houston

SPECIAL INTERESTS: All sports, golf course design

TURNED PROFESSIONAL: 1973 **Q SCHOOL:** Fall 1974

PLAYER PROFILE

CAREER EARNINGS: $3,731,261   **PLAYOFF RECORD:** 2-1.

TOUR VICTORIES: **1979** Wickes-Andy Williams San Diego Open, Masters. **1981** Colonial National
(TOTAL: 10) Invitation. **1983** Sea Pines Heritage Classic, Las Vegas Pro-Celebrity Classic. **1984** United States Open. **1985** Hertz Bay Hill Classic. **1986** AT&T Pebble Beach National Pro-Am, Sea Pines Heritage Golf Classic, Anheuser-Busch Golf Classic.

MONEY & POSITION:

1975--$ 7,318--146	1982--$126,512--28	1988--$209,564-- 51
1976--$ 52,557-- 56	1983--$417,597-- 2	1989--$217,742-- 65
1977--$ 76,417-- 40	1984--$157,460--40	1990--$199,629-- 79
1978--$109,055-- 20	1985--$244,003--15	1991--$385,139-- 42
1979--$196,951-- 9	1986--$358,115--13	1992--$125,003--114
1980--$ 95,531-- 46	1987--$222,921--44	1993--$378,175-- 39
1981--$151,571-- 19		

BEST 1993 FINISHES: 2--Buick Open; T3--MCI Heritage Classic; 4--Federal Express St. Jude Classic; T6--Honda Classic.

1993 SUMMARY: Tournaments entered--18; in money--17; top ten finishes--4.

1994 PGA TOUR CHARITY TEAM COMPETITION: THE PLAYERS Championship

NATIONAL TEAMS: Ryder Cup (3) 1979, 1983, 1985.

1993 SEASON: Continued to play limited schedule with positive results... Had back-to-back top-10 finishes in August, at Federal Express St. Jude Classic (4), followed very next week by runnerup placing (to Larry Mize) in Buick Open...Held four-shot advantage over Mize entering final round, when finished with 73 and 273 total for second...Shared 54-hole lead with eventual winner Nick Price at Memphis...Finished with 70 for 270 total, four strokes behind Price...Had two earlier top-10s... Opened with 66 in Honda Classic, finished T6 and finished T3 in MCI Heritage Classic...Best round of year recorded at Bob Hope Chrysler Classic, a third round 63.

CAREER HIGHLIGHTS: Has won two majors, 1979 Masters and 1984 U.S. Open...Latter came in 18 hole playoff with Greg Norman at Winged Foot... Accomplishilments came despite challenging medical history, principally back trouble tracing to high school basketball...Back problems became public knowledge prior to 1984 PGA Championship ...Could barely move on morning he was to play first round...Was rushed to hospital, where remained for nearly week ...Back condition worsened month later in Las Vegas, where was defending Panasonic Invitational title...Following surgery returned to TOUR end of February 1985, finished T46 in Doral-Eastern Open... Won Hertz Bay Hill Classic two weeks later...First win came in 1979 Andy Williams Open.

PERSONAL: Known for "whistling while he works"...Actively involved in golf course design, with one of primary projects being TPC at Summerlin, host course for Las Vegas Invitational...Member three Ryder Cup teams (1979-83-85) ...Winner 1973 Indiana State Amateur...1972 Florida State Junior College champion...Leader 1983 Seiko Grand Prix points...Winner 1985-86 Skins Games...Winner 1987 Merrill Lynch Shoot-Out Championship.

1993 PGA TOUR STATISTICS

Scoring Average	70.14 (12)
Driving Distance	273.3 (12T)
Driving Accuracy	72.2 (56)
Greens in Regulation	73.6 (1)
Putting	1.794 (82T)
All-Around	329 (6)
Sand Saves	55.2 (49T)
Total Driving	68 (4)
Eagles	10 (9T)
Birdies	265 (104T)

MISCELLANEOUS STATISTICS

Scoring Avg. (before cut)	70.26 (10)
Scoring Avg. (3rd round)	70.25 (25T)
Scoring Avg. (4th round)	70.76 (32)
Birdie Conversion	28.2 (69T)
Par Breakers	21.5 (5T)

1993 Low Round: 63: Hope Chrysler Classic/3
Career Low Round: 62: 1982 B.C. Open/2
Career Largest
Paycheck: $172,800/'91 PLAYERS Championship/2

RICHARD ZOKOL

EXEMPT STATUS: 1992 tournament winner

FULL NAME: Richard Francis Zokol

HEIGHT: 5' 9"   **WEIGHT:** 170

BIRTH DATE: August 21, 1958

BIRTHPLACE: Kitimat, B.C., Canada

RESIDENCE: Richmond, B.C., Canada

FAMILY: Wife, Joanie; Conor and Garrett (10/14/87); Hayley (6/25/90)

COLLEGE: Brigham Young University

SPECIAL INTERESTS: Hunting

TURNED PROFESSIONAL: 1981

Q-SCHOOL: Fall 1981, 1982, 1986, 1989, 1991

PLAYER PROFILE

CAREER EARNINGS: $1,323,173

TOUR VICTORIES: 1992 Greater Milwaukee Open
(TOTAL: 1)

MONEY & POSITION:

1982--$15,110--156	1986--$ 37,888--152	1990--$191,634-- 84
1983--$38,107--117	1987--$114,406-- 89	1991--$ 78,426--149
1984--$56,605-- 97	1988--$142,153-- 83	1992--$311,909-- 48
1985--$71,192--102	1989--$ 51,323--163	1993--$214,419-- 80

BEST 1993 FINISHES: T4--Greater Milwaukee Open; T6--Las Vegas Invitational.

1993 SUMMARY: Tournaments entered--25; in money--15; top ten finishes--2.

1994 PGA TOUR CHARITY TEAM COMPETITION: Honda Classic

1993 SEASON: Had struggling start to campaign, but finished strongly to record second-best money-won season of 12-year career...Closed with top-10 finishes in final two starts...Finished T4 in defense of Greater Milwaukee Open title, ended TOUR year with T6 in Las Vegas Invitational...Earned $90,900 in those two events...At GMO was never more than three shots off lead, trailed by single shot after 54 holes...With closing 68 and 271 total, finished one stroke out of Billy Mayfair-Mark Calcavecchia-Ted Schulz playoff...Week before placed T14 in NEC World Series of Golf.

CAREER HIGHLIGHTS: Captured first official PGA TOUR victory in September 1992, winning Greater Milwaukee Open by two strokes over Dick Mast... Earlier that year won unofficial Deposit Guaranty Golf Classic...GMO triumph provided largest payday of career, $180,000...Two wins combined to provide best earnings total of career, $311,909...Also went over $1 million in career earnings during 1992 campaign...Finished second in 1988 Hawaiian Open and 1990 Chattanooga Classic ...T5 in 1984 Canadian Open represented best finish by Canadian in their national championship in 26 years (Dave Barr subsequently finished T4 in 1988).

PERSONAL: Member 1980 Canada World Amateur Cup team...Winner 1980 International Champions (Morocco) ...Winner 1981 Canadian Amateur...Member 1981 Brigham Young University NCAA Championship team (roomed with Bobby Clampett for three years)... Winner 1982 British Columbia Open, 1984 Utah Open...Does column for Vancouver Sun, has syndicated television show in Canada...In November 1993 named director of golf for Intrawest Corp., Canada's largest resort development company.

1993 PGA TOUR STATISTICS

Scoring Average	71.36 (105T)
Driving Distance	253.2 (153T)
Driving Accuracy	70.3 (70T)
Greens in Regulation	62.9 (151T)
Putting	1.787 (61T)
All-Around	1005 (132)
Sand Saves	54.0 (64)
Total Driving	223 (143T)
Eagles	3 (116T)
Birdies	220 (142T)

MISCELLANEOUS STATISTICS

Scoring Avg. (before cut)	72.13 (128T)
Scoring Avg. (3rd round)	71.00 (73T)
Scoring Avg. (4th round)	71.64 (107T)
Birdie Conversion	26.4 (128T)
Par Breakers	16.9 (143T)

1993 Low Round: **66:** 2 times
Career Low Round: **63:** '87 Atlanta Golf Classic/2
Career Largest
Paycheck: **$180,000**/'92 Greater Milwaukee Open/1

A

ANDERSON, JC Birth Date 12/26/61 **Birthplace** Springfield, IL **Residence** Dallas, TX **Height** 6-1 **Weight** 185 **Special Interests** Reading, fishing **Family** Wife, Shelly **College** Lamar University **Turned Professional** 1984 **Q School** 1990, 1992. **Other Achievements** Winner, 1980 Illinois State High School Championship. Medalist at 1989 Canadian Tour Qualifying Tournament.
Exempt Status: 149th on 1993 money list
Best Ever Finish: 6 — 1993 Kemper Open
Money & Position: 1991 — $33,180 — 196   1993—$89,781—149
Best 1993 Finish: 6—Kemper Open
1993 Summary: Tournaments entered — 27; in money — 11; top ten finishes — 1.
Career Earnings: $122,962

ARMOUR III, Tommy Birth Date 10/8/59 **Birthplace** Denver, CO **Residence** Irving, TX **Height** 6-2 **Weight** 205 **Special Interests** Music, sports **Family** Single **College** University of New Mexico **Turned Professional** 1981 **Q School** Fall 1981, 1987. **Other Achievements** Winner,1981 New Mexico State Amateur; 1983 Mexican Open; 1981 William Tucker Intercollegiate.
Exempt Status: Past Champion
TOUR Victories: 1— 1990 Phoenix Open.

Money & Position:			
1982 — $ 4,254 — 208	1989 — $185,018 — 81	1992 — $ 47,218— 180
1987 — $ 970 — 290	1990 — $348,658 — 35	1993 — $ 52,011— 181
1988 — $175,461 — 66	1991 — $ 90,478 — 140	

Best 1993 Finish: T10—Kemper Open
1993 Summary: Tournaments entered — 20; in money — 7; top ten finishes — 1.
Career Earnings: $898,844

ARMSTRONG, Ty Birth Date 5/16/59 **Birthplace** Waxahachie, TX **Residence** Eden Prairie, MN **Height** 5-8 **Weight** 165 **Special Interests** Cross-country skiing **College** McNeese State University **Family** Wife, Mary; Patrick (11/16/92) **Turned Professional** 1986 **Q School** 1993 **Other Achievements** Several mini-tour victories. 1981 All-Southland Conference. High School All-State selection in baseball as a second baseman.
Exempt Status: T1 at 1993 Qualifying Tournament

B

BARRANGER, Todd Birth Date 10/19/68 **Birthplace** Phoenix, AZ **Residence** Orlando, FL **Height** 5-10 **Weight**175 **Special Interests** Golf, horses **College** Scottsdale Community College **Family** Wife, Tessa **Turned Professional** 1988 **Q School** 1993
Exempt Status: T11 at 1993 Qualifying Tournament

BEIERSDORF, Russell Birth Date 12/24/65 **Birthplace** Dallas,TX **Residence** Dallas, TX **Height** 6-5 **Weight** 200 **Special Interests** Sporting events **Family** Wife, Julie **College** Southern Methodist University(1988) **Turned Professional** 1986 **Q School** 1992 **Other Achievements** Winner, 1991 Ben Hogan Boise Open, 1992 Ben Hogan Greater Greenville Open and 1992 Ben Hogan Ft. Wayne Open. All-Southwest Conference in 1987.
Exempt Status: 133rd on 1993 money list
Best Ever Finish: T13—1993 BellSouth Classic
1993 Summary: Tournaments entered—30; in money—20; top ten finishes—0
1993 Best Finish: T13—BellSouth Classic
Money & Position: 1993—$111,750—133
Career Earnings: $111,750

BENEPE, Jim Birthdate 10/24/63 **Birthplace** Sheridan, WY **Residence** Jackson Hole, WY **Height** 5-7 **Weight** 150 **Special Interest** Hunting, fishing, reading, music **Family** Single **College** Northwestern University (1986, Psychology) **Turned Professional** 1986 **Q School** 1990 **Other Achievements** Winner, 1982 Wyoming State Amateur (stroke play); 1983 Wyoming State Amateur (medal play). Winner 1982 Western Junior Championship. Winner 1987 Canadian Tour Order of Merit. Named 1987 Canadian Tour Rookie of the Year. Winner 1988 Victorian (Australia) Open. Winner of four collegiate events for Northwestern, including co-champion 1986 Big Ten title. 1986 Collegiate All-American.
Exempt Status: Past Champion
TOUR Victories: 1-1988 Beatrice Western Open

Money & Position:	1988 — $176,055 — 65	1990 — $105,087 — 135	1993 — $ —0—
	1989 — $ 38,089 — 176	1991 — $ 62,082 — 164	

1993 Summary: Tournaments entered —2; in money — 0; top ten finishes — 0.
Career Earnings: $381,314

BOLDT, Rob Birth Date 5/5/63 **Birthplace** San Pablo, CA **Residence** Walnut Creek, CA **Height** 6-3 **Weight** 205 **Special Interests** All sports **Family** Wife, Terry **Turned Professional:** 1981 **Q School** 1993 **Other Achievements:** Played NIKE TOUR from 1990-93. Best-ever NIKE TOUR finish--T2-1991 Reno Open, which was a four-player playoff loss to John Flannery. Had eight top-ten finishes in 1991.
Exempt Status: T37 at 1993 Qualifying Tournament
1993 Summary: Tournaments entered —1; in money —0; top ten finishes —0.

BOROS, Guy Birth Date 9/4/64 **Birthplace** Ft. Lauderdale, FL **Residence** Ft. Lauderdale, FL **Height** 6-1 **Weight** 240 **Special Interests** Hunting, fishing **Family** Single **College** University of Iowa **Turned Professional** 1986 **Q School** 1993 **Other Achievements** Finished 13th on the 1993 NIKE TOUR money list with $75,104. Led 1991 Canadian Tour Order of Merit. All-Big Ten player 1984, 1985, and 1986. Played both the Canadian Tour and the Australasian Tour in 1992. Son of two-time U.S. Open winner Julius Boros.
Exempt Status: T18 at 1993 Qualifying Tournament

BRISKY, Mike Birth Date 5/28/65 **Birthplace** Brownsville, TX **Residence** Orlando, FL **Height** 6-1 **Weight** 185 **Special Interests** Fishing, movies, Bible study **Family** Wife, Judy **College** Pan American University **Turned Professional** 1987 **Q School** 1993 **Other Achievements** Two-time winner on the T.C. Jordan Tour.
Exempt Status: T37 at 1993 Qualifying Tournament

BRODIE, Steve Birth Date 1/24/65 **Birthplace** Compton, CA **Residence** Provo, UT **Height** 5-10 **Weight** 175 **Special Interests** Fishing, Chicago White Sox baseball **Family** Wife, Amy; Alexis (1983), Brooks (1986), Cassidy (1988), Chase (1989) **College** Long Beach State **Turned Professional** 1986 **Other Achievements** Played on the 1989 Australian Tour, winner of five mini-tour events. Member of 1990, 1991 and 1993 NIKE TOUR. Best-ever NIKE TOUR finish--T3-1991 Utah Classic.
Exempt Status: T26 at 1993 Qualifying Tournament

BROWNE, Olin Birth Date 4/22/59 **Birthplace** New York, NY **Residence** Jupiter, FL **Height** 5-9 **Weight** 165 **Special Interests** Fly fishing, the environment, some politics **Family** Wife; Pam; Olin Jr. (7/9/88), Alexandra Grace (10/24/91) **College** Occidental **Turned Professional** 1984 **Q School** 1991 **Other Achievements** Winner, 1991 Ben Hogan Bakersfield Open, Ben Hogan Hawkeye Open; 1993 NIKE Monterrey Open.
Exempt Status: 7th on 1993 NIKE TOUR money list
Best Ever Finish: T4—1992 Northern Telecom Open

Money & Position:	1992 — $84,152 — 147	1993 — $2,738 — 290

Best 1993 Finish: T58—AT&T Pebble Beach National Pro-Am
1993 Summary: Tournaments entered —2; in money — 1; top ten finishes — 0.
Career Earnings: $86,890

BURKE, Patrick Birth Date 3/17/62 **Birthplace** Hollywood, FL **Residence** Azusa, CA **Height** 5-5 **Weight** 165 **Special Interest** Ice hockey **Family** Wife, Jodi; Jamie (10/12/93) **College** Citrus College **Turned Professional** 1986 **Q School** 1989, 1991 **Other Achievements** Medalist in 1987 Australian Tour Qualifying School. Second team Division II All-American

Exempt Status: 144th on 1993 money list
Best Ever Finish: T6—1992 BellSouth Classic

Money and Position:

1990 — $ 5,228 — 247	1993 — $100,717 — 144	
1992 — $ 101,513 — 129		

1993 Best Finish: T9—Buick Invitational
1993 Summary: Tournaments entered—17; in money—11; top ten finishes—1
Career Earnings: $207,459

BURNS, Bob Birth Date 4/5/68 **Birthplace** Mission Hills, CA **Residence** Granada Hills, CA **Height** 5-8 **Weight** 150 **College** California State University-Northridge **Special Interests** Backpacking **Family** Single **Turned Professional** 1991 **Q-School** 1993 **Other Achievements** Winner, 1990 Division II Championship. NCAA All-American. Lost 1992 Ben Hogan South Texas Open to Brian Henninger on first extra playoff hole.
Exempt Status: T11 at 1993 Qualifying Tournament

BURNS III, George Birth Date 7/29/49 **Birthplace** Brooklyn, NY **Residence** Boynton Beach, FL **Height** 6-2 **Weight** 200 **Family** Wife, Irene; Kelly (4/2/76), Eileen (8/25/80) **College** University of Maryland **Turned Professional** 1975 **Q School** 1975, 1990 **Other Achievements** Winner 1973 Canadian Amateur and 1974 Porter Cup, North-South Amateur, and New York State Amateur. As professional, won 1975 Scandinavian Open and 1975 Kerrygold (Ireland). 1975 Walker Cup team and 1975 World Amateur Cup team. Winner, 1988 Chrysler Team Championship with Wayne Levi.

Exempt Status: Past Champion
TOUR Victories: 4-1979 Walt Disney World Team Championship (with Ben Crenshaw). 1980 Bing Crosby National Pro-Am. 1985 Bank of Boston Classic. 1987 Shearson Lehman Bros.-Andy Williams Open.

Money & Position:

1976 — $ 85,732 — 32	1982 — $181,864 — 18	1988 — $ 30,130 — 174
1977 — $102,026 — 2	1983 — $ 62,371 — 83	1989 — $ 5,645 — 230
1978 — $171,498 — 38	1984 — $198,848 — 37	1990 — $ 96,443 — 139
1979 — $107,830 — 33	1985 — $223,352 — 21	1992 — $ 6,864 — 254
1980 — $219,928 — 7	1986 — $ 77,474 —112	1993 — $ 2,550 — 298
1981 — $105,395 — 37	1987 — $216,257 — 45	

Best 1993 Finish: T67—AT&T Pebble Beach Pro-Am
1992 Summary: Tournaments entered —9; in money — 1; top ten finishes — 0.
Career Earnings: $1,763,208

BYRUM, Curt Birth Date 12/28/58 **Birthplace** Onida, SD **Residence** Scottsdale, AZ **Height** 6-2 **Weight** 190 **Special Interest** All sports **Family** Wife, Cyndi; Christina Suzanne (10/13/90) **College** University of New Mexico **Turned Professional** 1982 **Q School** 1982 **Other Achievements** Named All-American in 1980. Winner, 1979 Pacific Coast Amateur. Winner, South Dakota State Juniors four times, and South Dakota State Amateur five times. Winner, 1986 Showdown Classic on Senior PGA TOUR with Bobby Nichols.

Exempt Status: 10th on 1993 NIKE TOUR money list
TOUR Victories: 1-1989 Hardee's Golf Classic

Money & Position:

1983 — $ 30,772 — 130	1987 — $212,450 — 46	1991 — $ 78,725—148
1984 — $ 27,836 — 143	1988 — $208,853 — 55	1992 — $ 31,450—194
1985 — $ 6,943 — 193	1989 — $ 221,702— 64	1993 — $ —0—
1986 — $ 79,454 — 108	1990 — $ 117,134— 129	

Career Earnings: $1,015,319

BYRUM, Tom Birth Date 9/28/60 **Birthplace** Onida, SD **Residence** Ft. Worth, TX **Height** 5-10 **Weight** 175 **Special Interest** Hunting, fishing, all sports **Family** Wife, Dana; Brittni Rene (4/2/88), Corinne **College** New Mexico State University **Turned Professional** 1984 **Q School** 1985, 1991, 1992 **Other Achievements** Winner, 1983 New Mexico State Intercollegiate.

Exempt Status: 154th on 1993 money list
TOUR Victories: 1—1989 Kemper Open

Money and Position:

1986—$ 89,739— 93	1989—$ 320,939 — 32	1992—$ 94,399 —136
1987—$ 146,384— 76	1990—$ 136,910 —113	1993—$ 82,354 —154
1988—$ 174,378— 67	1991—$ 68,871 —153	

1993 Best Finish: T8—Anheuser-Busch Classic
1993 Summary: Tournaments entered—26; in money—12; top ten finishes—1
Career Earnings: $1,113,975

C

CALDWELL, Rex **Birth Date** 5/5/50 **Birthplace** Everett, WA **Residence** San Antonio, TX **Height** 6-2 **Weight** 225 **College** San Fernando Valley State **Special Interests** Basketball, jogging **Family** Wife, Jana **Turned Professional** 1972 **Other Achievements** College Division All-American in 1971-72. Winner 1978 California State Open. Winner of 1983 World Cup team title with John Cook as partner. Played two NIKE TOUR events in 1993, finishing T19 at South Texas Open and T41 at Texarkana Open for $2,250 total earnings last year.
Exempt Status: Past Champion
TOUR Victories: 1--1983 LaJet Classic

Money & Position:			
1975—$ 3,094 — 178	1980—$ 64,859 — 62	1985—$ 58,689— 114
1976—$ 24,912 — 87	1981—$ 33,945 — 102	1986—$ 39,674— 149
1977—$ 11,693 — 137	1982—$ 64,622 — 68	1987—$ 50,054— 153
1978—$ 66,451 — 42	1983—$ 284,434 — 6	1988—$ 15,896— 205
1979—$ 96,088 — 36	1984—$ 126,400 — 53	1989—$ 55,066— 161

1993 Best Finish: T16—Deposit Guaranty
1993 Summary: Tournaments entered —3; in money —1; top ten finish —0.
Career Earnings: $1,007,548

CLAMPETT, Bobby **Birth Date** 4/22/60 **Birthplace** Monterey, CA **Residence** Cary, NC **Height** 5-10 **Weight** 155 **Special Interest** Bible study, flying, snow skiing **Family** Wife, Ann; Katelyn (10/30/87), Daniel (8/11/89), Michael (12/29/91) **College** Brigham Young University **Turned Professional** 1980 **Q School** 1980, 1990 **Other Achievements** Winner 1978 and 1980 California State Amateur. Low Amateur, 1978 U.S. Open. Winner, 1978 World Amateur medal. Three-time All-American, 1978-80. Two-time Fred Haskins Award, presented to top collegiate player. Winner, 1978 Western Amateur and 1980 Sunnehanna Amateur.
Exempt Status: Past Champion
TOUR Victories: 1-1982 Southern Open

Money and Position:			
1980— $ 10,190 — 163	1985—$ 81,121— 94	1990— $ 29,268—194
1981— $ 184,710 — 14	1986—$ 97,178— 87	1991— $ 127,817—116
1982— $ 184,600 — 17	1987—$124,872— 84	1992— $ 29,175—199
1983— $ 86,575 — 64	1988—$ 88,067—118	1993— $ 112,293—131
1984— $ 41,837 — 117	1989—$ 68,868—148	

1993 Best Finish: T4— New England Classic
1993 Summary: Tournaments entered—16; in money—11; top ten finishes—3
Career Earnings: $1,226,573

CONNER, Frank **Birth Date** 1/11/46 **Birthplace** Vienna, Austria **Residence** San Antonio, TX **Height** 5-9 **Weight** 190 **Special Interests** Tennis **Family** Wife, Joy; Michelle (5/9/73), Nicole (1/28/75) **College** Trinity University (1969, Business Administration) **Turned Professional** 1971 **Other Achievements** Winner, 1982 King Hassan Open. Winner, 1988 Deposit Guaranty Classic. Winner, 1991 Ben Hogan Knoxville Open and Tulsa Open.
Exempt Status: Veteran member   **Playoff Record: 0-2**
Best Ever Finish: 2-1982 Sea Pines Heritage Classic; T2-1979 New Orleans Open, 1981 Quad Cities Open, 1984 Bank of Boston Classic.

Money & Position:			
1975 — $ 4,418 — 165	1982 — $ 72,181 — 58	1988 — $ 44,801 — 154
1976 — $ 9,273 — 147	1983 — $ 71,320 — 75	1989 — $ 3,052 — 244
1977 — $ 15,138 — 122	1984 — $ 55,405 — 98	1990 — $ 3,461 — 258
1978 — $ 11,325 — 136	1985 — $ 68,804 — 103	1991 — $ 18,318 — 207
1979 — $ 46,020 — 87	1986 — $ 35,729 — 155	1992 — $ 74,785 — 152
1980 — $ 37,149 — 87	1987 — $ 51,475 — 150	1993 — $ 34,154 — 195
1981 — $ 85,009 — 51		

Best 1993 Finish: T11— Canon Greater Hartford Open
1993 Summary: Tournaments entered —7; in money — 3; top ten finishes — 0.
Career Earnings: $741,818

D

DAY, Glen **Birth Date** 11/16/65 **Birthplace** Mobile, AL **Residence** Little Rock, AR **Height** 5-10 **Weight** 170 **College** University of Oklahoma **Special Interests** Hunting **Family** Wife, Jennifer Ralston-Day **Turned Professional** 1988 **Q-School** 1993 **Other Achievements** Winner, 1989 Malaysian Open. 1987 and 1988 All-American.
Exempt Status: T11at1993 Qualifying Tournament

DENNIS, Clark Birth Date 2/14/66 **Birthplace** Houston, TX **Residence** Ft. Worth, TX **Height** 5-11 **Weight** 180 **Special Interest** Fishing **Family** Wife, Vickie **College** Arkansas, Southern Methodist University **Turned Professional** 1986 **Q School** 1990, 1991, 1993 **Other Achievements** 1983 Texas State Junior Champion and 1988 Nevada State Open Champion. Winner, 1993 NIKE Bakersfield Open. Finished 22nd on the 1993 NIKE TOUR money list with $64,779. Winner, 1992 and '93 Newport Classic.

Exempt Status: T8 at 1993 Qualifying Tournament
Best Ever Finish: T3—1990 Hawaiian Open
Money and Position:

1990—$103,721—136	1992—$ 12,935—227	
1991—$ 57,760—170	1993—$ 6,050—259	

Best 1993 Finish: T45—Southwestern Bell Colonial
1993 Summary: Tournaments entered—2; in money—2; top ten finishes—0
Career Earnings: $161,440

DiMARCO, Chris Birth Date 8/23/68 **Birthplace** Huntington, NY **Residence** Altamonte Springs, FL **Height** 6-0 **Weight** 180 **Special Interest** Fishing, tennis **Family** Wife, Amy **College** University of Florida **Turned Professional** 1990 **Other Achievements** Member of NIKE TOUR in 1991, finished 53rd on money list with earnings of $23,333. Won 1992 Canadian Tour Order of Merit, also led the Canadian Tour in stroke average. NCAA All-American in 1990, SEC Player of Year in 1990, All-SEC in 1989-90. Winner, 1989 SEC Championship. Wife, Amy caddied for him in Canada and also on NIKE TOUR.

Exempt Status: 9th on 1993 NIKE TOUR money list
Best Ever Finish: T43—1989 Beatrice Western Open (amateur)

DONALD, Mike Birth Date 7/11/55 **Birthplace** Grand Rapids, MI **Residence** Hollywood, FL **Height** 5-11 **Weight** 200 **Family** Single **College** Broward Community College and Georgia Southern University **Turned Professional** 1978 **Q School** Fall 1979 **Other Achievements** Winner of the 1984 JCPenney Classic with Vicki Alvarez. Winner, 1974 National Junior College Championship while at Broward Community College and the 1973 Florida Junior Championship. Teamed with Fred Couples to win the 1990 Sazale Classic. Elected to a four-year term as a Player Director on the PGA TOUR Policy Board in 1987. Finished second to Hale Irwin in the 1990 U.S. Open. Both shot 74s in the playoff, and on the first sudden playoff hole in Open history, Irwin rolled in a 10-footer for birdie.

Exempt Status: Past Champion
TOUR Victories: 1—1989 Anheuser Busch Golf Classic
Money and Position

1980—$ 12,365 — 151	1985—$ 91,888— 46	1990—$ 348,328 — 36
1981—$ 50,665 — 83	1986—$108,772— 82	1991—$ 88,248 —142
1982—$ 39,967 — 101	1987—$137,734— 79	1992—$ 117,252 —120
1983—$ 72,343 — 73	1988—$118,509— 96	1993—$ 51,312 —183
1984—$ 146,324 — 46	1989—$430,232— 22	

1993 Best Finish: T10—Deposit Guaranty Golf Classic
1993 Summary: Tournaments entered—34; in money—11; top ten finishes—1
Career Earnings: $1,813,939

E

EASTWOOD, Bob Birth Date 4/9/46 **Birthplace** Providence, RI **Residence** Stockton, CA **Height** 5-10 **Weight** 175 **Special Interest** Hunting, fishing **Family** Wife, Connie; Scott (8/19/71); Steven (12/29/73) **College** San Jose State University **Turned Professional** 1969 **Q School** Spring 1969 **Other Achievements** Winner, 1973 mini-Kemper Open, 1976 Little Bing Crosby (both second Tour); 1965 Sacramento City Amateur, 1966 California State Amateur, 1968 West Coast Athletic Conference, 1981 Morocco Grand Prix. Medalist, Spring 1969 Qualifying School.

Exempt Status: Past Champion
TOUR Victories: 3—1984 USF&G Classic, Danny Thomas-Memphis Classic. 1985 Byron Nelson Classic.
Money and Position:

1972—$ 9,528	1980—$ 36,751 — 90	1987—$114,897 — 88
1973—$ 14,918	1981—$ 66,017 — 67	1988—$ 94,504 — 117
1974—$ 18,535—114	1982—$ 91,633 — 44	1989—$ 84,088 — 139
1975—$ 16,812—110	1983—$157,640 — 30	1990—$123,908 — 125
1976—$ 14,539—123	1984—$232,742 — 24	1991—$ 65,215 — 157
1977—$ 19,706—107	1985—$152,839 — 51	1992—$ 83,818 — 148
1978—$ 24,681—100	1986—$ 72,449 — 117	1993—$ 24,289 — 204
1979—$ 29,630—110		

1993 Best Finish: T18—United Airlines Hawaiian Open
1993 Summary: Tournaments entered—17; in money—3; top ten finishes—0
Career Earnings: $1,544,677

EDWARDS, Danny **Birth Date** 6/14/51 **Birthplace** Ketchikan, AK **Residence** Scottsdale, AZ **Height** 5-11 **Weight** 155 **College** Oklahoma State University **Family** Wife, Ann **Turned Professional** 1973 **Q School** Fall, 1974 **Playoff Record** 1-0 **Special Interests** Car collecting and skiing **Other Achievements** Collegiate All-American, 1972 & 1973. Winner 1972 North and South Amateur; member 1973 Walker Cup team, Low amateur 1973 British Open, Winner 1972 & 1973 Big Eight Conference, 1972 Southeastern Amateur; 1981 Toshiba Taiheiyo Masters.

Exempt status: Past Champion
TOUR Victories: 5—1977 Greater Greensboro Open. 1980 Walt Disney World National Team Play (with David Edwards) 1982 Greater Greensboro Open. 1983 Miller High Life-QCO 1985 Pensacola Open

Money & Position:			
1975 — $ 27,301 — 80	1981 — $ 66,567 — 66	1987 — $146,688 — 75
1976 — $ 25,859 — 85	1982 — $124,018 — 29	1988 — $ 36,637 — 160
1977 — $ 96,811 — 28	1983 — $104,942 — 54	1989 — $ 12,917 — 205
1978 — $ 55,343 — 60	1984 — $ 54,472 — 102	1990 — $ 8,343 — 240
1979 — $ 21,238 — 120	1985 — $206,891 — 25	1991 — $ 5,423 — 253
1980 — $ 73,196 — 57	1986 — $126,139 — 67	1992 — $ 10,852 — 237
		1993 — $ 1,557 — 323

1993 Best Finish: T32—Deposit Guaranty Golf Classic
1993 Summary: Tournaments entered—3; in money—1; top ten finishes—0.
Career Earnings: $1,205,194

F

FABEL, Brad Birth Date 11/30/55 **Birthplace** Louisville, KY **Residence** Nashville, TN **Height** 6-0 **Weight** 185 **Special Interests** Fishing, hunting **College** Western Kentucky University **Family** Wife, Beth; Austin (4/24/89), Morgan Scott (9/9/92) **Turned Professional** 1982 **Q School** Fall, 1984 **Other Achievements** Winner 1974 Kentucky State Amateur. Semi-finalist in 1974 Western Amateur. Winner of eight mini-tour events.

Exempt Status: Special Medical Extension
Best Ever Finish: T2—1990 Canon Greater Hartford Open

Money and Position:			
1985—$ 75,425—100	1988— $ 112,093 — 101	1991— $ 147,562 — 103
1986—$ 25,634—165	1989— $ 69,823 — 146	1992— $ 220,495 — 71
1987—$ 90,024—104	1990— $ 165,876 — 96	1993— $ 59,672 —175

Best 1993 Finish: T15—Freeport-McMoRan Classic
1993 Summary: Tournaments entered—27; in money—14; top ten finishes—0
Career Earnings: $965,605

FEHERTY, David Birth Date 8/13/58 **Birthplace** Bangor, Northern Ireland **Residence** Crawfordsburn Northern Ireland **Height** 5-11 **Weight** 175 **Special Interests** Music, cars **Family** Wife, Caroline; Shey (7/29/88), Rory (4/29/92) **Turned Professional** 1976 **Q School** 1993 **Other Achievements** Winner of four PGA European Tour events including the 1986 Italian and Scottish Opens, 1989 BMW International Open and 1991 Credit Lyonnais Cannes Open. Member, 1991 Ryder Cup; 1985, '86, '90 and '91 Dunhill Cup; 1990 World Cup.

Exempt Status: T11 at 1993 Qualifying Tournament
Best Ever Finish: T7—1991 B.C. Open
Money and Position: 1991—$38,000—187   1992—$11,668—231

FREEMAN, Robin Birth Date 5/7/59 **Birthplace** St. Charles, MO **Residence** Rancho Mirage, CA **Height** 6-0 **Weight** 185 **Special Interest** All sports **Family** Single **College** Central Oklahoma **Turned Professional** 1982 **Q School** 1988, 1991, 1992 **Other Achievements** Medalist 1988 and 1993 Qualifying Tournaments. 1981, 1982 first team NAIA All-American.
Exempt Status: T1 at 1993 Qualifying Tournament
Best Ever Finish: T3—1993 Northern Telecom

Money and Position:		
1989—$ 26,517—188	1993—$ 92,069—148
1992—$101,642—128	

1993 Best Finish: T3—Northern Telecom Open
1993 Summary: Tournaments entered—30; in money—14; top ten finishes—1
Career Earnings: $220,255

FURYK, Jim Birth Date 5/12/70 **Birthplace** West Chester, PA **Residence** Manheim, PA **Height** 6-2 **Weight** 200 **College** University of Arizona **Turned Professional** 1992 **Special Interests** All sports **Family** Single **Other Achievements** Two time collegiate All-American; twice named to First Team All-PAC-10. Won 1993 NIKE Mississippi Gulf Coast Classic on first playoff hole with Robert Friend. Lost to Clark Dennis in playoff of 1993 NIKE Bakersfield Open.
Exempt Status: T37 at 1993 Qualifying Tournament
1993 Summary: Tournaments entered —1; in money —0; top ten finishes —0.

FEZLER, Forrest Birth Date 9/23/49 **Birthplace** Hayward, CA **Residence** Hampton, VA **Height** 5-9 **Weight** 165 **Special Interests** Fishing, hunting **Family** Wife, Kathy; five children **College** San Jose Community College **Turned Professional** 1969 **Other Achievements** Winner, 1969 California Amateur; 1969 California Junior College Championship; runner-up 1974 U.S. Open. Named 1969 Junior College Player of the Year.

Exempt Status: Past Champion

TOUR Victories: 1—1974 Southern Open

Money & Position:			
1972 — $ 26,542 — 88	1979 — $ 11,427 — 148	1985 — $ 1,400 — 154
1973 — $106,390 — 12	1980 — $ 19,269 — 127	1986 — $ 2,080 — 244
1974 — $ 90,066 — 24	1981 — $ 13,064 — 158	1987 — $ 1,784 — 258
1975 — $ 52,157 — 43	1982 — $ 38,983 — 105	1988 — $ 3,477 — 207
1976 — $ 59,793 — 44	1983 — $ 24,452 — 143	1989 — $ 1,853 — 152
1977 — $ 30,812 — 82	1984 — $ 14,152 — 150	1993 — $ 2,610 — 295
1978 — $ 30,812 — 85		

1993 Best Finish: T41—Deposit Guaranty Classic
1993 Summary: Tournaments entered —7; in money —2; top ten finishes —0.
Career Earnings: $527,996

G

GARDNER, Buddy Birth Date 8/24/55 **Birthplace** Montgomery, AL **Residence** Birmingham, AL **Weight** 175 **Height** 5-11 **College** Auburn University **Family** Wife, Susan; Brooke Marie (2/1/87); Payton Webb (12/2/89) **Turned Professional** 1977 **Q School** Fall 1977, 1978, 1982 **Other Achievements** Winner, 1974 and '75 Alabama Amateur and 1976 Dixie Amateur. Claimed 1990 Ben Hogan Panama City Beach Classic. 1977 All-American.

Exempt Status: Veteran Member   **Playoff Record:** 0-1

Best Ever Finish: T2—1979 Tucson Open; 1979 Anheuser-Busch Classic; 2—1984 Houston Coca-Cola Open. 2—1987 Big "I" Houston Open.

Money and Position:			
1978 — $ 5,637 — 170	1984 — $ 118,945 — 55	1989 — $ 135,488 — 103
1979 — $ 71,468 — 56	1985 — $ 121,809 — 67	1990 — $ 159,737 — 99
1980 — $ 30,907 — 102	1986 — $ 92,006 — 91	1991 — $ 201,700 — 83
1981 — $ 14,635 — 151	1987 — $ 173,047 — 60	1992 — $ 113,394 — 124
1982 — $ 6,214 — 192	1988 — $ 130,589 — 91	1993 — $ 13,721 — 232
1983 — $ 56,529 — 91		

1993 Best Finish: T48—Buick Open; T48—Hardee's Golf Classic
1993 Summery: Tournaments entered—27; in money—7; top ten finishes—0
Career Earnings: $1,446,096

GARNER, Tom Birth Date 7/18/61 **Birthplace** Ft. Lauderdale, FL **Residence** Winter Park, FL **Height** 5-10 **Weight** 175 **Special Interests** Family, Sports **College** University of Alabama **Family** Wife, Julie **Turned Professional** 1984 **Q School** 1986, 1987, 1993 **Other Achievements** Winner, 1990 Ben Hogan Central New York Classic, 1992 Ben Hogan Bakersfield Open.

Exempt Status: T37 at 1993 Qualifying Tournament

Best Ever Finish: 37—1988 Georgia-Pacific Atlanta Classic

Money and Position:	
1987 — $12,226 — 202	1989 — $ 2,437 — 252
1988 — $ 5,148 — 243	1990 — $ 2,485 — 264

Career Earnings: $17,374

GONZALEZ, Ernie Birth Date 2/19/61 **Birthplace** San Diego, CA **Residence** San Diego CA **Height** 5-8 **Weight** 210 **College** United States International University **Special Interests** All Sports **Family** Wife, Judy **Turned Professional** 1983 **Q School** 1984, 1985, 1989 **Other Achievements** Winner 1981, 1982 San Diego County Amateur Match Play Championship; 1983 San Diego County Open (as an amateur); 1984, 1985 Queen Mary Open.

Exempt Status: Past Champion.

TOUR Victories: 1—1986 Pensacola Open.

Money & Position:			
1985 — $ 12,729 — 171	1988 — $ 14,135 — 207	1991 — $ 5,550 — 252
1986 — $125,548 — 68	1989 — $ 13,840 — 203	1992 — $ 5,485 — 262
1987 — $ 60,234 — 154	1990 — $ 13,540 — 221	1993 — $ 2,175 — 310

1993 Best Finish: T26— Deposit Guaranty Golf Classic
1993 Summary: Tournaments entered—2; in money—1; top ten finishes—0.
Career Earnings: $238,330

GOTSCHE, Steve Birth Date 8/24/61 **Birthplace** Wakeeny, KS **Residence** Great Bend, KS **Height** 6-2 **Weight** 200 **College** University of Nebraska **Special Interests** Fishing **Family** Wife, Linda; Adam (9/23/86), Ryan (7/16/90) **Turned Professional** 1984 **Q-School** 1993 **Other Achievements** 1990 National Assistants Champion. 1990-1993 Midwest Section Player of the Year. Winner, 1990 Kansas Open, 1988 Wyoming Open and 1986 Nebraska Open.
Exempt Status: T11 at 1993 Qualifying Tournament
Best Ever Finish: T55—1991 U.S. Open
Money and Position: 1991—$5,164—255   1993—$5,657—264
Best 1993 Finish: T68—U.S. Open
1993 Summary: Tournaments entered—1; in money—1; top ten finishes—0.

GOYDOS, Paul Birth Date 6/20/64 **Birthplace** Long Beach, CA **Residence** Long Beach, CA **Height** 5-9 **Weight** 190 **Special Interest** Sports **Family** Wife, Wendy; Chelsea Marie (8/21/90), Courtney (9/8/92) **College** Long Beach State **Turned Professional** 1989 **Q School** 1992,1993 **Other Achievements** Winner, 1990 Long Beach Open and 1992 Ben Hogan Yuma Open. Pacific Coast Athletic Association All-Conference 1985-86.
Exempt Status: T18 at 1993 Qualifying Tournament
Best Ever Finish: T13—Buick Classic
Money and Position: 1993—$87,803—152
1993 Best Finish: T13—Buick Classic
1993 Summary: Tournaments entered—30; in money—18; top ten finishes—0
Career Earnings: $87,803

GRAHAM, David Birth Date 5/23/46 **Birthplace** Windsor, Australia **Residence** Dallas, TX **Height** 5-10 **Weight** 162 **Special Interests** Hunting, golf club design, cars **Family** Wife, Maureen Burdett; Andrew (11/8/74); Michael (10/8/77) **Turned Professional** 1962 **Q School** Fall, 1971 **Other Achievements** Foreign victories include 1970 French Open, 1970 Thailand Open, 1971 Caracas Open, 1971 JAL Open, 1975 Wills Masters, 1976 Chunichi Crowns Invitational (Japan), 1976 Picadilly World Match Play, 1977 Australian Open and 1977 South African PGA. 1978 Mexico Cup. 1979 West Lakes Classic (Australia), New Zealand Open. 1980 Mexican Open, Rolex Japan, Brazilian Classic. 1981, 1982 Lancome (France). Winner, 1985 Queensland Open. **National Teams** Australian World Cup, 1970 (won team title with Bruce Devlin). U.S. vs. Japan, 1983. Australian Dunhill Cup, 1985, 1986, 1988.
Exempt Status: Past Champion **Playoff Record:** 2-1
TOUR Victories: 8-1972 Cleveland Open. 1976 Westchester Classic, American Golf Classic. 1979 PGA Championship 1980 Memorial Tournament. 1981 Phoenix Open, U.S. Open. 1983 Houston Coca-Cola Open.

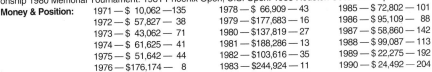

Money & Position:			
1971 — $ 10,062 —135	1978 — $ 66,909 — 43	1985 — $ 72,802 — 101
1972 — $ 57,827 — 38	1979 — $177,683 — 16	1986 — $ 95,109 — 88
1973 — $ 43,062 — 71	1980 — $137,819 — 27	1987 — $ 58,860 — 142
1974 — $ 61,625 — 41	1981 — $188,286 — 13	1988 — $ 99,087 — 113
1975 — $ 51,642 — 44	1982 — $103,616 — 35	1989 — $ 22,275 — 192
1976 — $176,174 — 8	1983 — $244,924 — 11	1990 — $ 24,492 — 204
1977 — $ 72,086 — 44	1984 — $116,627 — 58	

Career Earnings: $1,874,780

GUMP, Scott Birth Date 12/17/65 **Birthplace** Rockledge, FL **Residence** Orlando, FL **Height** 6-2 **Weight** 165 **Special Interest** Whitewater rafting **Family** Wife, Chris **College** University of Miami **Turned Professional** 1988 **Q School** 1990 **Other Achievements** Finished 50th on 1990 Ben Hogan Tour money list.
Exempt Status: 147th on 1993 money list
Best Ever Finish: T2—The International
Money and Position: 1991—$207,809— 80   1993—$96,822—147
                                   1992—$148,696—102
1993 Best Finish: T11—Cannon Greater Open
1993 Summary: Tournaments entered—31; in money—17; top ten finishes—0
Career Earnings: $453,326

H

HALLDORSON, Dan Birth Date 4/2/52 **Birthplace** Winnipeg, Canada **Residence** Cambridge,IL **Height** 5 -10 **Weight** 180 **Special Interests** Sports **Family** Wife, Pat; Angie (4/7/75) **Turned Professional** 1971 **Q School** 1974, 1978, 1990 **Other Achievements**In 1986 won the Deposit Guaranty Golf Classic, an unofficial PGA TOUR event. He defeated Paul Azinger by two strokes in Hattiesburg. A member of several Canadian World Cup teams. Winner of the 1983 Canadian Tour Order of Merit.
Exempt Status: Past Champion
TOUR Victories: 1—1980 Pensacola Open

Money & Position:

1975 — $ 619 —243	1984 — $ 55,215 — 99	1989 —$ 86,667—137
1979— $ 24,559 —116	1985 — $112,102 — 73	1990 —$ 18,155—215
1980— $111,553 — 36	1986 — $ 83,876 —101	1991 —$ 158,743— 97
1981— $ 90,064 — 47	1987 — $ 69,094 —125	1992 —$ 119,002—118
1982— $ 93,705 — 43	1988 — $ 96,079 —116	1993 —$ 24,284—205
1983— $ 21,458 —146		

1993 Best Finish: T31—Hardee's Golf Classic
1993 Summary: Tournaments entered —30; in money —9; top ten finishes —0.
Career Earnings: $1,165,919

HATALSKY, Morris Birth Date 11/10/51 **Birthplace** San Diego, CA **Residence** Ormond Beach, FL **Height** 5-11 **Weight** 165 **Special Interest** Family activities, TOUR Bible study, snow skiing **Family** Wife, Tracy; Daniel (12/11/80); Kenneth (12/11/80) **College** United States International University **Turned Professional** 1973 **Q School** Spring 1976, 1993 **Other Achievements** 1972 NAIA All-American. Captained 1972 U.S. International University team that won NAIA Championship. Winner, 1968 Mexico National Junior Championship.
Exempt Status: T8 at 1993 Qualifying Tournament
TOUR Victories: 4—1981 Hall of Fame Classic. 1983 Greater Milwaukee Open. 1988 Kemper Open. 1990 Bank of Boston Classic.

Money and Position:

1976—$ 249—288	1982—$ 66,128— 65	1988—$ 239,019 — 47
1977—$ 32,193— 79	1983—$102,567— 56	1989—$ 66,577 — 149
1978—$ 43,062— 114	1984—$ 50,957—107	1990—$ 253,639 — 59
1979—$ 61,625— 69	1985—$ 76,059— 96	1991—$ 106,265 — 132
1980—$ 47,107— 74	1986—$105,543— 83	1992—$ 55,042 — 170
1981—$ 70,186— 63	1987—$150,654— 70	1993—$ 111,057 — 135

1993 Best Finish: T2— Deposit Guaranty
1993 Summary: Tournaments entered—18; in money—13; top ten finishes—2
Career Earnings: $1,611,545

HAYES, Mark Birth Date 7/12/49 **Birthplace** Stillwater, OK **Residence** Edmond, OK **Height** 5-11 **Weight** 170 **Special Interest** Sports **Family** Wife,Jana; Kelly (12/9/79); Ryan (3/25/83) **College:** Oklahoma State University **Turned Professional** 1973 **Q School** 1973, 1988, 1989, 1990 **Other Achievements** 1967 and 1971 Oklahoma Amateur Champion. 1970 and 1971 Collegiate All-American.
Exempt Status: Past Champion
TOUR Victories: 3— 1976 Byron Nelson Classic, Pensacola Open. 1977 Tournament Players Championship.

Money & Position:

1973 — $ 8,637 — 160	1980 — $ 66,535 — 61	1987 — $ 76,666 — 116
1974 — $ 40,620 — 68	1981 — $ 91,624 — 46	1988 — $ 77,072 — 131
1975 — $ 49,297 — 47	1982 — $ 47,777 — 95	1989 — $ 87,689 — 134
1976 — $151,699 — 11	1983 — $ 63,431 — 81	1990 — $ 76,743 — 149
1977 — $115,749 — 19	1984 — $ 42,207 — 115	1991 — $ 36,370 — 191
1978 — $146,456 — 15	1985 — $ 61,988 — 108	1992— $ 50,324 — 175
1979 — $130,878 — 23	1986 — $117,837 — 74	1993 — $ 6,942 — 249

1993 Best Finish: T54—B.C. Open
1993 Summary: Tournaments entered — 9; in money —3; top ten finishes — 0.
Career Earnings: $1,544,836

HEINEN, Mike Birth Date 1/17/67 **Birthplace** Rayne, LA **Residence** Lake Charles, LA **Height** 6-1 **Weight** 195 **Special Interest** Hunting, fishing **Family** Wife, Kathy **College** University of Southwestern Louisiana **Turned Professional** 1989 **Q School** 1993 **Other Achievements** Earned $71,706 to finish 16th on the 1993 NIKE TOUR money list. Two-time NCAA Division I All-American.
Exempt Status: T26 at 1993 Qualifying Tournament

HEAFNER, Vance Birthdate 8/11/54 **Birthplace** Charlotte, NC **Residence** Raleigh, NC **Height** 6-0 **Weight** 170 **Special Interest** Fishing, hunting **Family** Wife, Paige; Elizabeth(10/13/85) **College** North Carolina State **Turned Professional** 1978 **Q School** 1980, 1989 **Other Achievements** All American at North Carolina State, 1984, 1985, 1986. Winner 1976 and 1978 Eastern Amateur titles; 1977 Porter Cup. 1977 Walker Cup team. Winner, 1977 Azalea Invitational, 1978, American Amateur Classic.
Exempt Status: Past Champion
TOUR Victories: 1-1981 Walt Disney World National Team Championship (w/ Mike Holland)

Money & Position:			
1980 — $ 11,398 — 156	1984 — $ 90,702— 71	1988 — $ 2,117 — 170
1981 — $ 73,244 — 60	1985 — $ 31,964 —142	1989 — $ 1,624 — 273
1982 — $113,717 — 33	1986— $ 28,763 —159	1990 — $ 6,525 — 256
1983 — $ 68,210 — 65	1987— $ 74,489 —119	

Career Earnings: $520,752

HENNINGER, Brian Birth Date 10/19/63 **Birthplace** Sacramento, CA **Residence** Lake Oswego, OR **Height** 5-8 **Weight** 155 **Special Interest** Hunting, fishing and horses **Family** Wife, Cathy **College** University of Southern California **Turned Professional** 1987 **Joined PGA TOUR** 1993 **Other Achievements** First on 1989 Golden State Order of Merit. Winner, 1992 Ben Hogan South Texas Open, 1992 Ben Hogan Macon Open, and 1992 Ben Hogan Knoxville Open. Finished second on 1992 Ben Hogan Tour money list.
Exempt Status: 130th on 1993 money list
Best Ever Finish: T4—1993 Sprint Western Open
Money and Position: 1993—$112,811—130
1993 Best Finish: T4—Sprint Western Open
1993 Summary: Tournaments entered—31; in money—16; top ten finishes—1.
Career Earnings: $112,811

HINKLE, Lon Birth Date 7/17/49 **Birthplace** Flint, MI **Residence** San Diego, CA **Height** 6-2 **Weight** 220 **Special Interests** Reading **Family** Monique (8/10/78), Danielle (3/20/82); Jake (9/6/85) **College** San Diego State University **Turned Professional** 1972 **Q School** 1972, 1991 **Other Achievements** Co-champion 1972 Pacific Coast Athletic Conference. Runner-up 1975 German Open and Sanpo Classic in Japan. Winner, 1978 JCPenney Classic with Pat Bradley. Runner-up 1980 European Open. 1981 National Long Drive Champion, 338 yds., 6 in.
Exempt Status: Past Champion
TOUR Victories: 3 —1978 New Orleans Open. 1979 Bing Crosby National Pro-Am, World Series of Golf

Money & Position:			
1972 — $ 7,350 — 145	1979 — $ 247,693 — 3	1986 — $ 97,610 — 86
1973 — $ 7,539 — 164	1980 — $ 134,913 — 29	1987 — $ 45,751 — 159
1974 — $ 6,509 — 162	1981 — $ 144,307 — 22	1989 — $151,828 — 92
1975 — $ 8,420 — 136	1982 — $ 55,406 — 81	1990 — $ 26,052 — 201
1976 — $ 11,058 — 138	1983 — $ 116,822 — 47	1991 — $ 49,692 — 174
1977 — $ 51,494 — 60	1984 — $ 89,850 — 73	1992 — $ 91,854 — 139
1978 — $138,388 — 16	1985 — $ 105,499 — 76	1993 —$ 8,621 — 244

1993 Best Finish: T58—AT&T Pebble Beach National Pro-Am
1993 Summary: Tournaments entered —13; in money—5 ; top ten finishes — 0.
Career Earnings: $ 1,595,836

HORGAN III, P.H. Birth Date 8/22/61 **Birthplace** Newport, RI **Residence** Newport, RI **Height** 5-10 **Weight** 180 **Special Interests** Water skiing, boating **Family** Single **College** University of Rhode Island **Turned Professional** 1984 **Q School** 1989, 1990 **Other Achievements** Winner, 1991 Ben Hogan Yuma Open and 1991 Macon Open. Finished third on the 1991 Ben Hogan Tour money list.
Exempt Status: 141st on 1993 money list
Best Ever Finish: T5—1989 USF&G Classic

Money and Position:		
1989 — $ 63,787 — 152	1991 — $ 2,912 — 267	
1990 — $ 72,898 — 154	1992 — $ 123,684 — 116	1993 — $105,571 — 141

1993 Best Finish: T7—Sprint Western Open
1993 Summary: Tournaments entered—31; in money—12; top ten finishes—3
Career Earnings: $368,851

J

JAECKEL, Barry   Birth Date 2/14/49 **Birthplace** Los Angeles, CA **Residence** Palm Desert, CA **Height** 5-11 **Weight** 160 **Special Interest** All sports **Family** Wife, Evelyn **College** Santa Monica J.C. **Turned Professional** 1971 **Q School** Spring 1975 **Other Achievements** 1968 Southern California Amateur champion. Winner, 1972 French Open.
Exempt Status: Past Champion
TOUR Victories: 1-1978 Tallahassee Open

Money and Position:

1975—$ 8,883— 133	1982—$ 62,940— 70	
1976—$ 36,888— 70	1983—$ 64,473— 80	
1978—$ 72,421— 37	1984—$ 49,308—110	1989—$ 64,782—151
1979—$ 46,541— 86	1985—$ 81,765— 92	1990—$ 63,590—168
1980—$ 25,501—116	1986—$ 80,646—105	1991—$ 59,216—167
1981—$ 87,931— 48	1987—$ 53,909—144	1992—$ 13,351—226
1982—$ 62,940— 70	1988—$ 39,227—173	1993—$ 15,584—226

1993 Best Finish: T4—Deposit Guaranty Golf Classic
1993 Summary: Tournaments entered—11; in money—3; top ten finishes—1
Career Earnings: $937,459

JENKINS, Tom Birth Date 12/14/47 **Birthplace** Houston, TX **Residence** Alachua, FL **Height** 5-11 **Weight** 175 **Special Interests** Camping, gardening **Family** Wife, Lynn, one child **College** University of Houston **Turned Professional** 1971 **Joined TOUR** 1972 **Other Achievements** Two time All-American. Member of 1970 NCAA Championship team at Houston.
Exempt Status: Past Champion   **Playoff Record:** 0-1
TOUR Victories: 1—1975 IVB-Philadelphia Classic

Money & Position:

1972 — $ 1,317 — 270	1978 — $ 2,902 — 186	
1973 — $ 38,241 — 80	1979 — $ 6,689 — 171	1984 — $ 53,200 — 103
1974 — $ 30,826 — 86	1980 — $ 16,178 — 137	1985 — $ 9,347 — 183
1975 — $ 45,267 — 52	1981 — $ 78,127 — 54	1986 — $ 995 — 275
1976 — $ 42,740 — 65	1982 — $ 64,753 — 67	1992 — $ 6,963 — 253
1977 — $ 15,780 — 120	1983 — $ 52,564 — 97	1993 — $ 4,302 — 277

Career Earnings: $456,669

JONES, Steve Birth Date 12/27/58 **Birthplace** Artesia, NM **Residence** Phoenix, AZ **Height** 6-4 **Weight** 185 **Special Interests** Snow skiing, basketball **Family** Wife, Bonnie, Cy Edmond (2/27/91) **College** University of Colorado **Turned Professional** 1981 **Q School** Fall 1981,1984,1986. **Other Achievements** Medalist in 1986 TOUR Qualifying Tournament. Semi-finalist in 1976 USGA Junior Championship, Second team All-American. Winner 1987 JCPenney Classic (with Jane Crafter).
Exempt Status: Past Champion   **Playoff Record:** 2-1
TOUR Victories: 4—1988 AT&T Pebble Beach Pro-Am. 1989 MONY Tournament of Champions, Bob Hope Chrysler Classic, Canadian Open.

Money & Position:

1982 — $ 1,986 — 229	1987 — $ 154,918 — 66	1990 — $350,982 — 34
1985 — $ 43,379 — 129	1988 — $ 241,877 — 45	1991 — $294,961 — 54
1986 — $ 51,473 — 136	1989 — $ 745,578 — 8	1992 — Did not play
		1993 — Did not play

Best 1993 Finish: Did Not Play
Career Earnings: $1,885,939

JORDAN, Pete Birth Date 6/10/64 **Birthplace** Elmhurst, IL **Residence** Valrico, FL **Height** 6-0 **Weight** 180 **Special Interests** Sports, music **Family** Wife, Kelly; Ryan (11/26/91) **College** Texas Christian University **Turned Professional** 1986 **Q School** 1993 **Other Achievements** 1986 NCAA All-American. Named All-Southwest Conference in 1985 and 1986. Member of NIKE TOUR 1991-'93.
Exempt Status: T4 at 1993 Qualifying Tournament
Best Ever Finish: T72--1993 U.S. Open
Money and Position: 1993--$5,405--269
1993 Summary: Tournaments entered--1; in money--1; top ten finishes--0

K

KENDALL, Skip Birth Date 9/9/64 **Birthplace** Milwaukee, WI **Residence** Oldsmar, FL **Height** 5-8 **Weight** 145 **Special Interests** Sports, movies **Family** Wife, Beth **College** University of Nevada-Las Vegas **Turned Professional** 1987 **Q School** 1992 **Other Achievements** Winner, 1988 and 1989 Wisconsin State Open. Co-medalist, 1992 Qualifying Tournament.
Exempt Status: 129th on 1993 money list
Best Ever Finish: 8—1993 The International
Money and Position: 1993—$115,189—129
1993 Best Finish: 8— The International
1993 Summary: Tournaments entered—32; in money—18; top ten finishes—1
Career Earnings: $115,189

KING, Brad **Birth Date** 11/13/65 **Birthplace** Northam, Western Australia **Residence** Marangaro, Perth, Australia **Height** 6-1 **Weight** 175 **Special Interests** Fishing **Family** Wife, Leanne **Turned Professional** 1987 **Q-School** 1993 **Other Achievements** Winner, 1989 Western PGA Championship.
Exempt Status: T37 at 1993 Qualifying Tournament

KIRBY, Ed **Birth Date** 11/24/62 **Birthplace** Providence, RI **Residence** Cumberland, RI **Height** 5-5 **Weight** 140 **Family** Single **College** Furman University **Turned Professional** 1985 **Q School** 1993 **Other Achievements** Winner, Rhode Island State Juniors, 1984 Southern Conference, 1985 New Hampshire Open, 1989 Rhode Island Open. All-American selection in 1984. Played Asian Tour in 1988-89 and NIKE TOUR in 1990 and 1992. Best-ever NIKE TOUR finish was a second at the 1992 New England Classic.
Exempt Status: T32 at 1993 Qualifying Tournament
Best-Ever Finish: T33--1989 U.S. Open   1993--$6,525--256
Money & Position: 1987--$3,178--242
                             1989--$7,577--221
Best 1993 Finish: T52—U.S. Open
1993 Summary: Tournaments entered— 2; in money— 1; top ten finishes— 0.

KITE, Chris **Birth Date** 2/5/64 **Birthplace** Taylorsville, NC **Residence** Huntersville, **Height** 5-9 **Weight** 150 **Special Interests** Music **Family** Single **College** Wake Forest University **Turned Professional** 1987 **Q School** 1993 **Other Achievements** Two-time first team All-American (1985-86). 1986 Wake Forest team won NCAA team championship. Runner-up, 1986 U.S. Amateur. Winner of Chris Schenkel Intercollegiate event.
Exempt Status: T37 at 1993 Qualifying Tournament
Best-Ever Finish: T11--1988 Anheuser-Busch Classic
Money & Position: 1988--$ 23,252--192   1989--$ 2,080--257
Career Earnings: $25,332

KNOX, Kenny **Birth Date** 8/15/56 **Birthplace** Columbus,GA **Residence** Tallahassee, FL **Height** 5-10 **Weight** 175 **Special Interests** Teaching juniors to play golf **Family** Wife, Karen; Michelle (12/24/80) **College** Florida State University, (1978. Physical Education) **Turned Professional** 1978 **Q School** Fall 1981,1983, 1984. **Other Achievements** 1977 and 1978 All-American. Winner, 1977 Southeastern Amateur.
Exempt Status: Past champion   **Playoff Record:** 1-1
TOUR Victories: 3-1986 Honda Classic. 1987 Hardee's Golf Classic. 1990 Buick Southern Open.

Money & Position:		
1982 — $ 6,919 — 186	1987 — $200,783 — 55	1991 — $423,025 — 32
1984 — $ 15,606 — 71	1988 — $168,099 — 70	1992 — $ 24,889 — 203
1985 — $ 26,968 — 41	1989 — $230,012 — 62	1993 — $ 3,630 — 282
1986 — $261,608 — 24	1990 — $209,679 — 73	

Best 1993 Finish: 74—Freeport-McMoRan Classic
1993 Summary: Tournaments entered —21; in money —2; top ten finishes — 0.
Career Earnings: $1,571,216

KOCH, Gary **Birth Date** 11/21/52 **Birthplace** Baton Rouge, LA **Residence** Tampa, FL **Height** 5-11 **Weight** 165 **Special Interests** Fishing, reading, music **Family** Wife, Donna; Patricia (4/1/81); Rachel (7/30/83) **College** University of Florida **Turned Professional** 1975 **Q School** Fall, 1975 **Other Achievements** Winner, 1968, 1969, 1970 Florida State Juniors; 1970 U.S. Juniors; 1969 Orange Bowl Juniors; 1969 Florida State Open; 1973 Trans-Mississippi Amateur; 1973, 1974 Southeastern Conference. First-team All-American, 1972, 1973, 1974. Member 1973 NCAA Championship team at Florida. Winner of 10 collegiate events. **National Teams** Walker Cup (2), 1973, 1975; U.S. World Amateur Cup Team 1974.
Exempt Status: Past Champion   **Playoff Record:** 2-0
TOUR Victories: 6-1976 Tallahassee Open. 1978 Florida Citrus Open. 1983 Doral Eastern Open. 1984 Isuzu-Andy Williams San Diego Open, Bay Hill Classic. 1988 Panasonic-Las Vegas Invitational.

Money & Position:		
1976 — $ 38,195 — 69	1982 — $ 43,449 — 98	1988 — $ 414,694 — 24
1977 — $ 58,383 — 52	1983 — $ 168,330 — 27	1989 — $ 86,348 — 138
1978 — $ 58,660 — 54	1984 — $ 262,679 — 17	1990 — $ 36,469 — 186
1979 — $ 46,809 — 84	1985 — $ 121,566 — 68	1991 — $ 7,189 — 243
1980 — $ 39,827 — 82	1986 — $ 180,693 — 50	1992 — $ 3,690 — 274
1981 — $ 11,999 — 162	1987 — $ 33,727 — 175	1993 — $ 702 — 329

1993 Best Finish: T51—Deposit Guaranty Golf Classic
1993 Summary: Tournaments entered —4; in money — 1; top ten finishes — 0.
Career Earnings: $1,613,407

Other Prominent Members of the PGA TOUR

KRATZERT, Bill Birth Date 6/29/52 **Birthplace** Quantico, VA **Residence** Ft. Wayne, IN **Height** 6-0 **Weight** 190 **Special Interests** Sports, Arabian horses **Family** Wife, Janie; Rebecca Brea (9/6/78), Tyler Brennie (12/5/80); Thomas Andrew (4/29/91) **College** University of Georgia **Turned Professional** 1974 **Q School** Spring 1976 **Other Achievements** Winner 1968 Indiana Amateur and 1969 Indiana Open. 1973 and 1974 All-American.

Exempt Status: T32 at 1993 Qualifying Tournament

TOUR Victories: 4--1976 Walt Disney World National Team Play (with Woody Blackburn), 1977 Greater Hartford Open. 1980 Greater Milwaukee Open. 1984 Pensacola Open

Money and Position:

1976—$ 21,253—102	1982—$ 22,779—139	1988—$ 43,519—158
1977—$134,758— 10	1983—$ 14,744—166	1989—$ 7,773—220
1978—$183,683— 8	1984—$149,827— 37	1990—$ 14,630—218
1979—$101,628— 35	1985—$180,331— 37	1991—$ 19,819—209
1980—$175,771— 12	1986—$ 47,421—139	1992—$ 16,439—217
1981—$ 55,513— 75	1987—$ 78,232—114	1993—$ 78,992—156

Best 1993 Finish T10--Nestle Invitational

1993 Summary Tournaments entered--15; in money--11; top ten finishes--1

Career Money $1,347,113

L

LAMONTAGNE, Steve Birth Date 6/27/65 **Birthplace** Izmir, Turkey **Residence** Melbourne, FL **Height** 5-9 **Weight** 175 **Special Interest** Sports **Family** Single **College** University of Florida **Turned Professional** 1987 **Q School** 1989, 1991 **Other Achievements** 1985 NJCAA Champion while at Brevard Community College.

Exempt Status: T32 1993 Qualifying Tournament

Best Ever Finish: T4—1992 Chattanooga Classic

Money and Position:

1990—$ 67,608—161	1992—$132,498—109
1991—$ 4,950—258	1993—$107,077—138

1993 Best Finish: T6—Buick Open

1993 Summary: Tournaments entered—33; in money—16; top ten finishes—1

Career Earnings: $307,182

LARDON, Brad Birth Date 4/29/65 **Birthplace** New York, NY **Residence** Kingwood, TX **Height** 5-9 **Weight** 170 **College** Rice University **Special Interests** Frisbee, bass fishing **Family** Wife, Kathie **Turned Professional** 1989 **Q-School** 1993 **Other Achievements** Winner, 1987 Sam Houston State Intercollegiate. Finished second in the Connecticut State Amateur in 1988 and second in the 1988 Houston State Amateur.

Exempt Status: T37 at 1993 Qualifying Tournament

Best Ever Finish: T18--1991 Independent Insurance Open

Money and Position: 1991—$20,928—205

LEVET, Thomas Birth Date 5/5/68 **Birthplace** Paris, France **Residence** Paris, France **Height** 5-9 **Weight** 160 **Special Interests** Soccer, music, animals, tennis **Family** Single **Turned Professional** 1988 **Q School** 1993 **Other Achievements** Winner 1988 and 1991 French PGA, 1992 French Championship.

Exempt Status: T18 at 1993 Qualifying Tournament

LYE, Mark Birth Date 11/13/52 **Birthplace** Vallejo, CA **Residence** Ft. Myers, FL **Height** 6-5 **Weight** 175 **Special Interest** Guitar, fishing **Family** Single **College** San Jose State **University Turned Professional** 1975 **Q School** Fall, 1976 **Other Achievements** Winner of the 1977 Australian Tour's Order of Merit and the 1976 Rolex Trophy tournament in Switzerland. Won the 1976 Champion of Champions Tournament in Australia. 1975 All-American.

Exempt Status: Special Medical Extension

TOUR Victories: 1—1983 Bank of Boston Classic

Money and Position:

1977—$ 22,034—100	1983—$164,506— 28	1989—$ 242,884— 56
1978—$ 13,648—125	1984—$152,356— 43	1990—$ 201,001— 77
1979—$ 51,184— 75	1985—$112,735— 72	1991—$ 147,530— 104
1980—$109,454— 39	1986—$ 78,960—111	1992—$ 9,921— 243
1981—$ 76,044— 56	1987—$ 73,625—121	1993—$ 106,935— 139
1982—$ 67,460— 61	1988—$106,972—108	

1993 Best Finish: T4—B.C. Open

1993 Summary: Tournaments entered—23; in money—13; top ten finishes—1

Career Earnings: $1,737,260

M

McCORD, Gary   Birth Date 5/23/48 **Birthplace** San Gabriel, CA **Residence** Escondido, CA **Height** 6-2 **Weight** 185 **College** University of California-Riverside (1971, Economics) **Special Interests** Enjoys spoofing people **Turned Professional** 1971 **Joined TOUR** Fall 1973; Fall 1982 **Other Achievements** Two-time All-American. 1970 NCAA Division II champion. Player Director on TOUR's Policy Board 1983-1986. Color analyst on CBS golf telecast. Winner, 1992 Ben Hogan Gateway Open.

Best-Ever Finish: 2—1975 Greater Milwaukee Open; T2—1977 Greater Milwaukee Open
Exempt Status: Veteran Member

Money & Position:			
1973 — $ 499 — 423	1980 — $ 13,521 — 146	1987 — $ 3,689 — 240
1974 — $ 33,640 — 78	1981 — $ 20,722 — 130	1988 — $ 15,502 — 204
1975 — $ 43,028 — 59	1982 — $ 27,380 — 130	1989 — $ 29,629 — 181
1976 — $ 26,479 — 84	1983 — $ 55,756 — 94	1990 — $ 32,249 — 191
1977 — $ 46,318 — 65	1984 — $ 68,213 — 85	1991 — $ 7,365 — 241
1978 — $ 15,280 —117	1985 — $ 32,198 — 140	1992 — $ 59,061 — 160
1979 — $ 36,843 —105	1986 — $ 27,747 — 160	1993 — $ 16,456 — 225

1993 Best Finish T32—Phoenix Open
1993 Summary Tournaments entered—8; in money—5; top ten finishes—0
Career Earnings $615,517

McCULLOUGH, Mike Birth Date 3/21/45 **Birthplace** Coshocton, OH **Residence** Scottsdale, AZ **Height** 5-9 **Weight** 170 **Special Interests** Flying, outdoor activities **Family** Wife, Marilyn; Jason (4/24/75); Michelle (5/13/86); Mark Andrew (6/7/89) **College** Bowling Green State University (1968, Education) **Turned Professional** 1970 **Joined TOUR** Fall 1972 **Other Achievements:** Winner of 1970 Ohio State Amateur. Winner of 1977 Magnolia Classic. 1974 Mini-Kemper Open.

Exempt Status: Veteran Member
Best-Ever Finish: 2—1977 Tournament Players Championship

Money & Position:		
1972 — $ 227 — 437	1980 — $ 19,588 —125	1988 — $ 27,561 — 181
1973 — $ 17,076 —114	1981 — $ 27,212 —115	1989 — $ 22,081 — 193
1974 — $ 31,961 — 83	1982 — $ 43,207 — 99	1990 — $ 20,870 — 210
1975 — $ 17,706 —109	1983 — $ 38,660 —116	1991 — $ 24,600 — 202
1976 — $ 29,491 — 76	1984 — $ 21,031 —153	1992 — $ 722 — 312
1977 — $ 79,413 —136	1985 — $ 27,257 —145	1993 — $ 2,011 — 314
1978 — $ 56,066 — 47	1986 — $ 60,586 —127	
1979 — $ 43,664 — 89	1987 — $ 75,890 —117	

1993 Best Finish: T48—B.C. Open
1993 Summary: Tournaments entered—3; in money—1; top ten finishes 0.
Career Earnings: $681,803

McGOWAN, Pat Birth Date 11/27/54 **Birthplace** Grand Forks, ND **Residence** Southern Pines, NC **Height** 5-11 **Weight** 170 **College** Brigham Young University **Special Interests** Reading, psycho-cybernetics, bird hunting **Family** Wife, Bonnie **Turned Professional** 1977 **Q School** 1977 **Other Achievements** Winner, 1971 Mexican International Junior, 1976 Air Force Academy Invitational, 1977 Pacific Coast Intercollegiate, 1984 Sacramento Classic (TPS). Former member of PGA TOUR Tournament Policy Board 1989-92.

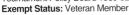

Exempt Status: Veteran Member
Best Ever Finish: 2-1978 Canadian Open, 1986 USF&G Classic; T2-1982 Quad Cities Open.

Money & Position:		
1978 — $ 47,091 — 67	1984 — $ 53,008 — 104	1990 — $ 66,738 — 164
1979 — $ 37,018 —104	1985 — $ 86,032 — 89	1991 — $ 21,098 — 204
1980 — $ 28,955 —106	1986 — $137,665 — 65	1992 — $ 4,065 — 271
1981 — $ 15,387 —147	1987 — $ 79,078 — 113	1993 — $ 6,650 — 253
1982 — $ 58,673 — 75	1988 — $ 74,156 — 135	
1983 — $100,508 — 57	1989 — $ 99,454 — 125	

1993 Best Finish: T10—Deposit Guaranty Golf Classic
1993 Summary: Tournaments entered—4; in money—1; top ten finishes —1.
Career Earnings: $915,577

MELNYK, Steve Birth Date 2/26/47 **Birthplace** Brunswick, GA **Residence** Amelia Island Plantation, FL **Height** 6-2 **Weight** 225 **College** University of Florida **Special Interests** Rare books, golf, art, bridge. **Family** Wife, Debby; Dalton (6/23/80) Butler (11/29/82) **Turned Professional** 1971 **Joined TOUR** Fall, 1971 **Other Achievements** Winner of nine collegiate tournaments, All-American 1967, 1968, 1969. 1969 U.S. Amateur champion. Winner, 1971 British Amateur, 1969 Western Amateur, 1970 Eastern Amateur. Member, 1969 Walker Cup team. **Best-Ever Finish:** 2nd five times. **Money Summary:** Started in 1972 winning $31,434 for 77th place. Best year was 1982 when he won $90,472 for 46th place. Last won money in 1984.

Career Earnings: $477,904

MICHEEL, Shaun Birth Date 1/5/69 **Birthplace** Orlando, FL **Residence** Memphis, TN **Height** 6-0 **Weight** 175 **Special Interests** Flying, scuba diving **Family** Single **College** Indiana University **Turned Professional** 1992 **Q School** 1993 **Other Achievements** 1991 First-team All-American.
Exempt Status: T37 at 1993 Qualifying Tournament

MILLER, Johnny   Birth Date 4/29/47 **Birthplace** San Francisco, CA **Residence** Napa, CA **Height** 6-2 **Weight** 180 **College** Brigham Young University (1969, Physical Education) **Special Interests** Fishing, church activities, golf course architecture, golf club design, television work **Family** Wife, Linda Strouse; John S. (6/2/70), Kelly (12/26/72), Casi (7/30/74), Scott (5/12/76), Brent (2/3/78), Todd (1/22/80) **Turned Professional** 1969 **Joined TOUR** Spring, 1969 **Playoff Record** 1-5 **Other Achievements** Winner, 1964 U.S. Juniors; 1974 Dunlop Phoenix (Japan); 1976 British Open; 1979 Lancome Trophy; 1983 Chrysler Team Championship (with Jack Nicklaus). Named 1974 PGA Player of the Year. **National Teams** Ryder Cup (2), 1975, 1981; World Cup (3), 1973, 1975, 1980, (individual winner in 1973 and 1975).
Exempt Status: Past Champion

TOUR Victories: 23—1971 Southern Open. 1972 Heritage Classic. 1973 U.S. Open. 1974 Bing Crosby Pro-Am, Phoenix Open, Dean Martin-Tucson Open, Heritage Classic, Tournament of Champions, Westchester Classic, World Open, Kaiser International. 1975 Phoenix Open, Dean Martin Tucson Open, Bob Hope Desert Classic, Kaiser International. 1976 NBC Tucson Open, Bob Hope Desert Classic. 1980 Jackie Gleason Inverrary Classic. 1981 Joe Garagiola Tucson Open, Glen Campbell Los Angeles Open. 1982 Wickes Andy Williams San Diego Open. 1983 Honda Inverrary Classic. 1987 AT&T Pebble Beach National Pro-Am.

Money & Position:			
	1969 — $ 8,364 —135	1977 — $ 61,025 — 48	1986 — $ 71,444 — 118
	1970 — $ 52,391 — 40	1978 — $ 17,740 — 111	1987 — $139,398 — 78
	1971 — $ 91,081 — 18	1980 — $127,117 — 30	1988 — $ 31,989 — 169
	1972 — $ 99,348 — 17	1981 — $193,167 — 12	1989 — $ 66,171 — 150
	1973 — $127,833 — 9	1982 — $169,065 — 20	1990 — $ 8,900 — 235
	1974 — $353,021 — 1	1983 — $230,186 — 14	1991 — $ 2,864 — 269
	1975 — $226,118 — 2	1984 — $139,422 — 47	1992 — $ 4,321 — 269
	1976 — $135,887 — 14	1985 — $126,616 — 64	1993 — $ —0—

Career Earnings: $2,521,425

MIZUMAKI, Yoshi   Birth Date 8/27/58 **Birthplace** Toyko, Japan **Residence** Toyko, Japan **Height** 5-11 **Weight** 170 **College** Hosel University (Japan) **Family** Wife, Jumko; Kento **Turned Professional** 1985 **Q School** 1993
Exempt Status: T11 at 1993 Qualifying Tournament
Best Ever Finish: T83--1993 Buick Invitational
Money & Position: 1993 — $1,718 — 321
1993 Summary: Tournaments entered--2; in money--1; top ten finishes--0

MOORE, Tommy Birth Date 12/23/62 **Birthplace** New Orleans, LA **Residence** New Orleans, LA **Height** 5-9 **Weight** 170 **College** Oklahoma State University (1984, Business) **Special Interest** Sports, stock market, music **Family** Wife, Tracy **Turned Professional** 1984 **Q School** 1989 **Other Achievements** Regained '94 PGA TOUR card by virtue of 6th place finish on 1993 NIKE TOUR money list, earning $102,004. Win at NIKE Boise Open career best outing. Three-time All-American at OSU (1982-84)
Exempt Status: 6th place on 1993 NIKE TOUR money list
Best Ever Finish: T4--1990 Buick Southern Open

Money & Position:			
	1990 — $99,276 —138	1991— $35,409 — 192	1992 — $630 — 316

Career Earnings: $135,315

N

NELFORD, Jim Birth Date 6/28/55 **Birthplace** Vancouver, BC **Residence** Gainey Ranch, Scottsdale, AZ **Height** 5-10 **Weight** 155 **College** Brigham Young University **Special Interests** Hockey, motorcycling, tennis, fishing **Family** Wife, Linda; Blake (7/84) **Turned Professional** 1977 **Joined TOUR** 1977,1987 **Other Achievements** Winner 1975 and 1976 Canadian Amateur, 1977 Western Amateur, 1977 French Nation's Cup, 1978 Cacherel Under 25. Member 1979, 1980 and 1983 Canada World Cup team. Winner of 1980 World Cup Team championship with Dan Halldorson. Winner of 1983 Essex International Classic (TPS) Commentator on ESPN broadcasts.

Exempt Status: Veteran Member   **Playoff Record:** 0-1
Best-Ever Finish: 2—1983 Sea Pines Heritage Classic, 1984 Bing Crosby National Pro Am

Money & Position:			
1978 — $ 29,959 — 87	1983 — $111,932 — 50	1988 — $ 20,209 — 200
1979 — $ 40,174 — 95	1984 — $ 80,470 — 76	1989 — $ 1,225 — 289
1980 — $ 33,769 — 98	1985 — $ 60,276 —112	1990 — $ 4,132 — 254
1981 — $ 20,275 —132	1986 — $ —0—	1991 — $ 3,510 — 263
1982 — $ 48,088 — 94	1987 — $ 24,097 —182	

Career Earnings: $478,816

NICOLETTE, Mike Birth Date 12/7/56 **Birthplace** Pittsburgh, PA **Residence** Scottsdale, AZ **Height** 5-9 **Weight** 155 **Special Interests** Skiing, fishing **Family** Wife, Denise; Mikey, Casey, Kelly **College** Rollins College **Turned Professional** 1978 **Q School** 1979, 1981,1985 **Other Achievements** Three-time Division II All-American

Exempt Status: Past Champion   **playoff Record:** 1-0
TOUR Victories: 1 — 1983 Bay Hill Classic

Money & Position:			
1979 — $ 9,140 — 161	1984 — $ 61,394 — 93	1989 $ 1,881 — 263
1980 — $ 13,196 — 147	1985 — $ 41,750 — 131	1990 — $ 4,200 — 252
1981 — $ 512 — 248	1986 — $ 12,197 — 197	1991 — $ 33,222 — 195
1982 — $ 38,084 — 106	1987 — $ 42,407 — 164	1992 — $ 22,065 — 208
1983 — $127,868 — 43	1988 — $ 24,342 — 199	1993 — $ 1,556 — 323

1993 Best Finish: T32—Deposit Guaranty Golf Classic
1993 Summary: Tournaments entered — 2; in money — 1; top ten finishes —0.
Career Earnings: $433,816

O

O'GRADY, Mac Birth Date 4/26/51 **Birthplace** Minneapolis, MN **Residence** Palm Springs, CA **Height** 6-0 **Weight** 165 **Special Interests** Modern times, sciences, history **Family** Wife, Fumiko Aoyagi **College** Santa Monica Junior College **Turned Professional** 1972 **Q School** 1982
Exempt Status: Past Champion
TOUR Victories: 2—1986 Canon-Sammy Davis Jr.-Greater Hartford Open. 1987 MONY Tournament of Champions

Money & Position:			
1983 — $ 50,379 — 101	1987 —$ 285,109 — 35	1991 — $ 14,102 — 220
1984 — $ 41,143 — 120	1988 — $ 116,153 — 98	1992 — $ 2,030 — 305
1985 — $ 223,808 — 20	1989 — $ 40,090 --170	1993 — $ 10,483 — 240
1986 — $ 256,344 — 26	1990 — $ — 0 —	

1993 Best Finish: T20—Hardee's Classic
1993 Summary: Tournaments entered — 4; in money — 1; top ten finishes — 0
Career Earnings: $1,039,586

P

PARNEVIK, Jesper Birth Date 3/7/65 **Birthplace** Stockholm, Sweden **Residence** South Palm Beach, FL **Height** 6-0 **Weight** 175 **College** Palm Beach Junior College **Special Interest** Tennis **Family** Single **Turned Professional** 1986 **Q School** 1993 **Other Achievements** Winner, 1988 Odense Open, 1988 Raklosia Open, 1990 Swedish Open, 1985 Dixie Amateur and 1993 Scottish Open.
Exempt Status: T4 at 1993 Qualifying Tournament

PATE, Jerry **Birth Date** 9/16/53 **Birthplace** Macon, GA **Residence** Pensacola FL; plays out of Tiger Point G&CC, Gulf Breeze, FL **Height** 6-0 **Weight** 175 **Special Interests** Water skiing **Family** Wife, Soozi; Jennifer (10/5/78); Wesley Nelson (9/5/80); James Kendrick (10/12/83) **College** University of Alabama **Turned Professional** 1975 **Q School** Fall 1975. **Other Achievements** Winner 1974 U.S. Amateur; winner 1974 Florida Amateur; winner 1976 Pacific Masters; 1977 Mixed Team Championship (with Hollis Stacy).

Exempt Status: Past Champion   **Playoff Record: 1-2**

TOUR Victories: 8-1976 U.S. Open, Canadian Open. 1977 Phoenix Open, Southern Open. 1978 Southern Open. 1981 Danny Thomas-Memphis Classic, Pensacola Open. 1982 Tournament Players Championship.

Money & Position:

1976 — $153,102 — 10	1982 — $280,141 — 9	1988 — $10,075 — 265
1977 — $ 98,152 — 27	1983 — $ 28,890 — 136	1989 — $ 9,168 — 213
1978 — $172,999 — 10	1984 — $ 41,746 — 118	1990 — $26,953 — 200
1979 — $193,707 — 11	1985 — $ 7,792 — 188	1991 — $ 6,249 — 248
1980 — $222,976 — 6	1986 — $ 1,445 — 260	1992 — $10,971 — 236
1981 — $280,627 — 6	1987 — $ 2,116 — 265	1993 — $ —0—

1993 Summary: Tournaments entered--2; in money--0; top ten finishes--0
Career Earnings: $1,550,360

PAULSON, Dennis **Birth Date** 9/27/62 **Birthplace** San Gabriel, CA **Residence** Palm Desert, CA **Height** 6-0 **Weight** 195 **College** San Diego State University **Special Interests** Bikes, fishing, shooting **Family** Wife, Linda **Turned Professional** 1985 **Q School** 1993 **Other Achievements** Winner, 1990 Philippine Open, 1990 California State Open and 1993 Utah State Open.
Exempt Status: 10th at 1993 Qualifying Tournament

PERRY, Chris **Birth Date** 9/27/61 **Birthplace** Edenton, NC **Residence** Columbus, OH **Height** 6-1 **Weight** 195 **College** Ohio State University **Special Interests** Snow skiing, family **Family** Single; Andrew (3/1/93) **Turned Professional** 1984 **Q-School** Fall, 1984 **Other Achievements** Named 1984 Collegiate Player of the Year. Three-time All-American, 1982, '83, and '84. Winner, 1983 Big Ten Championship, 1982 Northeast Amateur, 1982 and 1983 Minnesota State Amateur, 1984 Minnesota State Open, 1978, 1979 and 1980 Minnesota high school championships. Set Ohio State record with 14 victories. Father, Jim Perry, is former major league pitcher while uncle is Gaylord Perry.

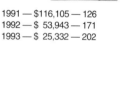

Exempt Status: Veteran Member
Best Ever Finish: T2--1987 Kemper Open; T2--1990 Cannon Greater Open

Money & Position:

1985 — $ 60,801 —110	1988 — $ 85,546 —121	1991 — $116,105 — 126
1986 — $ 75,212 —114	1989 — $206,932 — 67	1992 — $ 53,943 — 171
1987 — $197,593 — 56	1990 — $259,108 — 58	1993 — $ 25,332 — 202

1993 Best Finish: T21--B.C. Open
1993 Summary: Tournaments entered--9; in money--5; top ten finishes--0.
Career Earnings $1,080,573

PERSONS, Peter **Birth Date** 9/8/62 **Birthplace** Macon, GA **Residence** Macon, GA **Height** 5-7 **Weight** 155 **Special Interests** Tennis, Georgia football, hunting, reading **Family** Wife, Colyar; Pierce (8/15/91) **College** University of Georgia **Turned Professional** 1986 **Q School** Fall 1989 **Other Achievements** Runnerup 1985 U.S. Amateur. Three-time All-American, first team 1986. Winner 1985 Southeastern Conference championship, plus five collegiate events. Won both the 1979 Georgia State Junior and 1985 Georgia State Open.

Exempt Status: Past Champion
TOUR Victories: 1--1990 Chattanooga Classic

Money & Position:

1990 — $218,505 — 66	1992 — $203,625 — 75	1993 — $ 73,092 —164
1991 — $130,447 —114		

1993 Best Finish: T19--The International
1993 Summary: Tournaments entered--30; in money--16; top ten finishes--0.
Career Earnings $625,669

PFEIL, Mark Birth Date 7/18/51 **Birthplace** Chicago Heights, IL **Residence** La Quinta Hotel & CC, La Quinta, CA **Height** 5-11 **Weight** 175 **College** University of Southern California (BS, 1974) **Special Interests** Family activities **Family** Wife, Diana; Kimberly Ann (9/19/80); Kathryn (8/23/84) **Turned Professional** 1974 **Joined TOUR** Fall 1975 and Fall 1976 **Other Achievements** Won California Interscholastic Federation; 1973 Walker Cup team; All-American 1973, 1974. Winner Pacific Coast Amateur, 1972, 1974; Southern California Amateur, 1973; PAC-8, 1974. Winner 1983 Anderson-Pacific Classic (TPS). Winner, 1985 Jerry Ford Invitational. Winner, 1991 Concord General Pro-Am.
Exempt Status: Past Champion
TOUR Victories: 1—1980 Tallahassee Open
Money & Position:

1976 — $ 439 — 271	1981 — $ 62,663 — 71	1988 — $ 6,057 — 235
1977 — $ 9,924 — 149	1982 — $ 85,477 — 66	1989 — $ —0—
1978 — $ 13,943 — 123	1983 — $101,878 — 69	1990 — $ 3,383 — 260
1979 — $ 18,963 — 125	1985 — $ 54,098 —116	1991 — $ —0—
1980 — $ 52,704 — 72	1986 — $ 67,488 —122	1992 — $ 2,495 — 287
1981 — $ 28,951 — 112	1987 — $ 11,882 -- 203	1993 — $ 9,100 — 242

1993 Best Finish: T21—B.C. Open
1993 Summary: Tournaments entered —5; in money — 2; top ten finishes — 0.
Career Earnings: $529,414

PRIDE, Dicky Birth Date 7/15/69 **Birthplace** Tuscaloosa, AL **Residence** Orlando, FL **Height** 6-0 **Weight** 175 **Special Interests** Basketball, reading **Family** Single **College** University of Alabama **Turned Professional** 1992 **Q School** 1993 **Other Achievements** Two-time All-SEC. Semifinalist in 1991 U.S. Amateur.
Exempt Status: T24 at 1993 Qualifying Tournament

R

RANDOLPH, Sam Birth Date 5/13/64 **Birthplace** Santa Barbara, CA **Residence** McKinney, TX **Height** 6-0 **Weight** 175 **Special Interests** All Sports, Fishing **Family** Wife, Julie **College** University of Southern California **Turned Professional** 1986 **Q School** 1986, 1990 **Other Achievements** 1985 U.S. Amateur Champion. Winner of 1981 Junior World title. California State Amateur. Three time First-Team All-American. Winner of 13 collegiate titles. Awarded 1985 Fred Haskins Trophy as outstanding collegiate player.
Exempt Status: Past Champion
TOUR Victories: 1—1987 Bank of Boston Classic.
Money & Position:

1987 — $180,378 — 58	1989 — $ 35,561 — 178	1991 — $ 68,668 — 154
1988 — $117,132 — 97	1990 — $ 27,529 — 198	1992 — $ 49,085 — 176
		1993 — $ 4,460 — 275

1993 Best Finish: T63—New England Classic
1993 Summary: Tournaments entered—4; in money — 2; top ten finishes — 0.
Career Earnings: $482,814

RASSETT, Joey Birth Date 7/5/58 **Birthplace** Turlock, CA **Residence** Plantation, FL **Height** 6-0 **Weight** 190 **Special Interests** Automobiles, golf history, hunting **Family** Wife, Susan; Lauren, J.D. **Q School** 1983, 1984, 1988, 1993 **College** Oral Roberts University **Turned Professional** 1981 **Other Achievements** Low amateur in 1981 U.S. Open. Four-time NCAA All-American.
Exempt Status: 7th at 1993 Qualifying Tournament
Best Ever Finish: T16--1988 Provident Classic
Money & Position:

1983—$30,792 — 129	1987 — $ 2,315 — 257
1984—$11,220 — 176	1988 — $27,554 —182
1985—$ 3,450 — 213	

1993 Summary: Tournaments entered—1; in money — 0; top ten finishes — 0
Career Money $75,331

RAULERSON, Charles Birth Date 1/29/64 **Birthplace** Jacksonville, FL **Residence** Jacksonville, FL **Height** 6-0 **Weight** 160 **Special Interests** Reading **Family** Single **College** Clemson University, Louisiana State University **Turned Professional** 1987 **Q School** 1993
Exempt Status: T37 at 1993 Qualifying Tournament

Other Prominent Members of the PGA TOUR

RENNER, Jack Birth Date 7/6/56 **Birthplace** Palm Springs, CA **Residence** San Diego, CA **Height** 6-0 **Weight** 150 **College** College of the Desert **Special Interests** Reading, all sports **Family** Wife, Lisa; Jill Marie (6/10/90) **Turned Professional** 1976 **Q School** Spring 1977 **Other Achievements** Winner 1972 World Junior. Winner 1973 U.S Junior

Playoff Record: 1-0

Exempt Status: Past Champion

TOUR Victories: 3-1979-Manufacturers Hanover Westchester Classic, 1981-Pleasant Valley-Jimmy Fund Classic, 1984-Hawaiian Open

Money & Position:					
1977 — $ 12,837 — 128	1982 — $ 95,589 — 41	1988 — $ 82,046 — 128
1978 — $ 73,996 — 33	1983 — $133,290 — 41	1989 — $ —0—
1979 — $182,808 — 14	1984 — $260,153 — 19	1990 — $ 7,451 — 241
1980 — $ 97,501 — 45	1985 — $202,761 — 26	1991 — $ 13,612 — 222
1981 — $193,292 — 11	1986 — $ 84,028 — 100	1992 — $ 13,511 — 225
	1987 — $ 92,289 — 102	1993 — $ — 0 —

Career Earnings: $1,545,165

REESE, Don Birth Date 12/7/53 **Birthplace** O'Conta Falls, WI **Residence** Freeport, FL **Height** 6-0 **Weight** 190 **Special Interests** Hockey, fishing **College** Troy State University **Family** Single **Turned Professional** 1979 **Q School** 1988,1993 **Other Achievements** Winner, 1985 National PGA Match Play Championship; 1985, 1986 Metropolitan PGA Champion. 1976-77 NCAA All-American. All-Gulf South Conference in 1976 and 1977. Winner, 1991 Ben Hogan Lake City Classic.

Best Ever Finish: T5—1989 Hawaiian Open

Money and Position: 1982—$ 4,804—204

1989—$65,838—155   1990—$ 6,926—242

Exempt Status: T32 at 1993 Qualifying Tournament

Career Earnings: $72,569

RINTOUL, Steve Birth Date 6/7/63 **Birthplace** Bowrawl, Australia **Residence** Sarasota, FL **Height** 6-1 **Weight** 190 **Special Interest** Music, dining out, swimming **Family** Wife, Jill **College** University of Oregon **Turned Professional** 1988 **Q School** 1993 **Other Achievements** Winner, 1987-88 Oregon Stroke Play Amateur Championship, 1988 Oregon Amateur Champion and 1991 Northwest Oregon Champion. 1982 All-Australian schoolboys team. Three year NIKE TOUR veteran. Best year was 1993 when he earned $71,579 to place 17th on the NIKE money list.

Exempt Status: T11 at 1993 Qualifying Tournament

ROSBURG, Bob Birth Date 10/21/26 **Birthplace** San Francisco, CA **Residence** Rancho Mirage, CA **Height** 5-11 **Weight** 185 **College** Stanford University (1948) **Family** Wife, Eleanor; three children **Turned Professional** 1953 **Joined TOUR** 1953 **Other Achievements** 1958 Vardon Trophy winners. Member 1959 Ryder Cup team. Tournament Policy Board Player Director, 1972-73. Color commentator, ABC golf telecasts.

Exempt Status: Winner, 1959 PGA Championship

TOUR Victories: 7— 1954 Brawley Open, Miami Open. 1956 Motor City Open, San Diego Open. 1959 PGA Championship. 1961 Bing Crosby Pro-Am. 1972 Bob Hope Desert Classic.

Career Earnings: $436,466

ROSE, Clarence Birth Date 12/8/57 **Birthplace** Goldsboro, NC **Residence** Goldsboro, NC **Height** 5-8 **Weight** 175 **College** Clemson University **Special Interests** All sports, video games **Family** Wife, Jan; Clark (2/20/89) **Turned Professional** 1981 **Q School** Spring 1981 **Other Achievements** Winner, 1979 North Carolina Amateur. Quarterfinalist 1986 U.S. Amateur. All-American 1980 **Playoff Record:** 0-1

Exempt Status: Veteran Member

Best-Ever Finish: 2— 1985 Southern Open; 1986 Los Angeles Open; 1987 Greater Greensboro Open; 1988 GTE Byron Nelson Classic; 1989 The International; T2 — 1986 Honda Classic.

Money & Position:			
1981 — $ 965 — 233	1985 — $ 133,610 — 63	1989 — $ 267,141 — 49
1982 — $ 41,075 — 100	1986 — $ 189,387 — 44	1990 — $ 25,908 — 202
1983 — $ 45,271 — 109	1987 — $ 173,154 — 59	1991 — $ 9,564 — 228
1984 — $ 62,278 — 92	1988 — $ 228,976 — 48	1992 — $ 10,488 — 240
		1993 — $ 6,823 — 257

1993 Best Finish: T39—Anheuser-Busch Golf Classic

1993 Summary: Tournaments entered —8; in money — 3; top ten finishes — 0.

Career Earnings: $1,194,641

RUSSELL, D.A. Birth Date 11/6/57 **Birthplace** Kent, England **Residence** Calabasas, CA **Height** 6-3 **Weight** 225 **Special Interest** Fishing **Family** Wife, Sharon; Hayley (4/28/87), Holly (10/28/90) **Turned Professional** 1976 **Q School** 1993 **Other Achievements** Played the PGA European Tour since 1977.

Exempt Status: T26 at 1993 Qualifying Tournament

S

SANDER, Bill **Birth Date** 4/16/56 **Birthplace** Seattle,WA **Residence** Tallahassee,FL **Height** 6-2 **Weight** 185 **Special Interests** Fishing, guitar **Family** Wife,Lisa; Scully(the cat) **Turned Professional** 1977 **Q School** Fall 1977, 1984. **Other Achievements** Winner, 1976 United States Amateur. Three-time winner of Seattle City Amateur.
Exempt Status: Veteran Member
Best Ever Finish: 2—1991 Shearson Lehman Brothers Open
Money & Position:

1978 — $ 3,167 — 183	1983 — $ 9,416 — 181	1988 — $104,324 — 109
1979 — $ 9,826 — 154	1984 — $ 36,357 — 131	1989 — $105,083 — 122
1980 — $ 13,644 — 144	1985 — $ 54,707 — 115	1990 — $172,886 — 93
1981 — $ 11,034 — 165	1986 — $ 38,564 — 151	1991 — $139,444 — 110
1982 — $ 7,993 — 179	1987 — $ 95,921 — 101	1992 — $ 23,248 — 205
		1993 — $ 582 — 336

1993 Best Finish: 73—Deposit Guaranty Classic
1993 Summary: Tournaments entered —1; in money — 1; top ten finishes — 0.
Career Earnings: $823,428

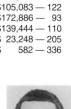

SILLS, Tony **Birth Date** 12/5/55 **Birthplace** Los Angeles, CA **Residence** Los Angeles, CA **Height** 5-10 **Weight** 165 **Special Interests** Running, weights, martial arts **Family** Single **College** University of Southern California **Turned Professional** 1980 **Q School** Fall 1982 **Other Achievements** Winner 1971 Los Angeles City Junior title; 1976 Southern California Amateur, 1981 Queen Mary Open; 1982 Coors (Kansas) Open.
Exempt Status: Past Champion **Playoff Record:** 1-0
TOUR Victories: 1—1990 Independent Insurance Agent Open
Money & Position:

1983 — $ 47,488 —104	1987 — $ 107,508 — 92	1991 — $ 13,914 — 223
1984 — $ 90,055 — 72	1988 — $ 76,689 — 132	1992 — $ 10,574 — 238
1985 — $114,895 — 66	1989 — $ 77,181 — 143	1993 — $ 11,686 — 233
1986 — $216,881 — 38	1990 — $ 243,350 — 61	

1993 Best Finish: T26—United Airlines Hawaiian Open
1993 Summary: Tournaments entered--5; in money--2; top ten finishes--0.
Career Earnings: $1,020,159

SILVEIRA, Larry **Birth Date** 10/12/65 **Birthplace** Walnut Creek, CA **Residence** Tucson, AZ **Height** 6-0 **Weight** 180 **College** University of Arizona **Special Interests** Hunting, fishing **Family** Wife, Beth **Turned Professional** 1987 **Q School** 1988,1989,1990 **Other Achievements** Regained PGA TOUR card by virtue of his eighth place finish on 1993 NIKE TOUR money list, earning $93,098. Three second place finishes best effort on NIKE TOUR. Member PGA TOUR from 1989-92. All-American selection in 1987-88, PAC-10 Player of Year in 1987. Winner of 1988 Arizona Open. Selected Athlete of Year at University of Arizona in 1987.
Exempt Status: 8th on 1993 NIKE TOUR money list
Money & Position: 1989 — $ 60,712 —156 1990 — $65,696 — 166 1991 — $ 93,893 — 138
1993 Summary: Tournaments entered--1; in money--0 ; top ten finishes--0
Career Earnings: $220,301

SIMPSON, Tim **Birth Date** 5/6/56 **Birthplace** Atlanta, GA **Residence** Dunwoody, GA **Height** 5-10 **Weight** 190 **Special Interests** Bow hunting, fishing **Family** Wife, Kathy; Christopher (1/5/84); Katie (9/24/86) **College** University of Georgia **Turned Professional** 1977 **Q School** Spring 1977 **Other Achievements** Winner 1976 Southern Amateur; All-Southeastern Conference and All-American. Winner of Georgia and Atlanta Junior Titles; 1981 World Under-25 Championship.
Exempt Status: Special Medical Extension
TOUR Victories: 4-1985 Southern Open. 1989 USF&G Classic, Walt Disney World/Oldsmobile Classic. 1990 Walt Disney World/Oldsmobile Classic.
Money & Position:

1977 — $ 2,778 — 193	1983 — $ 96,419 — 59	1989 — $761,597 — 6
1978 — $38,714 — 78	1984 — $157,082 — 41	1990 — $809,772 — 8
1979 — $36,223 — 106	1985 — $164,702 — 44	1991 — $196,582 — 85
1980 — $27,172 — 112	1986 — $240,911 — 31	1992 — $ 85,314 — 144
1981 — $63,063 — 70	1987 — $168,261 — 62	1993 — $111,435 — 134
1982 — $62,153 — 72	1988 — $200,748 — 56	

1993 Best Finish: T8—Hardee's Golf Classic
1993 Summary: Tournaments entered—28; in money—18; top ten finishes—1
Career Earnings: $3,221,926

Other Prominent Members of the PGA TOUR

SMITH, Mike **Birth Date** 8/25/50 **Birthplace** Selma, AL **Residence** Titusville, AL **Height** 5-11 **Weight** 175 **Special Interests** Family, hunting, fishing **Family** Wife, Monica; Christopher Michael (6/22/87) **College** Brevard Junior College **Turned Professional** 1973 **Q School** Spring 1973; Fall 1981, 1983, 1989 **Other Achievements** Winner, 1968 Dixie Junior, 1971 National Junior College Tournament.
Exempt Status: 137th on 1993 money list
Best Ever Finish: 2--1985 Panasonic Invitational

Money & Position:

1980 — $ 508 —246	1985 — $158,918 — 47	1991 — $149,613 —101
1981 — $ 19,682 —134	1986 — $ 19,159 —179	1992 — $178,964 — 84
1982 — $ 13,749 —161	1990 — $170,034 — 94	1993 — $107,375 —137
1984 — $ 42,045 —116		

1993 Best Finish: T5—Buick Classic
1993 Summary: Tournaments entered—33; in money—12; top ten finishes—2
Career Earnings: $893,681

SNEED, Ed **Birth Date** 8/6/44 **Birth Place** Roanoke, VA **Residence** Columbus, OH **Height** 6-2 **Weight** 185 **College** Ohio State University (1967 Marketing) **Special Interests** Bridge, running, reading **Family** Wife, Nancy Kay; Mary Elisa (8/16/74); Erica Kathryn (4/2177) **Turned Professional** 1967 **Joined TOUR** Fall, 1968 **Other Achievements** Winner, 1973 New South Wales Open; member 1977 Ryder Cup team; Player Director on Tournament Policy Board, 1977-78 and 1981-82; Winner, 1980 Morocco Grand Prix; 1965 Ohio Intercollegiate; Co-winner 1978 Jerry Ford Invitational.
Exempt Status: Past Champion
TOUR Victories: 4-1973 Kaiser International Open; 1974 Greater Milwaukee Open; 1977 Tallahassee Open; 1982 Michelob-Houston Open
Money Summary: Joined TOUR in 1969 and won $4,254 for 170th place. Best year was 1982 when he won $148,170 for 23rd on money list. Last won money in 1986.

STANKOWSKI Paul **Birth Date** 12/2/69 **Birthplace** Oxnard, CA **Residence** El Paso, TX **Height** 6-1 **Weight** 175 **College** University of Texas-El Paso **Special Interests** Relaxing, family **Family** Wife, Regina **Turned Professional** 1991 **Q School** 1993 **Other Achievements** Three-time NCAA All-American. 1990 Western Athletic Conference Champion and 1992 New Mexico Open champion.
Exempt Status: T26 at 1993 Qualifying Tournament

STOCKTON, Dave B. **Birth Date** 7/31/68 **Birthplace** Redlands, CA **Residence** La Quinta, CA **Height** 6-2 **Weight** 185 **Special Interests** Hunting, fishing, all sports **Family** Single **College** University of Southern California **Turned Professional** 1991 **Q School** 1993 **Other Achievements** All-American selection at USC. Winner, 1993 NIKE Connecticut Open and 1993 NIKE Hawkeye Open. Earned $64,214 to place 23rd on the 1993 NIKE TOUR money list.
Exempt Status T1 at 1993 Qualifying Tournament

STRECK, Ron **Birth Date** 6/17/54 **Birthplace** Tulsa, OK **Residence** Tulsa, OK **Height** 6-0 **Weight** 165 **College** University of Tulsa **Special Interests** Skiing, basketball **Turned Professional** 1976 **Q School** Fall 1976 **Other Achievements** Two-time winner Missouri Valley Conference title. Winner, 1993 NIKE Yuma Open. Finished 21st on 1993 NIKE TOUR with $65,718.
Exempt Status: Past Champion   **Playoff Record:** 0-1
TOUR Victories: 2—1978 San Antonio-Texas Open; 1981 Michelob-Houston Open

Money & Position:

1977 — $ 11,014 —143	1983 — $ 68,950 — 77	1989 — $ 50,444 — 164
1978 — $ 46,933 — 68	1984 — $ 82,235 — 81	1990 — $ 10,356 — 229
1979 — $ 39,484 — 99	1985 — $142,848 — 55	1991 — $ 13,914 — 221
1980 — $ 51,728 — 73	1986 — $ 21,605 — 172	1992 — $ 9,917 — 244
1981 — $114,895 — 29	1987 — $ 62,289 — 133	1993 -- $ 885 — 328
1982 — $ 67,962 — 60	1988 — $ 31,094 — 170	

1993 Best Finish: T44—Deposit Gauranty Classic
1993 Summary: Tournaments entered—2; in money—1; top ten finishes— 0.
Career Earnings: $815,019

STRICKER, Steve Birth Date 2/23/67 **Birthplace** Edgerton, WI **Residence** Edgerton, WI **Height** 6-0 **Weight** 185 **College** University of Illinois **Special Interests** Basketball, hunting **Family** Wife, Nicki **Turned Professional** 1990   **Q-School**1993
Other Achievements 1993 Canadian PGA Champion.
Exempt Status: T18 at 1993 Qualifying Tournament
Best Ever Finish: T4--1993 Canadian Open
Money and Position: 1990 — $3,973 — 255
                                               1992 — $5,550 — 261   1993 — $46,171 — 186
1993 Best Finish: T4--Canadian Open
1992 Summary: Tournaments entered— 6; in money—2; top ten finishes—1

SULLIVAN, Mike Birth Date 1/1/55 **Birthplace** Gary, IN **Residence** Ocala, FL **Height** 6-2 **Weight** 200 **Special Interest** Flying, fishing **Family** Wife, Sandy; Rebecca (6/13/85) **College** University of Florida **Turned Professional** 1975 **Q School** Fall 1976, 1985 **Other Achievements** Roommate of Andy Bean at the University of Florida.
Exempt Status: Past Champion
TOUR Victories: 2—1980 Southern Open. 1989 Independent Insurance Agent Open.
Money & Position:

1977 — $ 11,170 —142	1983 — $ 93,437 — 60	1989 — $273,963 — 47
1978 — $ 41,184 — 74	1984 — $111,415 — 63	1990 — $ 80,038 —147
1979 — $ 38,596 — 97	1985 — $ 45,032 —127	1991 — $106,048 —133
1980 — $147,759 — 22	1986 — $150,407 — 62	1992 — $115,441 —121
1981 — $ 94,844 — 41	1987 — $ 79,456 —112	1993 — $ 68,587 —167
1982 — $ 37,957 —108	1988 — $115,994 — 99	

1993 Best Finish: T12—Kmart Greater Greensboro Open
1993 Summary: Tournaments entered—15; in money—9; top ten finishes—0
Career Earnings: $1,611,327

T

TATAURANGI, Phil Birth Date 10/31/71 **Birthplace** Auckland, New Zealand **Residence** Auckland, New Zealand **Height** 5-11 **Weight** 160 **Special Interests** Music, fishing **Family** Single **Turned Professional** 1993 **Q School** 1993
Exempt status: T37 at 1993 Qualifying Tournament

TAYLOR, Harry Birth Date 11/03/54 **Birthplace** Detroit, MI **Residence** Old Hickory, TN **Height** 5-9 **Weight** 170 **Special Interests** Golf club design, classic cars. **Family** Wife, Saunora; Zachary (9/1/83), Brooke (12/19/87) **College** University of Tennessee (1979, Political Science) **Turned Professional** 1977 **Q School** 1980, 1985, 1986, 1987, 1989, 1992.
Exempt Status: 140th on 1993 money list
Best Ever Finish: T5—1990 Chattanooga Classic
Money & Position:

1986 — $ 27,017 —166	1988 — $ 34,132 — 167	1990 — $ 45,647 — 180
1987 — $ 54,843 —145	1989 — $ 6,081 — 229	1993 — $ 105,845 — 140

1993 Best Finish: T12 — Greater Milwaukee Open
1993 Summary: Tournaments entered—-30; in money—17; top ten finishes—0.
Career Earnings: $278,115

TEN BROECK, Lance Birth Date 3/21/56 **Birthplace** Chicago, IL **Residence** Jupiter, FL **Height** 6-3 **Weight** 195 **Special Interest** All sports **Family** Single **College** University of Texas **Turned Professional** 1977 **Other Achievements** Winner, 1984 Magnolia Classic, 1975 Southwest Conference, 1975 Chicago District Amateur, 1976 Harvey Penick Invitational.
Exempt Status: Veteran Member
Best Ever Finish: T3--1988 Deposit Guaranty Classic
Money & Position:

1980 — $ 10,230 —162	1984 — $ 40,185 — 123	1988 — $ 65,987 —138
1981 — $ 4,464	1985 — $ 23,591 — 153	1989 — $146,568 — 96
1982 — $ 25,049 —135	1986 — $ 18,165 — 181	1990 — $ 72,896 —155
1983 — $ 19,450 —152	1987 — $ 1,920 — 266	1993 — $ 88,262 —151

1993 Best Finish: T17--Shell Houston Open
1993 Summary: Tournaments entered--32; in money--16; top ten finishes--0.
Career Earnings: $731,585

THOMPSON, Leonard Birth Date 1/1/47 **Birthplace** Laurinburg, NC **Residence** Myrtle Beach, SC **Height** 6-2 **Weight** 200 **Special Interests** Fishing **Family** Wife, Lesley; Martha (6/7/67),Stephen (4/6/74). **College** Wake Forest University **Turned Professional** 1970 **Q School** Fall 1971. **Other Achievements** Winner 1975 Carolinas Open.

Exempt Status: Past Champion

TOUR Victories: 3—1974 Jackie Gleason-Inverrary Classic. 1977 Pensacola Open. 1989 Buick Open.

Money & Position:

1971 — $ 6,556 —153	1979 — $ 90,465 — 41	1987 — $ 52,326 — 147
1972 — $ 39,882 — 63	1980 — $138,826 — 25	1988 — $ 84,659 — 123
1973 — $ 91,158 — 15	1981 — $ 95,517 — 40	1989 — $261,397 — 52
1974 — $122,349 — 15	1982 — $ 60,998 — 73	1990 — $ 78,017 — 148
1975 — $ 48,748 — 48	1983 — $ 76,326 — 69	1991 — $114,275 — 128
1976 — $ 26,566 — 83	1984 — $ 36,920 — 126	1992 — $ 30,540 — 196
1977 — $107,293 — 23	1985 — $ 48,395 — 122	1993 — $ 15,152 — 228
1978 — $ 52,231 — 63	1986 — $ 83,420 — 102	

1993 Best Finish: T30—New England Classic
1993 Summary: Tournaments entered—12; in money—5; top ten finishes—0.
Career Earnings: $1,749,691

THORPE, Jim Birth Date 2/1/49 **Birthplace** Roxboro, NC **Residence** Buffalo, NY **Height** 6-0 **Weight** 200 **College** Morgan State University **Special Interests** Football, basketball, hunting **Family** Wife, Carol; Sheronne (3/6/77); Chera (12/3/88) **Turned Professional** 1972 **Joined TOUR** 1978 **Other Achievements** Winner, 1982 Canadian PGA, 1991 Jamaica Open. Comedalist 1978 TOUR Qualifying School. Winner, 1991 Amoco Centel Classic.

Exempt Status: Past Champion   **Playoff Record:** 0-1

TOUR Victories: 3 —1985 Greater Milwaukee Open, Seiko-Tucson Match Play Championship. 1986 Seiko-Tucson Match Play Championship.

Money & Position:

1976 — $ 2,000 —	1984 — $135,818 — 48	1989 — $104,704 — 123
1979 — $ 48,987 — 80	1985 — $379,091 — 4	1990 — $211,297 — 70
1980 — $ 33,671 — 99	1986 — $326,087 — 15	1991 — $ 46,039 — 179
1981 — $ 43,011 — 93	1987 — $ 57,198 —139	1992 — $ 28,235 — 200
1982 — $ 66,379 — 63	1988 — $ 4,028 —252	1993 — $ 70,375 — 166
1983 — $118,197 — 46		

1993 Best Finish: T14—H-E-B Texas Open
1993 Summary: Tournaments entered—19; in money—9; top ten finishes—0.
Career Earnings: $1,675,116

TOLEDO, Esteban Birth Date: 9/10/62 **Birthplace:** Mexicali, Mexico **Residence:** Milpitas, CA **Height:** 5-10 **Weight:** 160 **Family:** Single **Other Achievements:** Played Asian Tour 1988-90, NIKE TOUR from 1990-93. Best 1993 finish--T2 at NIKE White Rose Classic in York, PA., equals best-ever NIKE TOUR finish when he lost in playoff to John Flannery on fourth hole of 1991 Reno Open. Former professional boxer.

Exempt Status T26 at 1993 Qualifying Tournament

V

VENTURI, Ken Birth Date 5/15/31 **Birthplace** San Francisco, CA **Residence** Naples, FL **Height** 6-0 **Weight** 175 **College** San Jose State University (1953) **Special Interests** Hunting, fishing, cars. **Family** Wife, Beau; two children. **Turned Professional** 1956 **Joined TOUR** 1957 **Other Achievements** 1964 PGA Player of the Year. 1965 Ryder Cup team member Color commentator for CBS golf telecasts.

Exempt Status: 1964 U.S. Open winner

TOUR Victories: 14—1957 St. Paul Open, Miller Open; 1958 Thunderbird Invitational, Phoenix Open, Baton Rouge Open, Gleneagles Chicago Open; 1959 Gleneagles Chicago Open, Los Angeles Open; 1960 Bing Crosby Pro-Am, Milwaukee Open; 1964 U.S. Open, Insurance City Open, American Golf Classic; 1966 Lucky International.

Money Summary: Started in 1957 and won $18,781 for 10th place. Best year 1964 when he won $62,465 for 6th place. Last year he won money was in 1975.
Career Earnings: $268,293

VERPLANK, Scott Birth Date 7/9/64 **Birthplace** Dallas, TX **Residence** Edmond, OK **Height** 5-9 **Weight** 160 **College** Oklahoma State University **Special Interests** Hunting, fishing, football **Family** Wife, Kim **Turned Professional** 1986 **Other Achievements** Winner, 1984 United States Amateur. 1982,1984,1985 Texas State Amateur. 1982,1983,1984,1985 LaJet Amateur Classic in Abilene, TX; 1984 Western Amateur; 1984, 1985 Sunnehanna Amateur; 1984 Big Eight Conference. Two-Time All-America selection. 1985 Academic All-America team. Named 1982 American Junior Golf Association Player-of-the-Year; 1984 Player-of-the-Year by Golf Digest. Winner 1986 NCAA Championship. **National Teams** Walker Cup, 1985.
Exempt Status: Special medical extension   **Playoff Record:** 1-0
TOUR Victories: 2 —1985 Western Open, 1988 Buick Open

Money & Position:			
1986 — $ 19,575 — 177	1989 — $ 82,345 — 141	1992 — $ 1,760 — 309	
1987 — $ 34,136 — 173	1990 — $303,589 — 47	1993 — $ — 0 —	
1988 — $ 366,045 — 31	1991 — $ 3,195 — 266		

Career Earnings: $810,827

W

WADKINS, Bobby Birth Date 7/26/51 **Birthplace** Richmond, VA **Residence** Richmond, VA **Height** 6-1 **Weight** 195 **Special Interest** Duck and goose hunting, fishing **Family** Wife, Linda; Casey Tanner (2/14/90) **College** East Tennessee State University (1973, Health and Physical Education) **Turned Professional** 1973 **Q School** Fall 1974 **Other Achievements** Winner 1971 Virginia State Amateur, 1981-82 Virginia State Open. 1972-73 NCAA All-American at East Tennessee State. Along with brother, Lanny, kept Richmond, VA city junior title in family six straight years (Lanny 4, Bobby 2).
Exempt Status: Veteran Member   **Playoff Record:** 0-2
Best Ever Finish: 2 — 1979 IVB-Philadelphia Classic. 1985 Sea Pines Heritage Classic.

Money & Position:		
1975—$ 23,330— 90	1982—$ 69,400— 59	1989—$152,184— 91
1976—$ 23,510— 93	1983—$ 56,363— 92	1990—$190,613— 85
1977—$ 20,867—103	1984—$108,335— 67	1991—$206,503— 81
1978—$ 70,426— 41	1985—$ 84,542— 90	1992—$ 30,382—197
1979—$121,373— 28	1986—$226,079— 33	1993—$ 39,153—189
1980—$ 56,728— 67	1987—$342,173— 25	
1981—$ 58,346— 73	1988—$193,022— 59	

1993 Best Finish: T25—Memorial Tournament
1993 Summary: Tournaments entered—24; in money—8; top ten finishes—0.
Career Earnings: $2,073,328

WADSWORTH, Fred Birth Date 7/17/62 **Birthplace** Munich, Germany **Residence** Columbus, GA **Height** 6-3 **Weight** 170 **College** University of South Carolina **Special Interests** All sports, fishing **Family** Wife, Juli **Turned Professional** 1984 **Other Achievements** 1984 Eastern Amateur champion. 1984 All-American at South Carolina. Three mini-tour wins. South African Open champion.
Exempt Status: Past Champion
TOUR Victories: 1 —1986 Southern Open

Money & Position:		
1980 — $ 24,129 — 190	1987 — $ 80,585 — 109	1989 — $ 10,587— 208
1986 — $ 75,092 — 115	1988 — $ 24,129 — 190	1991 — $ 1,292 — 314
		1993 — $ 609 — 333

Best 1993 Finish: T68 — Deposit Gauranty Classic
1993 Summary: Tournaments entered--3; in money--1; top ten finishes--0
Career Earnings: $192,977

WALCHER, Rocky Birth Date 10/12/61 **Birthplace** Carnegie, OK **Residence** Oklahoma City, OK **Height** 6-0 **Weight** 185 **Special Interests** Reading, sports **Family** Wife Tracy; Tripp (11/16/91) **College** Southwest Oklahoma State **Turned Professional** 1985 **Q School** 1993 **Other Achievements** Winner, eight collegiate tournaments.
Exempt Status: T26 at 1993 Qualifying Tournament

WILSON, John Birth Date 2/23/59 **Birthplace** Ceres, CA **Residence** Palm Desert, CA **Height** 6-1 **Weight** 165 **Special Interests** Fishing, all sports **Family** Wife, Kathy; Christopher (2/26/78), Shannon (4/28/79), Spencer (12/10/91) **College** College of the Desert **Turned Professional** 1987 **Other Achievements** Played 1990 Australian Tour. Member PGA TOUR 1991, finished 180th on money list with $43,041. Finished T2 in 1991 Ben Hogan Mississippi Gulf Coast Classic.
Exempt Status: T18 at 1993 Qualifying Tournament
Best Ever Finish: T19— Deposit Guaranty Golf Classic, T19—Federal Express St. Jude Classic

Money & Position:	
1991— $43,041—180	1992 — $576 —318

Career Earnings: $43,041

WOODLAND, Jeff **Birth Date** 2/28/57 **Birthplace** Papua New Guinea **Residence** Queensland, Australia **Height** 6-0 **Weight** 170 **Special Interest** Surfing, sports and wine collecting **Family** Wife, Rita; Troy **Turned Professional** 1978 **Other Achievements** Winner, 1989 Fiji Open, Harvey Bay Open, Mt. ISA Open on Australian Tour. Won 1991 Ben Hogan Dakota Dunes Open, 1992 Ben Hogan Wichita Charity Classic and 1992 Ben Hogan Utah Open. Holds NIKE TOUR record for low 18 holes with a 12-under par 60 in 1991 Dakota Dunes Open.
Exempt Status: T4 at 1993 Qualifying Tournament
Best Ever Finish: T10--1993 Deposit Guaranty Golf Classic
Money & Position: 1991— $20,500—207 1993—$73,367—163
1993 Summary: Tournaments entered—27; in money—14; top ten finishes—1
Career Earnings: $73,367

WOODWARD, Jim **Birth Date** 6/5/57 **Birthplace** Wilmington, DE **Residence** Oklahoma City, OK **Height** 6-2 **Weight** 205 **Special Interests** Fishing, hunting, family activities **Family** Wife, Janet; Jacey (7/24/85); Sarah (7/8/88) **Turned Professional** 1979 **Q School** 1986, 1991 **Other Achievements** Winner, 1975 Oklahoma State High School Championship, 1975 Texas-Oklahoma Championship, 1978 Oklahoma State Amateur, 1978 Southern Amateur, 1986, 1988 California State Open.
Exempt Status: Special Medical Extension
Money & Position: 1990 — $118,462 — 128   1992 — $ 161,301 — 95
                     1991 — $ 28,307 — 199   1993 — $ 52,731 — 180
Best 1993 Finish: T11--Phoenix Open
1993 Summary: Tournaments entered--19; in money--8; top ten finishes--0
Career Earnings: $360,801

WRENN, Robert **Birth Date** 9/11/59 **Birthplace** Richmond, VA **Residence** Richmond, VA **Height** 5-10 **Weight** 170 **Special Interest** Reading, flying, thrill-seeking **Family** Wife, Kathy; Tucker (12/12/92) **College** Wake Forest University **Turned Professional** 1981 **Q School** Fall 1984, 1986 **Other Achievements** Winner 1981 Trans-Mississippi Amateur, 1983 Virginia State Open, 1983 Indonesian Open. All-Atlantic Coast Conference 1978-81. Among Wake Forest teammates was Scott Hoch.
Exempt Status: 143rd on 1993 money list
TOUR Victories: 1—1987 Buick Open
Money & Position: 1985 — $ 36,396 — 135   1989 — $ 243,638 — 55   1992 — $127,729 — 113
                     1986 — $ 22,869 — 171   1990 — $ 174,308 — 92   1993 — $103,928 — 143
                     1987 — $ 203,557 — 52   1991 — $ 141,255 —109
                     1988 — $ 209,404 — 52
1993 Best Finish: T3—Phoenix Open
1993 Summary: Tournaments entered—28; in money—13; top ten finishes—1
Career Earnings: $1,263,084

WURTZ, MARK **Birth Date** 10/31/64 **Birthplace** Yakima, WA **Residence** Port Ludlow, WA **Height** 5-9 **Weight** 155 **Special Interests** Movies, sports **Family** Single **College** University of New Mexico **Turned Professional** 1986 **Q School** 1993 **Other Achievements** Winner 1991 Canadian TPC, 1992 California State Open
Exempt Status: T24 at 1993 Qualifying Tournament

Robert Allenby

HEIGHT: 6'2" **WEIGHT:** 170 **BIRTH DATE:** July 12, 1971
BIRTHPLACE: Melbourne, Australia **RESIDENCE:** Melbourne, Australia
SPECIAL INTERESTS: Fishing, music
TURNED PROFESSIONAL: 1992
BEST EVER FINISH: T33--1993 U.S. Open
MONEY & POSITION: 1993-- $11,052--235
BEST 1993 FINISH: T33--U.S. Open
1993 SUMMARY: Tournaments entered--6; in money--1; top ten finishes--0.
OTHER ACHIEVEMENTS: Leader of Australian Order of Merit 1992,1993. Winner, 1992 Perak Masters and Johnnie Walker Classic. Winner, 1993 Optus Players Championship.
NATIONAL TEAMS: World Cup, 1993; Dunhill Cup, 1993.

Peter Baker

HEIGHT: 5'9" **WEIGHT:** 170 **BIRTH DATE:** October 7, 1967
BIRTHPLACE: Shifnal, England **RESIDENCE:** Tettenhall, England
FAMILY: Wife, Helen; Georgina
SPECIAL INTERESTS: Music, cars, sports, Wolversoccer
TURNED PROFESSIONAL: 1986
CAREER HIGHLIGHTS: Winner, 1993 Dunhill British Masters and Scandanavian Masters.
Winner, 1990 UAP under-25 Championship. Winner, 1988 Benson & Hedges International.
Placed seventh in 1993 PGA European Tour Order of Merit.
NATIONAL TEAMS: Walker Cup, 1985; Ryder Cup, 1993. Dunhill Cup, 1993

Seve Ballesteros

HEIGHT: 6' **WEIGHT:** 175 **BIRTH DATE:** April 9, 1957
BIRTHPLACE: Pedrena, Santander, Spain
RESIDENCE: Pedrena, Santander, Spain **FAMILY:** Wife, Carmen; Baldomero Javier
SPECIAL INTERESTS: Cycling
TURNED PROFESSIONAL: 1974 **PLAYOFF RECORD:** 1-2
TOUR VICTORIES: 6 — **1978** Greater Greensboro Open. **1980** Masters Tournament. **1983**
Masters Tournament, Manufacturers Hanover Westchester Classic. **1985** USF&G Classic.
1988 Manufacturers Hanover Westchester Classic.

MONEY & POSITION:			
	1983--$ 210,933-- 18	1987--$ 305,058-- 32	1991--$ 64,320--160
	1984--$ 132,660-- 52	1988--$ 165,202-- 71	1992--$ 39,206--184
	1985--$ 206,638-- 18	1989--$138,094--101	1993--$ 34,850--193
	1986--$ 45,877-- 141	1990--$ 84,584--144	

BEST 1993 FINISH: T11--Masters
1993 SUMMARY: Tournaments entered-3; in money--1; top ten finishes--0.
OTHER ACHIEVEMENTS: Winner of three British Opens, 1979, 1984, 1988. Winner of 60 tournaments worldwide including World Match Play, 1981, 1982, 1984, 1985; Lancome Trophy, 1976, 1983, 1986, 1988; Spanish Open, 1981, 1985; French Open, 1977, 1982, 1985, 1986; Dutch Open, 1976, 1980, 1986; Swiss Open, 1977, 1978, 1989; German Open, 1978, 1988; Irish Open, 1983, 1985, 1986; British Masters,1986, 1991; British PGA, 1983; Madrid Open, 1980, 1981, 1989; Japanese Open, 1977, 1978; Australian PGA, 1981; Dunlop Phoenix (Japan), 1977, 1981; Taiheiyo Masters (Japan), 1988; Kenya Open, 1978; Volvo PGA, 1991. Winner, 1992 Dubai Desert Classic and Turespana Open De Baleares. His string of 17 consecutive years with a victory on the European Tour ended in 1993.
NATIONAL TEAMS: European Ryder Cup (7), 1979, 1983, 1985, 1987, 1989, 1991, 1993. World Cup (4), 1975, 1976, 1977, 1992. Dunhill Cup (3), 1985, 1986, 1988.

Ernie Els

HEIGHT: 6'3" **WEIGHT:** 210 **BIRTH DATE:** October 17, 1969
BIRTHPLACE: Johannesburg, South Africa **RESIDENCE:** Johannesburg, South Africa
FAMILY: Single
BEST EVER FINISH: T7--1993 U. S. Open
MONEY & POSITION: 1992--$18,420--211   1993--$38,185--190
BEST 1993 FINISH: T7--U.S. Open
1993 SUMMARY: Tournaments entered--6; in money--2; top ten finishes--1.
OTHER ACHIEVEMENTS: Winner of 6 tournaments in Africa in 1992: Protea Assurance South African Open, Lexington PGA Championship, South African Masters, Hollard Royal Swazi Sun Classic, First National Bank Players Championship and Goodyear Classic.
NATIONAL TEAMS: Dunhill Cup, 1992. World Cup, 1993

Nick Faldo

HEIGHT: 6'3" **WEIGHT:** 195 **BIRTH DATE:** July 18, 1957
BIRTHPLACE: Hertfordshire, England **RESIDENCE:** Surrey, England
FAMILY: Wife, Gill; Natalie, Matthew **TURNED PROFESSIONAL:** 1976
PLAYOFF RECORD: 2-1
TOUR VICTORIES: 3— **1984** Sea Pines Heritage Classic. **1989** Masters Tournament.
1990 Masters Tournament.

MONEY & POSITION:

1981--$ 23,320--119	1985--$ 54,060--117	1989--$ 327,981-- 31
1982--$ 56,667-- 79	1986--$ 52,965--135	1990--$ 345,262-- 37
1983--$ 67,851-- 79	1987--$ 36,281--169	1991--$ 127,156--117
1984--$ 116,845-- 38	1988-$179,120---64	1992--$ 345,168-- 41
		1993--$ 188,886-- 91

BEST 1993 FINISHES: 3--PGA Championship, T6--Doral-Ryder Open
1993 SUMMARY: Tournaments entered--6; in money--6; top ten finishes--2.
OTHER ACHIEVEMENTS: Winner 1987, 1990, 1992 British Open. Winner 1975 British Youths Amateur and English Amateur Championships. Named 1977 European Tour Rookie of the Year. Winner British PGA Championship, 1978, 1980, 1981. Leading money winner on the European Tour in 1983 and 1992. Had 11 top ten finishes in 16 European starts in 1983 and compiled 69.03 stroke average. Winner 1984 Car Care Plan International (England); 1987 Spanish Open. Winner 1988 French Open, Volvo Masters. Winner of over 25 events worldwide. Winner 1989 Volvo PGA Championship, Dunhill British Masters, Peugeot French Open, Suntory World Match Play. Winner, 1991 Irish Open. Awarded MBE (Member British Empire) in 1987. Winner, 1992 Carroll's Irish Open, British Open, Scandinavian Masters, GA European Open, Toyota World Matchplay. Winner, 1993 Johnnie Walker Classic; Carroll's Irish Open.
NATIONAL TEAMS: European Ryder Cup (9), 1977, 1979, 1981, 1983, 1985, 1987, 1989, 1991, 1993. World Cup (2), 1977, 1991. Dunhill Cup (5), 1985, 1986, 1987,1988, 1991. Nissan Cup, 1986; Kirin Cup, 1987; Four Tours Championship, 1990.

Anders Forsbrand

HEIGHT: 6'1" **WEIGHT:** 162 **BIRTH DATE:** April 1, 1961
BIRTHPLACE: Filipstad, Sweden **RESIDENCE:** Marbella, Spain **FAMILY:** Single
SPECIAL INTERESTS: Ice hockey **TURNED PROFESSIONAL:** 1981
BEST EVER FINISH: T9--1992 PGA Championship
MONEY & POSITION: 1992--$50,531--172   1993--$34,850--193
BEST 1993 FINISH: T11--Masters
1993 SUMMARY: Tournaments entered--5; in money--1; top ten finishes--0.
OTHER ACHIEVEMENTS: Winner of six events on the PGA European Tour including the 1987 Ebel European Masters-Swiss Open, 1991 Volvo Open di Firenze, Benson & Hedges Trophy (with Helen Alfredsson), 1992 Volvo Open di Firenze, Credit Lyonnais Cannes Open and Equity & Law Challenge. Also winner of 1982 Swedish PGA Championship, 1983 Stiab GP and 1984 Swedish International, Gevalia Open.
NATIONAL TEAMS: Dunhill Cup (6), 1985, 1986, 1987, 1988, 1991, 1992; World Cup (4), 1984, 1985, 1988, 1991; Kirin Cup, 1984.

Joakim Haeggman

HEIGHT: 6'1" **WEIGHT:** 190   **BIRTH DATE:** August 28, 1969
BIRTHPLACE: Kalmar, Sweden **RESIDENCE:** London, England **FAMILY:** Single
SPECIAL INTERESTS: Fishing, skiing **TURNED PROFESSIONAL:** 1989
CAREER HIGHLIGHTS: Winner, 1993 Peugeot Spanish Open. Placed 15th on 1993 PGA European Tour Order of Merit. Winner, 1992 SI Compaq Open. Winner, 1990 Wermland Open.

NATIONAL TEAMS: Ryder Cup, 1993; World Cup, 1993. Dunhill Cup, 1993

Tony Johnstone

HEIGHT: 5'9" **WEIGHT:** 145 **BIRTH DATE:** May 2, 1956
BIRTHPLACE: Bulawayo, Zimbabwe **RESIDENCE:** Boksburg, South Africa
FAMILY: Wife, Karen; Dale, Lauren
SPECIAL INTERESTS: Hunting, gardening **TURNED PROFESSIONAL:** 1979
BEST EVER FINISH: T12--1984 B. C. Open
MONEY & POSITION: 1984--$ 6,600--193 1992--$25,800--202
1989--$12,092--206 1993--$10,892--237
BEST 1993 FINISH: T52--THE PLAYERS Championship
1993 SUMMARY: Tournaments entered--4; in money--2; top ten finishes--0.
OTHER ACHIEVEMENTS: Winner, 1984 Portuguese Open, South African Open, South
African Charity Classic and South African Masters; 1986 Goodyear Classic; 1987 ICL
International, Minolta Copiers Match Play and Wild Coast Classic; 1988 ICL International,
Minolta Copiers Match Play and Wild Coast Classic and Bloemfontein Classic; 1989
Lexington PGA Championship; 1990 Murphy's Cup and Palabora Classic; 1991 Murphy's
Classic; 1992 Volvo European PGA Championship
NATIONAL TEAMS: Hennessy Cognac Cup, 1992

Barry Lane

HEIGHT: 5'10" **WEIGHT:** 170 **BIRTH DATE:** June 21, 1960
BIRTHPLACE: Hayes, England **RESIDENCE:** Binfield, England
FAMILY: Wife, Melanie; Benjamin, Emma
SPECIAL INTERESTS: Cars, chess **TURNED PROFESSIONAL:** 1976
BEST EVER FINISH: T16--1993 U. S. Open
MONEY & POSITION: 1993--$24,088--206
BEST 1993 FINISH: T16--U. S. Open
1993 SUMMARY: Tournaments entered--2; in money--2; top ten finishes--0.
OTHER ACHIEVEMENTS: Winner of four European Tour Events: 1987 Equity & Law
Challenge, 1988 Bell's Scottish Open; 1992 Mercedes German Masters; 1993 Canon
European Masters. 5th on 1992 European Order of Merit, 10th in 1993. Winner, 1983
Jamaica Open.
NATIONAL TEAMS: European Ryder Cup, 1993. Dunhill Cup, 1988. World Cup, 1988.

Bernhard Langer

HEIGHT: 5'9" **WEIGHT:** 155 **BIRTH DATE:** August 27, 1957
BIRTHPLACE: Anhausen, Germany **RESIDENCE:** Anhausen, Germany
FAMILY: Wife, Vikki; Jackie Carol.
SPECIAL INTERESTS: All sports especially snow skiing, soccer.
TURNED PROFESSIONAL: 1972 **PLAYOFF RECORD:** 1-1
TOUR VICTORIES: 3— **1985** Masters, Sea Pines Heritage Classic. **1993** Masters
MONEY & POSITION: 1984--$ 82,465-- 75 1987--$366,430-- 23 1990--$
35,150--187
1985--$271,044-- 13 1988--$100,635--111 1991--$
112,539--129
1986--$379,800-- 10 1989--$195,973-- 73 1992--$
41,211--181
BEST 1993 FINISH: 1-- Masters 1993--$
626,938-- 23
1993 SUMMARY: Tournaments entered--6; in money--4; top ten finishes--3.
OTHER ACHIEVEMENTS: Winner of over 30 international tournaments including: 1980 Dunlop Masters,
Colombian Open; 1981, 1982, 1985 and 1986 German Open; 1981 Bob Hope British Classic; 1983 Italian Open;
1983 Glasgow Classic; TPC at St. Mellion; 1983 Johnnie Walker Tournament; 1983 Casio World (Japan); 1984,
1987 Irish Open; 1984 Dutch Open; 1984 French Open; 1984 Spanish Open; 1985 Australian Masters; 1985
European Open; 1985 Sun City Challenge; Co-winner Lancome Trophy. Winner of seven German National
Opens and two German National PGA's (Germans only). Leader in European Order of Merit, 1981 and 1984.
Winner 1987 PGA Championship in England, 1987 Belgian Classic. Winner 1988 European Epson Match Play.
Winner 1989 Peugeot Spanish Open, German Masters. Winner 1990 Madrid Open. Winner 1991 Benson &
Hedges Open. Winner 1992 Heineken Dutch Open and Honda Open. Winner, 1993 Volvo PGA Championship.
NATIONAL TEAMS: European Ryder Cup (7), 1981, 1983, 1985, 1987, 1989, 1991, 1993; World Cup (8), 1976,
1977, 1978, 1979, 1980, 1990, 1991, 1993; Nissan Cup (2), 1985, 1986 (captain both years); Kirin Cup, 1987
(captain in 1987); Four Tours World Championship, 1989 (captain).

Sandy Lyle

HEIGHT: 6'1" **WEIGHT:** 187 **BIRTH DATE:** February 9, 1958
BIRTHPLACE: Shrewsbury, England **RESIDENCE:** Surrey, England
FAMILY: Wife, Jolande; Stuart, James. **SPECIAL INTERESTS:** Motorcycles, cars, airplanes
TURNED PROFESSIONAL: 1977 **PLAYOFF RECORD:** 3-0
TOUR VICTORIES: 5—**1986** Greater Greensboro Open. **1987** Tournament Players Championship. **1988** Phoenix Open, Kmart Greater Greensboro Open, Masters Tournament.

MONEY & POSITION:			
1984--$ 15,532--169	1987--$286,176-- 34	1990--$ 51,280--175
1985--$ 40,452--132	1988--$726,934-- 7	1991--$ 59,794--166
1986--$143,415-- 64	1989--$292,292-- 43	1992--$ 73,459--154
		1993--$ 86,121--153

BEST 1993 FINISH: 5--Doral-Ryder Open
1993 SUMMARY: Tournaments entered--7; in money--5; top ten finishes--1.
OTHER ACHIEVEMENTS: Winner, 1985 British Open. Winner of 28 international events including 1978 Nigerian Open; 1979 Scandinavian Open, European Open; 1981 French Open; 1983 Madrid Open; 1984 Italian Open, Lancome Trophy, Kapalua International, Casio World (Japan); 1987 German Masters; 1988 Dunhill Masters, Suntory World Match Play; 1991 BMW International Open; 1992 Lancia Martini Italian Open.
NATIONAL TEAMS: European Ryder Cup (5), 1979, 1981, 1983, 1985, 1987; Nissan Cup (2), 1985, 1986 (medalist in 1985); Kirin Cup (2), 1987, 1988; Scotland World Cup (3), 1979, 1980, 1987 (medalist in 1980); British Walker Cup, 1977; Dunhill Cup (6), 1985, 1986, 1987, 1988, 1989, 1990.

Mark McNulty

HEIGHT: 5'10" **WEIGHT:** 158 **BIRTH DATE:** October 25, 1953
BIRTHPLACE: Zimbabwe **RESIDENCE:** Sunningdale, England **FAMILY:** Wife, Sue; Matthew, Carolina **SPECIAL INTERESTS:** Piano, snooker, cars, fine arts
TURNED PROFESSIONAL: 1977
BEST EVER FINISH: 4--1982 Danny Thomas Memphis Open; T4--1982 Sammy Davis Jr. Greater Hartford Open.

MONEY & POSITION:			
1982--$ 50,322-- 90	1986--$ 6,170--225	1990--$ 34,375-- 188
1983--$ 40,062--115	1987--$ 4,165--243	1991--$ 34,321-- 194
1984--$ 5,382--198	1988--$ 39,481--159	1992--$ 46,171-- 181
1985--$ 3,600- 217		

OTHER ACHIEVEMENTS: Winner of 33 events worldwide, including 11 on the PGA European Tour. Twice finished runner-up in the PGA European Tour Order of Merit, in 1987 and 1990.

Colin Montgomerie

HEIGHT: 6'1" **WEIGHT:** 191 **BIRTH DATE:** June 23, 1963
BIRTHPLACE: Glasgow, Scotland **RESIDENCE:** Walton-on-Thames, England
FAMILY: Wife, Eimear **SPECIAL INTERESTS:** Music, cars
TURNED PROFESSIONAL: 1987
BEST EVER FINISH: T3--1992 U.S. Open
MONEY & POSITION: 1992--$ 98,045--132   1993--$ 17,992--221
BEST 1993 FINISH: T33--U. S. Open
1993 SUMMARY: Tournaments entered--4; in money--3; top ten finishes--0.
OTHER ACHIEVEMENTS: Winner, 1993 Heineken Dutch Open, Volvo Masters. Winner, 1989 Portuguese Open, 1991 Scandinavian Masters. Winner 1985 Scottish Stroke Play, 1987 Scottish Amateur Championship. 1988 European Tour Rookie of the Year. Leader of 1993 Europeon Tour Order of Merit.
NATIONAL TEAMS: Walker Cup (2), 1985, 1987; Ryder Cup (2), 1991, 1993; Dunhill Cup (3), 1988, 1991, 1992; World Cup (2), 1988, 1991.

Tommy Nakajima

HEIGHT: 5'11" **WEIGHT:** 180 **BIRTH DATE:** October 24, 1954
BIRTHPLACE: Gunma, Japan **RESIDENCE:** Narita City, Japan
FAMILY: Wife, Ritsuko; Yoshino, Masao **SPECIAL INTERESTS:** Music, skiing
TURNED PROFESSIONAL: 1975
BEST EVER FINISH: 3--1988 PGA Championship

MONEY & POSITION:			
1983--$ 46,351--107	1987--$ 82,111--108		
1984--$ 78,796-- 77	1988--$148,304-- 81	1992--$ 16,951--215	
1985--$ 6,167--198	1989--$ 6,520--224	1993--$ 50,578--184	
1986--$ 37,847--153	1991--$ 35,150--193		

BEST 1993 FINISH: T15--The International
1993 SUMMARY: Tournaments entered--4; in money--3; top ten finishes--0.
OTHER ACHIEVEMENTS: Winner of over 50 events world wide, including the 1992 Pepsi Ube Kusan, NST Niigata Open and Japan Match Play Championship. Winner of four Japan Opens, three Japan PGA Championships, three Japan Match Play Championships and one Japan Series Championship.

Frank Nobilo

HEIGHT: 5'11" **WEIGHT:** 180 **BIRTH DATE:** May 14, 1960
BIRTHPLACE: Aucland, New Zealand **RESIDENCE:** Aucland, New Zealand
FAMILY: Wife, Gaynor; Bianca **SPECIAL INTERESTS:** Photography, squash
TURNED PROFESSIONAL: 1979
BEST EVER FINISH: T22--1993 PGA Championship
MONEY & POSITION: 1992--$ 7,000--252   1993--$ 14,500--230
BEST 1993 FINISH: T22--PGA Chamionship
1993 SUMMARY: Tournaments entered--1; in money--1; top ten finishes--0.
OTHER ACHIEVEMENTS: Winner of three PGA European Tour events: 1988 PLM Open, 1991 Lancome Trophy, 1993 Turespana Mediterranean Open. Winner, 1985 and 1987 New Zealand PGA. Winner, 1982 New South Wales PGA. Winner, 1978 New Zealand Amateur.
NATIONAL TEAMS: Dunhill Cup (7), 1985, 1986, 1987, 1989, 1990, 1992, 1993; World Cup (7), 1982, 1987, 1988, 1990, 1991, 1992, 1993; World Amateur Team 1978..

Jose Maria Olazabal

HEIGHT: 5'10"   **WEIGHT:** 160
BIRTH DATE: February 5, 1966   **BIRTHPLACE:** Fuenterrabia, Spain
RESIDENCE: Fuenterrabia, Spain **SPECIAL INTERESTS:** Music, cinema
TURNED PROFESSIONAL: 1985
TOUR VICTORIES: 2--**1990** NEC World Series of Golf. **1991** The International.

MONEY & POSITION:			
1987--$ 7,470--215	1990--$ 337,837-- 38	1992--$ 63,429--161
1989--$56,039--160	1991--$ 382,124-- 43	1993--$ 60,160--174

BEST 1993 FINISH: T7--Masters
1993 SUMMARY: Tournaments entered--6; in money--3; top ten finishes--1.
OTHER ACHIEVEMENTS: Winner 1983 Italian Amateur, Spanish Amateur; 1986 European Masters-Swiss Open, Sanyo Open; 1988 Belgian Open, German Masters; 1989 Tenerife Open, Dutch Open; 1990 Benson & Hedges International, Irish Open, Lancome Trophy, Visa Taiheyo Club Masters; 1991 Catalonia Open; 1992 Turespana Open de Tenerife and Open Mediterrania.
NATIONAL TEAMS: European Ryder Cup (4), 1987, 1989, 1991, 1993; Kirin Cup, 1987; Four Tours World Championship (2), 1989, 1990; World Cup, 1989; Dunhill Cup (5), 1986, 1987, 1988, 1989, 1992.

Masashi "Jumbo" Ozaki

HEIGHT: 6' 2" **WEIGHT:** 200 **BIRTH DATE:** January 27, 1947
BIRTHPLACE: Tokushima, Japan
RESIDENCE: Chiba, Japan **TURNED PROFESSIONAL:** 1970
BEST-EVER FINISH: T4--1993 Memorial Tournament

MONEY & POSITION:			
1987--$21,727--184	1990--$ 31,834--192		
1988--$ 6,321--233	1991--$ 15,765--218		
1989--$47,755--165	1992--$ 13,906--223	1993--$66,742--169	

BEST 1993 FINISH: T4--Memorial Tournament
1992 SUMMARY: Tournaments entered--4; in money--3; top ten finishes--1.
OTHER ACHIEVEMENTS: Winner of over 60 tournaments worldwide. Won six JPGA Tournaments in 1992: Dunlop Open, Chunichi Crowns, Philanthropy Cup, All Nippon Airways Open, Japan Open, Visa Taiheyo Masters. Has led the JPGA in earnings five times since 1973. Winner, 1990 Yonex Hiroshima Open, Maruman Open and Daiwa KBC Augusta.

Ronan Rafferty

HEIGHT: 5'11 1/2" **WEIGHT:** 195 **BIRTH DATE:** January 13, 1964
BIRTHPLACE: Newry, N. Ireland
RESIDENCE: Ascot, England **FAMILY:** Wife, Clare; Jonathan
SPECIAL INTERESTS: Snooker, cars, collecting fine wines.
TURNED PROFESSIONAL: 1981
BEST EVER FINISH: T14--1990 Masters Tournament.
MONEY & POSITION: 1989--$ 9,767--211 1990--$ 34,029--189 1992--$ 11,868--229
OTHER ACHIEVEMENTS: Winner of the 1993 Austrian Open; 1982 Venezuelan Open, Daiko Palm Meadows Cup, Portuguese Open; 1987 South Australian Open, New Zealand Open; 1988 Australian Match-Play Championship; Equity & Law Challenge; 1989 Lancia Italian Open, Scandinavian Enterprise Open, Volvo Masters; 1990 Melbourne Classic, 1990 PLM Open, Ebel European Masters; 1992 Portuguese Open. Leader 1989 PGA European Tour Order of Merit. Winner, 1979 British Boys Championship, 1980 English Open Amateur Strokeplay Championship.
NATIONAL TEAMS: European Ryder Cup, 1989; World Cup (6), 1983, 1984, 1987, 1988, 1990 1991; Dunhill Cup (7), 1986, 1987, 1988, 1989, 1990, 1991, 1992; Kirin Cup, 1988; Four Tours World Championship of Golf (3), 1989, 1990, 1991.

Steven Richardson

HEIGHT: 6'1" **WEIGHT:** 203 **BIRTH DATE:** July 24, 1966
BIRTHPLACE: Windsor, England **RESIDENCE:** Stubbington, Hants, England
TURNED PROFESSIONAL: 1989
BEST-EVER FINISH: T5--1991 PGA Championship
MONEY & POSITION: 1991--$ 60,000--165 1992--$15,737--219
OTHER ACHIEVEMENTS: Winner 1993 German Masters. Winner 1991 Girona Open, Portuguese Open. Winner 1989 English Amateur Championship.
NATIONAL TEAMS: Ryder Cup, 1991; Walker Cup, 1989; Dunhill Cup (2), 1991, 1992; Four Tour World Championship 1991.

Ian Woosnam

HEIGHT: 5'4" **WEIGHT:** 161 **BIRTH DATE:** March 2, 1958
BIRTHPLACE: Oswestry, Wales
RESIDENCE: Oswestry, Wales **FAMILY:** Wife, Glendryth; Daniel, Rebecca
SPECIAL INTERESTS: Fishing, sports, snooker **TURNED PROFESSIONAL:** 1976
TOUR VICTORIES: 2—**1991** USF&G Classic; Masters

MONEY & POSITION:			
	1986--$ 4,000--233	1988--$ 8,464--219	1991--$485,023-- 23
	1987--$ 3,980--236	1989--$146,323-- 97	1992--$ 52,046--171
		1990--$ 72,138--156	1993--$ 55,426--176

BEST 1993 FINISH: T17-- Masters
1993 SUMMARY: Tournaments entered--6; in money--4; top ten finishes--0.
OTHER ACHIEVEMENTS: Winner on the European Tour of the 1982 Swiss Open; winner of 1983 Silk Cut Masters; 1984 Scandinavian Enterprise Open; 1986 Lawrence Batley TPC; 1987 Jersey Open, Cespa Madrid Open, Bell's Scottish Open, Lancome Trophy, Suntory World Match Play Championship; 1988 Volvo PGA Championship, Carrolls Irish Open, Panasonic European Open; 1989 Carrolls Irish Open; 1990 Amex Mediterranean Open, Monte Carlo Open, Bell's Scottish Open, Epson Grand Prix, Suntory World Match Play Championship; 1991 Mediterranean Open, Monte Carlo Open; 1992 European Monte Carlo. Also has won the 1979 News of the World under-23 Match-play Championship, 1982 Cacherel under-25 Championship; 1985 Zambian Open; 1986 '555' Kenya Open; 1987 Hong Kong Open and World Cup Individual title; 1992 European Monte Carlo Open; 1993 Murphy's English Open and Lancom Trophy.
NATIONAL TEAMS: Ryder Cup (6), 1983, 1985, 1987, 1989, 1991, 1993; World Cup (10), 1980, 1982, 1983, 1984, 1985, 1987, 1990, 1991, 1992, 1993; Dunhill Cup (7), 1985, 1986, 1988, 1989, 1990, 1991, 1993; Nissan Cup (2), 1985, 1986; Kirin Cup, 1987; Four Tours World Championship of Golf (2), 1989, 1990.

Paul Azinger won three tournaments and
finished second on the money list in 1993.

INFINITI TOURNAMENT
OF CHAMPIONS

LaCosta Resort & Spa, Carlsbad, CA   **Purse: $800,000**
Par: 36-36--72   **Yards: 7,022**   **Jan. 7-10, 1993**

LEADERS: First Round--Paul Azinger fired a 7-under-par 65, and led by two strokes over Davis Love III. **Second Round**-- Azinger and Love at 10-under-par 134 led by four over Greg Norman. **Third Round** -- Love at 13-under-par 203 led by a stroke over Azinger.

PRO-AM: $10,000 total. All professionals received equal shares of $238.10. Rain cancelled play on Wednesday.

WEATHER: Due to heavy rains,Thursday's round was washed out completely. With the short field, the players played 36 holes on Friday in rainy conditions. Saturday was cloudy with occasional showers, as was Sunday.

Winner: Davis Love III 67- 67- 69- 69   272 $144,000.00

Tom Kite	2	69- 71- 69- 64	273	$86,400.00
Paul Azinger	T 3	65- 69- 70- 71	275	$46,400.00
Mark O'Meara	T 3	70- 70- 68- 67	275	$46,400.00
John Cook	T 5	73- 68- 68- 69	278	$31,000.00
Brad Faxon	T 5	71- 69- 67- 71	278	$31,000.00
Dan Forsman	T 7	68- 71- 69- 71	279	$27,225.00
Steve Pate	T 7	73- 66- 71- 69	279	$27,225.00
John Huston	9	70- 73- 68- 70	281	$24,825.00
Mark Calcavecchia	T10	68- 72- 70- 72	282	$23,025.00
Fred Couples	T10	70- 70- 72- 70	282	$23,025.00
Chip Beck	T12	71- 72- 69- 71	283	$20,625.00
Greg Norman	T12	68- 70- 71- 74	283	$20,625.00
Bill Glasson	14	67- 75- 70- 72	284	$19,225.00
Gary Hallberg	T15	70- 71- 69- 75	285	$17,625.00
David Peoples	T15	70- 71- 72- 72	285	$17,625.00
Craig Stadler	T15	73- 72- 71- 69	285	$17,625.00
Ben Crenshaw	T18	73- 72- 72- 70	287	$15,625.00
David Edwards	T18	71- 70- 74- 72	287	$15,625.00
Steve Elkington	T18	73- 69- 72- 73	287	$15,625.00
Fred Funk	21	72- 74- 70- 72	288	$14,425.00
Ray Floyd	T22	71- 72- 73- 73	289	$13,825.00
Richard Zokol	T22	70- 73- 72- 74	289	$13,825.00
Bruce Lietzke	24	74- 70- 73- 73	290	$13,225.00
Jay Haas	T25	72- 75- 73- 71	291	$12,625.00
Corey Pavin	T25	71- 74- 75- 71	291	$12,625.00
Lanny Wadkins	T25	71- 76- 70- 74	291	$12,625.00
Lee Janzen	28	76- 72- 74- 72	294	$12,225.00
Mark Carnevale	29	74- 71- 78- 76	299	$12,025.00
Billy Ray Brown	30	78- 79- 75- 72	304	$11,825.00

UNITED AIRLINES HAWAIIAN OPEN

Waialae CC, Honolulu, HI
Par: 36-36--72   Yards: 6,975

Purse: $1,200,000
January 14-17, 1993

Hawaiian Open

LEADERS: First Round-- Howard Twitty fired a 9-under-par 63 and led by two strokes over Bill Glasson. **Second Round**-- Twitty at 13-under-par 131 led by two over Fred Funk. **Third Round**-- Twitty moved to 15-under 201 and led Paul Azinger by three strokes.

CUT: 77 players at even par 144.

PRO-AM: $10,000. Individual-- Jeff Sluman, 67, $1,000. Team-- David Edwards, 53, $1,000.

WEATHER: Windy and overcast everyday, but no delays.

Winner: Howard Twitty 63- 68- 70- 68   269 $216,000.00

Player	Pos	Scores	Total	Money
Joey Sindelar	2	71- 68- 66- 68	273	$129,600.00
Paul Azinger	3	67- 68- 69- 70	274	$81,600.00
Keith Clearwater	T 4	72- 66- 68- 71	277	$49,600.00
Jeff Maggert	T 4	68- 71- 68- 70	277	$49,600.00
Brett Ogle	T 4	67- 70- 70- 70	277	$49,600.00
Nolan Henke	T 7	69- 71- 71- 67	278	$38,700.00
Davis Love III	T 7	69- 68- 71- 70	278	$38,700.00
Bill Glasson	T 9	65- 71- 73- 71	280	$31,200.00
Wayne Levi	T 9	72- 65- 69- 74	280	$31,200.00
Mark O'Meara	T 9	66- 73- 71- 70	280	$31,200.00
Duffy Waldorf	T 9	69- 69- 71- 71	280	$31,200.00
Brian Claar	T13	70- 74- 66- 71	281	$21,840.00
Russ Cochran	T13	72- 71- 68- 70	281	$21,840.00
David Edwards	T13	73- 71- 68- 70	281	$21,840.00
Fred Funk	T13	67- 66- 74- 74	281	$21,840.00
Corey Pavin	T13	68- 71- 72- 70	281	$21,840.00
Bob Eastwood	T18	69- 73- 67- 73	282	$16,200.00
John Flannery	T18	71- 69- 70- 72	282	$16,200.00
Steve Lowery	T18	67- 76- 69- 70	282	$16,200.00
Harry Taylor	T18	68- 69- 73- 72	282	$16,200.00
Dave Barr	T22	70- 70- 72- 71	283	$12,000.00
Chip Beck	T22	71- 71- 72- 69	283	$12,000.00
Ben Crenshaw	T22	66- 74- 73- 70	283	$12,000.00
Richard Zokol	T22	72- 71- 68- 72	283	$12,000.00
Brad Bryant	T26	73- 69- 70- 72	284	$9,060.00
Donnie Hammond	T26	70- 70- 70- 74	284	$9,060.00
Loren Roberts	T26	73- 69- 68- 74	284	$9,060.00
Tony Sills	T26	70- 71- 70- 73	284	$9,060.00
Mark Brooks	T30	71- 71- 71- 72	285	$6,410.00
Mike Donald	T30	74- 70- 70- 71	285	$6,410.00
John Elliott	T30	72- 68- 71- 74	285	$6,410.00
Bob Gilder	T30	71- 67- 76- 71	285	$6,410.00
Jay Haas	T30	74- 70- 71- 70	285	$6,410.00
Brian Henninger	T30	71- 70- 70- 74	285	$6,410.00
Hale Irwin	T30	70- 71- 71- 73	285	$6,410.00
Tom Lehman	T30	66- 73- 74- 72	285	$6,410.00
Mark Lye	T30	70- 72- 72- 71	285	$6,410.00
Jim McGovern	T30	72- 70- 69- 74	285	$6,410.00
Gene Sauers	T30	73- 70- 70- 72	285	$6,410.00
Craig Stadler	T30	72- 71- 70- 72	285	$6,410.00
Billy Andrade	T42	68- 71- 72- 75	286	$4,440.00
Robert Gamez	T42	70- 74- 72- 70	286	$4,440.00
Eddie Pearce	T42	70- 71- 70- 75	286	$4,440.00
Barry Cheesman	T45	70- 71- 73- 73	287	$3,513.60
Jim Gallagher, Jr.	T45	70- 71- 75- 71	287	$3,513.60
Neal Lancaster	T45	76- 68- 70- 73	287	$3,513.60
Craig Parry	T45	73- 66- 71- 77	287	$3,513.60
Scott Simpson	T45	74- 70- 72- 71	287	$3,513.60
Larry Mize	50	72- 70- 73- 73	288	$3,024.00
Marco Dawson	T51	72- 67- 73- 77	289	$2,764.80
Steve Elkington	T51	69- 71- 73- 76	289	$2,764.80
John Huston	T51	70- 72- 72- 75	289	$2,764.80
John Mahaffey	T51	71- 72- 69- 77	289	$2,764.80
Dave Peege	T51	72- 70- 72- 75	289	$2,764.80
Dave Rummells	T51	69- 68- 77- 75	289	$2,764.80
Jeff Sluman	T51	74- 70- 73- 72	289	$2,764.80
Mike Smith	T51	67- 74- 74- 74	289	$2,764.80
Mike Springer	T51	72- 72- 72- 73	289	$2,764.80
Lanny Wadkins	T51	72- 70- 73- 74	289	$2,764.80
Mike Schuchart	61	69- 72- 76- 73	290	$2,616.00
Bill Britton	T62	70- 74- 75- 72	291	$2,556.00
Rick Dalpos	T62	72- 71- 77- 71	291	$2,556.00
Ed Humenik	T62	71- 72- 75- 73	291	$2,556.00
Lee Porter	T62	71- 71- 76- 73	291	$2,556.00
Clark Dennis	T66	74- 70- 71- 78	293	$2,472.00
Kiyoshi Murota	T66	69- 74- 77- 73	293	$2,472.00
Neale Smith	T66	70- 74- 72- 77	293	$2,472.00
Steve Lamontagne	69	73- 71- 77- 73	294	$2,424.00
Kelly Gibson	T70	68- 76- 74- 77	295	$2,388.00
Jim Hallet	T70	71- 71- 77- 76	295	$2,388.00
Russell Beiersdorf	T72	68- 71- 77- 80	296	$2,316.00
Phil Blackmar	T72	73- 71- 74- 78	296	$2,316.00
Mark Carnevale	T72	72- 72- 77- 75	296	$2,316.00
Tad Rhyan	T72	72- 71- 76- 77	296	$2,316.00
Dan Halldorson	76	75- 69- 77- 77	298	$2,256.00
Skip Kendall	77	71- 73- 76- 79	299	$2,232.00

NORTHERN TELECOM OPEN

Tucson National, Tucson, AZ   Purse: $1,100,000
Par: 36-36--72   Yards: 7,148   January 21-24, 1993
Starr Pass Golf Course, Tucson, AZ
Par: 36-36--72   Yards: 7,010

LEADERS: First Round-- Billy Andrade (SP), with a 9-under-par 63, held a three-stroke lead over Dudley Hart (TN), Nolan Henke (SP) and Dick Mast (TN). **Second Round**-- Hart (SP) and Phil Mickelson (TN), each at 12-under-par 132, were two shots in front of Larry Mize (TN). (Rounds 3 and 4 at Tucson National). **Third Round**-- Hart and Mickelson, both at 15-under 201, continued to hold a two-stroke advantage over Mize, at 204.

CUT: 82 pros, 1 amateur at 2-under-par 142.

PRO-AM: Tucson National. $7,500. Individual--Payne Stewart, 66, $750. Team-- Dudley Hart, Gary McCord, 54, $675 each. Starr Pass. $7,500. Individual-- Gil Morgan, 65, $750. Team-- Roger Maltbie, 53, $750.

WEATHER: Sunny all four days, with cool temperatures early, turning mild later; varying amounts of wind each day, with gusts up to 25 mph Saturday.

Winner: Larry Mize   68- 66- 70- 67   271 $198,000.00

Name	Pos	Scores	Total	Money	Name	Pos	Scores	Total	Money
Jeff Maggert	2	70- 66- 70- 67	273	$118,800.00	Dan Halldorson	T41	73- 65- 76- 68	282	$3,850.00
Michael Allen	T 3	68- 70- 68- 68	274	$52,800.00	Steve Lowery	T41	69- 71- 71- 71	282	$3,850.00
Robin Freeman	T 3	71- 68- 69- 66	274	$52,800.00	Mark Lye	T41	72- 68- 71- 71	282	$3,850.00
Jim Gallagher, Jr.	T 3	75- 66- 67- 66	274	$52,800.00	Billy Mayfair	T41	72- 70- 69- 71	282	$3,850.00
Dudley Hart	T 3	66- 66- 69- 73	274	$52,800.00	Gene Sauers	T41	68- 68- 74- 72	282	$3,850.00
Billy Andrade	7	63- 73- 69- 70	275	$36,850.00	Dave Barr	T48	73- 69- 71- 70	283	$2,734.29
Lennie Clements	T 8	69- 67- 70- 70	276	$29,700.00	Brad Fabel	T48	72- 69- 70- 72	283	$2,734.29
Robert Gamez	T 8	69- 67- 72- 68	276	$29,700.00	Brian Kamm	T48	70- 67- 73- 73	283	$2,734.29
Roger Maltbie	T 8	70- 68- 70- 68	276	$29,700.00	Mike Standly	T48	70- 70- 73- 70	283	$2,734.29
Phil Mickelson	T 8	67- 65- 69- 75	276	$29,700.00	Ronnie Black	T48	70- 68- 75- 70	283	$2,734.28
Craig Parry	T 8	67- 72- 72- 65	276	$29,700.00	Marty Schiene	T48	74- 66- 74- 69	283	$2,734.28
John Flannery	T13	67- 69- 69- 72	277	$20,020.00	Mark Wiebe	T48	71- 67- 75- 70	283	$2,734.28
Donnie Hammond	T13	70- 71- 67- 69	277	$20,020.00	Russell Beiersdorf	T55	70- 72- 71- 71	284	$2,486.00
Nolan Henke	T13	66- 72- 70- 69	277	$20,020.00	Jim Hallet	T55	70- 70- 70- 74	284	$2,486.00
Payne Stewart	T13	71- 70- 68- 68	277	$20,020.00	Kenny Perry	T55	71- 69- 75- 69	284	$2,486.00
Curtis Strange	T13	71- 66- 71- 69	277	$20,020.00	Kirk Triplett	T55	71- 70- 70- 73	284	$2,486.00
Andy Bean	T18	69- 68- 72- 69	278	$12,466.67	Robert Wrenn	T55	72- 68- 72- 72	284	$2,486.00
Mark Brooks	T18	68- 68- 71- 71	278	$12,466.67	Michael Bradley	T60	69- 72- 70- 74	285	$2,343.00
Brian Claar	T18	67- 71- 72- 68	278	$12,466.67	Rick Dalpos	T60	68- 73- 71- 73	285	$2,343.00
Scott Gump	T18	67- 68- 72- 71	278	$12,466.67	Gary Hallberg	T60	70- 69- 69- 77	285	$2,343.00
Dan Pohl	T18	73- 67- 70- 68	278	$12,466.67	Larry Nelson	T60	72- 67- 72- 74	285	$2,343.00
Dave Rummells	T18	67- 69- 72- 70	278	$12,466.67	Dillard Pruitt	T60	68- 72- 72- 73	285	$2,343.00
Marco Dawson	T18	69- 68- 70- 71	278	$12,466.66	Joey Sindelar	T60	70- 70- 73- 72	285	$2,343.00
Harry Taylor	T18	70- 67- 69- 72	278	$12,466.66	Dennis Trixler	T60	72- 68- 75- 70	285	$2,343.00
Greg Twiggs	T18	68- 67- 70- 73	278	$12,466.66	Kim Young	T60	69- 70- 71- 75	285	$2,343.00
Trevor Dodds	T27	69- 71- 66- 73	279	$7,975.00	Russ Cochran	T68	71- 71- 76- 68	286	$2,189.00
Ed Dougherty	T27	69- 66- 74- 70	279	$7,975.00	Joel Edwards	T68	71- 68- 72- 75	286	$2,189.00
Paul Goydos	T27	71- 71- 68- 69	279	$7,975.00	Mike Hulbert	T68	70- 72- 70- 74	286	$2,189.00
Lee Janzen	T27	70- 68- 70- 71	279	$7,975.00	John Inman	T68	72- 70- 72- 72	286	$2,189.00
Rick Fehr	T31	69- 70- 75- 66	280	$6,820.00	Tad Rhyan	T68	69- 73- 71- 73	286	$2,189.00
Gil Morgan	T31	68- 68- 72- 72	280	$6,820.00	Ted Tryba	T68	70- 72- 72- 72	286	$2,189.00
Loren Roberts	T31	71- 69- 72- 68	280	$6,820.00	David Berganio	T68	73- 68- 70- 75	286	AMATEUR
Jeff Sluman	T34	71- 71- 70- 69	281	$5,437.15	Fulton Allem	T75	68- 70- 74- 75	287	$2,079.00
Duffy Waldorf	T34	70- 71- 70- 70	281	$5,437.15	Jay Delsing	T75	67- 74- 76- 70	287	$2,079.00
Bob Estes	T34	71- 67- 75- 68	281	$5,437.14	Kelly Gibson	T75	73- 69- 74- 71	287	$2,079.00
Neal Lancaster	T34	72- 68- 72- 69	281	$5,437.14	Brett Ogle	T75	69- 72- 73- 73	287	$2,079.00
Jim McGovern	T34	72- 70- 67- 72	281	$5,437.14	Brian Henninger	T79	71- 71- 71- 75	288	$2,013.00
Mike Springer	T34	70- 70- 68- 73	281	$5,437.14	Gary McCord	T79	68- 70- 77- 73	288	$2,013.00
Willie Wood	T34	70- 69- 74- 68	281	$5,437.14	Dick Mast	T81	66- 73- 75- 75	289	$1,969.00
John Adams	T41	70- 70- 72- 70	282	$3,850.00	Peter Persons	T81	75- 67- 74- 73	289	$1,969.00
Bruce Fleisher	T41	69- 71- 75- 67	282	$3,850.00	Hubert Green	83	72- 70- 74- 75	291	$1,936.00

PHOENIX OPEN

TPC of Scottsdale, Scottsdale, AZ   Purse: $1,000,000
Par: 35-36--71   Yards: 6,992   January 28-31,1993

PHOENIX OPEN

LEADERS: First Round-- Seven players-- Michael Allen, Mike Donald, David Frost, Jeff Maggert, Gary McCord, Scott Simpson and Robert Wrenn-- were deadlocked at five under-par 66; 10 other golfers were at 67. **Second Round**-- Frost and Lee Janzen, at 10-under-par 132, were two strokes in front of Wrenn and Steve Lowery, both at 134. **Third Round**--Wrenn, at 11-under-par 202, held a one-shot advantage over Frost and Andrew Magee, who fired a 7-under 64 to move into contention.

CUT: 78 players at 1-under-par 141.

PRO-AM: $7,500. Individual-- Mark O'Meara, 60, $750. Team-- John Daly, 51, $750.

WEATHER: Cool early Thursday, sunny and mild later. Early sun and cooler Friday, becoming partly cloudy with increasing wind later in the day. Partly sunny and cold with strong, gusting winds Saturday. Cloudy, overcast, and brisk Sunday, with winds up to 35 mph, a brief period of hail, and sunshine at day's end.

Winner: Lee Janzen   67- 65- 73- 68   273   **$180,000.00**

Player	Pos	Scores	Total	Money		Player	Pos	Scores	Total	Money
Andrew Magee	2	69- 70- 64- 72	275	$108,000.00		Brian Claar	T39	70- 71- 70- 73	284	$4,000.00
Michael Allen	T 3	66- 70- 70- 70	276	$48,000.00		Marco Dawson	T39	68- 70- 70- 76	284	$4,000.00
Mike Springer	T 3	70- 69- 68- 69	276	$48,000.00		Steve Elkington	T39	69- 72- 72- 71	284	$4,000.00
Kirk Triplett	T 3	69- 67- 69- 71	276	$48,000.00		Ed Humenik	T39	70- 69- 72- 73	284	$4,000.00
Robert Wrenn	T 3	66- 68- 68- 74	276	$48,000.00		Dillard Pruitt	T39	71- 68- 71- 74	284	$4,000.00
Keith Clearwater	T 7	68- 72- 71- 66	277	$32,250.00		Jim Carter	T45	70- 71- 75- 69	285	$2,752.50
Mark Wiebe	T 7	67- 70- 70- 70	277	$32,250.00		Robert Gamez	T45	69- 68- 73- 75	285	$2,752.50
Tom Lehman	T 9	69- 66- 73- 70	278	$28,000.00		Scott Gump	T45	69- 67- 77- 72	285	$2,752.50
Gil Morgan	T 9	71- 65- 74- 68	278	$28,000.00		Dudley Hart	T45	68- 72- 68- 77	285	$2,752.50
Ed Dougherty	T11	67- 69- 71- 72	279	$21,200.00		Bob Lohr	T45	69- 69- 75- 72	285	$2,752.50
Gary Hallberg	T11	70- 69- 67- 73	279	$21,200.00		Phil Mickelson	T45	67- 70- 78- 70	285	$2,752.50
Steve Lowery	T11	69- 65- 70- 75	279	$21,200.00		Steve Pate	T45	70- 67- 71- 77	285	$2,752.50
Jeff Maggert	T11	66- 70- 73- 70	279	$21,200.00		Tom Watson	T45	67- 68- 78- 72	285	$2,752.50
Jim Woodward	T11	67- 69- 72- 71	279	$21,200.00		Bill Glasson	T53	75- 66- 71- 74	286	$2,315.00
Chip Beck	T16	68- 70- 73- 69	280	$14,500.00		Peter Persons	T53	71- 67- 74- 74	286	$2,315.00
Russ Cochran	T16	69- 72- 70- 69	280	$14,500.00		Ted Schulz	T53	70- 70- 75- 71	286	$2,315.00
Joel Edwards	T16	70- 67- 72- 71	280	$14,500.00		Howard Twitty	T53	67- 74- 72- 73	286	$2,315.00
David Jackson	T16	69- 70- 71- 70	280	$14,500.00		Fred Funk	T57	72- 68- 68- 79	287	$2,200.00
Peter Jacobsen	T16	70- 70- 71- 69	280	$14,500.00		Tom Purtzer	T57	77- 64- 71- 75	287	$2,200.00
Mark O'Meara	T16	69- 70- 70- 71	280	$14,500.00		Jeff Sluman	T57	71- 70- 73- 73	287	$2,200.00
Tommy Armour	T22	69- 67- 74- 71	281	$9,600.00		Hal Sutton	T57	68- 73- 74- 72	287	$2,200.00
Phil Blackmar	T22	69- 72- 68- 72	281	$9,600.00		Lance Ten Broeck	T57	68- 69- 73- 77	287	$2,200.00
David Frost	T22	66- 66- 71- 78	281	$9,600.00		David Toms	T57	68- 70- 77- 72	287	$2,200.00
Mark McCumber	T22	72- 68- 70- 71	281	$9,600.00		Richard Zokol	T57	69- 72- 75- 71	287	$2,200.00
Scott Simpson	T22	66- 70- 74- 71	281	$9,600.00		Bob Estes	T64	69- 72- 70- 77	288	$2,110.00
Billy Andrade	T27	72- 68- 71- 71	282	$7,100.00		John Huston	T64	71- 69- 74- 74	288	$2,110.00
Mike Donald	T27	66- 71- 73- 72	282	$7,100.00		David Peoples	66	70- 69- 74- 76	289	$2,080.00
John Flannery	T27	70- 70- 69- 73	282	$7,100.00		Jay Delsing	T67	74- 67- 73- 76	290	$2,050.00
Bruce Fleisher	T27	70- 68- 71- 73	282	$7,100.00		Duffy Waldorf	T67	74- 67- 76- 73	290	$2,050.00
Larry Mize	T27	67- 71- 71- 73	282	$7,100.00		Bill Britton	T69	67- 71- 77- 76	291	$2,010.00
John Adams	T32	71- 70- 69- 73	283	$5,414.29		Skip Kendall	T69	68- 71- 75- 77	291	$2,010.00
Ronnie Black	T32	72- 67- 72- 72	283	$5,414.29		Brian Henninger	T71	72- 68- 78- 74	292	$1,950.00
Rick Fehr	T32	69- 68- 73- 73	283	$5,414.29		Perry Moss	T71	74- 67- 76- 75	292	$1,950.00
Gene Sauers	T32	72- 68- 71- 72	283	$5,414.29		Neale Smith	T71	72- 68- 77- 75	292	$1,950.00
R.W. Eaks	T32	72- 64- 70- 77	283	$5,414.28		Bobby Wadkins	T71	69- 69- 77- 77	292	$1,950.00
Gary McCord	T32	66- 69- 73- 75	283	$5,414.28		Nolan Henke	T75	72- 69- 73- 79	293	$1,890.00
Larry Rinker	T32	68- 72- 73- 70	283	$5,414.28		Ted Tryba	T75	69- 70- 75- 79	293	$1,890.00
Paul Azinger	T39	69- 70- 73- 72	284	$4,000.00						

AT&T PEBBLE BEACH NATIONAL PRO-AM

Pebble Beach GL,	Pebble Beach, CA	Purse: $1,250,000
(Host Course)	Par: 72 Yards: 6,799	$70,000 Pro-Am
Spyglass Hill CC	Par: 72 Yards: 6,810	February 4-7, 1993
Poppy Hills GC	Par: 72 Yards: 6,865	

LEADERS: First Round-- David Frost (PB), after an opening 6-under-par 66, held a one-shot lead over Mark Brooks (PB). **Second Round**--Brett Ogle (PH), at 8-under-par 136, had a one-stroke advantage over Brooks and Lennie Clements (both PH). **Third Round**-- Ogle (SG), at 11-under-par 205, was two shots in front of Billy Ray Brown (PB); Dan Forsman, shot a course record 64 at Spyglass Hill to move into a tie for third at 208.

CUT: 82 pros at 2-over-par 218, but only the low 60 pros and ties (69 players at 1-over 217) played final round. Team cut was 19-under-par 197 and 25 teams played (low 25 and ties)

WEATHER: Sunny and cool early Thursday, becoming overcast and windy later, with gusts up to 20 mph. High winds and cool Friday, with early overcast giving way to clear skies. Spectacular most of Saturday, becoming overcast mid-afternoon. Cloudy, overcast and cool Sunday, with rain arriving in the afternoon.

Winner: Brett Ogle   68- 68- 69- 71   276 $225,000.00

Player	Pos	Scores	Total	Money	Player	Pos	Scores	Total	Money
Billy Ray Brown	2	70- 68- 69- 72	279	$135,000.00	Jeff Wilson	T36	71- 71- 73- 72	287	$5,507.50
Trevor Dodds	T 3	70- 68- 70- 72	280	$65,000.00	Jay Delsing	T44	70- 71- 72- 75	288	$3,612.50
Joey Sindelar	T 3	69- 72- 70- 69	280	$65,000.00	Donnie Hammond	T44	72- 73- 72- 71	288	$3,612.50
Greg Twiggs	T 3	69- 72- 70- 69	280	$65,000.00	Peter Jacobsen	T44	74- 72- 70- 72	288	$3,612.50
Lee Janzen	6	71- 67- 72- 71	281	$45,000.00	Skip Kendall	T44	70- 73- 73- 72	288	$3,612.50
Chip Beck	T 7	72- 71- 69- 70	282	$40,312.50	Bill Kratzert	T44	70- 73- 68- 77	288	$3,612.50
Grant Waite	T 7	71- 70- 72- 69	282	$40,312.50	Bob Lohr	T44	68- 72- 74- 74	288	$3,612.50
Billy Andrade	T 9	70- 74- 68- 71	283	$27,968.75	David Ogrin	T44	70- 73- 74- 71	288	$3,612.50
Brandel Chamblee	T 9	72- 73- 68- 70	283	$27,968.75	Howard Twitty	T44	78- 71- 68- 71	288	$3,612.50
Bobby Clampett	T 9	73- 72- 68- 70	283	$27,968.75	Bill Britton	T52	74- 72- 71- 72	289	$2,900.00
Steve Elkington	T 9	68- 71- 74- 70	283	$27,968.75	Keith Clearwater	T52	69- 74- 69- 77	289	$2,900.00
John Flannery	T 9	70- 69- 70- 74	283	$27,968.75	John Cook	T52	70- 76- 71- 72	289	$2,900.00
Dan Forsman	T 9	73- 71- 64- 75	283	$27,968.75	Bob Friend	T52	69- 73- 71- 76	289	$2,900.00
Gil Morgan	T 9	69- 70- 69- 75	283	$27,968.75	Dave Peege	T52	72- 72- 71- 74	289	$2,900.00
Payne Stewart	T 9	72- 70- 71- 70	283	$27,968.75	Loren Roberts	T52	71- 72- 74- 72	289	$2,900.00
Emlyn Aubrey	T17	75- 70- 68- 71	284	$18,125.00	Olin Browne	T58	71- 74- 71- 74	290	$2,737.50
Mark Carnevale	T17	75- 70- 68- 71	284	$18,125.00	Brian Henninger	T58	71- 75- 70- 74	290	$2,737.50
David Frost	T17	66- 72- 71- 75	284	$18,125.00	Lon Hinkle	T58	70- 72- 75- 73	290	$2,737.50
Tom Watson	T17	71- 75- 71- 67	284	$18,125.00	Larry Mize	T58	70- 76- 69- 75	290	$2,737.50
Brad Bryant	T21	70- 72- 71- 72	285	$12,089.29	Perry Moss	T58	71- 72- 70- 77	290	$2,737.50
John Inman	T21	71- 74- 69- 71	285	$12,089.29	Chris Perry	T58	73- 72- 72- 73	290	$2,737.50
Tom Purtzer	T21	71- 73- 72- 69	285	$12,089.29	John Adams	T64	70- 78- 69- 74	291	$2,625.00
Fuzzy Zoeller	T21	69- 72- 73- 71	285	$12,089.29	Greg Cesario	T64	69- 73- 73- 76	291	$2,625.00
Mark Brooks	T21	67- 70- 73- 75	285	$12,089.28	John Mahaffey	T64	70- 75- 71- 75	291	$2,625.00
Fred Funk	T21	69- 69- 72- 75	285	$12,089.28	George Burns	T67	73- 71- 71- 78	293	$2,550.00
Ken Green	T21	70- 74- 69- 72	285	$12,089.28	Tim Loustalot	T67	75- 73- 68- 77	293	$2,550.00
Russell Beiersdorf	T28	70- 73- 70- 73	286	$7,961.25	David Toms	T67	70- 73- 70- 80	293	$2,550.00
Lennie Clements	T28	70- 67- 75- 74	286	$7,961.25	Paul Azinger	T70	72- 76- 70	218	$2,350.00
Tom Kite	T28	72- 74- 69- 71	286	$7,961.25	Brian Claar	T70	71- 74- 73	218	$2,350.00
Tom Lehman	T28	73- 74- 68- 71	286	$7,961.25	Rick Dalpos	T70	73- 73- 72	218	$2,350.00
Davis Love III	T28	68- 78- 71- 69	286	$7,961.25	John Elliott	T70	70- 76- 72	218	$2,350.00
Rocco Mediate	T28	71- 74- 69- 72	286	$7,961.25	Jim Hallet	T70	71- 76- 71	218	$2,350.00
Dillard Pruitt	T28	71- 72- 73- 70	286	$7,961.25	Ed Humenik	T70	75- 77- 66	218	$2,350.00
Kirk Triplett	T28	71- 70- 73- 72	286	$7,961.25	Roger Maltbie	T70	76- 72- 70	218	$2,350.00
Bob Gilder	T36	71- 77- 66- 73	287	$5,507.50	Dan Pohl	T70	70- 76- 72	218	$2,350.00
Jay Haas	T36	72- 72- 69- 74	287	$5,507.50	Sam Randolph	T70	68- 77- 73	218	$2,350.00
Brian Kamm	T36	72- 72- 70- 73	287	$5,507.50	Tom Sieckmann	T70	72- 78- 68	218	$2,350.00
Mark O'Meara	T36	71- 76- 69- 71	287	$5,507.50	Mike Smith	T70	75- 74- 69	218	$2,350.00
Larry Rinker	T36	71- 71- 74- 71	287	$5,507.50	Curtis Strange	T70	70- 74- 74	218	$2,350.00
Scott Simpson	T36	75- 73- 68- 71	287	$5,507.50	Richard Zokol	T70	72- 76- 70	218	$2,350.00
Stan Utley	T36	68- 71- 72- 76	287	$5,507.50					

BOB HOPE CHRYSLER CLASSIC

PGA West/Palmer (Host Course)   Purse: $1,100,000
La Quinta, CA   Par: 72   Yards: 6,901   (official)
Indian Wells CC   Par: 72   Yards: 6,478
Bermuda Dunes CC   Par: 72   Yards: 6,927
Tamarisk CC   Par: 72   Yards: 6,881   February 10-14, 1993

LEADERS: First Round-- Dave Rummells (PW) fired a 9-under-par 63 and led by two strokes over Mark Hayes (IW), Nolan Henke (IW) and Donnie Hammond (IW). **Second Round**-- Curtis Strange (IW) at 13-under-par 131 led by a stroke over Steve Elkington (PW), Rick Fehr (BD), Jay Haas (IW), Fred Couples (TC), and Rummells (BD). **Third Round**-- Tom Kite (IW) and Elkington (BD) at 18-under-par 198 led by two strokes over seven other golfers. **Fourth Round**-- Kite (PW) at 25-under-par 263 led by a stroke over Fehr (IW)

CUT: 76 players at 10-under-par 278.

PRO-AM: Overall $5,000. John Adams and Kelly Gibson, 59-under-par 229, $1,750 each.

WEATHER: Beautiful every day.

Winner: Tom Kite 67- 67- 64- 65- 62 325 $198,000.00

Player		Scores	Total	Money	Player		Scores	Total	Money
Rick Fehr	2	66- 66- 70- 62- 67	331	$118,800.00	Ted Tryba	T33	68- 67- 70- 69- 69	343	$5,451.11
Scott Simpson	3	71- 69- 66- 63- 66	335	$74,800.00	Grant Waite	T33	66- 71- 64- 72- 70	343	$5,451.11
Keith Clearwater	T 4	68- 66- 68- 70- 64	336	$43,312.50	Tommy Armour	T42	71- 66- 70- 69- 68	344	$4,180.00
Jim Gallagher, Jr.	T 4	69- 68- 67- 69- 63	336	$43,312.50	Greg Twiggs	T42	70- 68- 68- 68- 70	344	$4,180.00
Jay Haas	T 4	66- 66- 71- 65- 68	336	$43,312.50	Tim Simpson	T44	71- 69- 69- 65- 71	345	$3,246.58
Bob Lohr	T 4	68- 66- 66- 66- 70	336	$43,312.50	Bill Britton	T44	70- 65- 72- 70- 68	345	$3,246.57
Bill Glasson	8	70- 64- 66- 67- 70	337	$34,100.00	Jay Delsing	T44	68- 73- 66- 69- 69	345	$3,246.57
Fred Couples	T 9	68- 64- 68- 66- 72	338	$29,700.00	Bruce Fleisher	T44	71- 67- 68- 69- 70	345	$3,246.57
Steve Elkington	T 9	69- 63- 66- 68- 72	338	$29,700.00	Brian Henninger	T44	71- 72- 68- 65- 69	345	$3,246.57
Wayne Levi	T 9	68- 66- 66- 69- 69	338	$29,700.00	Jimmy Johnston	T44	68- 69- 69- 70- 69	345	$3,246.57
John Cook	T12	66- 67- 70- 65- 71	339	$20,271.43	Harry Taylor	T44	70- 68- 71- 67- 69	345	$3,246.57
Bob Estes	T12	67- 66- 72- 63- 71	339	$20,271.43	David Edwards	T51	69- 66- 69- 69- 73	346	$2,623.50
Kelly Gibson	T12	67- 67- 66- 69- 70	339	$20,271.43	David Jackson	T51	68- 70- 70- 66- 72	346	$2,623.50
Donnie Hammond	T12	65- 73- 64- 67- 70	339	$20,271.43	Skip Kendall	T51	70- 69- 66- 68- 73	346	$2,623.50
Davis Love III	T12	70- 70- 67- 65- 67	339	$20,271.43	Craig Stadler	T51	66- 72- 69- 67- 72	346	$2,623.50
Payne Stewart	T12	70- 66- 64- 67- 72	339	$20,271.43	Brian Claar	T55	66- 69- 70- 67- 75	347	$2,486.00
Gil Morgan	T12	69- 66- 67- 65- 72	339	$20,271.42	Lennie Clements	T55	71- 69- 69- 67- 71	347	$2,486.00
Scott Hoch	T19	70- 70- 68- 65- 67	340	$13,332.00	Joel Edwards	T55	66- 70- 67- 72- 72	347	$2,486.00
John Huston	T19	67- 70- 65- 67- 71	340	$13,332.00	Peter Jacobsen	T55	69- 68- 68- 66- 76	347	$2,486.00
Jodie Mudd	T19	68- 71- 66- 66- 69	340	$13,332.00	Steve Pate	T55	71- 67- 70- 70- 69	347	$2,486.00
Tad Rhyan	T19	68- 66- 69- 67- 70	340	$13,332.00	Russell Beiersdorf	T60	71- 70- 64- 71- 72	348	$2,365.00
Dennis Trixler	T19	67- 69- 69- 68- 67	340	$13,332.00	Ed Dougherty	T60	73- 67- 66- 69- 73	348	$2,365.00
Scott Gump	T24	68- 65- 67- 67- 74	341	$9,680.00	Fred Funk	T60	67- 72- 68- 68- 73	348	$2,365.00
Neal Lancaster	T24	72- 67- 68- 68- 66	341	$9,680.00	Robert Gamez	T60	71- 70- 69- 65- 73	348	$2,365.00
Lanny Wadkins	T24	69- 66- 66- 69- 71	341	$9,680.00	Tom Lehman	T60	69- 69- 70- 68- 72	348	$2,365.00
John Flannery	T27	71- 68- 65- 64- 74	342	$7,645.00	Jeff Sluman	T60	68- 67- 71- 65- 77	348	$2,365.00
Ed Humenik	T27	68- 67- 70- 67- 70	342	$7,645.00	Billy Ray Brown	T66	68- 68- 67- 70- 76	349	$2,244.00
Corey Pavin	T27	70- 70- 68- 67- 67	342	$7,645.00	Jaime Gomez	T66	70- 70- 66- 67- 76	349	$2,244.00
Mike Standly	T27	67- 70- 68- 68- 69	342	$7,645.00	Nolan Henke	T66	65- 70- 70- 73- 71	349	$2,244.00
Curtis Strange	T27	66- 65- 71- 70- 70	342	$7,645.00	Peter Persons	T66	66- 71- 70- 71- 71	349	$2,244.00
Fuzzy Zoeller	T27	76- 69- 63- 67- 67	342	$7,645.00	Hal Sutton	T66	71- 68- 71- 68- 71	349	$2,244.00
Ronnie Black	T33	67- 67- 69- 70- 70	343	$5,451.12	Robin Freeman	T71	67- 73- 69- 67- 74	350	$2,156.00
John Adams	T33	71- 65- 68- 68- 71	343	$5,451.11	Paul Goydos	T71	72- 67- 70- 66- 75	350	$2,156.00
Mike Donald	T33	67- 68- 69- 71- 68	343	$5,451.11	John Inman	T71	69- 73- 68- 68- 72	350	$2,156.00
Blaine McCallister	T33	71- 67- 71- 68- 66	343	$5,451.11	Steve Lowery	74	70- 72- 68- 68- 73	351	$2,112.00
Mark O'Meara	T33	70- 68- 64- 70- 71	343	$5,451.11	P.H. Horgan III	75	72- 70- 72- 64- 74	352	$2,090.00
Dave Rummells	T33	63- 69- 69- 69- 73	343	$5,451.11	Fulton Allem	76	68- 69- 67- 73- 77	354	$2,068.00
Mike Springer	T33	69- 70- 71- 66- 67	343	$5,451.11					

BUICK INVITATIONAL OF CALIFORNIA

Torrey Pines GC, LaJolla, CA

South Course:	Par: 36-36--72	Yards: 7,000	Purse: $1,000,000
North Course:	Par: 36-36--72	Yards: 6,592	February 18-21, 1993

LEADERS: First Round-- Jay Haas (NC) fired a 2-under-par 70 and led by two strokes over Payne Stewart (SC). **Second Round**-- Stewart at 6-under-par 138 led by three strokes over Dave Rummells (NC). **Third Round**-- Rummells at 4-under-par 212 led one over Phil Mickelson, Payne Stewart and Jay Haas.

CUT: 90 players at 7-over-par 151.

PRO-AM: North, $7,500. Individual-- John Daly, 66, $750. Team-- Dan Forsman, 54, $750. South, $7,500. Individual-- Jim McGovern, 68, $750. Team, Richard Zokol, Loren Roberts, Dudley Hart, Joey Sindelar, Brad Fabel, Donnie Hammond, Tom Byrum, John Adams, 58, $428.13.

WEATHER: Thursday was cold, overcast and extremely windy. Friday was marginally less extreme. Saturday was partly sunny and warmer. Sunday was partly sunny and cool.

Winner: Phil Mickelson 75- 69- 69- 65   278 $180,000.00

Player	Pos	Scores	Total	Money	Player	Pos	Scores	Total	Money
Dave Rummells	2	77- 64- 71- 70	282	$108,000.00	Joe Durant	T47	73- 77- 72- 71	293	$2,690.00
Payne Stewart	3	72- 66- 75- 70	283	$68,000.00	John Mahaffey	T47	74- 73- 76- 70	293	$2,690.00
Jay Don Blake	T4	73- 75- 70- 67	285	$41,333.34	Brad Sherfy	T47	75- 74- 72- 72	293	$2,690.00
Jay Haas	T4	70- 72- 71- 72	285	$41,333.33	Greg Whisman	T47	72- 77- 73- 71	293	$2,690.00
Greg Twiggs	T4	73- 73- 69- 70	285	$41,333.33	Michael Bradley	T51	76- 74- 71- 73	294	$2,340.00
Keith Clearwater	T7	75- 72- 70- 69	286	$32,250.00	Steve Lamontagne	T51	75- 76- 69- 74	294	$2,340.00
Joey Sindelar	T7	77- 68- 70- 71	286	$32,250.00	Neal Lancaster	T51	76- 72- 77- 69	294	$2,340.00
Patrick Burke	T9	74- 74- 68- 71	287	$24,000.00	Kirk Triplett	T51	76- 70- 73- 75	294	$2,340.00
Len Mattiace	T9	76- 68- 71- 72	287	$24,000.00	Dennis Trixler	T51	77- 74- 74- 69	294	$2,340.00
David Peoples	T9	77- 71- 69- 70	287	$24,000.00	Stan Utley	T51	79- 69- 74- 72	294	$2,340.00
Craig Stadler	T9	75- 68- 71- 73	287	$24,000.00	Willie Wood	T51	78- 71- 70- 75	294	$2,340.00
Hal Sutton	T9	73- 71- 74- 69	287	$24,000.00	Greg Cesario	T58	76- 73- 73- 73	295	$2,200.00
Mark Wiebe	T9	76- 73- 71- 67	287	$24,000.00	Morris Hatalsky	T58	76- 75- 73- 71	295	$2,200.00
Joel Edwards	T15	76- 74- 68- 70	288	$16,000.00	Peter Persons	T58	76- 71- 76- 72	295	$2,200.00
Tom Lehman	T15	79- 70- 68- 71	288	$16,000.00	Leonard Thompson	T58	79- 69- 75- 72	295	$2,200.00
Steve Pate	T15	75- 76- 65- 72	288	$16,000.00	Jim Thorpe	T58	77- 74- 72- 72	295	$2,200.00
Dan Pohl	T15	76- 74- 70- 68	288	$16,000.00	Dave Barr	T63	76- 73- 74- 73	296	$2,090.00
Tom Sieckmann	T15	76- 72- 71- 69	288	$16,000.00	John Cook	T63	77- 73- 72- 74	296	$2,090.00
Bruce Fleisher	T20	77- 71- 72- 69	289	$11,240.00	Mark Lye	T63	76- 75- 73- 72	296	$2,090.00
Jim Gallagher, Jr.	T20	81- 68- 68- 72	289	$11,240.00	Loren Roberts	T63	75- 76- 72- 73	296	$2,090.00
Donnie Hammond	T20	78- 71- 69- 71	289	$11,240.00	Marty Schiene	T63	75- 76- 73- 72	296	$2,090.00
John Huston	T20	76- 71- 70- 72	289	$11,240.00	Mike Standly	T63	74- 72- 73- 77	296	$2,090.00
Grant Waite	T20	77- 71- 69- 72	289	$11,240.00	Brad Fabel	T69	76- 73- 73- 75	297	$1,980.00
Rick Fehr	T25	75- 72- 72- 71	290	$7,975.00	Fred Funk	T69	76- 75- 75- 71	297	$1,980.00
Jim McGovern	T25	76- 74- 70- 70	290	$7,975.00	Jaime Gomez	T69	74- 77- 75- 71	297	$1,980.00
Jodie Mudd	T25	74- 72- 73- 71	290	$7,975.00	David Jackson	T69	76- 75- 68- 78	297	$1,980.00
Duffy Waldorf	T25	74- 69- 75- 72	290	$7,975.00	Mark Pfeil	T69	80- 71- 77- 69	297	$1,980.00
Michael Allen	T29	82- 67- 72- 70	291	$6,087.50	Tom Byrum	T74	78- 73- 76- 71	298	$1,870.00
Ronnie Black	T29	76- 69- 72- 74	291	$6,087.50	Dan Forsman	T74	76- 74- 69- 79	298	$1,870.00
Brandel Chamblee	T29	76- 74- 70- 71	291	$6,087.50	Scott Gump	T74	78- 72- 78- 70	298	$1,870.00
Bobby Clampett	T29	72- 76- 72- 71	291	$6,087.50	Jim Hallet	T74	77- 70- 74- 77	298	$1,870.00
Bob Estes	T29	76- 74- 71- 70	291	$6,087.50	Steve Lowery	T74	81- 70- 71- 76	298	$1,870.00
Perry Moss	T29	78- 69- 69- 75	291	$6,087.50	Lance Ten Broeck	T74	81- 67- 75- 75	298	$1,870.00
John Ross	T29	77- 71- 73- 70	291	$6,087.50	John Dowdall	T80	78- 72- 74- 75	299	$1,780.00
Jim Woodward	T29	76- 73- 73- 69	291	$6,087.50	Bob Tway	T80	79- 72- 76- 72	299	$1,780.00
Russell Beiersdorf	T37	74- 71- 77- 70	292	$4,000.00	Jeff Woodland	T80	78- 72- 75- 74	299	$1,780.00
Phil Blackmar	T37	75- 76- 73- 68	292	$4,000.00	Brad Bryant	T83	79- 72- 73- 76	300	$1,710.00
Gary Hallberg	T37	77- 72- 71- 72	292	$4,000.00	Ed Dougherty	T83	75- 73- 76- 76	300	$1,710.00
Lee Janzen	T37	81- 68- 73- 70	292	$4,000.00	Kenny Knox	T83	77- 73- 74- 76	300	$1,710.00
Rocco Mediate	T37	78- 73- 73- 68	292	$4,000.00	Yoshinori Mizumaki	T83	73- 78- 75- 74	300	$1,710.00
Bill Murchison	T37	76- 74- 70- 72	292	$4,000.00	Dave Eichelberger	T87	78- 73- 76- 75	302	$1,640.00
Dillard Pruitt	T37	76- 72- 73- 71	292	$4,000.00	Dan Halldorson	T87	81- 70- 75- 76	302	$1,640.00
Gene Sauers	T37	78- 72- 71- 71	292	$4,000.00	Bruce Zabriski	T87	78- 72- 77- 75	302	$1,640.00
Scott Simpson	T37	77- 74- 69- 72	292	$4,000.00	Jeff Cook	90	78- 73- 78- 74	303	$1,600.00
Robert Wrenn	T37	79- 71- 73- 69	292	$4,000.00					

NISSAN LOS ANGELES OPEN

Riviera CC, Pacific Palisades, CA   **Purse: $1,000,000**
Par: 35-36--71   **Yards: 6,946**   **February 25-28, 1993**

LEADERS: First Round-- Jim McGovern, Russell Beiersdorf, and Jay Don Blake at 4-under-par 67 led by one over Kelly Gibson, Scott Simpson, Hal Sutton, Ronnie Black, Lee Janzen, and Jeff Sluman.
Second Round-- Marco Dawson, Fred Couples, Donnie Hammond, and Payne Stewart at 4-under-par 138 led by one over Greg Twiggs, Rick Fehr, Blake, Jodie Mudd, McGovern, Jeff Cook, and Tom Kite.

CUT: 79 players at 3-over-par 145.

PRO-AM: $7,500. Individual-- Hale Irwin, 69, $750. Team-- Keith Clearwater, 55, $750.

WEATHER: Rainy early in the week, but Thursday's round had no delays and was beautiful. Friday's round was cancelled at 10:45 a.m., making the event a 54-hole tournament. Saturday and Sunday were beautiful.

Winner: Tom Kite 73- 66- 67   206 $180,000.00

Dave Barr	T 2	71- 72- 66	209	$66,000.00	Billy Mayfair	T37	73- 71- 71	215	$4,200.00
Fred Couples	T 2	71- 67- 71	209	$66,000.00	David Peoples	T37	71- 72- 72	215	$4,200.00
Donnie Hammond	T 2	69- 69- 71	209	$66,000.00	Mark Wiebe	T37	70- 73- 72	215	$4,200.00
Payne Stewart	T 2	72- 66- 71	209	$66,000.00	Jim Woodward	T37	71- 73- 71	215	$4,200.00
Paul Azinger	T 6	72- 68- 70	210	$28,187.50	Fulton Allem	T45	73- 70- 73	216	$2,580.00
Jay Don Blake	T 6	67- 72- 71	210	$28,187.50	Barry Cheesman	T45	73- 71- 72	216	$2,580.00
Rick Fehr	T 6	72- 67- 71	210	$28,187.50	Jay Haas	T45	70- 74- 72	216	$2,580.00
Peter Jacobsen	T 6	73- 68- 69	210	$28,187.50	Brian Kamm	T45	72- 72- 72	216	$2,580.00
Jeff Maggert	T 6	71- 73- 66	210	$28,187.50	Yoshinori Kaneko	T45	73- 71- 72	216	$2,580.00
Jodie Mudd	T 6	71- 68- 71	210	$28,187.50	Steve Pate	T45	70- 73- 73	216	$2,580.00
Greg Twiggs	T 6	72- 67- 71	210	$28,187.50	Tad Rhyan	T45	71- 72- 73	216	$2,580.00
Howard Twitty	T 6	70- 72- 68	210	$28,187.50	Marty Schiene	T45	72- 73- 71	216	$2,580.00
Ben Crenshaw	T14	72- 69- 70	211	$17,000.00	Tom Sieckmann	T45	73- 72- 71	216	$2,580.00
Lee Janzen	T14	68- 73- 70	211	$17,000.00	Scott Simpson	T45	68- 75- 73	216	$2,580.00
Steve Lowery	T14	71- 72- 68	211	$17,000.00	Jeff Sluman	T45	68- 75- 73	216	$2,580.00
Mark McCumber	T14	71- 70- 70	211	$17,000.00	Hal Sutton	T45	68- 75- 73	216	$2,580.00
Tom Purtzer	T14	73- 70- 68	211	$17,000.00	Grant Waite	T45	71- 71- 74	216	$2,580.00
Chip Beck	T19	70- 71- 71	212	$11,285.72	Russell Beiersdorf	T58	67- 75- 75	217	$2,170.00
Trevor Dodds	T19	73- 70- 69	212	$11,285.72	Bob Gilder	T58	76- 69- 72	217	$2,170.00
Hale Irwin	T19	72- 69- 71	212	$11,285.72	Gene Jones	T58	71- 73- 73	217	$2,170.00
Jeff Cook	T19	71- 68- 73	212	$11,285.71	Neal Lancaster	T58	73- 72- 72	217	$2,170.00
Marco Dawson	T19	71- 67- 74	212	$11,285.71	John Mahaffey	T58	69- 74- 74	217	$2,170.00
Jim McGovern	T19	67- 72- 73	212	$11,285.71	Rocco Mediate	T58	71- 71- 75	217	$2,170.00
Phil Mickelson	T19	70- 71- 71	212	$11,285.71	Gil Morgan	T58	73- 70- 74	217	$2,170.00
Keith Clearwater	T26	73- 69- 71	213	$7,400.00	Dillard Pruitt	T58	71- 70- 76	217	$2,170.00
John Daly	T26	70- 71- 72	213	$7,400.00	Ronnie Black	T66	68- 74- 76	218	$2,010.00
David Edwards	T26	73- 72- 68	213	$7,400.00	Carl Cooper	T66	74- 67- 77	218	$2,010.00
Kelly Gibson	T26	68- 76- 69	213	$7,400.00	Bob Estes	T66	75- 70- 73	218	$2,010.00
Ted Tryba	T26	71- 71- 71	213	$7,400.00	Robin Freeman	T66	72- 72- 74	218	$2,010.00
Michael Allen	T31	72- 68- 74	214	$5,800.00	Mike Hulbert	T66	71- 74- 73	218	$2,010.00
T.C. Chen	T31	71- 72- 71	214	$5,800.00	Hiroshi Makino	T66	74- 70- 74	218	$2,010.00
Rick Dalpos	T31	71- 71- 72	214	$5,800.00	Perry Moss	T66	73- 70- 75	218	$2,010.00
Jim Hallet	T31	71- 71- 72	214	$5,800.00	David Ogrin	T66	73- 69- 76	218	$2,010.00
Dan Pohl	T31	73- 69- 72	214	$5,800.00	Brian Henninger	T74	71- 73- 75	219	$1,910.00
Bob Tway	T31	73- 68- 73	214	$5,800.00	Dennis Trixler	T74	72- 73- 74	219	$1,910.00
Lennie Clements	T37	71- 74- 70	215	$4,200.00	John Flannery	76	71- 72- 77	220	$1,880.00
Paul Goydos	T37	72- 69- 74	215	$4,200.00	Tommy Armour	77	70- 71- 80	221	$1,860.00
Scott Gump	T37	70- 73- 72	215	$4,200.00	Jeff Woodland	78	69- 74- 80	223	$1,840.00
Steve Lamontagne	T37	72- 69- 74	215	$4,200.00	John Inman	79	74- 71- 79	224	$1,820.00

DORAL-RYDER OPEN

Doral Resort & CC, Miami, FL   **Purse: $1,400,000**
Par: 36-36--72 Yards: 6,939   **March 4-7, 1993**

LEADERS: First Round-- Greg Norman, with a 7-under-par 65, held a one-shot lead over Tom Kite and Dave Rummells. **Second Round**-- Norman and Paul Azinger, at 11-under-par 133, were a stroke in front of David Frost. **Third Round**-- Norman, after a course record tying 62, was at 21-under-par 195, good for a six-stroke advantage over Azinger.

CUT: 76 players at 1-under-par 143.

PRO-AM: $7,500. Individual-- Raymond Floyd, 67, $750. Team-- Paul Azinger, Bill Glasson, 57, $675 each.

WEATHER: Sunny and mild, with strong winds early diminishing late in the morning rounds Thursday. Continued sunny and mild with moderate winds Friday and Saturday. High clouds and overcast Sunday, with winds reversing direction.

Winner: Greg Norman 65- 68- 62- 70   265 $252,000.00

Paul Azinger	T 2	67- 66- 68- 68	269	$123,200.00	Neal Lancaster	T38	69- 70- 72- 71	282	$5,740.00
Mark McCumber	T 2	69- 67- 66- 67	269	$123,200.00	Jim McGovern	T38	70- 68- 73- 71	282	$5,740.00
David Frost	4	70- 64- 68- 68	270	$67,200.00	Dillard Pruitt	T38	73- 67- 69- 73	282	$5,740.00
Sandy Lyle	5	69- 67- 68- 68	272	$56,000.00	Tom Watson	T38	68- 71- 69- 74	282	$5,740.00
Fred Couples	T 6	68- 67- 71- 67	273	$48,650.00	Richard Zokol	T38	71- 71- 74- 66	282	$5,740.00
Nick Faldo	T 6	72- 65- 70- 66	273	$48,650.00	Brian Henninger	T45	69- 71- 69- 74	283	$4,099.20
Tom Kite	8	66- 73- 69- 67	275	$43,400.00	Steve Lamontagne	T45	73- 70- 70- 70	283	$4,099.20
Scott Hoch	9	71- 67- 69- 69	276	$40,600.00	Tom Purtzer	T45	68- 69- 72- 74	283	$4,099.20
Chip Beck	T10	70- 72- 72- 63	277	$31,033.34	Jeff Sluman	T45	72- 71- 70- 70	283	$4,099.20
Lee Janzen	T10	71- 71- 70- 65	277	$31,033.34	Lanny Wadkins	T45	70- 70- 71- 72	283	$4,099.20
John Adams	T10	72- 67- 70- 68	277	$31,033.33	Gil Morgan	T50	71- 70- 69- 74	284	$3,444.00
Steve Elkington	T10	68- 72- 67- 70	277	$31,033.33	Doug Tewell	T50	69- 73- 70- 72	284	$3,444.00
Ed Humenik	T10	67- 71- 69- 70	277	$31,033.33	Duffy Waldorf	T50	73- 70- 69- 72	284	$3,444.00
Jack Nicklaus	T10	69- 68- 67- 73	277	$31,033.33	Dan Halldorson	T53	70- 73- 70- 72	285	$3,241.00
Kelly Gibson	T16	73- 69- 68- 68	278	$19,005.00	Davis Love III	T53	75- 67- 73- 70	285	$3,241.00
Bill Glasson	T16	70- 69- 69- 70	278	$19,005.00	Eddie Pearce	T53	69- 69- 74- 73	285	$3,241.00
Wayne Grady	T16	71- 68- 70- 69	278	$19,005.00	Curtis Strange	T53	71- 71- 70- 73	285	$3,241.00
Ken Green	T16	69- 70- 68- 71	278	$19,005.00	Mark Carnevale	T57	71- 71- 71- 73	286	$3,122.00
Andrew Magee	T16	71- 69- 69- 69	278	$19,005.00	John Huston	T57	70- 72- 73- 71	286	$3,122.00
Kenny Perry	T16	71- 69- 70- 68	278	$19,005.00	David Jackson	T57	70- 69- 75- 72	286	$3,122.00
Nick Price	T16	70- 71- 67- 70	278	$19,005.00	Mark Lye	T57	74- 68- 74- 70	286	$3,122.00
Payne Stewart	T16	74- 67- 69- 68	278	$19,005.00	Ronnie Black	T61	72- 70- 73- 72	287	$2,996.00
Mark Calcavecchia	T24	77- 65- 67- 70	279	$11,620.00	Marco Dawson	T61	73- 68- 75- 71	287	$2,996.00
Peter Jacobsen	T24	68- 67- 74- 70	279	$11,620.00	Bob Lohr	T61	69- 74- 73- 71	287	$2,996.00
Billy Mayfair	T24	74- 67- 67- 71	279	$11,620.00	Mike Malizia	T61	76- 66- 73- 72	287	$2,996.00
Dave Rummells	T24	66- 72- 74- 67	279	$11,620.00	Gary Nicklaus	T61	72- 69- 73- 73	287	$2,996.00
Mike Standly	T24	70- 70- 66- 73	279	$11,620.00	Billy Andrade	T66	73- 68- 71- 76	288	$2,870.00
Keith Clearwater	T29	71- 65- 69- 75	280	$9,310.00	Tim Crockett	T66	73- 66- 74- 75	288	$2,870.00
John Daly	T29	70- 69- 69- 72	280	$9,310.00	Larry Nelson	T66	71- 71- 71- 75	288	$2,870.00
Bruce Lietzke	T29	71- 66- 75- 68	280	$9,310.00	Bob Tway	T66	73- 70- 79- 66	288	$2,870.00
Rocco Mediate	T29	70- 66- 69- 75	280	$9,310.00	Greg Cerulli	T70	70- 73- 73- 73	289	$2,786.00
Dave Barr	T33	71- 71- 68- 71	281	$7,560.00	Lance Ten Broeck	T70	70- 73- 71- 75	289	$2,786.00
Billy Ray Brown	T33	69- 72- 75- 65	281	$7,560.00	Robin Freeman	T72	68- 72- 71- 79	290	$2,716.00
Brian Claar	T33	70- 71- 71- 69	281	$7,560.00	Tom Shaw	T72	74- 69- 75- 72	290	$2,716.00
Ray Floyd	T33	72- 70- 68- 71	281	$7,560.00	Robert Wrenn	T72	68- 69- 76- 77	290	$2,716.00
Ted Tryba	T33	71- 70- 71- 69	281	$7,560.00	Andy Bean	75	70- 73- 69- 79	291	$2,660.00
Jay Don Blake	T38	69- 72- 70- 71	282	$5,740.00	Paul Trittler	76	72- 71- 79- 72	294	$2,632.00
Jim Gallagher, Jr.	T38	73- 69- 72- 68	282	$5,740.00					

HONDA CLASSIC

Weston Hills CC, Ft. Lauderdale, FL   **Purse: $1,100,000**
Par: 36-36--72   **Yards: 7,069**   **March 11-14, 1993**

LEADERS: First Round-- Fred Couples fired an 8-under-par 64 and led by one stroke over David Jackson and Phil Blackmar. **Second Round**-- Larry Mize at 8-under-par 136 led by one over David Frost, Dick Mast and Couples. **Third Round**--Cancelled due to windy conditions.

CUT: 77 players at 1-over-par.

PRO-AM: $7,500. Individual-- Steve Pate, Bruce Lietzke, 67, $675 each. Team-- Curtis Strange, 54, $750.

WEATHER: Near perfect conditions on Thursday. Increasingly windy on Friday. Saturday's round was cancelled due to the windy conditions. Sunday was windy and much cooler.

Winner: Fred Couples 64- 73- 70   207 $198,000.00
    (Won playoff with birdie on second extra hole)

Player	Pos	Scores	Total	Money	Player	Pos	Scores	Total	Money
Robert Gamez	2	68- 71- 68	207	$118,800.00	Brian Claar	T38	70- 75- 71	216	$4,180.00
Larry Mize	3	69- 67- 72	208	$74,800.00	Robin Freeman	T38	72- 70- 74	216	$4,180.00
Dick Mast	4	68- 69- 72	209	$52,800.00	Jim Gallagher, Jr.	T38	68- 73- 75	216	$4,180.00
Craig Parry	5	67- 71- 72	210	$44,000.00	Skip Kendall	T38	71- 72- 73	216	$4,180.00
Ed Dougherty	T 6	70- 74- 67	211	$32,135.72	Gary McCord	T38	70- 74- 72	216	$4,180.00
Mike Smith	T 6	69- 72- 70	211	$32,135.72	Larry Rinker	T38	72- 68- 76	216	$4,180.00
Fuzzy Zoeller	T 6	66- 75- 70	211	$32,135.72	Curtis Strange	T38	72- 70- 74	216	$4,180.00
David Frost	T 6	68- 69- 74	211	$32,135.71	Mike Sullivan	T38	70- 75- 71	216	$4,180.00
Jim McGovern	T 6	71- 69- 71	211	$32,135.71	Dave Barr	T48	70- 73- 74	217	$2,734.29
Rocco Mediate	T 6	71- 69- 71	211	$32,135.71	Bob Estes	T48	67- 77- 73	217	$2,734.29
Steve Pate	T 6	68- 71- 72	211	$32,135.71	Paul Goydos	T48	71- 73- 73	217	$2,734.29
Dudley Hart	T13	68- 73- 71	212	$22,000.00	Richard Zokol	T48	70- 73- 74	217	$2,734.29
John Inman	T13	70- 69- 73	212	$22,000.00	Bruce Fleisher	T48	70- 72- 75	217	$2,734.28
Nick Faldo	T15	69- 72- 72	213	$17,600.00	Steve Lamontagne	T48	71- 71- 75	217	$2,734.28
Corey Pavin	T15	70- 73- 70	213	$17,600.00	Tim Simpson	T48	70- 72- 75	217	$2,734.28
Don Pooley	T15	72- 72- 69	213	$17,600.00	Kelly Gibson	T55	70- 74- 74	218	$2,508.00
Joey Sindelar	T15	69- 70- 74	213	$17,600.00	Dave Peege	T55	68- 75- 75	218	$2,508.00
Bob Tway	T15	68- 72- 73	213	$17,600.00	Duffy Waldorf	T55	69- 74- 75	218	$2,508.00
John Daly	T20	69- 74- 71	214	$11,916.67	Ed Fiori	T58	71- 73- 75	219	$2,431.00
Joel Edwards	T20	69- 74- 71	214	$11,916.67	Tony Mollica	T58	69- 72- 78	219	$2,431.00
Bob Lohr	T20	72- 72- 70	214	$11,916.67	Gary Nicklaus	T58	69- 76- 74	219	$2,431.00
Gene Sauers	T20	66- 76- 72	214	$11,916.67	Leonard Thompson	T58	73- 72- 74	219	$2,431.00
Billy Andrade	T20	70- 68- 76	214	$11,916.66	Michael Bradley	T62	70- 75- 75	220	$2,310.00
Ed Humenik	T20	71- 70- 73	214	$11,916.66	Russ Cochran	T62	72- 73- 75	220	$2,310.00
Keith Clearwater	T26	71- 74- 70	215	$7,030.84	Rick Dalpos	T62	67- 78- 75	220	$2,310.00
John Flannery	T26	70- 74- 71	215	$7,030.84	Bob Gilder	T62	73- 71- 76	220	$2,310.00
Nick Price	T26	70- 74- 71	215	$7,030.84	Bill Glasson	T62	67- 76- 77	220	$2,310.00
David Toms	T26	70- 75- 70	215	$7,030.84	Massy Kuramoto	T62	72- 73- 75	220	$2,310.00
Phil Blackmar	T26	65- 77- 73	215	$7,030.83	Kenny Perry	T62	73- 71- 76	220	$2,310.00
Jeff Cook	T26	70- 72- 73	215	$7,030.83	Mike Hulbert	69	72- 70- 79	221	$2,222.00
Wayne Levi	T26	69- 75- 71	215	$7,030.83	Fulton Allem	T70	74- 71- 77	222	$2,156.00
Mark Lye	T26	69- 73- 73	215	$7,030.83	Scott Gump	T70	72- 72- 78	222	$2,156.00
Andrew Magee	T26	66- 76- 73	215	$7,030.83	David Jackson	T70	65- 80- 77	222	$2,156.00
Len Mattiace	T26	72- 72- 71	215	$7,030.83	Hal Sutton	T70	70- 75- 77	222	$2,156.00
Mike Standly	T26	70- 71- 74	215	$7,030.83	Willie Wood	T70	72- 73- 77	222	$2,156.00
Bobby Wadkins	T26	70- 72- 73	215	$7,030.83	Brad Fabel	T75	73- 72- 78	223	$2,079.00
Bill Britton	T38	73- 71- 72	216	$4,180.00	Brad Faxon	T75	70- 75- 78	223	$2,079.00
Mark Calcavecchia	T38	68- 73- 75	216	$4,180.00	Mark Brooks	77	71- 74- 80	225	$2,046.00

NESTLE INVITATIONAL

Bay Hill CC, Orlando, FL   Purse: $1,000,000
Par: 36-36--72 Yards: 7,114   March 18-21, 1993

LEADERS: First Round-- Rich Fehr, John Cook and Michael Allen, at 3-under-par 69, led by one over Fulton Allem, Curtis Strange, Jay Delsing, Dan Pohl, Vijay Singh, and Brad Bryant. **Second Round**-- Davis Love III at 4-under-par 140 led by one over Allen, Bernhard Langer, and Ben Crenshaw. **Third Round**-- Ben Crenshaw at 6-under-par 210 led by one over Love.

CUT: 75 players at 5-over-par 149.

PRO-AM: $7,500. Individual-- Duffy Waldorf, Lee Janzen, 67, $675 each. Team-- Duffy Waldorf, 53, $750.

WEATHER: Overcast, windy and cool all week long. There were some scattered showers during the week, with the final round being delayed from 12:48 p.m. to 1:45 p.m. due to rain and standing water on the course.

Winner: Ben Crenshaw   71- 70- 69- 70   280 $180,000.00

Rocco Mediate	T 2	72- 72- 70- 68	282	$74,666.67	Bill Britton	T39	77- 72- 71- 73	293	$4,000.00
Vijay Singh	T 2	70- 72- 71- 69	282	$74,666.67	Scott Hoch	T39	71- 74- 73- 75	293	$4,000.00
Davis Love III	T 2	71- 69- 71- 71	282	$74,666.66	Steve Pate	T39	74- 73- 73- 73	293	$4,000.00
Ed Humenik	5	73- 69- 72- 70	284	$40,000.00	David Peoples	T39	76- 73- 69- 75	293	$4,000.00
Bernhard Langer	T 6	71- 70- 71- 73	285	$33,500.00	Larry Rinker	T39	74- 72- 75- 72	293	$4,000.00
Mark McCumber	T 6	72- 71- 71- 71	285	$33,500.00	Kirk Triplett	T39	71- 71- 74- 77	293	$4,000.00
Mark O'Meara	T 6	71- 72- 72- 70	285	$33,500.00	Len Mattiace	T45	76- 72- 73- 73	294	$2,802.86
Joey Sindelar	9	72- 70- 73- 71	286	$29,000.00	Brett Ogle	T45	77- 71- 74- 72	294	$2,802.86
Billy Andrade	T10	72- 74- 70- 71	287	$21,428.58	Mike Springer	T45	73- 73- 75- 73	294	$2,802.86
Jay Haas	T10	71- 73- 71- 72	287	$21,428.57	Leonard Thompson	T45	72- 77- 72- 73	294	$2,802.86
Bill Kratzert	T10	72- 70- 70- 75	287	$21,428.57	Denis Watson	T45	74- 73- 74- 73	294	$2,802.86
Larry Mize	T10	74- 72- 70- 71	287	$21,428.57	Billy Ray Brown	T45	75- 70- 72- 77	294	$2,802.85
Greg Norman	T10	72- 73- 69- 73	287	$21,428.57	Tom Kite	T45	77- 72- 71- 74	294	$2,802.85
Dan Pohl	T10	70- 72- 70- 75	287	$21,428.57	Ian Baker-Finch	T52	75- 70- 75- 75	295	$2,360.00
Nick Price	T10	73- 75- 67- 72	287	$21,428.57	Bob Lohr	T52	75- 74- 76- 70	295	$2,360.00
Bruce Fleisher	T17	71- 75- 72- 70	288	$13,533.34	Corey Pavin	T52	74- 74- 73- 74	295	$2,360.00
Scott Simpson	T17	73- 72- 74- 69	288	$13,533.34	Dave Rummells	55	77- 70- 71- 78	296	$2,300.00
John Cook	T17	69- 77- 71- 71	288	$13,533.33	Rick Fehr	T56	69- 74- 76- 78	297	$2,250.00
Brad Faxon	T17	71- 72- 70- 75	288	$13,533.33	John Flannery	T56	76- 72- 76- 73	297	$2,250.00
Mark Lye	T17	73- 71- 72- 72	288	$13,533.33	Steve Lowery	T56	75- 71- 75- 76	297	$2,250.00
D.A. Weibring	T17	72- 75- 67- 74	288	$13,533.33	Ted Schulz	T56	76- 71- 76- 74	297	$2,250.00
Michael Allen	T23	69- 72- 73- 75	289	$8,650.00	Jim Gallagher, Jr.	T60	77- 70- 74- 77	298	$2,160.00
Peter Jacobsen	T23	76- 71- 71- 71	289	$8,650.00	Gary Hallberg	T60	73- 71- 77- 77	298	$2,160.00
Lee Janzen	T23	73- 72- 71- 73	289	$8,650.00	John Huston	T60	74- 73- 72- 79	298	$2,160.00
Massy Kuramoto	T23	73- 71- 72- 74	289	$8,650.00	Blaine McCallister	T60	73- 72- 75- 78	298	$2,160.00
Mike Sullivan	T23	74- 71- 72- 72	289	$8,650.00	Gene Sauers	T60	73- 73- 73- 79	298	$2,160.00
Fuzzy Zoeller	T23	73- 73- 70- 73	289	$8,650.00	Fulton Allem	T65	70- 75- 80- 74	299	$2,090.00
Mike Hulbert	T29	75- 74- 68- 73	290	$6,800.00	Robert Wrenn	T65	73- 75- 75- 76	299	$2,090.00
Curtis Strange	T29	70- 79- 70- 71	290	$6,800.00	Trevor Dodds	T67	76- 73- 73- 79	301	$2,030.00
Tom Watson	T29	76- 68- 70- 76	290	$6,800.00	Kelly Gibson	T67	76- 73- 75- 77	301	$2,030.00
Brad Bryant	T32	70- 74- 75- 72	291	$5,916.67	Nolan Henke	T67	74- 71- 78- 78	301	$2,030.00
Jay Delsing	T32	70- 73- 76- 72	291	$5,916.67	Joe Ozaki	T67	72- 76- 74- 79	301	$2,030.00
Dan Forsman	T32	73- 71- 71- 76	291	$5,916.66	Peter O'Malley	T71	75- 74- 75- 78	302	$1,970.00
Keith Clearwater	T35	74- 72- 74- 72	292	$5,037.50	Arnold Palmer	T71	73- 76- 78- 75	302	$1,970.00
John Daly	T35	77- 71- 70- 74	292	$5,037.50	Mark Carnevale	73	71- 76- 80- 77	304	$1,940.00
Ed Dougherty	T35	72- 73- 73- 74	292	$5,037.50	Hal Sutton	74	73- 76- 80- 76	305	$1,920.00
Payne Stewart	T35	75- 70- 76- 71	292	$5,037.50	Andy Bean	75	71- 76- 80- 80	307	$1,900.00

THE PLAYERS CHAMPIONSHIP

TPC at Sawgrass, Ponte Vedra, FL   Purse: $2,500,000
Par: 36-36--72   Yards: 6,896   March 25-28, 1993

LEADERS: First Round-- Kirk Triplett and Nick Price at 8-under-par 64 led by one stroke over Joey Sindelar and Bernhard Langer. **Second Round**-- Price at 12-under-par 132 led by two over Doug Tewell, Dave Rummells and Langer. **Third Round**-- Price at 13-under-par 203, led by one over Mark O'Meara, Greg Norman and Langer.

CUT: 72 players at 2-under-par.

WEATHER: Thursday was overcast and calm. Friday was overcast in the morning and cleared by late afternoon. There was a 55-minute delay from 3:45 to 4:40 p.m. due to lightning in the area. Saturday was clear and windy, as was Sunday

Winner: Nick Price   64- 68- 71- 67   270 $450,000.00

Bernhard Langer 2	65- 69- 70- 71	275	$270,000.00	Robert Wrenn T34	67- 73- 73- 72	285	$12,900.00
Gil Morgan .... T 3	68- 71- 72- 65	276	$145,000.00	Fuzzy Zoeller T34	67- 75- 74- 69	285	$12,900.00
Greg Norman .... T 3	66- 70- 68- 72	276	$145,000.00	Ian Baker-Finch T39	71- 71- 71- 73	286	$9,750.00
Mark O'Meara 5	67- 71- 66- 73	277	$100,000.00	Fred Couples T39	68- 69- 75- 74	286	$9,750.00
Paul Azinger .... T 6	68- 69- 68- 73	278	$80,937.50	Fred Funk T39	68- 73- 73- 72	286	$9,750.00
Ken Green .... T 6	70- 67- 69- 72	278	$80,937.50	Jim Gallagher, Jr. . T39	69- 69- 69- 79	286	$9,750.00
Rocco Mediate .... T 6	68- 71- 68- 71	278	$80,937.50	Mike Smith T39	70- 69- 74- 73	286	$9,750.00
Joe Ozaki .... T 6	72- 68- 68- 70	278	$80,937.50	Kirk Triplett T39	64- 78- 75- 69	286	$9,750.00
Tom Watson 10	70- 72- 69- 68	279	$67,500.00	Ian Woosnam T39	71- 70- 69- 76	286	$9,750.00
Joel Edwards T11	66- 69- 72- 73	280	$53,000.00	Marco Dawson T46	68- 73- 75- 71	287	$6,800.00
Dan Forsman T11	71- 67- 73- 69	280	$53,000.00	David Edwards T46	69- 70- 71- 77	287	$6,800.00
Mike Hulbert T11	71- 67- 72- 70	280	$53,000.00	Bruce Fleisher T46	74- 67- 72- 74	287	$6,800.00
Tom Lehman T11	69- 73- 69- 69	280	$53,000.00	Gary Hallberg T46	71- 71- 74- 71	287	$6,800.00
Payne Stewart T11	70- 70- 66- 74	280	$53,000.00	Larry Rinker T46	70- 72- 72- 73	287	$6,800.00
Steve Elkington T16	67- 70- 71- 73	281	$38,750.00	Jeff Sluman T46	71- 65- 80- 71	287	$6,800.00
Corey Pavin T16	69- 72- 67- 73	281	$38,750.00	Brad Bryant T52	69- 70- 72- 77	288	$5,771.43
Dave Rummells T16	69- 65- 74- 73	281	$38,750.00	Rick Fehr T52	67- 71- 74- 76	288	$5,771.43
Joey Sindelar T16	65- 71- 73- 72	281	$38,750.00	Billy Mayfair T52	73- 68- 72- 75	288	$5,771.43
Fulton Allem T20	70- 72- 73- 67	282	$26,071.43	Peter Persons T52	73- 68- 73- 74	288	$5,771.43
Billy Andrade T20	71- 70- 73- 68	282	$26,071.43	Duffy Waldorf T52	72- 66- 75- 75	288	$5,771.43
Bob Estes T20	70- 68- 72- 72	282	$26,071.43	Denis Watson T52	72- 66- 74- 76	288	$5,771.43
Andrew Magee T20	70- 71- 71- 70	282	$26,071.43	Tony Johnstone T52	70- 71- 70- 77	288	$5,771.42
Mark McCumber ... T20	68- 70- 70- 74	282	$26,071.43	Brad Fabel T59	68- 68- 77- 76	289	$5,525.00
Doug Tewell T20	67- 67- 74- 74	282	$26,071.43	Dick Mast T59	70- 70- 77- 72	289	$5,525.00
Jay Haas T20	69- 70- 68- 75	282	$26,071.42	Ed Dougherty T61	69- 71- 76- 74	290	$5,375.00
Russ Cochran 27	67- 72- 71- 73	283	$19,250.00	Brett Ogle T61	70- 72- 68- 80	290	$5,375.00
Ronnie Black T28	66- 70- 71- 77	284	$16,625.00	D.A. Weibring T61	69- 73- 72- 76	290	$5,375.00
Brian Claar T28	72- 69- 74- 69	284	$16,625.00	Mark Wiebe T61	71- 70- 74- 75	290	$5,375.00
Bruce Lietzke T28	69- 69- 72- 74	284	$16,625.00	Nolan Henke T65	70- 72- 73- 76	291	$5,225.00
Bob Lohr T28	71- 71- 70- 72	284	$16,625.00	Kenny Perry T65	70- 69- 76- 76	291	$5,225.00
Vijay Singh T28	69- 71- 72- 72	284	$16,625.00	Davis Love III T67	70- 69- 82- 72	293	$5,125.00
Howard Twitty T28	71- 70- 71- 72	284	$16,625.00	Mike Reid T67	68- 73- 72- 80	293	$5,125.00
Donnie Hammond . T34	66- 73- 73- 73	285	$12,900.00	Dillard Pruitt 69	70- 72- 72- 80	294	$5,050.00
Lee Janzen T34	70- 71- 71- 73	285	$12,900.00	Billy Ray Brown 70	68- 74- 78- 78	298	$5,000.00
Ted Schulz T34	71- 70- 73- 71	285	$12,900.00				

FREEPORT-McMoRAN GOLF CLASSIC

English Turn G&CC, New Orleans, LA   **Purse: $1,000,000**
Par: 36-36--72   **Yards: 7,116**   **April 1-4, 1993**

FREEPORT-
McMoRAN
Golf Classic

LEADERS: First Round-- Payne Stewart, at 2-under-par 70 (one of just five players under par), held a one-shot lead over Duffy Waldorf, MIke Standly, Ed Fiori, and Bill Kratzert. **Second Round**-- Stewart, after a second consecutive 70 and 4-under-par 140 total, had a two-stroke lead over Standly; Russ Cochran and Greg Kraft were tied for third at 1-under-par 143. **Third Round**-- Kraft, at 4-under-par 212, was one shot ahead of Cochran and Stewart.

CUT: 78 players at 8-over-par 152.

PRO-AM: $7,500. Individual-- Craig Stadler, 69, $750. Team-- Payne Stewart, Phil Blackmar, Russ Cochran, Billy Mayfair, 57, $581.25 each.

WEATHER: Sunny, mild and windy Thursday, with winds gusting to 35 mph. Continued sunny but cool with diminished winds Friday. Cloudy, overcast and windy with periods of light drizzle Saturday; winds picking up and turning cold mid-afternoon. Heavy rains overnight caused a 2-hour, 46-minute delay in Sunday starting times; play, which began at 10:20 a.m. with threesomes off two tees, was contested under threatening skies with cold, windy, wet conditions.

Winner: Mike Standly 71- 71- 72- 67   281 $180,000.00

Player	Pos	Scores	Total	Money	Player	Pos	Scores	Total	Money
Russ Cochran	T 2	75- 68- 70- 69	282	$88,000.00	Donnie Hammond	T39	74- 77- 71- 73	295	$4,000.00
Payne Stewart	T 2	70- 70- 73- 69	282	$88,000.00	David Jackson	T39	78- 73- 72- 72	295	$4,000.00
Greg Norman	4	77- 69- 70- 68	284	$48,000.00	Jim McGovern	T39	77- 67- 81- 70	295	$4,000.00
Vijay Singh	5	72- 73- 72- 68	285	$40,000.00	Eddie Pearce	T39	74- 72- 74- 75	295	$4,000.00
Scott Hoch	T 6	72- 74- 72- 69	287	$32,375.00	Dudley Hart	T45	73- 76- 74- 73	296	$2,860.00
Greg Kraft	T 6	72- 71- 69- 75	287	$32,375.00	Joe Ozaki	T45	76- 71- 74- 75	296	$2,860.00
Neal Lancaster	T 6	72- 73- 71- 71	287	$32,375.00	Mike Sullivan	T45	77- 71- 75- 73	296	$2,860.00
Dick Mast	T 6	76- 72- 70- 69	287	$32,375.00	Ted Tryba	T45	75- 74- 72- 75	296	$2,860.00
Mark Brooks	T10	73- 72- 71- 72	288	$24,000.00	Grant Waite	T45	78- 74- 72- 72	296	$2,860.00
Ed Fiori	T10	71- 75- 71- 71	288	$24,000.00	D.A. Weibring	T45	77- 74- 73- 72	296	$2,860.00
Jaime Gomez	T10	75- 70- 72- 71	288	$24,000.00	Russell Beiersdorf	T51	73- 78- 72- 74	297	$2,327.50
Duffy Waldorf	T10	71- 73- 72- 72	288	$24,000.00	Ronnie Black	T51	77- 75- 73- 72	297	$2,327.50
Kelly Gibson	14	73- 72- 73- 71	289	$19,000.00	John Daly	T51	75- 73- 74- 75	297	$2,327.50
Brad Fabel	T15	75- 69- 75- 71	290	$17,000.00	Ken Green	T51	78- 70- 76- 73	297	$2,327.50
Bill Kratzert	T15	71- 80- 68- 71	290	$17,000.00	Jim Hallet	T51	74- 74- 73- 76	297	$2,327.50
David Toms	T15	74- 72- 71- 73	290	$17,000.00	Peter Jacobsen	T51	75- 77- 74- 71	297	$2,327.50
Michael Bradley	T18	74- 74- 71- 72	291	$14,500.00	Lee Porter	T51	78- 73- 72- 74	297	$2,327.50
Bob Estes	T18	73- 71- 72- 75	291	$14,500.00	Mike Schuchart	T51	73- 78- 78- 68	297	$2,327.50
Steve Lowery	T20	75- 72- 74- 71	292	$10,833.34	Wayne Grady	T59	75- 72- 74- 77	298	$2,200.00
Greg Twiggs	T20	76- 75- 71- 70	292	$10,833.34	Morris Hatalsky	T59	80- 72- 75- 71	298	$2,200.00
JC Anderson	T20	78- 70- 73- 71	292	$10,833.33	Jose M. Olazabal	T59	78- 71- 77- 72	298	$2,200.00
Steve Elkington	T20	73- 73- 71- 75	292	$10,833.33	Andy Bean	T62	76- 75- 71- 77	299	$2,100.00
Ted Schulz	T20	77- 70- 70- 75	292	$10,833.33	Greg Cesario	T62	76- 76- 72- 75	299	$2,100.00
Richard Zokol	T20	75- 74- 70- 73	292	$10,833.33	Ben Crenshaw	T62	77- 75- 72- 75	299	$2,100.00
John Adams	T26	73- 75- 73- 72	293	$7,250.00	John Inman	T62	80- 72- 74- 73	299	$2,100.00
Ed Dougherty	T26	76- 74- 74- 69	293	$7,250.00	Peter Persons	T62	77- 74- 72- 76	299	$2,100.00
Robin Freeman	T26	79- 72- 71- 71	293	$7,250.00	Lance Ten Broeck	T62	76- 76- 75- 72	299	$2,100.00
Billy Mayfair	T26	74- 77- 67- 75	293	$7,250.00	Chris Tucker	T62	76- 75- 76- 72	299	$2,100.00
Peter O'Malley	T26	78- 74- 69- 72	293	$7,250.00	David Delong	T69	76- 76- 75- 73	300	$1,990.00
Jeff Woodland	T26	75- 76- 70- 72	293	$7,250.00	Jay Delsing	T69	74- 77- 76- 73	300	$1,990.00
Phil Blackmar	T32	79- 70- 71- 74	294	$5,414.29	Skip Kendall	T69	76- 76- 76- 72	300	$1,990.00
Brad Bryant	T32	76- 70- 74- 74	294	$5,414.29	Jodie Mudd	T69	72- 75- 77- 76	300	$1,990.00
Massy Kuramoto	T32	78- 73- 73- 70	294	$5,414.29	Mike Donald	73	78- 72- 76- 75	301	$1,940.00
Doug Tewell	T32	75- 76- 73- 70	294	$5,414.29	Kenny Knox	74	74- 77- 75- 76	302	$1,920.00
Fulton Allem	T32	78- 74- 73- 69	294	$5,414.28	Scott Gump	T75	76- 75- 78- 75	304	$1,880.00
Joel Edwards	T32	76- 73- 75- 70	294	$5,414.28	Eric Johnson	T75	76- 75- 75- 78	304	$1,880.00
Nick Faldo	T32	78- 71- 76- 69	294	$5,414.28	Denis Watson	T75	76- 72- 76- 80	304	$1,880.00
Dave Barr	T39	76- 74- 73- 72	295	$4,000.00	Tom Sieckmann	78	78- 74- 84- 82	308	$1,840.00
Patrick Burke	T39	74- 73- 76- 72	295	$4,000.00					

DEPOSIT GUARANTY GOLF CLASSIC

Hattiesburg CC, Hattiesburg, MS   **Purse: $300,000**
Par: 35-35--70   **Yards: 6,280**   **April 8-11, 1993**

LEADERS: First Round-- Jeff Cook and Jeff Woodland, at 6-under-par 64, held a one-shot lead over Len Mattiace, Ed Dougherty, Mike Donald and Greg Kraft. **Second Round**-- Cook, Woodland, Dougherty and Perry Moss were in a four-way tie for the lead at 8-under-par 132; Barry Jaeckel was one shot back at 133. **Third Round**-- Kraft and Jaeckel, at 11-under-par 199, were a stroke in front of Tad Rhyan, whose total was 200.

CUT: 74 players at one-over-par 141.

PRO-AM: $7,500. Individual-- Brad Fabel, 65, $750. Team-- Brad Fabel and John Ross, 55, $675 each.

WEATHER: Thursday, play was conducted under threatening skies. Lightning in the area caused a suspension at 1:30 p.m., with play being suspended for the day at 3 p.m. due to rain and an adverse forecast. The first round resumed at 7:40 a.m. The second round began at 11 a.m. Friday. Skies were partly cloudy Friday, with intermittent periods of sunshine; conditions were windy and cold. Play was suspended by darkness at 7:12, and the second round was completed Saturday morning. Ideal playing conditions both Saturday and Sunday.

Winner: Greg Kraft 65- 70- 64- 68   267 $54,000.00

Player	Pos	Scores	Total	Money
Morris Hatalsky	T 2	69- 65- 68- 66	268	$26,400.00
Tad Rhyan	T 2	66- 70- 64- 68	268	$26,400.00
Barry Jaeckel	T 4	68- 65- 66- 70	269	$11,310.00
Massy Kuramoto	T 4	69- 68- 66- 66	269	$11,310.00
Doug Martin	T 4	70- 66- 68- 65	269	$11,310.00
Len Mattiace	T 4	65- 70- 67- 67	269	$11,310.00
Grant Waite	T 4	72- 65- 69- 63	269	$11,310.00
Jeff Barlow	9	69- 69- 65- 67	270	$8,700.00
Bill Buttner	T10	68- 70- 67- 66	271	$6,650.00
Mike Donald	T10	65- 70- 69- 67	271	$6,650.00
J.P. Hayes	T10	68- 66- 68- 69	271	$6,650.00
Pat McGowan	T10	70- 69- 66- 66	271	$6,650.00
Stan Utley	T10	68- 66- 69- 68	271	$6,650.00
Jeff Woodland	T10	64- 68- 71- 68	271	$6,650.00
JC Anderson	T16	69- 68- 67- 68	272	$4,350.00
Rex Caldwell	T16	69- 67- 69- 67	272	$4,350.00
David Delong	T16	67- 67- 69- 69	272	$4,350.00
Paul Goydos	T16	69- 70- 65- 68	272	$4,350.00
David Ogrin	T16	68- 68- 67- 69	272	$4,350.00
Jim Thorpe	T16	69- 66- 67- 70	272	$4,350.00
Michael Bradley	T22	70- 64- 70- 69	273	$3,000.00
Brian Kamm	T22	69- 68- 71- 65	273	$3,000.00
Chris Perry	T22	68- 67- 69- 69	273	$3,000.00
John Ross	T22	70- 66- 69- 68	273	$3,000.00
Lennie Clements	T26	69- 67- 69- 69	274	$2,175.00
Ed Dougherty	T26	65- 67- 72- 70	274	$2,175.00
Ernie Gonzalez	T26	70- 66- 69- 69	274	$2,175.00
Steve Hart	T26	67- 68- 70- 69	274	$2,175.00
Steve Lamontagne	T26	68- 66- 72- 68	274	$2,175.00
Perry Moss	T26	66- 66- 72- 70	274	$2,175.00
David Canipe	T32	69- 70- 67- 69	275	$1,556.67
Brandel Chamblee	T32	70- 70- 68- 67	275	$1,556.67
Danny Edwards	T32	67- 69- 69- 70	275	$1,556.67
Jim Hallet	T32	71- 67- 68- 69	275	$1,556.67
Mike Nicolette	T32	67- 71- 71- 66	275	$1,556.67
Sonny Skinner	T32	66- 71- 67- 71	275	$1,556.67
Jeff Cook	T32	64- 68- 71- 72	275	$1,556.66
Harry Taylor	T32	67- 69- 67- 72	275	$1,556.66
Lance Ten Broeck	T32	71- 70- 65- 69	275	$1,556.66
John Dowdall	T41	72- 66- 71- 67	276	$1,170.00
Forrest Fezler	T41	69- 70- 69- 68	276	$1,170.00
Gene Jones	T41	67- 70- 70- 69	276	$1,170.00
Tommy Armour	T44	68- 72- 68- 69	277	$885.43
P.H. Horgan III	T44	66- 71- 70- 70	277	$885.43
Skip Kendall	T44	70- 69- 71- 67	277	$885.43
Bill Kratzert	T44	69- 72- 68- 68	277	$885.43
Clarence Rose	T44	71- 67- 71- 68	277	$885.43
Ron Streck	T44	69- 68- 68- 72	277	$885.43
Carl Cooper	T44	70- 71- 67- 69	277	$885.42
Rett Crowder	T51	72- 69- 69- 69	279	$702.00
Brad Fabel	T51	71- 68- 69- 71	279	$702.00
Buddy Gardner	T51	70- 69- 71- 69	279	$702.00
Tom Jenkins	T51	69- 72- 67- 71	279	$702.00
Gary Koch	T51	70- 71- 69- 69	279	$702.00
Greg Whisman	T51	66- 71- 70- 72	279	$702.00
Bob Wolcott	T51	69- 72- 68- 70	279	$702.00
Brian Henninger	T58	71- 70- 66- 73	280	$666.00
Lee Porter	T58	73- 67- 69- 71	280	$666.00
Mike Schuchart	T58	68- 70- 70- 72	280	$666.00
Russell Beiersdorf	T61	68- 71- 69- 73	281	$645.00
Tim Conley	T61	70- 70- 69- 72	281	$645.00
John Elliott	T61	72- 69- 68- 72	281	$645.00
Jaime Gomez	T61	70- 70- 72- 69	281	$645.00
Bob Friend	T65	68- 72- 72- 70	282	$624.00
Steve Lowery	T65	68- 73- 73- 68	282	$624.00
Ed Selser	T65	71- 68- 75- 68	282	$624.00
Dan Halldorson	T68	70- 71- 72- 70	283	$609.00
Fred Wadsworth	T68	67- 73- 71- 72	283	$609.00
Don Shirey, Jr.	T70	70- 70- 71- 73	284	$597.00
Steve Thomas	T70	67- 73- 72- 72	284	$597.00
Lon Hinkle	72	71- 68- 72- 75	286	$588.00
Bill Sander	73	73- 68- 78- 73	292	$582.00
Ed Sneed	74	70- 71- 79- 74	294	$576.00

MASTERS TOURNAMENT

Augusta National GC, Augusta, GA   Purse: $1,700,000
Par: 36-36--72   Yards: 6,905   April 8-11, 1993

LEADERS: First Round-- Lee Janzen, Jack Nicklaus, Tom Lehman, Corey Pavin and Larry Mize at 5-under-par 67, led by one stroke over John Huston, Ray Floyd and Bernhard Langer. **Second Round-**-Jeff Maggert at 7-under-par 137 led by one over Dan Forsman and Langer. **Third Round--** Langer at 9-under-par 207 led by four strokes over Chip Beck and Forsman.

CUT: 61 players at 3-over-par 147 from a starting field of 90. Cut was low 44 scores and ties and those within 10 strokes of the lead.

WEATHER: Thursday was beautiful with some wind. Friday was overcast and cool. Due to heavy rains, the round was suspended at 4:54 p.m. and called for the day at 5:55 p.m. The round resumed at 8:15 a.m. Saturday morning, with the third round starting at 10:00 a.m. The third round was sunny and windy. Sunday was beautiful with some light winds in the afternoon.

Winner: Bernhard Langer   68- 70- 69- 70   277 $306,000.00

Player	Pos	Rounds	Total	Money	Player	Pos	Rounds	Total	Money
Chip Beck	2	72- 67- 72- 70	281	$183,600.00	Andrew Magee	T31	75- 69- 70- 76	290	$10,533.00
John Daly	T3	70- 71- 73- 69	283	$81,600.00	Greg Norman	T31	74- 68- 71- 77	290	$10,533.00
Steve Elkington	T3	71- 70- 71- 71	283	$81,600.00	Bob Gilder	T34	69- 76- 75- 71	291	$8,975.00
Tom Lehman	T3	67- 75- 73- 68	283	$81,600.00	Phil Mickelson	T34	72- 71- 75- 73	291	$8,975.00
Lanny Wadkins	T3	69- 72- 71- 71	283	$81,600.00	Gene Sauers	T34	74- 71- 75- 71	291	$8,975.00
Dan Forsman	T7	69- 69- 73- 73	284	$54,850.00	Craig Stadler	T34	73- 74- 69- 75	291	$8,975.00
Jose Maria Olazabal	T7	70- 72- 74- 68	284	$54,850.00	Jay Haas	38	70- 73- 75- 74	292	$8,000.00
Brad Faxon	T9	71- 70- 72- 72	285	$47,600.00	Keith Clearwater	T39	74- 70- 75- 74	293	$6,817.00
Payne Stewart	T 9	74- 70- 72- 69	285	$47,600.00	John Cook	T39	76- 67- 75- 75	293	$6,817.00
Seve Ballesteros	T11	74- 70- 71- 71	286	$34,850.00	Nick Faldo	T39	71- 76- 79- 67	293	$6,817.00
Ray Floyd	T11	68- 71- 74- 73	286	$34,850.00	Lee Janzen	T39	67- 73- 76- 77	293	$6,817.00
Anders Forsbrand	T11	71- 74- 75- 66	286	$34,850.00	Ted Schulz	T39	69- 76- 76- 72	293	$6,817.00
Corey Pavin	T11	67- 75- 73- 71	286	$34,850.00	Duffy Waldorf	T39	72- 75- 73- 73	293	$6,817.00
Scott Simpson	T11	72- 71- 71- 72	286	$34,850.00	Jay Don Blake	T45	71- 74- 73- 76	294	$4,940.00
Fuzzy Zoeller	T11	75- 67- 71- 73	286	$34,850.00	Joe Ozaki	T45	74- 70- 78- 72	294	$4,940.00
Mark Calcavecchia	T17	71- 70- 74- 72	287	$24,650.00	Jumbo Ozaki	T45	75- 71- 77- 71	294	$4,940.00
Jeff Sluman	T17	71- 72- 71- 73	287	$24,650.00	Craig Parry	T45	69- 72- 75- 78	294	$4,940.00
Howard Twitty	T17	70- 71- 73- 73	287	$24,650.00	Tom Watson	T45	71- 75- 73- 75	294	$4,940.00
Ian Woosnam	T17	71- 74- 73- 69	287	$24,650.00	Gil Morgan	T50	72- 74- 72- 77	295	$4,250.00
Russ Cochran	T21	70- 69- 73- 76	288	$17,000.00	Brett Ogle	T50	70- 74- 71- 80	295	$4,250.00
Fred Couples	T21	72- 70- 74- 72	288	$17,000.00	Colin Montgomerie	T52	71- 72- 78- 75	296	$4,050.00
Sandy Lyle	T21	73- 71- 71- 73	288	$17,000.00	David Peoples	T52	71- 73- 78- 74	296	$4,050.00
Jeff Maggert	T21	70- 67- 75- 76	288	$17,000.00	Ian Baker-Finch	T54	73- 72- 73- 80	298	$3,900.00
Larry Mize	T21	67- 74- 74- 73	288	$17,000.00	David Edwards	T54	73- 73- 76- 76	298	$3,900.00
Mark O'Meara	T21	75- 69- 73- 71	288	$17,000.00	Davis Love III	T54	73- 72- 76- 77	298	$3,900.00
Nolan Henke	T27	76- 69- 71- 73	289	$12,350.00	Charles Coody	T57	74- 72- 75- 78	299	$3,800.00
Hale Irwin	T27	74- 69- 74- 72	289	$12,350.00	Gary Hallberg	T57	72- 74- 78- 75	299	$3,800.00
Jack Nicklaus	T27	67- 75- 76- 71	289	$12,350.00	John Huston	59	68- 74- 84- 75	301	$3,800.00
Joey Sindelar	T27	72- 69- 76- 72	289	$12,350.00	Gary Player	60	71- 76- 75- 80	302	$3,700.00
Bruce Lietzke	T31	74- 71- 71- 74	290	$10,533.00	Billy Andrade	61	73- 74- 80- 76	303	$3,700.00

MCI HERITAGE CLASSIC

Harbour Town GL, Hilton Head Island, SC   **Purse: $1,125,000**
Par: 36-35--71   Yards: 6,912   **April 15-18, 1993**

LEADERS: First Round-- Payne Stewart, at 6-under-par 65, held a one-shot lead over Mike Standly, Rocco Mediate, Lanny Wadkins and Dillard Pruitt. **Second Round**-- David Frost, Bernhard Langer and David Edwards, at 8-under-par 134, led Stewart and Bob Estes by a stroke. **Third Round**-- Edwards, Frost and Paul Azinger, at 9-under-par 204, were one shot ahead of John Cook.

CUT: 78 players at 1-over-par 143.

PRO-AM: $7,500. Individual-- Doug Tewell, Gene Sauers, 65, $675 each. Team-- Payne Stewart, 50, $750.

WEATHER: Windy, overcast and threatening Thursday. Early rain caused a 20-minute delay at 7:50 a.m. Friday, and was followed by sunny skies and swirling winds. Cool early Saturday, becoming sunny and mild with strong, gusty winds. Cold Sunday morning, with temperatures rising to near 70 under partly cloudy skies and continued wind.

Winner: David Edwards	68- 66- 70- 69	273	$202,500.00

Player	Pos	Scores	Total	Money
David Frost	2	67- 67- 70- 71	275	$121,500.00
Paul Azinger	T 3	70- 68- 66- 73	277	$50,737.60
Ian Baker-Finch	T 3	68- 70- 69- 70	277	$50,737.60
Mark McCumber	T 3	68- 68- 70- 71	277	$50,737.60
Don Pooley	T 3	67- 70- 70- 70	277	$50,737.60
Fuzzy Zoeller	T 3	70- 69- 68- 70	277	$50,737.60
John Cook	T 8	69- 67- 69- 73	278	$31,500.00
Tom Lehman	T 8	70- 70- 70- 68	278	$31,500.00
Gil Morgan	T 8	71- 72- 69- 66	278	$31,500.00
Steve Pate	T 8	71- 67- 68- 72	278	$31,500.00
Bob Estes	T12	68- 67- 75- 69	279	$22,781.25
Jodie Mudd	T12	69- 68- 69- 73	279	$22,781.25
Jeff Sluman	T12	68- 69- 70- 72	279	$22,781.25
Lanny Wadkins	T12	66- 70- 70- 73	279	$22,781.25
Rick Fehr	T16	71- 66- 70- 73	280	$17,437.50
Kelly Gibson	T16	74- 64- 72- 70	280	$17,437.50
Peter Jacobsen	T16	70- 70- 67- 73	280	$17,437.50
Bernhard Langer	T16	69- 65- 74- 72	280	$17,437.50
Billy Andrade	T20	70- 69- 70- 72	281	$12,645.00
Scott Hoch	T20	68- 73- 69- 71	281	$12,645.00
Hale Irwin	T20	68- 70- 71- 72	281	$12,645.00
Lee Janzen	T20	71- 66- 70- 74	281	$12,645.00
Kenny Perry	T20	69- 70- 72- 70	281	$12,645.00
Mark O'Meara	T25	69- 71- 74- 68	282	$9,187.34
Larry Nelson	T25	72- 68- 67- 75	282	$9,187.33
Doug Tewell	T25	69- 71- 70- 72	282	$9,187.33
Dick Mast	T28	71- 72- 68- 72	283	$7,649.80
Phil Mickelson	T28	70- 72- 72- 69	283	$7,649.80
Corey Pavin	T28	67- 70- 74- 72	283	$7,649.80
Dillard Pruitt	T28	66- 72- 72- 73	283	$7,649.80
Lance Ten Broeck	T28	70- 68- 72- 73	283	$7,649.80
Joel Edwards	T33	71- 69- 72- 72	284	$6,215.50
Dan Forsman	T33	69- 72- 71- 72	284	$6,215.50
Mike Standly	T33	66- 75- 67- 76	284	$6,215.50
Payne Stewart	T33	65- 70- 72- 77	284	$6,215.50
Russ Cochran	T37	74- 68- 71- 72	285	$5,400.50
Jim McGovern	T37	72- 69- 70- 74	285	$5,400.50
Mark Brooks	T39	71- 69- 72- 74	286	$4,275.50
Robert Gamez	T39	73- 69- 71- 73	286	$4,275.50
Jay Haas	T39	71- 72- 73- 70	286	$4,275.50
Nolan Henke	T39	68- 70- 81- 67	286	$4,275.50
Craig Parry	T39	70- 69- 73- 74	286	$4,275.50
Gene Sauers	T39	72- 71- 72- 71	286	$4,275.50
Howard Twitty	T39	70- 67- 74- 75	286	$4,275.50
Richard Zokol	T39	71- 71- 70- 74	286	$4,275.50
Dan Halldorson	T47	71- 72- 73- 71	287	$2,889.72
Craig Stadler	T47	69- 71- 74- 73	287	$2,889.72
Robert Wrenn	T47	73- 69- 72- 73	287	$2,889.72
Bill Britton	T47	70- 70- 73- 74	287	$2,889.71
Neal Lancaster	T47	71- 69- 71- 76	287	$2,889.71
Rocco Mediate	T47	66- 77- 70- 74	287	$2,889.71
Vijay Singh	T47	73- 70- 70- 74	287	$2,889.71
Billy Mayfair	T54	71- 72- 73- 72	288	$2,587.34
Chip Beck	T54	73- 69- 73- 73	288	$2,587.33
Nick Price	T54	71- 70- 73- 74	288	$2,587.33
Fred Funk	57	73- 69- 76- 71	289	$2,542.00
Dave Barr	T58	71- 72- 75- 72	290	$2,486.00
Marco Dawson	T58	72- 71- 71- 76	290	$2,486.00
Brad Faxon	T58	72- 67- 76- 75	290	$2,486.00
Ken Green	T58	74- 69- 72- 75	290	$2,486.00
Ed Fiori	T62	73- 70- 74- 74	291	$2,396.00
Buddy Gardner	T62	72- 71- 74- 74	291	$2,396.00
David Jackson	T62	72- 71- 72- 76	291	$2,396.00
D.A. Weibring	T62	70- 73- 74- 74	291	$2,396.00
Ed Humenik	T66	70- 73- 76- 73	292	$2,328.50
Mike Sullivan	T66	69- 70- 77- 76	292	$2,328.50
John Inman	T68	73- 70- 78- 72	293	$2,283.50
Barry Jaeckel	T68	73- 70- 77- 73	293	$2,283.50
Donnie Hammond	70	73- 69- 76- 76	294	$2,250.00
Tim Simpson	71	68- 70- 80- 77	295	$2,227.00
Tom Watson	72	71- 72- 76- 77	296	$2,205.00
Jay Delsing	73	71- 71- 79- 76	297	$2,182.00
Loren Roberts	74	71- 72- 78- 77	298	$2,160.00
Wayne Grady	75	71- 71- 75- 82	299	$2,137.00
Mike Springer	76	70- 73- 82- 76	301	$2,115.00
John Mahaffey	77	73- 69- 78- 85	305	$2,092.00
Jimmy Johnston	78	72- 71- 80- 84	307	$2,070.00

KMART GREATER GREENSBORO OPEN

Forest Oaks CC, Greensboro, NC   **Purse: $1,500,000**
Par: 36-36--72   **Yards: 6,958**   **April 22-25, 1993**

LEADERS: First Round-- Tom Purtzer and Mike Sullivan at 5-under-par 67, led by two over Jay Haas, Rick Lewallen, Jim Hallet, Jim McGovern and Chip Beck. **Second Round--** Sullivan at 9-under-par 135 led by two over Dudley Hart. **Third Round--** Steve Elkington and Sullivan at 8-under-par 208 led by one over Gil Morgan.

CUT: 84 players at 3-over-par.

PRO-AM: Due to darkness the pro-am, was divided into three separate events. The morning group completed 18 holes, while the afternoon segment was divided into two nine hole events. Morning Individual-- Brad Faxon, Tom Watson, John Cook, 68, $412.50 each. Morning Team-- Rick Fehr, 55, $450. Afternoon Front Nine Individual-- Fuzzy Zoeller, 34, $375. Afternoon Front Nine Team-- Sandy Lyle, 27, $450. Afternoon Back Nine Individual-- Jay Delsing, Nolan Henke, 34, $337.50. Afternoon Back Nine Team-- Ken Green, 25, $375.

WEATHER: Thursday and Friday were sunny, very cool and breezy. Saturday and Sunday were very pleasant with some wind

Winner: Rocco Mediate   74- 67- 71- 69   281 $270,000.00
(Won playoff with birdie on fourth extra hole)

Player	Pos	Rounds	Total	Money
Steve Elkington	2	71- 68- 69- 73	281	$162,000.00
Paul Azinger	T 3	73- 67- 70- 72	282	$78,000.00
Dudley Hart	T 3	72- 65- 74- 71	282	$78,000.00
Gil Morgan	T 3	71- 69- 69- 73	282	$78,000.00
David Edwards	T 6	70- 71- 70- 72	283	$50,250.00
Lee Janzen	T 6	71- 71- 70- 71	283	$50,250.00
Mark Wiebe	T 6	72- 73- 68- 70	283	$50,250.00
Billy Andrade	T 9	74- 72- 68- 70	284	$40,500.00
Vijay Singh	T 9	72- 67- 72- 73	284	$40,500.00
Jeff Sluman	T 9	78- 65- 71- 70	284	$40,500.00
Mark Brooks	T12	76- 68- 69- 72	285	$26,812.50
Mark Calcavecchia	T12	72- 69- 76- 68	285	$26,812.50
Peter Jacobsen	T12	70- 70- 75- 70	285	$26,812.50
Jim McGovern	T12	69- 72- 75- 69	285	$26,812.50
Mark O'Meara	T12	74- 68- 72- 71	285	$26,812.50
Gene Sauers	T12	74- 69- 76- 66	285	$26,812.50
Mike Sullivan	T12	67- 68- 73- 77	285	$26,812.50
Tom Watson	T12	75- 70- 72- 68	285	$26,812.50
Russell Beiersdorf	T20	75- 71- 69- 71	286	$16,250.00
Lennie Clements	T20	70- 68- 72- 76	286	$16,250.00
John Cook	T20	71- 73- 70- 72	286	$16,250.00
Jay Haas	T20	69- 73- 74- 70	286	$16,250.00
Donnie Hammond	T20	73- 72- 68- 73	286	$16,250.00
Howard Twitty	T20	72- 71- 70- 73	286	$16,250.00
Joel Edwards	26	70- 73- 71- 73	287	$12,000.00
Chip Beck	T27	69- 74- 74- 71	288	$10,425.00
John Huston	T27	73- 70- 72- 73	288	$10,425.00
Tom Lehman	T27	72- 73- 71- 72	288	$10,425.00
Davis Love III	T27	71- 74- 71- 72	288	$10,425.00
John Mahaffey	T27	70- 71- 70- 77	288	$10,425.00
Tom Purtzer	T27	67- 77- 74- 70	288	$10,425.00
Brian Claar	T33	72- 73- 75- 69	289	$7,925.00
Robert Gamez	T33	74- 72- 71- 72	289	$7,925.00
Wayne Levi	T33	75- 72- 70- 72	289	$7,925.00
Craig Parry	T33	71- 72- 74- 72	289	$7,925.00
Don Pooley	T33	74- 72- 70- 73	289	$7,925.00
Marty Schiene	T33	74- 71- 74- 70	289	$7,925.00
Roger Maltbie	T39	70- 71- 76- 73	290	$6,300.00
Lance Ten Broeck	T39	72- 70- 72- 76	290	$6,300.00
Jim Thorpe	T39	75- 71- 72- 72	290	$6,300.00
Grant Waite	T39	74- 73- 70- 73	290	$6,300.00
John Adams	T43	73- 67- 77- 74	291	$4,680.00
Rick Fehr	T43	73- 73- 71- 74	291	$4,680.00
Jim Gallagher, Jr.	T43	74- 73- 76- 68	291	$4,680.00
Brian Kamm	T43	74- 73- 73- 71	291	$4,680.00
Dick Mast	T43	70- 75- 68- 78	291	$4,680.00
Peter Persons	T43	73- 71- 74- 73	291	$4,680.00
Tom Sieckmann	T43	73- 73- 70- 75	291	$4,680.00
Jay Delsing	T50	72- 73- 75- 72	292	$3,485.46
John Flannery	T50	75- 72- 75- 70	292	$3,485.46
John Inman	T50	72- 73- 74- 73	292	$3,485.46
Sandy Lyle	T50	75- 70- 74- 73	292	$3,485.46
Harry Taylor	T50	72- 70- 78- 72	292	$3,485.46
Jaime Gomez	T50	75- 71- 72- 74	292	$3,485.45
Hale Irwin	T50	71- 73- 70- 78	292	$3,485.45
Len Mattiace	T50	73- 72- 74- 73	292	$3,485.45
Phil Mickelson	T50	77- 68- 73- 74	292	$3,485.45
Tim Simpson	T50	76- 71- 71- 74	292	$3,485.45
Fuzzy Zoeller	T50	74- 72- 71- 75	292	$3,485.45
Ronnie Black	T61	72- 73- 72- 76	293	$3,195.00
Kelly Gibson	T61	74- 72- 73- 74	293	$3,195.00
Ken Green	T61	73- 73- 71- 76	293	$3,195.00
Dave Peege	T61	71- 72- 76- 74	293	$3,195.00
Kenny Perry	T61	76- 71- 74- 72	293	$3,195.00
Mike Springer	T61	73- 74- 73- 73	293	$3,195.00
Brad Bryant	T67	71- 75- 74- 74	294	$3,045.00
Rick Dalpos	T67	70- 75- 71- 78	294	$3,045.00
Bruce Fleisher	T67	74- 71- 72- 77	294	$3,045.00
Loren Roberts	T67	72- 75- 75- 72	294	$3,045.00
Jim Hallet	T71	69- 75- 78- 73	295	$2,940.00
Nolan Henke	T71	72- 74- 75- 74	295	$2,940.00
Greg Kraft	T71	72- 71- 73- 79	295	$2,940.00
John Daly	T74	75- 72- 74- 75	296	$2,835.00
Mike Hulbert	T74	73- 73- 71- 79	296	$2,835.00
Skip Kendall	T74	71- 75- 73- 77	296	$2,835.00
Kirk Triplett	T74	74- 73- 76- 73	296	$2,835.00
Bob Estes	T78	76- 70- 78- 73	297	$2,715.00
Mark Lye	T78	74- 73- 73- 77	297	$2,715.00
Ted Schulz	T78	71- 71- 75- 80	297	$2,715.00
Joey Sindelar	T78	75- 72- 74- 76	297	$2,715.00
Mark Carnevale	82	73- 74- 77- 74	298	$2,640.00
Rick Lewallen	83	69- 74- 76- 80	299	$2,610.00
David Toms	84	77- 70- 77- 76	300	$2,580.00

SHELL HOUSTON OPEN

TPC at The Woodlands, The Woodlands, TX   **Purse: $1,300,000**
Par: 36-36-72   **Yards: 7,042**   **April 29-May 2, 1993**

LEADERS: First Round-- Blaine McCallister with an 8-under-par 64 led by one over John Huston and John Flannery. **Second Round**-- McCallister at 15-under-par 129 led by two strokes over Jim McGovern and Huston.

CUT: 77 pros and 1 amateur at 4-under-par 140.

PRO-AM: Individual-- Bill Britton, 65, $750. Team-- Hal Sutton, 53, $750.

WEATHER: The first round was delayed from 8:15 a.m. to 12:45 p.m. due to rain and lightning. Play was called at 7:30 p.m. with 78 players still on the course. Friday's round was delayed from 7:30 a.m. to 9:30 a.m. due to fog. The second round got underway at 1:00 p.m. Play was subsequently suspended at 6:15 p.m. due to lightning. Saturday's play got underway at 7:30 a.m. with the completion of the second round coming at approximately 11:15 a.m. The third round got underway at 12:03 p.m. Ten groups got onto the golf course, before rain and lightning halted play. The round was officially cancelled at 4:15 p.m., which made the tournament a 54-hole event.

Winner: Jim McGovern   **67- 64- 68**   **199**   **$234,000.00**
(Won playoff with birdie on second extra hole)

Player	Pos	Rounds	Total	Money		Player	Pos	Rounds	Total	Money
John Huston	2	65- 66- 68	199	$140,400.00		Perry Moss	T41	72- 66- 71	209	$4,115.10
Donnie Hammond	T 3	67- 65- 68	200	$67,600.00		Rick Dalpos	T41	66- 73- 70	209	$4,115.09
Blaine McCallister	T 3	64- 65- 71	200	$67,600.00		Trevor Dodds	T41	68- 71- 70	209	$4,115.09
Payne Stewart	T 3	66- 68- 66	200	$67,600.00		Rick Fehr	T41	70- 69- 70	209	$4,115.09
Larry Mize	6	68- 64- 69	201	$46,800.00		Ed Humenik	T41	69- 69- 71	209	$4,115.09
Fulton Allem	T 7	66- 70- 67	203	$39,162.50		J.L. Lewis	T41	69- 70- 70	209	$4,115.09
Steve Elkington	T 7	70- 65- 68	203	$39,162.50		Jeff Sluman	T41	68- 68- 73	209	$4,115.09
Loren Roberts	T 7	67- 67- 69	203	$39,162.50		Harry Taylor	T41	68- 69- 72	209	$4,115.09
Mike Springer	T 7	70- 69- 64	203	$39,162.50		Kirk Triplett	T41	71- 69- 69	209	$4,115.09
Tom Byrum	T11	70- 66- 68	204	$26,650.00		Ted Tryba	T41	71- 68- 70	209	$4,115.09
Ben Crenshaw	T11	67- 68- 69	204	$26,650.00		D.A. Weibring	T41	72- 68- 69	209	$4,115.09
Brian Kamm	T11	72- 64- 68	204	$26,650.00		Tim Simpson	T52	72- 66- 72	210	$3,001.15
Andrew Magee	T11	68- 68- 68	204	$26,650.00		Jim Woodward	T52	69- 69- 72	210	$3,001.15
Jeff Maggert	T11	66- 68- 70	204	$26,650.00		Jaime Gomez	T52	71- 68- 71	210	$3,001.14
Steve Pate	T11	67- 68- 69	204	$26,650.00		Scott Gump	T52	69- 70- 71	210	$3,001.14
Bill Britton	T17	67- 69- 69	205	$19,500.00		P.H. Horgan III	T52	69- 68- 73	210	$3,001.14
John Daly	T17	69- 70- 66	205	$19,500.00		Dennis Trixler	T52	70- 69- 71	210	$3,001.14
Lance Ten Broeck	T17	72- 67- 66	205	$19,500.00		Bobby Wadkins	T52	66- 71- 73	210	$3,001.14
Brian Henninger	T20	70- 68- 68	206	$14,083.34		Justin Leonard	T52	69- 68- 73	210	AMATEUR
Jeff Woodland	T20	70- 68- 68	206	$14,083.34		John Adams	T60	72- 68- 71	211	$2,821.00
Ronnie Black	T20	67- 68- 71	206	$14,083.33		Michael Allen	T60	70- 69- 72	211	$2,821.00
Jay Haas	T20	68- 67- 71	206	$14,083.33		Brad Fabel	T60	71- 69- 71	211	$2,821.00
Gil Morgan	T20	67- 70- 69	206	$14,083.33		Kelly Gibson	T60	69- 71- 71	211	$2,821.00
Peter Persons	T20	69- 68- 69	206	$14,083.33		Paul Goydos	T60	70- 70- 71	211	$2,821.00
Billy Ray Brown	T26	67- 72- 68	207	$9,230.00		Dillard Pruitt	T60	67- 72- 72	211	$2,821.00
John Dowdall	T26	66- 73- 68	207	$9,230.00		JC Anderson	T66	71- 69- 72	212	$2,691.00
Morris Hatalsky	T26	68- 70- 69	207	$9,230.00		Neal Lancaster	T66	72- 66- 74	212	$2,691.00
Scott Hoch	T26	68- 67- 72	207	$9,230.00		Eddie Pearce	T66	70- 68- 74	212	$2,691.00
Tom Sieckmann	T26	68- 69- 70	207	$9,230.00		David Peoples	T66	71- 67- 74	212	$2,691.00
Mike Sullivan	T26	68- 71- 68	207	$9,230.00		Lennie Clements	T70	71- 69- 73	213	$2,613.00
Willie Wood	T26	69- 70- 68	207	$9,230.00		Tim Conley	T70	68- 72- 73	213	$2,613.00
Dave Barr	T33	68- 71- 69	208	$6,581.25		Shane Bertsch	T72	69- 70- 75	214	$2,548.00
Michael Bradley	T33	69- 69- 70	208	$6,581.25		David Jackson	T72	70- 70- 74	214	$2,548.00
Keith Clearwater	T33	69- 70- 69	208	$6,581.25		Ed Sneed	T72	66- 73- 75	214	$2,548.00
Brad Faxon	T33	73- 65- 70	208	$6,581.25		Steve Lowery	T75	68- 71- 76	215	$2,483.00
John Flannery	T33	65- 70- 73	208	$6,581.25		David Ogrin	T75	67- 70- 78	215	$2,483.00
Dan Forsman	T33	69- 70- 69	208	$6,581.25		Chip Craig	T77	71- 69- 76	216	$2,431.00
Fred Funk	T33	69- 67- 72	208	$6,581.25		Rocco Mediate	T77	71- 69- 76	216	$2,431.00
Jim Gallagher, Jr.	T33	70- 68- 70	208	$6,581.25						

BELLSOUTH CLASSIC

Atlanta CC, Marietta, GA   Purse: $1,200,000
Par: 36-36--72   Yards: 7,018   May 6-9, 1993

LEADERS: First Round-- Steve Lowery shot a 7-under-par 65 and led by one stroke over Dillard Pruitt, Mike Hulbert, and Mark Carnevale. **Second Round--** Billy Andrade at 11-under-par 133 led by one over Tom Sieckmann, Mark Calcavecchia, and Pruitt. **Third Round--** Nick Price at 16-under-par 200 led by one stroke over Calcavecchia.

CUT: 79 players at 2-under-par 142.

PRO-AM: $7,500. Individual-- Mark McCumber, 66, $750. Team-- Jim Gallagher, Jr., 50, $750.

WEATHER: Sunny and warm every day with the exception of a few sprinkles on Saturday.

Winner: Nolan Henke 67- 69- 68- 67   271 $216,000.00

Player		Scores	Total	Money	Player		Scores	Total	Money
Mark Calcavecchia	T2	67- 67- 67- 72	273	$89,600.00	David Ogrin	T38	67- 75- 68- 73	283	$4,560.00
Nick Price	T2	69- 67- 64- 73	273	$89,600.00	Peter Persons	T38	70- 69- 71- 73	283	$4,560.00
Tom Sieckmann	T2	70- 64- 70- 69	273	$89,600.00	Mike Standly	T38	69- 70- 73- 71	283	$4,560.00
Fulton Allem	5	73- 68- 67- 66	274	$48,000.00	Harry Taylor	T38	72- 70- 69- 72	283	$4,560.00
Mike Springer	6	69- 66- 68- 72	275	$43,200.00	Grant Waite	T38	71- 70- 71- 71	283	$4,560.00
Billy Andrade	T7	67- 66- 73- 70	276	$33,700.00	D.A. Weibring	T38	73- 69- 69- 72	283	$4,560.00
Brian Claar	T7	70- 68- 67- 71	276	$33,700.00	Fuzzy Zoeller	T38	73- 69- 67- 74	283	$4,560.00
Jimmy Johnston	T7	71- 67- 64- 74	276	$33,700.00	Bill Britton	T48	71- 70- 68- 75	284	$3,096.00
Larry Mize	T7	69- 69- 68- 70	276	$33,700.00	Trevor Dodds	T48	69- 70- 71- 74	284	$3,096.00
Dillard Pruitt	T7	66- 68- 68- 74	276	$33,700.00	Mike Smith	T48	71- 70- 74- 69	284	$3,096.00
Kirk Triplett	T7	73- 69- 70- 64	276	$33,700.00	Curtis Strange	T48	73- 69- 68- 74	284	$3,096.00
Russell Beiersdorf	T13	67- 68- 71- 71	277	$21,840.00	Brad Bryant	T52	72- 66- 75- 72	285	$2,744.00
Brandel Chamblee	T13	70- 67- 69- 71	277	$21,840.00	Mark Carnevale	T52	66- 73- 76- 70	285	$2,744.00
Fred Funk	T13	71- 69- 73- 64	277	$21,840.00	Lennie Clements	T52	73- 69- 68- 75	285	$2,744.00
Hale Irwin	T13	71- 69- 71- 66	277	$21,840.00	Russ Cochran	T52	68- 67- 74- 76	285	$2,744.00
Corey Pavin	T13	69- 71- 70- 67	277	$21,840.00	Joel Edwards	T52	70- 71- 73- 71	285	$2,744.00
Patrick Burke	T18	68- 72- 72- 66	278	$17,400.00	Hubert Green	T52	70- 71- 73- 71	285	$2,744.00
Steve Lowery	T18	65- 72- 71- 70	278	$17,400.00	Brian Henninger	T52	71- 70- 72- 72	285	$2,744.00
John Adams	T20	68- 67- 72- 72	279	$15,000.00	Larry Nelson	T52	67- 72- 73- 73	285	$2,744.00
Davis Love III	T20	69- 69- 68- 73	279	$15,000.00	Willie Wood	T52	68- 68- 73- 76	285	$2,744.00
Phil Blackmar	T22	72- 69- 70- 69	280	$11,520.00	Tom Byrum	T61	72- 69- 71- 74	286	$2,544.00
David Frost	T22	71- 68- 69- 72	280	$11,520.00	Mike Donald	T61	70- 71- 71- 74	286	$2,544.00
Mike Hulbert	T22	66- 70- 71- 73	280	$11,520.00	Ed Dougherty	T61	73- 66- 73- 74	286	$2,544.00
John Huston	T22	67- 71- 69- 73	280	$11,520.00	John Elliott	T61	73- 78- 76- 69	286	$2,544.00
Scott Simpson	T22	68- 71- 72- 69	280	$11,520.00	Bill Glasson	T61	71- 69- 68- 78	286	$2,544.00
Wayne Grady	T27	70- 70- 69- 72	281	$8,520.00	Jim McGovern	T61	70- 71- 70- 75	286	$2,544.00
Morris Hatalsky	T27	69- 72- 69- 71	281	$8,520.00	Jodie Mudd	T61	70- 70- 74- 72	286	$2,544.00
Skip Kendall	T27	70- 70- 70- 71	281	$8,520.00	Tommy Armour	T68	68- 74- 73- 72	287	$2,436.00
Billy Mayfair	T27	71- 68- 71- 71	281	$8,520.00	Bobby Wadkins	T68	74- 68- 70- 75	287	$2,436.00
David Toms	T27	69- 70- 70- 72	281	$8,520.00	Andy Bean	70	70- 72- 72- 74	288	$2,400.00
Dave Barr	T32	68- 70- 69- 75	282	$6,640.00	Barry Cheesman	T71	71- 69- 75- 74	289	$2,328.00
Bob Eastwood	T32	68- 70- 71- 73	282	$6,640.00	Ed Fiori	T71	69- 73- 72- 75	289	$2,328.00
Brad Fabel	T32	69- 69- 73- 71	282	$6,640.00	Paul Goydos	T71	69- 68- 75- 77	289	$2,328.00
Blaine McCallister	T32	70- 68- 72- 72	282	$6,640.00	Ed Humenik	T71	72- 69- 75- 73	289	$2,328.00
Mark O'Meara	T32	71- 71- 71- 69	282	$6,640.00	Perry Moss	T71	69- 72- 74- 74	289	$2,328.00
Payne Stewart	T32	69- 71- 72- 70	282	$6,640.00	Mark Lye	T76	69- 73- 76- 72	290	$2,244.00
John Inman	T38	73- 69- 71- 70	283	$4,560.00	Ted Tryba	T76	73- 68- 73- 76	290	$2,244.00
Bill Kratzert	T38	68- 73- 69- 73	283	$4,560.00	David Delong	78	73- 68- 72- 80	293	$2,208.00
Neal Lancaster	T38	67- 73- 74- 69	283	$4,560.00	Lon Hinkle	79	71- 70- 79- 83	303	$2,184.00

GTE BYRON NELSON CLASSIC

TPC at Las Colinas, Irving, TX   **Purse:** $1,200,000
Par: 35-35--70   Yards: 6,742   May 13-16, 1993

LEADERS: First Round-- Scott Simpson, Dan Forsman and Russell Beiersdorf each shot five-under-par 65s to lead three players by one. **Second Round**-- Forsman, at 11-under 129, led Simpson by one and Billy Mayfair who fired a course-record 61,and Mark Calcavecchia by two. **Third Round**-- Simpson, at 11-under par 199, led Trevor Dodds by one and Forsman and Mayfair by two.

CUT: A total of 77 players (76 pros, 1 amateur) at one-over par 141.

PRO-AM: $7,500. Individual-- Mark Calcavecchia and Bruce Lietzke, 65, $675 each. Team-- Jay Don Blake, 50, $750.

WEATHER: Perfect each day although strong winds affected play on Thursday.

Winner: Scott Simpson	65- 66- 68- 71	270	$216,000.00

Player	Pos	Scores	Total	Money
Billy Mayfair	T 2	71- 61- 69- 70	271	$89,600.00
Corey Pavin	T 2	69- 68- 67- 67	271	$89,600.00
D.A. Weibring	T 2	68- 65- 69- 69	271	$89,600.00
Fred Couples	T 5	71- 63- 70- 68	272	$43,800.00
David Frost	T 5	68- 66- 69- 69	272	$43,800.00
Payne Stewart	T 5	70- 66- 68- 68	272	$43,800.00
Mark Calcavecchia	T 8	67- 65- 74- 67	273	$34,800.00
Ray Floyd	T 8	66- 69- 70- 68	273	$34,800.00
Larry Rinker	T 8	68- 69- 67- 69	273	$34,800.00
Fulton Allem	T11	69- 67- 70- 68	274	$22,400.00
John Cook	T11	67- 68- 67- 72	274	$22,400.00
Donnie Hammond	T11	71- 64- 71- 68	274	$22,400.00
Hale Irwin	T11	66- 72- 69- 67	274	$22,400.00
Davis Love III	T11	68- 66- 69- 71	274	$22,400.00
Larry Mize	T11	70- 67- 68- 69	274	$22,400.00
Nick Price	T11	68- 67- 68- 71	274	$22,400.00
Doug Tewell	T11	68- 66- 70- 70	274	$22,400.00
Dennis Trixler	T11	67- 69- 73- 65	274	$22,400.00
Bob Estes	T20	69- 69- 67- 70	275	$13,000.00
Dan Forsman	T20	65- 64- 72- 74	275	$13,000.00
Gil Morgan	T20	73- 66- 66- 70	275	$13,000.00
Dillard Pruitt	T20	71- 69- 69- 66	275	$13,000.00
Tim Simpson	T20	69- 71- 67- 68	275	$13,000.0C
Tom Watson	T20	68- 67- 68- 72	275	$13,000.00
Jay Don Blake	T26	69- 69- 65- 73	276	$8,520.00
Russ Cochran	T26	70- 70- 68- 68	276	$8,520.00
Jeff Cook	T26	74- 66- 71- 65	276	$8,520.00
Ed Fiori	T26	70- 68- 66- 72	276	$8,520.00
Jaime Gomez	T26	74- 66- 68- 68	276	$8,520.00
John Inman	T26	70- 71- 70- 65	276	$8,520.00
Loren Roberts	T26	68- 67- 70- 71	276	$8,520.00
Russell Beiersdorf	T33	65- 70- 72- 70	277	$5,820.00
Brandel Chamblee	T33	70- 69- 70- 68	277	$5,820.00
Ben Crenshaw	T33	70- 69- 73- 65	277	$5,820.00
Nolan Henke	T33	67- 74- 71- 65	277	$5,820.00
Bruce Lietzke	T33	71- 62- 70- 74	277	$5,820.00
Steve Lowery	T33	72- 67- 67- 71	277	$5,820.00
Blaine McCallister	T33	71- 66- 69- 71	277	$5,820.00
David Peoples	T33	72- 66- 70- 69	277	$5,820.00
Greg Twiggs	T33	68- 67- 71- 71	277	$5,820.00
Mark Wiebe	T33	74- 67- 69- 67	277	$5,820.00
Brad Bryant	T43	69- 66- 71- 72	278	$3,744.00
Jay Delsing	T43	71- 70- 70- 67	278	$3,744.00
Trevor Dodds	T43	69- 67- 64- 78	278	$3,744.00
John Dowdall	T43	69- 70- 72- 67	278	$3,744.00
Steve Elkington	T43	73- 68- 69- 68	278	$3,744.00
Dudley Hart	T43	71- 68- 68- 71	278	$3,744.00
Tom Sieckmann	T43	71- 67- 72- 68	278	$3,744.00
Michael Bradley	T50	70- 71- 66- 72	279	$2,872.00
Mark Brooks	T50	70- 69- 71- 69	279	$2,872.00
Gary Hallberg	T50	71- 69- 71- 68	279	$2,872.00
Brian Kamm	T50	73- 67- 71- 68	279	$2,872.00
Bob Lohr	T50	70- 69- 69- 71	279	$2,872.00
Howard Twitty	T50	66- 73- 67- 73	279	$2,872.00
Brian Claar	T56	69- 67- 71- 73	280	$2,712.00
Lennie Clements	T56	67- 68- 77- 68	280	$2,712.00
Brian Henninger	T56	72- 67- 70- 71	280	$2,712.00
Justin Leonard	T56	70- 67- 68- 75	280	AMATEUR
Mark Hayes	T60	70- 67- 71- 73	281	$2,640.00
Dave Peege	T60	71- 64- 74- 72	281	$2,640.00
Mike Schuchart	T60	71- 69- 71- 70	281	$2,640.00
Jay Haas	T63	70- 71- 70- 71	282	$2,556.00
Perry Moss	T63	72- 66- 72- 72	282	$2,556.00
Mike Smith	T63	72- 69- 72- 69	282	$2,556.00
Harry Taylor	T63	71- 69- 70- 72	282	$2,556.00
Marco Dawson	T67	70- 70- 69- 74	283	$2,460.00
Tom Lehman	T67	71- 67- 69- 76	283	$2,460.00
Jim McGovern	T67	72- 67- 72- 72	283	$2,460.00
Ted Schulz	T67	70- 69- 74- 70	283	$2,460.00
Steve Lamontagne	T71	71- 70- 69- 74	284	$2,388.00
John Mahaffey	T71	73- 68- 72- 71	284	$2,388.00
Neal Lancaster	T73	73- 68- 72- 72	285	$2,328.00
Tom Purtzer	T73	69- 72- 74- 70	285	$2,328.00
Hal Sutton	T73	70- 71- 72- 72	285	$2,328.00
Paul Goydos	T76	72- 69- 75- 71	287	$2,268.00
Len Mattiace	T76	76- 64- 70- 77	287	$2,268.00

KEMPER OPEN

KEMPER

OPEN

TPC at Avenel, Potomac, MD **Purse: $1,300,000**
Par: 36-35--71   **Yards: 7,005**   **May 20-23, 1993**

LEADERS: First Round-- Grant Waite fired a 5-under-par 66 to take a one-stroke lead over Ed Fiori, Tim Simpson, David Toms, Kelly Gibson, and Jeff Maggert. **Second Round**-- Waite, at 9-under-par 133, led by two over Tom Kite. **Third Round**-- Kite, at 9-under-par, 204 led by one over Waite.

CUT: 74 players at 2-over-par 144.

PRO-AM: $7,500. Individual-- Jim McGovern, Brett Ogle, 67, $675 each. Team-- Curtis Strange, 53, $750.

WEATHER: Rainy early in the week. Thursday was overcast and cool early. Sunny from Thursday afternoon on, with the exception of a 17-minute delay due to lightning Saturday afternoon.

Winner: Grant Waite   66- 67- 72- 70   275 $234,000.00

Player		Score	Total	Money	Player		Score	Total	Money
Tom Kite	2	70- 65- 69- 72	276	$140,400.00	Trevor Dodds	T38	70- 73- 74- 70	287	$4,940.00
Michael Bradley	T 3	69- 71- 69- 68	277	$75,400.00	John Flannery	T38	75- 69- 70- 73	287	$4,940.00
Scott Hoch	T 3	70- 69- 70- 68	277	$75,400.00	Fred Funk	T38	71- 73- 73- 70	287	$4,940.00
Bob Estes	5	68- 70- 74- 66	278	$52,000.00	Kelly Gibson	T38	67- 70- 74- 76	287	$4,940.00
JC Anderson	6	68- 73- 68- 70	279	$46,800.00	Neal Lancaster	T38	74- 70- 69- 74	287	$4,940.00
Billy Mayfair	T 7	70- 69- 72- 69	280	$40,516.67	Wayne Levi	T38	68- 74- 73- 72	287	$4,940.00
Craig Parry	T 7	71- 69- 71- 69	280	$40,516.67	Dick Mast	T38	73- 68- 74- 72	287	$4,940.00
Lee Janzen	T 7	71- 67- 70- 72	280	$40,516.66	Brett Ogle	T38	70- 71- 70- 76	287	$4,940.00
Tommy Armour	T10	68- 71- 70- 72	281	$31,200.00	Tim Simpson	T38	67- 76- 73- 71	287	$4,940.00
Ed Fiori	T10	67- 73- 70- 71	281	$31,200.00	Ronnie Black	T48	71- 69- 74- 74	288	$3,471.00
Morris Hatalsky	T10	72- 66- 75- 68	281	$31,200.00	Don Pooley	T48	72- 70- 73- 73	288	$3,471.00
John Inman	T10	71- 68- 69- 73	281	$31,200.00	Russell Beiersdorf	T50	71- 71- 71- 76	289	$3,135.60
Mark Carnevale	T14	69- 70- 71- 72	282	$24,050.00	Barry Cheesman	T50	71- 68- 73- 77	289	$3,135.60
Tim Conley	T14	68- 69- 72- 73	282	$24,050.00	Bobby Clampett	T50	70- 72- 77- 70	289	$3,135.60
Bob Gilder	T16	71- 69- 72- 71	283	$21,450.00	Mike Donald	T50	72- 70- 74- 73	289	$3,135.60
Peter Jacobsen	T16	69- 71- 71- 72	283	$21,450.00	John Ross	T50	69- 74- 71- 75	289	$3,135.60
Jay Delsing	T18	69- 71- 68- 76	284	$17,550.00	Billy Andrade	T55	71- 70- 76- 73	290	$2,951.00
Jim Hallet	T18	69- 69- 73- 73	284	$17,550.00	Ed Humenik	T55	72- 71- 74- 73	290	$2,951.00
Jeff Maggert	T18	67- 70- 76- 71	284	$17,550.00	Steve Lowery	T55	70- 73- 77- 70	290	$2,951.00
Howard Twitty	T18	70- 71- 72- 71	284	$17,550.00	Blaine McCallister	T55	74- 68- 78- 70	290	$2,951.00
Dave Barr	T22	69- 72- 74- 70	285	$10,600.91	Mark Calcavecchia	59	73- 69- 74- 75	291	$2,886.00
Frank Conner	T22	69- 74- 69- 73	285	$10,600.91	Ed Dougherty	T60	71- 72- 75- 74	292	$2,821.00
Jeff Cook	T22	74- 65- 73- 73	285	$10,600.91	Brad Faxon	T60	68- 71- 76- 77	292	$2,821.00
David Delong	T22	70- 72- 72- 71	285	$10,600.91	Mike Hulbert	T60	72- 72- 73- 75	292	$2,821.00
Donnie Hammond	T22	70- 72- 73- 70	285	$10,600.91	Len Mattiace	T60	71- 71- 78- 72	292	$2,821.00
David Ogrin	T22	69- 68- 72- 76	285	$10,600.91	Andy Bean	T64	72- 71- 78- 72	293	$2,730.00
Tom Sieckmann	T22	69- 73- 72- 71	285	$10,600.91	Gene Jones	T64	70- 73- 77- 73	293	$2,730.00
Jeff Sluman	T22	72- 69- 72- 72	285	$10,600.91	Mike Sullivan	T64	73- 70- 73- 77	293	$2,730.00
Curtis Strange	T22	71- 70- 73- 71	285	$10,600.91	Marco Dawson	T67	72- 71- 75- 76	294	$2,626.00
David Toms	T22	67- 72- 72- 74	285	$10,600.91	John Elliott	T67	71- 72- 78- 73	294	$2,626.00
Steve Lamontagne	T22	69- 68- 71- 77	285	$10,600.90	Robert Gamez	T67	69- 71- 78- 76	294	$2,626.00
Patrick Burke	T33	71- 73- 71- 71	286	$7,020.00	Tony Sills	T67	68- 76- 74- 76	294	$2,626.00
Rick Dalpos	T33	69- 71- 73- 73	286	$7,020.00	Harry Taylor	T67	72- 70- 76- 76	294	$2,626.00
Jay Haas	T33	71- 68- 75- 72	286	$7,020.00	Joey Sindelar	72	73- 70- 77- 75	295	$2,548.00
Skip Kendall	T33	72- 70- 72- 72	286	$7,020.00	Jay Overton	73	70- 74- 78- 76	298	$2,522.00
Bob Lohr	T33	69- 70- 79- 68	286	$7,020.00	Greg Kraft	74	70- 73- 82- 75	300	$2,496.00
Ian Baker-Finch	T38	73- 71- 73- 70	287	$4,940.00					

SOUTHWESTERN BELL COLONIAL

SOUTHWESTERN BELL
COLONIAL

Colonial CC, Fort Worth, TX **Purse: $1,300,000**
Par: 35-35--70 **Yards: 7,010** **May 27-30, 1993**

LEADERS: First Round-- Dick Mast fired a 6-under-par 64 and led by one over Jeff Maggert and Duffy Waldorf. **Second Round**-- Fulton Allem at 11-under-par 129 led by one over Mast. **Third Round**-- Greg Norman and Allem at 13-under-par 197 led by two over David Edwards and Mast.

CUT: 77 players at 2-over-par 142.

PRO-AM: $7,500. Individual-Craig Stadler, Jeff Maggert, 66,$675. Team-Craig Stadler, 53, $750.

WEATHER: Thursday was beautiful. Friday's round was delayed from 5:24 p.m. to 7:09 p.m. due to severe thunderstorm in the area. Saturday was partly cloudy, as was Sunday.

Winner: Fulton Allem **66- 63- 68- 67** **264** **$234,000.00**

Player	Pos	Scores	Total	Money	Player	Pos	Scores	Total	Money
Greg Norman	2	69- 64- 64- 68	265	$140,400.00	Mark Wiebe	T33	68- 71- 70- 68	277	$6,034.17
Jeff Maggert	3	65- 68- 68- 66	267	$88,400.00	Bruce Fleisher	T33	71- 71- 65- 70	277	$6,034.16
Loren Roberts	T 4	66- 70- 66- 66	268	$57,200.00	Greg Kraft	T33	71- 66- 68- 72	277	$6,034.16
Duffy Waldorf	T 4	65- 69- 69- 65	268	$57,200.00	Kenny Perry	T33	70- 70- 66- 71	277	$6,034.16
David Edwards	T 6	69- 67- 63- 70	269	$43,550.00	Fuzzy Zoeller	T33	69- 68- 70- 70	277	$6,034.16
John Huston	T 6	66- 70- 66- 67	269	$43,550.00	Michael Allen	T45	74- 68- 68- 68	278	$3,578.25
Tom Watson	T 6	69- 64- 71- 65	269	$43,550.00	Clark Dennis	T45	70- 67- 68- 73	278	$3,578.25
Keith Clearwater	T 9	71- 61- 69- 69	270	$36,400.00	Steve Elkington	T45	70- 68- 74- 66	278	$3,578.25
Corey Pavin	T 9	70- 65- 67- 68	270	$36,400.00	Larry Mize	T45	68- 71- 69- 70	278	$3,578.25
Mark Calcavecchia	T11	69- 64- 69- 69	271	$26,650.00	Jodie Mudd	T45	72- 68- 68- 70	278	$3,578.25
Hale Irwin	T11	68- 66- 69- 68	271	$26,650.00	Nick Price	T45	69- 70- 68- 71	278	$3,578.25
Lee Janzen	T11	70- 65- 75- 61	271	$26,650.00	Gene Sauers	T45	68- 69- 69- 72	278	$3,578.25
Tom Lehman	T11	72- 65- 65- 69	271	$26,650.00	Ted Schulz	T45	71- 69- 70- 68	278	$3,578.25
Gil Morgan	T11	67- 69- 69- 66	271	$26,650.00	Russell Beiersdorf	T53	72- 68- 69- 70	279	$2,995.20
D.A. Weibring	T11	66- 68- 68- 69	271	$26,650.00	Brian Claar	T53	69- 68- 71- 71	279	$2,995.20
David Frost	17	68- 66- 71- 67	272	$20,800.00	Brad Fabel	T53	73- 69- 69- 68	279	$2,995.20
Rick Fehr	T18	68- 71- 66- 68	273	$18,850.00	Brad Faxon	T53	69- 73- 68- 69	279	$2,995.20
Wayne Levi	T18	71- 68- 71- 63	273	$18,850.00	Blaine McCallister	T53	70- 70- 69- 70	279	$2,995.20
Mark Brooks	T20	72- 66- 68- 68	274	$16,250.00	Tom Kite	58	72- 66- 71- 71	280	$2,912.00
Russ Cochran	T20	66- 67- 77- 64	274	$16,250.00	Greg Twiggs	T59	72- 69- 69- 71	281	$2,873.00
Dan Forsman	T22	68- 69- 67- 71	275	$12,480.00	Stan Utley	T59	72- 69- 69- 71	281	$2,873.00
Dick Mast	T22	64- 66- 69- 76	275	$12,480.00	Phil Blackmar	T61	68- 74- 72- 68	282	$2,795.00
Billy Mayfair	T22	71- 68- 67- 69	275	$12,480.00	Gary Hallberg	T61	71- 70- 70- 71	282	$2,795.00
Jim Thorpe	T22	73- 68- 67- 67	275	$12,480.00	Jim McGovern	T61	72- 70- 70- 70	282	$2,795.00
Kirk Triplett	T22	71- 68- 67- 69	275	$12,480.00	Steve Pate	T61	67- 72- 76- 67	282	$2,795.00
Fred Funk	T27	70- 71- 71- 64	276	$9,035.00	Dave Barr	T65	68- 72- 73- 70	283	$2,678.00
Bill Glasson	T27	67- 70- 74- 65	276	$9,035.00	Tom Byrum	T65	72- 70- 72- 69	283	$2,678.00
Mike Hulbert	T27	68- 73- 72- 63	276	$9,035.00	Ed Dougherty	T65	75- 67- 71- 70	283	$2,678.00
Massy Kuramoto	T27	73- 67- 65- 71	276	$9,035.00	Davis Love III	T65	72- 70- 72- 69	283	$2,678.00
Craig Parry	T27	69- 69- 70- 68	276	$9,035.00	Brett Ogle	T65	70- 71- 70- 72	283	$2,678.00
Craig Stadler	T27	69- 68- 70- 69	276	$9,035.00	Wayne Grady	70	73- 69- 69- 73	284	$2,600.00
Ian Baker-Finch	T33	74- 67- 68- 68	277	$6,034.17	Steve Lowery	T71	73- 68- 70- 75	286	$2,561.00
Jay Don Blake	T33	71- 71- 69- 66	277	$6,034.17	Mark O'Meara	T71	69- 71- 73- 73	286	$2,561.00
Bill Britton	T33	70- 66- 72- 69	277	$6,034.17	Justin Leonard	T71	73- 69- 72- 72	286	AMATEUR
Ben Crenshaw	T33	72- 69- 68- 68	277	$6,034.17	Jim Gallagher, Jr.	74	71- 68- 73- 75	287	$2,522.00
Dudley Hart	T33	71- 69- 71- 66	277	$6,034.17	Tad Rhyan	75	70- 71- 72- 75	288	$2,496.00
Bruce Lietzke	T33	69- 72- 70- 66	277	$6,034.17	Mark Hayes	76	69- 72- 72- 77	290	$2,470.00
Roger Maltbie	T33	68- 68- 73- 68	277	$6,034.17					

THE MEMORIAL TOURNAMENT

Muirfield Village GC, Dublin, OH
Par:36-36--72   **Yards: 7,104**

Purse: $1,400,000
June 3-6, 1993

LEADERS: First Round--Davis Love III and Donnie Hammond, each with 6-under-par 66s, led by one over eight players. **Second Round**--Payne Stewart and Fred Couples, each at 9-under-par 135, led by one over Greg Norman. **Third Round**--Stewart, at 14-under-par 202, led by three over Paul Azinger and four over Love and Jim McGovern.

CUT: A total of 73 players at 1-over-par 145.

WEATHER: Cool and cloudy Thursday with some drizzle. Friday's round was suspended from 12:58 p.m to 4:30 p.m. due to lightning and heavy rains. Play was finally suspended for the day at 8:38 p.m. due to darkness with 18 players remaining on the course. The second round was completed Saturday morning beginning at 7:30 a.m. with the third round beginning at 10:05 a.m. It was cool and windy Saturday and absolutely beautiful on Sunday.

Winner: Paul Azinger   68- 69- 68- 69   274 $252,000.00

Player	Pos	Rounds	Total	Money
Corey Pavin	2	69- 70- 69- 67	275	$151,200.00
Payne Stewart	3	69- 66- 67- 74	276	$95,200.00
Fred Couples	T 4	67- 68- 73- 69	277	$50,750.00
Brad Faxon	T 4	69- 69- 70- 69	277	$50,750.00
Jay Haas	T 4	67- 70- 72- 68	277	$50,750.00
Jim McGovern	T 4	67- 71- 69- 70	277	$50,750.00
Greg Norman	T 4	68- 68- 74- 67	277	$50,750.00
Jumbo Ozaki	T 4	67- 70- 73- 67	277	$50,750.00
Bill Glasson	T10	69- 69- 68- 72	278	$36,400.00
Davis Love III	T10	66- 72- 69- 71	278	$36,400.00
Michael Allen	T12	70- 72- 70- 68	280	$28,350.00
John Cook	T12	67- 73- 71- 69	280	$28,350.00
Wayne Levi	T12	68- 69- 72- 71	280	$28,350.00
Jeff Maggert	T12	73- 72- 68- 67	280	$28,350.00
Dudley Hart	T16	67- 71- 70- 73	281	$22,400.00
Vijay Singh	T16	71- 69- 68- 73	281	$22,400.00
Fuzzy Zoeller	T16	71- 69- 73- 68	281	$22,400.00
Ben Crenshaw	T19	70- 69- 71- 72	282	$18,200.00
Kenny Perry	T19	67- 74- 69- 72	282	$18,200.00
Greg Twiggs	T19	70- 69- 71- 72	282	$18,200.00
Donnie Hammond	T22	66- 76- 69- 72	283	$14,560.00
Phil Mickelson	T22	73- 70- 72- 68	283	$14,560.00
D.A. Weibring	T22	72- 70- 72- 69	283	$14,560.00
David Frost	T25	75- 69- 71- 69	284	$10,920.00
Scott Hoch	T25	71- 70- 73- 70	284	$10,920.00
Joey Sindelar	T25	70- 72- 73- 69	284	$10,920.00
Bobby Wadkins	T25	68- 72- 72- 72	284	$10,920.00
Mark Wiebe	T25	69- 71- 73- 71	284	$10,920.00
Phil Blackmar	T30	69- 74- 72- 70	285	$8,890.00
Brian Claar	T30	70- 69- 74- 72	285	$8,890.00
Rocco Mediate	T30	69- 71- 73- 72	285	$8,890.00
Grant Waite	T30	69- 72- 74- 70	285	$8,890.00
Chip Beck	T34	71- 73- 74- 68	286	$7,070.00
Keith Clearwater	T34	70- 73- 72- 71	286	$7,070.00
Mike Hulbert	T34	69- 72- 74- 71	286	$7,070.00
Peter Jacobsen	T34	72- 70- 71- 73	286	$7,070.00
Steve Pate	T34	70- 72- 74- 70	286	$7,070.00
Loren Roberts	T34	72- 69- 74- 71	286	$7,070.00
Billy Andrade	T40	71- 72- 72- 72	287	$5,040.00
Ian Baker-Finch	T40	75- 69- 72- 71	287	$5,040.00
Russ Cochran	T40	70- 74- 72- 71	287	$5,040.00
Brad Fabel	T40	70- 71- 73- 73	287	$5,040.00
Dillard Pruitt	T40	70- 74- 72- 71	287	$5,040.00
Ted Schulz	T40	70- 71- 77- 69	287	$5,040.00
Craig Stadler	T40	73- 72- 73- 69	287	$5,040.00
Mike Standly	T40	69- 72- 74- 72	287	$5,040.00
John Huston	T48	70- 73- 73- 72	288	$3,738.00
Dave Rummells	T48	68- 73- 77- 70	288	$3,738.00
Michael Bradley	T50	72- 66- 76- 75	289	$3,328.00
David Edwards	T50	69- 75- 74- 71	289	$3,328.00
Bob Estes	T50	72- 71- 73- 73	289	$3,328.00
Lee Janzen	T50	72- 69- 78- 70	289	$3,328.00
John Mahaffey	T50	71- 74- 69- 75	289	$3,328.00
Tommy Nakajima	T50	70- 73- 74- 72	289	$3,328.00
Joe Ozaki	T50	67- 73- 76- 73	289	$3,328.00
Gary Hallberg	T57	70- 72- 73- 75	290	$3,136.00
Scott Simpson	T57	75- 70- 74- 71	290	$3,136.00
Curtis Strange	T57	72- 72- 76- 70	290	$3,136.00
Mark McCumber	T60	73- 72- 75- 71	291	$3,066.00
Larry Nelson	T60	71- 74- 72- 74	291	$3,066.00
Lanny Wadkins	62	73- 72- 73- 74	292	$3,024.00
Dave Barr	T63	68- 73- 73- 79	293	$2,982.00
Jay Don Blake	T63	71- 74- 76- 72	293	$2,982.00
Dan Forsman	65	72- 71- 77- 74	294	$2,940.00
Robert Gamez	T66	70- 72- 76- 77	295	$2,884.00
Gil Morgan	T66	72- 73- 75- 75	295	$2,884.00
Mark O'Meara	T66	70- 71- 77- 77	295	$2,884.00
David Peoples	69	70- 75- 76- 75	296	$2,828.00
John Daly	T70	70- 70- 79- 78	297	$2,786.00
Don Pooley	T70	74- 71- 78- 74	297	$2,786.00
Jack Nicklaus	72	70- 75- 81- 72	298	$2,744.00
Andrew Magee	73	72- 73- 81- 74	300	$2,716.00

BUICK CLASSIC

Westchester CC, Harrison, NY   **Purse: $1,000,000**
Par: 36-35--71   **Yards: 6,779**   **June 10-13, 1993**

LEADERS: First Round--Dudley Hart, at 5-under-par 66, held a one-stroke lead over Brandel Chamblee. **Second Round--**Tom Kite, Jeff Maggert and Duffy Waldorf, all at 3-under-par 139, led Vijay Singh by one shot. **Third Round--**Waldorf and Lee Janzen, both a 4-under-par 209, were three strokes ahead of Ian Baker-Finch and Loren Roberts.

CUT: 71 players at 5-over-par 147.

PRO-AM: Afternoon play cancelled due to rain, lighting and severe weather in the area. $7,500. Morning Individual--Loren Roberts, 66, $450. Morning Team--Corey Pavin, 55, $450. Afternoon--All players received equal shares of $144.23

WEATHER: Sunny and mild all four days, with strong and swirling winds Thursday and Friday. Winds diminishing Saturday and minimal Sunday.

Winner: Vijay Singh   72- 68- 74- 66   280 $180,000.00
(won playoff with birdie on third extra hole)

Mark Wiebe	2	72- 75- 67- 66	280	$108,000.00	Bob Tway	T34	68- 74- 72- 76	290	$5,275.00
David Frost	T 3	70- 72- 73- 66	281	$58,000.00	Brad Fabel	T38	72- 74- 73- 72	291	$4,200.00
Lee Janzen	T 3	69- 72- 68- 72	281	$58,000.00	Dudley Hart	T38	66- 77- 72- 76	291	$4,200.00
Tom Lehman	T 5	74- 69- 70- 69	282	$38,000.00	P.H. Horgan III	T38	74- 73- 71- 73	291	$4,200.00
Mike Smith	T 5	72- 73- 69- 68	282	$38,000.00	Jeff Maggert	T38	71- 68- 74- 78	291	$4,200.00
Chip Beck	T 7	71- 72- 74- 66	283	$31,166.67	Mark McCumber	T38	73- 73- 71- 74	291	$4,200.00
Payne Stewart	T 7	74- 72- 68- 69	283	$31,166.67	Ted Schulz	T38	76- 71- 73- 71	291	$4,200.00
Bob Gilder	T 7	72- 72- 69- 70	283	$31,166.66	Trevor Dodds	T44	74- 70- 71- 77	292	$2,890.00
Fred Funk	T10	69- 75- 71- 69	284	$25,000.00	Mike Donald	T44	75- 69- 71- 77	292	$2,890.00
Tom Kite	T10	68- 71- 75- 70	284	$25,000.00	Bruce Fleisher	T44	73- 72- 70- 77	292	$2,890.00
Duffy Waldorf	T10	69- 70- 70- 75	284	$25,000.00	Robin Freeman	T44	72- 74- 71- 75	292	$2,890.00
Brad Faxon	T13	69- 77- 71- 68	285	$19,333.34	Skip Kendall	T44	73- 72- 72- 75	292	$2,890.00
Ian Baker-Finch	T13	71- 72- 69- 73	285	$19,333.33	Colin Montgomerie	T44	76- 71- 72- 73	292	$2,890.00
Paul Goydos	T13	73- 73- 68- 71	285	$19,333.33	Peter Persons	T44	74- 70- 75- 73	292	$2,890.00
Phil Blackmar	T16	75- 71- 67- 73	286	$14,500.00	Hal Sutton	T44	75- 70- 74- 73	292	$2,890.00
Fred Couples	T16	72- 69- 72- 73	286	$14,500.00	Michael Allen	T52	73- 74- 71- 75	293	$2,360.00
Steve Lamontagne	T16	74- 73- 71- 68	286	$14,500.00	Massy Kuramoto	T52	70- 76- 70- 77	293	$2,360.00
Andy North	T16	74- 70- 72- 70	286	$14,500.00	Jim McGovern	T52	76- 71- 73- 73	293	$2,360.00
Loren Roberts	T16	72- 69- 71- 74	286	$14,500.00	Brian Claar	T55	75- 72- 72- 75	294	$2,260.00
Doug Tewell	T16	74- 71- 69- 72	286	$14,500.00	Marco Dawson	T55	71- 74- 73- 76	294	$2,260.00
Dave Barr	T22	77- 67- 72- 71	287	$10,000.00	John Flannery	T55	73- 72- 77- 72	294	$2,260.00
Bill Britton	T22	73- 74- 71- 69	287	$10,000.00	Bill Murchison	T55	74- 73- 77- 70	294	$2,260.00
Willie Wood	T22	72- 71- 72- 72	287	$10,000.00	Scott Simpson	T55	74- 73- 76- 71	294	$2,260.00
Jeff Woodland	T22	73- 71- 70- 73	287	$10,000.00	Barry Cheesman	T60	73- 73- 74- 75	295	$2,180.00
Steve Elkington	T26	75- 72- 67- 74	288	$7,400.00	Len Mattiace	T60	75- 72- 75- 73	295	$2,180.00
Rocco Mediate	T26	77- 69- 73- 69	288	$7,400.00	Jeff Sluman	T60	73- 72- 71- 79	295	$2,180.00
Corey Pavin	T26	73- 74- 72- 69	288	$7,400.00	Patrick Burke	T63	71- 74- 79- 73	297	$2,100.00
Larry Rinker	T26	72- 74- 70- 72	288	$7,400.00	Jay Delsing	T63	70- 74- 76- 77	297	$2,100.00
Mike Standly	T26	74- 70- 72- 72	288	$7,400.00	Jay Haas	T63	70- 75- 70- 82	297	$2,100.00
Lennie Clements	T31	74- 73- 72- 70	289	$6,200.00	Brian Kamm	T63	75- 68- 80- 74	297	$2,100.00
Mike Hulbert	T31	74- 73- 69- 73	289	$6,200.00	Mark Mielke	T63	73- 73- 73- 78	297	$2,100.00
David Ogrin	T31	75- 69- 72- 73	289	$6,200.00	Roger Maltbie	68	75- 72- 77- 74	298	$2,040.00
Mark Brooks	T34	76- 67- 73- 74	290	$5,275.00	Wayne Levi	69	71- 74- 78- 78	301	$2,020.00
Brandel Chamblee	T34	67- 74- 76- 73	290	$5,275.00	Greg Cesario	70	73- 74- 77- 83	307	$2,000.00
Morris Hatalsky	T34	75- 71- 73- 71	290	$5,275.00	Dennis Trixler	71	73- 74- 79- 82	308	$1,980.00

U.S. OPEN

Baltusrol GC, Springfield, NJ **Purse: $1,600,000**
Par: 34-36--70   **Yards: 7,152** **June 17-20, 1993**

LEADERS: First Round--Scott Hoch, Craig Parry and Joey Sindelar, all at 4-under-par 66, held a one-stroke lead over Lee Janzen and Craig Stadler. **Second Round--**Janzen, at 6-under-par 134 tying the U.S. Open 36-hole record, had a two-shot lead over Tom Watson and Payne Stewart. **Third Round--**Janzen, at 7-under-par 203 (again tying a U.S. Open mark), was one stroke ahead of Stewart.

CUT: 88 players (87 professionals and one amateur) at 4-over-par 144. Cut was low 60 and ties and anyone within 10 strokes of the lead.

WEATHER: Sunny, hot and humid Thursday and Friday. Similar conditions early Saturday, clouding up mid-afternoon with severe weather watch in effect, but no rain until after conclusion of play. Somewhat cooler but still humid Sunday with high overcast.

Winner: Lee Janzen   67- 67- 69- 69   272 $290,000.00

Payne Stewart	2	70- 66- 68- 70	274	$145,000.00
Paul Azinger	T 3	71- 68- 69- 69	277	$78,556.50
Craig Parry	T 3	66- 74- 69- 68	277	$78,556.50
Scott Hoch	T 5	66- 72- 72- 68	278	$48,730.00
Tom Watson	T 5	70- 66- 73- 69	278	$48,730.00
Ernie Els	T 7	71- 73- 68- 67	279	$35,481.25
Ray Floyd	T 7	68- 73- 70- 68	279	$35,481.25
Fred Funk	T 7	70- 72- 67- 70	279	$35,481.25
Nolan Henke	T 7	72- 71- 67- 69	279	$35,481.25
John Adams	T11	70- 70- 69- 71	280	$26,249.20
David Edwards	T11	70- 72- 66- 72	280	$26,249.20
Nick Price	T11	71- 66- 70- 73	280	$26,249.20
Loren Roberts	T11	70- 70- 71- 69	280	$26,249.20
Jeff Sluman	T11	71- 71- 69- 69	280	$26,249.20
Barry Lane	T16	74- 68- 70- 69	281	$21,576.67
Mike Standly	T16	70- 69- 70- 72	281	$21,576.67
Fred Couples	T16	68- 71- 71- 71	281	$21,576.66
Ian Baker-Finch	T19	70- 70- 70- 72	282	$18,071.67
Dan Forsman	T19	73- 71- 70- 68	282	$18,071.67
Tom Lehman	T19	71- 70- 71- 70	282	$18,071.67
Corey Pavin	T19	68- 69- 75- 70	282	$18,071.67
Blaine McCallister	T19	68- 73- 73- 68	282	$18,071.66
Steve Pate	T19	70- 71- 71- 70	282	$18,071.66
Chip Beck	T25	72- 68- 72- 71	283	$14,531.50
Mark Calcavecchia	T25	70- 70- 71- 72	283	$14,531.50
John Cook	T25	75- 66- 70- 72	283	$14,531.50
Wayne Levi	T25	71- 69- 69- 74	283	$14,531.50
Rocco Mediate	T25	68- 72- 73- 70	283	$14,531.50
Joe Ozaki	T25	70- 70- 74- 69	283	$14,531.50
Kenny Perry	T25	74- 70- 68- 71	283	$14,531.50
Curtis Strange	T25	73- 68- 75- 67	283	$14,531.50
Robert Allenby	T33	74- 69- 69- 72	284	$11,051.85
John Daly	T33	72- 68- 72- 72	284	$11,051.85
Mike Donald	T33	71- 72- 67- 74	284	$11,051.85
Steve Elkington	T33	71- 70- 69- 74	284	$11,051.85
Davis Love III	T33	70- 74- 68- 72	284	$11,051.85
Steve Lowery	T33	72- 71- 75- 66	284	$11,051.85
Craig Stadler	T33	67- 74- 71- 72	284	$11,051.85
Greg Twiggs	T33	72- 72- 70- 70	284	$11,051.85
Billy Andrade	T33	72- 67- 74- 71	284	$11,051.84
Bob Gilder	T33	70- 69- 75- 70	284	$11,051.84
Colin Montgomerie	T33	71- 72- 73- 68	284	$11,051.84
Jumbo Ozaki	T33	71- 71- 72- 70	284	$11,051.84
Lee Rinker	T33	70- 72- 71- 71	284	$11,051.84
Rick Fehr	T46	71- 72- 70- 72	285	$8,179.17
Mark McCumber	T46	70- 71- 73- 71	285	$8,179.17
Larry Nelson	T46	70- 71- 71- 73	285	$8,179.17
Scott Simpson	T46	70- 73- 72- 70	285	$8,179.17
Mark Brooks	T46	72- 68- 74- 71	285	$8,179.16
Brian Claar	T46	71- 70- 72- 72	285	$8,179.16
Fulton Allem	T52	71- 70- 74- 71	286	$6,525.60
Michael Christie	T52	70- 74- 71- 71	286	$6,525.60
Keith Clearwater	T52	71- 72- 71- 72	286	$6,525.60
Bob Estes	T52	71- 73- 69- 73	286	$6,525.60
Vance Heafner	T52	70- 72- 73- 71	286	$6,525.60
Edward Kirby	T52	72- 71- 72- 71	286	$6,525.60
Sandy Lyle	T52	70- 74- 70- 72	286	$6,525.60
Jeff Maggert	T52	69- 70- 73- 74	286	$6,525.60
Kirk Triplett	T52	70- 72- 75- 69	286	$6,525.60
Ian Woosnam	T52	70- 74- 72- 70	286	$6,525.60
Jay Don Blake	T62	72- 70- 71- 74	287	$5,940.50
Joel Edwards	T62	71- 73- 70- 73	287	$5,940.50
Mike Hulbert	T62	71- 73- 72- 71	287	$5,940.50
Hale Irwin	T62	73- 71- 71- 72	287	$5,940.50
Arden Knoll	T62	71- 70- 73- 73	287	$5,940.50
Mike Smith	T62	68- 72- 74- 73	287	$5,940.50
Brad Faxon	T68	72- 71- 70- 75	288	$5,657.00
Steve Gotsche	T68	70- 73- 71- 74	288	$5,657.00
Fuzzy Zoeller	T68	73- 67- 78- 70	288	$5,657.00
Justin Leonard	T68	69- 71- 73- 75	288	AMATEUR
Nick Faldo	T72	70- 74- 73- 72	289	$5,405.00
Peter Jordan	T72	71- 70- 73- 75	289	$5,405.00
Jack Nicklaus	T72	70- 72- 76- 71	289	$5,405.00
Grant Waite	T72	69- 73- 74- 73	289	$5,405.00
Duffy Waldorf	T72	71- 72- 71- 75	289	$5,405.00
Jay Haas	T77	71- 69- 75- 75	290	$5,121.50
Tony Johnstone	T77	71- 72- 74- 73	290	$5,121.50
Barney Thompson	T77	71- 73- 71- 75	290	$5,121.50
Mark Wiebe	T77	71- 72- 77- 70	290	$5,121.50
Wayne Grady	T81	69- 75- 70- 77	291	$4,932.50
Ted Schulz	T81	71- 73- 69- 78	291	$4,932.50
Steve Stricker	83	72- 72- 76- 72	292	$4,838.00
Stephen Flesch	84	71- 70- 78- 75	294	$4,775.00
John Flannery	T85	73- 69- 75- 78	295	$4,680.50
Doug Weaver	T85	70- 73- 77- 75	295	$4,680.50
Robert Wrenn	87	68- 73- 80- 76	297	$4,586.00
Robert Gamez	88	72- 70- 78- 78	298	$4,523.00

CANON GREATER HARTFORD OPEN

TPC at River Highlands, Cromwell, CT
Par: 35-35--70   **Yards: 6,820**

Purse: $1,000,000
June 24-27, 1993

LEADERS: First Round--Roger Maltbie and Craig Stadler, at 5-under-par 65, were a stroke in front of Keith Clearwater, Dan Forsman and John Huston. **Second Round--**Corey Pavin, at 8-under-par 132, held a two-shot lead over Clearwater and Mike Springer. **Third Round--**Pavin, at 5-under-par 205, was a stroke ahead of Don Pooley and Nick Price.

CUT: 80 players at 4-over-par 144.

PRO-AM: $7,500. Individual--John Cook, 65, $750. Team--Steve Pate, 54, $750.

WEATHER: Ideal playing conditions Thursday. Continued sunny and warm Friday, with strong afternoon winds. Winds continuing through Saturday along with sunny, hot and humid weather. Early morning rain Saturday resulted in 29-minute suspension of play due to wet grounds. Gradually clearing skies led to sunny, warm and virtually windless conditions most of the afternoon.

Winner: Nick Price   67- 70- 69- 65   271 $180,000.00

Dan Forsman	T 2	66- 69- 72- 65	272	$88,000.00	Greg Kraft	T38	72- 67- 72- 72	283	$3,800.00
Roger Maltbie	T 2	65- 71- 71- 65	272	$88,000.00	David Ogrin	T38	72- 71- 72- 68	283	$3,800.00
Corey Pavin	4	67- 65- 73- 69	274	$48,000.00	Jay Overton	T38	70- 69- 73- 71	283	$3,800.00
Kenny Perry	T 5	68- 69- 70- 68	275	$38,000.00	John Ross	T38	74- 67- 71- 71	283	$3,800.00
Mike Springer	T 5	69- 65- 73- 68	275	$38,000.00	Harry Taylor	T38	71- 73- 68- 71	283	$3,800.00
John Cook	T 7	73- 68- 71- 65	277	$30,125.00	Doug Tewell	T38	71- 70- 71- 71	283	$3,800.00
Brian Kamm	T 7	69- 75- 69- 64	277	$30,125.00	Dave Barr	T48	72- 71- 69- 72	284	$2,620.00
Rocco Mediate	T 7	68- 70- 72- 67	277	$30,125.00	Bob Gilder	T48	68- 72- 72- 72	284	$2,620.00
Don Pooley	T 7	70- 70- 66- 71	277	$30,125.00	Ed Humenik	T48	71- 69- 76- 68	284	$2,620.00
Frank Conner	T11	71- 70- 68- 69	278	$21,200.00	Tom Byrum	T51	71- 71- 68- 75	285	$2,340.00
Bruce Fleisher	T11	71- 65- 73- 69	278	$21,200.00	Trevor Dodds	T51	72- 70- 70- 73	285	$2,340.00
Scott Gump	T11	73- 67- 69- 69	278	$21,200.00	Paul Goydos	T51	70- 71- 76- 68	285	$2,340.00
John Huston	T11	66- 69- 72- 71	278	$21,200.00	Mike Hulbert	T51	69- 69- 77- 70	285	$2,340.00
Davis Love III	T11	72- 70- 68- 68	278	$21,200.00	Peter Persons	T51	71- 72- 72- 70	285	$2,340.00
Keith Clearwater	T16	66- 68- 73- 72	279	$15,500.00	Gene Sauers	T51	69- 71- 73- 72	285	$2,340.00
Brad Faxon	T16	67- 71- 75- 66	279	$15,500.00	Joey Sindelar	T51	67- 73- 72- 73	285	$2,340.00
Steve Lowery	T16	67- 68- 72- 72	279	$15,500.00	Carl Cooper	T58	70- 74- 72- 70	286	$2,190.00
Dave Peege	T16	71- 70- 72- 66	279	$15,500.00	Ed Fiori	T58	67- 73- 76- 70	286	$2,190.00
Patrick Burke	T20	68- 72- 72- 68	280	$10,833.34	Bill Glasson	T58	70- 73- 70- 73	286	$2,190.00
Hubert Green	T20	70- 70- 72- 68	280	$10,833.34	Billy Mayfair	T58	71- 70- 72- 73	286	$2,190.00
Fulton Allem	T20	70- 66- 74- 70	280	$10,833.33	Jim McGovern	T58	71- 73- 72- 70	286	$2,190.00
Jeff Sluman	T20	74- 68- 69- 69	280	$10,833.33	Willie Wood	T58	71- 72- 72- 71	286	$2,190.00
Lance Ten Broeck	T20	69- 68- 74- 69	280	$10,833.33	Marco Dawson	T64	72- 67- 74- 75	288	$2,090.00
Chris Tucker	T20	70- 72- 68- 70	280	$10,833.33	John Inman	T64	73- 71- 75- 69	288	$2,090.00
Dudley Hart	T26	71- 70- 71- 69	281	$7,550.00	David Jackson	T64	72- 72- 75- 69	288	$2,090.00
Bill Kratzert	T26	71- 67- 73- 70	281	$7,550.00	Jimmy Johnston	T64	71- 72- 74- 71	288	$2,090.00
Bob Lohr	T26	67- 73- 70- 71	281	$7,550.00	Barry Cheesman	T68	71- 72- 72- 74	289	$2,000.00
Kirk Triplett	T26	68- 69- 72- 72	281	$7,550.00	Donnie Hammond	T68	72- 70- 76- 71	289	$2,000.00
Brad Bryant	T30	70- 72- 69- 71	282	$5,812.50	Steve Lamontagne	T68	68- 70- 77- 74	289	$2,000.00
Mark Calcavecchia	T30	67- 71- 70- 74	282	$5,812.50	Dennis Trixler	T68	70- 74- 72- 73	289	$2,000.00
P.H. Horgan III	T30	72- 71- 68- 71	282	$5,812.50	Bobby Wadkins	T68	70- 74- 72- 73	289	$2,000.00
Craig Stadler	T30	65- 71- 76- 70	282	$5,812.50	Marty Schiene	73	69- 75- 74- 72	290	$1,940.00
Ted Tryba	T30	75- 69- 67- 71	282	$5,812.50	Michael Bradley	T74	73- 70- 76- 72	291	$1,900.00
Howard Twitty	T30	73- 66- 74- 69	282	$5,812.50	Mike Donald	T74	71- 70- 75- 75	291	$1,900.00
Jeff Woodland	T30	71- 71- 71- 69	282	$5,812.50	Mike Standly	T74	76- 68- 77- 70	291	$1,900.00
Bruce Zabriski	T30	74- 69- 72- 67	282	$5,812.50	Denis Watson	77	72- 70- 77- 74	293	$1,860.00
Brian Claar	T38	71- 69- 74- 69	283	$3,800.00	Michael Allen	T78	72- 71- 74- 77	294	$1,830.00
David Duval	T38	70- 72- 73- 68	283	$3,800.00	Lon Hinkle	T78	73- 70- 79- 72	294	$1,830.00
Kelly Gibson	T38	71- 70- 75- 67	283	$3,800.00	John Adams	80	77- 66- 77- 78	298	$1,800.00
Jay Haas	T38	70- 72- 71- 70	283	$3,800.00					

SPRINT WESTERN OPEN

Cog Hill G&CC (Dubsdread Course), Lemont, IL   Purse: $1,200,000
Par: 36-36--72   Yards: 7,073   July 1-4, 1993

LEADERS: First Round--Nick Price fired an 8-under-par 64 and led by one stroke over Mark Wiebe. **Second Round--**Price, at 9-under-par 135, led by two over Curtis Strange, Mike Hulbert, Greg Norman and John Huston. **Third Round--**Price at 14-under-par 202, led by two over Norman.

CUT: 82 pros and one amateur at even-par 144.

PRO-AM: Due to rainy conditions the pro-am was divided into two nine-hole events. Front Side Individual--Greg Norman 31, $450. Front Side Team--Joey Sindelar, 26, $450. Back Side Individual--Rick Fehr, 31, $450. Back Side Team--Mark Calcavecchia, Andrew Magee, Fred Funk, 28, $412.50 each.

WEATHER: Thursday was overcast but no delays. Friday's round was delayed from 2:00 p.m. to 5:30 p.m. due to lightning. The round was suspended at 8:22 p.m. due to darkness. The round was completed on Saturday morning with the third round starting at 10:38. Saturday was hot and humid as was Sunday.

Winner: Nick Price   64- 71- 67- 67   269 $216,000.00

Player	Pos	Scores	Total	Money
Greg Norman	2	69- 68- 67- 70	274	$129,600.00
Bob Lohr	3	72- 69- 67- 69	277	$81,600.00
John Adams	T 4	72- 71- 63- 72	278	$49,600.00
Brian Henninger	T 4	71- 73- 66- 68	278	$49,600.00
Mark Wiebe	T 4	65- 73- 71- 69	278	$49,600.00
Michael Allen	T 7	71- 68- 70- 70	279	$33,700.00
Rick Fehr	T 7	71- 68- 71- 69	279	$33,700.00
Dan Forsman	T 7	67- 73- 69- 70	279	$33,700.00
P.H. Horgan III	T 7	69- 74- 68- 68	279	$33,700.00
Curtis Strange	T 7	69- 68- 69- 73	279	$33,700.00
Doug Tewell	T 7	70- 69- 68- 72	279	$33,700.00
Mark Brooks	T13	69- 71- 69- 71	280	$21,200.00
Dudley Hart	T13	73- 66- 69- 72	280	$21,200.00
John Huston	T13	70- 67- 74- 69	280	$21,200.00
Larry Nelson	T13	70- 70- 67- 73	280	$21,200.00
Dillard Pruitt	T13	75- 69- 66- 70	280	$21,200.00
D.A. Weibring	T13	68- 75- 70- 67	280	$21,200.00
Chip Beck	T19	69- 71- 68- 73	281	$14,040.00
Keith Clearwater	T19	67- 71- 71- 72	281	$14,040.00
Russ Cochran	T19	67- 75- 69- 70	281	$14,040.00
Bruce Fleisher	T19	74- 67- 69- 71	281	$14,040.00
Loren Roberts	T19	70- 69- 69- 73	281	$14,040.00
Lance Ten Broeck	T19	71- 68- 72- 70	281	$14,040.00
Fred Couples	T25	68- 72- 70- 73	283	$9,570.00
Mike Hulbert	T25	67- 70- 72- 74	283	$9,570.00
Mark Lye	T25	72- 71- 70- 70	283	$9,570.00
Mark McCumber	T25	69- 71- 70- 73	283	$9,570.00
Justin Leonard	T25	70- 71- 69- 73	283	AMATEUR
Tom Byrum	T30	72- 72- 71- 69	284	$7,465.72
Ted Schulz	T30	71- 72- 71- 70	284	$7,465.72
Jeff Sluman	T30	73- 68- 74- 69	284	$7,465.72
David Duval	T30	72- 70- 69- 73	284	$7,465.71
Jaime Gomez	T30	71- 72- 69- 72	284	$7,465.71
Greg Kraft	T30	68- 72- 68- 76	284	$7,465.71
Tom Sieckmann	T30	69- 72- 69- 74	284	$7,465.71
Trevor Dodds	T37	72- 69- 72- 72	285	$5,530.00
John Flannery	T37	72- 69- 72- 72	285	$5,530.00
Brian Kamm	T37	67- 71- 73- 74	285	$5,530.00
Steve Lamontagne	T37	70- 72- 69- 74	285	$5,530.00
Dan Pohl	T37	69- 70- 73- 73	285	$5,530.00
Don Pooley	T37	70- 69- 70- 76	285	$5,530.00
JC Anderson	T43	72- 70- 72- 72	286	$3,966.86
Russell Beiersdorf	T43	67- 72- 76- 71	286	$3,966.86
Tim Conley	T43	71- 71- 71- 73	286	$3,966.86
Robin Freeman	T43	72- 72- 71- 71	286	$3,966.86
Howard Twitty	T43	71- 70- 74- 71	286	$3,966.86
Paul Goydos	T43	70- 72- 70- 74	286	$3,966.85
Andrew Magee	T43	68- 75- 69- 74	286	$3,966.85
Jeff Cook	T50	71- 73- 70- 73	287	$2,866.67
John Elliott	T50	70- 73- 75- 69	287	$2,866.67
Kelly Gibson	T50	69- 74- 73- 71	287	$2,866.67
Ed Humenik	T50	70- 74- 71- 72	287	$2,866.67
Hale Irwin	T50	72- 71- 74- 70	287	$2,866.67
Dennis Trixler	T50	74- 70- 74- 69	287	$2,866.67
Phil Blackmar	T50	71- 72- 69- 75	287	$2,866.66
Mark Carnevale	T50	70- 71- 70- 76	287	$2,866.66
Grant Waite	T50	68- 71- 72- 76	287	$2,866.66
Mark Calcavecchia	T59	70- 73- 71- 74	288	$2,640.00
Scott Hoch	T59	71- 68- 76- 73	288	$2,640.00
Tim Simpson	T59	73- 67- 72- 76	288	$2,640.00
Mike Springer	T59	72- 69- 73- 74	288	$2,640.00
Duffy Waldorf	T59	71- 71- 71- 75	288	$2,640.00
Barry Cheesman	T64	70- 74- 71- 74	289	$2,532.00
Joel Edwards	T64	72- 71- 72- 74	289	$2,532.00
Greg Twiggs	T64	75- 69- 73- 72	289	$2,532.00
Richard Zokol	T64	72- 70- 70- 77	289	$2,532.00
Brian Claar	T68	72- 71- 71- 76	290	$2,436.00
Ben Crenshaw	T68	74- 69- 75- 72	290	$2,436.00
Nolan Henke	T68	71- 70- 76- 73	290	$2,436.00
Willie Wood	T68	73- 68- 74- 75	290	$2,436.00
Robert Gamez	T72	69- 75- 76- 71	291	$2,352.00
Skip Kendall	T72	72- 72- 75- 72	291	$2,352.00
David Ogrin	T72	71- 71- 72- 77	291	$2,352.00
Marco Dawson	T75	73- 70- 72- 77	292	$2,268.00
Fred Funk	T75	71- 72- 75- 74	292	$2,268.00
Yoshinori Kaneko	T75	68- 73- 79- 72	292	$2,268.00
Billy Mayfair	T75	73- 71- 72- 76	292	$2,268.00
Dan Halldorson	79	70- 74- 76- 73	293	$2,208.00
Ed Fiori	T80	71- 71- 76- 76	294	$2,172.00
Mike Schuchart	T80	71- 73- 77- 73	294	$2,172.00
Eddie Pearce	82	74- 70- 77- 77	298	$2,136.00

ANHEUSER-BUSCH GOLF CLASSIC

Kingsmill GC, Williamsburg, VA
Par: 36-35--71   Yards: 6,797

Purse: $1,100,000
July 8-11, 1993

LEADERS: First Round--John Flannery, Trevor Dodds and Jim Gallagher, Jr., at 5-under-par 66, led by one over Brandel Chamblee, Curtis Strange, Morris Hatalsky, Lanny Wadkins, Keith Clearwater, Dave Rummells, Kirk Triplett and Richard Zokol. **Second Round--**Ted Tryba and John Adams, at 9-under-par 133, led by one over Tom Byrum, Blaine McCallister, Mark McCumber, John Cook and Gallagher. **Third Round--**Dillard Pruitt, at 13-under-par 200, led by one over John Adams.

CUT: 82 players at even-par 142.

PRO-AM: Due to an afternoon thunderstorm the afternoon portion of the pro-am was divided into two sections, with the morning group making up the other section. Morning Individual--Davis Love III, Fred Funk, Fuzzy Zoeller, 66, $1,100. Morning Team--Mark McCumber, Blaine McCallister, $1,150. Afternoon Front Nine Individual--Dillard Pruitt, 31, $1,000. Front Nine Team--Mike Donald, 26, $1,000. Back Nine Individual--Mark Wiebe, Hale Irwin, 33, $900. Back Nine Team--Mark Wiebe, John Adams, 27, $900.

WEATHER: Hot and humid every day.

Winner: Jim Gallagher, Jr.   66- 68- 70- 65   269 $198,000.00

Player	Pos	Scores	Total	Money	Player	Pos	Scores	Total	Money
Chip Beck	2	68- 68- 67- 68	271	$118,800.00	Scott Simpson	T39	72- 67- 69- 72	280	$4,290.00
Dave Rummells	T 3	67- 71- 66- 68	272	$57,200.00	Chris van der Velde	T39	71- 71- 69- 69	280	$4,290.00
Curtis Strange	T 3	67- 69- 68- 68	272	$57,200.00	D.A. Weibring	T39	70- 72- 69- 69	280	$4,290.00
Lanny Wadkins	T 3	67- 71- 64- 70	272	$57,200.00	Barry Cheesman	T46	71- 70- 71- 69	281	$2,941.72
Jim Hallet	T 6	70- 70- 68- 65	273	$38,225.00	John Inman	T46	71- 69- 71- 70	281	$2,941.72
Loren Roberts	T 6	70- 68- 69- 66	273	$38,225.00	Bill Murchison	T46	68- 74- 70- 69	281	$2,941.72
Tom Byrum	T 8	72- 62- 69- 71	274	$28,600.00	Brandel Chamblee	T46	67- 71- 67- 76	281	$2,941.71
Lennie Clements	T 8	70- 66- 69- 69	274	$28,600.00	Marco Dawson	T46	71- 70- 68- 72	281	$2,941.71
Fred Funk	T 8	70- 66- 67- 71	274	$28,600.00	Brian Henninger	T46	71- 70- 67- 73	281	$2,941.71
Bob Gilder	T 8	71- 69- 66- 68	274	$28,600.00	Billy Mayfair	T46	71- 67- 71- 72	281	$2,941.71
Dillard Pruitt	T 8	70- 68- 62- 74	274	$28,600.00	Russell Beiersdorf	T53	71- 67- 71- 73	282	$2,546.50
Ted Tryba	T 8	68- 65- 72- 69	274	$28,600.00	John Dowdall	T53	69- 70- 68- 75	282	$2,546.50
Mike Hulbert	T14	68- 72- 70- 65	275	$19,800.00	Larry Rinker	T53	70- 70- 73- 69	282	$2,546.50
Hale Irwin	T14	70- 67- 68- 70	275	$19,800.00	Fuzzy Zoeller	T53	74- 67- 71- 70	282	$2,546.50
Greg Lesher	T14	73- 69- 67- 66	275	$19,800.00	John Flannery	T57	66- 70- 76- 71	283	$2,464.00
John Adams	T17	68- 65- 68- 75	276	$13,915.00	Jaime Gomez	T57	71- 68- 75- 69	283	$2,464.00
Patrick Burke	T17	72- 70- 67- 67	276	$13,915.00	Lance Ten Broeck	T57	68- 73- 72- 70	283	$2,464.00
Jeff Cook	T17	68- 66- 72- 70	276	$13,915.00	Massy Kuramoto	T60	72- 68- 76- 68	284	$2,365.00
Jay Delsing	T17	70- 69- 68- 69	276	$13,915.00	David Peoples	T60	68- 70- 75- 71	284	$2,365.00
Scott Hoch	T17	69- 73- 66- 68	276	$13,915.00	John Ross	T60	69- 69- 75- 71	284	$2,365.00
Brian Kamm	T17	68- 68- 73- 67	276	$13,915.00	Mike Smith	T60	70- 70- 71- 73	284	$2,365.00
Blaine McCallister	T17	70- 64- 70- 72	276	$13,915.00	Dennis Trixler	T60	68- 69- 75- 72	284	$2,365.00
Mark McCumber	T17	69- 65- 69- 73	276	$13,915.00	Richard Zokol	T60	67- 71- 74- 72	284	$2,365.00
Mark Brooks	T25	72- 66- 69- 70	277	$8,772.50	Greg Cesario	T66	70- 72- 74- 69	285	$2,233.00
Keith Clearwater	T25	67- 70- 71- 69	277	$8,772.50	P.H. Horgan III	T66	68- 73- 74- 70	285	$2,233.00
Kelly Gibson	T25	70- 71- 65- 71	277	$8,772.50	Len Mattiace	T66	69- 73- 69- 74	285	$2,233.00
Kirk Triplett	T25	67- 70- 67- 73	277	$8,772.50	Eddie Pearce	T66	70- 71- 74- 70	285	$2,233.00
Mark Carnevale	T29	69- 68- 75- 66	278	$7,150.00	Mike Schuchart	T66	69- 72- 74- 70	285	$2,233.00
Robert Gamez	T29	71- 70- 69- 68	278	$7,150.00	Joey Sindelar	T66	72- 68- 72- 73	285	$2,233.00
Hubert Green	T29	70- 67- 69- 72	278	$7,150.00	John Elliott	T72	73- 65- 74- 74	286	$2,123.00
Jim Thorpe	T29	72- 66- 73- 67	278	$7,150.00	Bob Friend	T72	71- 69- 73- 73	286	$2,123.00
Bobby Wadkins	T29	73- 66- 70- 69	278	$7,150.00	Dick Mast	T72	73- 67- 73- 73	286	$2,123.00
Bill Kratzert	T34	71- 69- 70- 69	279	$5,676.00	Dave Peege	T72	72- 69- 73- 72	286	$2,123.00
Davis Love III	T34	71- 71- 69- 68	279	$5,676.00	Rick Dalpos	T76	73- 69- 74- 71	287	$2,046.00
Roger Maltbie	T34	73- 69- 69- 68	279	$5,676.00	David Ogrin	T76	72- 70- 73- 72	287	$2,046.00
Tom Sieckmann	T34	68- 69- 71- 71	279	$5,676.00	Jay Overton	T76	72- 68- 74- 73	287	$2,046.00
Bruce Zabriski	T34	72- 68- 70- 69	279	$5,676.00	Barry Jaeckel	T79	74- 68- 73- 74	289	$1,991.00
Trevor Dodds	T39	66- 70- 69- 75	280	$4,290.00	Neal Lancaster	T79	71- 69- 74- 75	289	$1,991.00
Webb Heintzelman	T39	72- 67- 70- 71	280	$4,290.00	Neale Smith	81	73- 67- 78- 73	291	$1,958.00
Ed Humenik	T39	69- 70- 72- 69	280	$4,290.00	Gary Hallberg	82	69- 71- 72- 80	292	$1,936.00
Clarence Rose	T39	70- 67- 67- 76	280	$4,290.00					

BRITISH OPEN

Royal St. George's GC, Sandwich, England **Purse: US$1,540,000**
Par: 35-35--70 **Yards: 6,860** **July 15-18, 1993**

LEADERS: First Round--Greg Norman, Peter Senior, Fuzzy Zoeller and Mark Calcavecchia, at 4-under-par 66, led by one over eight players. **Second Round**--Nick Faldo, at 8-under-par 132, led by one over Bernhard Langer, and by two over Fred Couples, Corey Pavin and Norman. **Third Round**--Pavin and Faldo, at 8-under-par 202, led by one over Norman and Langer.

CUT: 78 players at 3-over-par 143.

WEATHER: Thursday rain with a light breeze throughout the day. Friday, overcast with warm sunny spells and light breeze. Saturday, overcast and breezy, sunny later. Sunday, breezy with occasional showers, then clearing.

Winner: Greg Norman   **66-68-69-64**   **267**   **$154,000.00**

Player	Pos	Scores	Total	Money		Player	Pos	Scores	Total	Money
Nick Faldo	2	69-63-70-67	269	$123,200.00		Andrew Magee	T39	71-72-71-69	283	8,205.00
Bernhard Langer	3	67-66-70-67	270	103,180.00		Greg Turner	T39	67-76-70-70	283	8,205.00
Peter Senior	T4	66-69-70-67	272	77,770.00		Duffy Waldorf	T39	68-71-73-71	283	8,205.00
Corey Pavin	T4	68-66-68-70	272	77,770.00		Paul Moloney	T39	70-71-71-71	283	8,205.00
Nick Price	T6	68-70-67-69	274	51,077.00		Anders Sorenson	T39	69-70-72-72	283	8,205.00
Paul Lawrie	T6	72-68-69-65	274	51,077.00		Darren Clarke	T39	69-71-69-74	283	8,205.00
Ernie Els	T6	68-69-69-68	274	51,077.00		Christy O'Connor	T39	72-68-69-74	283	8,205.00
Fred Couples	T9	68-66-72-69	275	39,270.00		Steve Elkington	T48	72-71-71-70	284	7,469.00
Wayne Grady	T9	74-68-64-69	275	39,270.00		Lee Janzen	T48	69-71-73-71	284	7,469.00
Scott Simpson	T9	68-70-71-66	275	39,270.00		John Huston	T48	68-73-76-67	284	7,469.00
Payne Stewart	12	71-72-70-63	276	33,110.00		Ian Garbutt	T51	68-75-73-69	285	6,709.00
Barry Lane	13	70-68-71-68	277	31,570.00		Stephen Ames	T51	67-75-73-70	285	6,709.00
Mark Calcavecchia	T14	66-73-71-68	278	23,430.00		Miguel Jimenez	T51	69-74-72-70	285	6,709.00
Tom Kite	T14	72-70-68-68	278	23,430.00		Ian Woosnam	T51	72-71-72-70	285	6,709.00
Mark McNulty	T14	67-71-71-69	278	23,430.00		Sam Torrance	T51	72-70-72-71	285	6,709.00
Gil Morgan	T14	70-68-70-70	278	23,430.00		Frank Nobilo	T51	70-70-74-72	285	6,709.00
Jose Rivero	T14	68-73-67-70	278	23,430.00		Manuel Pinero	T51	70-72-71-72	285	6,709.00
Fuzzy Zoeller	T14	66-70-71-71	278	23,430.00		Jonathan Sewell	T51	70-72-69-74	285	6,709.00
John Daly	T14	71-66-70-71	278	23,430.00		Craig Parry	T59	72-69-71-74	286	6,198.00
Peter Baker	T21	70-67-74-68	279	15,400.00		Tom Lehman	T59	69-71-73-73	286	6,198.00
Jesper Parnevik	T21	68-74-68-69	279	15,400.00		Vijay Singh	T59	69-72-72-73	286	6,198.00
Howard Clark	T21	67-72-70-70	279	15,400.00		Paul Azinger	T59	69-73-74-70	286	6,198.00
Rodger Davis	T24	68-71-71-70	280	12,936.00		Ross Drummond	T63	73-67-76-71	287	5,929.00
David Frost	T24	69-73-70-68	280	12,936.00		Olle Karlsson	T63	70-71-73-73	287	5,929.00
Mark Roe	T24	70-71-73-66	280	12,936.00		James Spence	T63	69-72-72-74	287	5,929.00
Malcolm Mackenzie	T27	72-71-71-67	281	11,081.00		Tom Pernice	T66	73-70-70-75	288	5,659.00
Yoshinori Mizumaki	T27	69-69-73-70	281	11,081.00		James Cook	T66	71-71-74-72	288	5,659.00
Des Smyth	T27	67-74-70-70	281	11,081.00		Magnus Sunesson	T66	70-73-73-72	288	5,659.00
Larry Mize	T27	67-69-74-71	281	11,081.00		William Guy	T66	70-73-73-72	288	5,659.00
Mark James	T27	70-70-70-71	281	11,081.00		Mike Miller	T70	73-68-76-72	289	5,416.00
Iain Pyman	T27	68-72-70-71	281	AMATEUR		Tom Purtzer	T70	70-70-74-75	289	5,416.00
Seve Ballesteros	T27	68-73-69-71	281	11,081.00		Ian Baker-Finch	T70	73-69-67-80	289	5,416.00
Raymond Floyd	T34	70-72-67-73	282	9,517.00		Dan Forsman	T73	71-70-76-73	290	5,390.00
Howard Twitty	T34	71-71-67-73	282	9,517.00		Peter Fowler	T73	74-69-74-73	290	5,390.00
Wayne Westner	T34	67-73-72-70	282	9,517.00		Peter Mitchell	T73	73-70-72-75	290	5,390.00
Jean Van De Velde	T34	75-67-73-67	282	9,517.00		Mike Harwood	T73	72-70-72-76	290	5,390.00
Paul Broadhurst	T34	71-69-74-68	282	9,517.00		Mikael Krantz	77	77-66-72-77	292	5,390.00
Rocco Mediate	T39	71-71-72-69	283	8,205.00		Ricky Willison	78	73-70-74-76	292	5,390.00
Carl Mason	T39	69-73-72-69	283	8,205.00						

NEW ENGLAND CLASSIC

Pleasant Valley CC, Sutton, MA **Purse: $1,000,000**
Par: 36-35--71   Yards: 7,110   **July 22-25, 1993**

LEADERS: First Round--Bobby Clampett, with an 8-under-par 63, led Steve Lowery by three and Paul Azinger and Rick Fehr by four. **Second Round--**Willie Wood, at 9-under-par 133, led Clampett by one and four others by two. **Third Round--**Azinger, at 13-under-par 200, led Clampett by one and four others by three.

CUT: A total of 70 players at even-par 142.

PRO-AM: $7,500. Individual--Steve Pate, 64, $750. Team--Pate, Mark O'Meara, 53, $675 each.

WEATHER: Absolutely perfect each day with fairly strong winds on Thursday and lighter winds the remainder of the week.

Winner: Paul Azinger 67- 69- 64- 68   268 $180,000.00

Player		Scores	Total	Money
Jay Delsing	T 2	73- 67- 65- 67	272	$88,000.00
Bruce Fleisher	T 2	70- 67- 66- 69	272	$88,000.00
Bobby Clampett	T 4	63- 71- 67- 73	274	$44,000.00
Joey Sindelar	T 4	68- 67- 70- 69	274	$44,000.00
Brad Bryant	T 6	70- 65- 70- 70	275	$32,375.00
Peter Jacobsen	T 6	68- 71- 68- 68	275	$32,375.00
Curtis Strange	T 6	70- 70- 65- 70	275	$32,375.00
Willie Wood	T 6	68- 65- 70- 72	275	$32,375.00
Barry Cheesman	T10	69- 71- 67- 69	276	$25,000.00
Steve Lowery	T10	66- 69- 69- 72	276	$25,000.00
David Peoples	T10	72- 69- 62- 73	276	$25,000.00
Greg Kraft	T13	69- 70- 68- 70	277	$19,333.34
John Cook	T13	74- 67- 66- 70	277	$19,333.33
Bob Estes	T13	70- 65- 68- 74	277	$19,333.33
John Adams	T16	70- 69- 68- 71	278	$16,000.00
Nolan Henke	T16	71- 67- 69- 71	278	$16,000.00
Jim McGovern	T16	71- 66- 71- 70	278	$16,000.00
Mark Calcavecchia	T19	68- 70- 72- 69	279	$13,000.00
Jay Haas	T19	71- 69- 66- 73	279	$13,000.00
Brian Henninger	T19	73- 68- 70- 68	279	$13,000.00
Russell Beiersdorf	T22	71- 66- 71- 72	280	$8,775.00
Phil Blackmar	T22	71- 69- 70- 70	280	$8,775.00
Jaime Gomez	T22	72- 70- 74- 64	280	$8,775.00
Bob Lohr	T22	70- 72- 68- 70	280	$8,775.00
Bill Murchison	T22	71- 70- 67- 72	280	$8,775.00
Chris Perry	T22	71- 71- 67- 71	280	$8,775.00
Tim Simpson	T22	70- 70- 69- 71	280	$8,775.00
Greg Twiggs	T22	69- 72- 68- 71	280	$8,775.00
Lennie Clements	T30	72- 67- 70- 72	281	$5,688.89
Carl Cooper	T30	69- 73- 68- 71	281	$5,688.89
Steve Elkington	T30	73- 69- 68- 71	281	$5,688.89
Morris Hatalsky	T30	72- 67- 72- 70	281	$5,688.89
David Jackson	T30	71- 68- 69- 73	281	$5,688.89
Kenny Perry	T30	72- 70- 69- 70	281	$5,688.89
Hal Sutton	T30	71- 66- 71- 73	281	$5,688.89
Leonard Thompson	T30	69- 69- 73- 70	281	$5,688.89
Rick Fehr	T30	67- 69- 71- 74	281	$5,688.88
David Ogrin	T39	69- 70- 72- 71	282	$4,400.00
Craig Parry	T39	70- 70- 73- 69	282	$4,400.00
Jeff Cook	T41	70- 72- 68- 73	283	$3,600.00
Wayne Grady	T41	73- 68- 69- 73	283	$3,600.00
Wayne Levi	T41	70- 71- 71- 71	283	$3,600.00
Roger Maltbie	T41	72- 70- 71- 70	283	$3,600.00
John Ross	T41	71- 70- 75- 67	283	$3,600.00
Ted Schulz	T41	72- 70- 71- 70	283	$3,600.00
Tim Conley	T47	72- 68- 72- 72	284	$2,690.00
Dudley Hart	T47	73- 68- 71- 72	284	$2,690.00
Tom Lehman	T47	70- 71- 69- 74	284	$2,690.00
Chris Tucker	T47	74- 68- 70- 72	284	$2,690.00
Robin Freeman	T51	73- 68- 72- 72	285	$2,353.34
Steve Pate	T51	71- 69- 74- 71	285	$2,353.34
Frank Conner	T51	70- 71- 70- 74	285	$2,353.33
Massy Kuramoto	T51	69- 67- 74- 75	285	$2,353.33
Dana Quigley	T51	70- 71- 71- 73	285	$2,353.33
Mark Wiebe	T51	76- 66- 65- 78	285	$2,353.33
Mike Donald	T57	70- 72- 71- 73	286	$2,240.00
Fred Funk	T57	68- 74- 71- 73	286	$2,240.00
Mike Smith	T57	71- 70- 70- 75	286	$2,240.00
Michael Bradley	T60	74- 67- 74- 72	287	$2,180.00
Tom Byrum	T60	69- 67- 72- 79	287	$2,180.00
Ed Dougherty	T60	72- 70- 72- 73	287	$2,180.00
David Duval	T63	75- 67- 72- 74	288	$2,110.00
Scott Gump	T63	73- 69- 72- 74	288	$2,110.00
Sam Randolph	T63	76- 66- 69- 77	288	$2,110.00
Gene Sauers	T63	70- 71- 70- 77	288	$2,110.00
Lee Porter	T67	71- 71- 74- 73	289	$2,050.00
Harry Taylor	T67	71- 71- 77- 70	289	$2,050.00
Marco Dawson	69	69- 72- 70- 79	290	$2,020.00
Buddy Gardner	70	72- 70- 72- 78	292	$2,000.00

FEDERAL EXPRESS ST. JUDE CLASSIC

TPC at Southwind, Memphis, TN
Par: 36-35--71   Yards: 7,006

Purse: $1,100,000
July 29-August 1, 1993

LEADERS: First Round--Michael Bradley, with a 7-under-par 64, led by one over Jay Haas and Davis Love III. **Second Round--**Jeff Maggert at 10-under-par 132 led by a stroke over John Daly. **Third Round--**Nick Price and Fuzzy Zoeller at 13-under-par 200 led by two over Gil Morgan, Fred Funk and Rick Fehr.

CUT: 77 players at even-par 142.

PRO-AM: Individual--Tim Conley, 65, $750. Team--Paul Azinger, 50, $750.

WEATHER: Hot and humid all week. Sunday was overcast, rainy and humid.

Winner: Nick Price   69- 65- 66- 66   266 $198,000.00

Player	Pos	Scores	Total	Money	Player	Pos	Scores	Total	Money
Rick Fehr	T 2	68- 66- 68- 67	269	$96,800.00	Dan Forsman	T39	67- 73- 73- 67	280	$4,620.00
Jeff Maggert	T 2	67- 65- 71- 66	269	$96,800.00	Peter Jacobsen	T39	68- 72- 70- 70	280	$4,620.00
Fuzzy Zoeller	4	67- 68- 65- 70	270	$52,800.00	Jeff Woodland	T39	67- 70- 73- 70	280	$4,620.00
Gil Morgan	5	69- 69- 64- 69	271	$44,000.00	Jeff Cook	T43	70- 70- 71- 70	281	$3,432.00
Fred Funk	T 6	68- 69- 65- 70	272	$38,225.00	Ed Fiori	T43	68- 72- 71- 70	281	$3,432.00
Tom Kite	T 6	70- 67- 69- 66	272	$38,225.00	Gary Hallberg	T43	70- 70- 68- 73	281	$3,432.00
Jay Delsing	T 8	72- 69- 71- 61	273	$33,000.00	Mike Hulbert	T43	70- 69- 71- 71	281	$3,432.00
Curtis Strange	T 8	71- 66- 69- 67	273	$33,000.00	Skip Kendall	T43	69- 72- 73- 67	281	$3,432.00
Mark Brooks	T10	70- 69- 64- 71	274	$28,600.00	Dave Rummells	T43	67- 72- 68- 74	281	$3,432.00
Dan Pohl	T10	72- 68- 69- 65	274	$28,600.00	Willie Wood	T43	69- 70- 73- 69	281	$3,432.00
John Adams	T12	68- 68- 70- 69	275	$22,275.00	Gary McCord	T50	69- 71- 74- 68	282	$2,739.00
Dave Barr	T12	68- 69- 71- 67	275	$22,275.00	Kenny Perry	T50	69- 70- 71- 72	282	$2,739.00
Bob Gilder	T12	69- 69- 69- 68	275	$22,275.00	Phil Blackmar	T52	69- 69- 75- 70	283	$2,596.00
John Riegger	T12	69- 70- 68- 68	275	$22,275.00	Ben Crenshaw	T52	69- 71- 69- 74	283	$2,596.00
John Daly	T16	67- 66- 72- 71	276	$17,600.00	John Flannery	T52	68- 71- 75- 69	283	$2,596.00
Billy Mayfair	T16	70- 67- 69- 70	276	$17,600.00	Mark Calcavecchia	T55	71- 69- 69- 75	284	$2,497.00
Howard Twitty	T16	70- 68- 69- 69	276	$17,600.00	Mark Carnevale	T55	70- 69- 77- 68	284	$2,497.00
Ronnie Black	T19	69- 73- 68- 67	277	$13,805.00	John Cook	T55	70- 72- 71- 71	284	$2,497.00
David Duval	T19	71- 68- 66- 72	277	$13,805.00	David Toms	T55	72- 70- 68- 74	284	$2,497.00
Tim Simpson	T19	70- 70- 67- 70	277	$13,805.00	Jay Don Blake	T59	70- 72- 71- 72	285	$2,409.00
Bob Tway	T19	69- 71- 69- 68	277	$13,805.00	Paul Goydos	T59	70- 71- 72- 72	285	$2,409.00
Lennie Clements	T23	70- 69- 68- 71	278	$9,047.50	Tom Purtzer	T59	67- 71- 72- 75	285	$2,409.00
Joel Edwards	T23	73- 68- 67- 70	278	$9,047.50	Hal Sutton	T59	72- 70- 71- 72	285	$2,409.00
Jay Haas	T23	65- 72- 70- 71	278	$9,047.50	Andy Bean	T63	72- 68- 69- 77	286	$2,343.00
Scott Hoch	T23	71- 69- 67- 71	278	$9,047.50	Payne Stewart	T63	70- 71- 70- 75	286	$2,343.00
Davis Love III	T23	65- 72- 66- 75	278	$9,047.50	Bobby Clampett	T65	69- 72- 72- 74	287	$2,288.00
Mark McCumber	T23	72- 70- 70- 66	278	$9,047.50	Ed Dougherty	T65	70- 69- 73- 75	287	$2,288.00
Loren Roberts	T23	69- 67- 69- 73	278	$9,047.50	John Huston	T65	69- 70- 71- 77	287	$2,288.00
Doug Tewell	T23	67- 69- 73- 69	278	$9,047.50	Jim Ellis	T68	69- 69- 74- 76	288	$2,233.00
Michael Allen	T31	66- 72- 70- 71	279	$6,105.00	Jimmy Johnston	T68	75- 67- 72- 74	288	$2,233.00
Brad Bryant	T31	70- 66- 72- 71	279	$6,105.00	Jeff Sluman	T70	68- 71- 73- 77	289	$2,189.00
Brandel Chamblee	T31	70- 72- 68- 69	279	$6,105.00	Robert Wrenn	T70	72- 69- 73- 75	289	$2,189.00
Jim Gallagher, Jr.	T31	73- 68- 67- 71	279	$6,105.00	Craig Lee	T72	71- 70- 71- 78	290	$2,145.00
Neal Lancaster	T31	66- 73- 67- 73	279	$6,105.00	Gene Sauers	T72	70- 72- 74- 74	290	$2,145.00
Jodie Mudd	T31	70- 68- 69- 72	279	$6,105.00	Jim McGovern	T74	73- 65- 77- 76	291	$2,101.00
Kirk Triplett	T31	71- 70- 65- 73	279	$6,105.00	Denis Watson	T74	72- 70- 73- 76	291	$2,101.00
Jim Woodward	T31	71- 71- 68- 69	279	$6,105.00	Ted Schulz	76	71- 71- 75- 76	293	$2,068.00
Bob Estes	T39	69- 70- 69- 72	280	$4,620.00	Michael Bradley	77	64- 74- 82- 76	296	$2,046.00

BUICK OPEN

Warwick Hills G&CC, Grand Blanc, MI
Par: 36-36--72   Yards: 7,105

Purse: $1,000,000
August 5-8, 1993

LEADERS: First Round--Larry Mize, at 8-under-par 64, held a two-stroke lead over Paul Goydos, John Huston and Payne Stewart. **Second Round--**Mize, at 11-under-par 133, was one stroke in front of Fuzzy Zoeller. **Third Round--**Zoeller, following a 66, stood at 16-under-par 200 and had a four-stroke advantage over Mize.

CUT: 79 players at even-par 144.

PRO-AM: $7,500. Individual--Russ Cochran, 67, $750. Team--Billy Andrade, Phil Mickelson, Howard Twitty, 55, $625 each.

WEATHER: Cool early Thursday, becoming sunny and mild with ideal playing conditions most of the day. Overcast and cool Friday morning, becoming rainy and windy in the afternoon. Cool early, becoming sunny and warmer Saturday and Sunday.

Winner: Larry Mize   64- 69- 71- 68   272 $180,000.00

Fuzzy Zoeller	2	69- 65- 66- 73	273	$108,000.00	Lennie Clements .	T40	70- 72- 70- 72	284	$3,600.00
Greg Norman	3	68- 73- 68- 65	274	$68,000.00	John Cook	T40	72- 71- 71- 70	284	$3,600.00
Jay Don Blake	T 4	69- 71- 67- 69	276	$44,000.00	Ed Dougherty	T40	72- 71- 71- 70	284	$3,600.00
Corey Pavin	T 4	71- 65- 71- 69	276	$44,000.00	Joel Edwards	T40	75- 68- 73- 68	284	$3,600.00
Steve Elkington	T 6	67- 72- 70- 68	277	$33,500.00	Paul Goydos	T40	66- 71- 72- 75	284	$3,600.00
Fred Funk	T 6	68- 71- 67- 71	277	$33,500.00	Mark McCumber .	T40	71- 70- 72- 71	284	$3,600.00
Steve Lamontagne .	T 6	67- 70- 70- 70	277	$33,500.00	Tom Sieckmann ..	T40	70- 70- 71- 73	284	$3,600.00
Neal Lancaster	T 9	69- 71- 71- 67	278	$27,000.00	Keith Clearwater .	T48	69- 72- 72- 72	285	$2,544.00
Payne Stewart	T 9	66- 71- 71- 70	278	$27,000.00	Buddy Gardner	T48	75- 68- 71- 71	285	$2,544.00
David Toms	T 9	73- 67- 68- 70	278	$27,000.00	Phil Mickelson	T48	70- 74- 69- 72	285	$2,544.00
John Flannery	12	71- 70- 68- 70	279	$23,000.00	Kenny Perry	T48	70- 71- 68- 76	285	$2,544.00
Fred Couples	T13	72- 69- 67- 72	280	$20,000.00	Kirk Triplett	T48	73- 71- 71- 70	285	$2,544.00
Jim McGovern	T13	69- 71- 68- 72	280	$20,000.00	Ian Baker-Finch ...	T53	70- 73- 74- 69	286	$2,304.00
John Huston	T15	66- 77- 66- 72	281	$16,500.00	Jimmy Johnston .	T53	72- 72- 72- 70	286	$2,304.00
Wayne Levi	T15	72- 71- 66- 72	281	$16,500.00	David Ogrin	T53	70- 72- 72- 72	286	$2,304.00
Hal Sutton	T15	72- 70- 71- 68	281	$16,500.00	David Peoples	T53	71- 71- 71- 73	286	$2,304.00
Tom Watson	T15	70- 71- 70- 70	281	$16,500.00	Peter Persons	T53	69- 73- 73- 71	286	$2,304.00
Jay Haas	T19	74- 70- 69- 69	282	$10,875.00	Dave Barr	T58	72- 71- 71- 73	287	$2,200.00
Dudley Hart	T19	69- 72- 70- 71	282	$10,875.00	Bobby Clampett ..	T58	72- 72- 72- 71	287	$2,200.00
Andrew Magee	T19	73- 69- 73- 67	282	$10,875.00	Trevor Dodds	T58	70- 71- 76- 70	287	$2,200.00
Rocco Mediate	T19	71- 68- 72- 71	282	$10,875.00	Jeff Sluman	T58	72- 71- 70- 74	287	$2,200.00
Steve Pate	T19	70- 72- 69- 71	282	$10,875.00	Dennis Trixler	T58	67- 77- 72- 71	287	$2,200.00
Warren Schutte	T19	70- 68- 73- 71	282	$10,875.00	Brad Faxon	T63	69- 71- 69- 79	288	$2,120.00
Craig Stadler	T19	71- 70- 70- 71	282	$10,875.00	Gil Morgan	T63	72- 72- 71- 73	288	$2,120.00
Willie Wood	T19	72- 72- 70- 68	282	$10,875.00	Lance Ten Broeck	T63	72- 72- 69- 75	288	$2,120.00
Mark Brooks	T27	71- 71- 71- 70	283	$5,992.31	JC Anderson	66	72- 71- 74- 72	289	$2,080.00
Russ Cochran	T27	70- 74- 70- 69	283	$5,992.31	Michael Bradley ..	T67	71- 73- 72- 74	290	$2,040.00
Ed Fiori	T27	70- 71- 73- 69	283	$5,992.31	Tim Conley	T67	69- 73- 71- 77	290	$2,040.00
Peter Jacobsen	T27	71- 69- 72- 71	283	$5,992.31	Kelly Gibson	T67	73- 69- 74- 74	290	$2,040.00
Skip Kendall	T27	70- 71- 71- 71	283	$5,992.31	Michael Allen	T70	70- 74- 71- 76	291	$1,940.00
Steve Lowery	T27	70- 71- 71- 71	283	$5,992.31	Chip Beck	T70	70- 74- 74- 73	291	$1,940.00
Mark O'Meara	T27	69- 67- 75- 72	283	$5,992.31	Marco Dawson ...	T70	71- 73- 76- 71	291	$1,940.00
Ted Tryba	T27	75- 69- 69- 70	283	$5,992.31	Craig Parry	T70	71- 72- 74- 74	291	$1,940.00
Lanny Wadkins	T27	69- 73- 71- 70	283	$5,992.31	Bob Tway	T70	68- 74- 74- 75	291	$1,940.00
Jim Woodward	T27	71- 73- 72- 67	283	$5,992.31	Grant Waite	T70	71- 72- 73- 75	291	$1,940.00
Scott Gump	T27	68- 71- 71- 73	283	$5,992.30	Mike Weir	T70	73- 69- 73- 76	291	$1,940.00
John Inman	T27	70- 69- 71- 73	283	$5,992.30	Dillard Pruitt	77	71- 72- 77- 72	292	$1,860.00
Davis Love III	T27	67- 73- 71- 72	283	$5,992.30	Perry Moss	78	71- 71- 75- 76	293	$1,840.00
Brad Bryant	T40	70- 71- 71- 72	284	$3,600.00	Steve Brady	79	72- 71- 74- 79	296	$1,820.00

PGA CHAMPIONSHIP

Inverness Club, Toledo, OH
Par: 35-36--71   Yards: 7,024

Purse: $1,700,000
August 12-15, 1993

LEADERS: First Round--Scott Simpson, with a 7-under-par 64, held a one-stroke lead over Lanny Wadkins. **Second Round--**Vijay Singh, with a course-record 63 and 11-under-par 131 total, had a one-stroke lead over Wadkins and Steve Elkington. **Third Round--**Greg Norman, at 10-under-par 203, was one shot in front of six players: Paul Azinger, Bob Estes, Hale Irwin, Singh, Wadkins and Tom Watson.

CUT: 74 players at 1-over-par 145.

WEATHER: Sunny and mild Thursday. Early-morning fog produced a 90-minute start delay Friday, with play getting underway at 8:40 a.m.; sunny and warm once the fog lifted. Ideal playing conditions Saturday. Increasing high overcast and mild Sunday.

Winner: Paul Azinger   69- 66- 69- 68   272 $300,000.00
(won playoff with par on second extra hole)

Player	Pos	Scores	Total	Money	Player	Pos	Scores	Total	Money
Greg Norman	2	68- 68- 67- 69	272	$155,000.00	Craig Parry	T31	70- 73- 68- 72	283	$7,057.69
Nick Faldo	3	68- 68- 69- 68	273	$105,000.00	Nick Price	T31	74- 66- 72- 71	283	$7,057.69
Vijay Singh	4	68- 63- 73- 70	274	$90,000.00	Hal Sutton	T31	69- 72- 70- 72	283	$7,057.69
Tom Watson	5	69- 65- 70- 72	276	$75,000.00	Tom Wargo	T31	71- 70- 71- 71	283	$7,057.69
John Cook	T 6	72- 66- 68- 71	277	$47,812.50	Fuzzy Zoeller	T31	72- 70- 71- 70	283	$7,057.69
Bob Estes	T 6	69- 66- 69- 73	277	$47,812.50	Fred Funk	T44	72- 66- 76- 70	284	$4,607.15
Dudley Hart	T 6	66- 68- 71- 72	277	$47,812.50	D.A. Weibring	T44	68- 74- 72- 70	284	$4,607.15
Nolan Henke	T 6	72- 70- 67- 68	277	$47,812.50	Russ Cochran	T44	69- 74- 70- 71	284	$4,607.14
Scott Hoch	T 6	74- 68- 68- 67	277	$47,812.50	Dan Forsman	T44	67- 75- 70- 72	284	$4,607.14
Hale Irwin	T 6	68- 69- 67- 73	277	$47,812.50	John Huston	T44	68- 69- 75- 72	284	$4,607.14
Phil Mickelson	T 6	67- 71- 69- 70	277	$47,812.50	Joe Ozaki	T44	73- 68- 66- 77	284	$4,607.14
Scott Simpson	T 6	64- 70- 71- 72	277	$47,812.50	Payne Stewart	T44	71- 70- 70- 73	284	$4,607.14
Steve Elkington	T14	67- 66- 74- 71	278	$25,000.00	John Daly	T51	71- 68- 73- 73	285	$3,600.00
Brad Faxon	T14	70- 70- 65- 73	278	$25,000.00	Hubert Green	T51	70- 71- 69- 75	285	$3,600.00
Bruce Fleisher	T14	69- 74- 67- 68	278	$25,000.00	Andrew Magee	T51	71- 72- 74- 68	285	$3,600.00
Gary Hallberg	T14	70- 69- 68- 71	278	$25,000.00	Jeff Maggert	T51	72- 69- 71- 73	285	$3,600.00
Lanny Wadkins	T14	65- 68- 71- 74	278	$25,000.00	Peter Senior	T51	69- 70- 70- 76	285	$3,600.00
Richard Zokol	T14	66- 71- 71- 70	278	$25,000.00	Rick Fehr	T56	70- 71- 72- 73	286	$3,110.00
Jay Haas	T20	69- 68- 70- 72	279	$18,500.00	Tom Kite	T56	73- 69- 71- 73	286	$3,110.00
Eduardo Romero	T20	67- 67- 74- 71	279	$18,500.00	Sandy Lyle	T56	69- 73- 70- 74	286	$3,110.00
Lee Janzen	T22	70- 68- 71- 72	281	$14,500.00	Larry Nelson	T56	73- 67- 74- 72	286	$3,110.00
Jim McGovern	T22	71- 67- 69- 74	281	$14,500.00	Jose Maria Olazabal	T56	73- 69- 73- 71	286	$3,110.00
Frank Nobilo	T22	69- 66- 74- 72	281	$14,500.00	Michael Allen	T61	73- 70- 75- 69	287	$2,800.00
Gene Sauers	T22	68- 74- 70- 69	281	$14,500.00	Ben Crenshaw	T61	70- 70- 73- 74	287	$2,800.00
Greg Twiggs	T22	70- 69- 70- 72	281	$14,500.00	Donnie Hammond	T61	73- 70- 68- 76	287	$2,800.00
Ian Woosnam	T22	70- 71- 68- 72	281	$14,500.00	Jeff Sluman	T61	74- 69- 72- 72	287	$2,800.00
Peter Jacobsen	T28	71- 67- 74- 70	282	$10,166.67	Mike Standly	T61	72- 71- 68- 76	287	$2,800.00
Billy Mayfair	T28	68- 73- 70- 71	282	$10,166.67	Ian Baker-Finch	66	73- 69- 70- 76	288	$2,650.00
Loren Roberts	T28	67- 67- 76- 72	282	$10,166.66	Mark Wiebe	67	74- 69- 73- 73	289	$2,625.00
Mark Calcavecchia	T31	68- 70- 77- 68	283	$7,057.70	Bob Ford	T68	70- 71- 78- 71	290	$2,587.50
Davis Love III	T31	70- 72- 72- 69	283	$7,057.70	Rocco Mediate	T68	70- 73- 74- 73	290	$2,587.50
Mark McCumber	T31	67- 72- 75- 69	283	$7,057.70	Steve Pate	70	73- 70- 72- 77	292	$2,550.00
Fulton Allem	T31	70- 71- 70- 72	283	$7,057.69	Kevin Burton	T71	69- 73- 76- 76	294	$2,512.50
Fred Couples	T31	70- 68- 71- 74	283	$7,057.69	Barry Lane	T71	67- 74- 77- 76	294	$2,512.50
Mike Hulbert	T31	67- 72- 72- 72	283	$7,057.69	Bob Borowicz	73	72- 71- 80- 72	295	$2,475.00
Stu Ingraham	T31	74- 69- 71- 69	283	$7,057.69	John Adams	74	72- 70- 76- 78	296	$2,450.00
Wayne Levi	T31	69- 73- 66- 75	283	$7,057.69					

THE INTERNATIONAL

Castle Pines GC, Castle Rock, CO
Par: 36-36--72   **Yards: 7,559**

Purse: $1,300,000
August 19-22, 1993

FORMAT: Modified Stableford with points awarded as follows: Double eagle +8; eagle +5; birdie +2; par 0; bogey -1; double bogey or worse -3.

LEADERS: First Round--Steve Pate with 14 points led by one point over Mark O'Meara and Brad Faxon. **Second Round--**O'Meara with 22 points led by a point over Skip Kendall and Phil Blackmar. **Third Round--**Phil Mickelson with 29 points led by three over Blackmar.

CUT: Starting field of 144 players cut to 72 after 36 holes. Trevor Dodds, Lee Janzen, P.H. Horgan, Barry Cheesman and Jimmy Johnston played off for one spot. Janzen advanced with a birdie on the first extra hole. After 54 holes the field was reduced to 24 players. There was no playoff.

PRO-AM: Due to inclement weather, the afternoon portion of the pro-am was only able to complete nine holes. $10,000. Morning Individual--Donnie Hammond, 15, $600. Morning Team--Andrew Magee, Bruce Lietzke, 36, $575 each. Afternoon Front Nine Individual--Jack Nicklaus, 8, $500. Afternoon Front Nine Team--Greg Norman, 26, $500. Afternoon Back Nine Individual--Mark Brooks, 7, $500. Afternoon Back Nine Team--Mark O'Meara, 23, $500.

WEATHER: There was no delay on Thursday. Friday's playoff was delayed from 6:25 p.m. to 6:37 p.m. due to lightning in the area. Saturday's round was delayed from 1:46 p.m. to 2:43 p.m. due to lightning, and again from 4:26 p.m. to 6:12 p.m. due to lightning.

Winner: Phil Mickelson	11 — 7 — 11— 16	45	$234,000.00
Mark Calcavecchia 2	0 — 4 — 14— 18	37	$140,000.00
Phil Blackmar 3	6 — 15 — 5— 7	33	88,400.00
Greg Norman T4	11 — 6 — 5— 9	31	57,200.00
Scott Simpson T4	2 — 13 — 8— 8	31	57,200.00
Steve Pate T6	14 — 1 — 5— 8	28	41,175.00
Brad Faxon T6	13 — 7 — 2— 6	28	41,175.00
Skip Kendall 8	12 — 9 — 1— 4	26	40,300.00
Rocco Mediate 9	8 — 1 — 5— 11	25	37,700.00
Craig Parry 10	4 — 3 — 12— 4	23	35,100.00
Hale Irwin T11	4 — 4 — 7— 7	22	31,200.00
Brian Claar T11	7 — 9 — 1— 5	22	31,200.00
Larry Rinker T13	10 — 5 — 1— 5	21	26,000.00
Mark O'Meara T13	13 — 9 — 1—(-2)	21	26,000.00
Tommy Nakajima ... T15	2 — 12 — 4— 1	19	22,100.00
Steve Elkington T15	5 — 2 — 10— 2	19	22,100.00
Vijay Singh T15	2 — 4 — 15—(-2)	19	22,100.00
Mike Hulbert 18	5 — 1 — 8— 4	18	19,500.00
Brett Ogle T19	2 — 3 — 8— 4	16	16,900.00
Peter Persons T19	1 — 4 — 10— 1	16	16,900.00
Tom Purtzer T19	2 — 12 — 5—(-3)	16	16,900.00
Neal Lancaster 22	(-2) — 10 — 5— 1	14	14,560.00
Perry Moss 23	(-1) — 10 — 9—(-5)	13	13,520.00
Marco Dawson 24	4 — 9 — 0—(-4)	9	12,480.00

NEC WORLD SERIES OF GOLF

WORLD SERIES OF GOLF
FIRESTONE C.C.

Firestone CC (South Course), Akron, OH   Purse: $2,000,000
Par: 35-35--70   Yards: 7,149   August 26-29, 1993

LEADERS: First Round--David Edwards and Jim Gallagher, Jr., each fired 4-under-par 66s, and led by two over Massy Kuramoto, John Huston, Fulton Allem and David Frost. **Second Round--**Edwards at 5-under-par 135 led by one over Steve Elkington, Nick Price and Allem. **Third Round--**Greg Norman, Price, Edwards and Gallagher at 3-under-par 207 led by one over Craig Stadler, Frost, Allem and Elkington.

PRO-AM: $10,000. Individual--Phil Mickelson, 67, $1,000. Team--Paul Azinger, 54, $1,000.

WEATHER: Hot and humid on Thursday and Friday. A little cooler on Saturday and Sunday.

Winner:	Fulton Allem	68- 68- 72- 62	270	$360,000.00
Craig Stadler	T 2	71- 69- 68- 67	275	$149,333.34
Jim Gallagher, Jr.	T 2	66- 75- 66- 68	275	$149,333.33
Nick Price	T 2	69- 67- 71- 68	275	$149,333.33
Vijay Singh	5	73- 70- 68- 66	277	$80,000.00
David Edwards	6	66- 69- 72- 72	279	$72,000.00
Steve Elkington	T 7	69- 67- 72- 72	280	$62,366.67
David Frost	T 7	68- 69- 71- 72	280	$62,366.67
Greg Norman	T 7	69- 69- 69- 73	280	$62,366.66
Grant Waite	10	72- 70- 75- 65	282	$54,100.00
Fred Couples	T11	77- 77- 65- 67	286	$46,100.00
John Daly	T11	72- 73- 70- 71	286	$46,100.00
Tom Kite	T11	72- 71- 72- 71	286	$46,100.00
Lee Janzen	T14	75- 70- 73- 69	287	$37,100.00
Richard Zokol	T14	73- 71- 71- 72	287	$37,100.00
Isao Aoki	T16	74- 72- 69- 73	288	$32,500.00
Gary Hallberg	T16	74- 69- 72- 73	288	$32,500.00
John Huston	T16	68- 74- 78- 68	288	$32,500.00
Bradley Hughes	T19	73- 73- 69- 74	289	$28,125.00
Larry Mize	T19	75- 72- 70- 72	289	$28,125.00
Joe Ozaki	21	76- 74- 68- 72	290	$26,550.00
Jim McGovern	T22	73- 76- 71- 71	291	$25,150.00
Tommy Nakajima	T22	71- 75- 71- 74	291	$25,150.00
Mike Standly	T22	75- 72- 76- 68	291	$25,150.00
Ben Crenshaw	T25	74- 70- 75- 73	292	$22,500.00
Nolan Henke	T25	73- 72- 77- 70	292	$22,500.00
Davis Love III	T25	75- 71- 75- 71	292	$22,500.00
Rocco Mediate	T25	74- 69- 76- 73	292	$22,500.00
Craig Parry	T25	74- 71- 76- 71	292	$22,500.00
Howard Twitty	T25	71- 76- 73- 72	292	$22,500.00
Paul Azinger	31	72- 72- 75- 75	294	$20,900.00
Ron McDougal	T32	72- 75- 72- 76	295	$20,375.00
Brian Watts	T32	70- 76- 73- 76	295	$20,375.00
Massy Kuramoto	34	68- 74- 81- 74	297	$19,850.00
Brett Ogle	35	75- 75- 77- 72	299	$19,500.00
Phil Mickelson	T36	77- 75- 71- 77	300	$19,200.00
Clinton Whitelaw	T36	71- 79- 72- 78	300	$19,200.00

GREATER MILWAUKEE OPEN

Tuckaway CC, Franklin, WI
Par: 36-36--72   **Yards: 7,020**

Purse: $1,000,000
September 2-5, 1993

LEADERS: First Round--Morris Hatalsky, with an 8-under-par 64, held a one-stroke lead over Steve Pate. **Second Round--**Billy Mayfair and Harry Taylor, at 11-under-par 133, were one stroke ahead of Donnie Hammond, Russell Beiersdorf, Jim McGovern, Dave Rummells and Gil Morgan. **Third Round--**Mayfair, at 14-under-par 202, had a one-stroke edge over Mark Calcavecchia, Richard Zokol and McGovern.

CUT: 82 players at 3-under-par 141.

PRO-AM: $7,500. Individual--Duffy Waldorf, Bruce Fleisher, Jay Delsing, 65, $625 each. Team--Andy North, Roger Maltbie, Ian Baker-Finch, Nolan Henke, 56, all $581.25 each.

WEATHER: Cool each morning, with temperatures moderating throughout the day, and windy every day. Cloudy and overcast Thursday, with some light rain. Mostly sunny Friday and Saturday. Partly sunny early Sunday, becoming cloudy and overcast later; turning chilly with some late rain.

Winner: Billy Mayfair 67- 66- 69- 68   270 $180,000.00
(won playoff with birdie on fourth extra hole)

Player		Scores	Total	Money	Player		Scores	Total	Money
Mark Calcavecchia	T 2	72- 64- 67- 67	270	$88,000.00	Jay Haas	T41	66- 73- 72- 70	281	$3,405.00
Ted Schulz	T 2	69- 67- 68- 66	270	$88,000.00	Nolan Henke	T41	67- 69- 71- 74	281	$3,405.00
Bruce Lietzke	T 4	69- 66- 69- 67	271	$44,000.00	Greg Kraft	T41	68- 68- 75- 70	281	$3,405.00
Richard Zokol	T 4	67- 68- 68- 68	271	$44,000.00	Dick Mast	T41	69- 69- 73- 70	281	$3,405.00
Ken Green	6	69- 66- 69- 68	272	$36,000.00	Gene Sauers	T41	69- 69- 75- 70	281	$3,405.00
Donnie Hammond	7	69- 65- 70- 69	273	$33,500.00	Mark Wiebe	T41	67- 69- 73- 72	281	$3,405.00
Hale Irwin	T 8	70- 66- 70- 68	274	$28,000.00	Roger Maltbie	T49	71- 70- 72- 69	282	$2,443.34
Brian Kamm	T 8	69- 69- 69- 67	274	$28,000.00	Robert Wrenn	T49	71- 70- 70- 71	282	$2,443.34
Gil Morgan	T 8	69- 65- 70- 70	274	$28,000.00	Robin Freeman	T49	71- 69- 69- 73	282	$2,443.33
Craig Parry	T 8	70- 66- 69- 69	274	$28,000.00	Paul Goydos	T49	69- 70- 71- 72	282	$2,443.33
Ronnie Black	T12	69- 67- 68- 71	275	$20,250.00	David Peoples	T49	71- 69- 70- 72	282	$2,443.33
Jim McGovern	T12	67- 67- 69- 72	275	$20,250.00	Tim Simpson	T49	68- 72- 71- 71	282	$2,443.33
Harry Taylor	T12	67- 66- 76- 66	275	$20,250.00	Jay Don Blake	T55	70- 71- 71- 71	283	$2,240.00
Duffy Waldorf	T12	72- 67- 69- 67	275	$20,250.00	Brad Bryant	T55	70- 71- 73- 69	283	$2,240.00
David Frost	T16	69- 68- 72- 67	276	$16,000.00	Brian Claar	T55	71- 68- 73- 71	283	$2,240.00
Bill Glasson	T16	70- 69- 71- 66	276	$16,000.00	Jay Delsing	T55	75- 65- 74- 69	283	$2,240.00
Howard Twitty	T16	69- 67- 72- 68	276	$16,000.00	John Flannery	T55	74- 67- 72- 70	283	$2,240.00
Ed Dougherty	T19	69- 67- 73- 68	277	$12,120.00	Kenny Perry	T55	71- 70- 73- 69	283	$2,240.00
Rick Fehr	T19	71- 66- 71- 69	277	$12,120.00	Dave Rummells	T55	68- 66- 74- 75	283	$2,240.00
Jim Gallagher, Jr.	T19	70- 68- 71- 68	277	$12,120.00	Brandel Chamblee	T62	68- 71- 75- 70	284	$2,130.00
Andrew Magee	T19	68- 70- 70- 69	277	$12,120.00	Bobby Clampett	T62	68- 70- 71- 75	284	$2,130.00
Steve Pate	T19	65- 70- 69- 73	277	$12,120.00	Scott Gump	T62	72- 69- 73- 70	284	$2,130.00
Russell Beiersdorf	T24	66- 68- 72- 72	278	$8,525.00	Bob Tway	T62	73- 68- 74- 69	284	$2,130.00
Scott Hoch	T24	67- 68- 76- 67	278	$8,525.00	Jeff Cook	T66	69- 68- 73- 75	285	$2,040.00
Massy Kuramoto	T24	73- 68- 69- 68	278	$8,525.00	Dan Halldorson	T66	68- 73- 77- 67	285	$2,040.00
Blaine McCallister	T24	72- 69- 69- 68	278	$8,525.00	Steve Lowery	T66	69- 68- 77- 71	285	$2,040.00
Fred Funk	T28	67- 69- 73- 70	279	$7,100.00	David Ogrin	T66	71- 70- 72- 72	285	$2,040.00
Mark Lye	T28	68- 68- 70- 73	279	$7,100.00	Doug Tewell	T66	69- 70- 75- 71	285	$2,040.00
Corey Pavin	T28	67- 68- 71- 73	279	$7,100.00	Keith Clearwater	T71	68- 72- 74- 72	286	$1,960.00
John Adams	T31	67- 71- 69- 73	280	$5,320.00	Dan Forsman	T71	71- 69- 76- 70	286	$1,960.00
Fulton Allem	T31	70- 69- 70- 71	280	$5,320.00	Peter Persons	T71	69- 70- 77- 70	286	$1,960.00
Michael Bradley	T31	74- 66- 72- 68	280	$5,320.00	David DeLong	T74	70- 70- 74- 73	287	$1,910.00
Gary Hallberg	T31	67- 69- 72- 72	280	$5,320.00	John Dowdall	T74	70- 70- 75- 72	287	$1,910.00
Morris Hatalsky	T31	64- 73- 72- 71	280	$5,320.00	Tommy Armour	T76	70- 71- 76- 71	288	$1,850.00
Bill Kratzert	T31	67- 73- 69- 71	280	$5,320.00	Mark Carnevale	T76	69- 71- 74- 74	288	$1,850.00
Steve Lamontagne	T31	70- 70- 73- 67	280	$5,320.00	Ed Fiori	T76	69- 72- 75- 72	288	$1,850.00
Mark McCumber	T31	68- 70- 69- 73	280	$5,320.00	Buddy Gardner	T76	72- 67- 73- 76	288	$1,850.00
Nick Price	T31	68- 68- 71- 73	280	$5,320.00	JC Anderson	80	69- 72- 79- 69	289	$1,800.00
Tom Sieckmann	T31	66- 73- 70- 71	280	$5,320.00	David Edwards	T81	69- 69- 78- 74	290	$1,770.00
Chip Beck	T41	69- 70- 71- 71	281	$3,405.00	Len Mattiace	T81	71- 70- 76- 73	290	$1,770.00
John Elliott	T41	69- 67- 71- 74	281	$3,405.00					

CANADIAN OPEN

Glen Abbey GC, Oakville, Ontario　　**Purse: $1,000,000**
Par: 36-36--72　　**Yards: 7,112**　　**September 9-12, 1993**

LEADERS: First Round--Steve Stricker, at 6-under-par 66, had a two-stroke lead over Scott Gump, Brad Bryant, Nick Price, Phil Mickelson and Jimmy Johnston. **Second Round--**Stricker, at 9-under-par 135, held a three-stroke advantage over Brad Bryant. **Third Round--**Bryant, at 8-under-par 208, was one stroke in front of Stricker.

CUT: 75 players at 4-over-par 148.

PRO-AM: $7,500. Individual--Brad Faxon, 66, $750. Team--Scott Hoch, 53, $750.

WEATHER: Some light rain and cool early Thursday, becoming sunny and warmer; wind picking up midday, becoming stronger later. A 21-minute delay due to wet grounds early Friday was followed by a one-hour, 20-minute delay shortly after noon; intermittent sun, rain, wind and cold throughout the day. Play was suspended by darkness at 7:45 p.m., with the completion of Round 2 starting at 9:30 a.m. Saturday. Round 3 began at 11:15 a.m. Mostly sunny early Saturday, becoming overcast later, continued windy and cold. Partly cloudy and overcast Sunday, with somewhat warmer but still windy conditions.

Winner:　David Frost　72- 70- 69- 68　　279　　$180,000.00

Player	Pos	Scores	Total	Money	Player	Pos	Scores	Total	Money
Fred Couples	2	70- 71- 70- 69	280	$108,000.00	Don Pooley	T35	73- 75- 70- 74	292	$4,930.00
Brad Bryant	3	68- 70- 70- 74	282	$68,000.00	JC Anderson	T40	73- 73- 72- 75	293	$3,900.00
Craig Stadler	T 4	71- 73- 71- 69	284	$41,333.34	Bob Estes	T40	76- 70- 74- 73	293	$3,900.00
Bruce Lietzke	T 4	71- 72- 71- 70	284	$41,333.33	John Flannery	T40	76- 71- 73- 73	293	$3,900.00
Steve Stricker	T 4	66- 69- 74- 75	284	$41,333.33	Donnie Hammond	T40	71- 75- 73- 74	293	$3,900.00
Bill Glasson	7	70- 73- 71- 71	285	$33,500.00	Billy Mayfair	T40	73- 75- 71- 74	293	$3,900.00
Phil Blackmar	T 8	69- 71- 72- 74	286	$30,000.00	Patrick Burke	T45	71- 74- 76- 73	294	$2,670.00
Dudley Hart	T 8	69- 71- 74- 72	286	$30,000.00	Mark Calcavecchia	T45	73- 72- 77- 72	294	$2,670.00
Brandel Chamblee	T10	70- 70- 76- 71	287	$22,166.67	Jay Delsing	T45	73- 70- 76- 75	294	$2,670.00
Jim Gallagher, Jr.	T10	73- 74- 68- 72	287	$22,166.67	Brad Fabel	T45	70- 77- 78- 69	294	$2,670.00
P.H. Horgan III	T10	72- 73- 72- 70	287	$22,166.67	Gary Hallberg	T45	72- 70- 74- 78	294	$2,670.00
Nick Price	T10	68- 74- 71- 74	287	$22,166.67	Mark O'Meara	T45	76- 68- 73- 77	294	$2,670.00
Ed Dougherty	T10	71- 70- 70- 76	287	$22,166.66	Mike Standly	T45	74- 74- 73- 73	294	$2,670.00
Kenny Perry	T10	70- 71- 70- 76	287	$22,166.66	Ray Stewart	T45	72- 75- 73- 74	294	$2,670.00
Ian Baker-Finch	T16	69- 75- 74- 70	288	$15,500.00	Ted Tryba	T45	75- 71- 74- 74	294	$2,670.00
Brad Faxon	T16	74- 72- 72- 70	288	$15,500.00	Greg Twiggs	T45	75- 73- 73- 73	294	$2,670.00
Scott Gump	T16	68- 75- 72- 73	288	$15,500.00	Blaine McCallister	55	72- 76- 72- 75	295	$2,300.00
Mark McCumber	T16	73- 72- 69- 74	288	$15,500.00	Bobby Clampett	T56	72- 73- 76- 75	296	$2,270.00
Mike Hulbert	T20	74- 71- 73- 71	289	$12,500.00	Gene Sauers	T56	75- 71- 75- 75	296	$2,270.00
Tom Lehman	T20	78- 70- 69- 72	289	$12,500.00	Arden Knoll	T58	71- 74- 73- 79	297	$2,230.00
Jay Don Blake	T22	75- 72- 70- 73	290	$8,775.00	Mark Wiebe	T58	77- 68- 71- 81	297	$2,230.00
Mark Brooks	T22	73- 74- 72- 71	290	$8,775.00	Tim Conley	T60	72- 76- 78- 72	298	$2,130.00
Paul Goydos	T22	71- 72- 71- 76	290	$8,775.00	Kelly Gibson	T60	70- 78- 74- 76	298	$2,130.00
John Huston	T22	75- 72- 70- 73	290	$8,775.00	Lee Janzen	T60	72- 76- 76- 74	298	$2,130.00
Jimmy Johnston	T22	68- 72- 71- 79	290	$8,775.00	Perry Moss	T60	69- 75- 74- 80	298	$2,130.00
Bob Lohr	T22	74- 69- 72- 75	290	$8,775.00	Tim Simpson	T60	73- 72- 78- 75	298	$2,130.00
Steve Lowery	T22	75- 70- 74- 71	290	$8,775.00	Jim Thorpe	T60	71- 77- 77- 73	298	$2,130.00
Jim McGovern	T22	70- 73- 75- 72	290	$8,775.00	Kirk Triplett	T60	69- 78- 71- 80	298	$2,130.00
Russell Beiersdorf	T30	74- 72- 72- 73	291	$6,210.00	D.A. Weibring	T60	70- 71- 77- 80	298	$2,130.00
Keith Clearwater	T30	74- 72- 71- 74	291	$6,210.00	Skip Kendall	T68	75- 72- 77- 75	299	$2,020.00
Marco Dawson	T30	70- 72- 74- 75	291	$6,210.00	Tom Sieckmann	T68	72- 74- 79- 74	299	$2,020.00
Ed Fiori	T30	70- 76- 71- 74	291	$6,210.00	Bob Tway	T68	71- 74- 70- 84	299	$2,020.00
Denis Watson	T30	73- 71- 71- 76	291	$6,210.00	John Elliott	T71	74- 72- 79- 75	300	$1,960.00
Andy Bean	T35	70- 76- 72- 74	292	$4,930.00	Massy Kuramoto	T71	74- 74- 72- 80	300	$1,960.00
Rick Fehr	T35	74- 71- 71- 76	292	$4,930.00	Dick Mast	T71	71- 75- 77- 77	300	$1,960.00
Ed Humenik	T35	74- 72- 72- 74	292	$4,930.00	Ted Schulz	74	71- 77- 80- 73	301	$1,920.00
Corey Pavin	T35	71- 76- 72- 73	292	$4,930.00	Len Mattiace	75	73- 75- 77- 78	303	$1,900.00

HARDEE'S GOLF CLASSIC

Hardee's GOLF CLASSIC

Oakwood CC, Coal Valley, IL
Par: 35-35--70   Yards: 6,755

Purse: $1,000,000
September 16-19, 1993

LEADERS: First Round--Jeff Woodland, with a 7-under-par 63, had a two-stroke lead over Jeff Maggert, Ed Dougherty, Dave Barr and Kenny Perry. **Second Round--**Barr, D.A. Weibring and David Frost at 9-under-par 131, were one stroke ahead of Dougherty **Third Round--**Frost, at 15-under-par 195, was two strokes ahead of Weibring.

CUT: 74 players at 2-under-par 138.

PRO-AM: $7,500. Individual--Ted Schulz, Andrew Magee, Mark O'Meara, Bob Tway, 66, $581.25 each. Team--John Huston, Bob Estes, Hal Sutton, Bob Tway, 53, $581.25 each.

WEATHER: Cloudy and cold Thursday. Cool early Friday, becoming sunny and mild. Some intermittent light drizzle Saturday morning, giving way to overcast and cool conditions. Chilly Sunday, with rain early, briefly heavy; mostly cloudy remainder of day.

Winner: David Frost   68- 63- 64- 64   259 $180,000.00

Player	Pos	Scores	Total	Money	Player	Pos	Scores	Total	Money
Payne Stewart	T 2	66- 68- 67- 65	266	$88,000.00	Bill Britton	T39	71- 65- 70- 69	275	$3,700.00
D.A. Weibring	T 2	66- 65- 66- 69	266	$88,000.00	Ed Dougherty	T39	65- 67- 72- 71	275	$3,700.00
Bob Tway	4	69- 67- 67- 65	268	$48,000.00	Robert Gamez	T39	68- 66- 72- 69	275	$3,700.00
John Huston	T 5	70- 68- 66- 65	269	$36,500.00	Greg Kraft	T39	69- 69- 68- 69	275	$3,700.00
David Ogrin	T 5	66- 70- 68- 65	269	$36,500.00	Tom Lehman	T39	69- 69- 70- 67	275	$3,700.00
Mike Schuchart	T 5	69- 65- 69- 66	269	$36,500.00	Chris Perry	T39	68- 67- 68- 72	275	$3,700.00
P.H. Horgan III	T 8	68- 68- 66- 68	270	$26,000.00	Harry Taylor	T39	70- 67- 68- 70	275	$3,700.00
Andrew Magee	T 8	68- 66- 67- 69	270	$26,000.00	Lance Ten Broeck	T39	68- 68- 68- 71	275	$3,700.00
Kenny Perry	T 8	65- 70- 64- 71	270	$26,000.00	Bruce Zabriski	T39	67- 70- 69- 69	275	$3,700.00
Larry Rinker	T 8	69- 67- 65- 69	270	$26,000.00	Brad Bryant	T48	67- 70- 68- 71	276	$2,485.72
Tim Simpson	T 8	70- 66- 68- 66	270	$26,000.00	Steve Elkington	T48	70- 68- 67- 71	276	$2,485.72
Willie Wood	T 8	66- 69- 67- 68	270	$26,000.00	Brad Fabel	T48	69- 67- 69- 71	276	$2,485.72
Brandel Chamblee	T14	71- 64- 68- 68	271	$16,500.00	David Berganio	T48	68- 69- 71- 68	276	$2,485.71
Jay Delsing	T14	66- 71- 67- 67	271	$16,500.00	Buddy Gardner	T48	66- 70- 72- 68	276	$2,485.71
David Edwards	T14	67- 68- 66- 70	271	$16,500.00	Jay Haas	T48	69- 69- 71- 67	276	$2,485.71
Bob Estes	T14	68- 69- 69- 65	271	$16,500.00	Tom Sieckmann	T48	67- 69- 70- 70	276	$2,485.71
Kelly Gibson	T14	69- 69- 67- 66	271	$16,500.00	Bobby Clampett	T55	67- 67- 70- 73	277	$2,250.00
Jeff Maggert	T14	65- 70- 69- 67	271	$16,500.00	Morris Hatalsky	T55	66- 70- 72- 69	277	$2,250.00
Ed Fiori	T20	69- 68- 69- 66	272	$10,428.58	Neal Lancaster	T55	70- 68- 68- 71	277	$2,250.00
Dave Barr	T20	65- 66- 72- 69	272	$10,428.57	Steve Lowery	T55	70- 68- 71- 68	277	$2,250.00
Lennie Clements	T20	69- 69- 66- 68	272	$10,428.57	Billy Mayfair	T55	70- 68- 71- 68	277	$2,250.00
Scott Hoch	T20	70- 67- 67- 68	272	$10,428.57	Dillard Pruitt	T55	68- 69- 71- 69	277	$2,250.00
Gene Jones	T20	69- 67- 68- 68	272	$10,428.57	Robin Freeman	T61	69- 68- 72- 69	278	$2,170.00
Brian Kamm	T20	67- 71- 69- 65	272	$10,428.57	Hal Sutton	T61	70- 67- 68- 73	278	$2,170.00
Mac O'Grady	T20	66- 68- 70- 68	272	$10,428.57	Barry Cheesman	T63	66- 71- 71- 71	279	$2,110.00
Peter Jacobsen	T27	69- 67- 69- 68	273	$7,250.00	Russ Cochran	T63	69- 69- 69- 72	279	$2,110.00
Curtis Strange	T27	72- 66- 67- 68	273	$7,250.00	John Elliott	T63	67- 69- 70- 73	279	$2,110.00
Jeff Woodland	T27	63- 70- 69- 71	273	$7,250.00	Peter Persons	T63	70- 68- 72- 69	279	$2,110.00
Robert Wrenn	T27	67- 69- 68- 69	273	$7,250.00	Jeff Cook	T67	67- 70- 72- 71	280	$2,050.00
Ronnie Black	T31	68- 67- 65- 74	274	$5,550.00	Bruce Fleisher	T67	68- 69- 69- 74	280	$2,050.00
Mark Brooks	T31	68- 70- 69- 67	274	$5,550.00	Grant Waite	69	66- 71- 72- 72	281	$2,020.00
Dan Halldorson	T31	68- 70- 67- 69	274	$5,550.00	Bill Murchison	70	69- 69- 73- 71	282	$2,000.00
David Jackson	T31	70- 68- 69- 67	274	$5,550.00	Keith Clearwater	71	71- 67- 76- 69	283	$1,980.00
Bill Kratzert	T31	68- 70- 68- 68	274	$5,550.00	Brian Henninger	T72	69- 68- 74- 73	284	$1,940.00
Doug Martin	T31	66- 68- 69- 71	274	$5,550.00	Marty Schiene	T72	68- 70- 70- 76	284	$1,940.00
Dick Mast	T31	68- 68- 72- 66	274	$5,550.00	Rob Sullivan	T72	69- 67- 73- 75	284	$1,940.00
Loren Roberts	T31	68- 68- 70- 68	274	$5,550.00					

B.C. OPEN

En-Joie GC, Endicott, NY
Par: 37-34--71   Yards: 6,966

Purse: $800,000
September 23-26, 1993

LEADERS: First Round--Bill Glasson and Ed Humenik at 5-under-par 66 led by one stroke over Mark Lye and Brian Claar. **Second Round**--Jim McGovern at 6-under-par 136 led by one over Peter Jacobsen. **Third Round**--Blaine McCallister at 9-under-par 204 led by one over McGovern.

CUT: 81 players at 2-over-par 144.

PRO-AM: $7,500. Individual--Nolan Henke, 66, $750. Team--Bill Britton, Blaine McCallister, Jay Haas, 54, $525 each.

WEATHER: Thursday's round was suspended at 4:45 p.m. due to rain. The round resumed on Friday, and the field was cut on Friday. Saturday was sunny and cool. Sunday's round was delayed from 9:47 a.m. to 11:20 a.m due to rain.

Winner: Blaine McCallister   68- 71- 65- 67   271 $144,000.00

Player	Pos	Scores	Total	Money		Player	Pos	Scores	Total	Money
Denis Watson	2	69- 70- 68- 65	272	$86,400.00		John Elliott	T41	71- 69- 73- 71	284	$2,800.00
Bill Glasson	3	66- 72- 68- 67	273	$54,400.00		Brad Fabel	T41	70- 73- 73- 68	284	$2,800.00
Greg Kraft	T 4	70- 70- 68- 67	275	$33,066.67		Morris Hatalsky	T41	68- 74- 73- 69	284	$2,800.00
Mark Lye	T 4	67- 71- 69- 68	275	$33,066.67		Gene Jones	T41	75- 69- 71- 69	284	$2,800.00
David Ogrin	T 4	71- 71- 64- 69	275	$33,066.66		Brett Ogle	T41	70- 72- 72- 70	284	$2,800.00
Dick Mast	7	68- 72- 71- 65	276	$26,800.00		Jeff Sluman	T41	72- 69- 70- 73	284	$2,800.00
Rick Fehr	T 8	70- 71- 67- 69	277	$24,000.00		Robin Freeman	T48	71- 72- 71- 71	285	$2,010.67
Chris Smith	T 8	70- 71- 66- 70	277	$24,000.00		Neal Lancaster	T48	70- 70- 72- 73	285	$2,010.67
Billy Mayfair	T10	70- 71- 69- 68	278	$17,733.34		Mike McCullough	T48	72- 69- 73- 71	285	$2,010.67
David Toms	T10	71- 70- 71- 66	278	$17,733.34		Mike Springer	T48	73- 70- 71- 71	285	$2,010.67
Bobby Clampett	T10	70- 70- 69- 69	278	$17,733.33		Stephen Flesch	T48	71- 73- 73- 68	285	$2,010.66
Ed Dougherty	T10	71- 69- 70- 68	278	$17,733.33		Robert Wrenn	T48	72- 68- 70- 75	285	$2,010.66
Ed Humenik	T10	66- 75- 67- 70	278	$17,733.33		Andy Bean	T54	70- 74- 73- 69	286	$1,832.00
Peter Jacobsen	T10	69- 68- 70- 71	278	$17,733.33		Brad Faxon	T54	71- 72- 72- 71	286	$1,832.00
Jim Thorpe	16	73- 69- 70- 67	279	$13,600.00		Dudley Hart	T54	69- 75- 72- 70	286	$1,832.00
Patrick Burke	T17	72- 69- 70- 69	280	$11,600.00		Mark Hayes	T54	71- 72- 67- 76	286	$1,832.00
Fred Funk	T17	69- 74- 69- 68	280	$11,600.00		John Daly	T58	71- 72- 71- 73	287	$1,744.00
Bill Murchison	T17	71- 69- 72- 68	280	$11,600.00		Buddy Gardner	T58	72- 70- 72- 73	287	$1,744.00
Harry Taylor	T17	72- 69- 69- 70	280	$11,600.00		Paul Goydos	T58	72- 72- 70- 73	287	$1,744.00
Bill Britton	T21	68- 72- 72- 69	281	$7,120.00		Brian Kamm	T58	71- 70- 76- 70	287	$1,744.00
Lennie Clements	T21	68- 74- 70- 69	281	$7,120.00		Rocco Mediate	T58	72- 71- 73- 71	287	$1,744.00
Nolan Henke	T21	68- 71- 72- 70	281	$7,120.00		Larry Mize	T58	69- 74- 69- 75	287	$1,744.00
Steve Lamontagne	T21	72- 71- 69- 69	281	$7,120.00		Mike Schuchart	T58	71- 73- 72- 71	287	$1,744.00
Jim McGovern	T21	69- 67- 69- 76	281	$7,120.00		Tim Conley	T65	70- 73- 72- 73	288	$1,648.00
Perry Moss	T21	69- 72- 72- 68	281	$7,120.00		Doug Martin	T65	73- 71- 73- 71	288	$1,648.00
Chris Perry	T21	74- 67- 67- 73	281	$7,120.00		Lee Porter	T65	69- 70- 74- 75	288	$1,648.00
Mark Pfeil	T21	69- 71- 72- 69	281	$7,120.00		Clarence Rose	T65	72- 72- 74- 70	288	$1,648.00
Tom Purtzer	T21	70- 72- 70- 69	281	$7,120.00		Marty Schiene	T65	72- 71- 72- 73	288	$1,648.00
Howard Twitty	T21	69- 72- 71- 69	281	$7,120.00		Neale Smith	70	71- 71- 74- 73	289	$1,600.00
Bill Kratzert	T31	68- 74- 71- 69	282	$4,537.15		Marco Dawson	T71	72- 72- 75- 71	290	$1,576.00
Jeff Woodland	T31	69- 71- 72- 70	282	$4,537.15		P.H. Horgan III	T71	71- 71- 73- 75	290	$1,576.00
Brad Bryant	T31	68- 71- 68- 75	282	$4,537.14		Tom Byrum	T73	68- 73- 74- 76	291	$1,520.00
Ed Fiori	T31	69- 70- 72- 71	282	$4,537.14		Brian Claar	T73	67- 74- 75- 75	291	$1,520.00
Deane Pappas	T31	69- 73- 73- 67	282	$4,537.14		Greg Lesher	T73	74- 69- 73- 75	291	$1,520.00
Lance Ten Broeck	T31	70- 69- 71- 72	282	$4,537.14		Bob Lohr	T73	73- 71- 75- 72	291	$1,520.00
Jim Woodward	T31	71- 70- 70- 71	282	$4,537.14		Len Mattiace	T73	74- 70- 75- 72	291	$1,520.00
John Inman	T38	72- 71- 69- 71	283	$3,600.00		Jaime Gomez	T78	70- 73- 71- 78	292	$1,464.00
Tom Jenkins	T38	70- 71- 71- 71	283	$3,600.00		Richie Karl	T78	77- 66- 77- 72	292	$1,464.00
Dillard Pruitt	T38	70- 74- 69- 70	283	$3,600.00		Forrest Fezler	80	75- 68- 79- 71	293	$1,440.00
Mark Carnevale	T41	72- 72- 72- 68	284	$2,800.00		John Ross	81	72- 70- 83- 76	301	$1,424.00

BUICK SOUTHERN OPEN

Callaway Gardens Resort, Pine Mountain, GA
Par: 36-36--72　　　　**Yards: 7,057**

Purse: $700,000
Sept. 30-Oct. 3, 1993

LEADERS: First Round--Jim Hallet shot a 5-under-par 67 and led nine players by a stroke. **Second Round--**Tom Lehman shot a course-record 7-under-par 65, and finished with a 9-under-par 135 total. He led Billy Andrade and Peter Persons by three strokes. **Third Round--**Bob Estes at 10-under-par 206 led John Inman by two.

CUT: 86 players at 2-over-par 146.

PRO-AM: $7,500. Individual--Jay Delsing, Brian Claar, Dillard Pruitt, 67, $625 each. Team--John Huston, Gary Hallberg, Kirk Triplett, 56, $625 each.

WEATHER: Beautiful every day.

Winner:　John Inman　71- 73- 64- 70　　　278　　$126,000.00
(won playoff with birdie on second extra hole)

Player		Scores	Total	Money	Player		Scores	Total	Money
Billy Andrade	T 2	68- 70- 73- 67	278	$46,200.00	Jodie Mudd	T36	73- 73- 70- 70	286	$2,873.18
Mark Brooks	T 2	72- 70- 72- 64	278	$46,200.00	Dan Pohl	T36	76- 67- 72- 71	286	$2,873.18
Brad Bryant	T 2	69- 72- 70- 67	278	$46,200.00	Doug Tewell	T36	74- 70- 72- 70	286	$2,873.18
Bob Estes	T 2	70- 69- 67- 72	278	$46,200.00	Tom Byrum	T47	73- 70- 74- 70	287	$1,850.80
Russ Cochran	T 6	74- 71- 65- 69	279	$24,325.00	Greg Lesher	T47	73- 73- 72- 69	287	$1,850.80
Tom Lehman	T 6	70- 65- 76- 68	279	$24,325.00	Larry Mize	T47	68- 72- 72- 75	287	$1,850.80
Bill Glasson	T 8	71- 73- 69- 67	280	$20,300.00	Perry Moss	T47	68- 73- 71- 75	287	$1,850.80
David Toms	T 8	72- 69- 74- 65	280	$20,300.00	Gene Sauers	T47	73- 69- 75- 70	287	$1,850.80
Willie Wood	T 8	69- 70- 71- 70	280	$20,300.00	Phil Blackmar	T52	74- 70- 72- 72	288	$1,608.25
Neal Lancaster	T11	68- 71- 73- 69	281	$16,800.00	Scott Gump	T52	74- 71- 69- 74	288	$1,608.25
Mike Springer	T11	72- 69- 69- 71	281	$16,800.00	Craig Parry	T52	71- 69- 73- 75	288	$1,608.25
Mark Calcavecchia	T13	73- 72- 69- 68	282	$13,533.34	Mike Schuchart	T52	77- 69- 71- 71	288	$1,608.25
Mark Carnevale	T13	72- 71- 70- 69	282	$13,533.33	Tom Sieckmann	T52	71- 74- 70- 73	288	$1,608.25
Rick Fehr	T13	73- 71- 69- 69	282	$13,533.33	Tim Simpson	T52	75- 71- 69- 73	288	$1,608.25
Jay Don Blake	T16	74- 72- 66- 71	283	$11,200.00	Ted Tryba	T52	72- 74- 73- 69	288	$1,608.25
Len Mattiace	T16	70- 73- 69- 71	283	$11,200.00	Jim Woodward	T52	75- 69- 73- 71	288	$1,608.25
Kenny Perry	T16	69- 77- 68- 69	283	$11,200.00	Barry Cheesman	T60	73- 72- 73- 71	289	$1,519.00
Ed Fiori	T19	70- 71- 72- 71	284	$7,900.00	John Elliott	T60	72- 74- 73- 70	289	$1,519.00
Fred Funk	T19	68- 71- 71- 74	284	$7,900.00	Steve Lamontagne	T60	74- 71- 72- 72	289	$1,519.00
Skip Kendall	T19	72- 71- 68- 73	284	$7,900.00	David Ogrin	T60	71- 73- 70- 75	289	$1,519.00
Dick Mast	T19	69- 73- 69- 73	284	$7,900.00	Ronnie Black	T64	73- 73- 72- 72	290	$1,449.00
Loren Roberts	T19	68- 73- 70- 73	284	$7,900.00	Brandel Chamblee	T64	68- 75- 74- 73	290	$1,449.00
Kirk Triplett	T19	76- 70- 69- 69	284	$7,900.00	Brian Claar	T64	72- 74- 74- 70	290	$1,449.00
Mark Wiebe	T19	75- 70- 70- 69	284	$7,900.00	Bob Eastwood	T64	70- 75- 74- 71	290	$1,449.00
Patrick Burke	T26	69- 73- 73- 70	285	$4,665.50	Brett Ogle	T64	71- 75- 72- 72	290	$1,449.00
Jim Gallagher, Jr.	T26	71- 73- 72- 69	285	$4,665.50	Dillard Pruitt	T64	74- 72- 73- 71	290	$1,449.00
Mike Hulbert	T26	72- 70- 73- 70	285	$4,665.50	P.H. Horgan III	T70	71- 74- 74- 72	291	$1,393.00
John Huston	T26	71- 69- 74- 71	285	$4,665.50	John Mahaffey	T70	75- 71- 74- 71	291	$1,393.00
Wayne Levi	T26	73- 71- 75- 66	285	$4,665.50	Joe Durant	T72	74- 70- 76- 72	292	$1,365.00
Peter Persons	T26	72- 66- 74- 73	285	$4,665.50	Bill Murchison	T72	71- 74- 77- 70	292	$1,365.00
Scott Simpson	T26	69- 71- 72- 73	285	$4,665.50	John Flannery	T74	72- 73- 75- 73	293	$1,323.00
Lance Ten Broeck	T26	69- 76- 69- 71	285	$4,665.50	Gene Jones	T74	72- 74- 72- 75	293	$1,323.00
Jim Thorpe	T26	73- 73- 68- 71	285	$4,665.50	Blaine McCallister	T74	68- 76- 75- 74	293	$1,323.00
Bobby Wadkins	T26	70- 73- 72- 70	285	$4,665.50	Neale Smith	T74	71- 74- 74- 74	293	$1,323.00
Morris Hatalsky	T36	77- 68- 72- 69	286	$2,873.19	Marco Dawson	T78	72- 72- 74- 76	294	$1,281.00
Doug Martin	T36	74- 71- 74- 67	286	$2,873.19	Lon Hinkle	T78	72- 69- 76- 77	294	$1,281.00
Jay Delsing	T36	72- 74- 69- 71	286	$2,873.18	Gary Hallberg	80	72- 71- 77- 75	295	$1,260.00
Ed Dougherty	T36	71- 72- 73- 70	286	$2,873.18	Hubert Green	81	71- 75- 75- 75	296	$1,246.00
Robin Freeman	T36	74- 70- 69- 73	286	$2,873.18	Greg Cesario	T82	75- 71- 76- 75	297	$1,211.00
Jaime Gomez	T36	74- 70- 68- 74	286	$2,873.18	Tad Rhyan	T82	70- 73- 78- 76	297	$1,211.00
Jim Hallet	T36	67- 72- 72- 75	286	$2,873.18	Greg Twiggs	T82	73- 73- 76- 75	297	$1,211.00
Bill Kratzert	T36	68- 73- 74- 71	286	$2,873.18	Jeff Woodland	T82	71- 75- 78- 73	297	$1,211.00

WALT DISNEY WORLD/ OLDSMOBILE GOLF CLASSIC

Three Disney Courses, Lake Buena Vista, FL
Magnolia: 7,190
Palm: 6,967
Lake Buena Vista: 6,829

Purse: $1,100,000
October 7-10, 1993

All Par: 36-36--72

LEADERS: First Round--Keith Clearwater (M), Tom Purtzer (LBV) and Ted Tryba (P), at 8-under-par 64, held a one-shot lead over seven players. **Second Round**--Clearwater (P), Jeff Maggert (M) and Skip Kendall (M), all at 13-under-par 131, had a one-stroke advantage over Purtzer (M), Tryba (LBV) and Mark McCumber (LBV). **Third Round**--Maggert (P), at 19-under-par 197, was two shots in front of Kendall (P), Tryba (M) and Clearwater (LBV).

CUT: 75 players at 7-under-par 209.

WEATHER: Partly sunny and mild Thursday. Mostly cloudy conditions early Friday led to lightning and rain later, producing two afternoon delays and an eventual suspension for the day at 6 p.m. Length of first delay at M and P: 55 minutes; LBV 1:15. Start time for second delays (leading to final suspension): LBV 4:10 p.m.; M and P 4:25 p.m. Saturday resumption of Round 2: LBV 8 a.m., M and P 8:20 a.m. Mostly sunny skies much of Saturday gave way to showers, lighting and yet another suspension at 3:01 p.m. Play suspended for day at 5 p.m. Round 3 resumed at 7:30 a.m. early Sunday; only nine players completed play Saturday. Round 4 began at 12:06 p.m. Sunday. Mostly sunny skies early in the day gave way to thunderstorms and suspension at 1:22 p.m.; play resumed at 2:35 p.m. and continued under partly sunny skies.

Winner: Jeff Maggert   66- 65- 66- 68   265 $198,000.00

Greg Kraft 2	69- 69- 64- 66	268	$118,800.00
Ken Green .... T 3	70- 68- 63- 69	270	$52,800.00
Loren Roberts .... T 3	66- 68- 67- 69	270	$52,800.00
Craig Stadler .... T 3	68- 67- 68- 67	270	$52,800.00
Ted Tryba .... T 3	64- 68- 67- 71	270	$52,800.00
John Cook 7	70- 67- 65- 69	271	$36,850.00
Billy Mayfair .... T 8	68- 68- 71- 65	272	$33,000.00
Tom Purtzer .... T 8	64- 68- 71- 69	272	$33,000.00
Keith Clearwater T10	64- 67- 68- 74	273	$23,571.43
Jay Delsing T10	69- 67- 71- 66	273	$23,571.43
Larry Mize T10	66- 70- 66- 71	273	$23,571.43
David Ogrin T10	74- 69- 65- 65	273	$23,571.43
Tom Sieckmann T10	69- 66- 69- 69	273	$23,571.43
Curtis Strange T10	65- 70- 69- 69	273	$23,571.43
Scott Hoch T10	66- 69- 68- 70	273	$23,571.42
Barry Cheesman ... T17	68- 67- 65- 74	274	$14,394.29
Dan Forsman T17	67- 70- 69- 68	274	$14,394.29
Dennis Trixler T17	66- 72- 67- 69	274	$14,394.29
Mark Wiebe T17	66- 67- 68- 73	274	$14,394.29
Brian Claar T17	67- 67- 69- 71	274	$14,394.28
Skip Kendall T17	65- 66- 68- 75	274	$14,394.28
Mark McCumber ... T17	65- 67- 70- 72	274	$14,394.28
JC Anderson T24	65- 71- 66- 73	275	$7,965.00
Ronnie Black T24	69- 68- 67- 71	275	$7,965.00
Robert Gamez T24	71- 70- 66- 68	275	$7,965.00
Bill Glasson T24	67- 68- 71- 69	275	$7,965.00
Jaime Gomez T24	70- 65- 69- 71	275	$7,965.00
Jay Haas T24	65- 69- 71- 70	275	$7,965.00
Lee Janzen T24	65- 69- 69- 72	275	$7,965.00
Davis Love III T24	70- 66- 70- 69	275	$7,965.00
Perry Moss T24	69- 67- 66- 73	275	$7,965.00
Larry Rinker T24	70- 69- 68- 68	275	$7,965.00
Tim Simpson T24	69- 68- 70- 68	275	$7,965.00
Ed Humenik T35	69- 64- 70- 73	276	$4,968.34
Rocco Mediate T35	71- 64- 68- 73	276	$4,968.34
Scott Simpson T35	71- 69- 67- 69	276	$4,968.34
Phil Blackmar T35	65- 71- 67- 73	276	$4,968.33
John Huston T35	69- 68- 67- 72	276	$4,968.33
David Jackson T35	70- 66- 69- 71	276	$4,968.33
Andrew Magee T35	71- 67- 68- 70	276	$4,968.33
Dick Mast T35	70- 69- 66- 71	276	$4,968.33
Gene Sauers T35	68- 70- 67- 71	276	$4,968.33
Billy Andrade T44	68- 68- 69- 72	277	$3,325.67
Fred Funk T44	66- 69- 69- 73	277	$3,325.67
Mike Hulbert T44	67- 69- 69- 72	277	$3,325.67
Mike Schuchart T44	70- 67- 68- 72	277	$3,325.67
Nolan Henke T44	68- 67- 70- 72	277	$3,325.66
Corey Pavin T44	70- 69- 70- 68	277	$3,325.66
Dave Barr T50	69- 67- 71- 71	278	$2,653.20
Tom Lehman T50	67- 67- 70- 74	278	$2,653.20
Blaine McCallister . T50	73- 71- 65- 69	278	$2,653.20
Kenny Perry T50	70- 70- 69- 69	278	$2,653.20
Kirk Triplett T50	72- 69- 69- 68	278	$2,653.20
Chip Beck T55	68- 72- 68- 71	279	$2,486.00
John Inman T55	70- 71- 68- 70	279	$2,486.00
Steve Lowery T55	70- 70- 69- 70	279	$2,486.00
Mike Sullivan T55	67- 74- 68- 70	279	$2,486.00
Howard Twitty T55	69- 70- 68- 72	279	$2,486.00
Fulton Allem T60	67- 69- 70- 74	280	$2,387.00
Paul Azinger T60	70- 70- 67- 73	280	$2,387.00
Mark Carnevale T60	70- 71- 67- 72	280	$2,387.00
David Peoples T60	75- 69- 65- 71	280	$2,387.00
Robin Freeman T64	70- 70- 69- 72	281	$2,277.00
Hubert Green T64	66- 71- 70- 74	281	$2,277.00
John Mahaffey T64	69- 68- 72- 72	281	$2,277.00
Mike Smith T64	70- 68- 69- 74	281	$2,277.00
Lanny Wadkins T64	74- 68- 67- 72	281	$2,277.00
D.A. Weibring T64	70- 69- 67- 75	281	$2,277.00
Brad Bryant T70	69- 73- 67- 73	282	$2,189.00
Greg Twiggs T70	70- 70- 67- 75	282	$2,189.00
Bob Lohr T72	70- 67- 71- 76	284	$2,145.00
Harry Taylor T72	70- 67- 71- 76	284	$2,145.00

H-E-B TEXAS OPEN

Oak Hills CC, San Antonio, TX   Purse: $1,000,000
Par: 35-36--71   Yards: 6,650   October 14-17, 1993

LEADERS: First Round--Mike Smith, after a par-71 course record-tying 62, held a two-stroke lead over Lanny Wadkins, Mark Wiebe and Dan Forsman. **Second Round--**Forsman, Bob Lohr, Billy Andrade and Gil Morgan, all at 10-under-par 132, had a one-shot advantage over Jay Haas. **Third Round--**Forsman, Haas, Lohr and Tom Lehman, each at 14-under-par 199, were one stroke in front of David Edwards.

CUT: 78 players at 2-under-par 140.

PRO-AM: $7,500 (Due to morning rain all groups played only nine holes.) Front Nine Individual--Billy Andrade, 30, $450. Back Nine Individual--Steve Elkington, Tom Lehman, Mark O'Meara, Mark Wiebe, 33, $393.75 each. Front Nine Team--Keith Clearwater, 24, $450. Back Nine Team--Steve Elkington, David Toms, 25, $431.25 each.

WEATHER: Sunny and warm Thursday. Some light drizzle early Friday, with skies changing from cloudy and overcast to partly sunny during the day; wins picking up in the afternoon. Mostly cloudy with variable winds early Saturday, becoming mostly sunny, hot and humid with virtually no wind in the afternoon. Sunday mostly cloudy early with some light fog, becoming mostly sunny in the afternoon.

Winner Jay Haas 68- 65- 66- 64   263 $180,000.00
(won playoff with birdie on second extra hole)

Player	Pos	Rounds	Total	Money		Player	Pos	Rounds	Total	Money
Bob Lohr	2	68- 64- 67- 64	263	$108,000.00		T. Gene Jones	T37	71- 67- 68- 70	276	$3,900.00
Billy Andrade	3	66- 66- 69- 66	267	$68,000.00		Mark O'Meara	T37	68- 66- 71- 71	276	$3,900.00
Bob Estes	4	66- 71- 64- 67	268	$48,000.00		Corey Pavin	T37	70- 66- 69- 71	276	$3,900.00
Marco Dawson	T 5	69- 67- 65- 68	269	$32,750.00		Tim Simpson	T37	66- 71- 68- 71	276	$3,900.00
David Edwards	T 5	68- 66- 66- 69	269	$32,750.00		Mike Smith	T37	62- 73- 70- 71	276	$3,900.00
Dan Forsman	T 5	64- 68- 67- 70	269	$32,750.00		Dennis Trixler	T37	67- 69- 73- 67	276	$3,900.00
Tom Lehman	T 5	71- 63- 65- 70	269	$32,750.00		D.A. Weibring	T37	70- 68- 71- 67	276	$3,900.00
Gil Morgan	T 5	66- 66- 70- 67	269	$32,750.00		Blaine McCallister	T48	68- 70- 74- 65	277	$2,513.34
Mike Standly	T 5	66- 71- 65- 67	269	$32,750.00		Jeff Woodland	T48	68- 70- 72- 67	277	$2,513.34
John Elliott	T11	70- 68- 69- 63	270	$23,000.00		Patrick Burke	T48	72- 68- 67- 70	277	$2,513.33
Scott Hoch	T11	68- 66- 68- 68	270	$23,000.00		Barry Cheesman	T48	67- 73- 71- 66	277	$2,513.33
Mark Wiebe	T11	64- 70- 70- 66	270	$23,000.00		P.H. Horgan III	T48	69- 69- 70- 69	277	$2,513.33
Tim Conley	T14	67- 72- 67- 65	271	$17,500.00		Ted Tryba	T48	67- 71- 67- 72	277	$2,513.33
Tom Kite	T14	66- 70- 65- 70	271	$17,500.00		John Flannery	T54	73- 67- 74- 64	278	$2,300.00
Jim Thorpe	T14	71- 69- 66- 65	271	$17,500.00		Brian Kamm	T54	70- 66- 71- 71	278	$2,300.00
Lanny Wadkins	T14	64- 70- 68- 69	271	$17,500.00		Denis Watson	T54	70- 68- 69- 71	278	$2,300.00
Russ Cochran	T18	68- 69- 69- 66	272	$13,500.00		Bobby Clampett	T57	69- 71- 67- 72	279	$2,230.00
Rick Fehr	T18	66- 69- 68- 69	272	$13,500.00		Steve Elkington	T57	67- 73- 66- 73	279	$2,230.00
Bruce Lietzke	T18	67- 70- 68- 67	272	$13,500.00		Gary Hallberg	T57	69- 71- 72- 67	279	$2,230.00
Mark Lye	T18	69- 66- 66- 71	272	$13,500.00		Jeff Sluman	T57	73- 65- 70- 71	279	$2,230.00
Brad Faxon	T22	70- 65- 72- 66	273	$9,600.00		Ben Crenshaw	T61	67- 73- 69- 71	280	$2,170.00
Paul Goydos	T22	68- 71- 68- 66	273	$9,600.00		Larry Nelson	T61	68- 69- 71- 72	280	$2,170.00
John Huston	T22	71- 69- 66- 67	273	$9,600.00		Howard Twitty	63	74- 65- 76- 66	281	$2,140.00
David Ogrin	T22	70- 66- 67- 70	273	$9,600.00		Gary McCord	T64	70- 70- 70- 72	282	$2,110.00
Dillard Pruitt	T22	74- 64- 69- 66	273	$9,600.00		Neale Smith	T64	69- 70- 69- 74	282	$2,110.00
Brad Bryant	T27	69- 68- 71- 66	274	$7,100.00		Phil Blackmar	T66	70- 70- 71- 72	283	$2,030.00
Brandel Chamblee	T27	69- 70- 68- 67	274	$7,100.00		Ed Fiori	T66	70- 69- 70- 74	283	$2,030.00
Donnie Hammond	T27	72- 68- 65- 69	274	$7,100.00		Bob Gilder	T66	70- 70- 72- 71	283	$2,030.00
Morris Hatalsky	T27	71- 67- 68- 68	274	$7,100.00		Steve Lowery	T66	70- 69- 75- 69	283	$2,030.00
Willie Wood	T27	69- 68- 69- 68	274	$7,100.00		Perry Moss	T66	72- 66- 76- 69	283	$2,030.00
Jim Kane	T32	66- 70- 68- 71	275	$5,660.00		Leonard Thompson	T66	69- 71- 72- 71	283	$2,030.00
Jeff Maggert	T32	70- 67- 70- 68	275	$5,660.00		Tom Byrum	T72	67- 73- 71- 73	284	$1,940.00
Steve Pate	T32	68- 69- 71- 67	275	$5,660.00		David Jackson	T72	69- 71- 74- 70	284	$1,940.00
Lee Porter	T32	69- 66- 70- 70	275	$5,660.00		Lance Ten Broeck	T72	68- 72- 69- 75	284	$1,940.00
Mike Schuchart	T32	71- 68- 65- 71	275	$5,660.00		Dave Peege	75	68- 72- 76- 69	285	$1,900.00
Russell Beiersdorf	T37	67- 70- 72- 67	276	$3,900.00		JC Anderson	76	71- 66- 75- 74	286	$1,880.00
Brian Claar	T37	68- 72- 71- 65	276	$3,900.00		J.L. Lewis	T77	71- 69- 75- 73	288	$1,850.00
Jeff Cook	T37	69- 71- 68- 68	276	$3,900.00		Chris Tucker	T77	68- 71- 76- 73	288	$1,850.00
Scott Gump	T37	67- 67- 70- 72	276	$3,900.00						

LAS VEGAS INVITATIONAL

LAS VEGAS INVITATIONAL

TPC at Summerlin	Yards: 7,243	Purse: $1,400,000
Desert Inn CC	Yards: 7,111	October 20-24, 1993
Las Vegas CC	Yards: 7,164	
Las Vegas, NV	All Par: 36-36--72	

LEADERS: First Round--Jeff Woodland (DI), Gil Morgan and Bob Lohr (both TPC), at 8-under-par 64, had a one-stroke lead over Phil Mickelson (TPC) and Howard Twitty (LVCC). **Second Round**--Lohr, Morgan, Blaine McCallister and Keith Clearwater (all LVCC) were tied at 12-under-par 132, one stroke ahead of Craig Stadler (LVCC), Davis Love III and Paul Azinger (both DI). **Third Round**--Clearwater (DI), at 17-under-par 199, held a one-stroke lead over Love (TPC). (All Saturday/Sunday play at TPC at Summerlin) **Fourth Round**--Love, at 23-under-par 265, had a six-stroke margin over Bob Estes.

CUT: 76 players at 5-under-par 211.

WEATHER: Cool each morning, with virtually no wind throughout. Sunny and mild Wednesday. Partly cloudy with high overcast Thursday. Sunny and warm Friday through Sunday, with some afternoon cloudiness Sunday.

Winner: Davis Love III   67- 66- 67- 65- 66   331 $252,000.00

Player	Pos	Scores	Total	Money	Player	Pos	Scores	Total	Money
Craig Stadler	2	67- 66- 69- 72- 65	339	$151,200.00	Fuzzy Zoeller	T34	73- 70- 68- 69- 70	350	$6,626.67
Paul Azinger	T 3	66- 67- 72- 68- 67	340	$72,800.00	John Inman	T34	67- 72- 70- 69- 72	350	$6,626.66
David Edwards	T 3	72- 66- 68- 67- 67	340	$72,800.00	Billy Mayfair	T34	68- 68- 72- 69- 73	350	$6,626.66
Bob Estes	T 3	68- 68- 68- 67- 69	340	$72,800.00	Willie Wood	T34	70- 70- 69- 68- 73	350	$6,626.66
John Huston	T 6	69- 66- 69- 71- 67	342	$46,900.00	Marco Dawson	T43	71- 68- 68- 70- 74	351	$4,760.00
Bob Tway	T 6	71- 68- 68- 67- 68	342	$46,900.00	Ed Dougherty	T43	70- 65- 69- 74- 73	351	$4,760.00
Richard Zokol	T 6	68- 67- 68- 69- 70	342	$46,900.00	Paul Goydos	T43	69- 71- 71- 68- 72	351	$4,760.00
Gil Morgan	9	64- 68- 72- 70- 69	343	$40,600.00	John Mahaffey	T43	70- 66- 73- 71- 71	351	$4,760.00
Robert Gamez	T10	66- 70- 68- 69- 71	344	$35,000.00	JC Anderson	T47	72- 63- 75- 71- 71	352	$3,515.56
Brian Kamm	T10	68- 70- 69- 69- 68	344	$35,000.00	Brian Claar	T47	68- 69- 72- 71- 72	352	$3,515.56
Dick Mast	T10	72- 68- 66- 68- 70	344	$35,000.00	Bruce Fleisher	T47	67- 69- 70- 77- 69	352	$3,515.56
Michael Allen	T13	71- 64- 71- 70- 69	345	$26,250.00	Scott Gump	T47	66- 71- 73- 73- 69	352	$3,515.56
Jay Don Blake	T13	71- 70- 66- 68- 70	345	$26,250.00	Blaine McCallister	T47	67- 65- 78- 73- 69	352	$3,515.56
Russ Cochran	T13	68- 70- 68- 69- 70	345	$26,250.00	Russell Beiersdorf	T47	75- 67- 67- 70- 73	352	$3,515.56
Vijay Singh	T13	68- 69- 72- 69- 67	345	$26,250.00	Bill Britton	T47	73- 69- 65- 72- 73	352	$3,515.55
Keith Clearwater	T17	67- 65- 67- 74- 73	346	$21,700.00	David Peoples	T47	70- 69- 64- 73- 76	352	$3,515.55
Tom Lehman	T17	70- 70- 71- 70- 65	346	$21,700.00	Tim Simpson	T47	70- 71- 66- 71- 74	352	$3,515.55
Scott Hoch	T19	69- 70- 68- 72- 68	347	$17,570.00	Wayne Levi	T56	68- 70- 71- 73- 71	353	$3,150.00
Phil Mickelson	T19	65- 69- 68- 71- 74	347	$17,570.00	Bob Lohr	T56	64- 68- 73- 71- 77	353	$3,150.00
Kirk Triplett	T19	71- 72- 66- 71- 67	347	$17,570.00	Perry Moss	T56	68- 71- 72- 75- 67	353	$3,150.00
Grant Waite	T19	69- 69- 69- 68- 72	347	$17,570.00	Mike Springer	T56	67- 68- 73- 71- 74	353	$3,150.00
John Cook	T23	66- 73- 70- 73- 66	348	$12,460.00	Joel Edwards	T60	72- 69- 69- 69- 75	354	$3,038.00
Brad Faxon	T23	66- 71- 71- 70- 70	348	$12,460.00	Tom Sieckmann	T60	67- 72- 72- 69- 74	354	$3,038.00
Rick Fehr	T23	70- 68- 72- 70- 68	348	$12,460.00	Harry Taylor	T60	71- 69- 68- 72- 74	354	$3,038.00
Ken Green	T23	69- 66- 68- 72- 73	348	$12,460.00	Jeff Woodland	T60	64- 73- 69- 76- 72	354	$3,038.00
Bill Murchison	T23	73- 71- 66- 67- 71	348	$12,460.00	David Toms	T64	74- 69- 68- 71- 73	355	$2,940.00
Tim Conley	T28	71- 68- 69- 72- 69	349	$9,310.00	Howard Twitty	T64	65- 73- 73- 77- 67	355	$2,940.00
Bill Glasson	T28	69- 66- 69- 74- 71	349	$9,310.00	Duffy Waldorf	T64	70- 68- 73- 73- 71	355	$2,940.00
Roger Maltbie	T28	69- 72- 68- 70- 70	349	$9,310.00	Jim McGovern	67	68- 71- 72- 75- 70	356	$2,884.00
Mark McCumber	T28	68- 68- 71- 71- 71	349	$9,310.00	Steve Lowery	T68	66- 71- 72- 76- 72	357	$2,842.00
Mark O'Meara	T28	71- 69- 68- 71- 70	349	$9,310.00	Steve Pate	T68	70- 72- 69- 72- 74	357	$2,842.00
Mike Sullivan	T28	71- 75- 64- 72- 67	349	$9,310.00	Kelly Gibson	70	70- 70- 70- 75- 73	358	$2,800.00
Ronnie Black	T34	72- 68- 70- 73- 67	350	$6,626.67	Jay Delsing	T71	69- 69- 72- 72- 77	359	$2,758.00
Gary Hallberg	T34	68- 68- 72- 75- 67	350	$6,626.67	Brian Henninger	T71	70- 72- 69- 73- 75	359	$2,758.00
Steve Lamontagne	T34	71- 66- 71- 74- 68	350	$6,626.67	Tom Byrum	73	69- 68- 71- 80- 73	361	$2,716.00
Gene Sauers	T34	68- 71- 71- 69- 71	350	$6,626.67	Ben Crenshaw	T74	75- 68- 68- 75- 77	363	$2,674.00
D.A. Weibring	T34	70- 71- 70- 71- 68	350	$6,626.67	John Flannery	T74	68- 67- 76- 78- 74	363	$2,674.00

TOUR CHAMPIONSHIP

The Olympic Club (Lake Course)
San Francisco, CA
Par: 35-36--71   Yards: 7,005

Purse: $3,000,000
October 28-31, 1993

THE TOUR
CHAMPIONSHIP

LEADERS: First Round--Jim Gallagher, Jr., fired a course-record 8-under-par 63 and led by five over Scott Simpson, Corey Pavin and David Frost. **Second Round--**Frost and Gallagher at 6-under-par 136 led by one over Tom Kite. **Third Round--**Frost at 8-under-par 205 led by two over Greg Norman.

PRO-AM: $10,000. Individual--Corey Pavin, Phil Mickelson, Scott Simpson, Nolan Henke, 66, $775 each. Team--Steve Elkington, 54. $1,000.

WEATHER: Near ideal conditions every day.

Winner: Jim Gallagher, Jr.		**63- 73- 72- 69**	**277**	**$540,000.00**
David Frost	T 2	68- 68- 69- 73	278	$198,750.00
John Huston	T 2	72- 68- 68- 70	278	$198,750.00
Greg Norman	T 2	72- 67- 68- 71	278	$198,750.00
Scott Simpson	T 2	68- 70- 70- 70	278	$198,750.00
Rick Fehr	6	69- 69- 70- 71	279	$108,000.00
Mark Calcavecchia	T 7	69- 69- 75- 67	280	$96,000.00
Tom Kite	T 7	69- 68- 72- 71	280	$96,000.00
Corey Pavin	T 7	68- 73- 72- 67	280	$96,000.00
Fred Couples	T10	74- 72- 70- 65	281	$83,100.00
Jay Haas	T10	70- 69- 72- 70	281	$83,100.00
Fulton Allem	T12	69- 72- 71- 71	283	$73,200.00
Chip Beck	T12	71- 70- 70- 72	283	$73,200.00
David Edwards	T12	71- 72- 68- 72	283	$73,200.00
Jeff Maggert	15	71- 74- 69- 70	284	$66,000.00
Jim McGovern	T16	71- 70- 73- 71	285	$62,400.00
Vijay Singh	T16	70- 71- 74- 70	285	$62,400.00
Larry Mize	T18	69- 76- 71- 70	286	$58,800.00
Gil Morgan	T18	70- 71- 71- 74	286	$58,800.00
Nick Price	T18	72- 68- 75- 71	286	$58,800.00
Paul Azinger	21	72- 71- 72- 73	288	$56,400.00
Lee Janzen	22	73- 68- 74- 74	289	$55,200.00
Steve Elkington	T23	74- 71- 72- 73	290	$52,800.00
Nolan Henke	T23	69- 72- 74- 75	290	$52,800.00
Rocco Mediate	T23	78- 70- 70- 72	290	$52,800.00
Payne Stewart	26	74- 72- 73- 73	292	$50,400.00
Davis Love III	27	77- 72- 73- 71	293	$49,800.00
Phil Mickelson	28	71- 75- 74- 74	294	$49,200.00
Craig Stadler	29	71- 75- 73- 77	296	$48,600.00
Billy Mayfair	30	77- 77- 74- 71	299	$48,000.00

LINCOLN-MERCURY
KAPALUA INTERNATIONAL

Plantation Club, Kapalua Resort
Par: 36-37--73 Yards: 7,263
Bay Course, Kapalua Resort
Par: 35-36--71 Yards: 6,600
Kapalua, Maui, Hawaii

Purse: $1,000,000
Nov. 4-7, 1993

Lincoln / Mercury
Kapalua International

LEADERS: First Round—Andrew Magee, with a 6-under-par 67 on the Plantation Course, had his total matched at the Bay Course by Scott Hoch and Peter Jacobsen, both of whom were 4-under-par. **Second Round**—Mike Hulbert (B), at 9-under-par 135, held a one-stroke lead over Loren Roberts (B); Fred Couples (P) was third at 7-under-par 137. **Third Round**—With the pro-am portion of the tournament over and all play at the Plantation Course, Couples, at 13-under-par 204, held a two-stroke advantage over Hulbert.

WEATHER: Sunny, mild and windy all four days with temperatures in the low 80s.

WNNER: FRED COUPLES   69-68-67-70 274 $180,000

Blaine McCallister	2	74-66-70-68	278	$104,000.00	Donnie Hammond	T27	72-77-68-77	294	9,175.00
Davis Love III	3	70-72-69-68	279	65,000.00	Bob Estes	T27	71-70-76-77	294	9,175.00
Peter Jacobsen	4	67-74-67-73	281	42,500.00	Sean Murphy	T27	71-75-74-74	294	9,175.00
Nolan Henke	T5	69-73-67-73	282	34,000.00	Chip Beck	T27	76-72-72-74	294	9,175.00
David Peoples	T5	73-65-69-75	282	34,000.00	Bruce Fleischer	T27	76-70-75-73	294	9,175.00
Loren Roberts	7	70-66-77-70	282	28,000.00	Mark Brooks	T27	74-72-75-73	294	9,175.00
Tom Purtzer	T8	71-69-77-67	284	21,600.00	Grant Waite	T27	72-75-74-73	294	9,175.00
Scott Simpson	T8	73-72-71-68	284	21,600.00	Bob Gilder	T35	72-72-74-77	295	8,463.00
Keith Clearwater	T8	71-69-72-72	284	21,600.00	Howard Twitty	T35	78-71-70-76	295	8,463.00
Andrew Magee	T8	67-72-70-75	284	21,600.00	Steve Pate	T35	75-72-74-74	295	8,463.00
Mike Hulbert	T8	70-65-71-78	284	21,600.00	Ed Humenik	T35	72-73-76-74	295	8,463.00
Tom Lehman	13	70-75-72-68	285	18,000.00	Billy Mayfair	39	72-79-72-74	297	8,300.00
Scott Hoch	14	67-75-71-73	286	17,000.00	David Duval	40	76-71-72-79	298	8,250.00
Hale Irwin	T15	69-73-70-75	287	15,500.00	Fulton Allem	T41	78-72-72-77	299	8,175.00
Dave Stockton	T15	73-68-70-76	287	15,500.00	Fred Funk	T41	73-76-76-74	299	8,175.00
Lee Trevino	17	73-68-74-73	288	14,100.00	Mike Standly	43	75-75-76-74	300	8,100.00
Jim McGovern	18	78-69-74-68	289	13,600.00	Robert Gamez	44	74-78-74-76	302	8,050.00
Mark Calcavecchia	T19	77-65-74-74	290	12,850.00	Michael Allen	45	75-73-74-81	303	8,000.00
John Cook	T19	75-70-71-74	290	12,850.00	Bob Lohr	46	73-70-78-83	304	7,950.00
Ben Crenshaw	21	72-74-69-76	291	12,100.00	Greg Twiggs	47	69-82-80-76	307	7,900.00
Russ Cochran	T22	74-73-73-72	292	11,200.00	Jeff Maggert	48	73-79-75-81	308	7,850.00
Gary McCord	T22	77-68-72-75	292	11,200.00	Billy Andrade	49	78-75-74-82	309	7,800.00
Kirk Triplett	T22	72-72-72-76	292	11,200.00	John Adams	50	70-79-80-85	314	7,750.00
Andy Bean	T25	76-70-73-74	293	10,250.00	Mark Rolfing	51	78-82-83-85	328	7,700.00
Dave Rummells	T25	74-71-74-74	293	10,250.00	John Daly		71-DQ		
Roger Maltbie	T27	75-69-74-76	294	9,175.00					

WORLD CUP OF GOLF BY HEINEKEN

Heineken
WORLD CUP GOLF

Lake Nona GC, Orlando, FL
Par: 36-36--72   **Yards: 7,011**

Purse: $1,200,000
Nov. 11-14, 1993

TEAM LEADERS: First Round—Fred Couples-Davis Love III, United States, shot 7-under-par 137 and led by three strokes over Ernie Els-Retief Goosen of South Africa and Jean Van de Velde-Marc-Antoine Farry of France. Couples shot 66 and Love 71. **Second Round**—Couples-Love moved to 11-under-par 211 and led by one stroke over Nick Price-Mark McNulty of South Africa. Couples shot 71 and Love, 69.**Third Round**—Couples-Love maintained their a 3-stroke lead with a score of 14-under-par 418. Price-McNulty were alone in second place at 11-under-par 421. Couples shot 70 and Love, 71.

INDIVIDUAL: First Round—Fred Couples of the U.S. and Jean Van de Velde of France shot 6-under-par 66s. **Second Round**—Van de Velde remained in the lead with 66-70--136, 8-under-par. Couples, Bernhard Langer of Germany and Sam Torrance of Scotland were tied at 7-under-par 137.**Third Round**—Langer added a 6-under-par 66 for a 13-under-par 203. Couples and Van de Velde were four strokes back at 9-under-par 207.

WEATHER: Beautiful every day, with some wind each day.

WINNER : UNITED STATES - 556 (-20)

Fred Couples	66-71-70-68—275	$130,000
Davis Love III	71-69-71-70—281	$130,000

2- ZIMBABWE - 561 (-15)			
Nick Price	70-69-71-68—278	$ 75,000	
Mark McNulty	71-68-72-72—283	$ 75,000	
3- SCOTLAND - 565 (-11)			
Sam Torrance	68-69-71-73—281	$ 50,000	
Colin Montgomerie	75-70-69-70—284	$ 50,000	
4- AUSTRALIA - 566 (-10)			
Robert Allenby	72-68-70-70—280	$ 37,500	
Rodger Davis	70-70-72-74—286	$ 37,500	
5- SPAIN - 567(-9)			
Miguel Angel Jimenez	72-70-72-68—282	$ 30,000	
Jose Rivero	73-72-66-74—285	$ 30,000	
T6- SOUTH AFRICA - 568 (-8)			
Ernie Els	69-71-72-66—278	$ 18,750	
Retief Goosen	71-74-69-76—290	$ 18,750	
T6- NEW ZEALAND - 568 (-8)			
Frank Nobilo	74-69-69-71—283	$ 18,750	
Greg Turner	73-73-64-75—285	$ 18,750	
8- GERMANY - 571 (-5)			
Bernhard Langer	69-68-66-69—272	$ 12,500	
Sven Struver	74-75-74-76—299	$ 12,500	
T9- IRELAND - 573 (-3)			
Ronan Rafferty	71-69-73-71—284	$ 9,250	
Paul McGinley	72-71-73-73—289	$ 9,250	
T9- ITALY - 573 (-3)			
Costantino Rocca	71-75-67-70—283	$ 9,250	
Silvio Grappasonni	74-72-69-75—290	$ 9,250	
T11- CANADA - 574 (-2)			
Dave Barr	74-70-70-71—285	$ 7,000	
Richard Zokol	76-71-70-72—289	$ 7,000	
T11- ENGLAND - 574 (-2)			
David Gilford	69-73-72-72—286	$ 7,000	
Mark James	76-74-68-70—288	$ 7,000	
T13- FRANCE - 575 (-1)			
Jean Van de Velde	66-70-71-72—279	$ 5,250	
Marc-Antoine Farry	74-78-72-72—296	$ 5,250	
T13- SWEDEN - 575 (-1)			
Anders Forsbrand	71-69-74-68—282	$ 5,250	
Joakim Haeggman	72-77-72-72—293	$ 5,250	
15- PARAGUAY - 579 (+3)			
Pedro Rodolfo Martinez	74-73-69-71—287	$ 4,500	
Felix Ramon Franco	73-73-69-77—292	$ 4,500	
16- WALES - 582 (+6)			
Mark Mouland	68-70-75-73—286	$ 4,000	
Ian Woosnam	74-79-74-69—296	$ 4,000	
17- BRAZIL - 583 (+7)			
Antonio Barcellos	76-70-70-71—287	$ 3,500	
Joao Corteiz	75-70-75-76—296	$ 3,500	
18- JAPAN - 588 (+12)			
Katsuyoshi Tomori	74-73-72-73—292	$ 3,500	
Hideto Shigenobu	70 77 76 73—296	$ 3,500	

19- ARGENTINA - 592 (+16)			
Eduardo Romero	71-70-72-75—288	$ 3,500	
Luis Carbonetti	73-80-77-74—304	$ 3,500	
T20- HONG KONG - 597 (+21)			
Richard Kan	74-72-75-76—297	$ 3,500	
Yau Sui Ming	73-74-76-77—300	$ 3,500	
T20- MEXICO - 597 (+21)			
Rodolfo Cazaubon	68-79-75-76—298	$ 3,500	
Efren Serna	78-75-72-74—299	$ 3,500	
22- HOLLAND - 602 (+26)			
Chris Van Der Velde	74-72-73-81—300	$ 3,500	
Constant Van Waesberghe	78-75-75-74—302	$ 3,500	
23- GREECE - 603 (+27)			
George Nikitaides	77-75-73-75—300	$ 3,500	
Vassilios Karatzias	74-75-79-75—303	$ 3,500	
24- CHINESE TAIPEI - 609 (+33)			
Yu-Shu Hsieh	76-72-76-77—301	$ 3,500	
Liang-Hsi Chen	80-78-79-71—308	$ 3,500	
25- BERMUDA - 617 (+41)			
Kim Swan	76-76-72-79—303	$ 3,500	
Dwayne Pearman	78-79-76-81—314	$ 3,500	
26- PUERTO RICO - 629 (+53)			
Rafael Castrillo	78-77-76-77—308	$ 3,500	
Juan M. Rodriguez	85-77-77-82—321	$ 3,500	
27- FIJI - 646 (+70)			
Dharam Prakash	80-79-74-71—314	$ 3,500	
Vilikesa Kalou	89-79-82-82—332	$ 3,500	
28- JAMAICA - 652 (+76)			
Seymour Rose	88-75-72-75—310	$ 3,500	
Christian Bernard	86-79-89-88—342	$ 3,500	
29- ISRAEL - 682 (+106)			
Rami Assyag	80-82-82-84—328	$ 3,500	
Jacob Avnaim	94-85-88-87—354	$ 3,500	
DENMARK			
Steen Tinning	76-76-70-69—291	$ 3,500	
Anders Sorensen	Withdrew, injury	$ 3,500	
CHILE			
Guillermo Encina	79-77-69-73—298	$ 3,500	
Roy Mackenzie	71-Withdrew, injury	$ 3,500	
KOREA			
Kang-Sun Lee	73-74-74-75—296	$ 3,500	
Nam Sin Park	DQ-Signed for wrong score.	$ 3,500	

INTERNATIONAL TROPHY

1. Bernhard Langer, Germany	69-68-66-69—272	$ 75,000	
2. Fred Couples, USA	66-71-70-68—275	$ 50,000	
T3. Ernie Els, South Africa	69-71-72-66—278	$ 35,000	
T3. Nick Price, Zimbabwe	70-69-71-68—278	$ 35,000	
5. Jean Van de Velde, France	66-70-71-72—279	$ 20,000	
6. Robert Allenby, Australia	72-68-70-70—280	$ 15,000	

FRANKLIN FUNDS
SHARK SHOOTOUT

Franklin Funds
SHARK **SHOOTOUT**
HOSTED BY GREG NORMAN
S H E R W O O D   C O U N T R Y   C L U B

Sherwood CC, Thousand Oaks, CA
Par: 36-36--72   Yards: 7,025

Purse: $1,100,000
Nov. 19-21,1993

LEADERS: First Round—Steve Elkington/Raymond Floyd and Mark Calcavecchia/Brad Faxon, at 10-under-par 62 in the better-ball format, held a one-stroke lead over Tom Kite/Davis Love III and Hale Irwin/Bruce Lietzke. **Second Round**—Elkington/Floyd, after a combined 64 in the alternate-shot format, were at 18-under-par 126, good for a two-stroke advantage over Irwin/Lietzke heading into the final-round scramble format.

WEATHER: Cool early Friday and Saturday, becoming sunny and mild each day. Overcast and cool throughout Sunday.

WINNERS: Steve Elkington/Raymond Floyd   62-64-62   188 $150,000 each

Hale Irwin/Bruce Lietzke	T2	63-65-61	189	$57,125 each
Mark O'Meara/Curtis Strange	T2	64-65-60	189	$57,125 each
Mark Calcavecchia/Brad Faxon	T2	62-68-59	189	$57,125 each
Tom Kite/Davis Love III	T2	63-70-56	189	$57,125 each
Greg Norman/Nick Price	T6	67-69-55	191	$37,750 each
Chip Beck/Corey Pavin	T6	64-68-59	191	$37,750 each
Ben Crenshaw/Fulton Allem	8	66-69-62	197	$34,000 each
John Cook/Payne Stewart	9	66-68-64	198	$32,000 each
Peter Jacobsen/Arnold Palmer	10	69-70-64	203	$30,000 each

THE SKINS GAME

Bighorn GC, Palm Desert, CA
Par: 36-36--72   **Yards: 6,850**

Purse: $540,000
Nov. 27-28,1993

WEATHER: High overcast and cool Saturday. Partly sunny and cool early Sunday, warming later.

Holes 1-6:	Worth $20,000
Holes 7-12:	Worth $30,000
Holes 13-18:	Worth $40,000

Hole No. 1:	Couples and Palmer halve with birdies
Hole No. 2:	Stewart wins with birdie/collects $40,000 (two skins)
Hole No. 3:	Stewart wins with birdie/collects $20,000 (one skin)
Hole No. 4:	Stewart, Azinger, Palmer and Couples halve with pars
Hole No. 5:	Azinger and Palmer halve with birdies
Hole No. 6:	Couples wins with birdie/collects $60,000 (three skins)
Hole No. 7:	Couples, Palmer and Azinger halve with pars
Hole No. 8:	Couples, Palmer and Stewart halve with pars
Hole No. 9:	Couples wins with birdie/collects $90,000 (three skins)

Hole No. 10:	Couples wins with birdie/collects $30,000 (one skin)
Hole No. 11:	Azinger and Couples halve with birdies
Hole No. 12:	Stewart and Palmer halve with birdies
Hole No. 13:	Stewart wins with birdie/collects $100,000 (three skins)
Hole No. 14:	Azinger and Stewart halve with pars
Hole No. 15:	Palmer and Couples halve with birdies
Hole No. 16:	Stewart wins with birdie/collects $120,000 (three skins)
Hole No. 17:	Stewart and Couples halve with pars
Hole No. 18:	Couples wins with birdie/collects $80,000 (two skins)

Final Results

Payne Stewart	(nine skins)	$280,000
Fred Couples	(nine skins)	$260,000
Arnold Palmer	(zero skins)	$0
Paul Azinger	(zero skins)	$0

JCPENNEY CLASSIC

The JCPenney Classic
...on Florida's Suncoast

Innisbrook Hilton Resort, Tarpon Springs, FL
Par: 36-35--71   **Yards: 7,065 (Men)**
                             6,394 (Women)

Purse: $1,200,000
Dec. 2-5,1993

LEADERS: First Round— Tom Sieckmann and Deborah McHaffie fired an 8-under-par 63 and led by two strokes over Tom Purtzer-Beth Daniel, Dan Forsman-Dottie Mochrie and Kenny Perry-Sherri Steinhauer. **Second Round—** Sieckmann and McHaffie at 10-under-par 132 led by one over Perry-Steinhauer and Fred Funk-Tina Barrett. **Third Round—** Mike Springer-Melissa McNamara and Sieckmann-McHaffie at 14-under 199 led by one over Perry-Steinhauer.

PRO-AM: $10,000 Tuesday: Individual— Tom Purtzer, 65, $300. Team— John Huston, 50, $300. Wednesday: Individual— Billy Andrade, 64, $300. Team— Ted Schulz, 48, $300.

WEATHER: Sunny and mild all week.

WINNERS: Mike Springer/Melissa McNamara 67-69-63-66 265 $120,000 (each)

John Huston/Amy Benz	T2	68-70-66-65	265	$42,638.00
Robert Gamez/Helen Alfredsson	T2	67-71-66-65	269	42,638.00
Fred Funk/Tina Barrett	T2	68-65-68-68	269	42,638.00
Kenny Perry/Sherri Steinhauer	T2	65-68-67-69	269	42,638.00
Tom Sieckmann/Deborah McHaffie	T2	63-69-67-70	269	42,638.00
Tom Wargo/Nancy Scranton	7	69-66-66-70	271	20,730.00
Tom Purtzer/Beth Daniel	T8	65-70-69-68	272	15,817.50
Gary Koch/Tammie Green	T8	68-68-68-68	272	15,817.50
Rocco Mediate/Missie Berteotti	T10	69-69-70-65	273	10,497.50
Bill Glasson/Pat Bradley	T10	70-69-65-69	273	l0,497.50
Dudley Hart/Dawn Coe-Jones	T10	71-66-66-70	273	10,497.50
Bob Gilder/Cindy Rarick	T10	72 66-65-70	273	10,497.50
Billy Andrade/Kris Tschetter	T14	68-70-67-69	274	8,180.00
Greg Kraft/Michelle McGann	T14	69-69-67-69	274	8,180.00
Dan Forsman/Dottie Mochrie	T14	65-71-68-70	274	8,180.00
Michael Allen/Dana Lofland-Dormann	T17	71-69-67-68	275	6,276.25
Dick Mast/Deb Richard	T17	73-68-65-69	275	6,276.25
David Peoples/Barb Mucha	T17	70-68-71-66	275	6,276.25
Jay Overton/Cindy Schreyer	T17	70-70-66-69	275	6,276.25
Roger Maltbie/Rosie Jones	T21	67-69-70-70	276	5,030.00
Jay Delsing/Judy Dickinson	T21	71-68-69-68	276	5,030.00
John Adams/Alice Ritzman	T21	69-67-70-70	276	5,030.00
Jim Dent/Kris Monaghan	T21	68-70-68-70	276	5,030.00
Scott Hoch/Kelly Robbins	T21	69-71-66-70	276	5,030.00
Jay Don Blake/Page Dunlap	T21	68-70-67-71	276	5,030.00
Steve Pate/Meg Mallon	T21	69-65-70-72	276	5,030.00
John Inman/Donna Andrews	T28	70-68-69-70	277	4,315.00
Marco Dawson/Jan Stephenson	T28	70-70-67-70	277	4,315.00
Mike Standly/Val Skinner	T28	66-70-71-70	277	4,315.00
Kirk Triplett/Julie Larsen	T28	69-68-71-69	277	4,315.00
Mark McCumber/Debbie Massey	T28	70-70-69-68	277	4,315.00
Ken Green/Barb Bunkowsky	T28	70-72-67-68	277	4,315.00
Willie Wood/Cathy Johnston-Forbes	T34	68-70-69-71	278	3,765.00
Billy Mayfair/Brandie Burton	T34	68-70-71-69	278	3,765.00
D.A. Weibring/Florence Descampe	T34	72-68-69-69	278	3,765.00
David Ogrin/Hollis Stacy	T34	71-72-66-69	278	3,765.00
Steve Lowery/Nancy Ramsbottom	T38	74-67-68-70	279	3,440.00
Bryan Claar/Kristi Albers	T38	70-71-68-70	279	3,440.00
Jim McGovern/Dale Eggeling	T38	69-72-68-70	279	3,440.00
Ted Schulz/Jane Crafter	T41	69-73-66-72	280	3,302.50
Chi Chi Rodriguez/ Danielle Ammaccapane	T41	73-72-67-68	280	3,302.50
Bob Estes/Cindy Figg-Currier	T43	71-69-70-71	281	3,192.50
Ed Humenik/Elaine Crosby	T43	70-73-70-68	281	3,192.50
Ed Dougherty/Shelley Hamlin	T45	66-72-72-72	282	3,082.50
Joel Edwards/Missie McGeorge	T45	71-72-67-72	282	3,082.50
Brian Kamm/Colleen Walker	T47	67-73-74-69	283	2,945.00
Andy North/JoAnne Carner	T47	74-70-70-69	283	2,945.00
Brad Bryant/Trish Johnson	T47	73-72-69-69	283	2,945.00
Mike Hulbert/Laura Davies	50	70-71-72-71	284	2,835.00
Larry Rinker/Laurie Rinker-Graham	T51	70-70-71-74	285	2,752.50
Bruce Fleisher/Tracy Kerdyk	T51	72-70-72-71	285	2,752.50

1993 PGA TOUR QUALIFYING TOURNAMENT GRADUATES

La Quinta Resort (Dunes Course), La Quinta, CA
Par: 37-35--72   Yards: 6,861
PGA West (Nicklaus Resort Course), La Quinta, CA
Par: 36-36--72   Yards: 7,126

December 1-6, 1993

More than 800 applications were accepted with 13 regionals held to reduce the field to 191 players for the final tournament.

RANK	NAME	SCORE	TOTAL
1.	Ty Armstrong	71-70-68-71-67-68	415
	Dave Stockton, Jr.	68-72-66-68-70-71	415
	Robin Freeman	70-68-68-68-70-71	415
4.	Jesper Parnevik	65-66-79-67-67-72	416
	Jeff Woodland	68-69-71-69-68-71	416
	Pete Jordan	71-65-69-72-68-71	416
7.	Joey Rassett	74-71-66-66-72-68	417
8.	Clark Dennis	69-72-70-68-69-71	419
	Morris Hatalsky	69-71-70-71-68-70	419
10.	Dennis Paulson	70-70-71-69-69-71	420
11.	Glen Day	69-71-71-73-68-69	421
	David Feherty	76-70-69-66-68-72	421
	Yoshi Mizumaki	73-74-67-67-71-69	421
	Todd Barranger	67-73-71-68-73-69	421
	Steve Rintoul	68-71-68-72-73-69	421
	Bob Burns	70-69-67-70-67-78	421
	Steve Gotsche	74-68-74-68-67-70	421
18.	Tim Simpson	71-71-71-68-67-74	422
	Guy Boros	72-70-68-70-71-71	422
	Paul Goydos	71-71-72-65-72-71	422
	John Wilson	70-70-70-73-68-71	422
	Thomas Levet	67-71-66-76-72-70	422
	Steve Stricker	71-73-73-69-65-71	422
24.	Mark Wurtz	74-69-69-68-72-71	423
	Dicky Pride	70-71-65-72-68-77	423
26.	Esteban Toledo	70-68-73-70-70-73	424
	Paul Stankowski	66-71-74-70-71-72	424
	Steve Brodie	70-73-71-72-73-65	424
	Rocky Walcher	72-69-73-68-70-72	424
	D.A. Russell	73-71-67-72-67-74	424
	Mike Heinen	68-70-75-67-76-68	424
32.	Don Reese	71-67-76-72-69-70	425
	Ed Kirby	75-66-72-69-71-72	425
	Steve Lamontagne	73-71-72-70-70-69	425
	Bill Britton	73-75-66-68-74-69	425
	Bill Kratzert	70-71-73-70-72-69	425
37.	Charles Raulerson	70-72-71-70-69-74	426
	Rob Boldt	70-72-73-71-72-68	426
	Shaun Micheel	73-68-69-76-73-67	426
	Mike Brisky	69-69-72-72-69-75	426
	Chris Kite	68-75-71-71-69-72	426
	Brad Lardon	73-69-72-70-73-69	426
	Phil Tataurangi	68-72-69-75-71-71	426
	Jim Furyk	70-71-74-71-69-71	426
	Brad King	68-74-70-67-73-74	426
	Tom Garner	71-70-71-68-74-72	426

SUMMARY OF QUALIFYING TOURNAMENTS

DATE	SITE	MEDALIST	CARDS GRANTED	APPLICANTS	FINAL FIELD	FORMAT
1965	PGA National G.C. Palm Beach Gardens, FL	John Schlee	17	49	49	144 holes
1966	PGA National G.C. Palm Beach Gardens, FL	Harry Toscano	32	99	99	144 holes
1967	PGA National G.C. Palm Beach Gardens, FL	Bobby Cole	30	111	111	144 holes
Spring 1968	PGA National G.C. Palm Beach Gardens, FL	Bob Dickson	15	81	81	144 holes
Fall 1968	PGA National G.C. Palm Beach Gardens, FL	Grier Jones	30	79	79	144 holes
Spring 1969	PGA National G.C. Palm Beach Gardens, FL	Bob Eastwood	15	91	91	144 holes
Fall 1969	PGA National G.C. Palm Beach Gardens, FL	Doug Olson	12	182	48	144 holes
1970	Tucson C.C. Tucson, AZ	Robert Barbarossa	18	250	60	72 holes, after nine 54-hole District Qualifiers
1971	PGA National G.C. Palm Beach Gardens, FL	Bob Zender	23	357	75	108 holes, after three 72-hole Regional Qualifiers
1972	Silverado C.C. Napa, CA	Larry Stubblefield John Adams	25	468	81	108 holes, after three 72-hole Regional Qualifiers
1973	Perdido Bay C.C. Pensacola, FL Dunes G.C. N. Myrtle Beach, SC	Ben Crenshaw	23	373	78	144 holes, after three 72-hole Regional Qualifiers
1974	Silverado C.C. Napa CA Canyon C.C. Palm Springs, CA	Fuzzy Zoeller	19	447	78	144 holes, after three 72-hole Regional Qualifiers
Spring 1975	Bay Tree Plantation N. Myrtle Beach, SC	Joey Dills	13	233	233	108 holes
Fall 1975	Walt Disney World Lake Buena Vista, FL	Jerry Pate	25	380	380	108 holes
Spring 1976	Bay Tree Plantation N. Myrtle Beach, SC	Bob Shearer Woody Blackburn	15	276	276	108 holes
Fall 1976	Rancho Viejo C.C. Valley International C.C. Brownsville, TX	Keith Fergus	29	349	349	108 holes

Qualifying Tournament Summary (cont'd.)

DATE	SITE	MEDALIST	CARDS GRANTED	APPLICANTS	FINAL FIELD	FORMAT
Spring 1977	Pinehurst C.C. Pinehurst, NC	Phil Hancock	26	408	408	108 holes
Fall 1977	Pinehurst C.C. Pinehurst, NC	Ed Fiori	34	660	144	72 holes, after Sectional Qualifiers
Spring 1978	U. of New Mexico G.C. Albuquerque, NM	Wren Lum	28	502	150	72 holes, after five 72-hole Regional Qualifiers
Fall 1978	Waterwood National C.C. Huntsville, TX	Jim Thorpe John Fought	27	606	120	72 holes, after five 72-hole Regional Qualifiers
Spring 1979	Pinehurst C.C. Pinehurst, NC	Terry Mauney	25	521	150	72 holes, after five 72-hole Regional Qualifiers
Fall 1979	Waterwood National C.C. Huntsville, TX	Tom Jones	27	652	120	72 holes, after five 72-hole Regional Qualifiers
Spring 1980	Pinehurst C.C. Pinehurst, NC	Jack Spradlin	27	553	150	72 holes, after five 72-hole Regional Qualifiers
Fall 1980	Fort Washington G&CC Fresno, Calif.	Bruce Douglass	27	621	120	72 holes, after five 72-hole Regional Qualifiers
Spring 1981	Walt Disney World Golf Resort Lake Buena Vista, FL	Billy Glisson	25	556	150	72 holes, after five 72-hole Regional Qualifiers
Fall 1981	Waterwood National C.C. Huntsville, TX	Robert Thompson Tim Graham	34	513	120	72 holes, after six 72-hole Regional Qualifiers
1982	Tournament Players Club & Sawgrass Country Club Ponte Vedra, FL	Donnie Hammond	50	696	200	108 holes after eight Regional Qualifiers
1983	Tournament Players Club Ponte Vedra, FL	Willie Wood	57	624	144	108 holes after nine Regional Qualifiers
1984	La Quinta Hotel and G.C. Mission Hills C.C. La Quinta, CA	Paul Azinger	50	800	160	108 holes after ten Regional Qualifiers
1985	Grenelefe Golf and Tennis Club Haines City, FL	Tom Sieckmann	50	825	162	108 holes after 11 Regional Qualifiers
1986	PGA West (Stadium Golf Course) La Quinta Hotel Golf & Tennis Resort (Dunes Course) La Quinta, CA	Steve Jones	53	750	186	108 holes after 14 Regionals

Qualifying Tournament Summary (cont'd.)

DATE	SITE	MEDALIST	CARDS GRANTED	APPLICANTS	FINAL FIELD	FORMAT
1987	Matanzas Woods GC Pine Lakes CC Palm Coast, FL	John Huston	54	800	183	108 holes after 11 Regionals
1988	La Quinta Hotel (Dunes Course) PGA West Jack Nicklaus Resort Course La Quinta, CA	Robin Freeman	52	750	183	108 holes after 11 Regionals
1989	TPC at The Woodlands The Woodlands Inn & CC The Woodlands, TX	David Peoples	59	825	180	108 holes after 11 Regionals
1990	La Quinta Hotel (Dunes Course) PGA West Jack Nicklaus Resort Course La Quinta, CA	Duffy Waldorf	49	835	182	108 holes after 11 Regionals
1991	Grenelefe Resort & Conference Center Haines City, FL	Mike Standly	48	850	181	108 holes, after 12 regionals
1992	TPC at The Woodlands The Woodlands Inn & CC The Woodlands, TX	Massy Kuramato Skip Kendall Brett Ogle Perry Moss Neale Smith	43	800	186	108 holes, after 13 Regionals
1993	La Quinta Hotel (Dunes Course) PGA West Jack Nicklaus Resort Course La Quinta, CA	Ty Armstrong Dave Stockton, Jr. Robin Freeman	46	800	191	108 holes after 13 Regionals

NOTE: The American Professional Golfers also held a School in the fall of 1968, graduating 21. The 144-hole competition was played at Doral C.C. The medalist was Martin Roesink.

Lee Janzen won two tournaments in 1993,
the Phoenix Open and the U.S. Open.

1993 OFFICIAL PGA TOUR MONEY LIST

	Name	Events	Money		Name	Events	Money
1.	NICK PRICE	18	$1,478,557	67.	DAVE RUMMELLS#	28	$247,963
2.	PAUL AZINGER	24	1,458,456	68.	LANNY WADKINS	22	244,544
3.	GREG NORMAN	15	1,359,653	69.	JOHN INMAN	32	242,140
4.	JIM GALLAGHER, JR.	27	1,078,870	70.	ROBERT GAMEZ	25	236,458
5.	DAVID FROST	22	1,030,717	71.	JAY DELSING	29	233,484
6.	PAYNE STEWART	26	982,875	72.	GREG TWIGGS#	29	231,823
7.	LEE JANZEN	26	932,335	73.	MICHAEL ALLEN#	27	231,072
8.	TOM KITE	20	887,811	74.	BRAD BRYANT	31	230,139
9.	FULTON ALLEM	28	851,345	75.	KEN GREEN	22	229,750
10.	FRED COUPLES	19	796,579	76.	JOHN DALY	24	225,591
11.	JEFF MAGGERT	28	793,023	77.	PETER JACOBSEN	23	222,291
12.	DAVIS LOVE III	26	777,059	78.	JOHN ADAMS	29	221,753
13.	LARRY MIZE	22	724,660	79.	MIKE SPRINGER	30	214,729
14.	SCOTT SIMPSON	22	707,166	80.	RICHARD ZOKOL	25	214,419
15.	JOHN HUSTON	30	681,441	81.	BRUCE FLEISHER	28	214,279
16.	ROCCO MEDIATE	24	680,623	82.	DICK MAST	28	210,125
17.	STEVE ELKINGTON	23	675,383	83.	PHIL BLACKMAR	30	207,310
18.	COREY PAVIN	24	675,087	84.	DUFFY WALDORF	25	202,638
19.	VIJAY SINGH	14	657,831	85.	BRIAN CLAAR	32	202,624
20.	DAVID EDWARDS	21	653,086	86.	JAY DON BLAKE	26	202,482
21.	MARK CALCAVECCHIA	30	630,366	87.	TOM SIECKMANN	31	201,429
22.	PHIL MICKELSON	24	628,735	88.	KENNY PERRY	29	196,863
23.	BERNHARD LANGER *	6	626,938	89.	MIKE HULBERT	31	193,833
24.	GIL MORGAN	24	610,312	90.	KIRK TRIPLETT	27	189,418
25.	CHIP BECK	27	603,376	91.	NICK FALDO *	6	188,886
26.	JAY HAAS	29	601,603	92.	STEVE LOWERY @	32	188,287
27.	JIM MCGOVERN	34	587,495	93.	JEFF SLUMAN	27	187,841
28.	RICK FEHR	26	556,322	94.	BRIAN KAMM @	27	183,185
29.	CRAIG STADLER	24	553,623	95.	WAYNE LEVI	25	179,521
30.	BILLY MAYFAIR	32	513,072	96.	DAVE BARR	28	179,264
31.	NOLAN HENKE	26	502,375	97.	BILLY RAY BROWN	15	173,662
32.	BOB ESTES	28	447,187	98.	DILLARD PRUITT	26	168,053
33.	TOM LEHMAN	28	422,761	99.	ED DOUGHERTY	34	167,651
34.	HOWARD TWITTY	29	416,833	100.	TED SCHULZ	31	164,260
35.	GRANT WAITE#	30	411,405	101.	BRUCE LIETZKE	16	163,241
36.	DAN FORSMAN	25	410,150	102.	JOHN FLANNERY @	31	161,234
37.	SCOTT HOCH	28	403,742	103.	ROGER MALTBIE	20	155,454
38.	JOEY SINDELAR	22	391,649	104.	DAVID OGRIN#	28	155,016
39.	FUZZY ZOELLER	18	378,175	105.	ED HUMENIK	31	152,562
40.	BILLY ANDRADE	29	365,759	106.	JOEL EDWARDS	30	150,623
41.	MARK MCCUMBER	21	363,269	107.	NEAL LANCASTER	32	149,381
42.	MARK WIEBE	27	360,213	108.	BOB GILDER	27	148,496
43.	MARK O'MEARA	26	349,516	109.	BOB TWAY	25	148,120
44.	KEITH CLEARWATER	31	348,763	110.	KELLY GIBSON	33	148,003
45.	JOHN COOK	23	342,321	111.	GARY HALLBERG	27	147,706
46.	TOM WATSON	16	342,023	112.	WILLIE WOOD#	25	146,206
47.	DONNIE HAMMOND	23	340,432	113.	LENNIE CLEMENTS#	26	141,526
48.	BRETT OGLE#	18	337,374	114.	IAN BAKER-FINCH	20	140,621
49.	MIKE STANDLY	30	323,886	115.	JOE OZAKI	12	139,784
50.	CRAIG PARRY	23	323,068	116.	TED TRYBA @	33	136,670
51.	BEN CRENSHAW	22	318,605	117.	DOUG TEWELL	21	132,478
52.	DUDLEY HART	30	316,750	118.	LARRY RINKER	28	130,613
53.	LOREN ROBERTS	28	316,506	119.	BRANDEL CHAMBLEE#	29	126,940
54.	BOB LOHR	26	314,982	120.	RAY FLOYD	6	126,516
55.	BRAD FAXON	25	312,023	121.	MICHAEL BRADLEY#	26	126,160
56.	FRED FUNK	34	309,435	122.	DON POOLEY	15	123,105
57.	BILL GLASSON	22	299,799	123.	DAVID TOMS	32	120,952
58.	D.A. WEIBRING	22	299,293	124.	MARCO DAWSON	32	120,462
59.	RUSS COCHRAN	27	293,868	125.	RONNIE BLACK	28	120,041
60.	GREG KRAFT#	24	290,581	126.	TREVOR DODDS#	30	119,436
61.	BLAINE MCCALLISTER	27	290,434	127.	ED FIORI	31	117,617
62.	ANDREW MAGEE	25	269,986	128.	GENE SAUERS	28	117,608
63.	CURTIS STRANGE	24	262,697	129.	SKIP KENDALL#	32	115,189
64.	STEVE PATE	28	254,841	130.	BRIAN HENNINGER @	31	112,811
65.	HALE IRWIN	21	252,686	131.	BOBBY CLAMPETT	16	112,293
66.	MARK BROOKS	31	249,696	132.	DENIS WATSON	25	111,977

* Non-PGA TOUR Member　　@ 1992 NIKE TOUR Grad　　# 1992 Qualifying Tournament Grad

Name	Events	Money	Name	Events	Money
133. RUSSELL BEIERSDORF @	30	$111,750	199. HUBERT GREEN	19	$29,786
134. TIM SIMPSON	28	111,436	200. BRADLEY HUGHES *	2	28,125
135. MORRIS HATALSKY	18	111,057	201. DAVID DUVAL *	5	27,181
136. TOM PURTZER	21	107,570	202. CHRIS PERRY	9	25,333
137. MIKE SMITH	33	107,375	203. GENE JONES#	20	24,522
138. STEVE LAMONTAGNE	33	107,077	204. BOB EASTWOOD	17	24,289
139. MARK LYE	23	106,936	205. DAN HALLDORSON	30	24,284
140. HARRY TAYLOR#	30	105,845	206. BARRY LANE *	2	24,089
141. P.H. HORGAN III	31	105,571	207. CHRIS SMITH *	3	24,000
142. DAVID PEOPLES	29	105,309	208. JOHN ROSS	15	23,412
143. ROBERT WRENN	28	103,928	209. BRIAN WATTS *	3	23,235
144. PATRICK BURKE	17	100,717	210. GREG LESHER	14	23,171
145. MARK CARNEVALE	32	100,046	211. JOHN RIEGGER *	1	22,275
146. DAN POHL	20	97,830	212. DOUG MARTIN	5	21,381
147. SCOTT GUMP	31	96,822	213. DAVID DELONG#	22	21,059
148. ROBIN FREEMAN#	30	92,096	214. MARTY SCHIENE#	25	20,857
149. JC ANDERSON#	27	89,782	215. JOHN DOWDALL#	22	20,381
150. JODIE MUDD	20	89,366	216. RON MCDOUGAL *	5	20,375
151. LANCE TEN BROECK	32	88,262	217. CLINTON WHITELAW *	1	19,200
152. PAUL GOYDOS#	30	87,804	218. EDDIE PEARCE#	27	18,741
153. SANDY LYLE *	7	86,121	219. EDUARDO ROMERO *	1	18,500
154. TOM BYRUM#	26	82,355	220. EMLYN AUBREY *	1	18,125
155. JIM HALLET	34	80,366	221. COLIN MONTGOMERIE *	4	17,992
156. BILL KRATZERT	15	78,993	222. CHRIS TUCKER	14	17,473
157. JAIME GOMEZ @	30	77,495	223. STAN UTLEY	5	17,371
158. DENNIS TRIXLER#	29	75,032	224. BRUCE ZABRISKI	8	16,829
159. BILL BRITTON	30	74,748	225. GARY MCCORD	8	16,456
160. LEN MATTIACE#	26	74,521	226. BARRY JAECKEL	11	15,585
161. HAL SUTTON	29	74,144	227. GREG CESARIO#	25	15,333
162. MASSY KURAMOTO#	21	74,133	228. LEONARD THOMPSON	12	15,153
163. JEFF WOODLAND @	27	73,367	229. LEE PORTER#	19	14,908
164. PETER PERSONS	30	73,092	230. FRANK NOBILO *	1	14,500
165. JEFF COOK#	29	72,398	230. ANDY NORTH	4	14,500
166. JIM THORPE	19	70,376	232. BUDDY GARDNER	27	13,722
167. MIKE SULLIVAN	15	68,587	233. TONY SILLS	5	11,686
168. BARRY CHEESMAN#	30	66,748	234. NEALE SMITH#	22	11,413
169. JUMBO OZAKI *	4	66,742	235. ROBERT ALLENBY *	6	11,052
170. TIM CONLEY *	22	66,593	235. LEE RINKER *	1	11,052
171. PERRY MOSS#	29	63,565	237. TONY JOHNSTONE *	4	10,893
172. MIKE SCHUCHART#	24	61,492	238. WARREN SCHUTTE *	6	10,875
173. JOHN ELLIOTT#	28	60,378	239. CARL COOPER#	19	10,774
174. JOSE MARIA OLAZABAL *	6	60,160	240. MAC O'GRADY	4	10,429
175. BRAD FABEL	27	59,672	241. PETER O'MALLEY *	3	9,220
176. IAN WOOSNAM *	6	55,426	242. MARK PFEIL	5	9,100
177. LARRY NELSON	18	54,870	243. JEFF BARLOW *	1	8,700
178. JIMMY JOHNSTON#	28	54,419	244. LON HINKLE	13	8,621
179. DAVID JACKSON @	31	53,563	245. JAY OVERTON#	13	8,368
180. JIM WOODWARD	19	52,731	246. ARDEN KNOLL *	2	8,171
181. TOMMY ARMOUR	20	52,011	247. STU INGRAHAM *	1	7,058
182. JACK NICKLAUS	10	51,532	247. TOM WARGO *	1	7,058
183. MIKE DONALD	34	51,313	249. MARK HAYES	9	6,942
184. TOMMY NAKAJIMA *	4	50,578	250. CHRIS VAN DER VELDE *	2	6,854
185. TAD RHYAN#	32	50,524	251. CLARENCE ROSE	4	6,823
186. STEVE STRICKER *	6	46,171	252. STEPHEN FLESCH *	1	6,786
187. WAYNE GRADY	20	45,959	253. BILL BUTTNER *	1	6,650
188. BILL MURCHISON#	19	45,402	253. J.P. HAYES *	1	6,650
189. BOBBY WADKINS	24	39,153	253. PAT MCGOWAN *	4	6,650
190. ERNIE ELS *	6	38,185	256. MICHAEL CHRISTIE *	1	6,526
191. ANDY BEAN	21	37,292	256. VANCE HEAFNER *	3	6,526
192. JOHN MAHAFFEY	28	36,913	256. EDWARD KIRBY *	2	6,526
193. SEVE BALLESTEROS *	3	34,850	259. CLARK DENNIS *	2	6,050
193. ANDERS FORSBRAND *	5	34,850	260. MIGUEL MARTIN *	1	6,019
195. FRANK CONNER	7	34,154	261. J.L. LEWIS *	3	5,965
196. DAVE PEEGE#	22	33,531	262. T.C. CHEN *	1	5,800
197. ISAO AOKI	1	32,500	263. JIM KANE *	2	5,660
198. RICK DALPOS @	28	31,585	264. STEVE GOTSCHE *	1	5,657

* Non-PGA TOUR Member   @ 1992 NIKE TOUR Grad   # 1992 Qualifying Tournament Grad

1993 OFFICIAL PGA TOUR MONEY LIST (cont.)

	Name	Events	Money
265.	ROBERT FRIEND	10	$5,647
266.	JEFF WILSON *	3	5,508
267.	GARY NICKLAUS *	6	5,427
268.	R.W. EAKS *	1	5,414
269.	PETER JORDAN *	1	5,405
270.	MIKE REID	5	5,125
271.	BARNEY THOMPSON *	1	5,122
272.	YOSHINORI KANEKO *	3	4,848
273.	DOUG WEAVER *	1	4,681
274.	DEANE PAPPAS *	3	4,537
275.	SAM RANDOLPH	4	4,460
276.	REX CALDWELL	2	4,350
277.	TOM JENKINS	4	4,302
278.	WEBB HEINTZELMAN *	2	4,290
279.	JOE DURANT#	18	4,055
280.	CHARLES COODY	1	3,800
281.	GARY PLAYER	1	3,700
282.	KENNY KNOX	21	3,630
283.	PETER SENIOR *	3	3,600
284.	GREG WHISMAN	2	3,392
285.	ED SNEED	3	3,124
286.	MIKE MALIZIA *	1	2,996
287.	TIM CROCKETT *	1	2,870
288.	GREG CERULLI *	2	2,786
289.	JIM CARTER *	1	2,753
290.	OLIN BROWNE	2	2,738
291.	TOM SHAW	2	2,716
292.	BRAD SHERFY *	2	2,690
293.	RAY STEWART *	1	2,670
294.	PAUL TRITTLER *	2	2,632
295.	FORREST FEZLER	7	2,610
295.	RICK LEWALLEN *	1	2,610
297.	BOB FORD *	1	2,588
298.	GEORGE BURNS	9	2,550
298.	TIM LOUSTALOT *	1	2,550
300.	SHANE BERTSCH *	1	2,548
301.	KEVIN BURTON *	2	$2,513
302.	DAVID BERGANIO *	4	2,486
303.	BOB BOROWICZ *	1	2,475
304.	KIYOSHI MUROTA *	1	2,472
305.	CHIP CRAIG *	1	2,431
305.	TONY MOLLICA *	1	2,431
307.	DANA QUIGLEY *	2	2,353
308.	KIM YOUNG#	17	2,343
309.	JIM ELLIS *	1	2,233
310.	ERNIE GONZALEZ	2	2,175
310.	STEVE HART *	1	2,175
312.	CRAIG LEE *	1	2,145
313.	MARK MIELKE *	3	2,100
314.	MIKE MCCULLOUGH	3	2,011
315.	HIROSHI MAKINO *	1	2,010
316.	ARNOLD PALMER	5	1,970
317.	ROB SULLIVAN *	1	1,940
317.	MIKE WEIR *	2	1,940
319.	ERIC JOHNSON *	2	1,880
320.	STEVE BRADY *	1	1,820
321.	YOSHINORI MIZUMAKI *	2	1,710
322.	DAVE EICHELBERGER	5	1,640
323.	DAVID CANIPE *	2	1,557
323.	DANNY EDWARDS	3	1,557
323.	MIKE NICOLETTE	2	1,557
323.	SONNY SKINNER *	1	1,557
327.	RICHIE KARL	1	1,464
328.	RON STRECK	2	885
329.	RETT CROWDER *	1	702
329.	GARY KOCH	4	702
329.	BOB WOLCOTT *	3	702
332.	ED SELSER *	1	624
333.	FRED WADSWORTH	3	609
334.	DON SHIREY, JR. *	3	597
334.	STEVE THOMAS *	1	597
336.	BILL SANDER	1	582

* Non-PGA TOUR Member

\# 1992 Qualifying Tournament Graduate

1993 PGA TOUR FACTS AND FIGURES

LOW 9:   28 (7-under)   *Keith Clearwater, Wayne Levi,* SW Bell Colonial
                    29 (7-under)   *Fuzzy Zoeller, Tom Kite,* Hope Chrysler; *Greg Norman,* Buick Open; *Dan Halldorson,* GMO

LOW 18:   61 (10-under)   *Jay Delsing,* FESJC
                    61 (9-under)   *Billy Mayfair,* GTE Byron Nelson; *Keith Clearwater, Lee Janzen,* SW Bell Colonial

LOW FIRST 18:   62 (9-under)   *Mike Smith,* H-E-B Texas Open
                    63 (9-under)   *Howard Twitty,* United Airlines Hawaiian; *Billy Andrade,* N. Telecom
                    63 (8-under)   *Jim Gallagher, Jr.,* TOUR Championship
                    63 (7-under)   *Jeff Woodland,* Hardee's

LOW FIRST 36:   129 (15-under)   *Blaine McCallister,* Shell Houston Open
                    129 (11-under)   *Dan Forsman,* GTE Byron Nelson; *Fulton Allem,* SW Bell Colonial

LOW 36:   127 (17-under)   *Tom Kite* (65-62), Hope Chrysler, rounds 4-5
(Any Rounds)   127 (13-under)   *David Frost* (63-64), Hardees, Rounds 2-3

LOW FIRST 54:   195 (21-under)   *Greg Norman* (65-68-62), Doral-Ryder
                    195 (15-under)   *David Frost* (68-63-64), Hardee's

LOW 54:   191 (25-under)   *Tom Kite* (64-65-62), Hope Chrysler, rounds 3-4-5
(Any rounds)   191 (19-under)   *David Frost* (63-64-64), Hardee's, rounds 2-3-4

LOW FIRST 72:   259 (21-under)   *David Frost,* Hardee's
                    263 (25-under)   *Tom Kite,* Hope Chrysler

LOW 90:   325 (35-under)   *Tom Kite,* Hope Chrysler

HIGH WINNING SCORE: 281 (7-under)   *Mike Standly,* Freeport-McMoRan; *Rocco Mediate,* Kmart GGO
                           280 (4-under)   *Vijay Singh,* Buick Classic

LARGEST WINNING MARGIN: 8 strokes   *Davis Love III,* Las Vegas Invitational

LOW START BY WINNER: 63 (9-under)   *Howard Twitty,* United Airlines Hawaiian
                            63 (8-under)   *Jim Gallagher, Jr.,* TOUR Championship

HIGH START BY WINNER: 75 (3-over)   *Phil Mickelson,* Buick Invitational

LOW FINISH BY WINNER: 62 (10-under)   *Tom Kite,* Hope Chrysler
                             62 (8-under)   *Fulton Allem,* NEC WSOG

HIGH FINISH BY WINNER: 71 (1-under)   *Brett Ogle,* AT&T Pebble Beach
                              71 (1 over)   *Scott Simpson,* GTE Byron Nelson

LARGEST 18-HOLE LEAD: 5 strokes   *Jim Gallagher, Jr.,* TOUR Championship

LARGEST 36-HOLE LEAD: 3 strokes   *Payne Stewart,* Buick Invitational; *Steve Stricker,* Canadian Open; *Tom Lehman,* Buick Southern

LARGEST 54-HOLE LEAD: 6 strokes   *Greg Norman,* Doral-Ryder

LOW 36-HOLE CUT: 140 (4-under)   Shell Houston Open
                        140 (2-under)   H-E-B Texas Open

HIGH 36-HOLE CUT: 152 (8-over)   Freeport-McMoRan

FEWEST TO MAKE 36-HOLE CUT: 70 at New England

MOST TO MAKE 36-HOLE CUT: 90 at Buick Invitational

LOW 54-HOLE CUT: 209 (7-under)   Walt Disney World/Oldsmobile Classic

HIGH 54-HOLE CUT: 217 (1-over)   AT&T Pebble Beach National Pro-Am

FEWEST TO MAKE 54-HOLE CUT: 73 @ Walt Disney World/Oldsmobile Classic

MOST TO MAKE 54-HOLE CUT: 82 @ AT&T Pebble Beach National Pro-Am

MOST CONSECUTIVE EVENTS IN THE MONEY: *Steve Elkington,* 25

CONSECUTIVE YEARS W/WIN: 7 by Paul Azinger (1987 thru 1993)

HOLES-IN-ONE (25):   *Carl Cooper*, United Airlines Hawaiian; *Larry Nelson, Mark Lye*, N. Telecom; *Dave Rummells*, DoralRyder; *Bobby Wadkins*, Honda; *John Ross, Doug Martin*, Deposit Guaranty; *Scott Gump, Robin Freeman*, BellSouth; *Loren Roberts*, SW Bell Colonial & Walt Disney World/Oldsmobile Cl.; *Lanny Wadkins*, Memorial; *Mike Gilmore*, Buick Classic; *Mike Hulbert, Sandy Lyle*, U.S. Open; *Patrick Burke*, A-B Classic; *John Inman*, Buick Open; *Len Mattiace*, GMO; *Tom Lehman, Dudley Hart*, Canadian Open; *Morris Hatalsky, Willie Wood*, Hardee's; *Chris Perry*, B.C. Open; *Howard Twitty*, H-E-B Texas Open; *Jay Haas*, Las Vegas Invitational

DOUBLE EAGLES: *Massy Kuramoto*, Deposit Guaranty (Hattiesburg CC, #3, 482 yards, driver/2-iron)
Tom Sieckmann, Kmart GGO (Forest Oaks CC, #9, 574 yards, driver/3-wood)
Bobby Wadkins, Memorial (Muirfield Village GC, #15, 490 yards, driver/3-wood)
Darrell Kestner, PGA Championship (Inverness Club, #13, 515 yards, driver/5-wood)

TWO EAGLES ONE ROUND: *Billy Andrade*, United Airlines Hawaiian; *Gene Sauers*, N. Telecom; *Fred Couples, Steve Lowery*, *Keith Clearwater*, Hope Chrysler; *Jimmy Johnston*, BellSouth; *Tad Rhyan*, New England; *Jay Delsing*, FESJC; *John Inman*, Buick Open; *Mark Calcavecchia*, International; *Tom Lehman*, Buick Southern; *Jeff Cook, P.H. Horgan*, H-E-B Texas Open; *Davis Love III*, Las Vegas Invitational

BEST BIRDIE STREAK: 7 by *Keith Clearwater*, SW Bell Colonial

EAGLE/BIRDIE STREAK: *Rick Fehr*, birdie, eagle-3, 3 birdies, Hope Chrysler

BEST COME FROM BEHIND LAST DAY TO WIN: 5 strokes, *Vijay Singh*, Buick Classic

FIRST-TIME WINNERS: *Brett Ogle*, AT&T Pebble Beach National Pro-Am; *Mike Standly*, Freeport-McMoRan Classic; *Jim McGovern*, Shell Houston Open; *Grant Waite*, Kemper Open; *Vijay Singh*, Buick Classic; *Billy Mayfair*, GMO; *Jeff Maggert*, Walt Disney World/Oldsmobile Classic

WIRE-TO-WIRE WINNERS: *Howard Twitty*, Hawaii
(no ties)   *Nick Price*, Sprint Western Open

MULTIPLE WINNERS: *Nick Price* (4), PLAYERS, Canon GHO, Sprint Western & FESJC; *Paul Azinger* (3), Memorial, New England &PGA Championship; *Tom Kite* (2), Hope Chrysler &Nissan Los Angeles; *Lee Janzen* (2), Phoenix Open & U.S. Open; *Larry Mize* (2), N. Telecom & Buick Open; *Phil Mickelson* (2), Buick Invitational & The International; *Fulton Allem* (2), SW Bell Colonial & NEC WSOG; *David Frost* (2), Canadian Open & Hardee's; *Davis Love III* (2), Tournament of Champions & Las Vegas Invitational; *Jim Gallagher, Jr.* (2), Anheuser-Busch Classic & TOUR Championship

LONGEST PERIOD SINCE PREVIOUS WIN: *Howard Twitty*, United Airlines Hawaii/12 years 7 months

COURSE RECORDS: 64 (8-under), *Dan Forsman*, Spyglass Hill, AT&T Pebble Beach
(no ties)   62 (10-under), *Tom Kite*, PGA West, Bob Hope Chrysler Classic
61 (9-under), *Billy Mayfair*, TPC at Las Colinas, GTE Byron Nelson
61 (9-under), *Keith Clearwater*, Colonial CC (later tied by Lee Janzen), SW Bell Colonial
61 (10-under), *Jay Delsing*, TPC at Southwind, FESJC
63 (8-under), *Vijay Singh*, Inverness Club, PGA Championship
65 (7-under), *Tom Lehman*, Callaway Gardens, Buick Southern
64 (8-under), *John Inman*, Callaway Gardens, Buick Southern (later tied by Mark Brooks)
63 (8-under), *Jim Gallagher*, Jr., Olympic Club, TOUR Championship

TOURNAMENT RECORDS: 325 (35-under), *Tom Kite*, Bob Hope Chrysler Classic
(no ties)   265 (23-under), *Greg Norman*, Doral-Ryder Open
269 (19-under), *Nick Price*, Western
259 (21-under), *David Frost*, Hardee's
270 (18-under), *Nick Price*, PLAYERS
264 (16-under), *Fulton Allem*, Colonial

MOST CONSECUTIVE ROUNDS PAR OR LESS IN 1993:
18 by *Corey Pavin* (2 Shell Houston, 4 BellSouth, 4 Byron Nelson, 4 SW Bell Colonial, 4 Memorial)

SINGLE-SEASON MONEY RECORD: *Nick Price*, $1,478,557

PLAYOFFS:
Honda Classic	*Fred Couples* def. *Robert Gamez*, par on second extra hole
Kmart Greater Greensboro Open	*Rocco Mediate* def. *Steve Elkington*, birdie on fourth extra hole
Shell Houston Open	*Jim McGovern* def. *John Huston*, birdie on second extra hole
Buick Classic	*Vijay Singh* def. *Mark Wiebe*, birdie on third extra hole
Greater Milwaukee Open	*Billy Mayfair* def. *Mark Calcavecchia*, birdie on fourth extra hole
Buick Southern Open	*John Inman* def. *Bob Estes*, birdie on second extra hole
H-E-B Texas Open	*Jay Haas* def. *Bob Lohr*, birdie on second extra hole

THE LAST TIME

WINNERS:

Last to win back-to-back events .... David Frost, 1993 Canadian Open, Hardee's Golf Classic
Last to win three consecutive events .... Gary Player, 1978 Masters, T of C, Houston Open
Last to win three consecutive starts ...... Nick Price, 1993 Hartford, Western, FedEx St. Jude
Last to defend title .... David Frost, 1992, 1993 Hardee's Golf Classic
Last lefthander to win .... Phil Mickelson, 1993 The International
Last Monday Open Qualifier to win .... Fred Wadsworth, 1986 Southern Open
Last rookie to win .... Vijay Singh, 1993 Buick Classic
Last rookie to win twice .... Robert Gamez, 1990 Northern Telecom Tucson Open and
                                                              Nestle Invitational
Last amateur to win .... Phil Mickelson, 1991 Northern Telecom Open
Last to win in first-ever TOUR start .... Jim Benepe, 1988 Beatrice Western Open
Last to win in first start as official
  member of PGA TOUR .... Robert Gamez, 1990 Northern Telecom Tucson Open
Last wire-to-wire winner (no ties) .... Nick Price, 1993 Sprint Western Open
Last player to win with over-par score ... Bruce Lietzke, 1981 Byron Nelson Classic, plus-1
Last time player shot 80 and won .... Kenny Knox, 1986 Honda Classic (third round)
Last to repeat as money leader .... Curtis Strange, 1987, 1988

TOURNAMENT FINISHES

Last 36-hole event .... 1986 Pensacola Open
Last 54-hole event .... 1993 Shell Houston Open
Last Monday finish .... 1988 Canadian Open
Last Monday finish for playoff .... 1991 Doral-Ryder Open
Last Monday U.S. Open playoff finish ... 1991 Payne Stewart defeated Scott Simpson 75-77
Last Tuesday finish .... 1980 Joe Garagiola-Tucson Open
Last 36-hole final day .... 1987 Beatrice Western Open
Last time cut made after 18 holes .... 1987 Beatrice Western Open

WEATHER

Last time tournament rained out .... 1991 Independent Insurance Agent Open
Last time it snowed during tournament.. 1987 Greater Greensboro Open

DOUBLE EAGLES, ACES & EAGLES

Last time back-to-back eagles .... David Toms, 1992 Chattanooga Classic
Last time double eagle .... Darrell Kestner, 1993 PGA Championship
Last time three eagles in same round ... Don Pooley, 1992 H-E-B Texas Open.
Last time four aces same day,
  same hole .... 1989 U.S. Open, Doug Weaver, Mark Wiebe, Jerry Pate,
                                                              Nick Price on hole No. 6, 160 yards, all used a 7-iron.

PLAYOFF

Last one-hole playoff .... 1992 Colonial (Bruce Lietzke def. Corey Pavin)
Last two-hole playoff .... 1993 H-E-B Texas Open (Jay Haas def. Bob Lohr)
Last three-hole playoff .... 1993 Buick Classic (Vijay Singh def. Mark Wiebe)
Last four-hole playoff .... 1993 Greater Milwaukee Open (Billy Mayfair def. Mark
                                                              Calcavecchia and Ted Schulz)
Last five-hole playoff .... 1989 Las Vegas Invitational (Scott Hoch def. Robert Wrenn)
Last six-hole playoff .... 1986 Kemper Open (Greg Norman def. Larry Mize)
Last seven-hole playoff .... 1991 New England Classic (Bruce Fleisher def. Ian Baker-
                                                              Finch)
Last eight hole playoff .... 1983 Phoenix Open (Bob Gilder def. Johnny Miller, Mark
                                                              O'Meara and Rex Caldwell)
Last 11-hole playoff (TOUR record
  for sudden death) .... 1949 Motor City Open (Middlecoff and Mangrum co-winners)
Last 18-hole playoff .... 1991 U.S. Open (Payne Stewart def. Scott Simpson, 75-77)
Last playoff won with eagle .... 1992 Bob Hope Chrysler Classic (John Cook defeated Gene
                                                              Sauers, Tom Kite, Mark O'Meara and Rick Fehr)
Last playoff won with birdie .... 1993 H-E-B Texas Open (Jay Haas def. Bob Lohr)
Last playoff won with bogey .... 1988 Phoenix Open (Sandy Lyle def. Fred Couples, third
                                                              extra hole)
Last two-man playoff .... 1993 H-E-B Texas Open (Jay Haas def. Bob Lohr)
Last three-man playoff .... 1993 Greater Milwaukee Open (Billy Mayfair def. Mark
                                                              Calcavecchia and Ted Schulz)
Last four-man playoff .... 1990 Doral Ryder Open (Greg Norman def. Paul Azinger,
                                                              Mark Calcavecchia and Tim Simpson)
Last five-man playoff .... 1993 Buick Southern Open (John Inman def. Bob Estes, Billy
                                                              Andrade, Brad Bryant and Mark Brooks)
Last five-TEAM playoff .... 1985 Chrysler Team Championship

1993 PGA TOUR TOURNAMENT SUMMARY

*Denotes first time winner

	TOURNAMENT	COURSE	WINNER	SCORE	UNDER PAR	MARGIN	MONEY	RUNNERS-UP
1.	Infiniti Tournament of Champions	LaCosta Resort Carlsbad, CA	Davis Love III	272	16	1	$144,000	Tom Kite
2.	United Airlines Hawaiian Open	Waialae CC Honolulu, HI	Howard Twitty	269	19	4	$216,000	Joey Sindelar
3.	Northern Telecom Open	Tucson National Starr Pass Tucson, AZ	Larry Mize	271	17	2	$198,000	Jeff Maggert
4.	Phoenix Open	TPC of Scottsdale Scottsdale, AZ	Lee Janzen	273	11	2	$180,000	Andrew Magee
5.	AT&T Pebble Beach National Pro-Am	Pebble Beach GL Spyglass Hill GC Poppy Hills GC Pebble Beach, CA	Brett Ogle*	276	12	3	$225,000	Billy Ray Brown
6.	Bob Hope Chrysler Classic	PGA West/Palmer Course Indian Wells CC Bermuda Dunes CC Tamarisk CC La Quinta, CA	Tom Kite	325	35	6	$198,000	Rick Fehr
7.	Buick Invitational of California	Torrey Pines GC La Jolla, CA	Phil Mickelson	278	10	4	$180,000	Dave Rummells
8.	Nissan Los Angeles Open	Riviera CC Pacific Palisades, CA	Tom Kite (2) (event shortened to 54 holes due to rain)	206	7	3	$180,000	Fred Couples Payne Stewart Donnie Hammond Dave Barr
9.	Doral-Ryder Open	Doral Resort & CC Miami, FL	Greg Norman	265	23	4	$252,000	Paul Azinger Mark McCumber
10.	Honda Classic	Weston Hills CC Ft. Lauderdale, FL	Fred Couples (won playoff with par on 2nd extra hole) (event shortened to 54 holes due to wind)	207	9	Playoff	$198,000	Robert Gamez
11.	Nestle Invitational	Bay Hill Club & Lodge Orlando, FL	Ben Crenshaw	280	8	2	$180,000	Rocco Mediate Davis Love III Vijay Singh
12.	THE PLAYERS Championship	TPC at Sawgrass Ponte Vedra, FL	Nick Price	270	18	5	$450,000	Bernhard Langer
13.	Freeport-McMoRan Classic	English Turn G & CC New Orleans, LA	Mike Standly*	281	7	1	$180,000	Russ Cochran Payne Stewart
14a.	The Masters	Augusta National GC Augusta, GA	Bernhard Langer	277	11	4	$306,000	Chip Beck
14b.	Deposit Guaranty Golf Classic	Hattiesburg CC Hattiesburg, MS	Greg Kraft	267	13	1	$54,000 (unofficial)	Morris Hatalsky Tad Rhyan
15.	MCI Heritage Classic	Harbour Town GL Hilton Head Island, SC	David Edwards	273	11	2	$202,500	David Frost
16.	Kmart Greater Greensboro Open	Forest Oaks CC Greensboro, NC	Rocco Mediate (won playoff with birdie on 4th extra hole)	281	7	Playoff	$270,000	Steve Elkington
17.	Shell Houston Open	TPC at The Woodlands The Woodlands, TX	Jim McGovern* (won playoff with birdie on 2nd extra hole)	199	17	Playoff	$234,000	John Huston
18.	BellSouth Classic	Atlanta CC Marietta, GA	Nolan Henke	271	17	2	$216,000	Tom Sieckmann Nick Price Mark Calcavecchia
19.	GTE Byron Nelson Classic	TPC at Las Colinas Irving, TX	Scott Simpson	270	10	1	$216,000	Billy Mayfair Corey Pavin D.A. Weibring
20.	Kemper Open	TPC at Avenel Potomac, MD	Grant Waite*	275	9	1	$234,000	Tom Kite
21.	Southwestern Bell Colonial	Colonial CC Ft. Worth, TX	Fulton Allem	264	16	1	$234,000	Greg Norman
22.	Memorial	Muirfield Village GC Dublin, OH	Paul Azinger	274	14	1	$252,000	Corey Pavin
23.	Buick Classic	Westchester CC Harrison, NY	Vijay Singh* (won playoff with birdie on 3rd extra hole)	280	4	Playoff	$180,000	Mark Wiebe

1993 PGA TOUR TOURNAMENT SUMMARY * Denotes first time winner

TOURNAMENT	COURSE	WINNER	SCORE	UNDER PAR	MARGIN	MONEY	RUNNERS-UP
24. U.S. Open	Baltusrol GC Springfield, NJ	Lee Janzen (2)	272	8	2	$290,000	Payne Stewart
25. Canon Greater Hartford Open	TPC at River Highlands Cromwell, CT	Nick Price (2)	271	9	1	$180,000	Dan Forsman Roger Maltbie
26. Sprint Western Open	Cog Hill G&CC (Dubsdread Course) Lemont, IL	Nick Price (3)	269	19	5	$216,000	Greg Norman
27. Anheuser-Busch Classic	Kingsmill GC (River Course) Williamsburg, VA	Jim Gallagher, Jr.	269	15	2	$198,000	Chip Beck
28. New England Classic	Pleasant Valley CC Sutton, MA	Paul Azinger (2)	268	16	4	$180,000	Jay Delsing Bruce Fleisher
29. Federal Express St. Jude Classic	TPC at Southwind Memphis, TN	Nick Price (4)	266	18	3	$198,000	Jeff Maggert Rick Fehr
30. Buick Open	Warwick Hills G&CC Grand Blanc, MI	Larry Mize (2)	272	16	1	$180,000	Fuzzy Zoeller
31. PGA Championship	Inverness Club Toledo, OH	Paul Azinger (3) (won playoff with par on 2nd extra hole)	272	12	Playoff	$300,000	Greg Norman
32. The International	Castle Pines GC Castle Rock, CO	Phil Mickelson (2)	45 points	—	8	$234,000	Mark Calcavecchia
33. NEC World Series of Golf	Firestone CC (South Course) Akron, OH	Fulton Allem (2)	270	10	5	$360,000	Craig Stadler Jim Gallagher, Jr. Nick Price
34. Greater Milwaukee Open	Tuckaway CC Franklin, WI	Billy Mayfair* (won playoff with birdie on 4th extra hole)	270	18	Playoff	$180,000	Mark Calcavecchia Ted Schulz
35. Canadian Open	Glen Abbey GC Oakville, Ontario	David Frost	279	9	1	$180,000	Fred Couples
36. Hardee's Golf Classic	Oakwood CC Coal Valley, IL	David Frost (2)	259	21	7	$180,000	D.A. Weibring Payne Stewart
37. B.C. Open	En-Joie GC Endicott, NY	Blaine McCallister	271	13	1	$144,000	Denis Watson
38. Buick Southern Open	Callaway Gardens (Mountain Course) Pine Mountain, GA	John Inman (won playoff with birdie on 2nd extra hole)	278	10	Playoff	$126,000	Bob Estes Mark Brooks Brad Bryant Billy Andrade
39. Walt Disney World/ Oldsmobile Classic	Walt Disney Resort Lake Buena Vista, FL	Jeff Maggert	265	23	3	$180,000	Greg Kraft
40. H-E-B Texas Open	Oak Hills CC San Antonio, TX	Jay Haas (won playoff with birdie on 2nd extra hole)	263	21	Playoff	$180,000	Bob Lohr
41. Las Vegas Invitational	TPC at Summerlin Desert Inn & CC Las Vegas CC Las Vegas, NV	Davis Love III	331	29	8	$234,000	Craig Stadler
42. THE TOUR Championship	The Olympic Club (Lake Course) San Francisco, CA	Jim Gallagher, Jr. (2)	277	7	1	$540,000	Scott Simpson Greg Norman David Frost John Huston
43. Lincoln Mercury Kapalua International	Kapalua Resort (Plantation Course, Bay Course) Kapalua, Maui, HI	Fred Couples	274	16	4	$180,000	Blaine McCallister
44. World Cup of Golf	Lake Nona Resort Orlando, FL	United States	556	20	5	$130,000 each	Zimbabwe
45. Franklin Funds Shark Shootout	Sherwood CC Thousands Oaks, CA	Steve Elkington/ Ray Floyd	188	28	1	$150,000 each	four teams
46. The Skins Game	Bighorn GC Palm Desert, CA	Payne Stewart	—	—	—	$280,000	Fred Couples
47. JCPenney Classic	Innisbrook Resort Tarpon Springs, FL	Mike Springer/ Melissa McNamara	265	19	4	$120,000 each	five teams

1993 PGA TOUR STATISTICAL LEADERS

DRIVING DISTANCE

	NAME	YARDS
1.	JOHN DALY	288.9
2.	DAVIS LOVE III	280.2
3.	DAVID JACKSON	278.7
4.	BARRY CHEESMAN	278.6
5.	JOHN ADAMS	277.6
6.	BRETT OGLE	276.9
7.	FRED COUPLES	275.0
8.	JAY DELSING	274.8
9.	GREG NORMAN	274.4
10.	JOHN ELLIOTT	274.2
11.	NICK PRICE	273.9
12.	PAUL AZINGER	273.3
12.	JODIE MUDD	273.3
12.	FUZZY ZOELLER	273.3
15.	ED HUMENIK	272.7
16.	PHIL BLACKMAR	271.4
17.	KELLY GIBSON	270.9
18.	JC ANDERSON	270.6
18.	JOHN HUSTON	270.6
20.	DAN POHL	270.5
21.	STEVE LAMONTAGNE	270.3
22.	MIKE STANDLY	269.9
23.	TOM LEHMAN	269.5
24.	DUFFY WALDORF	269.3
25.	PHIL MICKELSON	269.2
26.	KENNY PERRY	269.1
26.	PAYNE STEWART	269.1
26.	TOM WATSON	269.1
29.	MICHAEL BRADLEY	268.8
30.	JIM GALLAGHER, JR.	268.7
30.	HOWARD TWITTY	268.7
32.	TOM PURTZER	268.4
33.	CRAIG STADLER	268.2
34.	BRAD BRYANT	268.1
35.	BILL GLASSON	267.9
36.	MARCO DAWSON	267.8
37.	STEVE ELKINGTON	267.5
38.	JIM MCGOVERN	267.1
38.	JOEY SINDELAR	267.1
40.	STEVE LOWERY	267.0
41.	DAVE RUMMELLS	266.4
42.	NEAL LANCASTER	266.2
43.	MIKE SPRINGER	266.1
44.	NEALE SMITH	265.7
45.	NOLAN HENKE	265.5
46.	GIL MORGAN	265.4
47.	ANDY BEAN	265.2
47.	MARK CALCAVECCHIA	265.2
47.	DUDLEY HART	265.2
50.	DAVID PEOPLES	265.1

DRIVING ACCURACY

	NAME	PCT.
1.	DOUG TEWELL	82.5
2.	DILLARD PRUITT	81.7
3.	FRED FUNK	80.6
4.	HALE IRWIN	79.8
5.	DAVID EDWARDS	78.3
6.	D.A. WEIBRING	77.9
7.	FULTON ALLEM	77.6
8.	ED FIORI	77.3
9.	LOREN ROBERTS	77.2
10.	TOM BYRUM	76.9
11.	BOB LOHR	76.8
12.	BRUCE LIETZKE	76.6
12.	COREY PAVIN	76.6
14.	JEFF MAGGERT	76.3
15.	BILLY MAYFAIR	76.2
16.	GIL MORGAN	76.1
17.	MORRIS HATALSKY	76.0
18.	BRUCE FLEISHER	75.6
19.	BLAINE MCCALLISTER	75.5
19.	CURTIS STRANGE	75.5
21.	JOHN DOWDALL	75.2
22.	JOHN INMAN	75.1
23.	DAVID OGRIN	75.0
23.	DAVE PEEGE	75.0
25.	DONNIE HAMMOND	74.9
26.	JOHN MAHAFFEY	74.8
27.	HUBERT GREEN	74.7
27.	LARRY MIZE	74.7
29.	MARK CARNEVALE	74.6
30.	PAUL GOYDOS	74.5
31.	TIM SIMPSON	74.3
32.	LENNIE CLEMENTS	73.9
32.	PETER JACOBSEN	73.9
32.	GREG NORMAN	73.9
32.	NICK PRICE	73.9
36.	ROCCO MEDIATE	73.8
36.	HARRY TAYLOR	73.8
38.	JOHN COOK	73.7
38.	BILL GLASSON	73.7
40.	BRIAN CLAAR	73.6
41.	TIM CONLEY	73.4
42.	JIM MCGOVERN	73.2
43.	IAN BAKER-FINCH	73.1
43.	JAIME GOMEZ	73.1
43.	WAYNE LEVI	73.1
46.	MARK BROOKS	73.0
46.	PETER PERSONS	73.0
48.	ROBERT GAMEZ	72.7
49.	RICK FEHR	72.6
49.	TOM WATSON	72.6

1993 PGA TOUR Statistical Leaders *(cont'd.)*

GREENS IN REGULATION

	NAME	PCT.
1.	FUZZY ZOELLER	73.6
2.	BILL GLASSON	72.3
3.	DAVID EDWARDS	72.1
4.	JOHN COOK	71.7
5.	DAN POHL	71.5
6.	NICK PRICE	71.3
7.	SCOTT HOCH	71.2
8.	GIL MORGAN	71.1
8.	DILLARD PRUITT	71.1
10.	COREY PAVIN	70.9
11.	DAVE BARR	70.7
12.	PAUL AZINGER	70.6
13.	BLAINE MCCALLISTER	70.3
14.	DAVID PEOPLES	70.2
15.	BILLY MAYFAIR	70.1
16.	GREG NORMAN	70.0
17.	BRUCE LIETZKE	69.9
18.	TIM SIMPSON	69.8
19.	JAY HAAS	69.7
20.	MARK MCCUMBER	69.5
21.	TOM KITE	69.4
21.	PAYNE STEWART	69.4
23.	BILL KRATZERT	69.2
24.	STEVE ELKINGTON	69.0
24.	JEFF MAGGERT	69.0
26.	LOREN ROBERTS	68.9
27.	LENNIE CLEMENTS	68.8
28.	HARRY TAYLOR	68.7
29.	TOM LEHMAN	68.6
29.	CRAIG STADLER	68.6
31.	RICK FEHR	68.5
31.	PETER JACOBSEN	68.5
31.	ROCCO MEDIATE	68.5
31.	DAVID OGRIN	68.5
35.	DONNIE HAMMOND	68.4
35.	JOHN HUSTON	68.4
37.	FRED COUPLES	68.3
37.	HALE IRWIN	68.3
39.	FRED FUNK	68.2
40.	RUSS COCHRAN	68.1
41.	BOB ESTES	67.9
41.	ANDREW MAGEE	67.9
41.	JOHN MAHAFFEY	67.9
41.	KENNY PERRY	67.9
45.	DAN FORSMAN	67.8
45.	ED HUMENIK	67.8
47.	FULTON ALLEM	67.7
47.	JIM GALLAGHER, JR.	67.7
47.	DAVIS LOVE III	67.7
50.	KIRK TRIPLETT	67.6

PUTTING LEADERS

	NAME	AVG.
1.	DAVID FROST	1.739
2.	BRAD FAXON	1.741
3.	KEN GREEN	1.750
4.	GREG NORMAN	1.751
5.	SCOTT SIMPSON	1.752
6.	JOHN FLANNERY	1.753
7.	DICK MAST	1.754
8.	BEN CRENSHAW	1.755
9.	DONNIE HAMMOND	1.758
9.	WAYNE LEVI	1.758
11.	RUSS COCHRAN	1.760
11.	GREG KRAFT	1.760
11.	COREY PAVIN	1.760
14.	LANNY WADKINS	1.764
14.	DENIS WATSON	1.764
16.	BOB LOHR	1.765
16.	PAYNE STEWART	1.765
18.	LEE JANZEN	1.766
18.	NICK PRICE	1.766
18.	TOM WATSON	1.766
21.	JOHN HUSTON	1.768
21.	TOM KITE	1.768
21.	LARRY MIZE	1.768
24.	DAN FORSMAN	1.769
24.	CURTIS STRANGE	1.769
26.	PAUL AZINGER	1.770
26.	RUSSELL BEIERSDORF	1.770
26.	CRAIG PARRY	1.770
29.	GARY HALLBERG	1.771
29.	LANCE TEN BROECK	1.771
31.	FRED COUPLES	1.774
31.	NOLAN HENKE	1.774
33.	RICK FEHR	1.775
33.	JOHN INMAN	1.775
33.	BRIAN KAMM	1.775
33.	TOM SIECKMANN	1.775
37.	STEVE LOWERY	1.776
37.	MARK WIEBE	1.776
39.	FULTON ALLEM	1.777
39.	BILLY ANDRADE	1.777
39.	BRIAN CLAAR	1.777
39.	MORRIS HATALSKY	1.777
39.	JIM MCGOVERN	1.777
39.	D.A. WEIBRING	1.777
45.	DAVIS LOVE III	1.778
46.	HOWARD TWITTY	1.779
47.	MICHAEL BRADLEY	1.780
47.	MARK CALCAVECCHIA	1.780
47.	STEVE ELKINGTON	1.780
47.	SCOTT HOCH	1.780
47.	KIRK TRIPLETT	1.780

1993 PGA TOUR Statistical Leaders *(cont'd.)*

TOTAL DRIVING

NAME	TOTAL
1. GREG NORMAN	41
2. NICK PRICE	43
3. GIL MORGAN	62
4. FUZZY ZOELLER	68
5. BLAINE MCCALLISTER	70
6. JEFF MAGGERT	71
7. BILL GLASSON	73
8. TOM WATSON	75
9. PAUL AZINGER	78
10. JIM MCGOVERN	80
11. PETER JACOBSEN	100
12. BRUCE LIETZKE	101
13. MARK MCCUMBER	107
14. KENNY PERRY	108
15. ROCCO MEDIATE	109
15. PAYNE STEWART	109
17. DONNIE HAMMOND	117
18. WAYNE LEVI	120
19. TOM KITE	121
20. LARRY MIZE	122
21. FULTON ALLEM	123
22. DAN POHL	126
23. BOB ESTES	127
23. DAVID PEOPLES	127
23. CRAIG STADLER	127
26. STEVE ELKINGTON	129
26. SCOTT GUMP	129
28. TOM LEHMAN	134
29. RICK FEHR	135
29. ANDREW MAGEE	135
31. KELLY GIBSON	136
31. HOWARD TWITTY	136
33. ED HUMENIK	140
34. ROBERT GAMEZ	141
35. DILLARD PRUITT	143
36. MARK CARNEVALE	145
37. NOLAN HENKE	147
38. BRIAN HENNINGER	150
38. JODIE MUDD	150
40. JOEY SINDELAR	151
41. DOUG TEWELL	152
42. RUSS COCHRAN	153
42. HALE IRWIN	153
42. DUFFY WALDORF	153
45. GRANT WAITE	155
46. PATRICK BURKE	156
46. DAVE RUMMELLS	156
48. PAUL GOYDOS	157
48. SKIP KENDALL	157
48. MARK O'MEARA	157
48. TOM PURTZER	157

EAGLE LEADERS

NAME	TOTAL
1. DAVIS LOVE III	15
2. JAY DELSING	13
3. JOHN DALY	12
3. ED HUMENIK	12
3. NEAL LANCASTER	12
6. KEITH CLEARWATER	11
6. TOM LEHMAN	11
6. DAVE RUMMELLS	11
9. MARK CALCAVECCHIA	10
9. KELLY GIBSON	10
9. STEVE LAMONTAGNE	10
9. STEVE LOWERY	10
9. ANDREW MAGEE	10
9. JIM MCGOVERN	10
9. FUZZY ZOELLER	10
16. MARCO DAWSON	9
16. BRIAN HENNINGER	9
16. MIKE HULBERT	9
16. PETER JACOBSEN	9
16. GIL MORGAN	9
16. TAD RHYAN	9
16. GENE SAUERS	9
16. TOM SIECKMANN	9
16. KIRK TRIPLETT	9
25. MICHAEL ALLEN	8
25. JC ANDERSON	8
25. CHIP BECK	8
25. PHIL BLACKMAR	8
25. FRED COUPLES	8
25. BOB ESTES	8
25. JAY HAAS	8
25. GARY HALLBERG	8
25. BRETT OGLE	8
25. TOM PURTZER	8
25. MIKE STANDLY	8
25. GREG TWIGGS	8
37. JOHN ADAMS	7
37. DAVE BARR	7
37. RUSSELL BEIERSDORF	7
37. BRAD BRYANT	7
37. RUSS COCHRAN	7
37. BRAD FABEL	7
37. LEE JANZEN	7
37. MASSY KURAMOTO	7
37. WAYNE LEVI	7
37. JEFF MAGGERT	7
37. NEALE SMITH	7
37. DENNIS TRIXLER	7
37. MARK WIEBE	7
50. 17 PLAYERS TIED WITH	6

BIRDIE LEADERS

	NAME	TOTAL
1.	JOHN HUSTON	426
2.	JIM MCGOVERN	412
3.	FRED FUNK	394
4.	KEITH CLEARWATER	384
5.	JAY HAAS	374
6.	STEVE LOWERY	372
7.	JOHN FLANNERY	370
8.	PAYNE STEWART	365
9.	BRIAN CLAAR	364
10.	DAVIS LOVE III	361
11.	BILLY MAYFAIR	356
12.	BRAD BRYANT	353
13.	RUSSELL BEIERSDORF	350
14.	SCOTT HOCH	347
15.	RUSS COCHRAN	344
16.	BOB ESTES	343
16.	RICK FEHR	343
18.	ED DOUGHERTY	341
19.	LEE JANZEN	340
20.	NOLAN HENKE	339
21.	JEFF MAGGERT	337
21.	COREY PAVIN	337
23.	NEAL LANCASTER	335
24.	MARK CALCAVECCHIA	333
25.	BLAINE MCCALLISTER	328
26.	KELLY GIBSON	325
27.	TOM LEHMAN	324
27.	TOM SIECKMANN	324
29.	HOWARD TWITTY	323
30.	FULTON ALLEM	322
31.	STEVE ELKINGTON	317
31.	TED TRYBA	317
33.	BILLY ANDRADE	316
33.	GENE SAUERS	316
35.	MIKE HULBERT	315
36.	JAY DELSING	314
37.	JIM GALLAGHER, JR.	312
38.	MARCO DAWSON	311
38.	DICK MAST	311
40.	BRAD FAXON	310
40.	KIRK TRIPLETT	310
42.	DAN FORSMAN	309
42.	DONNIE HAMMOND	309
44.	GARY HALLBERG	308
44.	GREG TWIGGS	308
46.	BRIAN KAMM	307
46.	DAVID OGRIN	307
46.	KENNY PERRY	307
46.	LOREN ROBERTS	307
46.	LANCE TEN BROECK	307
46.	MARK WIEBE	307

SAND SAVES

	NAME	PCT.
1.	KEN GREEN	64.4
2.	MORRIS HATALSKY	63.7
3.	JIMMY JOHNSTON	63.6
3.	NICK PRICE	63.6
5.	GARY HALLBERG	63.3
6.	LARRY MIZE	62.7
7.	CHIP BECK	62.6
8.	GREG NORMAN	62.4
9.	STEVE PATE	61.9
10.	MICHAEL BRADLEY	61.7
10.	DICK MAST	61.7
12.	JODIE MUDD	61.4
13.	BOB GILDER	60.6
13.	BRUCE LIETZKE	60.6
15.	DUDLEY HART	60.4
16.	KEITH CLEARWATER	59.9
17.	TOM WATSON	59.3
18.	ED FIORI	59.2
19.	SCOTT SIMPSON	58.9
19.	D.A. WEIBRING	58.9
21.	KELLY GIBSON	58.8
22.	BRIAN KAMM	58.7
23.	FRED COUPLES	58.6
24.	PAYNE STEWART	58.4
25.	BRAD FAXON	58.3
26.	LENNIE CLEMENTS	58.1
27.	BEN CRENSHAW	58.0
28.	JEFF WOODLAND	57.8
29.	DAVID FROST	57.4
30.	DAVE PEEGE	57.3
31.	DAVID EDWARDS	57.0
31.	BOB LOHR	57.0
31.	LOREN ROBERTS	57.0
34.	PAUL AZINGER	56.8
34.	BILL BRITTON	56.8
36.	BUDDY GARDNER	56.5
36.	JOHN INMAN	56.5
36.	GIL MORGAN	56.5
39.	GREG CESARIO	56.3
40.	PATRICK BURKE	56.2
41.	DAVIS LOVE III	56.1
42.	MARK CALCAVECCHIA	56.0
43.	BRIAN CLAAR	55.9
44.	BILL KRATZERT	55.7
44.	TIM SIMPSON	55.7
46.	COREY PAVIN	55.6
46.	LEE PORTER	55.6
48.	JAY HAAS	55.3
49.	JOHN DALY	55.2
49.	JEFF SLUMAN	55.2
49.	FUZZY ZOELLER	55.2

SCORING AVERAGE

	NAME	AVG.
1.	GREG NORMAN	68.90
2.	NICK PRICE	69.11
3.	DAVID FROST	69.48
4.	TOM KITE	69.74
5.	PAUL AZINGER	69.75
6.	PAYNE STEWART	69.82
7.	FRED COUPLES	69.85
8.	STEVE ELKINGTON	69.97
9.	COREY PAVIN	70.00
10.	RICK FEHR	70.09
11.	GIL MORGAN	70.12
12.	FUZZY ZOELLER	70.14
13.	TOM LEHMAN	70.18
13.	LARRY MIZE	70.18
15.	TOM WATSON	70.19
16.	LEE JANZEN	70.21
17.	JEFF MAGGERT	70.24
18.	BOB ESTES	70.25
19.	MARK MCCUMBER	70.27
20.	DAVIS LOVE III	70.28
21.	HALE IRWIN	70.30
22.	DAVID EDWARDS	70.32
22.	JAY HAAS	70.32
22.	BILL KRATZERT	70.32
25.	SCOTT SIMPSON	70.33
26.	SCOTT HOCH	70.36
27.	DAN FORSMAN	70.38
27.	PETER JACOBSEN	70.38
29.	JOHN COOK	70.45
30.	BILL GLASSON	70.49
31.	DONNIE HAMMOND	70.51
31.	CURTIS STRANGE	70.51
33.	KEITH CLEARWATER	70.53
34.	MORRIS HATALSKY	70.55
35.	MARK BROOKS	70.58
36.	ROCCO MEDIATE	70.59
37.	JOHN HUSTON	70.60
37.	CRAIG STADLER	70.60
39.	LOREN ROBERTS	70.61
40.	JOEY SINDELAR	70.65
41.	MARK CALCAVECCHIA	70.66
42.	BRAD FAXON	70.68
43.	HOWARD TWITTY	70.70
44.	JIM MCGOVERN	70.71
45.	LENNIE CLEMENTS	70.73
46.	PATRICK BURKE	70.75
46.	D.A. WEIBRING	70.75
48.	RUSS COCHRAN	70.76
48.	BOB LOHR	70.76
50.	CHIP BECK	70.77

ALL AROUND

	NAME	TOTAL
1.	GIL MORGAN	252
2.	PAYNE STEWART	266
3.	PAUL AZINGER	286
4.	NICK PRICE	296
5.	JEFF MAGGERT	328
6.	FUZZY ZOELLER	329
7.	GREG NORMAN	374
8.	DAVIS LOVE III	381
9.	STEVE ELKINGTON	384
10.	JIM MCGOVERN	389
11.	LARRY MIZE	397
12.	RUSS COCHRAN	405
13.	BILL GLASSON	434
14.	FULTON ALLEM	439
15.	KEITH CLEARWATER	440
16.	TOM LEHMAN	448
17.	TOM WATSON	451
18.	BOB ESTES	463
19.	JAY HAAS	478
20.	PETER JACOBSEN	480
21.	RICK FEHR	491
22.	COREY PAVIN	493
23.	LEE JANZEN	494
24.	FRED COUPLES	495
25.	MARK MCCUMBER	515
26.	SCOTT HOCH	521
27.	BLAINE MCCALLISTER	526
28.	WAYNE LEVI	534
29.	DAN FORSMAN	537
30.	JOHN HUSTON	539
31.	DONNIE HAMMOND	544
31.	STEVE LOWERY	544
33.	KIRK TRIPLETT	553
34.	BRIAN KAMM	563
35.	BRUCE LIETZKE	568
36.	LOREN ROBERTS	570
37.	HOWARD TWITTY	572
38.	DAVID FROST	573
39.	LENNIE CLEMENTS	579
40.	KELLY GIBSON	585
41.	FRED FUNK	593
42.	TOM KITE	596
43.	DAVID EDWARDS	603
44.	NOLAN HENKE	604
45.	MARK CALCAVECCHIA	610
46.	ROCCO MEDIATE	611
47.	BRAD BRYANT	613
48.	ANDREW MAGEE	616
49.	RUSSELL BEIERSDORF	624
49.	CRAIG STADLER	624

YEAR BY YEAR STATISTICAL LEADERS

SCORING AVERAGE
1980	Lee Trevino	69.73
1981	Tom Kite	69.80
1982	Tom Kite	70.21
1983	Raymond Floyd	70.61
1984	Calvin Peete	70.56
1985	Don Pooley	70.36
1986	Scott Hoch	70.08
1987	David Frost	70.09
1988	Greg Norman	69.38
1989	Payne Stewart	*69.485
1990	Greg Norman	69.10
1991	Fred Couples	69.59
1992	Fred Couples	69.38
1993	Greg Norman	68.90

DRIVING DISTANCE
1980	Dan Pohl	274.3
1981	Dan Pohl	280.1
1982	Bill Calfee	275.3
1983	John McComish	277.4
1984	Bill Glasson	276.5
1985	Andy Bean	278.2
1986	Davis Love III	285.7
1987	John McComish	283.9
1988	Steve Thomas	284.6
1989	Ed Humenik	280.9
1990	Tom Purtzer	279.6
1991	John Daly	288.9
1992	John Daly	283.4
1993	John Daly	288.9

DRIVING ACCURACY
1980	Mike Reid	79.5%
1981	Calvin Peete	81.9
1982	Calvin Peete	84.6
1983	Calvin Peete	81.3
1984	Calvin Peete	77.5
1985	Calvin Peete	80.6
1986	Calvin Peete	81.7
1987	Calvin Peete	83.0
1988	Calvin Peete	82.5
1989	Calvin Peete	82.6
1990	Calvin Peete	83.7
1991	Hale Irwin	78.3
1992	Doug Tewell	82.3
1993	Doug Tewell	82.5

GREENS IN REGULATION
1980	Jack Nicklaus	72.1%
1981	Calvin Peete	73.1
1982	Calvin Peete	72.4
1983	Calvin Peete	71.4
1984	Andy Bean	72.1
1985	John Mahaffey	71.9
1986	John Mahaffey	72.0
1987	Gil Morgan	73.3
1988	John Adams	73.9
1989	Bruce Lietzke	72.6
1990	Doug Tewell	70.9
1991	Bruce Lietzke	73.3
1992	Tim Simpson	74.0
1993	Fuzzy Zoeller	73.6

PUTTING
1980	Jerry Pate	28.81
1981	Alan Tapie	28.70
1982	Ben Crenshaw	28.65
1983	Morris Hatalsky	27.96
1984	Gary McCord	28.57
1985	Craig Stadler	* 28.627
1986	Greg Norman	1.736
1987	Ben Crenshaw	1.743
1988	Don Pooley	1.729
1989	Steve Jones	1.734
1990	Larry Rinker	*1.7467
1991	Jay Don Blake	*1.7326
1992	Mark O'Meara	1.731
1993	David Frost	1.739

ALL-AROUND
1987	Dan Pohl	170
1988	Payne Stewart	170
1989	Paul Azinger	250
1990	Paul Azinger	162
1991	Scott Hoch	283
1992	Fred Couples	256
1993	Gil Morgan	252

SAND SAVES
1980	Bob Eastwood	65.4%
1981	Tom Watson	60.1
1982	Isao Aoki	60.2
1983	Isao Aoki	62.3
1984	Peter Oosterhuis	64.7
1985	Tom Purtzer	60.8
1986	Paul Azinger	63.8
1987	Paul Azinger	63.2
1988	Greg Powers	63.5
1989	Mike Sullivan	66.0
1990	Paul Azinger	67.2
1991	Ben Crenshaw	64.9
1992	Mitch Adcock	66.9
1993	Ken Green	64.4

PAR BREAKERS (category discontinued)
1980	Tom Watson	.213
1981	Bruce Lietzke	.225
1982	Tom Kite	*.2154
1983	Tom Watson	.211
1984	Craig Stadler	.220
1985	Craig Stadler	.218
1986	Greg Norman	.248
1987	Mark Calcavecchia	.221
1988	Ken Green	.236
1989	Greg Norman	.224
1990	Greg Norman	.219

TOTAL DRIVING
1991	Bruce Lietzke	42
1992	Bruce Lietzke	50
1993	Greg Norman	41

EAGLES
1980	Dave Eichelberger	16
1981	Bruce Lietzke	12
1982	Tom Weiskopf	10
	J.C. Snead	10
	Andy Bean	10
1983	Chip Beck	15
1984	Gary Hallberg	15
1985	Larry Rinker	14
1986	Joey Sindelar	16
1987	Phil Blackmar	20
1988	Ken Green	21
1989	Lon Hinkle	14
	Duffy Waldorf	14
1990	Paul Azinger	14
1991	Andy Bean	15
	John Huston	15
1992	Dan Forsman	18
1993	Davis Love III	15

BIRDIES
1980	Andy Bean	388
1981	Vance Heafner	388
1982	Andy Bean	392
1983	Hal Sutton	399
1984	Mark O'Meara	419
1985	Joey Sindelar	411
1986	Joey Sindelar	415
1987	Dan Forsman	409
1988	Dan Forsman	465
1989	Ted Schulz	415
1990	Mike Donald	401
1991	Scott Hoch	446
1992	Jeff Sluman	417
1993	John Huston	426

* had to be carried a decimal further
to determine winner

1993 PGA TOUR STATISTICAL HIGH/LOWS

Those with 50 rounds or more based on 189 ranked players.

STATISTICAL CATEGORY	HIGHEST	AVERAGE	LOWEST
Driving Distance	288.9	260.3	240.9
Driving Accuracy	82.5%	68.8%	53.0%
Greens in Regulation	73.6%	65.5%	52.3%
Putting	1.739	1.798	1.885
Par Breakers	23.1%	18.3%	12.9%
Eagles	15	4	0
Birdies	426	263	122
Scoring Average	69.48	71.58	74.23
Sand Saves	64.4%	51.7%	35.8%

1980-1993 CUMULATIVE STATISTICS RANKINGS (min. of 350 rounds)

SCORING LEADERS

1	TOM KITE	70.53
2	GREG NORMAN	70.63
3	PAYNE STEWART	70.73
4	COREY PAVIN	70.75
5	TOM WATSON	70.76
6	LEE JANZEN	70.78
7	BRUCE LIETZKE	70.80
T8	STEVE ELKINGTON	70.85
T8	PAUL AZINGER	70.85
10	SCOTT HOCH	70.91

DRIVING DISTANCE

1	DAVIS LOVE III	277.5
2	GREG NORMAN	276.2
T3	FRED COUPLES	274.9
T3	ED HUMENIK	274.9
5	DUFFY WALDORF	273.7
6	DAN POHL	273.5
7	BILL GLASSON	273.3
T8	LON HINKLE	272.6
T8	NEAL LANCASTER	272.6
10	TOM PURTZER	272.5

DRIVING ACCURACY

1	CALVIN PEETE	.817
2	MIKE REID	.768
3	FRED FUNK	.757
T4	DILLARD PRUITT	.748
T4	FULTON ALLEM	.748
6	DAVID EDWARDS	.746
7	JACK RENNER	.745
T8	LARRY MIZE	.739
T8	DOUG TEWELL	.739
10	2 TIED WITH	.732

GREENS IN REGULATION

1	BRUCE LIETZKE	.710
2	DILLARD PRUITT	.708
3	JOHN MAHAFFEY	.707
4	BILLY MAYFAIR	.706
5	KENNY PERRY	.703
6	DAN POHL	.702
7	CALVIN PEETE	.701
8	DAVE BARR	.698
T9	TIM SIMPSON	.696
T9	HAL SUTTON	.696

PUTTING LEADERS

1	MORRIS HATALSKY	28.44
2	TOM PERNICE	28.64
3	LEE JANZEN	28.65
4	FRANK CONNER	28.70
5	GIBBY GILBERT	28.71
6	ROD CURL	28.75
7	WILLIE WOOD	28.76
8	BRIAN CLAAR	28.79
9	BERNHARD LANGER	28.84
10	2 TIED WITH	28.85

PAR BREAKERS

1	GREG NORMAN	.217
T2	DAVIS LOVE III	.210
T2	FRED COUPLES	.210
4	JOHN HUSTON	.208
5	PAYNE STEWART	.207
6	TOM WATSON	.206
T7	PAUL AZINGER	.205
T7	JAY DON BLAKE	.205
9	CRAIG STADLER	.203
10	TOM KITE	.202

EAGLE LEADERS

1	FRED COUPLES	119
2	CRAIG STADLER	109
3	CHIP BECK	105
4	BRUCE LIETZKE	99
5	BUDDY GARDNER	98
6	TOM PURTZER	96
T7	ANDY BEAN	95
T7	JOEY SINDELAR	95
T7	JOHN ADAMS	95
10	FUZZY ZOELLER	92

BIRDIE LEADERS

1	JAY HAAS	4,607
2	TOM KITE	4,529
3	MIKE DONALD	4,526
4	BOBBY WADKINS	4,485
5	HOWARD TWITTY	4,458
6	SCOTT HOCH	4,447
7	TIM SIMPSON	4,370
8	CURTIS STRANGE	4,294
9	CHIP BECK	4,289
10	FRED COUPLES	4,283

SAND-SAVES

1	DAVID FROST	.592
2	JOHN INMAN	.568
3	BOB EASTWOOD	.565
4	ISAO AOKI	.564
5	MORRIS HATALSKY	.561
6	BILLY MAYFAIR	.556
T7	LARRY MIZE	.555
T7	PAUL AZINGER	.555
9	JEFF SLUMAN	.554
10	PETER PERSONS	.553

TOUGHEST HOLES ON THE 1993 PGA TOUR

RANK	GOLF COURSE	HOLE #	PAR	AVG. SCORE	AVG. OVER PAR	EAGLES	BIRDIES	PARS	BOGEYS	DOUBLE BOGEYS	TRIPLE BOGEY+	TOURN. NAME
1	TORREY PINES - NORTH	6	3	3.576	.576		9	60	69	12	1	BUICK INVITATIONAL OF CALIFORNIA
2	BAY HILL CLUB	18	4	4.548	.548		24	189	119	46	7	THE NESTLE INVITATIONAL
3	ENGLISH TURN G&CC	18	4	4.454	.454		25	234	147	32	5	FREEPORT-MCMORAN CLASSIC
4	WESTCHESTER CC	12	4	4.447	.447		21	225	187	16	1	BUICK CLASSIC
5	FIRESTONE CC	4	4	4.444	.444		11	74	59	7	2	NEC WORLD SERIES OF GOLF
6	TORREY PINES - SOUTH	7	4	4.442	.442		18	170	124	14	4	BUICK INVITATIONAL OF CALIFORNIA
7	WESTCHESTER CC	11	4	4.440	.440		23	239	159	27	2	BUICK CLASSIC
8	BAY HILL CLUB	11	4	4.429	.429		19	225	104	31	6	THE NESTLE INVITATIONAL
8	AUGUSTA NATIONAL GC	12	3	3.429	.429		30	169	59	34	9	THE MASTERS TOURNAMENT
10	EN-JOIE GC	15	4	4.416	.416		29	238	169	14	7	B.C. OPEN
11	WESTCHESTER CC	4	4	4.411	.411	1	26	250	137	32	4	BUICK CLASSIC
12	SPYGLASS HILL GC	16	4	4.408	.408	1	10	94	65	8	1	AT&T PEBBLE BEACH NATIONAL PRO-AM
13	TORREY PINES - SOUTH	1	4	4.406	.406		13	186	116	14	1	BUICK INVITATIONAL OF CALIFORNIA
13	RIVIERA CC	2	4	4.406	.406		22	189	134	14	2	NISSAN LOS ANGELES OPEN
15	BAY HILL CLUB	1	4	4.403	.403		12	217	145	11		THE NESTLE INVITATIONAL
16	PEBBLE BCH GOLF LINK	9	4	4.394	.394		14	135	88	12		AT&T PEBBLE BEACH NATIONAL PRO-AM
17	TUCSON NAT'L GOLF	10	4	4.391	.391		23	181	90	23	3	NORTHERN TELECOM OPEN
18	TPC AT LAS COLINAS	3	4	4.388	.388	1	29	257	144	26	4	GTE BYRON NELSON GOLF CLASSIC
19	WESTCHESTER CC	15	4	4.382	.382	1	27	254	140	23	5	BUICK CLASSIC
20	ENGLISH TURN G&CC	7	4	4.375	.375		36	230	153	23	1	FREEPORT-MCMORAN CLASSIC
21	GLEN ABBEY GC	14	4	4.364	.364		23	271	127	28	1	CANADIAN OPEN
21	TORREY PINES - NORTH	5	4	4.364	.364		4	93	49	5		BUICK INVITATIONAL OF CALIFORNIA
23	FIRESTONE CC	9	4	4.359	.359		9	86	52	6		NEC WORLD SERIES OF GOLF
24	WESTCHESTER CC	8	4	4.351	.351		21	271	139	17	2	BUICK CLASSIC
25	GLEN ABBEY GC	17	4	4.347	.347		33	252	148	12	5	CANADIAN OPEN
26	TPC AT AVENEL	12	4	4.344	.344		42	259	120	31	5	KEMPER OPEN
26	POPPY HILLS	1	4	4.344	.344		7	116	48	6	3	AT&T PEBBLE BEACH NATIONAL PRO-AM
28	TPC OF SOUTHWIND	14	3	3.343	.343		52	252	119	38	5	FEDERAL EXPRESS ST. JUDE CLASSIC
29	OAKWOOD CC	4	4	4.336	.336		25	266	155	12		HARDEE'S GOLF CLASSIC
30	TORREY PINES - SOUTH	12	4	4.330	.330		24	190	101	13	2	BUICK INVITATIONAL OF CALIFORNIA
31	ENGLISH TURN G&CC	10	4	4.327	.327		32	258	134	16	3	FREEPORT-MCMORAN CLASSIC
32	TUCSON NAT'L GOLF	18	4	4.325	.325		18	204	79	15	4	NORTHERN TELECOM OPEN
32	THE OLYMPIC CLUB	3	3	3.325	.325		4	74	41	1		TOUR CHAMPIONSHIP
34	WESTON HILLS CC	15	4	4.322	.322		26	231	78	21	7	HONDA CLASSIC
35	SPYGLASS HILL GC	6	4	4.318	.318		16	96	62	4	1	AT&T PEBBLE BEACH NATIONAL PRO-AM
36	ARNOLD PALMER COURSE	9	4	4.317	.317		14	132	42	12	2	BOB HOPE CHRYSLER CLASSIC
36	WESTON HILLS CC	16	4	4.317	.317		33	212	91	24	3	HONDA CLASSIC
38	TPC OF SCOTTSDALE	14	4	4.314	.314	1	24	257	112	17	3	PHOENIX OPEN
38	RIVIERA CC	15	4	4.314	.314	1	31	202	110	17		NISSAN LOS ANGELES OPEN
40	WAIALAE CC	4	3	3.310	.310		29	271	120	20	2	UNITED AIRLINES HAWAIIAN OPEN
41	TORREY PINES - NORTH	7	4	4.305	.305		13	84	49	5		BUICK INVITATIONAL OF CALIFORNIA
42	TORREY PINES - SOUTH	4	4	4.303	.303		29	186	104	8	3	BUICK INVITATIONAL OF CALIFORNIA
43	ENGLISH TURN G&CC	5	4	4.302	.302		26	270	134	13		FREEPORT-MCMORAN CLASSIC
43	SPYGLASS HILL GC	13	4	4.302	.302		9	115	49	4	2	AT&T PEBBLE BEACH NATIONAL PRO-AM
45	TORREY PINES - SOUTH	5	4	4.300	.300		26	198	91	12	3	BUICK INVITATIONAL OF CALIFORNIA
45	FOREST OAKS CC	3	4	4.300	.300		22	306	132	15	1	KMART GREATER GREENSBORO OPEN
47	COG HILL G&CC	18	4	4.299	.299	1	37	280	129	24	1	SPRINT WESTERN OPEN
48	TORREY PINES - NORTH	8	4	4.298	.298		11	89	47	3	1	BUICK INVITATIONAL OF CALIFORNIA
49	SPYGLASS HILL GC	8	4	4.296	.296		21	95	53	9	1	AT&T PEBBLE BEACH NATIONAL PRO-AM
50	MUIRFIELD VILLAGE GC	2	4	4.295	.295		25	227	105	10	3	MEMORIAL TOURNAMENT
50	PLEASANT VALLEY CC	10	4	4.295	.295		23	278	132	11		THE NEW ENGLAND CLASSIC

PLAYER PERFORMANCE CHART

TOP THIRTY MONEY WINNERS ON THE 1993 PGA TOUR

LEGEND:

- ☐ Did not play
- T7 Final position
- ①② Involved in play-off
- DQ Disqualified
- MC Missed cut
- WD Withdrew

Players:
1. Nick Price
2. Paul Azinger
3. Greg Norman
4. Jim Gallagher, Jr.
5. David Frost
6. Payne Stewart
7. Lee Janzen
8. Tom Kite
9. Fulton Allem
10. Fred Couples
11. Jeff Maggert
12. Davis Love III
13. Larry Mize
14. Scott Simpson
15. John Huston
16. Rocco Mediate
17. Steve Elkington
18. Corey Pavin
19. Vijay Singh
20. David Edwards
21. Mark Calcavecchia
22. Phil Mickelson
23. Bernhard Langer
24. Gil Morgan
25. Chip Beck
26. Jay Haas
27. Jim McGovern
28. Rick Fehr
29. Craig Stadler
30. Billy Mayfair

Tournament	1	2	3	4	5	6	7	8	9	10	11	12	13	14	15	16	17	18	19	20	21	22	23	24	25	26	27	28	29	30
Infiniti Tournament of Ch.		T3	T12			T28	2		10		1			9		T18	T25		T18	T10				12	T25				T15	
United Airlines Hawaiian Open	3		T45	MC	MC				T4	T7	50	T45	T51			T51	T13		T13	MC				T22	T30	T30			T30	MC
Northern Telecom Open			T3		T13	T27		T15		2		1		WD			MC	T8		T31						T34	T31			T41
Phoenix Open	T39		MC	T22		1		MC		T11		T27	T22	T64		T39			MC	T45		T9	T16		MC	T32				MC
AT&T Pebble Bch Ntl Pro-Am	T70			T17	T9	6	T28	MC		MC	T28	T58	T36		T28	T9	MC		MC	MC		T9	T7	T36	MC					
Bob Hope Chrysler Classic			T4		T12		1	76	T9		T12		3	T19	MC	T9	T27		T51		MC		T12		T4	MC	2		T51	MC
Buick Invitational of California			T20		3	T37		MC						T37	T20	T37					1			MC	T4	T25	T25	9	MC	
Nissan Los Angeles Open	T6				T2	T14	1	T45	T2	T6	MC		T45			T58			T26	MC	T19		T58	T19	T45	T19	T6	MC	T37	
Doral-Ryder Open	T16	T2	1	T38	4	T16	T10	8	MC	T6	MC	T53		T57	T29	T10		MC	T24	MC		T50	T10		T38					T24
Honda Classic	T26		T38	T6				T10	①	MC		3			T6		T15		T38							T6				MC
Nestle Invitational	T10	MC	T10	T60		T35	T23	T45	T65	MC		T2	T10	T17	T60	T2		T52	T2		MC		T6		T10		T56	MC		
THE PLAYERS Championship	1	T6	T3	T39	MC	T11	T34	MC	T20	T39	MC	T67	MC	MC	MC	T6	T16	T16	T28	T46	MC	MC	2	T3	MC	T20	MC	T52	MC	T52
Freeport-McMoRan Classic		4		MC	T2			T32		MC					T20			5						MC		T39			MC	T26
Masters Tournament	MC	MC	T31	MC	MC	T9	T39	MC		T21	T21	T54	T21	T11	59		T3	T11		T54	T17	T34	1	T50	2	38			T34	
Deposit Guaranty Classic																														
MCI Heritage Classic	T54	T3			2	T33	T20	MC			MC				T47		T28	T47	1	MC	T28	T16	8	T54	T39	T37	T16	T47	T54	
Kmart Gr. Greensboro Open		T3		T43	MC			T6		MC	MC	MC	T27			T27		①	②		T9	T6	T12	T50	T3	T27	T20	T12	T43	MC
Shell Houston Open			T33	MC	T3			T7		T11		6				②	T17	T7	MC					T20		T20	①	T41		MC
BellSouth Classic	T2	MC	WD	T22	T32		5			T20	T7	T22	T22			T13		T2								T61				T27
GTE Byron Nelson Classic	T11			T5	T5			MC	T11	5	MC	T11	T11	1		T43	T2		T8	MC		T20	MC	T63	T67	MC	MC			T7
Kemper Open							T7	2		T18									59							T33	MC			T7
Southwestern Bell Colonial	T45	2	74	17	DQ	T11	58	1		3	T65	T45		T6	MC	T45	T9	T6	T11	MC		T11	MC			T61	T18	T27	T22	
Memorial Tournament		1	T4	MC	T25	3	T50		MC	T4	T12	T10	MC	T57	T48	T30		2	T16	T50	WD	T22		T66	T34	T4	T4	MC	T40	
Buick Classic	MC		MC	T3	T7	T3		T10	MC	T16	T38		T55			T26	T26	T26	①			MC			T7	T63	T52			MC
U.S. Open	T11	T3	MC	MC	MC	2	1		MC	T52	T16	T52	T33	MC	T46	MC	T25	T33	T19	MC	T11	T25		MC	MC	T25	T77		T46	T33
Canon Greater Hartford Open	1	MC						T20		T11		T11	T7		4		T30									T38	T58	MC	T30	T58
Sprint Western Open	1	2	MC		MC	MC	MC		T25	MC			DQ	T13			T59	MC			T19							T7		T75
Anheuser-Busch Classic			1									T34		T39				MC				2								T46
New England Classic	1														T30			T19			MC					T19	T16	T30	MC	
Federal-Express St. Jude Cl.	1	MC		T31		T63		T6			T2	T23	MC		T65			MC	T55			5			T23	T74	T2			T16
Buick Open		3			T9		MC		T13	MC	T27	1		T15	T19	T6	T4	MC		T48					T63	T70	T19	T13	T19	MC
PGA Championship	T31	①	②	MC	MC	T44	T22	T56	T31	T31	T51	T31	MC	T6	T44	T68	T14	MC	4	MC	T31	T6	MC	MC	MC	T20	T22	T56	MC	T28
The International		T4			T29	MC					T4			9	T15		T15	2	1					T25		T34		T34		
NEC World Series of Golf	T2	31	T7	T2	T7		T14	T11	1	T11		T25	T19	DQ	T16	T25	T7		5	6		T36		T22	T2					
Greater Milwaukee Open	T31			T19	T16	MC		T31					MC		T28				T81	②			T8	T41	T41	T12	T19			①
Canadian Open	T10	MC		T10	1		T60		2	MC	MC		T22			T35			T45	DQ				MC		T22	T35	T4	T40	
Hardee's Golf Classic				1	T2						T14				T5		T48		T14					MC		T48				T55
B.C. Open									T58						T58				MC						MC	T21	T8			T10
Buick Southern Open			T26						WD			T47	T26	26			T13										MC	T13		
Walt Disney World/Olds Cl.	T60			MC	T24		T60			1	T24	T10	T35	T35	T35		T34		T5						T55	T24	WD		T3	8
H-E-B Texas Open								T14		T32			T22	T57	T37			T5				①						T18	MC	
Las Vegas Invitational		T3	MC						MC	1			T6	WD			T13	T3		T19		9	MC	MC	MC	67	T23	2	T34	
THE TOUR Championship	T18	21	T2	1	T2	26	22	T7	T12	T10	15	27	T18	T2	T2	T23	T23	T7	T16	T12	T7	28		T18	T12	T10	T16	6	29	30

276

Tom Kite won two events in 1993 and became the
first player to surpass $8 million in career earnings

ALL-TIME PGA TOUR RECORDS

All Information Based On Official PGA TOUR Co-Sponsored or Approved Events

SCORING RECORDS

72 holes:

257—(60-68-64-65) by **Mike Souchak**, at Brackenridge Park Golf Course, San Antonio, TX, in 1955 Texas Open (27-under-par).

258—(65-64-65-64) by **Donnie Hammond**, at Oak Hills CC, San Antonio, TX, in 1989 Texas Open Presented by Nabisco (22-under-par).

259—(62-68-63-66) by **Byron Nelson**, at Broadmoor Golf Club. Seattle, WA, in 1945 Seattle Open (21-under-par).

259—(70-63-63-63) by **Chandler Harper,** at Brackenridge Park Golf Course, San Antonio, TX, in 1954 Texas Open (25-under-par).

259—(63-64-66-66) by **Tim Norris**, at Wethersfield CC, Hartford, CT, in 1982 Sammy Davis Greater Hartford Open (25-under-par)

259—(64-63-66-66) by **Corey Pavin**, at Oak Hills CC, San Antonio, TX, in 1988 Texas Open Presented by Nabisco (21-under-par).

259—(68-63-64-64) by **David Frost,** at Oakwood CC, Coal Valley, IL, in 1993 Hardee's Golf Classic (21-under-par).

90 holes:

325—(67-67-64-65-62) by **Tom Kite,** at four courses, Palm Springs, CA, in the 1993 Bob Hope Chrysler Classic (35-under-par)

329—(69-65-67-62-66) by **Andrew Magee**, at three courses, Las Vegas, NV, in the 1991 Las Vegas Invitational (31-under-par).

329—(70-64-65-64-66) by **D.A. Weibring**, at three courses, Las Vegas, NV, in the 1991 Las Vegas Invitational (31-under-par).

Most shots under par:
72 holes:

27— **Mike Souchak** in winning the 1955 Texas Open with 257.

27— **Ben Hogan** in winning the 1945 Portland Invitational with 261.

26— **Gay Brewer** in winning the 1967 Pensacola Open with 262.

26— **Robert Wrenn** in winning the 1987 Buick Open with 262.

26— **Chip Beck** in winning the 1988 USF&G Classic with 262.

26— **John Huston** in winning the 1992 Walt Disney World/Oldsmobile Classic with 262.

90 holes:

35— **Tom Kite** in winning the 1993 Bob Hope Chrysler Classic with 325.

31— **Andrew Magee** in winning the 1991 Las Vegas Invitational with 329.

31— **D.A. Weibring** in finishing second in the 1991 Las Vegas Invitational with 329 (lost playoff).

54 holes:
Opening rounds:

191—(66-64-61) by **Gay Brewer,** at Pensacola CC, Pensacola, FL, in winning 1967 Pensacola Open (25-under-par).

192—(60-68-64) by **Mike Souchak**, at Brackenridge Park Golf Course. San Antonio, TX, in 1955 Texas Open (21-under-par).

192—(64-63-65) by **Bob Gilder**, at Westchester CC, Harrison, NY, in 1982 Manufacturers Hanover Westchester Classic (18-under-par).

Consecutive rounds

189—(63-63-63) by **Chandler Harper** in the last three rounds of the 1954 Texas Open at Brackenridge (24-under-par).

36 holes:
Opening rounds

126—(64-62) by **Tommy Bolt,** at Cavalier Yacht & Country Club, Virginia Beach, VA, in 1954Virginia Beach Open (12-under-par).

126—(64-62) by **Paul Azinger**, at Oak Hills CC, San Antonio, TX, in 1989 Texas Open Presented by Nabisco (14-under-par).

ALL-TIME PGA TOUR RECORDS

All Information Based On Official PGA TOUR Co-Sponsored or Approved Events

Consecutive rounds

125— (64-61) by **Gay Brewer** in the middle rounds of the 1967 Pensacola Open at Pensacola CC, Pensacola, FL (19-under-par).

125— (63-62) by **Ron Streck** in the last two rounds of the 1978 Texas Open at Oak Hills Country Club, San Antonio, TX (15-under-par).

125— (62-63) by **Blaine McCallister** in the middle two rounds of the 1988 Hardee's Golf Classic at Oakwood CC, Coal Valley, IL (15-under-par).

126— (62-64) by **Johnny Palmer** in the last two rounds of the 1948 Tucson Open at El Rio Country Club, Tucson, AZ (14-under-par).

126— (63-63) by **Sam Snead** in the last two rounds of the 1950 Texas Open at Brackenridge Park GC, San Antonio, TX (16-under-par).

126— (63-63) by **Chandler Harper** in the middle rounds and last two rounds of the 1954 Texas Open at Brackenridge Park GC, San Antonio, TX (16-under-par).

126— (60-66) by **Sam Snead** in the middle rounds of the 1957 Dallas Open at Glen Lakes Country Club, Dallas, TX (16-under-par).

126— (61-65) by **Jack Rule, Jr.,** in the middle rounds of the 1963 St. Paul Open at Keller Golf Club, St. Paul, MN (18-under-par).

126— (63-63) by **Mark Pfeil,** in the middle rounds of the 1983 Texas Open at Oak Hills CC, San Antonio, TX (14-under-par).

18 holes:

59— by **Al Geiberger,** at Colonial Country Club, Memphis, TN, in second round of 1977 Memphis Classic (13-under-par).

59— by **Chip Beck,** at Sunrise Golf Club, Las Vegas, NV, in third round of 1991 Las Vegas Invitational (13-under-par).

60— by **Al Brosch,** at Brackenridge Park Golf Course, San Antonio, TX, in third round of 1951 Texas Open (11-under-par).

60— by **Bill Nary,** at El Paso Country Club, El Paso, TX, in third round of 1952 El Paso Open (11-under-par).

60— by **Ted Kroll,** at Brackenridge Park Golf Course, San Antonio, TX, in third round of 1954 Texas Open (11-under-par).

60— by **Wally Ulrich,** at Cavalier Yacht and Country Club, Virginia Beach, VA, in second round of 1954 Virginia Beach Open (9-under-par).

60— by **Tommy Bolt,** at Wethersfield Country Club, Hartford, CT, in second round of 1954 Insurance City Open (11-under-par).

60— by **Mike Souchak** at Brackenridge Park Golf Course, San Antonio, TX, in first round of 1955 Texas Open (11-under-par).

60— by **Sam Snead,** at Glen Lakes Country Club, Dallas, TX, in second round of 1957 Dallas Open (11-under-par).

60— by **David Frost,** at Randolph Park Golf Course, Tucson, AZ, in second round of 1990 Northern Telecom Tucson Open (12-under-par).

9 holes:

27— by **Mike Souchak,** at Brackenridge Park Golf Course, San Antonio, TX, on par-35 second nine of first round in 1955 Texas Open.

27— by **Andy North** at En-Joie Golf Club, Endicott, NY, on par-34 second nine of first round in 1975 B.C. Open.

Best Vardon Trophy scoring average:

Non-adjusted:

69.23—**Sam Snead** in 1950 (6646 strokes, 96 rounds).

69.30—**Ben Hogan** in 1948 (5267 strokes, 76 rounds).

69.37—**Sam Snead** in 1949 (5064 strokes, 73 rounds).

Adjusted (since 1988):

69.10—**Greg Norman** in 1990.

69.11—**Nick Price** in 1993.

Most consecutive rounds under 70:

ALL-TIME PGA TOUR RECORDS

All Information Based On Official PGA TOUR Co-Sponsored or Approved Events

19— **Byron Nelson** in 1945.

Most birdies in a row:

8— **Bob Goalby** at Pasadena Golf Club, St. Petersburg FL, during fourth round of 1961 St. Petersburg Open.

Fuzzy Zoeller, at Oakwood Country Club, Coal Valley, IL, during first round of 1976 Quad Cities Open.

Dewey Arnette, Warwick Hills GC, Grand Blanc, MI, during first round of the 1987 Buick Open.

Best birdie-eagle streak:

7— **Al Geiberger**, 6 birdies and 1 eagle, at Colonial Country Club, Memphis, TN, during second round of 1977 Danny Thomas Memphis Classic.

Webb Heintzelman, 5 birdies, eagle and 1 birdie, in 1989 Las Vegas Invitational.

Most birdies in a row to win:

5— by **Jack Nicklaus** to win 1978 Jackie Gleason Inverrary Classic (last 5 holes).

VICTORY RECORDS

Most victories during career (PGA TOUR co-sponsored and/or approved tournaments only):

81— **Sam Snead**
70— **Jack Nicklaus**
63— **Ben Hogan**
60— **Arnold Palmer**
52— **Byron Nelson**
51— **Billy Casper**

Most consecutive years winning at least one tournament:

17— **Jack Nicklaus** (1962-78)
17— **Arnold Palmer** (1955-71)
16— **Billy Casper** (1956-71)

Most consecutive victories:

11— **Byron Nelson**, from Miami Four Ball March 8-11, 1945, through Canadian Open, August 2-4, 1945. Tournament, site, dates, score, purse-Miami Four Ball, Miami Springs Course, Miami, FL, March 8-11, won 8-6, $1,500; Charlotte Open, Myers Park Golf Club, Charlotte, NC, March 16-19, 272, $2000; Greensboro Open, Starmount Country Club, Greensboro, NC, March 23-25, 271, $1000; Durham Open, Hope Valley Country Club, Durham, NC, March 30-April 1, 276, $1000; Atlanta Open, Capital City Course, Atlanta, GA, April 5-8, 263, $2000; Montreal Open, Islemere Golf and Country Club, Montreal, Que., June 7-10, 268, $2000; Philadelphia Inquirer Invitational, Llanerch Country Club, Phila., PA, June 14-17, 269, $3000; Chicago Victory National Open, Calumet Country Club, Chicago, IL, June 29-July 1, 275, $2000; PGA Championship, Moraine Country Club, Dayton, OH, July 9-15,4-3, $3750; Tam O'Shanter Open, Tam O'Shanter Country Club, Chicago, IL, July 26-29 269, $10,000; Canadian Open,Thornhill Country Club, Toronto, Ont., August 2-4, 280, $2000; Winnings for streak $30,250. NOTE: Nelson won a 12th event in Spring Lake, NJ which is not accounted as official as its $2,500 purse was below the PGA $3000 minimum.

4— **Jackie Burke, Jr.**, in 1952: From February 14 to March 9-Texas Open, Houston Open, Baton Rouge Open, St. Petersburg Open.

3— **Byron Nelson** in 1944, 1945-46.

Sam Snead in 1945.

Ben Hogan in 1946.

Bobby Locke in 1947.

ALL-TIME PGA TOUR RECORDS

All Information Based On Official PGA TOUR Co-Sponsored or Approved Events

Most consecutive victories cont.:

3— **Jim Ferrier** in 1951.
Billy Casper in 1960.
Arnold Palmer in 1960, 1962.
Johnny Miller in 1974.
Hubert Green in 1976.
Gary Player in 1978.
Tom Watson in 1980.
Nick Price in 1993.

Most victories in a single event:

8— **Sam Snead**, Greater Greensboro Open: 1938, 1946, 1949, 1950, 1955, 1956, 1960, and 1965

6— **Sam Snead**, Miami Open: 1937, 1939, 1946, 1950, 1951, and 1955.

6— **Jack Nicklaus**, Masters: 1963, 1965, 1966, 1972, 1975 and 1986.

5— **Walter Hagen**, PGA Championship:1921, 1924 1925, 1926, and 1927.
Ben Hogan Colonial NIT: 1946 1947, 1952, 1953, and 1959.
Arnold Palmer, Bob Hope Desert Classic: 1960, 1962, 1968, 1971, and 1973.
Jack Nicklaus Tournament of Champions: 1963, 1964, 1971, 1973, and 1977.
Jack Nicklaus, PGA Championship: 1963, 1971, 1973, 1975, and 1980.
Walter Hagen, Western Open: 1916, 1921, 1926, 1927, 1932.

Most consecutive victories in a single event:

4— **Walter Hagen**, PGA Championship, 1924-1927.

3— **Willie Anderson**, U.S. Open, 1903-1905.

3— **Ralph Guldahl**, Western Open, 1936-1938.

3— **Gene Littler**, Tournament of Champions, 1955-1957.

3— **Billy Casper**, Portland Open, 1959-1961.

3— **Arnold Palmer**, Texas Open, 1960-1962, Phoenix Open, 1961-1963.

3— **Jack Nicklaus**, Disney World Golf Classic, 1971-1973.

3— **Johnny Miller**, Tucson Open, 1974-1976.

3— **Tom Watson**, Byron Nelson Classic, 1978-1980.

Most victories in a calendar year:

18— **Byron Nelson** (1945)

13— **Ben Hogan** (1946)

11— **Sam Snead** (1950)

10— **Ben Hogan** (1948)

Most victories in a calendar year cont.:

8— **Byron Nelson** (1944)

8— **Lloyd Mangrum** (1948)

8— **Arnold Palmer** (1960)

8— **Johnny Miller** (1974)

8— **Sam Snead** (1938)

7— 11 times

Most first-time winners during one calendar year:

14— 1991

12— 1979, 1980, 1986

11— 1977, 1985, 1988

10— 1968, 1969, 1971, 1974, 1983, 1987, 1990

Most years between victories:

13— **Howard Twitty** (1980-1993)

12— **Leonard Thompson** (1977-1989)

11— **Bob Murphy** (1975-1986)

ALL-TIME PGA TOUR RECORDS

All Information Based On Official PGA TOUR Co-Sponsored or Approved Events

Most years from first victory to last:
- 29— by **Ray Floyd** (1963-1992)
- 29— by **Sam Snead** (1936-1965)
- 24— by **Jack Nicklaus** (1962-1986)
- 23— by **Gene Littler** (1954-1977)
- 22— by **Art Wall** (1953-1975)

Youngest winners:
- **Johnny McDermott,** 19 years and 10 months, 1911 U.S. Open.
- **Gene Sarazen**, 20 years and 4 months, 1922, U.S. Open.
- **Horton Smith**, 20 years and 5 months, 1928 Oklahoma City Open.
- **Ray Floyd**, 20 years and 6 months, 1963 St. Petersburg Open.
- **Phil Mickelson**, 20 years and 6 months, 1991 Northern Telecom Open.
- **Seve Ballesteros**, 20 years and 11 months, 1978 Greater Greensboro Open.

Oldest winners:
- **Sam Snead**, 52 years and 10 months, 1965 Greater Greensboro Open.
- **Art Wall**, 51 years and 10 months, 1975 Greater Milwaukee Open.
- **John Barnum**, 51 years and 1 month, 1962 Cajun Classic.
- **Jim Barnes**, 50 years, 1937 Long Island Open.
- **Ray Floyd**, 49 years and 6 months, 1992 Doral-Ryder Open.

Widest winning margin: Strokes
- 16— **Bobby Locke**, 1948 Chicago Victory National Championship.
- 14— **Ben Hogan**, 1945 Portland Invitational.
  - **Johnny Miller**, 1975 Phoenix Open.
- 13— **Byron Nelson,** 1945 Seattle Open.
  - **Gene Littler**, 1955 Tournament of Champions
- 12— **Arnold Palmer**, 1962 Phoenix Open.
  - **Jose Maria Olazabal**, 1990 NEC World Series of Golf.

PLAYOFF RECORDS

Longest sudden death playoffs: Holes:
- 11— **Cary Middlecoff** and **Lloyd Mangrum** were declared co-winners by mutual agreement in the 1949 Motor City Open.
- 8— **Dick Hart** defeated **Phil Rodgers** in the 1965 Azalea Open.
- 8— **Lee Elder** defeated **Lee Trevino** in the 1978 Greater Milwaukee Open.
- 8— **Dave Barr** defeated **Woody Blackburn, Dan Halldorson, Frank Conner, Victor Regalado** in the 1981Quad Cities Open.
- 8— **Bob Gilder** defeated **Rex Caldwell, Johnny Miller, Mark O'Meara** in the 1983 Phoenix Open.

Most players in a sudden-death playoff:
- 5— 1948 Tacoma Open—**Ed Oliver** defeated **Cary Middlecoff, Fred Haas, Charles Congdon** and **Vic Ghezzi.**
- 5— 1953 Houston Open—**Cary Middlecoff** defeated **Shelly Mayfield, Jim Ferrier, Earl Stewart** and **Bill Nary** (18-hole playoff).
- 5— 1981 Bing Crosby—**John Cook** defeated **Hale Irwin, Bobby Clampett, Ben Crenshaw** and **Barney Thompson.**
- 5— 1981 Quad Cities Open— **Dave Barr** defeated **Frank Conner, Woody Blackburn, Dan Halldorson** and **Victor Regalado.**
- 5— 1983 Kemper Open—**Fred Couples** defeated **T.C. Chen, Barry Jaeckel, Gil Morgan** and **Scott Simpson.**
- 5— Teams at 1985 Chrysler Team Championship.
- 5— 1992 Bob Hope Chrysler Classic—**John Cook** defeated **Mark O'Meara, Tom Kite, Rick Fehr** and **Gene Sauers.**
- 5— 1993 Buick Southern Open—**John Inman** defeated **Billy Andrade, Brad Bryant, Mark Brooks** and **Bob Estes.**

ALL-TIME PGA TOUR RECORDS

All Information Based On Official PGA TOUR Co-Sponsored or Approved Events

Most Playoffs, season:
- **16—** 1988, 1991
- **15—** 1972

PUTTING RECORDS

Fewest putts, one round:
- **18— Sam Trahan**, at Whitemarsh Valley Country Club, in final round of 1979 IVB Philadelphia Golf Classic.
- **18— Mike McGee**, at Colonial CC, in first round of 1987 Federal Express St. Jude Classic.
- **18— Kenny Knox**, at Harbour Town GL, in first round of 1989 MCI Heritage Classic.
- **18— Andy North**, at Kingsmill GC, in second round of 1990 Anheuser Busch Golf Classic.
- **18— Jim McGovern,** at TPC at Southwind, in second round of 1992 Federal Express St. Jude Classic.

Fewest putts, four rounds:
- **93— Kenny Knox** in 1989 MCI Heritage Classic at Harbour Town Golf Links.
- **94— George Archer** in 1980 Sea Pines Heritage Classic at Harbour Town Golf Links.
- **99— Bob Menne** in 1977 Tournament Players Championship at Sawgrass.
- **99— Steve Melnyk** in 1980 Sea Pines Heritage Classic at Harbour Town Golf Links.
- **99— Greg Norman** in 1990 USF&G Classic at English Turn G&CC.

Fewest putts, nine holes:
- **8— Jim Colbert**, at the Deerwood Club, on front nine of last round in 1967 Greater Jacksonville Open.
- **8— Sam Trahan**, at Whitemarsh Valley Country Club, on the back nine of the last round in the1979 IVB Philadelphia Golf Classic.
- **8— Bill Calfee**, at Forest Oaks CC, on the back nine of the third round of the 1980 Greater Greensboro Open.
- **8— Kenny Knox**, at Harbour Town GL, on the back nine of the first round of the 1989 MCI Heritage Classic.

MISCELLANEOUS RECORDS

Most consecutive events without missing cut:
- **113— Byron Nelson**, during the 1940s.
- **105— Jack Nicklaus**, from Sahara Open, November 1970, through World Series of Golf, September 1976 (missed cut in 1976 World Open).
- **86— Hale Irwin**, from Tucson Open, February 1975, through conclusion of 1978 season.
- **72— Dow Finsterwald**, from Carling Golf Classic, September 1955, through Houston Invitational, February, 1958.

Youngest pro shooting age:
- **66—** (4 under), **Sam Snead** (age 67), 1979 Quad Cities Open.

MONEY WINNING RECORDS

Most money won in a single season:
- $1,478,557 by **Nick Price** in 1993
- $1,458,456 by **Paul Azinger** in 1993
- $1,395,278 by **Tom Kite** in 1989.

Most money won by a rookie:
- $657,831 by **Vijay Singh** in 1993.
- $574,783 by **John Daly** in 1991.
- $461,407 by **Robert Gamez** in 1990.

ALL-TIME PGA TOUR RECORDS

All Information Based On Official PGA TOUR Co-Sponsored or Approved Events

Most money won by a second-year player:
$693,658 by **Billy Mayfair** in 1990.
$652,780 by **Bob Tway** in 1986.
$426,668 by **Hal Sutton** in 1985.

Most money won in first two seasons:
$962,238 by **John Daly** (1991-1992)
$818,804 by **Bob Tway** (1985-1986)
$805,650 by **Billy Mayfair** (1989-1990)

Most consecutive years $100,000 or more:
20— **Tom Watson** (1974-present)
18— **Tom Kite** (1976-present)
17— **Bruce Lietzke** (1977-present)

Most consecutive years $200,000 or more:
13— **Tom Kite** (1981-present)
12— **Curtis Strange** (1980-1991)
12— **Tom Watson** (1977-1988)
10— **Payne Stewart** (1984-present)
10— **Mark O'Meara** (1984-present)

Most consecutive years $300,000 or more:
8— **Payne Stewart** (1986-present)
8— **Tom Kite** (1986-present)
7— **Paul Azinger** (1987-present)
7— **Mark Calcavecchia** (1987-present)
7— **Fred Couples** (1987-present)

Most consecutive years $400,000 or more:
7— **Paul Azinger** (1987-present)
7— **Chip Beck** (1987-present)
6— **Payne Stewart** (1986-1991)

Most consecutive years $500,000 or more:
7— **Paul Azinger** (1987-present)
7— **Chip Beck** (1987-present)
5— **Fred Couples** (1989-present)
5— **Payne Stewart** (1986-1990)
5— **Greg Norman** (1986-1990)

Most consecutive years $600,000 or more:
5— **Paul Azinger** (1989-present)
5— **Fred Couples** (1989-present)

$1 million in two seasons:
Nick Price (1992, 1993)
Greg Norman (1990, 1993)

Most consecutive years Top 10 Money List:
17— **Jack Nicklaus** (1962-1978)
15— **Arnold Palmer** (1957-1971)

Most years Top 10 Money List:
18— **Jack Nicklaus**
15— **Arnold Palmer, Sam Snead**

ALL-TIME PGA TOUR RECORDS

All Information Based On Official PGA TOUR Co-Sponsored or Approved Events

Most years leading Money List:
 8— **Jack Nicklaus**
Most consecutive years leading Money List:
 4— **Tom Watson** (1977-1980)
Most money won in a single season without a victory:
 $982,875 by **Payne Stewart** in 1993.

$1 MILLION IN A SINGLE SEASON

1.	Nick Price	$1,478,557	1993
2.	Paul Azinger	1,458,456	1993
3.	Tom Kite	1,395,278	1989
4.	Greg Norman	1,359,653	1993
5.	Fred Couples	1,344,188	1992
6.	Payne Stewart	1,201,301	1989
7.	Davis Love III	1,191,630	1992
8.	John Cook	1,165,606	1992
9.	Greg Norman	1,165,477	1990
10.	Curtis Strange	1,147,644	1988
11.	Nick Price	1,135,773	1992
12	Jim Gallagher, Jr.	1,078,870	1993
13.	David Frost	1,030,717	1993
14.	Wayne Levi	1,024,647	1990

FIRST-YEAR PLAYERS TO EARN $200,000 OR MORE

1.	Vijay Singh	$657,831	1993
2.	John Daly	574,783	1991
3.	Robert Gamez	461,407	1990
4.	Brett Ogle	337,374	1993
5.	Keith Clearwater	320,007	1987
6.	Corey Pavin	260,536	1984
7.	Jeff Maggert	240,940	1991
8.	Hal Sutton	237,434	1982
9.	Mark Carnevale	220,922	1992
10.	Peter Persons	218,505	1990
11.	Scott Gump	207,809	1991

BIGGEST ONE SEASON GAINS

	Season	Money	Season	Money	Gain
1. Curtis Strange	1986	$237,700	1987	$925,941	+$688,241
2. Hale Irwin	1989	$150,977	1990	$838,249	+$687,272
3. Greg Norman	1992	$676,443	1993	$1,359,653	+$683,210
4. Payne Stewart	1988	$553,571	1989	$1,201,301	+$646,720
5. Fulton Allem	1992	$209,982	1993	$851,345	+$641,363

ALL-TIME PGA TOUR RECORDS

All Information Based On Official PGA TOUR Co-Sponsored or Approved Events

NUMBER OF $100,000 WINNERS IN A SINGLE YEAR

1963—2	1970—16	1976—24	1982—36	1988—112
1964—2	1971—12	1977—25	1983—57	1989—124
1965—2	1972—16	1978—24	1984—69	1990—136
1966—3	1973—14	1979—35	1985—78	1991—136
1967—7	1974—20	1980—44	1986—83	1992—130
1968—14	**1975—14**	1981—38	1987—96	1993—145
1969—11				

$200,000

1968—1	1975—4	1980—9	1985—26	1990—78
1971—3	1976—4	1981—9	1986—41	1991—84
1972—2	1977—5	1982—15	1987—55	1992—76
1973—5	1978—6	1983—21	1988—56	1993—87
1974—4	1979—7	1984—28	1989—71	

$300,000

1972—1	1978—1	1982—7	1986—19	1990—47
1973—1	1979—1	1983—5	1987—32	1991—53
1974—1	1980—2	1984—9	1988—32	1992—49
1977—1	1981—5	1985—10	1989—39	1993—56

$400,000

1979—1	1982—1	1985—2	1988—25	1991—37
1980—1	1983—2	1986—6	1989—29	1992—34
1981—0	1984—4	1987—19	1990—30	1993—37

$500,000

1980—1	1983—0	1986—3	1989—15	1992—27
1981—0	1984—0	1987—14	1990—22	1993—31
1982—0	1985—1	1988—19	1991—29	

$600,000

1986—2	1988—10	1990—16	1992—22	1993—26
1987—5	1989—13	1991—14		

$700,000

1987—2	1989—8	1991—7	1992—16	1993—14
1988—7	1990—11			

$800,000

1987—2	1989—5	1991—1	1992—8	1993—9
1988—3	1990—8			

$900,000

1987—1	1989—3	1991—1	1992—7	1993—7
1988—2	1990—5			

ALL-TIME PGA TOUR RECORDS

All Information Based On Official PGA TOUR Co-Sponsored or Approved Events

$1,000,000

1988—1 1989—2	1990—2	1991—0	1992—4	1993—5

$1,100,000

1988—1 1989—2	1990—1	1991—0	1992—4	1993—3

$1,200,000

1989—2	1990—0	1991—0	1992—1	1993—3

$1,300,000

1989—1	1990—0	1991—0	1992—1	1993—3

$1,400,000

1993—2

GROWTH OF TOUR PURSES

YEAR	NO. OF EVENTS	TOTAL PURSE	YEAR	NO. OF EVENTS	TOTAL PURSE
1938	38	$158,000	1966	36	3,704,445
1939	28	121,000	1967	37	3,979,162
1940	27	117,000	1968	45	5,077,600
1941	30	169,200	1969	47	5,465,875
1942	21	116,650	1970	55	6,751,523
1943	3	17,000	1971	63	7,116,000
1944	22	150,500	1972	71	7,596,749
1945	36	435,380	1973	75	8,657,225
1946	37	411,533	1974	57	8,165,941
1947	31	352,500	1975	51	7,895,450
1948	34	427,000	1976	49	9,157,522
1949	25	338,200	1977	48	9,688,977
1950	33	459,950	1978	48	10,337,332
1951	30	460,200	1979	46	12,801,200
1952	32	498,016	1980	45	13,371,786
1953	32	562,704	1981	45	14,175,393
1954	26	600,819	1982	46	15,089,576
1955	36	782,010	1983	45	17,588,242
1956	36	847,070	1984	46	21,251,382
1957	32	820,360	1985	47	25,290,526
1958	39	1,005,800	1986	46	25,442,242
1959	43	1,225,205	1987	46	32,106,093
1960	41	1,335,242	1988	47	36,959,307
1961	45	1,461,830	1989	44	41,288,787
1962	49	1,790,320	1990	44	46,251,831
1963	43	2,044,900	1991	44	49,628,203
1964	41	2,301,063	1992	44	49,386,906
1965	36	2,848,515	1993	43	53,203,611

LEADERS IN CAREER MONEY EARNINGS

1.	TOM KITE	$8,500,729
2.	PAUL AZINGER	6,761,306
3.	GREG NORMAN	6,607,562
4.	PAYNE STEWART	6,377,573
5.	TOM WATSON	6,370,949
6.	FRED COUPLES	6,263,494
7.	CURTIS STRANGE	6,042,561
8.	LANNY WADKINS	5,877,256
9.	BEN CRENSHAW	5,448,507
10.	JACK NICKLAUS	5,360,662
11.	CHIP BECK	5,304,632
12.	NICK PRICE	5,226,491
13.	CRAIG STADLER	5,131,605
14.	RAY FLOYD	5,033,996
15.	MARK O'MEARA	4,998,267
16.	COREY PAVIN	4,929,138
17.	BRUCE LIETZKE	4,875,942
18.	HALE IRWIN	4,839,626
19.	MARK CALCAVECCHIA	4,489,962
20.	DAVID FROST	4,428,831
21.	GIL MORGAN	4,426,178
22.	DAVIS LOVE III	4,037,672
23.	JAY HAAS	4,011,175
24.	WAYNE LEVI	3,990,815
25.	LARRY MIZE	3,908,681
26.	SCOTT HOCH	3,868,695
27.	JOHN COOK	3,845,252
28.	FUZZY ZOELLER	3,731,261
29.	SCOTT SIMPSON	3,665,272
30.	JOHN MAHAFFEY	3,606,019
31.	LEE TREVINO	3,478,449
32.	HAL SUTTON	3,391,692
33.	STEVE PATE	3,280,181
34.	PETER JACOBSEN	3,260,745
35.	JOEY SINDELAR	3,247,940
36.	ANDY BEAN	3,234,265
37.	TIM SIMPSON	3,221,926
38.	MARK MCCUMBER	3,215,569
39.	LARRY NELSON	3,206,418
40.	JIM GALLAGHER, JR.	3,200,722
41.	KEN GREEN	3,019,069
42.	JEFF SLUMAN	2,995,571
43.	STEVE ELKINGTON	2,976,192
44.	DAVID EDWARDS	2,961,573
45.	TOM PURTZER	2,942,809
46.	BOB TWAY	2,914,016
47.	MIKE REID	2,874,570
48.	D.A. WEIBRING	2,839,550
49.	JODIE MUDD	2,735,887
50.	DAN POHL	2,721,117
51.	DAN FORSMAN	$2,684,806
52.	HUBERT GREEN	2,575,609
53.	JOHNNY MILLER	2,521,424
54.	DON POOLEY	2,507,341
55.	BRAD FAXON	2,452,804
56.	GENE SAUERS	2,440,343
57.	MARK BROOKS	2,410,031
58.	HOWARD TWITTY	2,393,070
59.	JOHN HUSTON	2,381,943
60.	MIKE HULBERT	2,345,965
61.	BOB GILDER	2,342,243
62.	CALVIN PEETE	2,302,363
63.	RUSS COCHRAN	2,283,493
64.	TOM WEISKOPF	2,241,687
65.	J.C. SNEAD	2,219,171
66.	ROCCO MEDIATE	2,215,680
67.	DOUG TEWELL	2,201,210
68.	ANDREW MAGEE	2,144,914
69.	DONNIE HAMMOND	2,131,142
70.	BILL GLASSON	2,129,022
71.	MARK WIEBE	2,120,874
72.	LOREN ROBERTS	2,115,727
73.	LEE JANZEN	2,088,842
74.	BLAINE MCCALLISTER	2,088,043
75.	BOBBY WADKINS	2,073,328
76.	ROGER MALTBIE	2,034,729
77.	IAN BAKER-FINCH	1,916,751
78.	ARNOLD PALMER	1,904,667
79.	RICK FEHR	1,898,467
80.	STEVE JONES	1,885,939
81.	DAVID GRAHAM	1,874,780
82.	DAVE BARR	1,837,220
83.	KEITH CLEARWATER	1,818,238
84.	GARY PLAYER	1,814,950
85.	MIKE DONALD	1,813,939
86.	FULTON ALLEM	1,810,872
87.	GARY HALLBERG	1,804,014
88.	GEORGE BURNS	1,763,208
89.	LEONARD THOMPSON	1,749,691
90.	BOB LOHR	1,747,794
91.	MARK LYE	1,737,260
92.	ED FIORI	1,723,564
93.	NOLAN HENKE	1,699,629
94.	BILLY MAYFAIR	1,696,274
95.	BILLY ANDRADE	1,692,587
96.	BILLY CASPER	1,691,583
97.	WAYNE GRADY	1,687,520
98.	JIM THORPE	1,675,116
99.	BILL BRITTON	1,668,609
100.	BOB MURPHY	1,642,861

PAST LEADING MONEY-WINNERS

1934	Paul Runyan	$6,767.00		1964	Jack Nicklaus	$113,284.50
1935	Johnny Revolta	9,543.00		1965	Jack Nicklaus	140,752.14
1936	Horton Smith	7,682.00		1966	Billy Casper	121,944.92
1937	Harry Cooper	14,138.69		1967	Jack Nicklaus	188,998.08
1938	Sam Snead	19,534.49		1968	Billy Casper	205,168.67
1939	Henry Picard	10,303.00		1969	Frank Beard	164,707.11
1940	Ben Hogan	10,655.00		1970	Lee Trevino	157,037.63
1941	Ben Hogan	18,358.00		1971	Jack Nicklaus	244,490.50
1942	Ben Hogan	13,143.00		1972	Jack Nicklaus	320,542.26
1943	No Statistics Compiled			1973	Jack Nicklaus	308,362.10
1944	Byron Nelson (War Bonds)	37,967.69		1974	Johnny Miller	353,021.59
1945	Byron Nelson (War Bonds)	63,335.66		1975	Jack Nicklaus	298,149.17
1946	Ben Hogan	42,556.16		1976	Jack Nicklaus	266,438.57
1947	Jimmy Demaret	27,936.83		1977	Tom Watson	310,653.16
1948	Ben Hogan	32,112.00		1978	Tom Watson	362,428.93
1949	Sam Snead	31,593.83		1979	Tom Watson	462,636.00
1950	Sam Snead	35,758.83		1980	Tom Watson	530,808.33
1951	Lloyd Mangrum	26,088.83		1981	Tom Kite	375,698.84
1952	Julius Boros	37,03297		1982	Craig Stadler	446,462.00
1953	Lew Worsham	34,002.00		1983	Hal Sutton	426,668.00
1954	Bob Toski	65,819.81		1984	Tom Watson	476,260.00
1955	Julius Boros	63,121.55		1985	Curtis Strange	542,321.00
1956	Ted Kroll	72,835.83		1986	Greg Norman	653,296.00
1957	Dick Mayer	65,835.00		1987	Curtis Strange	925,941.00
1958	Arnold Palmer	42,607.50		1988	Curtis Strange	1,147,644.00
1959	Art Wall	53,167.60		1989	Tom Kite	1,395,278.00
1960	Arnold Palmer	75,262.85		1990	Greg Norman	1,165,477.00
1961	Gary Player	64,540.45		1991	Corey Pavin	979,430.00
1962	Arnold Palmer	81,448.33		1992	Fred Couples	1,344,188.00
1963	Arnold Palmer	128,230.00		1993	Nick Price	1,478,557.00

*TOTAL MONEY LISTED BEGINNING IN 1968 THROUGH 1974.   ** OFFICIAL MONEY LISTED BEGINNING IN 1975.

ALL-TIME TOUR WINNERS

1.	Sam Snead	81		Craig Wood	21
2.	Jack Nicklaus	70		Lanny Wadkins	21
3.	Ben Hogan	63	T30.	James Barnes	20
4.	Arnold Palmer	60		Doug Sanders	20
5.	Byron Nelson	52	T32.	Doug Ford	19
6.	Billy Casper	51		Hubert Green	19
T7.	Walter Hagen	40		Hale Irwin	19
	Cary Middlecoff	40		Tom Kite	19
9.	Gene Sarazen	38	T36.	Julius Boros	18
10.	Lloyd Mangrum	36		Jim Ferrier	18
T11.	Horton Smith	32		Johnny Revolta	18
	Tom Watson	32	T39.	Jack Burke	17
T13.	Harry Cooper	31		Ben Crenshaw	17
	Jimmy Demaret	31		Bobby Cruickshank	17
15.	Leo Diegel	30		Harold McSpaden	17
T16.	Gene Littler	29		Curtis Strange	17
	Paul Runyan	29	44.	Ralph Guldahl	16
18.	Lee Trevino	27	T45.	Tommy Bolt	15
19.	Henry Picard	26		Ed Dudley	15
T20.	Tommy Armour	24		Denny Shute	15
	Macdonald Smith	24		Mike Souchak	15
22.	Johnny Miller	23		Tom Weiskopf	15˙
T23.	Johnny Farrell	22	T50.	Bruce Crampton	14
	Ray Floyd	22		Dave Hill	14
T25.	Willie Macfarlane	21		Joe Turnesa	14
	Bill Mehlhorn	21		Ken Venturi	14
	Gary Player	21		Art Wall	14

MOST TOUR WINS YEAR BY YEAR

Year	Player	Wins	Year	Player	Wins
1916	James Barnes	3	1961	Arnold Palmer	5
	Walter Hagen	3		Doug Sanders	5
1917	James Barnes	2	1962	Arnold Palmer	7
	Mike Brady	2	1963	Arnold Palmer	7
1918	Jock Hutchison	1	1964	Jack Nicklaus	4
	Walter Hagen	..1		Billy Casper	4
	Patrick Doyle	1		Tony Lema	...4
1919	James Barnes	5	1965	Jack Nicklaus	5
1920	Jock Hutchison	4	1966	Billy Casper	4
1921	James Barnes	4	1967	Jack Nicklaus	5
1922	Gene Sarazen	3	1968	Billy Casper	6
	Walter Hagen	3	1969	Dave Hill	3
1923	Walter Hagen	5		Billy Casper	3
	Joe Kirkwood, Sr	5		Jack Nicklaus	3
1924	Joe Kirkwood, Sr	4		Ray Floyd	3
	Walter Hagen	4	1970	Billy Casper	4
1925	Leo Diegel	5	1971	Jack Nicklaus	5
1926	Bill Mehlhorn	5		Lee Trevino	5
	Macdonald Smith	5	1972	Jack Nicklaus	7
1927	Johnny Farrell	7	1973	Jack Nicklaus	7
1928	Bil Mehlhorn	7	1974	Johnny Miller	8
1929	Horton Smith	8	1975	Jack Nicklaus	5
1930	Gene Sarazen .	8	1976	Ben Crenshaw	3
1931	Wiffy Cox .	4		Hubert Green	3
1932	Craig Wood	...3	1977	Tom Watson	4
	Gene Sarazen	3	1978	Tom Watson	5
	Olin Dutra	3	1979	Tom Watson	5
	Mike Turnesa	...3	1980	Tom Watson	6
	Tommy Armour	3	1981	Tom Watson	3
1933	Paul Runyan	9		Bruce Lietzke	3
1934	Paul Runyan	...7		Ray Floyd	3
1935	Johnny Revolta	5		Bill Rogers.	3
	Henry Picard	5	1982	Craig Stadler	4
1936	Ralph Guldahl	3		Calvin Peete	4
	Henry Picard.	3	1983	Fuzzy Zoeller	2
	Jimmy Hines	...3		Lanny Wadkins	2
1937	Harry Cooper	8		Calvin Peete	2
1938	Sam Snead	8		Hal Sutton	2
1939	Henry Picard	8		Gil Morgan	2
1940	Jimmy Demaret	6		Mark McCumber	2
1941	Sam Snead	7		Jim Colbert	2
1942	Ben Hogan	6		Seve Ballesteros	2
1943	Sam Byrd	1	1984	Tom Watson	3
	Harold McSpaden	1		Denis Watson	.3
	Steve Warga	1	1985	Lanny Wadkins	3
1944	Byron Nelson	8		Curtis Strange	3
1945	Byron Nelson	18	1986	Bob Tway	4
1946	Ben Hogan .	... 13	1987	Curtis Strange	.3
1947	Ben Hogan .	..7		Paul Azinger	3
1948	Ben Hogan	10	1988	Curtis Strange	4
1949	Cary Middlecoff	7	1989	Tom Kite	. 3
1950	Sam Snead	11		Steve Jones	. 3
1951	Cary Middlecoff	...6	1990	Wayne Levi	4
1952	Jack Burke, Jr	 5	1991	Ian Woosnam	2
	Sam Snead	5		Corey Pavin	2
1953	Ben Hogan	4		Billy Andrade	2
	Lloyd Mangrum	...4		Tom Purtzer	2
1954	Bob Toski	4		Mark Brooks	2
1955	Cary Middlecoff	6		Nick Price	2
1956	Mike Souchak	4		Fred Couples	2
1957	Arnold Palmer	4		Andrew Magee	2
1958	Ken Venturi	4	1992	Fred Couples	3
1959	Gene Littler	5		Davis Love III	3
1960	Arnold Palmer	8		John Cook	3
			1993	Nick Price	4

INDIVIDUAL PLAYOFF RECORDS

AARON,Tommy—0-4: 1963: Lost toTony Lema, Memphis Open Invit; Lost to Arnold Palmer, Cleveland Open. 1972: Lost to George Archer, L.A. Open; Lost to George Archer, Greater Greensboro Open.

ADAMS, John—0-1: 1982: Lost to Jay Haas, Hall of Fame Tournament.

ALLIN, Bud—1-0: 1971: Defeated Rod Funseth, Dave Eichelberger, Greater Greensboro Open.

ANDRADE, Billy—1-1: 1991: Defeated Jeff Sluman, Kemper Open. 1993: Lost to John Inman, Buick Southern Open.

ARCHER, George—4-3: 1965: Defeated Bob Charles, Lucky Internat'l Open. 1969: Lost to Jack Nicklaus, Kaiser Internat'l Open. 1970: Lost to George Knudson, Robinson Open. 1971: Defeated J.C. Snead, Lou Graham, Hartford Open. 1972: Defeated Tommy Aaron, Dave Hill, L.A. Open; Lost to Miller Barber, Tucson Open; Defeated Tommy Aaron, Greater Greensboro Open.

AZINGER, Paul—1-2: 1989: Lost to Steve Jones, Bob Hope Chrysler Classic. 1990: Lost to Greg Norman, Doral Ryder Open. 1993: Defeated Greg Norman, PGA Championship.

BAIRD, Butch—1-0: 1976: Defeated Miller Barber, San Antonio Texas Open.

BAKER-FINCH, Ian—0-1: 1991: Lost to Bruce Fleisher, New England Classic.

BALLESTEROS, Seve—1-2: 1987: Lost to Larry Mize, The Masters; Lost to J. C. Snead, Manufacturers Hanover Westchester Classic. 1988: Defeated David Frost, Ken Green, Greg Norman, Manufacturers Hanover Westchester Classic.

BARBER, Miller—3-4: 1964: Lost to Gary Player, Pensacola Open Invit. 1967: Defeated Gary Player, Oklahoma City Open. 1970: Defeated Bob Charles, Howie Johnson, New Orleans. 1972: Defeated George Archer, Tucson Open. 1973: Lost to Jack Nicklaus, New Orleans; Lost to Bert Greene, Liggett & Myers Open. 1976: Lost to Butch Baird, San Antonio Texas Open.

BARR, Dave—1-2: 1981: Defeated Frank Conner, Woody Blackburn, Dan Halldorson, Victor Regalado Quad Cities Open. 1986: Lost to Corey Pavin, Greater Milwaukee Open. 1988: Lost to Mark Brooks, Canon SDJ Greater Hartford Open.

BEAN, Andy—3-3: 1979: Lost to Lon Hinkle, Crosby. 1981: Defeated Lee Trevino, Memphis Classic; Defeated Bill Rogers, Western Open. 1984: Lost to Bruce Lietzke, Honda Classic; Lost to Jack Nicklaus, Memorial. 1986: Defeated Hubert Green, Doral-Eastern Open

BEARD, Frank—0-3: 1968: Lost to Jack Nicklaus, American Golf Classic. 1969: Lost to Larry Hinson, New Orleans. 1974: Lost to Johnny Miller, World Open.

BECK, Chip—0-2: 1988: Lost to Bob Lohr, Walt Disney. 1991: Lost to Brad Faxon, Buick Open.

BIES, Don—1-0: 1975: Defeated Hubert Green, Hartford Open.

BLACK, Ronnie—1-1: 1983: Defeated Sam Torrance, Southern Open. 1989: Lost to Wayne Grady, Manufacturers Hanover Westchester Classic.

BLACKBURN, Woody—2-1: 1976: Defeated Gay Brewer/Bobby Nichols, Walt Disney Team Championship with Bill Kratzert. 1981: Lost to Dave Barr, Quad Cities Open. 1985: Defeated Ron Streck, Isuzu Andy Williams San Diego Open.

BLACKMAR, Phil—2-0: 1985: Defeated Jodie Mudd, Dan Pohl, Canon Sammy Davis, Jr -Greater Hartford Open. 1988: Defeated Payne Stewart, Provident Classic.

BLANCAS, Homero—1-1: 1969: Lost to Larry Ziegler, Michigan Classic. 1972: Defeated Lanny Wadkins, Phoenix Open.

BOROS, Julius—4-5: 1952: Defeated Cary Middlecoff, World Championship of Golf. 1954: Defeated George Fazio, Carling's Open 1958: Lost to Sam Snead, Dallas Open Invitational. 1959: Lost to Jack Burke, Houston Classic. 1963: Defeated Arnold Palmer, Jacky Cupit, U.S. Open; Lost to Arnold Palmer, Western Open . 1964: Defeated Doug Sanders, Greater Greensboro Open. 1969: Lost to Gene Littler, Greater Greensboro Open. 1975: Lost to Gene Littler, Westchester Classic.

BREWER, Gay—2-6: 1959: Lost to Arnold Palmer, West Palm Beach Open. 1965: Defeated Doug Sanders, Greater Seattle Open Invitational. Defeated Bob Goalby, Hawaiian Open Invit. 1966: Lost to Jack Nicklaus, Masters; Lost to Arnold Palmer, Tournament of Champions. 1969: Lost to Dave Hill, IVB-Philadelphia Classic. 1974: Lost to Jim Colbert, American Golf Classic. 1976: Lost to Woody Blackburn/Bill Kratzert, Disney Team Championship.

BRITTON, Bill—0-1: 1982: Lost to Hal Sutton, Walt Disney World Golf Classic.

BROOKS,Mark—2-2: 1988: Defeated Dave Barr, Joey Sindelar, Canon SDJ Greater Hartford Open; Lost to Tom Purtzer, Southwest Classic. 1991: Defeated Gene Sauers, Kmart Greater Greensboro Open. 1993: Lost to John Inman, Buick Southern Open.

INDIVIDUAL PLAYOFF RECORDS (cont'd.)

BROWN, Billy Ray— 2-0: 1991: Defeated Corey Pavin, Rick Fehr, Canon Greater Hartford Open. 1992: Defeated Ray Floyd, Bruce Lietzke, Ben Crenshaw, GTE Byron Nelson Classic.

BROWN, Pete—1-1: 1964: Lost to Billy Casper, Almaden Open Invit. 1970: Defeated Tony Jacklin, San Diego Open.

BRYANT, Brad—0-1: 1993: Lost to John Inman, Buick Southern Open.

BURNS, George —0-2: 1984: Lost to Gary Koch, Bay Hill Classic. 1985: Lost to Roger Maltbie, Manufacturers Hanover Westchester Classic.

BYMAN, Bob—1-0: 1979: Defeated John Schroeder, Bay Hill.

CADLE, George—0-1: 1983: Lost to Morris Hatalsky, Greater Milwaukee Open.

CALCAVECCHIA, Mark—0-3: 1987: Lost to Fred Couples, Byron Nelson Golf Classic.1990: Lost to Greg Norman, Doral Ryder Open. 1993: Lost to Billy Mayfair, Greater Milwaukee Open.

CALDWELL, Rex—0-2: 1983: Lost to Keith Fergus, Bob Hope Desert Classic; Lost to Bob Gilder, Phoenix Open.

CASPER, Billy—8-8: Defeated Ken Venturi, Greater New Orleans.1961: Lost to Jack Burke,Buick Open. 1964: Defeated Pete Brown, Jerry Steelsmith, Almaden Open Invit. 1965: Lost to Wes Ellis, San Diego Open; Defeated Johnny Pott, Insurance City Invit. 1966: Defeated Arnold Palmer, U.S. Open. 1967: Defeated Art Wall, Canadian Open; Defeated Al Geiberger, Carling World Open; Lost to Dudley Wysong, Hawaiian Open. 1968: Lost to Johnny Pott, Bing Crosby National Pro-Am. 1969: Lost to Jack Nicklaus, Kaiser. 1970: Defeated Hale Irwin, L. A. Open; Defeated Gene Littler, Masters. 1971: Lost to Bob Lunn, L.A. Open. 1972: Lost to Chi Chi Rodriguez, Byron Nelson. 1975: Lost to Jack Nicklaus, World Open.

CHARLES, Bob—0-2: 1965: Lost to George Archer, Lucky International Open. 1970: Lost to Miller Barber, New Orleans Open.

CHEN, Tze-Chung —1-1: 1983: Lost to Fred Couples, Kemper Open. 1987: Defeated Ben Crenshaw, Los Angeles Open presented by Nissan.

CLAMPETT, Bobby—0-2: 1981: Lost to John Cook, Crosby Pro-Am; Lost to Hale Irwin, Buick Open.

COCHRAN, Russ—0-1: 1991: Lost to Craig Stadler, THE TOUR Championship.

COLBERT, Jim—2-0: 1974: Defeated Ray Floyd, Gay Brewer, Forrest Fezler, American Golf Classic. 1983: Defeated Fuzzy Zoeller, Colonial National Invitation.

CONNER, Frank—0-2: 1981: Lost to Dave Barr, Quad Cities Open. 1982: Lost to Tom Watson, Heritage Classic.

COOK, John—3-3: 1981: Defeated Hale Irwin, Bobby Clampett, Ben Crenshaw, Barney Thompson, Crosby Pro-Am. 1983: Defeated Johnny Miller, Canadian Open 1986: Lost to Donnie Hammond, Bob Hope Chrysler Classic. 1990: Lost to Tom Kite, Federal Express St. Jude Classic; Lost to Bob Tway, Las Vegas Invitational. 1992: Defeated Tom Kite, Gene Sauers, Rick Fehr, Mark O'Meara, Bob Hope Chrysler Classic.

COUPLES, Fred—4-3: 1983: Defeated Tze-Chung Chen, Barry Jaeckel, Gil Morgan, Scott Simpson, Kemper Open. 1986: Lost to Tom Kite, Western Open. 1987: Defeated Mark Calcavecchia, Byron Nelson Golf Classic. 1988: Lost to Sandy Lyle, Phoenix Open. 1992: Defeated Davis Love III, Nissan Los Angeles; Lost to Corey Pavin, Honda Classic. 1993: Defeated Robert Gamez, Honda Classic.

COURTNEY, Chuck—0-1: 1972: Lost to DeWitt Weaver, Southern Open.

CRAMPTON, Bruce—0-2: 1970: Lost to Gibby Gilbert, Houston Champions. 1974: Lost to Richie Karl, B.C. Open.

CRENSHAW, Ben—0-8: 1978: Lost to Tom Watson, Bing Crosby National Pro-Am. 1979: Lost to Larry Nelson,Western; Lost to David Graham, PGA. 1981: Lost to John Cook, Crosby Pro-Am; Lost to Bill Rogers, Texas Open. 1987: Lost toTze-Chung Chen, Los Angeles Open presented by Nissan. 1989: Lost to David Frost, NEC World Series of Golf. 1992: Lost to Billy Ray Brown, GTE Byron Nelson Classic.

DEVLIN, Bruce—0-3: 1968: Lost to Johnny Pott, Bing Crosby National Pro Am. 1969: Lost to Bert Yancey, Atlanta Classic. 1972: Lost to David Graham, Cleveland Open.

DIEHL, Terry—0-1: 1976: Lost to Tom Kite, IVB-Bicentennial Golf Classic.

DONALD, Mike—1-1: 1989: Defeated Tim Simpson and Hal Sutton, Anheuser Busch Classic. 1990: Lost to Hale Irwin, U.S. Open.

DOUGLASS, Dale—0-3: 1968: Lost to Chi Chi Rodriguez, Sahara Invitational. 1970: Lost to Don

INDIVIDUAL PLAYOFF RECORDS (cont'd.)

January, Jacksonville Open. 1971: Lost to Tom Weiskopf, Kemper Open.

DOUGHERTY, Ed—0-1: 1990: Lost to Jim Gallagher, Greater Milwaukee Open.

EASTWOOD, Bob—1-0: 1985: Defeated Payne Stewart, Byron Nelson Classic.

EDWARDS, Danny—1-0: 1983: Defeated Morris Hatalsky, Miller High Life QCO.

EDWARDS, David— 1-0: 1992: Defeated Rick Fehr, Memorial Tournament.

EICHELBERGER, Dave—1-1: 1971: Lost to Bud Allin, Greater Greensboro Open. 1981: Defeated Bob Murphy, Mark O'Meara, Tallahassee Open.

ELDER, Lee—2-2: 1968: Lost to Jack Nicklaus, American Golf Classic. 1972: Lost to Lee Trevino, Hartford Open. 1974: Defeated Peter Oosterhuis, Monsanto Open. 1978: Defeated Lee Trevino, Greater Milwaukee Open; Lost to Nick Price, H.E.B Texas Open.

ERSKINE, Randy—0-1: 1976: Lost to Ed Sabo, Buick Open.

ELKINGTON, Steve--- 1-3: 1992: Defeated Brad Faxon, Infiniti Tournament of Champions; Lost to Dan Forsman, Buick Open; Lost to Nick Price H-E-B Texas Open. 1993: Lost to Rocco Mediate, Kmart Greater Greensboro Open.

ESTES, Bob—0-2: 1989: Lost to Mike Hulbert, B.C. Open. 1993: Lost to John Inman, Buick Southern Open.

FALDO, Nick—2-1: 1988: Lost to Curtis Strange, U.S. Open. 1989: Defeated Scott Hoch, The Masters. 1990: Defeated Ray Floyd, The Masters.

FAXON, Brad—1-2: 1991: Defeated Chip Beck, Buick Open. 1992: Lost to Steve Elkington, Infiniti Tournament of Champions; Lost to Dan Forsman, Buick Open.

FEHR, Rick— 0-3: 1991: Lost to Billy Ray Brown, Canon Greater Hartford Open. 1992: Lost to John Cook, Bob Hope Chrysler Classic; Lost to David Edwards, Memorial.

FERGUS, Keith—2-0: 1982: Defeated Raymond Floyd, Georgia Pacific Atlanta Classic. 1983: Defeated Rex Caldwell, Bob Hope Desert Classic.

FEZLER, Forrest—0-1: 1974: Lost to Jim Colbert, American Golf Classic.

FINSTERWALD, Dow—2-4: 1956: Lost to Doug Sanders, Canadian Open. 1957: Defeated Don Whitt, Tucson Open Invit. 1958: Lost to Art Wall, Rubber City Open. 1959: Lost to Art Wall, Buick Open; Defeated Don Fairfield, Kansas City Open Invit. 1962: Lost to Arnold Palmer, Masters.

FIORI, Ed—2-0: 1979: Defeated Tom Weiskopf, Southern Open. 1982: Defeated Tom Kite, Bob Hope Desert Classic.

FLECKMAN, Marty—1-0: 1967: Defeated Jack Montgomery, Cajun Classic.

FLEISHER, Bruce—1-0: 1991: Defeated Ian Baker Finch, New England Classic.

FLOYD, Ray—5-10: 1969: Defeated Gardner Dickinson, Greater Jacksonville Open. 1971: Lost to Arnold Palmer, Bob Hope Desert Classic. 1973: Lost to Jack Nicklaus, Bing Crosby National Pro-Am. 1974: Lost to Jim Colbert, American Golf Classic. 1975: Lost to J. C. Snead, Andy Williams San Diego Open. 1976: Defeated Jerry McGee, World Open. 1980: Defeated Jack Nicklaus, Doral. 1981: Lost to Bruce Lietzke, Andy Williams-San Diego Open; Defeated Barry Jaeckel, Curtis Strange, TPC. 1982: Lost to Keith Fergus, Georgia-Pacific Atlanta Classic; Lost to Craig Stadler, World Series of Golf. 1985: Lost to Roger Maltbie, Manufacturers Hanover Westchester Classic. 1986: Defeated Lon Hinkle, Mike Sullivan, Walt Disney World/Oldsmobile Classic. 1990: Lost to Nick Faldo, The Masters. 1992: Lost to Billy Ray Brown, GTE Byron Nelson Classic.

FORD, Doug—5-7: 1951: Lost to E. J. Harrison, Texas Open; Lost to Cary Middlecoff, Kansas City Open. 1952: Defeated Sam Snead, Jacksonville Open. 1953: Lost to Earl Steward, Greensboro Open. 1954: Defeated Marty Furgol, Greensboro Open. 1955: Lost to Henry Ransom, Rubber City Open; Lost to Ted Kroll, Philadelphia Daily News Open. 1956: Lost to Mike Fetchick, Western Open. 1957: Lost to Arnold Palmer, Rubber City Open; Defeated George Bayer, Gene Littler, Billy Maxwell, Western Open. 1961: Defeated Arnold Palmer, "500" Festival Open Invit. 1962: Defeated Joe Campbell, Bing Crosby National.

FORSMAN, Dan—1-0: 1992: Defeated Steve Elkington, Brad Faxon, Buick Open.

FOUGHT, John—1-0: 1979: Defeated Jim Simons, Buick.

FROST, David—2-2: 1986: Lost to Tom Kite, Western Open. 1988: Lost to Seve Ballesteros, Manufacturers Hanover Westchester Classic; Defeated Bob Tway, Southern Open. 1989: Defeated Ben Crenshaw, NEC World Series of Golf.

FUNSETH, Rod—0-1: 1971: Lost to Bud Allin, Greater Greensboro Open.

GALLAGHER, Jim—1-1: 1990: Defeated Ed Dougherty, Billy Mayfair, Greater Milwaukee Open. 1991:

293

Lost to Tom Purtzer, NEC World Series of Golf.

GAMEZ, Robert—0-1: 1993: Lost to Fred Couples, Honda Classic

GARDNER,Buddy—0-2: 1979: Lost to Bobby Walzel, Magnolia Classic.1987: Lost to Jay Haas,Big I Houston Open.

GEIBERGER, Al—1-1: 1967: Lost to Billy Casper, Carling World Open. 1975: Defeated Gary Player, Tournament of Champions.

GILBERT, Gibby—1-0: 1970: Defeated Bruce Crampton, Houston Champions.

GILDER, Bob—1-0: 1983: Defeated Rex Caldwell, Johnny Miller, Mark O'Meara, Phoenix Open

GOALBY, Bob—2-1: 1962: Defeated Art Wall, Insurance City Open. 1965: Lost to Gay Brewer, Hawaiian Open Invit. 1969: Defeated Jim Wiechers, Robinson Open.

GRADY, Wayne—1-0: 1989: Defeated Ronnie Black, Manufacturers Hanover Westchester Classic.

GRAHAM,David—2-1: 1972: Defeated Bruce Devlin, Cleveland Open; Lost to Lou Graham, Liggett & Myers Open. 1979: Defeated Ben Crenshaw, PGA Championship.

GRAHAM, Lou—3-1: 1971: Lost to George Archer, Hartford Open. 1972: Defeated Hale Irwin, Larry Ziegler, David Graham, Liggett & Myers Open. 1975: Defeated John Mahaffey, U.S. Open. 1979: Defeated Bobby Wadkins, Philadelphia.

GREEN, Hubert—2-3: 1971: Defeated Don January, Houston Champions. 1975: Lost to Don Bies, Hartford Open. 1978: Defeated Bill Kratzert, Hawaiian Open; Lost to Gil Morgan, World Series of Golf. 1986: Lost to Andy Bean, Doral-Eastern Open.

GREEN, Ken—0-2: 1988: Lost to Sandy Lyle, Greater Greensboro Open; Lost to Seve Ballesteros, Manufacturers Hanover Westchester Classic.

HAAS, Jay—3-0: 1982: Defeated John Adams, Hall of Fame Tournament. 1987: Defeated Buddy Gardner, Big I Houston Open. 1993: Defeated Bob Lohr, H-E-B Texas Open.

HALLBERG, Gary—0-2: 1984: Lost to Gary Koch, Isuzu-Andy Williams San Diego Open. 1991: Lost to Blaine McCallister, H.E.B. Texas Open.

HALLDORSON, Dan—0-1: 1981: Lost to Dave Barr, Quad Cities Open.

HALLET, Jim—-0-2: 1990: Lost to Kenny Knox, Buick Southern Open. 1991: Lost to Ian Woosnam, USF&G Classic.

HAMMOND, Donnie—1-0: 1986: Defeated John Cook, Bob Hope Chrysler Classic.

HARRIS, Labron—1-1: 1968: Lost to Bob Murphy, Philadelphia Golf Classic. 1971: Defeated Bert Yancey, Robinson Open .

HATALSKY, Morris—2-1: 1983: Defeated George Cadle, Greater Milwaukee Open; Lost to Danny Edwards, Miller High Life QCO. 1988: Defeated Tom Kite, Kemper Open.

HAYES, Mark—0-2: 1979: Lost to Lon Hinkle, Crosby. 1981: Lost to Larry Nelson, Greater Greensboro.

HEARD, Jerry—0-1: 1974: Lost to Bob Menne, Kemper Open.

HEBERT, Lionel—1-1: 1956: Lost to Mike Fetchick, St. Petersburg Open. 1962: Defeated Gary Player, Gene Littler, Memphis Open Invit.

HILL, Dave—4-2: 1961: Defeated Tommy Bolt, Bud Sullivan, Home of the Sun Open . 1963: Defeated Mike Souchak, Hot Springs Open. 1969: Defeated Gay Brewer, Tom Jacobs, R. H. Sikes, IVB-Philadelphia; Lost to Bob Lunn, Hartford Open. 1972: Lost to George Archer, L.A. Open. 1975: Defeated Rik Massengale, Sahara Invit.

HINKLE, Lon—1-2: 1977: Lost to Ed Sneed, Tallahassee Open. 1979: Defeated Mark Hayes, Andy Bean, Crosby. 1986: Lost to Ray Floyd, Walt Disney World/Oldsmobile Classic.

HINSON, Larry—1-1: 1969: Defeated Frank Beard, New Orleans. 1975: Lost to Don January, San Antonio-Texas.

HISKEY, Babe—1-0: 1965: Defeated Dudley Wysong, Cajun Classic.

HOCH, Scott—1-1: 1989: Lost to Nick Faldo, The Masters; Defeated Robert Wrenn, Las Vegas Invitational.

HULBERT, Mike—2-0: 1989: Defeated Bob Estes, B.C. Open. 1991: Defeated Kenny Knox, Anheuser Busch Golf Classic.

HUSTON, John—0-1: 1993: Lost to Jim McGovern, Shell Houston Open.

INMAN, John—1-0: 1993: Defeated Billy Andrade, Mark Brooks, Brad Bryant, Bob Estes, Buick Southern Open.

IRWIN, Hale—4-5: 1970: Lost to Billy Casper, L.A. Open. 1972: Lost to Lou Graham, Liggett & Myers Open. 1976: Defeated Kermit Zarley, Florida Citrus Open; Lost to Roger Maltbie, Memorial. 1981:

Lost to John Cook, Crosby Pro-Am; Defeated Bobby Clampett, Peter Jacobsen, Gil Morgan, Buick Open. 1984: Defeated Jim Nelford, Bing Crosby Pro-Am. 1990: Defeated Mike Donald, U.S. Open. 1991: Lost to Kenny Perry, Memorial.

JACKLIN, Tony—1-1: 1970: Lost to Pete Brown, San Diego Open. 1972: Defeated John Jacobs, Jacksonville Open.

JACOBSEN, Peter—1-3: 1981: Lost to Hale Irwin, Buick Open. 1984: Defeated Payne Stewart, Colonial National Invitation. 1985: Lost to Curtis Strange, Honda Classic. 1989: Lost to Mark McCumber, Beatrice Western Open.

JAECKEL, Barry—1-2: 1978: Defeated Bruce Lietzke, Tallahassee Open. 1981: Lost to Ray Floyd, TPC 1983: Lost to Fred Couples, Kemper Open.

JANUARY, Don—3-5: 1956: Lost to Mike Fetchick, Western Open. 1961: Lost to Jerry Barber, PGA Championship 1964: Lost to Chi Chi Rodriguez, Lucky Internat'l Open. 1967: Defeated Don Massengale, PGA Championship. 1969: Lost to Jack Nicklaus, Kaiser International. 1970: Defeated Dale Douglass, Jacksonville Open. 1971: Lost to Hubert Green, Houston Champions. 1975: Defeated Larry Hinson, San Antonio Texas Open.

JENKINS, Tom—0-1: 1981: Lost to Bruce Lietzke, Williams-San Diego Open.

JONES, Grier—2-0: 1972: Defeated Bob Murphy, Hawaiian Open; Defeated Dave Marad, Robinson's Fall Classic .

JONES, Steve—2-1: 1988: Defeated Bob Tway, AT&T Pebble Beach Pro-Am. 1989: Defeated Sandy Lyle and Paul Azinger, Bob Hope Chrysler Classic. 1990: Lost to Payne Stewart, MCI Heritage Classic.

KARL, Richie—1-0: 1974: Defeated Bruce Crampton, B.C. Open.

KITE, Tom—6-4: 1976: Defeated Terry Diehl, Philadelphia Classic. 1982: Lost to Ed Fiori, Bob Hope Desert Classic; Defeated Jack Nicklaus, Denis Watson, Bay Hill Classic. 1986: Defeated Fred Couples, David Frost, Nick Price, Western Open. 1988: Lost to Morris Hatalsky, Kemper Open; Lost to Curtis Strange, Nabisco Championships. 1989: Defeated Davis Love III, The Nestle Invitational; Defeated Payne Stewart, Nabisco Championships. 1990: Defeated John Cook, Federal Express St. Jude Classic. 1992: Lost to John Cook, Bob Hope Chrysler Classic.

KNOX, Kenny—1-1: 1990: Defeated Jim Hallet, Buick Southern Open. 1991: Lost to Mike Hulbert, Anheuser Busch Golf Classic.

KNUDSON, George—4-0: 1962: Defeated Jim Ferree, Maracaibo Open Invit. 1963: Defeated Mason Rudolph, Portland Open Invitational. 1964: Defeated Al Balding, Fresno Open Invit. 1970: Defeated George Archer, Robinson Open.

KOCH, Gary—2-0: 1984: Defeated Gary Hallberg, Isuzu Andy Williams San Diego Open; Defeated George Burns, Bay Hill Classic.

KRATZERT, Bill—1-1: 1976: Defeated Gay Brewer/Bobby Nichols, Walt Disney Team Championship with Woody Blackburn. 1978: Lost to Hubert Green, Hawaiian Open.

LANGER, Bernhard—1-1: 1985: Defeated Bobby Wadkins, Sea Pines Heritage Classic. 1986: Lost to Bob Tway, Shearson Lehman Andy Williams Open.

LEVI, Wayne—2-1: 1980: Defeated Gil Morgan, Pleasant Valley Jimmy Fund. 1984: Lost to Jack Renner, Hawaiian Open. 1985: Defeated Steve Pate, Georgia-Pacific Atlanta Classic.

LIETZKE, Bruce—6-4: 1977: Defeated Gene Littler, Tucson Open; Lost to Jack Nicklaus, Tournament of Champions. 1978: Lost to Barry Jaeckel, Tallahassee Open. 1981: Defeated Ray Floyd, Tom Jenkins, Andy Williams-San Diego Open; Defeated Tom Watson, Byron Nelson Classic. 1984: Defeated Andy Bean, Honda Classic. 1988: Defeated Clarence Rose, GTE Byron Nelson Classic. 1992: Lost to Billy Ray Brown, GTE Byron Nelson Classic; Defeated Corey Pavin, Southwestern Bell Colonial; Lost to Greg Norman, Canadian Open.

LITTLER, Gene—3-8: 1955: Defeated Stan Leonard, Labatt Open. 1956: Lost to Peter Thomson, Texas Internat'l Open. 1957: Lost to Doug Ford, Western Open. 1960: Lost to Tommy Bolt, Memphis Open. 1962: Lost to Lionel Hebert, Memphis Open Invit. 1966: Lost to Joe Campbell, Tucson Open. 1969: Defeated Orville Moody, Julius Boros, Tom Weiskopf, Greater Greensboro Open. 1970: Lost to Billy Casper, Masters. 1975: Defeated Julius Boros, Westchester Classic. 1977: Lost to Bruce Lietzke, Tucson Open; Lost to Lanny Wadkins, PGA Championship.

LOHR, Bob—1-1: 1988: Defeated Chip Beck, Walt Disney World Oldsmobile Classic. 1993: Lost to Jay

Haas, H-E-B Texas Open.

LOVE III, Davis—0-3: 1989; Lost to Tom Kite, The Nestle Invitational. 1991: Lost to Tom Purtzer, NEC World Series of Golf. 1992: Lost to Fred Couples, Nissan Los Angeles Open.

LUNN, Bob—2-0: 1969: Defeated Dave Hill, Hartford Open. 1971: Defeated Billy Casper, L.A. Open.

LYLE, Sandy—3-1:1987: Defeated Jeff Sluman, Tournament Players Championship. 1988: Defeated Fred Couples, Phoenix Open; Defeated Ken Green, Greater Greensboro Open. 1989: Lost to Steve Jones, Bob Hope Chrysler Classic.

MAGEE, Andrew—1-0: 1991: Defeated D.A. Weibring, Las Vegas invitational.

McCALLISTER, Blaine—1-1: 1986: Lost to Gene Sauers, Bank of Boston Classic. 1991: Defeated Gary Hallberg, H.E.B. Texas Open.

McCUMBER, Mark—1-0: 1989: Defeated Peter Jacobsen, Beatrice Western Open.

McGEE, Jerry—0-1: 1976: Lost to Ray Floyd, World Open.

McGOVERN, Jim—1-0: 1993: Defeated John Huston, Shell Houston Open.

McLENDON, Mac—1-0: 1978: Defeated Mike Reid, Pensacola Open.

MAHAFFEY, John—3-2: 1975: Lost to Lou Graham, U.S. Open. 1978: Defeated Tom Watson and Jerry Pate, PGA Championship. 1984: Defeated Jim Simons, Bob Hope Classic. 1985: Lost to Mark Wiebe, Anheuser Busch Classic; Defeated Jodie Mudd, Texas Open.

MALTBIE, Roger—2-1: 1976: Defeated Hale Irwin, Memorial Tournament. 1985: Defeated George Burns, Ray Floyd, Manufacturers Hanover Westchester Classic. 1986: Lost to Mac O'Grady, Canon Sammy Davis, Jr.-Greater Hartford Open.

MARAD, Dave—0-1: 1972: Lost to Grier Jones, Robinson's Fall Classic.

MARR, Dave—2-0:1961: Defeated Bob Rosburg, Jacky Cupit, Greater Seattle Open Invitational. 1962: Defeated Jerry Steelsmith, Azalea Open.

MASSENGALE, Don—0-1: 1967: Lost to Don January, PGA Championship.

MASSENGALE, Rik—0-1: 1975: Lost to Dave Hill, Sahara Open.

MAXWELL, Billy—1-2: 1955: Lost to Bo Wininger, Baton Rouge Open. 1957: Lost to Doug Ford, Western Open. 1961: Defeated Ted Kroll, Insurance City Open Invit.

MAYFAIR, Billy—1-2: 1990: Lost to Jim Gallagher, Greater Milwaukee Open; Lost to Jodie Mudd, Nabisco Championship. 1993: Defeated Mark Calcavecchia and Ted Schulz, Greater Milwaukee Open.

MEDIATE, Rocco—2-0: 1991: Defeated Curtis Strange, Doral Ryder Open. 1993: Defeated Steve Elkington, Kmart Greater Greensboro Open.

MENNE, Bob—1-1: 1970: Lost to Lee Trevino, National Airlines Open. 1974: Defeated Jerry Heard, Kemper Open.

MILLER, Johnny—1-5: 1972: Lost to Jack Nicklaus, Bing Crosby National Pro-Am. 1974: Defeated Frank Beard, Jack Nicklaus, Bob Murphy, World Open. 1979: Lost to Tom Watson, Hall of Fame. 1982: Lost to Tom Watson, Glen Campbell Los Angeles Open. 1983: Lost to Bob Gilder, Phoenix Open. Lost to John Cook, Canadian Open

MITCHELL, Bobby—1-0: 1972: Defeated Jack Nicklaus, Tournament of Champions.

MIZE, Larry—1-2: 1986: Lost to Greg Norman, Kemper Open. 1987: Defeated Greg Norman, Seve Ballesteros, Masters. 1990: Lost to Payne Stewart, MCI Heritage Classic.

MOODY, Orville—0-2: 1969: Lost to Gene Littler,Greater Greensboro Open. 1973: Lost to Jack Nicklaus, Bing Crosby National Pro-Am.

MORGAN, Gil—3-3: 1978: Defeated Hubert Green, World Series of Golf. 1979: Defeated Larry Nelson, Memphis. 1980: Lost to Wayne Levi, Pleasant Valley Jimmy Fund. 1981: Lost to Hale Irwin, Buick Open 1983: Defeated Lanny Wadkins, Curtis Strange, Joe Garagiola-Tucson Open; Lost to Fred Couples, Kemper Open.

MUDD, Jodie—2-2: 1985: Lost to Phil Blackmar, Canon Sammy Davis, Jr -Greater Hartford Open; Lost to John Mahaffey, Texas Open. 1989: Defeated Larry Nelson, GTE Byron Nelson Classic. 1990: Defeated Billy Mayfair, Nabisco Championships.

MURPHY, Bob—1-5: 1968: Defeated Labron Harris, Philadelphia Golf Classic. 1970: Lost to Lee Trevino, Tucson Open. 1972: Lost to Grier Jones, Hawaiian Open. 1973: Lost to Bobby Nichols, Westchester Classic. 1974: Lost to Johnny Miller, World Open. 1981: Lost to Dave Eichelberger, Tallahassee Open.

NELFORD, Jim—0-1: 1984: Lost to Hale Irwin, Bing Crosby Pro-Am.

NELSON, Larry—2-2: 1979: Lost to Gil Morgan, Memphis; Defeated Ben Crenshaw, Western Open. 1981: Defeated Mark Hayes, Greater Greensboro Open. 1989: Lost to Jodie Mudd, GTE Byron Nelson Classic.

NEWTON, Jack—1-0: 1978: Defeated Mike Sullivan, Buick-Goodwrench Open.

NICHOLS, Bobby—2-3: 1961: Lost to Eric Monti, Ontario Open. 1962: Defeated Dan Sikes, Jack Nicklaus, Houston Classic. 1973: Defeated Bob Murphy, Westchester Classic. 1975: Lost to J. C. Snead, Andy Williams San Diego Open. 1976: Lost to Woody Blackburn/Bill Kratzert, Walt Disney Team Championship.

NICKLAUS, Jack—13-10: 1962: Lost to Bobby Nichols, Houston Classic; Defeated Arnold Palmer, U.S. Open. 1963: Defeated Gary Player, Palm Springs Golf Classic; Lost to Arnold Palmer, Western Open. 1965: Lost to Doug Sanders, Pensacola Open; Defeated Johnny Pott, Memphis Open. 1966: Defeated Tom Jacobs, Gay Brewer, Masters. 1968: Defeated Frank Beard, Lee Elder, American Golf Classic. 1969: Defeated George Archer, Billy Casper, Don January, Kaiser International. 1970: Defeated Arnold Palmer, Byron Nelson Classic. 1971: Lost to Gardner Dickinson, Atlanta Golf Classic; Lost to Lee Trevino, U.S. Open. 1972: Defeated Johnny Miller, Bing Crosby Pro-Am; Lost to Bobby Mitchell, Tournament of Champions. 1973: Defeated Orville Moody, Ray Floyd, Bing Crosby Pro-Am; Defeated Miller Barber, New Orleans. 1974: Lost to Johnny Miller, World Open. 1975: Lost to Tom Weiskopf, Canadian Open; Defeated Billy Casper, World Open. 1977: Defeated Bruce Lietzke, Tournament of Champions. 1980: Lost to Ray Floyd, Doral. 1982: Lost to Tom Kite, Bay Hill Classic. 1984: Defeated Andy Bean, Memorial.

NICOLETTE, Mike—1-0: 1983: Defeated Greg Norman, Bay Hill Classic.

NORMAN, Greg—3-7: 1983: Lost to Mike Nicolette, Bay Hill Classic. 1984: Lost to Fuzzy Zoeller, U.S. Open; Lost to Tom Watson, Western Open. 1986: Defeated Larry Mize, Kemper Open. 1987: Lost to Larry Mize, The Masters. 1988: Lost to Curtis Strange, Independent Insurance Agent Open; Lost to Seve Ballesteros, Manufacturers Hanover Westchester Classic. 1990: Defeated Paul Azinger, Mark Calcavecchia, Tim Simpson, Doral Ryder Open. 1992: Defeated Bruce Lietzke, Canadian Open. 1993: Lost to Paul Azinger, PGA Championship.

O'GRADY, Mac—1-0: 1986: Defeated Roger Maltbie, Canon Sammy Davis, Jr.-Greater Hartford Open

O'MEARA, Mark—1-4: 1981: Lost to Dave Eichelberger, Tallahassee Open. 1983: Lost to Bob Gilder, Phoenix Open. 1991: Lost to Corey Pavin, Bob Hope Chrysler Classic. 1992: Lost to John Cook, Bob Hope Chrysler; Defeated Jeff Sluman , AT&T Pebble Beach National Pro-am.

OGRIN, David—0-1: 1985: Lost to Hal Sutton, St. Jude Memphis Classic.

OOSTERHUIS, Peter—0-1: 1974: Lost to Lee Elder, Monsanto Open.

PALMER, Arnold—14-10: 1956: Defeated Ted Kroll, Insurance City Open. 1957: Defeated Doug Ford, Rubber City Open. 1958: Lost to Howie Johnson, Azalea Open International. 1959: Defeated Gay Brewer, Peter Cooper, West Palm Beach Open Invit. 1960: Lost to Bill Collins, Houston Classic; Defeated Bill Collins, Jack Fleck, Insurance City Open. 1961: Defeated Al Balding, San Diego Open; Defeated Doug Sanders, Phoenix Open; Lost to Doug Ford, "500" Festival Open. 1962: Defeated Gary Player, Dow Finsterwald, Masters; Defeated Johnny Pott, Colonial Nat'l Invitational; Lost to Jack Nicklaus, U.S. Open. 1963: Defeated Paul Harney, Thunderbird Classic; Lost to Julius Boros, U.S. Open; Defeated Tommy Aaron, Tony Lema, Cleveland Open; Defeated Julius Boros, Jack Nicklaus, Western Open. 1964: Lost to Gary Player, Pensacola Open; Lost to Tony Lema, Cleveland Open. 1966: Lost to Doug Sanders, Bob Hope Desert Classic; Defeated Gay Brewer, Tournament of Champions; Lost to Billy Casper, U.S. Open. 1968: Defeated Deane Beman, Bob Hope Desert Classic. 1970: Lost to Jack Nicklaus, Byron Nelson Golf Classic. 1971: Defeated Ray Floyd, Bob Hope Desert Classic.

PATE, Jerry—1-2: 1977: Defeated Dave Stockton, Phoenix Open. 1978: Lost to John Mahaffey, PGA Championship. 1980: Lost to Doug Tewell, Heritage.

PATE, Steve—0-2: 1985: Lost to Wayne Levi, Georgia-Pacific Atlanta Classic. 1991: Lost to Corey Pavin, BellSouth Atlanta Classic.

PAVIN, Corey—5-2: 1986: Defeated Dave Barr, Greater Milwaukee Open. 1987: Defeated Craig

Stadler, Hawaiian Open. 1991: Defeated Mark O'Meara, Bob Hope Chrysler Classic; Defeated Steve Pate, BellSouth Atlanta Classic; Lost to Billy Ray Brown, Canon Greater Hartford Open. 1992: Defeated Fred Couples, Honda Classic; Lost to Bruce Lietzke, Southwestern Bell Colonial.

PEETE, Calvin—0-1: 1986: Lost to Curtis Strange, Houston Open.

PERRY, Kenny—1-0: 1991: Defeated Hale Irwin, Memorial.

PLAYER, Gary—3 -11: 1958: Lost to Sam Snead, Greenbrier Invit.; Lost to Sam Snead, Dallas Open Invit. 1959: Lost to Don Whitt, Memphis Open Invit. 1961: Lost to Jay Hebert, American Golf Classic. 1962: Lost to Arnold Palmer, Masters; Lost to Lionel Hebert , Memphis Open. 1963: Lost to Jack Nicklaus, Palm Springs Golf Classic. 1964: Defeated Arnold Palmer, Miller Barber, Pensacola Open. 1965: Defeated Kel Nagle, U.S. Open. 1967: Lost to Miller Barber, Oklahoma City Open. 1968: Lost to Steve Reid, Azalea Open. 1971: Defeated Hal Underwood, Jacksonville Open; Lost to Tom Weiskopf, Kemper Open. 1975: Lost to Al Geiberger, Tournament of Champions.

POHL, Dan—1-2: 1982: Lost to Craig Stadler, Masters. 1985: Lost to Phil Blackmar, Canon Sammy Davis, Jr.-Greater Hartford Open. 1986: Defeated Payne Stewart, Colonial NIT.

PRICE, Nick—1-1: 1986: Lost to Tom Kite, Western Open. 1992: Defeated Steve Elkington, H-E-B Texas Open.

PURTZER, Tom—2-0: 1988: Defeated Mark Brooks, Southwest Classic. 1991: Defeated Davis Love III, Jim Gallagher, Jr., NEC World Series of Golf.

REGALADO, Victor—0-1: 1981: Lost to Dave Barr, Quad Cities Open.

REID, Mike—1-2: 1978: Lost to Mac McLendon, Pensacola Open. 1985: Lost to Hal Sutton, Southwest Golf Classic. 1988: Defeated Tom Watson, NEC World Series of Golf.

RENNER, Jack—1-0: 1984: Defeated Wayne Levi, Hawaiian Open.

RODGERS, Phil—0-1: 1965: Lost to Dick Hart, Azalea Open.

RODRIGUEZ, Chi Chi—3-1: 1964: Defeated Don January, Lucky International Open. 1966: Lost to Jacky Cupit, Cajun Classic. 1968: Defeated Dale Douglass, Sahara Invit. 1972: Defeated Billy Casper, Byron Nelson Golf Classic.

ROGERS, Bill—1-2: 1978: Lost to Andy Bean, Western Open. 1979: Lost to Tom Watson, Byron Nelson. 1981: Defeated Ben Crenshaw, Texas Open.

ROSE, Clarence—0-1: 1988: Lost to Bruce Lietzke, GTE Byron Nelson Classic.

RUDOLPH, Mason—0-1: 1963: Lost to George Knudson, Portland Open Invit.

SAUERS, Gene—1-2: 1986: Defeated Blaine McCallister, Bank of Boston Classic. 1991: Lost to Mark Brooks, Kmart Greater Greensboro Open. 1992: Lost to John Cook, Bob Hope Chrysler Classic.

SCHLEE, John—0-1: 1973: Lost to Ed Sneed, Kaiser Open.

SCHROEDER, John—0-1: 1979: Lost to Bob Byman, Bay Hill.

SCHULZ, Ted—0-1: 1993: Lost to Billy Mayfair, Greater Milwaukee Open.

SHEARER, Bob—0-1: 1982: Lost to Ed Sneed, Michelob-Houston Open.

SIECKMANN, Tom—1-0: 1988: Defeated Mark Wiebe, Anheuser-Busch.

SIFFORD, Charles—2-0: 1957: Defeated Eric Monti, Long Beach Open. 1969: Defeated Harold Henning, L.A. Open.

SIKES, Dan—0-2: 1962: Lost to Bobby Nichols, Houston Classic. 1973: Lost to Lanny Wadkins, Byron Nelson Classic.

SIKES, R. H.—0-1: 1969: Lost to Dave Hill, IVB-Philadelphia Classic.

SILLS, Tony—1-0: 1990: Defeated Gil Morgan, Independent Insurance Agent Open.

SIMONS, Jim—0-3: 1979: Lost to John Fought, Buick. 1980: Lost to Howard Twitty, Hartford. 1984: Lost to John Mahaffey, Bob Hope Classic.

SIMPSON, Scott—1-2: 1983: Lost to Fred Couples, Kemper Open. 1989: Defeated Bob Tway, BellSouth Atlanta Classic. 1991: Lost to Payne Stewart, U.S. Open.

SIMPSON, Tim—0-2: 1989: Lost to Mike Donald, Anheuser Busch Classic. 1990: Lost to Greg Norman, Doral Ryder Open.

SINDELAR, Joey—1-1: 1988: Lost to Mark Brooks, Canon SDJ Greater Hartford Open. 1990: Defeated Willie Wood, Hardee's Golf Classic.

SINGH, Vijay—1-0: 1993: Defeated Mark Wiebe, Buick Classic.

SLUMAN, Jeff—0-3: 1987: Lost to Sandy Lyle, Tournament Players Championship. 1991: Lost to Billy Andrade, Kemper Open. 1992: Lost to Mark O'Meara, AT&T Pebble Beach National Pro-Am.

SNEAD, J. C.—3-1: 1971: Lost to George Archer, Hartford Open. 1975: Defeated Ray Floyd, Bobby Nichols, Andy Williams San Diego Open. 1981: Defeated Mike Sullivan, Southern Open. 1987: Defeated Seve Ballesteros, Manufacturers Hanover Westchester Classic.

SNEAD, Sam—8-6: 1945: Defeated Byron Nelson, Gulfport Open; Lost to Byron Nelson, Charlotte Open. 1947: Lost to Lew Worsham, U. S. Open. 1949: Defeated Lloyd Mangrum, Greater Greensboro Open. 1950: Defeated Ben Hogan, L.A. Open; Tied with Jack Burke, Dave Douglass, Smiley Quick, Crosby Pro-Am (no playoff, equal money); Lost to Jim Ferrier, St. Paul Open. 1952: Lost by forfeit to Doug Ford, Jacksonville Open. 1953: Lost to Earl Steward, Greensboro Open. 1954: Defeated Ben Hogan, Masters. 1955: Defeated Tommy Bolt, Miami Beach Open 1956: Defeated Fred Wampler, Greensboro Open. 1958: Defeated Gary Player, Greenbrier Invitational; Defeated Gary Player, Julius Boros, John McMullin, Dallas Open Invitational; Lost to George Bayer, Havana International.

SNEED, Ed—3-1: 1973: Defeated John Schlee, Kaiser International Open. 1977: Defeated Lon Hinkle, Tallahassee Open. 1979: Lost to Fuzzy Zoeller, Masters. 1982: Defeated Bob Shearer, Michelob-Houston Open.

STADLER, Craig—3-2: 1982: Defeated Dan Pohl, Masters; Defeated Raymond Floyd, World Series of Golf. 1985: Lost to Lanny Wadkins, Bob Hope Classic. 1987: Lost to Corey Pavin, Hawaiian Open. 1991: Defeated Russ Cochran, THE TOUR Championship.

STEWART, Payne—2-5: 1984: Lost to Peter Jacobsen, Colonial National Invitation. 1985: Lost to Bob Eastwood, Byron Nelson Classic. 1986: Lost to Dan Pohl, Colonial NIT. 1988: Lost to Phil Blackmar, Provident. 1989: Lost to Tom Kite, Nabisco Championships. 1990: Defeated Steve Jones, Larry Mize, MCI Heritage Classic. 1991: Defeated Scott Simpson, U.S. Open.

STILL, Ken—1-0: 1970: Defeated Bert Yancey, Lee Trevino, Kaiser International Open.

STOCKTON, Dave—0-1: 1977: Lost to Jerry Pate, Phoenix Open.

STRANGE, Curtis—6-3: 1980: Defeated Lee Trevino, Houston. 1981: Lost to Ray Floyd, TPC. 1983: Lost to Gil Morgan, Joe Garagiola-Tucson Open. 1985: Defeated Peter Jacobsen, Honda Classic. 1986: Defeated Calvin Peete, Houston Open. 1988: Defeated Greg Norman, Independent Insurance Agent Open; Defeated Nick Faldo, U.S. Open; Defeated Tom Kite, Nabisco Championships. 1991: Lost to Rocco Mediate, Doral Ryder Open.

STRECK, Ron—0-1: 1985: Lost to Woody Blackburn, Isuzu-Andy Williams San Diego Open.

SULLIVAN, Mike—0-3: 1978: Lost to Jack Newton, Buick Goodwrench Open. 1981: Lost to J. C. Snead, Southern Open. 1986: Lost to Ray Floyd, Walt Disney World/Oldsmobile Classic.

SUTTON, Hal—3-1: 1982: Defeated Bill Britton, Walt Disney World Golf Classic. 1985: Defeated David Ogrin, St. Jude Memphis Classic; Defeated Mike Reid, Southwest Golf Classic. 1989: Lost to Mike Donald, Anheuser-Busch Classic.

TEWELL, Doug—1-0: 1980: Defeated Jerry Pate, Heritage.

THOMPSON, Barney—0-1: 1981: Lost to John Cook, Crosby Pro-Am.

THORPE, Jim—0-1: 1985: Lost to Scott Verplank, Western Open.

TREVINO, Lee—5-5: 1970: Defeated Bob Murphy, Tucson Open; Defeated Bob Menne, National Airlines Open; Lost to Ken Still, Internat'l Open. 1971: Defeated Jack Nicklaus, U.S. Open; Lost to Tom Weiskopf, Kemper Open; Defeated Art Wall, Canadian Open. 1972: Defeated Lee Elder, Hartford Open. 1978: Lost to Andy Bean, Memphis Classic; Lost to Lee Elder, Greater Milwaukee Open. 1980: Lost to Curtis Strange, Houston.

TWAY, Bob—2-3: 1986: Defeated Bernhard Langer, Shearson Lehman Andy Williams Open. 1988: Lost to Steve Jones, AT&T Pebble Beach Pro-Am; Lost to David Frost, Southern Open. 1989: Lost to Scott Simpson, BellSouth Atlanta Classic. 1990: Defeated John Cook, Las Vegas Invitational.

TWITTY, Howard—1-0: 1980: Defeated Jim Simons, Hartford.

VALENTINE, Tommy—0-1: 1981: Lost to Tom Watson, Atlanta Classic.

VERPLANK, Scott—1-0: 1985: Defeated Jim Thorpe, Western Open.

WADKINS, Bobby—0-2: 1979: Lost to Lou Graham, Philadelphia. 1985: Lost to Bernhard Langer, Sea Pines Heritage Classic.

WADKINS, Lanny—3-2: 1972: Lost to Homero Blancas, Phoenix Open. 1973: Defeated Dan Sikes, Byron Nelson Golf Classic. 1977: Defeated Gene Littler, PGA Championship. 1983: Lost to Gil Morgan, Joe Garagiola-Tucson Open. 1985: Defeated Craig Stadler, Bob Hope Classic.

INDIVIDUAL PLAYOFF RECORDS (cont'd.)

WALL, Art—6-5: 1953: Lost to Earl Steward, Greensboro Open; Defeated Cary Middlecoff, Fort Wayne Open. 1956: Defeated Bill Trombley, Gardner Dickinson, Fort Wayne Open. 1958: Defeated Jack Burke, Bob Rosburg, Eastern Open Invitational; Defeated Dow Finsterwald, Rubber City Open. 1959: Defeated Dow Finsterwald, Buick Open. 1960: Lost to Stan Leonard, Western Open. 1962: Lost to Bob Goalby, Insurance City Open. 1964: Defeated Jay Dolan, Puerto Rico Open. 1967: Lost to Billy Casper, Canadian Open. 1971: Lost to Lee Trevino, Canadian Open.

WATSON, Denis—0-1: 1982: Lost to Tom Kite, Bay Hill Classic.

WATSON, Tom—8-4: 1978: Defeated Ben Crenshaw, Bing Crosby National Pro-Am; Lost to John Mahaffey, PGA Championship. 1979: Lost to Fuzzy Zoeller, Masters; Defeated Bill Rogers, Byron Nelson; Defeated Johnny Miller, Hall of Fame. 1980: Defeated D. A. Weibring, San Diego. 1981: Lost to Bruce Lietzke, Byron Nelson Classic; Defeated Tommy Valentine, Atlanta Classic. 1982: Defeated Johnny Miller, Glen Campbell, Los Angeles Open; Defeated Frank Conner, Heritage Classic. 1984: Defeated Greg Norman, Western Open. 1988: Lost to Mike Reid, NEC World Series of Golf .

WEAVER, DeWitt—1-0: 1972: Defeated Chuck Courtney, Southern Open.

WEIBRING, D. A.—0-2: 1980: Lost to Tom Watson, San Diego. 1991: Lost to Andrew Magee, Las Vegas Invitational.

WEISKOPF, Tom—2-3: 1966: Lost to Doug Sanders, Greensboro Open. 1969: Lost to Gene Littler, Greater Greensboro Open. 1971: Defeated Dale Douglass, Gary Player, Lee Trevino, Kemper Open. 1975: Defeated Jack Nicklaus, Canadian Open. 1979: Lost to Ed Fiori, Southern.

WIEBE, Mark—1-2: 1985: Defeated John Mahaffey, Anheuser-Busch Classic. 1988: Lost to Tom Sieckmann, Anheuser-Busch. 1993: Lost to Vijay Singh, Buick Classic.

WIECHERS, Jim—0-1: 1969: Lost to Bob Goalby, Robinson Open.

WOOD, Willie—0-1: 1990: Lost to Joey Sindelar, Hardee's Golf Classic.

WOOSNAM, Ian—1-0: 1991: Defeated Jim Hallet, USF&G Classic.

YANCEY, Bert—2-2: 1969: Defeated Bruce Devlin, Atlanta Classic. 1970: Lost to Ken Still, Kaiser Internat'l. 1971: Lost to Labron Harris, Robinson Open. 1972: Defeated Tom Ulozas, American Golf Classic.

ZARLEY, Kermit—0-1: 1976: Lost to Hale Irwin, Florida Citrus Open.

ZIEGLER, Larry—1-1: 1969: Defeated Homero Blancas, Michigan Golf Classic. 1972: Lost to Lou Graham, Liggett & Myers Open.

ZOELLER, Fuzzy—2-1: 1979: Defeated Ed Sneed and Tom Watson, Masters. 1983: Lost to Jim Colbert, Colonial National Invitation. 1984: Defeated Greg Norman, U.S. Open.

Greg Norman won both the Doral-Ryder Open and the British Open for the second time in 1993.

MERCEDES CHAMPIONSHIPS

Year	Winner	Score	Location	Par/Yards
TOURNAMENT OF CHAMPIONS				
1953	Al Besselink	280	Desert Inn CC, Las Vegas, NV	72/7209
1954	Art Wall	278	Desert Inn CC, Las Vegas, NV	72/7209
1955	Gene Littler	280	Desert Inn CC, Las Vegas, NV	72/7209
1956	Gene Littler	281	Desert Inn CC, Las Vegas, NV	72/7209
1957	Gene Littler	285	Desert Inn CC, Las Vegas, NV	72/7209
1958	Stan Leonard	275	Desert Inn CC, Las Vegas, NV	72/7209
1959	Mike Souchak	281	Desert Inn CC, Las Vegas, NV	72/7209
1960	Jerry Barber	268	Desert Inn CC, Las Vegas, NV	72/7209
1961	Sam Snead	273	Desert Inn CC, Las Vegas, NV	72/7209
1962	Arnold Palmer	276	Desert Inn CC, Las Vegas, NV	72/7209
1963	Jack Nicklaus	273	Desert Inn CC, Las Vegas, NV	72/7209
1964	Jack Nicklaus	279	Desert Inn CC, Las Vegas, NV	72/7209
1965	Arnold Palmer	277	Desert Inn CC, Las Vegas, NV	72/7209
1966	*Arnold Palmer	283	Desert Inn CC, Las Vegas, NV	72/7209
1967	Frank Beard	278	Stardust CC, Las Vegas, NV	71/6725
1968	Don January	276	Stardust CC, Las Vegas, NV	71/6725
1969	Gary Player	284	LaCosta CC, Carlsbad, CA	72/6911
1970	Frank Beard	273	LaCosta CC, Carlsbad, CA	72/6911
1971	Jack Nicklaus	279	LaCosta CC, Carlsbad, CA	72/6911
1972	*Bobby Mitchell	280	LaCosta CC, Carlsbad, CA	72/6911
1973	Jack Nicklaus	276	LaCosta CC, Carlsbad, CA	72/6911
1974	Johnny Miller	280	LaCosta CC, Carlsbad, CA	72/6911
MONY TOURNAMENT OF CHAMPIONS				
1975	*Al Geiberger	277	LaCosta CC, Carlsbad, CA	72/6911
1976	Don January	277	LaCosta CC, Carlsbad, CA	72/6911
1977	*Jack Nicklaus	281	LaCosta CC, Carlsbad, CA	72/6911
1978	Gary Player	281	LaCosta CC, Carlsbad, CA	72/6911
1979	Tom Watson	275	LaCosta CC, Carlsbad, CA	72/6911
1980	Tom Watson	276	LaCosta CC, Carlsbad, CA	72/6911
1981	Lee Trevino	273	LaCosta CC, Carlsbad, CA	72/6911
1982	Lanny Wadkins	280	LaCosta CC, Carlsbad, CA	72/6911
1983	Lanny Wadkins	280	LaCosta CC, Carlsbad, CA	72/6911
1984	Tom Watson	274	LaCosta CC, Carlsbad, CA	72/7022
1985	Tom Kite	275	LaCosta CC, Carlsbad, CA	72/7022
1986	Calvin Peete	267	LaCosta CC, Carlsbad, CA	72/7022
1987	Mac O'Grady	278	LaCosta CC, Carlsbad, CA	72/7022
1988	~Steve Pate	202	LaCosta CC, Carlsbad, CA	72/7022
1989	Steve Jones	279	LaCosta CC, Carlsbad, CA	72/7022
INFINITI TOURNAMENT OF CHAMPIONS				
1990	Paul Azinger	272	LaCosta CC, Carlsbad, CA	72/7022
1991	Tom Kite	272	LaCosta CC, Carlsbad, CA	72/7022
1992	*Steve Elkington	279	LaCosta CC, Carlsbad, CA	72/7022
1993	Davis Love III	272	LaCosta CC, Carlsbad, CA	72/7022

UNITED AIRLINES HAWAIIAN OPEN

Year	Winner	Score	Location	Par/Yards
HAWAIIAN OPEN				
1965	*Gay Brewer	281	Waialae CC, Honolulu, HI	72/7234
1966	Ted Makalena	271	Waialae CC, Honolulu, HI	72/7234
1967	*Dudley Wysong	284	Waialae CC, Honolulu, HI	72/7234
1968	Lee Trevino	272	Waialae CC, Honolulu, HI	72/7234
1969	Bruce Crampton	274	Waialae CC, Honolulu, HI	72/7234
1970	No Tournament			
1971	Tom Shaw	273	Waialae CC, Honolulu, HI	72/7234
1972	*Grier Jones	274	Waialae CC, Honolulu, HI	72/7234

KEY * = Playoff # = Amateur ~ = Rain-curtailed

Past Winners of PGA TOUR Events (cont'd.)

Year	Winner	Score	Location	Par/Yards
1973	John Schlee	273	Waialae CC, Honolulu, HI	72/7234
1974	Jack Nicklaus	271	Waialae CC, Honolulu, HI	72/7234
1975	Gary Groh	274	Waialae CC, Honolulu, HI	72/7234
1976	Ben Crenshaw	270	Waialae CC, Honolulu, HI	72/7234
1977	Bruce Lietzke	273	Waialae CC, Honolulu, HI	72/7234
1978	*Hubert Green	274	Waialae CC, Honolulu, HI	72/7234
1979	Hubert Green	267	Waialae CC, Honolulu, HI	72/7234
1980	Andy Bean	266	Waialae CC, Honolulu, HI	72/7234
1981	Hale Irwin	265	Waialae CC, Honolulu, HI	72/7234
1982	Wayne Levi	277	Waialae CC, Honolulu, HI	72/7234
1983	Isao Aoki	268	Waialae CC, Honolulu, HI	72/7234
1984	*Jack Renner	271	Waialae CC, Honolulu, HI	72/7234
1985	Mark O'Meara	267	Waialae CC, Honolulu, HI	72/6975
1986	Corey Pavin	272	Waialae CC, Honolulu, HI	72/6975
1987	*Corey Pavin	270	Waialae CC, Honolulu, HI	72/6975
1988	Lanny Wadkins	271	Waialae CC, Honolulu, HI	72/6975
1989	~Gene Sauers	197	Waialae CC, Honolulu, HI	72/6975
1990	David Ishii	279	Waialae CC, Honolulu, HI	72/6975

UNITED HAWAIIAN OPEN

Year	Winner	Score	Location	Par/Yards
1991	Lanny Wadkins`	270	Waialae CC, Honolulu, HI	72/6975

UNITED AIRLINES HAWAIIAN OPEN

Year	Winner	Score	Location	Par/Yards
1992	John Cook	265	Waialae CC, Honolulu, HI	72/6975
1993	Howard Twitty	269	Waialae CC, Honolulu, HI	72/6975

NORTHERN TELECOM OPEN

Year	Winner	Score	Location	Par/Yards

TUCSON OPEN

Year	Winner	Score	Location	Par/Yards
1945	Ray Mangrum	268	El Rio G&CC, Tucson, AZ	70/6418
1946	Jimmy Demaret	268	El Rio G&CC, Tucson, AZ	70/6418
1947	Jimmy Demaret	264	El Rio G&CC, Tucson, AZ	70/6418
1948	Skip Alexander	264	El Rio G&CC, Tucson, AZ	70/6418
1949	Lloyd Mangrum	263	El Rio G&CC, Tucson, AZ	70/6418
1950	Chandler Harper	267	El Rio G&CC, Tucson, AZ	70/6418
1951	Lloyd Mangrum	269	El Rio G&CC, Tucson, AZ	70/6418
1952	Henry Williams	274	El Rio G&CC, Tucson, AZ	70/6418
1953	Tommy Bolt	265	El Rio G&CC, Tucson, AZ	70/6418
1954	No Tournament			
1955	Tommy Bolt	265	El Rio G&CC, Tucson, AZ	70/6418
1956	Ted Kroll	264	El Rio G&CC, Tucson, AZ	70/6418
1957	Dow Finsterwald	269	El Rio G&CC, Tucson, AZ	70/6418
1958	Lionel Hebert	265	El Rio G&CC, Tucson, AZ	70/6418
1959	Gene Littler	266	El Rio G&CC, Tucson, AZ	70/6418
1960	Don January	271	El Rio G&CC, Tucson, AZ	70/6418

HOME OF THE SUN INVITATIONAL

Year	Winner	Score	Location	Par/Yards
1961	*Dave Hill	269	El Rio G&CC, Tucson, AZ	70/6418

TUCSON OPEN

Year	Winner	Score	Location	Par/Yards
1962	Phil Rodgers	263	El Rio G&CC, Tucson, AZ	70/6418
1963	Don January	266	49er CC, Tucson, AZ	72/6722
1964	Jack Cupit	274	49er CC, Tucson, AZ	72/6722
1965	Bob Charles	271	Tucson National GC, Tucson, AZ	72/7305
1966	*Joe Campbell	278	Tucson National GC, Tucson, AZ	72/7305
1967	Arnold Palmer	273	Tucson National GC, Tucson, AZ	72/7305
1968	George Knudson	273	Tucson National GC, Tucson, AZ	72/7305
1969	Lee Trevino	271	Tucson National GC, Tucson, AZ	72/7305
1970	*Lee Trevino	275	Tucson National GC, Tucson, AZ	72/7305
1971	J.C. Snead	273	Tucson National GC, Tucson, AZ	72/7305
1972	Miller Barber	273	Tucson National GC, Tucson, AZ	72/7305

DEAN MARTIN TUCSON OPEN

Year	Winner	Score	Location	Par/Yards
1973	Bruce Crampton	277	Tucson National GC, Tucson, AZ	72/7305
1974	Johnny Miller	272	Tucson National GC, Tucson, AZ	72/7305
1975	Johnny Miller	263	Tucson National GC, Tucson, AZ	72/7305

KEY * = Playoff # = Amateur ~ = Rain-curtailed

Past Winners of PGA TOUR Events (cont'd.)

Year	Winner	Score	Location	Par/Yards
NBC TUCSON OPEN				
1976	Johnny Miller	274	Tucson National GC, Tucson, AZ	72/7305
JOE GARAGIOLA TUCSON OPEN				
1977	*Bruce Lietzke	275	Tucson National GC, Tucson, AZ	72/7305
1978	Tom Watson	276	Tucson National GC, Tucson, AZ	72/7305
1979	Bruce Lietzke	265	Randolph Park Muncipal GC, (North), Tucson, AZ	70/6860
1980	Jim Colbert	270	Tucson National GC, Tucson, AZ	72/7305
1981	Johnny Miller	265	Randolph Park Municipal GC, (North), Tucson, AZ	70/6860
1982	Craig Stadler	266	Randolph Park Municipal GC, (North), Tucson, AZ	70/6860
1983	*Gil Morgan	271	Randolph Park Municipal GC, (North), Tucson, AZ	70/6860
SEIKO-TUCSON MATCH PLAY CHAMPIONSHIPS				
1984	Tom Watson	2&1	Randolph Park Municipal GC, (North), Tucson, AZ	70/6860
1985	Jim Thorpe	4&3	Randolph Park Municipal GC, (North), Tucson, AZ	70/6860
1986	Jim Thorpe	67	Randolph Park Municipal GC, (North), Tucson, AZ	70/6860
SEIKO-TUCSON OPEN				
1987	Mike Reid	268	TPC at StarPass, Tucson, AZ	72/7010
NORTHERN TELECOM TUCSON OPEN				
1988	David Frost	266	TPC at StarPass, Tucson, AZ	72/7010
1989	No Tournament held due to the change on schedule from end of year to beginning of year.			
1990	Robert Gamez	270	TPC at StarPass, Tucson, AZ	72/7010
			Randolph Park Municipal GC, Tucson, AZ	72/6902
NORTHERN TELECOM OPEN				
1991	#Phil Mickelson	272	TPC at StarPass, Tucson, AZ	72/7010
			Tucson National GC, Tucson, AZ	72/7305
1992	Lee Janzen	270	TPC at StarPass, Tucson, AZ	72/7010
			Tucson National GC, Tucson, AZ	72/7305
1993	Larry Mize	271	Tucson National GC, Tucson, AZ	72/7148
			StarrPass GC, Tucson, AZ	72/7010

PHOENIX OPEN

Year	Winner	Score	Location	Par/Yards
PHOENIX OPEN INVITATIONAL				
1935	Ky Laffoon	281	Phoenix CC, Phoenix, AZ	71/6726
1936-				
1938	No Tournaments			
1939	Byron Nelson	198	Phoenix CC, Phoenix, AZ	71/6726
1940	Ed Oliver	205	Phoenix CC, Phoenix, AZ	71/6726
1941-				
1943	No Tournaments			
1944	*Harold McSpaden	273	Phoenix CC, Phoenix, AZ	71/6726
1945	Byron Nelson	274	Phoenix CC, Phoenix, AZ	71/6726
1946	*Ben Hogan	273	Phoenix CC, Phoenix, AZ	71/6726
1947	Ben Hogan	270	Phoenix CC, Phoenix, AZ	71/6726
1948	Bobby Locke	268	Phoenix CC, Phoenix, AZ	71/6726
1949	*Jimmy Demaret	278	Phoenix CC, Phoenix, AZ	71/6726
1950	Jimmy Demaret	269	Phoenix CC, Phoenix, AZ	71/6726
1951	Lew Worsham	272	Phoenix CC, Phoenix, AZ	71/6726
1952	Lloyd Mangrum	274	Phoenix CC, Phoenix, AZ	71/6726
1953	Lloyd Mangrum	272	Phoenix CC, Phoenix, AZ	71/6726
1954	*Ed Furgol	272	Phoenix CC, Phoenix, AZ	71/6726
1955	Gene Littler	275	Arizona CC, Phoenix, AZ	70/6216
1956	Cary Middlecoff	276	Phoenix CC, Phoenix, AZ	71/6726
1957	Billy Casper	271	Arizona CC, Phoenix, AZ	70/6216
1958	Ken Venturi	274	Phoenix CC, Phoenix, AZ	71/6726
1959	Gene Littler	268	Arizona CC, Phoenix, AZ	70/6216
1960	*Jack Fleck	273	Phoenix CC, Phoenix, AZ	71/6726
1961	*Arnold Palmer	270	Arizona CC, Phoenix, AZ	70/6216
1962	Arnold Palmer	269	Phoenix CC, Phoenix, AZ	71/6726
1963	Arnold Palmer	273	Arizona CC, Phoenix, AZ	70/6216
1964	Jack Nicklaus	271	Phoenix CC, Phoenix, AZ	71/6726
1965	Rod Funseth	274	Arizona CC, Phoenix, AZ	70/6216

KEY * = Playoff # = Amateur ~ = Rain-curtailed

Year	Winner	Score	Location	Par/Yards
1966	Dudley Wysong	278	Phoenix CC, Phoenix, AZ	71/6726
1967	Julius Boros	272	Arizona CC, Phoenix, AZ	70/6216
1968	George Knudson	272	Phoenix CC, Phoenix, AZ	71/6726
1969	Gene Littler	263	Arizona CC, Phoenix, AZ	70/6216
1970	Dale Douglass	271	Phoenix CC, Phoenix, AZ	71/6726
1971	Miller Barber	261	Arizona CC, Phoenix, AZ	70/6216
1972	Homero Blancas	273	Phoenix CC, Phoenix, AZ	71/6726
1973	Bruce Crampton	268	Arizona CC, Phoenix, AZ	70/6216
1974	Johnny Miller	271	Phoenix CC, Phoenix, AZ	71/6726
1975	Johnny Miller	260	Phoenix CC, Phoenix, AZ	71/6726
1976	Bob Gilder	268	Phoenix CC, Phoenix, AZ	71/6726
1977	*Jerry Pate	277	Phoenix CC, Phoenix, AZ	71/6726
1978	Miller Barber	272	Phoenix CC, Phoenix, AZ	71/6726
1979	~Ben Crenshaw	199	Phoenix CC, Phoenix, AZ	71/6726
1980	Jeff Mitchell	272	Phoenix CC, Phoenix, AZ	71/6726
1981	David Graham	268	Phoenix CC, Phoenix, AZ	71/6726
1982	Lanny Wadkins	263	Phoenix CC, Phoenix, AZ	71/6726
1983	*Bob Gilder	271	Phoenix CC, Phoenix, AZ	71/6726
1984	Tom Purtzer	268	Phoenix CC, Phoenix, AZ	71/6726
1985	Calvin Peete	270	Phoenix CC, Phoenix, AZ	71/6726
1986	Hal Sutton	267	Phoenix CC, Phoenix, AZ	71/6726
1987	Paul Azinger	268	TPC of Scottsdale, Scottsdale, AZ	71/6992
1988	*Sandy Lyle	269	TPC of Scottsdale, Scottsdale, AZ	71/6992
1989	Mark Calcavecchia	263	TPC of Scottsdale, Scottsdale, AZ	71/6992
1990	Tommy Armour III	267	TPC of Scottsdale, Scottsdale, AZ	71/6992
1991	Nolan Henke	268	TPC of Scottsdale, Scottsdale, AZ	71/6992
1992	Mark Calcavecchia	264	TPC of Scottsdale, Scottsdale, AZ	71/6992
1993	Lee Janzen	273	TPC of Scottsdale, Scottsdale, AZ	71/6992

AT&T PEBBLE BEACH NATIONAL PRO-AM

Year	Winner	Score	Location	Par/Yards
BING CROSBY PROFESSIONAL-AMATEUR				
1937	Sam Snead	68	Rancho Santa Fe CC, San Diego, CA	73/6769
1938	Sam Snead	139	Rancho Santa Fe CC, San Diego, CA	73/6769
1939	Dutch Harrison	138	Rancho Santa Fe CC, San Diego, CA	73/6769
1940	Ed Oliver	135	Rancho Santa Fe CC, San Diego, CA	73/6769
1941	Sam Snead	136	Rancho Santa Fe CC, San Diego, CA	73/6769
1942	Tie-Lloyd Mangrum			
	Leland Gibson	133	Rancho Santa Fe CC, San Diego, CA	73/6769
1943—1946 No Tournaments				
1947	Tie-Ed Furgol	213	Cypress Point CC, Monterey Peninsula, CA	72/6506
	George Fazio		Monterey Peninsula CC, Monterey Peninsula, CA	71/6356
			Pebble Beach GL, Monterey Peninsula, CA	72/6815
1948	Lloyd Mangrum	205	Cypress Point CC, Monterey Peninsula, CA	72/6506
			Monterey Peninsula CC, Monterey Peninsula, CA	71/6356
			Pebble Beach GL, Monterey Peninsula, CA	72/6815
1949	Ben Hogan	208	Cypress Point CC, Monterey Peninsula, CA	72/6506
			Monterey Peninsula CC, Monterey Peninsula, CA	71/6356
			Pebble Beach GL, Monterey Peninsula, CA	72/6815
1950	Tie-Sam Snead	214	Cypress Point CC, Monterey Peninsula, CA	72/6506
	Jack Burke, Jr		Monterey Peninsula CC, Monterey Peninsula, CA	71/6356
	Smiley Quick		Pebble Beach GL, Monterey Peninsula, CA	72/6815
	Dave Douglas			
1951	Byron Nelson	209	Cypress Point CC, Monterey Peninsula, CA	72/6506
			Monterey Peninsula CC, Monterey Peninsula, CA	71/6356
			Pebble Beach GL, Monterey Peninsula, CA	72/6815
1952	Jimmy Demaret	145	Cypress Point CC, Monterey Peninsula, CA	72/6506
			Monterey Peninsula CC, Monterey Peninsula, CA	71/6356
			Pebble Beach GL, Monterey Peninsula, CA	72/6815

KEY * = Playoff # = Amateur ~ = Rain-curtailed

Past Winners of PGA TOUR Events *(cont'd.)*

Year	Winner	Score	Location	Par/Yards

THE BING CROSBY PROFESSIONAL-AMATEUR INVITATIONAL

Year	Winner	Score	Location	Par/Yards
1953	Lloyd Mangrum	204	Cypress Point CC, Monterey Peninsula, CA	72/6506
			Pebble Beach GL, Monterey Pennsula, CA	72/6815
1954	Dutch Harrison	210	Cypress Point CC, Monterey Peninsula, CA	72/6506
			Monterey Peninsula CC, Monterey Peninsula, CA	71/6356
			Pebble Beach GL, Monterey Peninsula, CA	72/6815
1955	Cary Middlecoff	209	Cypress Point CC, Monterey Peninsula, CA	72/6506
			Monterey Peninsula CC, Monterey Peninsula, CA	71/6356
			Pebble Beach GL, Monterey Peninsula, CA	72/6815

BING CROSBY NATIONAL PROFESSIONAL-AMATEUR GOLF CHAMPIONSHIP

Year	Winner	Score	Location	Par/Yards
1956	Cary Middlecoff	202	Cypress Point CC, Monterey Peninsula, CA	72/6506
			Monterey Peninsula CC, Monterey Peninsula, CA	71/6356
			Pebble Beach GL, Monterey Peninsula, CA	72/6815
1957	Jay Hebert	213	Cypress Point CC, Monterey Peninsula, CA	72/6506
			Monterey Peninsula CC, Monterey Peninsula, CA	71/6356
			Pebble Beach GL, Monterey Peninsula, CA	72/6815
1958	Billy Casper	277	Cypress Point CC, Monterey Peninsula, CA	72/6506
			Monterey Peninsula CC, Monterey Peninsula, CA	71/6356
			Pebble Beach GL, Monterey Peninsula, CA	72/6815

BING CROSBY NATIONAL

Year	Winner	Score	Location	Par/Yards
1959	Art Wall	279	Cypress Point CC, Monterey Peninsula, CA	72/6506
			Monterey Peninsula CC, Monterey Peninsula, CA	71/6356
			Pebble Beach GL, Monterey Peninsula, CA	72/6815
1960	Ken Venturi	286	Cypress Point CC, Monterey Peninsula, CA	72/6506
			Monterey Peninsula CC, Monterey Peninsula, CA	71/6356
			Pebble Beach GL, Monterey Peninsula, CA	72/6815
1961	Bob Rosburg	282	Cypress Point CC, Monterey Peninsula, CA	72/6506
			Monterey Peninsula CC, Monterey Peninsula, CA	71/6356
			Pebble Beach GL, Monterey Peninsula, CA	72/6815
1962	*Doug Ford	286	Cypress Point CC, Monterey Peninsula, CA	72/6506
			Monterey Peninsula CC, Monterey Peninsula, CA	71/6356
			Pebble Beach GL, Monterey Peninsula, CA	72/6815
1963	Billy Casper	285	Cypress Point CC, Monterey Peninsula, CA	72/6506
			Monterey Peninsula CC, Monterey Peninsula, CA	71/6356
			Pebble Beach GL, Monterey Peninsula, CA	72/6815

BING CROSBY NATIONAL PROFESSIONAL-AMATEUR

Year	Winner	Score	Location	Par/Yards
1964	Tony Lema	284	Cypress Point CC, Monterey Peninsula, CA	72/6506
			Monterey Peninsula CC, Monterey Peninsula, CA	71/6356
			Pebble Beach GL, Monterey Peninsula, CA	72/6815
1965	Bruce Crampton	284	Cypress Point CC, Monterey Peninsula, CA	72/6506
			Monterey Peninsula CC, Monterey Peninsula, CA	71/6356
			Pebble Beach GL, Monterey Peninsula, CA	72/6815
1966	Don Massengale	283	Cypress Point CC, Monterey Peninsula, CA	72/6506
			Monterey Peninsula CC, Monterey Peninsula, CA	71/6356
			Pebble Beach GL, Monterey Peninsula, CA	72/6815
1967	Jack Nicklaus	284	Pebble Beach GL, Monterey Peninsula, CA	72/6815
			Cypress Point CC, Monterey Peninsula, CA	72/6506
			Spyglass Hill GC, Monterey Peninsula, CA	72/6810
1968	*Johnny Pott	285	Pebble Beach GL, Monterey Peninsula, CA	72/6815
			Cypress Point CC, Monterey Peninsula, CA	72/6506
			Spyglass Hill GC, Monterey Peninsula, CA	72/6810
1969	George Archer	283	Pebble Beach GL, Monterey Peninsula, CA	72/6815
			Cypress Point CC, Monterey Peninsula, CA	72/6506
			Spyglass Hill GC, Monterey Peninsula, CA	72/6810
1970	Bert Yancey	278	Pebble Beach GL, Monterey Peninsula, CA	72/6815
			Cypress Point CC, Monterey Peninsula, CA	72/6506
			Spyglass Hill GC, Monterey Peninsula, CA	72/6810
1971	Tom Shaw	278	Pebble Beach GL, Monterey Peninsula, CA	72/6815
			Cypress Point CC, Monterey Peninsula, CA	72/6506
			Spyglass Hill GC, Monterey Peninsula, CA	72/6810
1972	*Jack Nicklaus	284	Pebble Beach GL, Monterey Peninsula, CA	72/6815
			Cypress Point CC, Monterey Peninsula, CA	72/6506
			Spyglass Hill GC, Monterey Peninsula, CA	72/6810

KEY * = Playoff # = Amateur ~ = Rain-curtailed

Year	Winner	Score	Location	Par/Yards
1973	*Jack Nicklaus	282	Pebble Beach GL, Monterey Peninsula, CA	72/6815
			Cypress Point CC, Monterey Peninsula, CA	72/6506
			Spyglass Hill GC, Monterey Peninsula, CA	72/6810
1974	~Johnny Miller	208	Pebble Beach GL, Monterey Peninsula, CA	72/6815
			Cypress Point CC, Monterey Peninsula, CA	72/6506
			Spyglass Hill GC, Monterey Peninsula, CA	72/6810
1975	Gene Littler	280	Pebble Beach GL, Monterey Peninsula, CA	72/6815
			Cypress Point CC, Monterey Peninsula, CA	72/6506
			Spyglass Hill GC, Monterey Peninsula, CA	72/6810
1976	Ben Crenshaw	281	Pebble Beach GL, Monterey Peninsula, CA	72/6815
			Cypress Point CC, Monterey Peninsula, CA	72/6506
			Spyglass Hill GC, Monterey Peninsula, CA	72/6810
1977	Tom Watson	273	Pebble Beach GL, Monterey Peninsula, CA	72/6815
			Cypress Point CC, Monterey Peninsula, CA	72/6506
			Monterey Peninsula CC, Monterey Peninsula, CA	71/6400
1978	*Tom Watson	280	Pebble Beach GL, Monterey Peninsula, CA	72/6815
			Cypress Point CC, Monterey Peninsula, CA	72/6506
			Spyglass Hill GC, Monterey Peninsula, CA	72/6810
1979	Lon Hinkle	284	Pebble Beach GL, Monterey Peninsula, CA	72/6815
			Cypress Point CC, Monterey Peninsula, CA	72/6506
			Spyglass Hill GC, Monterey Peninsula, CA	72/6810
1980	George Burns	280	Pebble Beach GL, Monterey Peninsula, CA	72/6815
			Cypress Point CC, Monterey Peninsula, CA	72/6506
			Spyglass Hill GC, Monterey Peninsula, CA	72/6810
1981	~*John Cook	209	Pebble Beach GL, Monterey Peninsula, CA	72/6815
			Cypress Point CC, Monterey Peninsula, CA	72/6506
			Spyglass Hill GC, Monterey Peninsula, CA	72/6810
1982	Jim Simons	274	Pebble Beach GL, Monterey Peninsula, CA	72/6815
			Cypress Point CC, Monterey Peninsula, CA	72/6506
			Spyglass Hill GC, Monterey Peninsula, CA	72/6810
1983	Tom Kite	276	Pebble Beach GL, Monterey Peninsula, CA	72/6815
			Cypress Point CC, Monterey Peninsula, CA	72/6506
			Spyglass Hill GC, Monterey Peninsula CA	72/6810
1984	*Hale Irwin	278	Pebble Beach GL, Monterey Peninsula, CA	72/6815
			Cypress Point CC, Monterey Peninsula, CA	72/6506
			Spyglass Hill GC, Monterey Peninsula, CA	72/6810
1985	Mark O'Meara	283	Pebble Beach GL, Monterey Peninsula, CA	72/6815
			Cypress Point CC, Monterey Peninsula, CA	72/6506
			Spyglass Hill GC, Monterey Peninsula, CA	72/6810

AT&T PEBBLE BEACH NATIONAL PRO-AM

Year	Winner	Score	Location	Par/Yards
1986	~Fuzzy Zoeller	205	Pebble Beach GL, Monterey Peninsula, CA	72/6815
			Cypress Point CC, Monterey Peninsula, CA	72/6506
			Spyglass Hill GC, Monterey Peninsula, CA	72/6810
1987	Johnny Miller	278	Pebble Beach GL, Monterey Peninsula, CA	72/6815
			Cypress Point CC, Monterey Peninsula, CA	72/6506
			Spyglass Hill GC, Monterey Peninsula, CA	72/6810
1988	*Steve Jones	280	Pebble Beach GL, Monterey Peninsula, CA	72/6815
			Cypress Point CC, Monterey Peninsula, CA	72/6506
			Spyglass Hill GC, Monterey Peninsula, CA	72/6810
1989	Mark O'Meara	277	Pebble Beach GL, Monterey Peninsula, CA	72/6815
			Cypress Point CC, Monterey Peninsula, CA	72/6506
			Spyglass Hill GC, Monterey Peninsula, CA	72/6810
1990	Mark O'Meara	281	Pebble Beach GL, Monterey Peninsula, CA	72/6815
			Cypress Point CC, Monterey Peninsula, CA	72/6506
			Spyglass Hill GC, Monterey Peninsula, CA	72/6810
1991	Paul Azinger	274	Pebble Beach GL, Monterey Peninsula, CA	72/6815
			Spyglass Hill GC, Monterey Peninsula, CA	72/6810
			Poppy Hills GC, Monterey Peninsula, CA	72/6865
1992	*Mark O'Meara	275	Pebble Beach GL, Monterey Peninsula, CA	72/6815
			Spyglass Hill GC, Monterey Peninsula, CA	72/6810
			Poppy Hills GC, Monterey Peninsula, CA	72/6865

KEY * = Playoff # = Amateur ~ = Rain-curtailed

Past Winners of PGA TOUR Events (cont'd.)

Year	Winner	Score	Location	Par/Yards
1993	Brett Ogle	276	Pebble Beach GL, Monterey Peninsula, CA	72/6815
			Spyglass Hill GC, Monterey Peninsula, CA	72/6810
			Poppy Hills GC, Monterey Peninsula, CA	72/6865

NISSAN LOS ANGELES OPEN

Year	Winner	Score	Location	Par/Yards
LOS ANGELES OPEN				
1926	Harry Cooper	279	Los Angeles CC, Los Angeles, CA	71/6895 (North)
1927	Bobby Cruikshank	282	El Caballero CC, Los Angeles, CA	71/6830
1928	Mac Smith	284	Wilshire CC, Los Angeles, CA	71/6442
1929	Mac Smith	285	Riviera CC, Pacific Palisades, CA	71/7029
1930	Densmore Shute	296	Riviera CC, Pacific Palisades, CA	71/7029
1931	Ed Dudley	285	Wilshire CC, Los Angeles, CA	71/6442
1932	Mac Smith	281	Hillcrest CC, Los Angeles, CA	71/6911
1933	Craig Wood	281	Wilshire CC, Los Angeles, CA	71/6442
1934	Mac Smith	280	Los Angeles CC, Los Angeles, CA	71/6895 (North)
1935	*Vic Ghezzi	285	Los Angeles CC, Los Angeles, CA	71/6895 (North)
1936	Jimmy Hines	280	Los Angeles CC, Los Angeles, CA	71/6895 (North)
1937	Harry Cooper	274	Griffith Park, Los Angeles, CA	
			Wilson-72/6802, Harding-72/6488	
1938	Jimmy Thomson	273	Griffith Park, Los Angeles, CA	
			Wilson-72/6802, Harding-72/6488	
1939	Jimmy Demaret	274	Griffith Park, Los Angeles, CA	
			Wilson-72/6802, Harding-72/6488	
1940	Lawson Little	282	Los Angeles CC, Los Angeles, CA	71/6895 (North)
1941	Johnny Bulla	281	Riviera CC, Pacific Palisades, CA	71/7029
1942	*Ben Hogan	282	Hillcrest CC, Los Angeles, CA	71/6911
1943	No Tournament			
1944	Harold McSpaden	278	Wilshire CC, Los Angeles, CA	71/6442
1945	Sam Snead	283	Riviera CC, Pacific Palisades, CA	71/7029
1946	Byron Nelson	284	Riviera CC, Pacific Palisades, CA	71/7029
1947	Ben Hogan	280	Riviera CC, Pacific Palisades, CA	71/7029
1948	Ben Hogan	275	Riviera CC, Pacific Palisades, CA	71/7029
1949	Lloyd Mangrum	284	Riviera CC, Pacific Palisades, CA	71/7029
1950	*Sam Snead	280	Riviera CC, Pacific Palisades, CA	71/7029
1951	Lloyd Mangrum	280	Riviera CC, Pacific Palisades, CA	71/7029
1952	Tommy Bolt	289	Riviera CC, Pacific Palisades, CA	71/7029
1953	Lloyd Mangrum	280	Riviera CC, Pacific Palisades, CA	71/7029
1954	Fred Wampler	281	Fox Hills CC, Culver City, CA	N/A
1955	Gene Littler	276	Inglewood CC, Inglewood, CA	N/A
1956	Lloyd Mangrum	272	Rancho Municipal GC, Los Angeles, CA	71/6827
1957	Doug Ford	280	Rancho Municipal GC, Los Angeles, CA	71/6827
1958	Frank Stranahan	275	Rancho Municipal GC, Los Angeles, CA	71/6827
1959	Ken Venturi	278	Rancho Municipal GC, Los Angeles, CA	71/6827
1960	Dow Finsterwald	280	Rancho Municipal GC, Los Angeles, CA	71/6827
1961	Bob Goalby	275	Rancho Municipal GC, Los Angeles, CA	71/6827
1962	Phil Rodgers	268	Rancho Municipal GC, Los Angeles, CA	71/6827
1963	Arnold Palmer	274	Rancho Municipal GC, Los Angeles, CA	71/6827
1964	Paul Harney	280	Rancho Municipal GC, Los Angeles, CA	71/6827
1965	Paul Harney	276	Rancho Municipal GC, Los Angeles, CA	71/6827
1966	Arnold Palmer	273	Rancho Municipal GC, Los Angeles, CA	71/6827
1967	Arnold Palmer	269	Rancho Municipal GC, Los Angeles, CA	71/6827
1968	Billy Casper	274	Brookside GC, Pasadena, CA	71/7021
1969	*Charles Sifford	276	Rancho Municipal GC, Los Angeles, CA	71/6827
1970	*Billy Casper	276	Rancho Municipal GC. Los Angeles, CA	71/6827
GLEN CAMPBELL LOS ANGELES OPEN				
1971	*Bob Lunn	274	Rancho Municipal GC, Los Angeles, CA	7 i/6827
1972	*George Archer	270	Rancho Municipal GC, Los Angeles, CA	71/6827
1973	Rod Funseth	276	Riviera CC, Pacific Palisades, CA	71/7029
1974	Dave Stockton	276	Riviera CC, Pacific Palisades, CA	71/7029
1975	Pat Fitzsimons	275	Riviera CC, Pacific Palisades, CA	71/7029

KEY * = Playoff # = Amateur ~ = Rain-curtailed

Year	Winner	Score	Location	Par/Yards
1976	Hale Irwin	272	Riviera CC, Pacific Palisades, CA	71/7029
1977	Tom Purtzer	273	Riviera CC, Pacific Palisades, CA	71/7029
1978	Gil Morgan	278	Riviera CC, Pacific Palisades, CA	71/7029
1979	Lanny Wadkins	276	Riviera CC, Pacific Palisades, CA	71/7029
1980	Tom Watson	276	Riviera CC, Pacific Palisades, CA	71/7029
1981	Johnny Miller	270	Riviera CC, Pacific Palisades, CA	71/7029
1982	*Tom Watson	271	Riviera CC, Pacific Palisades, CA	71/7029
1983	Gil Morgan	270	Rancho Municipal GC, Los Angeles, CA	71/6827
LOS ANGELES OPEN				
1984	David Edwards	279	Riviera CC, Pacific Palisades, CA	71/7029
1985	Lanny Wadkins	264	Riviera CC, Pacific Palisades, CA	71/7029
1986	Doug Tewell	270	Riviera CC, Pacific Palisades, CA	71/7029
LOS ANGELES OPEN PRESENTED BY NISSAN				
1987	*Tze-Chung Chen	275	Riviera CC, Pacific Palisades, CA	71/7029
1988	Chip Beck	267	Riviera CC, Pacific Palisades, CA	71/7029
NISSAN LOS ANGELES OPEN				
1989	Mark Calcavecchia	272	Riviera CC, Pacific Palisades, CA	71/7029
1990	Fred Couples	266	Riviera CC, Pacific Palisades, CA	71/7029
1991	Ted Schulz	272	Riviera CC, Pacific Palisades, CA	71/7029
1992	*Fred Couples	269	Riviera CC, Pacific Palisades, CA	71/7029
1993	~Tom Kite	206	Riviera CC, Pacific Palisades, CA	71/7029

BOB HOPE CHRYSLER CLASSIC

Year	Winner	Score	Location	Par/Yards
PALM SPRINGS GOLF CLASSIC				
1960	Arnold Palmer	338	Bermuda Dunes CC, Palm Springs, CA	72/6837
			Indian Wells CC, Indian Wells, CA	72/6478
			Tamarisk CC, Palm Springs, CA	72/6869
			Thunderbird CC, Palm Springs, CA	N/A
1961	Billy Maxwell	345	Bermuda Dunes CC, Palm Springs, CA	72/6837
			Indian Wells CC, Indian Wells, CA	72/6478
			Tamarisk CC, Palm Springs, CA	72/6869
			Thunderbird CC, Palm Springs, CA	N/A
			Eldorado CC, Palm Springs, CA	72/6708
1962	Arnold Palmer	342	Bermuda Dunes CC, Palm Springs, CA	72/6837
			Indian Wells CC, Indian Wells, CA	72/6478
			Tamarisk CC, Palm Springs, CA	72/6869
			Thunderbird CC, Palm Springs, CA	N/A
			Eldorado CC, Palm Springs, CA	72/6708
1963	*Jack Nicklaus	345	Bermuda Dunes CC, Palm Springs, CA	72/6837
			Indian Wells CC, Indian Wells, CA	72/6478
			Tamarisk CC, Palm Springs, CA	72/6869
			Eldorado CC, Palm Springs, CA	72/6708
1964	*Tommy Jacobs	348	Bermuda Dunes CC, Palm Springs, CA	72/6837
			Indian Wells CC, Indian Wells, CA	72/6478
			Eldorado CC, Palm Springs, CA	72/6708
			La Quinta CC, La Quinta, CA	72/6911
BOB HOPE DESERT CLASSIC				
1965	Billy Casper	348	Bermuda Dunes CC, Palm Springs, CA	72/6837
			Indian Wells CC, Indian Wells, CA	72/6478
			Eldorado CC, Palm Springs, CA	72/6708
			La Quinta CC, La Quinta, CA	72/6911
1966	*Doug Sanders	349	Bermuda Dunes CC, Palm Springs, CA	72/6837
			Indian Wells CC, Indian Wells, CA	72/6478
			Eldorado CC, Palm Springs, CA	72/6708
			La Quinta CC, La Quinta. CA	72/6911
1967	Tom Nieporte	349	Bermuda Dunes CC, Palm Springs, CA	72,6837
			Indian Wells CC, Indian Wells, CA	72/6478
			Eldorado CC, Palm Springs, CA	72/6708
			La Quinta CC, La Quinta, CA	72/6911

KEY * = Playoff # = Amateur ~ = Rain-curtailed

Past Winners of PGA TOUR Events *(cont'd.)*

Year	Winner	Score	Location	Par/Yards
1968	*Arnold Palmer	348	Bermuda Dunes CC, Palm Springs, CA	72/6837
			Indian Wells CC, Indian Wells, CA	72/6478
			Eldorado CC, Pa!m Springs, CA	72/6708
			La Quinta CC, La Quinta, CA	72/6911
1969	Billy Casper	345	Bermuda Dunes CC, Palm Springs, CA	72/6837
			Indian Wells CC, Indian Wells, CA	72/6478
			Tamarisk CC, Palm Springs, CA	72/6869
			La Quinta CC, La Quinta, CA	72/6911
1970	Bruce Devlin	339	Bermuda Dunes CC, Palm Springs, CA	72/6837
			Indian Wells CC, Indian Wells, CA	72/6478
			Eldorado CC, Palm Springs, CA	72/6708
			La Quinta CC, La Quinta, CA	72/6911
1971	*Arnold Palmer	342	Bermuda Dunes CC, Palm Springs, CA	72/6837
			Indian Wells CC, Indian Wells, CA	72/6478
			Tamarisk CC, Palm Springs, CA	72/6869
			La Quinta CC, La Quinta, CA	72/6911
1972	Bob Rosburg	344	Bermuda Dunes CC, Palm Springs, CA	72/6837
			Indian Wells CC, Indian Wells, CA	72/6478
			Eldorado CC, Palm Springs, CA	72/6708
			La Quinta CC, La Quinta, CA	72/6911
1973	Arnold Palmer	343	Bermuda Dunes CC, Palm Springs, CA	72/6837
			Indian Wells CC, Indian Wells, CA	72/6478
			Tamarisk CC, Palm Springs, CA	72/6869
			La Quinta CC, La Quinta, CA	72/6911
1974	Hubert Green	341	Bermuda Dunes CC, Palm Springs, CA	72/6837
			Indian Wells CC, Indian Wells, CA	72/6478
			Eldorado CC, Palm Springs, CA	72/6708
			La Quinta CC, La Quinta, CA	72/6911
1975	Johnny Miller	339	Bermuda Dunes CC, Palm Springs, CA	72/6837
			Indian Wells CC, Indian Wells, CA	72/6478
			Tamarisk CC, Palm Springs, CA	72/6869
			La Quinta CC, La Quinta, CA	72/6911
1976	Johnny Miller	344	Bermuda Dunes CC, Palm Springs, CA	72/6837
			Indian Wells CC, Indian Wells, CA	72/6478
			Eldorado CC, Palm Springs, CA	72/6708
			La Quinta CC, La Quinta, CA	72/6911
1977	Rik Massengale	337	Bermuda Dunes CC, Palm Springs, CA	72/6837
			Indian Wells CC, Indian Wells, CA	72/6478
			Tamarisk CC, Palm Springs, CA	72/6869
			La Quinta CC, La Quinta, CA	72/6911
1978	Bill Rogers	339	Bermuda Dunes CC, Palm Springs, CA	72/6837
			Indian Wells CC, Indian Wells, CA	72/6478
			Eldorado CC, Palm Springs, CA	72/6708
			La Quinta CC, La Quinta, CA	72/6911
1979	John Mahaffey	343	Bermuda Dunes CC, Palm Springs, CA	72/6837
			Indian Wells CC, Indian Wells, CA	72/6478
			Tamarisk CC, Palm Springs, CA	72/6869
			La Quinta CC, La Quinta, CA	72/6911
1980	Craig Stadler	343	Bermuda Dunes CC, Palm Springs, CA	72/6837
			Indian Wells CC, Indian Wells, CA	72/6478
			Eldorado CC, Palm Springs, CA	72/6708
			La Quinta CC, La Quinta, CA	72/6911
1981	Bruce Lietzke	335	Bermuda Dunes CC, Palm Springs, CA	72/6837
			Indian Wells CC, Indian Wells, CA	72/6478
			Tamarisk CC, Palm Springs, CA	72/6869
			La Quinta CC, La Quinta, CA	72/6911
1982	*Ed Fiori	335	Bermuda Dunes CC, Palm Springs, CA	72/6837
			Indian Wells CC, Indian Wells, CA	72/6478
			Eldorado CC, Palm Springs, CA	72/6708
			La Quinta CC, La Quinta, CA	72/6911

KEY * = Playoff # = Amateur ~ = Rain-curtailed

Past Winners of PGA TOUR Events *(cont'd.)*

Year	Winner	Score	Location	Par/Yards
1983	*Keith Fergus	335	Bermuda Dunes CC, Palm Springs, CA	72/6837
			Indian Wells CC, Indian Wells, CA	72/6478
			Tamarisk CC, Palm Springs, CA	72/6869
			La Quinta CC, La Quinta, CA	72/6911
BOB HOPE CLASSIC				
1984	*John Mahaffey	340	Bermuda Dunes CC, Palm Springs, CA	72/6837
			Indian Wells CC, Indian Wells, CA	72/6478
			Eldorado CC, Palm Springs, CA	72/6708
			La Quinta CC, La Quinta, CA	72/6911
1985	*Lanny Wadkins	333	Bermuda Dunes CC, Palm Springs, CA	72/6837
			Indian Wells CC, Indian Wells, CA	72/6478
			Tamarisk CC, Palm Springs, CA	72/6869
			La Quinta CC, La Quinta, CA	72/6911
BOB HOPE CHRYSLER CLASSIC				
1986	*Donnie Hammond	335	Bermuda Dunes CC, Palm Springs, CA	72/6837
			Indian Wells CC, Indian Wells, CA	72/6478
			Eldorado CC, Palm Springs, CA	72/6708
			La Quinta CC, La Quinta, CA	72/6911
1987	Corey Pavin	341	Bermuda Dunes CC, Palm Springs, CA	72/6837
			Indian Wells CC, Indian Wells, CA	72/6478
			Tamarisk CC, Palm Springs, CA	72/6869
			TPC at PGA West, La Quinta, CA	72/7002
1988	Jay Haas	338	Bermuda Dunes CC, Palm Springs, CA	72/6837
			Indian Wells CC, Indian Wells, CA	72/6478
			La Quinta CC, La Quinta, CA	72/6911
			Palmer Course at PGA West, La Quinta, CA	72/6924
1989	*Steve Jones	343	Bermuda Dunes CC, Palm Springs, CA	72/6837
			Indian Wells CC, Indian Wells, CA	72/6478
			Eldorado CC, Palm Springs, CA	72/6708
			PGA West/Palmer Course, La Quinta, CA	72/6924
1990	Peter Jacobsen	339	PGA West/Palmer Course, La Quinta, CA	72/6924
			Bermuda Dunes CC, Palm Springs, CA	72/6927
			Indian Wells CC, Indian Wells, CA	72/6478
			Tamarisk CC, Palm Springs, CA	72/6875
1991	*Corey Pavin	331	PGA West/Palmer Course, La Quinta, CA	72/6924
			Bermuda Dunes CC, Palm Springs, CA	72/6927
			Indian Wells CC, Indian Wells, CA	72/6478
			La Quinta CC, La Quinta, CA	72/6911
1992	*John Cook	336	PGA West/Palmer Course, La Quinta, CA	72/6924
			Bermuda Dunes CC, Palm Springs, CA	72/6927
			Indian Wells CC, Indian Wells, CA	72/6478
			La Quinta CC, La Quinta, CA	72/6911
1993	Tom Kite	325	PGA West/Palmer Course, La Quinta, CA	72/6924
			Bermuda Dunes CC, Palm Springs, CA	72/6927
			Indian Wells CC, Indian Wells, CA	72/6478
			Tamarisk CC, La Quinta, CA	72/6881

BUICK INVITATIONAL OF CALIFORNIA

Year	Winner	Score	Location	Par/Yards
SAN DIEGO OPEN				
1952	Ted Kroll	276	San Diego CC, San Diego, CA	72/6931
1953	Tommy Bolt	274	San Diego CC, San Diego, CA	72/6931
1954	#Gene Littler	274	Rancho Santa Fe GC, San Diego, CA	72/6797
CONVAIR-SAN DIEGO OPEN				
1955	Tommy Bolt	274	Mission Valley CC, San Diego, CA	72/6619
1956	Bob Rosburg	270	Singing Hills GC, San Diego, CA	72/6573
SAN DIEGO OPEN INVITATIONAL				
1957	Arnold Palmer	271	Mission Valley CC, San Diego, CA	72/6619
1958	No Tournament			
1959	Marty Furgol	274	Mission Valley CC, San Diego, CA	72/6619
1960	Mike Souchak	269	Mission Valley CC, San Diego, CA	72/6619
1961	*Arnold Palmer	271	Mission Valley CC, San Diego, CA	72/6619

KEY * = Playoff # = Amateur ~ = Rain-curtailed

Year	Winner	Score	Location	Par/Yards
1962	*Tommy Jacobs	277	Stardust CC, San Diego, CA	71/6725
1963	Gary Player	270	Stardust CC, San Diego, CA	71/6725
1964	Art Wall	274	Rancho Bernardo CC, San Diego, CA	72/6455
1965	*Wes Ellis	267	Stardust CC, San Diego, CA	71/6725
1966	Billy Casper	268	Stardust CC, San Diego, CA	71/6725
1967	Bob Goalby	269	Stardust CC, San Diego, CA	71/6725

ANDY WILLIAMS-SAN DIEGO OPEN INVITATIONAL

Year	Winner	Score	Location	Par/Yards
1968	Tom Weiskopf	273	Torrey Pines GC, San Diego, CA	72/N-6659, S-7021
1969	Jack Nicklaus	284	Torrey Pines GC, San Diego, CA	72/N-6659, S-7021
1970	*Pete Brown	275	Torrey Pines GC, San Diego, CA	72/N-6659, S-7021
1971	George Archer	272	Torrey Pines GC, San Diego, CA	72/N-6659, S-7021
1972	Paul Harney	275	Torrey Pines GC, San Diego, CA	72/N-6659, S-7021
1973	Bob Dickson	278	Torrey Pines GC, San Diego, CA	72/N-6659, S-7021
1974	Bobby Nichols	275	Torrey Pines GC, San Diego, CA	72/N-6659, S-7021
1975	*J. C. Snead	279	Torrey Pines GC, San Diego, CA	72/N-6659, S-7021
1976	J. C. Snead	272	Torrey Pines GC, San Diego, CA	72/N-6659, S-7021
1977	Tom Watson	269	Torrey Pines GC, San Diego, CA	72/N-6659, S-7021
1978	Jay Haas	278	Torrey Pines GC, San Diego, CA	72/N-6659, S-7021
1979	Fuzzy Zoeller	282	Torrey Pines GC, San Diego, CA	72/N-6659, S-7021
1980	*Tom Watson	275	Torrey Pines GC, San Diego, CA	72/N-6659, S-7021

WICKES/ANDY WILLIAMS SAN DIEGO OPEN

Year	Winner	Score	Location	Par/Yards
1981	*Bruce Lietzke	278	Torrey Pines GC, San Diego, CA	72/N-6659, S-7021
1982	Johnny Miller	270	Torrey Pines GC, San Diego, CA	72/N-6659, S-7021

ISUZU/ANDY WILLIAMS SAN DIEGO OPEN

Year	Winner	Score	Location	Par/Yards
1983	Gary Hallberg	271	Torrey Pines GC, San Diego, CA	72/N-6659, S-7021
1984	*Gary Koch	272	Torrey Pines GC, San Diego, CA	72/N-6659, S-7021
1985	*Woody Blackburn	269	Torrey Pines GC, San Diego, CA	72/N-6659, S-7021

SHEARSON LEHMAN BROTHERS ANDY WILLIAMS OPEN

Year	Winner	Score	Location	Par/Yards
1986	~*Bob Tway	204	Torrey Pines GC, San Diego, CA	72/N-6659, S-7021
1987	George Burns	266	Torrey Pines GC, San Diego, CA	72/N-6659, S-7021

SHEARSON LEHMAN HUTTON ANDY WILLIAMS OPEN

Year	Winner	Score	Location	Par/Yards
1988	Steve Pate	269	Torrey Pines GC, San Diego, CA	72/N-6659, S-7021

SHEARSON LEHMAN HUTTON OPEN

Year	Winner	Score	Location	Par/Yards
1989	Greg Twiggs	271	Torrey Pines GC, San Diego, CA	72/N-6659, S-7021
1990	Dan Forsman	275	Torrey Pines GC, San Diego, CA	72/N-6659, S-7021

SHEARSON LEHMAN BROTHERS OPEN

Year	Winner	Score	Location	Par/Yards
1991	Jay Don Blake	268	Torrey Pines GC, San Diego, CA	72/N-6659, S-7021

BUICK INVITATIONAL OF CALIFORNIA

Year	Winner	Score	Location	Par/Yards
1992	~Steve Pate	200	Torrey Pines GC, San Diego, CA	72/N-6659, S-7021
1993	Phil Mickelson	278	Torrey Pines GC, San Diego, CA	72/N-6659, S-7021

DORAL-RYDER OPEN

Year	Winner	Score	Location	Par/Yards

DORAL CC OPEN INVITATIONAL

Year	Winner	Score	Location	Par/Yards
1962	Billy Casper	283	Doral CC (Blue), Miami, FL	72/6939
1963	Dan Sikes	283	Doral CC (Blue), Miami, FL	72/6939
1964	Billy Casper	277	Doral CC (Blue), Miami, FL	72/6939
1965	Doug Sanders	274	Doral CC (Blue), Miami, FL	72/6939
1966	Phil Rodgers	278	Doral CC (Blue), Miami, FL	72/6939
1967	Doug Sanders	275	Doral CC (Blue), Miami, FL	72/6939
1968	Gardner Dickinson	275	Doral CC (Blue), Miami, FL	72/6939
1969	Tom Shaw	276	Doral CC (Blue), Miami, FL	72/6939

DORAL-EASTERN OPEN INVITATIONAL

Year	Winner	Score	Location	Par/Yards
1970	Mike Hill	279	Doral CC (Blue), Miami, FL	72/6939
1971	J.C. Snead	275	Doral CC (Blue), Miami, FL	72/6939
1972	Jack Nicklaus	276	Doral CC (Blue), Miami, FL	72/6939
1973	Lee Trevino	276	Doral CC (Blue), Miami, FL	72/6939
1974	Brian Allin	272	Doral CC (Blue), Miami, FL	72/6939
1975	Jack Nicklaus	276	Doral CC (Blue), Miami, FL	72/6939
1976	Hubert Green	270	Doral CC (Blue), Miami, FL	72/6939
1977	Andy Bean	277	Doral CC (Blue), Miami, FL	72/6939

KEY * = Playoff # = Amateur ~ = Rain-curtailed

Year	Winner	Score	Location	Par/Yards
1978	Tom Weiskopf	272	Doral CC (Blue), Miami, FL	72/6939
1979	Mark McCumber	279	Doral CC (Blue), Miami, FL	72/6939
1980	*Raymond Floyd	279	Doral CC (Blue), Miami, FL	72/6939
1981	Raymond Floyd	273	Doral CC (Blue), Miami, FL	72/6939
1982	Andy Bean	278	Doral CC (Blue), Miami, FL	72/6939
1983	Gary Koch	271	Doral CC (Blue), Miami, FL	72/6939
1984	Tom Kite	272	Doral CC (Blue), Miami, FL	72/6939
1985	Mark McCumber	284	Doral CC (Blue), Miami, FL	72/6939
1986	*Andy Bean	276	Doral CC (Blue), Miami, FL	72/6939
DORAL-RYDER OPEN				
1987	Lanny Wadkins	277	Doral CC (Blue), Miami, FL	72/6939
1988	Ben Crenshaw	274	Doral CC (Blue), Miami, FL	72/6939
1989	Bill Glasson	275	Doral CC (Blue), Miami, FL	72/6939
1990	*Greg Norman	273	Doral CC (Blue), Miami, FL	72/6939
1991	*Rocco Mediate	276	Doral CC (Blue), Miami, FL	72/6939
1992	Raymond Floyd	271	Doral CC (Blue), Miami, FL	72/6939
1993	Greg Norman	265	Doral CC (Blue), Miami, FL	72/6939

HONDA CLASSIC

Year	Winner	Score	Location	Par/Yards
JACKIE GLEASON'S INVERRARY CLASSIC				
1972	Tom Weiskopf	278	Inverrary G&CC (East), Lauderhill, FL	72/7128
JACKIE GLEASON'S INVERRARY NATIONAL AIRLINES CLASSIC				
1973	Lee Trevino	279	Inverrary G&CC (East), Lauderhill, FL	72/7128
JACKIE GLEASON'S INVERRARY CLASSIC				
1974	Leonard Thompson	278	Inverrary G&CC (East), Lauderhill, FL	72/7128
1975	Bob Murphy	273	Inverrary G&CC (East), Lauderhill, FL	72/7128
1976	Hosted Tournament Players Championship			
1977	Jack Nicklaus	275	Inverrary G&CC (East), Lauderhill, FL	72/7128
1978	Jack Nicklaus	276	Inverrary G&CC (East), Lauderhill, FL	72/7128
1979	Larry Nelson	274	Inverrary G&CC (East), Lauderhill, FL	72/7128
1980	Johnny Miller	274	Inverrary G&CC (East), Lauderhill, FL	72/7128
AMERICAN MOTORS INVERRARY CLASSIC				
1981	Tom Kite	274	Inverrary G&CC (East), Lauderhill, FL	72/7128
HONDA INVERRARY CLASSIC				
1982	Hale Irwin	269	Inverrary G&CC (East), Lauderhill, FL	72/7128
1983	Johnny Miller	278	Inverrary G&CC (East), Lauderhill, FL	72/7128
HONDA CLASSIC				
1984	*Bruce Lietzke	280	TPC at Eagle Trace, Coral Springs, FL	72/7030
1985	*Curtis Strange	275	TPC at Eagle Trace, Coral Springs, FL	72/7030
1986	Kenny Knox	287	TPC at Eagle Trace, Coral Springs, FL	72/7030
1987	Mark Calcavecchia	279	TPC at Eagle Trace, Coral Springs, FL	72/7030
1988	Joey Sindelar	276	TPC at Eagle Trace, Coral Springs, FL	72/7030
1989	Blaine McCallister	266	TPC at Eagle Trace, Coral Springs, FL	72/7030
1990	John Huston	282	TPC at Eagle Trace, Coral Springs, FL	72/7030
1991	Steve Pate	279	TPC at Eagle Trace, Coral Springs, FL	72/7030
1992	*Corey Pavin	273	Weston Hills G&CC, Ft. Lauderdale, FL	72/7069
1993	~*Fred Couples	207	Weston Hills G&CC, Ft. Lauderdale, FL	72/7069

THE NESTLE INVITATIONAL

Year	Winner	Score	Location	Par/Yards
FLORIDA CITRUS OPEN INVITATIONAL				
1966	Lionel Hebert	279	Rio Pinar CC, Orlando, FL	72/7012
1967	Julius Boros	274	Rio Pinar CC, Orlando, FL	72/7012
1968	Dan Sikes	274	Rio Pinar CC, Orlando, FL	72/7012
1969	Ken Still	278	Rio Pinar CC, Orlando, FL	72/7012
1970	Bob Lunn	271	Rio Pinar CC, Orlando, FL	72/7012
1971	Arnold Palmer	270	Rio Pinar CC, Orlando, FL	72/7012
1972	Jerry Heard	276	Rio Pinar CC, Orlando, FL	72/7012
1973	Brian Allin	265	Rio Pinar CC, Orlando, FL	72/7012

KEY * = Playoff # = Amateur ~ = Rain-curtailed

Past Winners of PGA TOUR Events (cont'd.)

Year	Winner	Score	Location	Par/Yards
1974	Jerry Heard	273	Rio Pinar CC, Orlando, FL	72/7012
1975	Lee Trevino	276	Rio Pinar CC, Orlando, FL	72/7012
1976	*Hale Irwin	270	Rio Pinar CC, Orlando, FL	72/7012
1977	Gary Koch	274	Rio Pinar CC, Orlando, FL	72/7012
1978	Mac McLendon	271	Rio Pinar CC, Orlando, FL	72/7012
BAY HILL CITRUS CLASSIC				
1979	*Bob Byman	278	Bay Hill Club, Orlando, FL	71/7103
BAY HILL CLASSIC				
1980	Dave Eichelberger	279	Bay Hill Club, Orlando, FL	71/7103
1981	Andy Bean	266	Bay Hill Club, Orlando, FL	71/7103
1982	*Tom Kite	278	Bay Hill Club, Orlando, FL	71/7103
1983	*Mike Nicolette	283	Bay Hill Club, Orlando, FL	71/7103
1984	*Gary Koch	272	Bay Hill Club, Orlando, FL	71/7103
HERTZ BAY HILL CLASSIC				
1985	Fuzzy Zoeller	275	Bay Hill Club, Orlando, FL	71/7103
1986	~Dan Forsman	202	Bay Hill Club, Orlando, FL	71/7103
1987	Payne Stewart	264	Bay Hill Club, Orlando, FL	71/7103
1988	Paul Azinger	271	Bay Hill Club, Orlando, FL	71/7103
THE NESTLE INVITATIONAL				
1989	*Tom Kite	278	Bay Hill Club, Orlando, FL	71/7103
1990	Robert Gamez	274	Bay Hill Club, Orlando, FL	71/7103
1991	~Andrew Magee	203	Bay Hill Club, Orlando, FL	71/7103
1992	Fred Couples	269	Bay Hill Club, Orlando, FL	71/7103
1993	Ben Crenshaw	280	Bay Hill Club, Orlando, FL	71/7103

THE PLAYERS CHAMPIONSHIP

Year	Winner	Score	Location	Par/Yards
TOURNAMENT PLAYERS CHAMPIONSHIP				
1974	Jack Nicklaus	272	Atlanta CC, Atlanta, GA	72/6883
1975	Al Geiberger	270	Colonial CC, Fort Worth, TX	70/7160
1976	Jack Nicklaus	269	Inverrary G&CC, Lauderhill, FL	72/7127
1977	Mark Hayes	289	Sawgrass, Ponte Vedra, FL	72/7174
1978	Jack Nicklaus	289	Sawgrass, Ponte Vedra, FL	72/7174
1979	Lanny Wadkins	283	Sawgrass, Ponte Vedra, FL	72/7174
1980	Lee Trevino	278	Sawgrass, Ponte Vedra, FL	72/7174
1981	*Raymond Floyd	285	Sawgrass, Ponte Vedra, FL	72/7174
1982	Jerry Pate	280	TPC at Sawgrass, Ponte Vedra, FL	72/6857
1983	Hal Sutton	283	TPC at Sawgrass, Ponte Vedra, FL	72/6857
1984	Fred Couples	277	TPC at Sawgrass, Ponte Vedra, FL	72/6857
1985	Calvin Peete	274	TPC at Sawgrass, Ponte Vedra, FL	72/6857
1986	John Mahaffey	275	TPC at Sawgrass, Ponte Vedra, FL	72/6857
1987	*Sandy Lyle	274	TPC at Sawgrass, Ponte Vedra, FL	72/6857
THE PLAYERS CHAMPIONSHIP				
1988	Mark McCumber	273	TPC at Sawgrass, Ponte Vedra, FL	72/6857
1989	Tom Kite	279	TPC at Sawgrass, Ponte Vedra, FL	72/6857
1990	Jodie Mudd	278	TPC at Sawgrass, Ponte Vedra, FL	72/6857
1991	Steve Elkington	276	TPC at Sawgrass, Ponte Vedra, FL	72/6857
1992	Davis Love III	273	TPC at Sawgrass, Ponte Vedra, FL	72/6857
1993	Nick Price	270	TPC at Sawgrass, Ponte Vedra, FL	72/6857

FREEPORT-MCMORAN CLASSIC

Year	Winner	Score	Location	Par/Yards
GREATER NEW ORLEANS OPEN INVITATIONAL				
1938	Harry Cooper	285	City Park GC, New Orleans, LA	72/6656
1939	Henry Picard	284	City Park GC, New Orleans, LA	72/6656
1940	Jimmy Demaret	286	City Park GC, New Orleans, LA	72/6656
1941	Henry Picard	276	City Park GC, New Orleans, LA	72/6656
1942	Lloyd Mangrum	281	City Park GC, New Orleans, LA	72/6656
1943	No Tournament			
1944	Sammy Byrd	285	City Park GC, New Orleans, LA	72/6656
1945	*Byron Nelson	284	City Park GC, New Orleans, LA	72/6656

KEY * = Playoff # = Amateur ~ = Rain-curtailed

Past Winners of PGA TOUR Events *(cont'd.)*

Year	Winner	Score	Location	Par/Yards
1946	Byron Nelson	277	City Park GC, New Orleans, LA	72/6656
1947	No Tournament			
1948	Bob Hamilton	280	City Park GC. New Orleans, LA	72/6656
1949-				
1957	No Tournaments			
1958	*Billy Casper	278	City Park GC, New Orleans, LA	72/6656
1959	Bill Collins	280	City Park GC, New Orleans, LA	72/6656
1960	Dow Finsterwald	270	City Park GC, New Orleans, LA	72/6656
1961	Doug Sanders	272	City Park GC, New Orleans, LA	72/6656
1962	Bo Wininger	281	City Park GC, New Orleans, LA	72/6656
1963	Bo Wininger	279	Lakewood CC, New Orleans, LA	72/7080
1964	Mason Rudolph	283	Lakewood CC, New Orleans, LA	72/7080
1965	Dick Mayer	273	Lakewood CC, New Orleans, LA	72/7080
1966	Frank Beard	276	Lakewood CC, New Orleans, LA	72/7080
1967	George Knudson	277	Lakewood CC, New Orleans, LA	72/7080
1968	George Archer	271	Lakewood CC, New Orleans, LA	72/7080
1969	*Larry Hinson	275	Lakewood CC, New Orleans, LA	72/7080
1970	*Miller Barber	278	Lakewood CC, New Orleans, LA	72/7080
1971	Frank Beard	276	Lakewood CC, New Orleans, LA	72/7080
1972	Gary Player	279	Lakewood CC, New Orleans, LA	72/7080
1973	*Jack Nicklaus	280	Lakewood CC, New Orleans, LA	72/7080
1974	Lee Trevino	267	Lakewood CC, New Orleans, LA	72/7080

FIRST NBC NEW ORLEANS OPEN

Year	Winner	Score	Location	Par/Yards
1975	Billy Casper	271	Lakewood CC, New Orleans, LA	72/7080
1976	Larry Ziegler	274	Lakewood CC, New Orleans, LA	72/7080
1977	Jim Simons	273	Lakewood CC, New Orleans, LA	72/7080
1978	Lon Hinkle	271	Lakewood CC, New Orleans, LA	72/7080
1979	Hubert Green	273	Lakewood CC, New Orleans, LA	72/7080

GREATER NEW ORLEANS OPEN

Year	Winner	Score	Location	Par/Yards
1980	Tom Watson	273	Lakewood CC, New Orleans, LA	72/7080

USF&G NEW ORLEANS OPEN

Year	Winner	Score	Location	Par/Yards
1981	Tom Watson	270	Lakewood CC, New Orleans, LA	72/7080

USF&G CLASSIC

Year	Winner	Score	Location	Par/Yards
1982	~Scott Hoch	206	Lakewood CC, New Orleans, LA	72/7080
1983	Bill Rogers	274	Lakewood CC, New Orleans, LA	72/7080
1984	Bob Eastwood	272	Lakewood CC, New Orleans, LA	72/7080
1985	~Seve Ballesteros	205	Lakewood CC, New Orleans, LA	72/7080
1986	Calvin Peete	269	Lakewood CC, New Orleans, LA	72/7080
1987	Ben Crenshaw	268	Lakewood CC, New Orleans, LA	72/7080
1988	Chip Beck	262	Lakewood CC, New Orleans, LA	72/7080
1989	Tim Simpson	274	English Turn G&CC, New Orleans, LA	72/7106
1990	David Frost	276	English Turn G&CC, New Orleans, LA	72/7106
1991	*Ian Woosnam	275	English Turn G&CC, New Orleans, LA	72/7106

FREEPORT-MCMORAN CLASSIC

Year	Winner	Score	Location	Par/Yards
1992	Chip Beck	276	English Turn G&CC, New Orleans, LA	72/7106
1993	Mike Standly	281	English Turn G&CC, New Orleans, LA	72/7106

MCI HERITAGE CLASSIC

Year	Winner	Score	Location	Par/Yards

HERITAGE CLASSIC

Year	Winner	Score	Location	Par/Yards
1969	Arnold Palmer	283	Harbour Town GL, Hilton Head, SC	71/6657
1970	Bob Goalby	280	Harbour Town GL, Hilton Head, SC	71/6657

SEA PINES HERITAGE CLASSIC

Year	Winner	Score	Location	Par/Yards
1971	Hale Irwin	279	Harbour Town GL, Hilton Head, SC	71/6657
1972	Johnny Miller	281	Ocean Course, Hilton Head, SC (first two rounds)	72/6600
			Harbour Town GL, Hilton Head, SC (second two rounds)	71/6657
1973	Hale Irwin	272	Harbour Town GL, Hilton Head, SC	71/6657
1974	Johnny Miller	276	Harbour Town GL, Hilton Head, SC	71/6657
1975	Jack Nicklaus	271	Harbour Town GL, Hilton Head, SC	71/6657
1976	Hubert Green	274	Harbour Town GL, Hilton Head, SC	71/6657
1977	Graham Marsh	273	Harbour Town GL, Hilton Head, SC	71/6657
1978	Hubert Green	277	Harbour Town GL, Hilton Head, SC	71/6657

KEY * = Playoff # = Amateur ~ = Rain-curtailed

Past Winners of PGA TOUR Events (cont'd.)

Year	Winner	Score	Location	Par/Yards
1979	Tom Watson	270	Harbour Town GL, Hilton Head, SC	71/6657
1980	*Doug Tewell	280	Harbour Town GL, Hilton Head, SC	71/6657
1981	Bill Rogers	278	Harbour Town GL, Hilton Head, SC	71/6657
1982	*Tom Watson	280	Harbour Town GL, Hilton Head, SC	71/6657
1983	Fuzzy Zoeller	275	Harbour Town GL, Hilton Head, SC	71/6657
1984	Nick Faldo	270	Harbour Town GL, Hilton Head, SC	71/6657
1985	*Bernhard Langer	273	Harbour Town GL, Hilton Head, SC	71/6657
1986	Fuzzy Zoeller	276	Harbour Town GL, Hilton Head, SC	71/6657
MCI HERITAGE CLASSIC				
1987	Davis Love III	271	Harbour Town GL, Hilton Head, SC	71/6657
1988	Greg Norman	271	Harbour Town GL, Hilton Head, SC	71/6657
1989	Payne Stewart	268	Harbour Town GL, Hilton Head, SC	71/6657
1990	*Payne Stewart	276	Harbour Town GL, Hilton Head, SC	71/6657
1991	Davis Love III	271	Harbour Town GL, Hilton Head, SC	71/6657
1992	Davis Love III	269	Harbour Town GL, Hilton Head, SC	71/6657
1993	David Edwards	273	Harbour Town GL, Hilton Head, SC	71/6657

KMART GREATER GREENSBORO OPEN

Year	Winner	Score	Location	Par/Yards
GREATER GREENSBORO OPEN				
1938	Sam Snead	272	Starmount Forest CC, Greensboro, NC	71/6630
			Sedgefield CC, Greensboro, NC	70/6680
1939	Ralph Guldahl	280	Starmount Forest CC, Greensboro, NC	71/6630
			Sedgefield CC, Greensboro, NC	70/6680
1940	Ben Hogan	270	Starmount Forest CC, Greensboro, NC	71/6630
			Sedgefield CC, Greensboro, NC	70/6680
1941	Byron Nelson	276	Starmount Forest CC, Greensboro, NC	71/6630
			Sedgefield CC, Greensboro, NC	70/6680
1942	Sam Byrd	279	Starmount Forest CC, Greensboro, NC	71/6630
1943-				
1944	No Tournaments			
1945	Byron Nelson	271	Starmount Forest CC, Greensboro, NC	71/6630
1946	Sam Snead	270	Sedgefield CC, Greensboro, NC	70/6680
1947	Vic Ghezzi	286	Starmount Forest CC, Greensboro, NC	71/6630
1948	Lloyd Mangrum	278	Sedgefield CC, Greensboro, NC	70/6680
1949	*Sam Snead	276	Starmount Forest CC, Greensboro, NC	71/6630
1950	Sam Snead	269	Sedgefield CC, Greensboro, NC	70/6680
1951	Art Doering	279	Starmount Forest CC, Greensboro, NC	71/6630
1952	Dave Douglas	277	Starmount Forest CC, Greensboro, NC	71/6630
1953	*Earl Stewart	275	Sedgefield CC, Greensboro, NC	70/6680
1954	*Doug Ford	283	Starmount Forest CC, Greensboro, NC	71/6630
1955	Sam Snead	273	Sedgefield CC, Greensboro, NC	70/6680
1956	*Sam Snead	279	Starmount Forest CC, Greensboro, NC	71/6630
1957	Stan Leonard	276	Sedgefield CC, Greensboro, NC	70/6680
1958	Bob Goalby	275	Starmount Forest CC, Greensboro, NC	71/6630
1959	Dow Finsterwald	278	Starmount Forest CC, Greensboro, NC	71/6630
1960	Sam Snead	270	Starmount Forest CC, Greensboro, NC	71/6630
1961	Mike Souchak	276	Sedgefield CC, Greensboro, NC	70/6680
1962	Billy Casper	275	Sedgefield CC, Greensboro, NC	70/6680
1963	Doug Sanders	270	Sedgefield CC, Greensboro, NC	70/6680
1964	*Julius Boros	277	Sedgefield CC, Greensboro, NC	70/6680
1965	Sam Snead	273	Sedgefield CC, Greensboro, NC	70/6680
1966	*Doug Sanders	276	Sedgefield CC, Greensboro, NC	70/6680
1967	George Archer	267	Sedgefield CC, Greensboro, NC	70/6680
1968	Billy Casper	267	Sedgefield CC, Greensboro, NC	70/6680
1969	*Gene Littler	274	Sedgefield CC, Greensboro, NC	70/6680
1970	Gary Player	271	Sedgefield CC, Greensboro, NC	71/7034
1971	*Bud Allin	275	Sedgefield CC, Greensboro, NC	71/7034
1972	*George Archer	272	Sedgefield CC, Greensboro, NC	71/7034
1973	Chi Chi Rodriguez	267	Sedgefield CC, Greensboro, NC	71/7012

KEY * = Playoff # = Amateur ~ = Rain-curtailed

Year	Winner	Score	Location	Par/Yards
1974	Bob Charles	270	Sedgefield CC, Greensboro, NC	71/7012
1975	Tom Weiskopf	275	Sedgefield CC, Greensboro, NC	71/6643
1976	Al Geiberger	268	Sedgefield CC, Greensboro, NC	71/6643
1977	Danny Edwards	276	Forest Oaks CC, Greensboro, NC	72/7075
1978	Seve Ballesteros	282	Forest Oaks CC, Greensboro, NC	72/6958
1979	Raymond Floyd	282	Forest Oaks CC, Greensboro, NC	72/6958
1980	Craig Stadler	275	Forest Oaks CC, Greensboro, NC	72/6958
1981	*Larry Nelson	281	Forest Oaks CC, Greensboro, NC	72/6984
1982	Danny Edwards	285	Forest Oaks CC, Greensboro, NC	72/6984
1983	Lanny Wadkins	275	Forest Oaks CC, Greensboro, NC	72/6984
1984	Andy Bean	280	Forest Oaks CC, Greensboro, NC	72/6984
1985	Joey Sindelar	285	Forest Oaks CC, Greensboro, NC	72/6984
1986	Sandy Lyle	275	Forest Oaks CC, Greensboro, NC	72/6984
1987	Scott Simpson	282	Forest Oaks CC, Greensboro, NC	72/6984

KMART GREATER GREENSBORO OPEN

Year	Winner	Score	Location	Par/Yards
1988	*Sandy Lyle	271	Forest Oaks CC, Greensboro, NC	72/6984
1989	Ken Green	277	Forest Oaks CC, Greensboro, NC	72/6984
1990	Steve Elkington	282	Forest Oaks CC, Greensboro, NC	72/6984
1991	*Mark Brooks	275	Forest Oaks CC, Greensboro, NC	72/6984
1992	Davis Love III	272	Forest Oaks CC, Greensboro, NC	72/6984
1993	*Rocco Mediate	281	Forest Oaks CC, Greensboro, NC	72/6984

SHELL HOUSTON OPEN

Year	Winner	Score	Location	Par/Yards
TOURNAMENT OF CHAMPIONS				
1946	Byron Nelson	274	River Oaks CC, Houston, TX	71/6588
1947	Bobby Locke	277	Memorial Park GC, Houston, TX	72/7421
1948	No Tournament			
1949	John Palmer	272	Pine Forest CC, Houston, TX	72/6510
HOUSTON OPEN				
1950	Cary Middlecoff	277	Brae Burn CC, Houston, TX	72/6725
1951	Marty Furgol	277	Memorial Park GC, Houston, TX	70/7212
1952	Jack Burke, Jr.	277	Memorial Park GC, Houston, TX	70/7212
1953	*Cary Middlecoff	283	Memorial Park GC, Houston, TX	70/7212
1954	Dave Douglas	277	Memorial Park GC, Houston, TX	70/7212
1955	Mike Souchak	273	Memorial Park GC, Houston, TX	70/7212
1956	Ted Kroll	277	Memorial Park GC, Houston, TX	70/7212
1957	Arnold Palmer	279	Memorial Park GC, Houston, TX	70/7212
1958	Ed Oliver	281	Memorial Park GC, Houston, TX	70/7212
HOUSTON CLASSIC				
1959	*Jack Burke, Jr.	277	Memorial Park GC, Houston, TX	70/7212
1960	*Bill Collins	280	Memorial Park GC, Houston, TX	70/7212
1961	*Jay Hebert	276	Memorial Park GC, Houston, TX	72/7122
1962	*Bobby Nichols	278	Memorial Park GC, Houston, TX	72/7201
1963	Bob Charles	268	Memorial Park GC, Houston, TX	72/7201
1964	Mike Souchak	278	Sharpstown CC, Houston, TX	71/7201
1965	Bobby Nichols	273	Sharpstown CC, Houston, TX	71/7201
HOUSTON CHAMPION INTERNATIONAL				
1966	Arnold Palmer	275	Champions GC, Houston, TX	71/7166
1967	Frank Beard	274	Champions GC, Houston, TX	71/7166
1968	Roberto De Vicenzo	274	Champions GC, Houston, TX	71/7166
1969	Hosted U.S. Open			70/6967
1970	*Gibby Gilbert	282	Champions GC, Houston, TX	70/6967
1971	*Hubert Green	280	Champions GC, Houston, TX	70/6967
HOUSTON OPEN				
1972	Bruce Devlin	278	Westwood CC, Houston, TX	72/6998
1973	Bruce Crampton	277	Quail Valley GC, Houston, TX	72/6905
1974	Dave Hill	276	Quail Valley GC, Houston, TX	72/6905
1975	Bruce Crampton	273	Woodlands CC, The Woodlands, TX	72/6929
1976	Lee Elder	278	Woodlands CC, The Woodlands, TX	72/6997
1977	Gene Littler	276	Woodlands CC, The Woodlands, TX	72/6997
1978	Gary Player	270	Woodlands CC, The Woodlands, TX	72/6997

KEY * = Playoff # = Amateur ~ = Rain-curtailed

Past Winners of PGA TOUR Events *(cont'd.)*

Year	Winner	Score	Location	Par/Yards
1979	Wayne Levi	268	Woodlands CC, The Woodlands, TX	71/6918
MICHELOB HOUSTON OPEN				
1980	*Curtis Strange	266	Woodlands CC, The Woodlands, TX	71/6918
1981	~Ron Streck	198	Woodlands CC, The Woodlands, TX	71/7071
1982	*Ed Sneed	275	Woodlands CC, The Woodlands, TX	71/7031
HOUSTON COCA-COLA OPEN				
1983	David Graham	275	Woodlands CC, The Woodlands, TX	71/7031
1984	Corey Pavin	274	Woodlands CC, The Woodlands, TX	71/7031
HOUSTON OPEN				
1985	Raymond Floyd	277	TPC at The Woodlands, The Woodlands, TX	72/7042
1986	*Curtis Strange	274	TPC at The Woodlands, The Woodlands, TX	72/7045
BIG I HOUSTON OPEN				
1987	*Jay Haas	276	TPC at The Woodlands, The Woodlands, TX	72/7045
INDEPENDENT INSURANCE AGENT OPEN				
1988	*Curtis Strange	270	TPC at The Woodlands, The Woodlands, TX	72/7042
1989	Mike Sullivan	280	TPC at The Woodlands, The Woodlands, TX	72/7042
1990	~*Tony Sills	204	TPC at The Woodlands, The Woodlands, TX	72/7042
1991	Fulton Allem	273	TPC at The Woodlands, The Woodlands, TX	72/7042
SHELL HOUSTON OPEN				
1992	Fred Funk	272	TPC at The Woodlands, The Woodlands, TX	72/7042
1993	~*Jim McGovern	199	TPC at The Woodlands, The Woodlands, TX	72/7042

BELLSOUTH CLASSIC

Year	Winner	Score	Location	Par/Yards
ATLANTA CLASSIC				
1967	Bob Charles	282	Atlanta CC, Atlanta, GA	72/7007
1968	Bob Lunn	280	Atlanta CC, Atlanta, GA	72/7007
1969	*Bert Yancey	277	Atlanta CC, Atlanta, GA	72/7007
1970	Tommy Aaron	275	Atlanta CC, Atlanta, GA	72/7007
1971	*Gardner Dickinson	275	Atlanta CC, Atlanta, GA	72/7007
1972	Bob Lunn	275	Atlanta CC, Atlanta, GA	72/7007
1973	Jack Nicklaus	272	Atlanta CC, Atlanta, GA	72/7007
1974	Hosted TPC			
1975	Hale Irwin	271	Atlanta CC, Atlanta, GA	72/7007
1976	Hosted U.S. Open			
1977	Hale Irwin	273	Atlanta CC, Atlanta, GA	72/7007
1978	Jerry Heard	269	Atlanta CC, Atlanta, GA	72/7007
1979	Andy Bean	265	Atlanta CC, Atlanta, GA	72/7007
1980	Larry Nelson	270	Atlanta CC, Atlanta, GA	72/7007
1981	*Tom Watson	277	Atlanta CC, Atlanta, GA	72/7007
GEORGIA-PACIFIC ATLANTA GOLF CLASSIC				
1982	*Keith Fergus	273	Atlanta CC, Atlanta, GA	72/7007
1983	~*Calvin Peete	206	Atlanta CC, Atlanta, GA	72/7007
1984	Tom Kite	269	Atlanta CC, Atlanta, GA	72/7007
1985	*Wayne Levi	273	Atlanta CC, Atlanta, GA	72/7007
1986	Bob Tway	269	Atlanta CC, Atlanta, GA	72/7007
1987	Dave Barr	265	Atlanta CC, Atlanta, GA	72/7007
1988	Larry Nelson	268	Atlanta CC, Atlanta, GA	72/7007
BELLSOUTH ATLANTA GOLF CLASSIC				
1989	*Scott Simpson	278	Atlanta CC, Atlanta, GA	72/7007
1990	Wayne Levi	275	Atlanta CC, Atlanta, GA	72/7007
1991	*Corey Pavin	272	Atlanta CC, Atlanta, GA	72/7007
BELLSOUTH CLASSIC				
1992	Tom Kite	272	Atlanta CC, Atlanta, GA	72/7007
1993	Nolan Henke	271	Atlanta CC, Atlanta, GA	72/7007

GTE BYRON NELSON CLASSIC

Year	Winner	Score	Location	Par/Yards
DALLAS OPEN				
1944	Byron Nelson	276	Lakewood CC, Dallas, TX	N/A
1945	Sam Snead	276	Dallas CC, Dallas, TX	N/A

KEY * = Playoff # = Amateur ~ = Rain-curtailed

Past Winners of PGA TOUR Events *(cont'd.)*

Year	Winner	Score	Location	Par/Yards
1946	Ben Hogan	284	Brook Hollow CC, Dallas, TX	N/A
1947-				
1955	No Tournaments			
1956	Don January	268	Preston Hollow CC, Dallas, TX	N/A
1956A	*Peter Thomson	267	Preston Hollow CC, Dallas, TX	N/A
1957	Sam Snead	264	Glen Lakes CC, Dallas, TX	N/A
1958	*Sam Snead	272	Oak Cliffs CC, Dallas, TX	71/6836
1959	Julius Boros	274	Oak Cliffs CC, Dallas, TX	71/6836
1960	*Johnny Pott	275	Oak Cliffs CC, Dallas, TX	71/6836
1961	Earl Stewart, Jr.	278	Oak Cliffs CC, Dallas, TX	71/6836
1962	Billy Maxwell	277	Oak Cliffs CC, Dallas, TX	71/6836
1963	No Tournament			
1964	Charles Coody	271	Oak Cliffs CC, Dallas, TX	71/6836
1965	No Tournament			
1966	Roberto De Vicenzo	276	Oak Cliffs CC, Dallas, TX	71/6836
1967	Bert Yancey	274	Oak Cliffs CC, Dallas, TX	71/6836
BYRON NELSON GOLF CLASSIC				
1968	Miller Barber	270	Preston Trail Golf Club, Dallas, TX	70/6993
1969	Bruce Devlin	277	Preston Trail Golf Club, Dallas, TX	70/6993
1970	*Jack Nicklaus	274	Preston Trail Golf Club, Dallas, TX	70/6993
1971	Jack Nicklaus	274	Preston Trail Golf Club, Dallas, TX	70/6993
1972	*Chi Chi Rodriquez	273	Preston Trail Golf Club, Dallas, TX	70/6993
1973	*Lanny Wadkins	277	Preston Trail Golf Club, Dallas, TX	70/6993
1974	Brian Allin	269	Preston Trail Golf Club, Dallas, TX	70/6993
1975	Tom Watson	269	Preston Trail Golf Club, Dallas, TX	70/6993
1976	Mark Hayes	273	Preston Trail Golf Club, Dallas, TX	70/6993
1977	Raymond Floyd	276	Preston Trail Golf Club, Dallas, TX	70/6993
1978	Tom Watson	272	Preston Trail Golf Club, Dallas, TX	70/6993
1979	*Tom Watson	275	Preston Trail Golf Club, Dallas, TX	70/6993
1980	Tom Watson	274	Preston Trail Golf Club, Dallas, TX	70/6993
1981	*Bruce Lietzke	281	Preston Trail Golf Club, Dallas, TX	70/6993
1982	Bob Gilder	266	Preston Trail Golf Club, Dallas, TX	70/6993
1983	Ben Crenshaw	273	Las Colinas Sports Club, Irving, TX	71/6982
1984	Craig Stadler	276	Las Colinas Sports Club, Irving, TX	71/6982
1985	*Bob Eastwood	272	Las Colinas Sports Club, Irving, TX	71/6982
1986	Andy Bean	269	TPC at Las Colinas, Irving, TX	70/6767
1987	*Fred Couples	266	TPC at Las Colinas, Irving, TX	70/6767
GTE BYRON NELSON GOLF CLASSIC				
1988	*Bruce Lietzke	271	TPC at Las Colinas, Irving, TX	70/6767
1989	*Jodie Mudd	265	TPC at Las Colinas, Irving, TX	70/6767
1990	~Payne Stewart	202	TPC at Las Colinas, Irving, TX	70/6767
1991	Nick Price	270	TPC at Las Colinas, Irving, TX	70/6767
1992	*~Billy Ray Brown	199	TPC at Las Colinas, Irving, TX	70/6850
1993	Scott Simpson	270	TPC at Las Colinas, Irving, TX	70/6850

THE MEMORIAL TOURNAMENT

Year	Winner	Score	Location	Par/Yards
THE MEMORIAL TOURNAMENT				
1976	*Roger Maltbie	288	Muirfield Village GC, Dublin, OH	72/7027
1977	Jack Nicklaus	281	Muirfield Village GC, Dublin, OH	72/7101
1978	Jim Simons	284	Muirfield Village GC, Dublin, OH	72/7101
1979	Tom Watson	285	Muirfield Village GC, Dublin, OH	72/7101
1980	David Graham	280	Muirfield Village GC, Dublin, OH	72/7116
1981	Keith Fergus	284	Muirfield Village GC, Dublin, OH	72/7116
1982	Raymond Floyd	281	Muirfield Village GC, Dublin, OH	72/7116
1983	Hale Irwin	281	Muirfield Village GC, Dublin, OH	72/7116
1984	*Jack Nicklaus	280	Muirfield Village GC, Dublin, OH	72/7116
1985	Hale Irwin	281	Muirfield Village GC, Dublin, OH	72/7106
1986	Hal Sutton	271	Muirfield Village GC, Dublin, OH	72/7106
1987	Don Pooley	272	Muirfield Village GC, Dublin, OH	72/7104
1988	Curtis Strange	274	Muirfield Village GC, Dublin, OH	72/7104

KEY * = Playoff # = Amateur ~ = Rain-curtailed A = Second tournament that year

Year	Winner	Score	Location	Par/Yards
1989	Bob Tway	277	Muirfield Village GC, Dublin, OH	72/7104
1990	~Greg Norman	216	Muirfield Village GC, Dublin, OH	72/7104
1991	*Kenny Perry	273	Muirfield Village GC, Dublin, OH	72/7104
1992	*David Edwards	273	Muirfield Village GC, Dublin, OH	72/7104
1993	Paul Azinger	274	Muirfield Village GC, Dublin, OH	72/7104

SOUTHWESTERN BELL COLONIAL

Year	Winner	Score	Location	Par/Yards
COLONIAL NATIONAL INVITATION TOURNAMENT				
1946	Ben Hogan	279	Colonial CC, Fort Worth, TX	70/7035
1947	Ben Hogan	279	Colonial CC, Fort Worth, TX	70/7035
1948	Clayton Heafner	272	Colonial CC, Fort Worth, TX	70/7035
1949	No Tournament			
1950	Sam Snead	277	Colonial CC, Fort Worth, TX	70/7035
1951	Cary Middlecoff	282	Colonial CC, Fort Worth, TX	70/7035
1952	Ben Hogan	279	Colonial CC, Fort Worth, TX	70/7035
1953	Ben Hogan	282	Colonial CC, Fort Worth, TX	70/7035
1954	Johnny Palmer	280	Colonial CC, Fort Worth, TX	70/7035
1955	Chandler Harper	276	Colonial CC, Fort Worth, TX	70/7035
1956	Mike Souchak	280	Colonial CC, Fort Worth, TX	70/7035
1957	Roberto De Vicenzo	284	Colonial CC, Fort Worth, TX	70/7021
1958	Tommy Bolt	282	Colonial CC, Fort Worth, TX	70/7021
1959	*Ben Hogan	285	Colonial CC, Fort Worth, TX	70/7021
1960	Julius Boros	280	Colonial CC, Fort Worth, TX	70/7021
1961	Doug Sanders	281	Colonial CC, Fort Worth, TX	70/7021
1962	*Arnold Palmer	281	Colonial CC, Fort Worth, TX	70/7021
1963	Julius Boros	279	Colonial CC, Fort Worth, TX	70/7021
1964	Billy Casper	279	Colonial CC, Fort Worth, TX	70/7021
1965	Bruce Crampton	276	Colonial CC, Fort Worth, TX	70/7021
1966	Bruce Devlin	280	Colonial CC, Fort Worth, TX	70/7021
1967	Dave Stockton	278	Colonial CC, Fort Worth, TX	70/7021
1968	Billy Casper	275	Colonial CC, Fort Worth, TX	70/7021
1969	Gardner Dickinson	278	Colonial CC, Fort Worth, TX	70/7142
1970	Homero Blancas	273	Colonial CC, Fort Worth, TX	70/7142
1971	Gene Littler	283	Colonial CC, Fort Worth, TX	70/7142
1972	Jerry Heard	275	Colonial CC, Fort Worth, TX	70/7142
1973	Tom Weiskopf	276	Colonial CC, Fort Worth, TX	70/7142
1974	Rod Curl	276	Colonial CC, Fort Worth, TX	70/7142
1975	Hosted TPC			
1976	Lee Trevino	273	Colonial CC, Fort Worth, TX	70/7142
1977	Ben Crenshaw	272	Colonial CC, Fort Worth, TX	70/7142
1978	Lee Trevino	268	Colonial CC, Fort Worth, TX	70/7142
1979	Al Geiberger	274	Colonial CC, Fort Worth, TX	70/7096
1980	Bruce Lietzke	271	Colonial CC, Fort Worth, TX	70/7096
1981	Fuzzy Zoeller	274	Colonial CC, Fort Worth, TX	70/7096
1982	Jack Nicklaus	273	Colonial CC, Fort Worth, TX	70/7096
1983	*Jim Colbert	278	Colonial CC, Fort Worth, TX	70/7096
1984	*Peter Jacobsen	270	Colonial CC, Fort Worth, TX	70/7096
1985	Corey Pavin	266	Colonial CC, Fort Worth, TX	70/7096
1986	*~Dan Pohl	205	Colonial CC, Fort Worth, TX	70/7096
1987	Keith Clearwater	266	Colonial CC, Fort Worth, TX	70/7096
1988	Lanny Wadkins	270	Colonial CC, Fort Worth, TX	70/7096
SOUTHWESTERN BELL COLONIAL				
1989	Ian Baker-Finch	270	Colonial CC, Fort Worth, TX	70/7096
1990	Ben Crenshaw	272	Colonial CC, Fort Worth, TX	70/7096
1991	Tom Purtzer	267	Colonial CC, Fort Worth, TX	70/7096
1992	*Bruce Lietzke	267	Colonial CC, Fort Worth, TX	70/7096
1993	Fulton Allem	264	Colonial CC, Fort Worth, TX	70/7096

KEY * = Playoff # = Amateur ~ = Rain-curtailed

Past Winners of PGA TOUR Events *(cont'd.)*

KEMPER OPEN

Year	Winner	Score	Location	Par/Yards
KEMPER OPEN				
1968	Arnold Palmer	276	Pleasant Valley CC, Sutton, MA	71/7205
1969	Dale Douglass	274	Quail Hollow CC, Charlotte, NC	72/7205
1970	Dick Lotz	278	Quail Hollow CC, Charlotte, NC	72/7205
1971	*Tom Weiskopf	277	Quail Hollow CC, Charlotte, NC	72/7205
1972	Doug Sanders	275	Quail Hollow CC, Charlotte, NC	72/7205
1973	Tom Weiskopf	271	Quail Hollow CC, Charlotte, NC	72/7205
1974	*Bob Menne	270	Quail Hollow CC, Charlotte, NC	72/7205
1975	Raymond Floyd	278	Quail Hollow CC, Charlotte, NC	72/7205
1976	Joe Inman	277	Quail Hollow CC, Charlotte, NC	72/7205
1977	Tom Weiskopf	277	Quail Hollow CC, Charlotte, NC	72/7205
1978	Andy Bean	273	Quail Hollow CC, Charlotte, NC	72/7205
1979	Jerry McGee	272	Quail Hollow CC, Charlotte, NC	72/7205
1980	John Mahaffey	275	Congressional CC, Bethesda, MD	72/7173
1981	Craig Stadler	270	Congressional CC, Bethesda, MD	72/7173
1982	Craig Stadler	275	Congressional CC, Bethesda, MD	72/7173
1983	*Fred Couples	287	Congressional CC, Bethesda, MD	72/7173
1984	Greg Norman	280	Congressional CC, Bethesda, MD	72/7173
1985	Bill Glasson	278	Congressional CC, Bethesda, MD	72/7173
1986	*Greg Norman	277	Congressional CC, Bethesda, MD	72/7173
1987	Tom Kite	270	TPC at Avenel, Potomac, MD	71/6864
1988	*Morris Hatalsky	274	TPC at Avenel, Potomac, MD	71/6864
1989	Tom Byrum	268	TPC at Avenel, Potomac, MD	71/6864
1990	Gil Morgan	274	TPC at Avenel, Potomac, MD	71/6864
1991	*Billy Andrade	263	TPC at Avenel, Potomac, MD	71/6864
1992	Bill Glasson	276	TPC at Avenel, Potomac, MD	71/6864
1993	Grant Waite	275	TPC at Avenel, Potomac, MD	71/6864

BUICK CLASSIC

Year	Winner	Score	Location	Par/Yards
WESTCHESTER CLASSIC				
1967	Jack Nicklaus	272	Westchester CC, Harrison, NY	72/6573
1968	Julius Boros	272	Westchester CC, Harrison, NY	72/6648
1969	Frank Beard	275	Westchester CC, Harrison, NY	72/6677
1970	Bruce Crampton	273	Westchester CC, Harrison, NY	72/6700
1971	Arnold Palmer	270	Westchester CC, Harrison, NY	72/6700
1972	Jack Nicklaus	270	Westchester CC, Harrison, NY	72/6700
1973	*Bobby Nichols	272	Westchester CC, Harrison, NY	72/6614
1974	Johnny Miller	269	Westchester CC, Harrison, NY	72/6614
1975	*Gene Littler	271	Westchester CC, Harrison, NY	72/6614
AMERICAN EXPRESS WESTCHESTER CLASSIC				
1976	David Graham	272	Westchester CC, Harrison, NY	71/6603
1977	Andy North	272	Westchester CC, Harrison, NY	71/6603
1978	Lee Elder	274	Westchester CC, Harrison, NY	71/6603
MANUFACTURERS HANOVER WESTCHESTER CLASSIC				
1979	Jack Renner	277	Westchester CC, Harrison, NY	71/6603
1980	Curtis Strange	273	Westchester CC, Harrison, NY	71/6603
1981	Raymond Floyd	275	Westchester CC, Harrison, NY	71/6603
1982	Bob Gilder	261	Westchester CC, Harrison, NY	70/6329
1983	Seve Ballesteros	276	Westchester CC, Harrison, NY	71/6687
1984	Scott Simpson	269	Westchester CC, Harrison, NY	71/6687
1985	*Roger Maltbie	275	Westchester CC, Harrison, NY	71/6722
1986	Bob Tway	272	Westchester CC, Harrison, NY	71/6723
1987	*J.C. Snead	276	Westchester CC, Harrison, NY	71/6769
1988	*Seve Ballesteros	276	Westchester CC, Harrison, NY	71/6779
1989	*Wayne Grady	277	Westchester CC, Harrison, NY	71/6779
BUICK CLASSIC				
1990	Hale Irwin	269	Westchester CC, Harrison, NY	71/6779

KEY * = Playoff # = Amateur ~ = Rain-curtailed

Past Winners of PGA TOUR Events *(cont'd.)*

Year	Winner	Score	Location	Par/Yards
1991	Billy Andrade	273	Westchester CC, Harrison, NY	71/6779
1992	David Frost	268	Westchester CC, Harrison, NY	71/6779
1993	*Vijay Singh	280	Westchester CC, Harrison, NY	71/6779

CANON GREATER HARTFORD OPEN

Year	Winner	Score	Location	Par/Yards
INSURANCE CITY OPEN				
1952	Ted Kroll	273	Wethersfield CC, Hartford, CT	71/6568
1953	Bob Toski	269	Wethersfield CC, Hartford, CT	71/6568
1954	*Tommy Bolt	271	Wethersfield CC, Hartford, CT	71/6568
1955	Sam Snead	269	Wethersfield CC, Hartford, CT	71/6568
1956	*Arnold Palmer	274	Wethersfield CC, Hartford, CT	71/6568
1957	Gardner Dickinson	272	Wethersfield CC, Hartford, CT	71/6568
1958	Jack Burke, Jr.	268	Wethersfield CC, Hartford, CT	71/6568
1959	Gene Littler	272	Wethersfield CC, Hartford, CT	71/6568
1960	*Arnold Palmer	270	Wethersfield CC, Hartford, CT	71/6568
1961	*Billy Maxwell	271	Wethersfield CC, Hartford, CT	71/6568
1962	*Bob Goalby	271	Wethersfield CC, Hartford, CT	71/6568
1963	Billy Casper	271	Wethersfield CC, Hartford, CT	71/6568
1964	Ken Venturi	273	Wethersfield CC, Hartford, CT	71/6568
1965	*Billy Casper	274	Wethersfield CC, Hartford, CT	71/6568
1966	Art Wall	266	Wethersfield CC, Hartford, CT	71/6568
GREATER HARTFORD OPEN INVITATIONAL				
1967	Charlie. Sifford	272	Wethersfield CC, Hartford, CT	71/6568
1968	Billy Casper	266	Wethersfield CC, Hartford, CT	71/6568
1969	*Bob Lunn	268	Wethersfield CC, Hartford, CT	71/6568
1970	Bob Murphy	267	Wethersfield CC, Hartford, CT	71/6568
1971	*George Archer	268	Wethersfield CC, Hartford, CT	71/6568
1972	*Lee Trevino	269	Wethersfield CC, Hartford, CT	71/6568
SAMMY DAVIS JR. GREATER HARTFORD OPEN				
1973	Billy Casper	264	Wethersfield CC, Hartford, CT	71/6568
1974	Dave Stockton	268	Wethersfield CC, Hartford, CT	71/6568
1975	*Don Bies	267	Wethersfield CC, Hartford, CT	71/6568
1976	Rik Massengale	266	Wethersfield CC, Hartford, CT	71/6568
1977	Bill Kratzert	265	Wethersfield CC, Hartford, CT	71/6568
1978	Rod Funseth	264	Wethersfield CC, Hartford, CT	71/6568
1979	Jerry McGee	267	Wethersfield CC, Hartford, CT	71/6568
1980	*Howard Twitty	266	Wethersfield CC, Hartford, CT	71/6568
1981	Hubert Green	264	Wethersfield CC, Hartford, CT	71/6568
1982	Tim Norris	259	Wethersfield CC, Hartford, CT	71/6568
1983	Curtis Strange	268	Wethersfield CC, Hartford, CT	71/6568
1984	Peter Jacobsen	269	TPC of Connecticut, Cromwell, CT	71/6786
1985	*Phil Blackmar	271	TPC of Connecticut, Cromwell, CT	71/6786
CANON SAMMY DAVIS JR.GREATER HARTFORD OPEN				
1986	*Mac O'Grady	269	TPC of Connecticut, Cromwell, CT	71/6786
1987	Paul Azinger	269	TPC of Connecticut, Cromwell, CT	71/6786
1988	*Mark Brooks	269	TPC of Connecticut, Cromwell, CT	71/6786
CANON GREATER HARTFORD OPEN				
1989	Paul Azinger	267	TPC of Connecticut, Cromwell, CT	71/6786
1990	Wayne Levi	267	TPC of Connecticut, Cromwell, CT	70/6531
1991	*Billy Ray Brown	271	TPC at River Highlands, Cromwell, CT	70/6820
1992	Lanny Wadkins	274	TPC at River Highlands, Cromwell, CT	70/6820
1993	Nick Price	271	TPC at River Highlands, Cromwell, CT	70/6820

MOTOROLA

Year	Winner	Score	Location	Par/Yards
WESTERN OPEN				
1899	*Willie Smith	156	Glenview GC, Chicago, IL	72/6362
1900	No Tournament			
1901	Laurie Auchterlonie	160	Midlothian CC, Chicago, IL	71/6654
1902	Willie Anderson	299	Euclid Club, Cleveland, OH	N/A

KEY * = Playoff # = Amateur ~ = Rain-curtailed

Year	Winner	Score	Location	Par/Yards
1903	Alex Smith	318	Milwaukee CC, Milwaukee, WI	72/6867
1904	Willie Anderson	304	Kent CC, Grand Rapids, MI	71/6514
1905	Arthur Smith	278	Cincinnati GC, Cincinnati, OH	71/6231
1906	Alex Smith	306	Homewood CC, Chicago, IL	70/6311
1907	Robert Simpson	307	Hinsdale GC, Hinsdale, IL	71/6475
1908	Willie Anderson	299	Normancie GC, St. Louis, MO	71/6534
1909	Willie Anderson	288	Skokie CC, Chicago, IL	72/6913
1910	#Chick Evans, Jr.	6&5	Beverly CC, Chicago, IL	72/6754
1911	Robert Simpson	2&1	Kent CC, Grand Rapids, MI	71/6514
1912	Mac Smith	299	Idlewild CC, Chicago, IL	72/6754
1913	John McDermott	295	Memphis CC, Memphis, TN	70/6695
1914	Jim Barnes	293	Interlachen CC, Minneapolis, MN	73/6733
1915	Tom McNamara	304	Glen Oak CC, Chicago, IL	72/6503
1916	Walter Hagen	286	Blue Mound CC, Chicago, IL	N/A
1917	Jim Barnes	283	Westmoreland CC, Chicago, IL	72/6798
1918	No Tournament			
1919	Jim Barnes	283	Mayfield CC, Cleveland, OH	72/6609
1920	Jock Hutchinson	296	Olympia Fields CC, Chicago, IL	71/6749
1921	Walter Hagen	287	Oakwood Club, Cleveland, OH	71/6709
1922	Mike Brady	291	Oakland Hills CC, Detroit, MI	72/7052
1923	Jock Hutchinson	281	Colonial CC, Memphis, TN	70/7116
1924	Bill Mehlhorn	293	Calumet CC, Chicago, IL	72/6524
1925	Mac Smith	281	Youngstown CC, Youngstown, OH	71/6597
1926	Walter Hagen	279	Highland G&CC, Indianapolis, IN	70/6501
1927	Walter Hagen	281	Olympia Fields CC, Chicago, IL	71/6749
1928	Abe Espinosa	291	North Shore GC, Chicago, IL	72/7024
1929	Tommy Armour	273	Ozaukee CC, Milwaukee, WI	70/6553
1930	Gene Sarazen	278	Indianwood G&CC, Detroit, MI	N/A
1931	Ed Dudley	280	Miami Valley GC, Dayton, OH	71/6589
1932	Walter Hagen	287	Canterbury GC, Cleveland, OH	72/6877
1933	Mac Smith	282	Olympia Fields CC, Chicago, IL	71/6749
1934	*Harry Cooper	274	Country Club of Peoria, Peoria, IL	70/6068
1935	John Revolta	290	South Bend CC, South Bend, IN	71/6455
1936	Ralph Guldahl	274	Davenport CC, Davenport, IA	71/6458
1937	*Ralph Guldahl	288	Canterbury CC, Cleveland, OH	72/6877
1938	Ralph Guldahl	279	Westwood CC, St. Louis, MO	72/6785
1939	Byron Nelson	281	Medinah CC, Chicago, IL	71/7104
1940	*Jimmy Demaret	293	River Oaks CC, Houston, TX	72/6868
1941	Ed Oliver	275	Phoenix GC, Phoenix, AZ	71/6726
1942	Herman Barron	276	Phoenix GC, Phoenix, AZ	71/6726
1943-				
1945	No Tournaments			
1946	Ben Hogan	271	Sunset CC, St. Louis, MO	72/6323
1947	Johnny Palmer	270	Salt Lake City CC, Salt Lake City, UT	72/6891
1948	*Ben Hogan	281	Brookfield CC, Buffalo, NY	72/6813
1949	Sam Snead	268	Keller GC, St. Paul, MN	72/6542
1950	Sam Snead	282	Brentwood CC, Los Angeles, CA	72/6729
1951	Marty Furgol	270	Davenport CC, Davenport, IA	71/6450
1952	Lloyd Mangrum	274	Westwood CC, St. Louis, MO	72/6785
1953	Dutch Harrison	278	Bellerive CC, St. Louis, MO	71/7305
1954	*Lloyd Mangrum	277	Kenwood CC, Cincinnati, OH	72/6950
1955	Cary Middlecoff	272	Portland GC, Portland, OR	72/6564
1956	*Mike Fetchick	284	Presidio CC, San Francisco, CA	72/6488
1957	*Doug Ford	279	Plum Hollow GC, Detroit, MI	72/6854
1958	Doug Sanders	275	Red Run GC, Royal Oak, MI	72/6801
1959	Mike Souchak	272	Pittsburgh Field Club, Fox Chapel, PA	71/6586
1960	*Stan Leonard	278	Western G & CC, Detroit, MI	72/6808
1961	Arnold Palmer	271	Blythefield CC, Grand Rapids, MI	71/6730
1962	Jacky Cupit	281	Medinah CC, Medinah, IL	71/7014
1963	*Arnold Palmer	280	Beverly CC, Chicago, IL	71/6923
1964	Chi Chi Rodriquez	268	Tam O'Shanter CC, Niles, IL	71/6686
1965	Billy Casper	270	Tam O'Shanter CC, Niles, IL	71/6686

KEY * = Playoff # = Amateur ~ = Rain-curtailed A = Second tournament that year

Year	Winner	Score	Location	Par/Yards
1966	Billy Casper	283	Medinah CC, Medinah, IL	71/7014
1967	Jack Nicklaus	274	Beverly CC, Chicago, IL	71/6923
1968	Jack Nicklaus	273	Olympia Fields CC, Olympia Fields, IL	71/6749
1969	Billy Casper	276	Midlothia CC, Midlothia, IL	71/6654
1970	Hugh Royer	273	Beverly CC, Chicago, IL	71/6923
1971	Bruce Crampton	279	Olympia Fields CC, Olympia Fields, IL	71/6749
1972	Jim Jamieson	271	Sunset Ridge, Winnetka, IL	71/6716
1973	Billy Casper	272	Midlothian CC, Midlothian, IL	71/6654
1974	Tom Watson	287	Butler National GC, Oak Brook, IL	71/7002
1975	Hale Irwin	283	Butler National GC, Oak Brook, IL	71/7002
1976	Al Geiberger	288	Butler National GC, Oak Brook, IL	71/7002
1977	Tom Watson	283	Butler National GC, Oak Brook, IL	72/7097
1978	*Andy Bean	282	Butler National GC, Oak Brook, IL	72/7097
1979	*Larry Nelson	286	Butler National GC, Oak Brook, IL	72/7097
1980	Scott Simpson	281	Butler National GC, Oak Brook, IL	72/7097
1981	Ed Fiori	277	Butler National GC, Oak Brook, IL	72/7097
1982	Tom Weiskopf	276	Butler National GC, Oak Brook, IL	72/7097
1983	Mark McCumber	284	Butler National GC, Oak Brook, IL	72/7097
1984	*Tom Watson	280	Butler National GC, Oak Brook, IL	72/7097
1985	#Scott Verplank	279	Butler National GC, Oak Brook, IL	72/7097
1986	*Tom Kite	286	Butler National GC, Oak Brook, IL	72/7097

BEATRICE WESTERN OPEN

Year	Winner	Score	Location	Par/Yards
1987	~D. A. Weibring	207	Butler National GC, Oak Brook, IL**	72/6752

** Rain forced play to be held on nine holes of Butler National and nine holes at adjacent Oak Brook Village course.

Year	Winner	Score	Location	Par/Yards
1988	Jim Benepe	278	Butler National GC, Oak Brook, IL	72/7097
1989	*Mark McCumber	275	Butler National GC, Oak Brook, IL	72/7097

CENTEL WESTERN OPEN

Year	Winner	Score	Location	Par/Yards
1990	Wayne Levi	275	Butler National GC, Oak Brook, IL	72/7097
1991	Russ Cochran	275	Cog Hill CC (Dubsdread), Lemont, IL	72/7040
1992	Ben Crenshaw	276	Cog Hill CC (Dubsdread), Lemont, IL	72/7040

SPRINT WESTERN OPEN

Year	Winner	Score	Location	Par/Yards
1993	Nick Price	269	Cog Hill CC (Dubsdread), Lemont, IL	72/7040

ANHEUSER-BUSCH GOLF CLASSIC

KAISER INTERNATIONAL OPEN INVITATIONAL

Year	Winner	Score	Location	Par/Yards
1968	Kermit Zarley	273	Silverado CC, Napa, CA	N-72/6849, S-71/6602
1969	~Miller Barber	135	Silverado CC, Napa, CA	N-72/6849, S-71/6602
1969A	*Jack Nicklaus	273	Silverado CC, Napa, CA	N-72/6849, S-71/6602
1970	*Ken Still	278	Silverado CC, Napa, CA	N-72/6849, S-71/6602
1971	Billy Casper	269	Silverado CC, Napa, CA	N-72/6849, S-71/6602
1972	George Knudson	271	Silverado CC, Napa, CA	N-72/6849, S-71/6602
1973	*Ed Sneed	275	Silverado CC, Napa, CA	N-72/6849, S-71/6602
1974	Johnny Miller	271	Silverado CC, Napa, CA	N-72/6849, S-71/6602
1975	Johnny Miller	272	Silverado CC, Napa, CA	N-72/6849, S-71/6602
1976	J. C. Snead	274	Silverado CC, Napa, CA	N-72/6849, S-71/6602

ANHEUSER-BUSCH GOLF CLASSIC

Year	Winner	Score	Location	Par/Yards
1977	Miller Barber	272	Silverado CC, Napa, CA	N-72/6849, S-71/6602
1978	Tom Watson	270	Silverado CC, Napa, CA	N-72/6849, S-71/6602
1979	John Fought	277	Silverado CC, Napa, CA	N-72/6849, S-72/6619
1980	Ben Crenshaw	272	Silverado CC, Napa, CA	N-72/6849, S-72/6619
1981	John Mahaffey	276	Kingsmill GC, Kingsmill, VA	71/6776
1982	~Calvin Peete	203	Kingsmill GC, Kingsmill, VA	71/6776
1983	Calvin Peete	276	Kingsmill GC, Kingsmill, VA	71/6776
1984	Ronnie Black	267	Kingsmill GC, Kingsmill, VA	71/6776
1985	*Mark Wiebe	273	Kingsmill GC, Kingsmill, VA	71/6776
1986	Fuzzy Zoeller	274	Kingsmill GC, Kingsmill, VA	71/6776
1987	Mark McCumber	267	Kingsmill GC, Kingsmill, VA	71/6776
1988	*Tom Sieckmann	270	Kingsmill GC, Kingsmill, VA	71/6776
1989	*Mike Donald	268	Kingsmill GC, Kingsmill, VA	71/6776

KEY * = Playoff # = Amateur ~ = Rain-curtailed

Past Winners of PGA TOUR Events *(cont'd.)*

Year	Winner	Score	Location	Par/Yards
1990	Lanny Wadkins	266	Kingsmill GC, Kingsmill, VA	71/6776
1991	*Mike Hulbert	266	Kingsmill GC, Kingsmill, VA	71/6776
1992	David Peoples	271	Kingsmill GC, Kingsmill, VA	71/6776
1993	Jim Gallagher, Jr.	269	Kingsmill GC, Kingsmill, VA	71/6776

DEPOSIT GUARANTY GOLF CLASSIC

Year	Winner	Score	Location	Par/Yards
MAGNOLIA STATE CLASSIC				
1968	*B.R. McLendon	269	Hattiesburg CC, Hattiesburg, MS	70/6280
1969	Larry Mowry	272	Hattiesburg CC, Hattiesburg, MS	70/6280
1970	Chris Blocker	271	Hattiesburg CC, Hattiesburg, MS	70/6280
1971	Roy Pace	270	Hattiesburg CC, Hattiesburg, MS	70/6280
1972	Mike Morey	269	Hattiesburg CC, Hattiesburg, MS	70/6280
1973	Dwight Nevil	268	Hattiesburg CC, Hattiesburg, MS	70/6280
1974	~Dwight Nevil	133	Hattiesburg CC, Hattiesburg, MS	70/6280
1975	Bob Wynn	270	Hattiesburg CC, Hattiesburg, MS	70/6280
1976	Dennis Meyer	271	Hattiesburg CC, Hattiesburg, MS	70/6280
1977	Mike McCullough	269	Hattiesburg CC, Hattiesburg, MS	70/6280
1978	Craig Stadler	268	Hattiesburg CC, Hattiesburg, MS	70/6280
1979	Bobby Walzel	272	Hattiesburg CC, Hattiesburg, MS	70/6280
1980	~*Roger Maltbie	65	Hattiesburg CC, Hattiesburg, MS	70/6280
1981	*Tom Jones	268	Hattiesburg CC, Hattiesburg, MS	70/6280
1982	Payne Stewart	270	Hattiesburg CC, Hattiesburg, MS	70/6280
1983	~Russ Cochran	203	Hattiesburg CC, Hattiesburg, MS	70/6280
1984	~*Lance Ten Broeck	201	Hattiesburg CC, Hattiesburg, MS	70/6280
1985	~*Jim Gallagher, Jr.	131	Hattiesburg CC, Hattiesburg, MS	70/6280
DEPOSIT GUARANTY CLASSIC				
1986	Dan Halldorson	263	Hattiesburg CC, Hattiesburg, MS	72/6594
1987	David Ogrin	267	Hattiesburg CC, Hattiesburg, MS	72/6594
1988	Frank Conner	267	Hattiesburg CC, Hattiesburg, MS	72/6594
1989	~*Jim Booros	199	Hattiesburg CC, Hattiesburg, MS	72/6594
1990	Gene Sauers	268	Hattiesburg CC, Hattiesburg, MS	72/6594
1991	*Larry Silveira	266	Hattiesburg CC, Hattiesburg, MS	72/6594
1992	Richard Zokol	267	Hattiesburg CC, Hattiesburg, MS	72/6594
1993	Greg Kraft	267	Hattiesburg CC, Hattiesburg, MS	72/6594

Note: 1983-85 TPS Event

NEW ENGLAND CLASSIC

Year	Winner	Score	Location	Par/Yards
CARLING WORLD OPEN				
1965	Tony Lema	279	Pleasant Valley CC, Sutton, MA	71/7110
KEMPER OPEN				
1968	Arnold Palmer	276	Pleasant Valley CC, Sutton, MA	71/7110
AVCO GOLF CLASSIC				
1969	Tom Shaw	280	Pleasant Valley CC, Sutton, MA	71/7110
1970	Billy Casper	277	Pleasant Valley CC, Sutton, MA	71/7110
MASSACHUSETTS CLASSIC				
1971	Dave Stockton	275	Pleasant Valley CC, Sutton, MA	72/7241
USI CLASSIC				
1972	Bruce Devlin	275	Pleasant Valley CC, Sutton, MA	72/7241
1973	Lanny Wadkins	279	Pleasant Valley CC, Sutton, MA	72/7241
PLEASANT VALLEY CLASSIC				
1974	Victor Regalado	278	Pleasant Valley CC, Sutton, MA	71/7110
1975	Roger Maltbie	276	Pleasant Valley CC, Sutton, MA	71/7110
1976	Bud Allin	277	Pleasant Valley CC, Sutton, MA	71/7110
1977	Raymond Floyd	271	Pleasant Valley CC, Sutton, MA	71/7110
AMERICAN OPTICAL CLASSIC				
1978	John Mahaffey	270	Pleasant Valley CC, Sutton, MA	71/7110
1979	Lou Graham	275	Pleasant Valley CC, Sutton, MA	71/7110
PLEASANT VALLEY JIMMY FUND CLASSIC				
1980	*Wayne Levi	273	Pleasant Valley CC, Sutton, MA	71/7110

KEY * = Playoff # = Amateur ~ = Rain-curtailed

Past Winners of PGA TOUR Events *(cont'd.)*

Year	Winner	Score	Location	Par/Yards
1981	Jack Renner	273	Pleasant Valley CC, Sutton, MA	71/7110
BANK OF BOSTON CLASSIC				
1982	Bob Gilder	271	Pleasant Valley CC, Sutton, MA	71/7110
1983	Mark Lye	273	Pleasant Valley CC, Sutton, MA	71/7110
1984	George Archer	270	Pleasant Valley CC, Sutton, MA	71/7110
1985	George Burns	267	Pleasant Valley CC, Sutton, MA	71/7110
1986	*Gene Sauers	274	Pleasant Valley CC, Sutton, MA	71/7110
1987	~Sam Randolph	199	Pleasant Valley CC, Sutton, MA	71/7110
1988	Mark Calcavecchia	274	Pleasant Valley CC, Sutton, MA	71/7110
1989	Blaine McCallister	271	Pleasant Valley CC, Sutton, MA	71/7110
1990	Morris Hatalsky	275	Pleasant Valley CC, Sutton, MA	71/7110
NEW ENGLAND CLASSIC				
1991	*Bruce Fleisher	268	Pleasant Valley CC, Sutton, MA	71/7110
1992	Brad Faxon	268	Pleasant Valley CC, Sutton, MA	71/7110
1993	Paul Azinger	268	Pleasant Valley CC, Sutton, MA	71/7110

FEDERAL EXPRESS ST. JUDE CLASSIC

Year	Winner	Score	Location	Par/Yards
MEMPHIS INVITATIONAL OPEN				
1958	Billy Maxwell	267	Colonial CC, Memphis, TN	70/6466
1959	*Don Whitt	272	Colonial CC, Memphis, TN	70/6466
1960	*Tommy Bolt	273	Colonial CC, Memphis, TN	70/6466
1961	Cary Middlecoff	266	Colonial CC, Memphis, TN	70/6466
1962	*Lionel Hebert	267	Colonial CC, Memphis, TN	70/6466
1963	*Tony Lema	270	Colonial CC, Memphis, TN	70/6466
1964	Mike Souchak	270	Colonial CC, Memphis, TN	70/6466
1965	*Jack Nicklaus	271	Colonial CC, Memphis, TN	70/6466
1966	Bert Yancey	265	Colonial CC, Memphis, TN	70/6466
1967	Dave Hill	272	Colonial CC, Memphis, TN	70/6466
1968	Bob Lunn	268	Colonial CC, Memphis, TN	70/6466
1969	Dave Hill	265	Colonial CC, Memphis, TN	70/6466
DANNY THOMAS MEMPHIS CLASSIC				
1970	Dave Hill	267	Colonial CC, Memphis, TN	70/6466
1971	Lee Trevino	268	Colonial CC, Memphis, TN	70/6466
1972	Lee Trevino	281	Colonial CC, Cordova, TN	S-72/6883
1973	Dave Hill	283	Colonial CC, Cordova, TN	S-72/7282
1974	Gary Player	273	Colonial CC, Cordova, TN	S-72/7282
1975	Gene Littler	270	Colonial CC, Cordova, TN	S-72/7282
1976	Gibby Gilbert	273	Colonial CC, Cordova, TN	S-72/7282
1977	Al Geiberger	273	Colonial CC, Cordova, TN	S-72/7282
1978	*Andy Bean	277	Colonial CC, Cordova, TN	S-72/7282
1979	*Gil Morgan	278	Colonial CC, Cordova, TN	S-72/7282
1980	Lee Trevino	272	Colonial CC, Cordova, TN	S-72/7282
1981	Jerry Pate	274	Colonial CC, Cordova, TN	S-72/7282
1982	Raymond Floyd	271	Colonial CC, Cordova, TN	S-72/7282
1983	Larry Mize	274	Colonial CC, Cordova, TN	S-72/7282
1984	Bob Eastwood	280	Colonial CC, Cordova, TN	S-72/7282
ST. JUDE MEMPHIS CLASSIC				
1985	*Hal Sutton	279	Colonial CC, Cordova, TN	S-72/7282
FEDERAL EXPRESS ST. JUDE CLASSIC				
1986	Mike Hulbert	280	Colonial CC, Cordova, TN	S-72/7282
1987	Curtis Strange	275	Colonial CC, Cordova, TN	S-72/7282
1988	Jodie Mudd	273	Colonial CC, Cordova, TN	S-72/7282
1989	John Mahaffey	272	TPC at Southwind, Germantown, TN	71/7006
1990	*Tom Kite	269	TPC at Southwind, Germantown, TN	71/7006
1991	Fred Couples	269	TPC at Southwind, Germantown, TN	71/7006
1992	Jay Haas	263	TPC at Southwind, Germantown, TN	71/7006
1993	Nick Price	266	TPC at Southwind, Germantown, TN	71/7006

KEY * = Playoff # = Amateur ~ = Rain-curtailed 2T = Second Tour

Past Winners of PGA TOUR Events *(cont'd.)*

BUICK OPEN

Year	Winner	Score	Location	Par/Yards
BUICK OPEN INVITATIONAL				
1958	Billy Casper	285	Warwick Hills CC, Grand Blanc, MI	72/7014
1959	Art Wall	282	Warwick Hills CC, Grand Blanc, MI	72/7014
1960	Mike Souchak	282	Warwick Hills CC, Grand Blanc, MI	72/7014
1961	Jack Burke, Jr.	284	Warwick Hills CC, Grand Blanc, MI	72/7014
1962	Bill Collins	284	Warwick Hills CC, Grand Blanc, MI	72/7014
1963	Julius Boros	274	Warwick Hills CC, Grand Blanc, MI	72/7014
1964	Tony Lema	277	Warwick Hills CC, Grand Blanc, MI	72/7014
1965	Tony Lema	280	Warwick Hills CC, Grand Blanc, MI	72/7014
1966	Phil Rodgers	284	Warwick Hills CC, Grand Blanc, MI	72/7014
1967	Julius Boros	283	Warwick Hills CC, Grand Blanc, MI	72/7014
1968	Tom Weiskopf	280	Warwick Hills CC, Grand Blanc, MI	72/7014
1969	Dave Hill	277	Warwick Hills CC, Grand Blanc, MI	72/7014
VERN PARSELL BUICK OPEN				
1972	Gary Groh	273	Flint Elks CC, Flint, MI	72/6902
LAKE MICHIGAN CLASSIC				
1973	(2T) Wilf Homenuik	215	Benton Harbor Elks CC, Benton Harbor, MI	71/6690
FLINT ELKS OPEN				
1974	(2T) Bryan Abbott	135	Flint Elks CC, Flint, MI	72/6902
1975	(2T) Spike Kelley	208	Flint Elks CC, Flint, MI	72/6902
1976	(2T) Ed Sabo	279	Flint Elks CC, Flint, MI	72/6902
1977	Bobby Cole	271	Flint Elks CC, Flint, MI	72/6902
BUICK GOODWRENCH OPEN				
1978	*Jack Newton	280	Warwick Hills CC, Grand Blanc, MI	72/7014
1979	*John Fought	280	Warwick Hills CC, Grand Blanc, MI	72/7014
1980	Peter Jacobsen	276	Warwick Hills CC, Grand Blanc, MI	72/7014
BUICK OPEN				
1981	*Hale Irwin	277	Warwick Hills CC, Grand Blanc, MI	72/7014
1982	Lanny Wadkins	273	Warwick Hills CC, Grand Blanc, MI	72/7014
1983	Wayne Levi	272	Warwick Hills CC, Grand Blanc, MI	72/7014
1984	Denis Watson	271	Warwick Hills CC, Grand Blanc, MI	72/7014
1985	Ken Green	268	Warwick Hills CC, Grand Blanc, MI	72/7014
1986	Ben Crenshaw	270	Warwick Hills CC, Grand Blanc, MI	72/7014
1987	Robert Wrenn	262	Warwick Hills CC, Grand Blanc, MI	72/7014
1988	Scott Verplank	268	Warwick Hills CC, Grand Blanc, MI	72/7014
1989	Leonard Thompson	273	Warwick Hills CC, Grand Blanc, MI	72/7014
1990	Chip Beck	272	Warwick Hills CC, Grand Blanc, MI	72/7014
1991	*Brad Faxon	271	Warwick Hills CC, Grand Blanc, MI	72/7014
1992	*Dan Forsman	276	Warwick Hills CC, Grand Blanc, MI	72/7014
1993	Larry Mize	272	Warwick Hills CC, Grand Blanc, MI	72/7014

THE INTERNATIONAL

Year	Winner	Score	Location	Par/Yards
1986	Ken Green	Plus 12	Castle Pines GC, Castle Rock, CO	72/7503
1987	John Cook	Plus 11	Castle Pines GC, Castle Rock, CO	72/7503
1988	Joey Sindelar	Plus 17	Castle Pines GC, Castle Rock, CO	72/7503
1989	Greg Norman	Plus 13	Castle Pines GC, Castle Rock, CO	72/7503
1990	Davis Love III	Plus 14	Castle Pines GC, Castle Rock, CO	72/7503
1991	Jose Maria Olazabal	Plus 10	Castle Pines GC, Castle Rock, CO	72/7503
1992	Brad Faxon	Plus 14	Castle Pines GC, Castle Rock, CO	72/7503
1993	Phil Mickelson	Plus 45	Castle Pines GC, Castle Rock, CO	72/7503

(Note: Prior to 1993, winning score was for fourth round only. Beginning in 1993, winning score was total for four rounds)

NEC WORLD SERIES OF GOLF

Year	Winner	Score	Location	Par/Yards
WORLD SERIES OF GOLF				
1976	Jack Nicklaus	275	Firestone CC (South Course), Akron, OH	70/7149
1977	Lanny Wadkins	267	Firestone CC (South Course), Akron, OH	70/7149

KEY * = Playoff # = Amateur ~ = Rain-curtailed

Past Winners of PGA TOUR Events (cont'd.)

Year	Winner	Score	Location	Par/Yards
1978*	Gil Morgan	278	Firestone CC (South Course), Akron, OH	70/7149
1979	Lon Hinkle	272	Firestone CC (South Course), Akron, OH	70/7149
1980	Tom Watson	270	Firestone CC (South Course), Akron, OH	70/7149
1981	Bill Rogers	275	Firestone CC (South Course), Akron, OH	70/7149
1982*	Craig Stadler	278	Firestone CC (South Course), Akron, OH	70/7149
1983	Nick Price	270	Firestone CC (South Course), Akron, OH	70/7149
NEC WORLD SERIES OF GOLF				
1984	Denis Watson	271	Firestone CC (South Course), Akron, OH	70/7149
1985	Roger Maltbie	268	Firestone CC (South Course), Akron, OH	70/7149
1986	Dan Pohl	277	Firestone CC (South Course), Akron, OH	70/7149
1987	Curtis Strange	275	Firestone CC (South Course), Akron, OH	70/7149
1988*	Mike Reid	275	Firestone CC (South Course), Akron, OH	70/7149
1989*	David Frost	276	Firestone CC (South Course), Akron, OH	70/7149
1990	Jose Maria Olazabal	262	Firestone CC (South Course), Akron, OH	70/7149
1991*	Tom Purtzer	279	Firestone CC (South Course), Akron, OH	70/7149
1992	Craig Stadler	273	Firestone CC (South Course), Akron, OH	70/7149
1993	Fulton Allem	270	Firestone CC (South Course), Akron, OH	70/7149

GREATER MILWAUKEE OPEN

Year	Winner	Score	Location	Par/Yards
GREATER MILWAUKEE OPEN				
1968	Dave Stockton	275	Northshore CC, Mequon, WI	71/7075
1969	Ken Still	277	Northshore CC, Mequon, WI	71/7075
1970	Deane Beman	276	Northshore CC, Mequon, WI	71/7075
1971	Dave Eichelberger	270	Tripoli GC, Milwaukee, WI	71/6514
1972	Jim Colbert	271	Tripoli GC, Milwaukee, WI	71/6514
1973	Dave Stockton	276	Tuckaway CC, Franklin, WI	72/7030
1974	Ed Sneed	276	Tuckaway CC, Franklin, WI	72/7030
1975	Art Wall	271	Tuckaway CC, Franklin, WI	72/7030
1976	Dave Hill	270	Tuckaway CC, Franklin, WI	72/7030
1977	Dave Eichelberger	278	Tuckaway CC, Franklin, WI	72/7030
1978	*Lee Elder	275	Tuckaway CC, Franklin, WI	72/7030
1979	Calvin Peete	269	Tuckaway CC, Franklin, WI	72/7030
1980	Bill Kratzert	266	Tuckaway CC, Franklin, WI	72/7030
1981	Jay Haas	274	Tuckaway CC, Franklin, WI	72/7030
1982	Calvin Peete	274	Tuckaway CC, Franklin, WI	72/7030
1983	*Morris Hatalsky	275	Tuckaway CC, Franklin, WI	72/7030
1984	Mark O'Meara	272	Tuckaway CC, Franklin, WI	72/7030
1985	Jim Thorpe	274	Tuckaway CC, Franklin, WI	72/7030
1986	*Corey Pavin	272	Tuckaway CC, Franklin, WI	72/7030
1987	Gary Hallberg	269	Tuckaway CC, Franklin, WI	72/7030
1988	Ken Green	268	Tuckaway CC, Franklin, WI	72/7030
1989	Greg Norman	269	Tuckaway CC, Franklin, WI	72/7030
1990	*Jim Gallagher, Jr.	271	Tuckaway CC, Franklin, WI	72/7030
1991	Mark Brooks	270	Tuckaway CC, Franklin, WI	72/7030
1992	Richard Zokol	269	Tuckaway CC, Franklin, WI	72/7030
1993	*Billy Mayfair	270	Tuckaway CC, Franklin, WI	72/7030

BELL CANADIAN OPEN

Year	Winner	Score	Location	Par/Yards
1904	J. H. Oke	156	Royal Montreal GC, Montreal, Quebec	N/A
1905	George Cumming	148	Toronto GC, Toronto, Ontario	N/A
1906	Charles Murray	170	Royal Ottawa GC, Ottawa, Ontario	N/A
1907	Percy Barrett	306	Lambton GC, Toronto, Ontario	N/A
1908	Albert Murray	300	Royal Montreal GC, Montreal, Quebec	N/A
1909	Karl Keffer	309	Toronto GC, Toronto, Ontario	N/A
1910	Daniel Kenny	303	Lambton GC, Toronto, Ontario	70/N/A
1911	Charles Murray	314	Royal Ottawa GC, Ottawa, Ontario	N/A
1912	George Sargent	299	Rosedale GC, Toronto, Ontario	N/A
1913	Albert Murray	295	Royal Montreal GC, Montreal, Quebec	N/A

KEY * = Playoff   # = Amateur   ~ = Rain-curtailed

Past Winners of PGA TOUR Events *(cont'd.)*

Year	Winner	Score	Location	Par/Yards
1914	Karl Keffer	300	Toronto GC, Toronto, Ontario	N/A
1915-				
1918	No Tournaments			
1919	J. Douglas Edgar	278	Hamilton GC, Hamilton, Ontario	N/A
1920	*J. Douglas Edgar	298	Rivermead GC, Ottawa, Ontario	N/A
1921	W. H. Trovinger	293	Toronto GC, Toronto, Ontario	N/A
1922	Al Watrous	303	Mt. Bruno GC, Montreal, Quebec	72/6643
1923	C. W. Hackney	295	Lakeview CG, Toronto, Ontario	N/A
1924	Leo Diegel	285	Mt. Bruno GC, Montreal, Quebec	72/6643
1925	Leo Diegel	295	Lambton GC, Toronto, Ontario	N/A
1926	Mac Smith	283	Royal Montreal GC, Montreal, Quebec	N/A
1927	Tommy Armour	288	Toronto GC, Toronto, Ontario	N/A
1928	Leo Diegel	282	Rosedale GC, Toronto, Ontario	N/A
1929	Leo Diegel	274	Kanawaki GC, Montreal, Quebec	N/A
1930	*Tommy Armour	273	Hamilton GC, Hamilton, Ontario	N/A
1931	*Walter Hagen	292	Mississauga G & CC, Toronto, Ontario	N/A
1932	Harry Cooper	290	Ottawa Hunt Club, Ottawa, Ontario	N/A
1933	Joe Kirkwood	282	Royal York CG, Toronto, Ontario	N/A
1934	Tommy Armour	287	Lakeview CG, Toronto, Ontario	N/A
1935	Gene Kunes	280	Summerlea GC, Montreal, Quebec	N/A
1936	Lawson Little	271	St. Andrews GC, Toronto, Ontario	70/N/A
1937	Harry Cooper	285	St. Andrews GC, Toronto, Ontario	70/N/A
1938	*Sam Snead	277	Mississauga G&CC, Toronto, Ontario	N/A
1939	Harold McSpaden	282	Riverside GC, St. John, New Brunswick	70/6231
1940	*Sam Snead	281	Scarborough G&CC, Toronto, Ontario	/6685
1941	Sam Snead	274	Lambton GC, Toronto, Ontario	70/N/A
1942	Craig Wood	275	Mississauga G&CC, Toronto, Ontario	N/A
1943-				
1944	No Tournaments			
1945	Byron Nelson	280	Thornhill GC, Toronto, Ontario	N/A
1946	*George Fazio	278	Beaconsfield GC, Montreal, Quebec	N/A
1947	Bobby Locke	268	Scarborough G&CC, Toronto, Ontario	N/A
1948	C. W. Congdon	280	Shaugnessy Heights GC, Vancouver, B.C.	N/A
1949	Dutch Harrison	271	St. Georges G&CC, Toronto, Ontario	N/A
1950	Jim Ferrier	271	Royal Montreal GC, Montreal, Quebec	N/A
1951	Jim Ferrier	273	Mississauga G & CC, Toronto, Ontario	N/A
1952	John Palmer	263	St. Charles CC, Winnipeg, Manitoba	N/A
1953	Dave Douglas	273	Scarborough G&CC, Toronto, Ontario	N/A
1954	Pat Fletcher	280	Point Grey GC, Vancouver, B.C.	N/A
1955	Arnold Palmer	265	Weston GC, Toronto, Ontario	N/A
1956	#Doug Sanders	273	Beaconsfield GC, Montreal, Quebec	N/A
1957	George Bayer	271	Westmount G&CC, Kitchener, Ontario	N/A
1958	Wesley Ellis, Jr.	267	Mayfair G&CC, Edmonton, Alberta	N/A
1959	Doug Ford	276	Islesmere G&CC, Montreal, Quebec	N/A
1960	Art Wall, Jr.	269	St. Georges G&CC, Toronto, Ontario	N/A
1961	Jacky Cupit	270	Niakwa GC, Winnipeg, Manitoba	N/A
1962	Ted Kroll	278	Laval sue-le-Lac, Montreal, Quebec	N/A
1963	Doug Ford	280	Scarborough G&CC, Toronto, Ontario	N/A
1964	Kel Nagle	277	Pinegrove CC, St. Luc, Quebec	N/A
1965	Gene Littler	273	Mississauga G&CC, Toronto, Ontario	N/A
1966	Don Massengale	280	Shaughnessy G&CC, Toronto, Ontario	N/A
1967	*Billy Casper	279	Montreal Municipal GC, Montreal, Quebec	N/A
1968	Bob Charles	274	St. Georges G&CC, Toronto, Ontario	70/6792
1969	*Tommy Aaron	275	Pinegrove G&CC, St. Luc, Quebec	72/7076
1970	Kermit Zarley	279	London Hunt & CC, London, Ontario	72/7168
1971	*Lee Trevino	275	Richelieu Valley GC, Montreal, Quebec	72/6920
1972	Gay Brewer	275	Cherry Hill Club, Ridgeway, Ontario	71/6751
1973	Tom Weiskopf	278	Reichelieu Valley G&CC, Ste. Julie de Vercheres, Que.	72/6905
1974	Bobby Nichols	270	Mississaugua G&CC, Mississauga, Ontario	70/6788
1975	*Tom Weiskopf	274	Royal Montreal GC, Ile Bizard, Quebec	70/6628

KEY * = Playoff # = Amateur ~ = Rain-curtailed

Past Winners of PGA TOUR Events *(cont'd.)*

Year	Winner	Score	Location	Par/Yards
1976	Jerry Pate	267	Essex G&CC,Windsor, Ontario.	70/6696
1977	Lee Trevino	280	Glen Abbey GC, Oakville, Ontario	72/7096
1978	Bruce Lietzke	283	Glen Abbey GC, Oakville, Ontario	71/7050
1979	Lee Trevino	281	Glen Abbey GC, Oakville, Ontario	71/7059
1980	Bob Gilder	274	Royal Montreal GC, Ile Bizard, Quebec	70/6628
1981	Peter Oosterhuis	280	Glen Abbey GC, Oakville, Ontario	71/7060
1982	Bruce Lietzke	277	Glen Abbey GC, Oakville, Ontario	71/7060
1983	*John Cook	277	Glen Abbey GC, Oakville, Ontario	71/7055
1984	Greg Norman	278	Glen Abbey GC, Oakville, Ontario	72/7102
1985	Curtis Strange	279	Glen Abbey GC, Oakville, Ontario	72/7102
1986	Bob Murphy	280	Glen Abbey GC, Oakville, Ontario	72/7102
1987	Curtis Strange	276	Glen Abbey GC, Oakville, Ontario	72/7102
1988	Ken Green	275	Glen Abbey GC, Oakville, Ontario	72/7102
1989	Steve Jones	271	Glen Abbey GC, Oakville, Ontario	72/7102
1990	Wayne Levi	278	Glen Abbey GC, Oakville, Ontario	72/7102
1991	Nick Price	273	Glen Abbey GC, Oakville, Ontario	72/7102
1992	*Greg Norman	280	Glen Abbey GC, Oakville, Ontario	72/7102
1993	David Frost	279	Glen Abbey GC, Oakville, Ontario	72/7102

HARDEE'S GOLF CLASSIC

Year	Winner	Score	Location	Par/Yards
QUAD CITIES OPEN				
1972	Deane Beman	279	Crow Valley CC, Bettendorf, IA	71/6501
1973	Sam Adams	268	Crow Valley CC, Bettendorf, IA	71/6501
1974	Dave Stockton	271	Crow Valley CC, Bettendorf, IA	71/6501
ED MCMAHON-JAYCEES QUAD CITY OPEN				
1975	Roger Maltbie	275	Oakwood CC, Coal Valley, IL	70/6602
1976	John Lister	268	Oakwood CC, Coal Valley, IL	70/6602
1977	Mike Morley	267	Oakwood CC, Coal Valley, IL	70/6602
1978	Victor Regalado	269	Oakwood CC, Coal Valley, IL	70/6602
1979	D. A. Weibring	266	Oakwood CC, Coal Valley, IL	70/6602
QUAD CITIES OPEN				
1980	Scott Hoch	266	Oakwood CC, Coal Valley, IL	70/6602
1981	*Dave Barr	270	Oakwood CC, Coal Valley, IL	70/6602
MILLER HIGH-LIFE QUAD CITIES OPEN				
1982	Payne Stewart	268	Oakwood CC, Coal Valley, IL	70/6602
1983	*Danny Edwards	266	Oakwood CC, Coal Valley, IL	70/6602
1984	Scott Hoch	266	Oakwood CC, Coal Valley, IL	70/6602
LITE QUAD CITIES OPEN				
1985	Dan Forsman	267	Oakwood CC, Coal Valley, IL	70/6602
HARDEE'S GOLF CLASSIC				
1986	Mark Wiebe	268	Oakwood CC, Coal Valley, IL	70/6602
1987	Kenny Knox	265	Oakwood CC, Coal Valley, IL	70/6606
1988	Blaine McCallister	261	Oakwood CC, Coal Valley, IL	70/6606
1989	Curt Byrum	268	Oakwood CC, Coal Valley, IL	70/6606
1990	*Joey Sindelar	268	Oakwood CC, Coal Valley, IL	70/6606
1991	D. A. Weibring	267	Oakwood CC, Coal Valley, IL	70/6796
1992	David Frost	266	Oakwood CC, Coal Valley, IL	70/6796
1993	David Frost	259	Oakwood CC, Coal Valley, IL	70/6796

B. C. OPEN

Year	Winner	Score	Location	Par/Yards
BROOME COUNTY OPEN				
1971	*Claude Harmon, Jr.	69	En Joie GC, Endicott, NY	71/6966
B. C. OPEN				
1972	Bob Payne	136	En Joie GC, Endicott, NY	71/6966
1973	Hubert Green	266	En Joie GC, Endicott, NY	71/6966
1974	*Richie Karl	273	En Joie GC, Endicott, NY	71/6966

KEY * = Playoff # = Amateur ~ = Rain-curtailed

330

Year	Winner	Score	Location	Par/Yards
1975	Don Iverson	274	En Joie GC, Endicott, NY	71/6966
1976	Bob Wynn	271	En Joie GC, Endicott, NY	71/6966
1977	Gil Morgan	270	En Joie GC, Endicott, NY	71/6966
1978	Tom Kite	267	En Joie GC, Endicott, NY	71/6966
1979	Howard Twitty	270	En Joie GC, Endicott, NY	71/6966
1980	Don Pooley	271	En Joie GC, Endicott, NY	71/6966
1981	Jay Haas	270	En Joie GC, Endicott, NY	71/6966
1982	Calvin Peete	265	En Joie GC, Endicott, NY	71/6966
1983	Pat Lindsey	268	En Joie GC, Endicott, NY	71/6966
1984	Wayne Levi	275	En Joie GC, Endicott, NY	71/6966
1985	Joey Sindelar	274	En Joie GC, Endicott, NY	71/6966
1986	Rick Fehr	267	En Joie GC, Endicott, NY	71/6966
1987	Joey Sindelar	266	En Joie GC, Endicott, NY	71/6966
1988	Bill Glasson	268	En Joie GC, Endicott, NY	71/6966
1989	*Mike Hulbert	268	En Joie GC, Endicott, NY	71/6966
1990	Nolan Henke	268	En Joie GC, Endicott, NY	71/6966
1991	Fred Couples	269	En Joie GC, Endicott, NY	71/6966
1992	John Daly	266	En Joie GC, Endicott, NY	71/6966
1993	Blaine McCallister	271	En Joie GC, Endicott, NY	71/6966

BUICK SOUTHERN OPEN

Year	Winner	Score	Location	Par/Yards

GREEN ISLAND OPEN INVITATIONAL

Year	Winner	Score	Location	Par/Yards
1970	Mason Rudolph	274	Green Island CC, Columbus, GA	70/6791

SOUTHERN OPEN INVITATIONAL

Year	Winner	Score	Location	Par/Yards
1971	Johnny Miller	267	Green Island CC, Columbus, GA	70/6791
1972	*DeWitt Weaver	276	Green Island CC, Columbus, GA	70/6791
1973	Gary Player	270	Green Island CC, Columbus, GA	70/6791
1974	Forrest Fezler	271	Green Island CC, Columbus, GA	70/6791
1975	Hubert Green	264	Green Island CC, Columbus, GA	70/6791
1976	Mac McClendon	274	Green Island CC, Columbus, GA	70/6791
1977	Jerry Pate	266	Green Island CC, Columbus, GA	70/6791
1978	Jerry Pate	269	Green Island CC, Columbus, GA	70/6791
1979	*Ed Fiori	274	Green Island CC, Columbus, GA	70/6791
1980	Mike Sullivan	269	Green Island CC, Columbus, GA	70/6791
1981	*J. C. Snead	271	Green Island CC, Columbus, GA	70/6791
1982	Bobby Clampett	266	Green Island CC, Columbus, GA	70/6791
1983	*Ronnie Black	271	Green Island CC, Columbus, GA	70/6791
1984	Hubert Green	265	Green Island CC, Columbus, GA	70/6791
1985	Tim Simpson	264	Green Island CC, Columbus, GA	70/6791
1986	Fred Wadsworth	269	Green Island CC, Columbus, GA	70/6791
1987	Ken Brown	266	Green Island CC, Columbus, GA	70/6791
1988	*David Frost	270	Green Island CC, Columbus, GA	70/6791
1989	Ted Schulz	266	Green Island CC, Columbus, GA	70/6791

BUICK SOUTHERN OPEN

Year	Winner	Score	Location	Par/Yards
1990	*Kenny Knox	265	Green Island CC, Columbus, GA	70/6791
1991	David Peoples	276	Callaway Gardens Resort, Pine Mountain, GA	72/7057
1992	~Gary Hallberg	206	Callaway Gardens Resort, Pine Mountain, GA	72/7057
1993	*John Inman	278	Callaway Gardens Resort, Pine Mountain, GA	72/7057

WALT DISNEY WORLD/OLDSMOBILE CLASSIC

Year	Winner	Score	Location	Par/Yards

WALT DISNEY WORLD OPEN INVITATIONAL

Year	Winner	Score	Location	Par/Yards
1971	Jack Nicklaus	273	Magnolia, Walt Disney World, Lake Buena Vista, FL	72/7190
1972	Jack Nicklaus	267	Palm, Walt Disney World, Lake Buena Vista, FL	72/6941
			Magnolia, Walt Disney World, Lake Buena Vista, FL	72/7190
1973	Jack Nicklaus	275	Palm, Walt Disney World, Lake Buena Vista, FL	72/6941
			Magnolia, Walt Disney World, Lake Buena Vista, FL	72/7190

WALT DISNEY WORLD NATIONAL TEAM CHAMPIONSHIP

Year	Winner	Score	Location	Par/Yards
1974	Hubert Green/	255	Palm, Walt Disney World, Lake Buena Vista, FL	72/6941
	Mac McClendon		Magnolia, Walt Disney World, Lake Buena Vista, FL	72/7190

KEY * = Playoff # = Amateur ~ = Rain-curtailed

1975	Jim Colbert/	252	Palm, Walt Disney World, Lake Buena Vista, FL	72/6941
	Dean Refram		Magnolia, Walt Disney World, Lake Buena Vista, FL	72/7190
1976	*Woody Blackburn/	260	Palm, Walt Disney World, Lake Buena Vista, FL	72/6941
	Bill Kratzert		Magnolia, Walt Disney World, Lake Buena Vista, FL	72/7190
1977	Gibby Gilbert/	253	Palm, Walt Disney World, Lake Buena Vista, FL	72/6941
	Grier Jones		Magnolia, Walt Disney World, Lake Buena Vista, FL	72/7190
1978	Wayne Levi/	254	Palm, Walt Disney World, Lake Buena Vista, FL	72/6941
	Bob Mann		Magnolia, Walt Disney World, Lake Buena Vista, FL	72/7190
1979	George Burns/	255	Palm, Walt Disney World, Lake Buena Vista, FL	72/6941
	Ben Crenshaw		Magnolia, Walt Disney World, Lake Buena Vista, FL	72/7190
1980	Danny Edwards/	253	Palm, Walt Disney World, Lake Buena Vista, FL	72/6941
	Dave Edwards		Magnolia, Walt Disney World, Lake Buena Vista, FL	72/7190
1981	Vance Heafner/	275	Palm, Walt Disney World, Lake Buena Vista, FL	72/6941
	Mike Holland		Magnolia, Walt Disney World, Lake Buena Vista, FL	72/7190

WALT DISNEY WORLD GOLF CLASSIC

1982	*Hal Sutton	269	Palm, Walt Disney World, Lake Buena Vista, FL	72/6941
			Magnolia, Walt Disney World, Lake Buena Vista, FL	72/7190
			Lake Buena Vista CC, Lake Buena Vista, FL	72/6706
1983	Payne Stewart	269	Palm, Walt Disney World, Lake Buena Vista, FL	72/6941
			Magnolia, Walt Disney World, Lake Buena Vista, FL	72/7190
			Lake Buena Vista CC, Lake Buena Vista, FL	72/6706
1984	Larry Nelson	266	Palm, Walt Disney World, Lake Buena Vista, FL	72/6941
			Magnolia, Walt Disney World, Lake Buena Vista, FL	72/7190
			Lake Buena Vista CC, Lake Buena Vista, FL	72/6706

WALT DISNEY WORLD OLDSMOBILE CLASSIC

1985	Lanny Wadkins	267	Palm, Walt Disney World, Lake Buena Vista, FL	72/6941
			Magnolia, Walt Disney World, Lake Buena Vista, FL	72/7190
			Lake Buena Vista CC, Lake Buena Vista, FL	72/6706
1986	*Ray Floyd	275	Palm, Walt Disney World, Lake Buena Vista, FL	72/6941
			Magnolia, Walt Disney World, Lake Buena Vista, FL	72/7190
			Lake Buena Vista CC, Lake Buena Vista, FL	72/6706
1987	Larry Nelson	268	Palm, Walt Disney World, Lake Buena Vista, FL	72/6941
			Magnolia, Walt Disney World, Lake Buena Vista, FL	72/7190
			Lake Buena Vista CC, Lake Buena Vista, FL	72/6706
1988	*Bob Lohr	263	Palm, Walt Disney World, Lake Buena Vista, FL	72/6941
			Magnolia, Walt Disney World, Lake Buena Vista, FL	72/7190
			Lake Buena Vista CC, Lake Buena Vista, FL	72/6706
1989	Tim Simpson	272	Palm, Walt Disney World, Lake Buena Vista, FL	72/6941
			Magnolia, Walt Disney World, Lake Buena Vista, FL	72/7190
			Lake Buena Vista CC, Lake Buena Vista, FL	72/6706
1990	Tim Simpson	264	Palm, Walt Disney World, Lake Buena Vista, FL	72/6941
			Magnolia, Walt Disney World, Lake Buena Vista, FL	72/7190
			Lake Buena Vista CC, Lake Buena Vista, FL	72/6706
1991	Mark O'Meara	267	Palm, Walt Disney World, Lake Buena Vista, FL	72/6941
			Magnolia, Walt Disney World, Lake Buena Vista, FL	72/7190
			Lake Buena Vista CC, Lake Buena Vista, FL	72/6706
1992	John Huston	262	Palm, Walt Disney World, Lake Buena Vista, FL	72/6941
			Magnolia, Walt Disney World, Lake Buena Vista, FL	72/7190
			Lake Buena Vista CC, Lake Buena Vista, FL	72/6706
1993	Jeff Maggert	265	Palm, Walt Disney World, Lake Buena Vista, FL	72/6941
			Magnolia, Walt Disney World, Lake Buena Vista, FL	72/7190
			Lake Buena Vista CC, Lake Buena Vista, FL	72/6706

TEXAS OPEN

Year	Winner	Score	Location	Par/Yards
TEXAS OPEN				
1922	Bob MacDonald	281	Brackenridge Park GC, San Antonio, TX	71/6185
1923	Walter Hagen	279	Brackenridge Park GC, San Antonio, TX	71/6185
1924	Joe Kirkwood	279	Brackenridge Park GC, San Antonio, TX	71/6185
1925	Joe Turnesa	284	Brackenridge Park GC, San Antonio, TX	71/6185
1926	Mac Smith	288	Brackenridge Park GC, San Antonio, TX	71/6185

KEY * = Playoff # = Amateur ~ = Rain-curtailed

Year	Winner	Score	Location	Par/Yards
1927	Bobby Cruikshank	272	Willow Springs GC, San Antonio, TX	72/6930
1928	Bill Mehlhorn	297	Willow Springs GC, San Antonio, TX	72/6930
1929	Bill Mehlhorn	277	Brackenridge Park GC, San Antonio, TX	71/6185
1930	Denny Shute	277	Brackenridge Park GC, San Antonio, TX	71/6185
1931	Abe Espinosa	281	Brackenridge Park GC, San Antonio, TX	71/6185
1932	Clarence Clark	287	Brackenridge Park GC, San Antonio, TX	71/6185
1933	No Tournament			
1934	Wiffy Cox	283	Brackenridge Park GC, San Antonio, TX	71/6185
1935-				
1938	No Tournaments			
1939	Dutch Harrison	271	Brackenridge Park GC, San Antonio, TX	71/6185
1940	Byron Nelson	271	Brackenridge Park GC, San Antonio, TX	71/6185
1941	Lawson Little	273	Willow Springs GC, San Antonio, TX	72/6930
1942	*Chick Harbert	272	Willow Springs GC, San Antonio, TX	72/6930
1943	No Tournament			
1944	Johnny Revolta	273	Willow Springs GC, San Antonio, TX	72/6930
1945	Sam Byrd	268	Willow Springs GC, San Antonio, TX	72/6930
1946	Ben Hogan	264	Willow Springs GC, San Antonio, TX	72/6930
1947	Ed Oliver	265	Willow Springs GC, San Antonio, TX	72/6930
1948	Sam Snead	264	Willow Springs GC, San Antonio, TX	72/6930
1949	Dave Douglas	268	Willow Springs GC, San Antonio, TX	72/6930
1950	Sam Snead	265	Brackenridge Park GC, San Antonio, TX	71/6185
			Ft. Sam Houston GC, San Antonio, TX	72/6566
1951	*Dutch Harrison	265	Brackenridge Park GC, San Antonio, TX	71/6185
			Ft. Sam Houston GC, San Antonio, TX	72/6566
1952	Jack Burke, Jr.	260	Brackenridge Park GC, San Antonio, TX	71/6185
1953	Tony Holguin	264	Brackenridge Park GC, San Antonio, TX	71/6185
1954	Chandler Harper	259	Brackenridge Park GC, San Antonio, TX	71/6185
1955	Mike Souchak	257	Brackenridge Park GC, San Antonio, TX	71/6185
1956	Gene Littler	276	Ft. Sam Houston GC, San Antonio, TX	72/6566
1957	Jay Hebert	271	Brackenridge Park GC, San Antonio, TX	71/6185
1958	Bill Johnston	274	Brackenridge Park GC, San Antonio, TX	71/6185
1959	Wes Ellis	276	Brackenridge Park GC, San Antonio, TX	71/6185
1960	Arnold Palmer	276	Ft. Sam Houston GC, San Antonio, TX	72/6566
1961	Arnold Palmer	270	Oak Hills CC, San Antonio, TX	70/6576
1962	Arnold Palmer	273	Oak Hills CC, San Antonio, TX	70/6576
1963	Phil Rodgers	268	Oak Hills CC, San Antonio, TX	70/6576
1964	Bruce Crampton	273	Oak Hills CC, San Antonio, TX	70/6576
1965	Frank Beard	270	Oak Hills CC, San Antonio, TX	70/6576
1966	Harold Henning	272	Oak Hills CC, San Antonio, TX	70/6576
1967	Chi Chi Rodriquez	277	Pecan Valley CC, San Antonio, TX	71/7183
1968	No Tournament			
1969	*Deane Beman	274	Pecan Valley CC, San Antonio, TX	71/7183

SAN ANTONIO TEXAS OPEN

Year	Winner	Score	Location	Par/Yards
1970	Ron Cerrudo	273	Pecan Valley CC, San Antonio, TX	71/7183
1971	No Tournament			
1972	Mike Hill	273	Woodlake GC, San Antonio, TX	72/7143
1973	Ben Crenshaw	270	Woodlake GC, San Antonio, TX	71/6990
1974	Terry Diehl	269	Woodlake GC, San Antonio, TX	72/7143
1975	*Don January	275	Woodlake GC, San Antonio, TX	72/7143
1976	*Butch Baird	273	Woodlake GC, San Antonio, TX	72/7143
1977	Hale Irwin	266	Oak Hills CC, San Antonio, TX	70/6576
1978	Ron Streck	265	Oak Hills CC, San Antonio, TX	70/6576
1979	Lou Graham	268	Oak Hills CC, San Antonio, TX	70/6576
1980	Lee Trevino	265	Oak Hills CC, San Antonio, TX	70/6576

TEXAS OPEN

Year	Winner	Score	Location	Par/Yards
1981	*Bill Rogers	266	Oak Hills CC, San Antonio, TX	70/6576
1982	Jay Haas	262	Oak Hills CC, San Antonio, TX	70/6576
1983	Jim Colbert	261	Oak Hills CC, San Antonio, TX	70/6576
1984	Calvin Peete	266	Oak Hills CC, San Antonio, TX	70/6576
1985	*John Mahaffey	268	Oak Hills CC, San Antonio, TX	70/6576

KEY * = Playoff # = Amateur ~ = Rain-curtailed

Past Winners of PGA TOUR Events *(cont'd.)*

Year	Winner	Score	Location	Par/Yards
VANTAGE CHAMPIONSHIP				
1986	~Ben Crenshaw	196	Oak Hills CC, San Antonio, TX	70/6576
NABISCO CHAMPIONSHIPS OF GOLF				
1987	Tom Watson	268	Oak Hills CC, San Antonio, TX	70/6576
TEXAS OPEN PRESENTED BY NABISCO				
1988	Corey Pavin	259	Oak Hills CC, San Antonio, TX	70/6576
1989	Donnie Hammond	258	Oak Hills CC, San Antonio, TX	70/6576
H-E-B TEXAS OPEN				
1990	Mark O'Meara	261	Oak Hills CC, San Antonio, TX	70/6576
1991	*Blaine McCallister	269	Oak Hills CC, San Antonio, TX	70/6576
1992	*Nick Price	263	Oak Hills CC, San Antonio, TX	71/6650
1993	*Jay Haas	263	Oak Hills CC, San Antonio, TX	71/6650

LAS VEGAS INVITATIONAL

Year	Winner	Score	Location	Par/Yards
PANASONIC LAS VEGAS PRO-CELEBRITY CLASSIC				
1983	Fuzzy Zoeller	340	Las Vegas CC, Las Vegas, NV	72/7162
			Desert Inn CC, Las Vegas, NV	72/7111
			Dunes CC, Las Vegas, NV	72/7240
			Showboat CC, Las Vegas, NV	72/7045
PANASONIC LAS VEGAS INVITATIONAL				
1984	Denis Watson	341	Las Vegas CC, Las Vegas, NV	72/7162
			Desert Inn CC, Las Vegas, NV	72/7111
			Showboat CC, Las Vegas, NV	72/7045
			Tropicana CC, Las Vegas, NV	71/6481
1985	Curtis Strange	338	Las Vegas CC, Las Vegas, NV	72/7162
			Desert Inn CC, Las Vegas, NV	72/7111
			Tropicana CC, Las Vegas, NV	71/6481
1986	Greg Norman	333	Las Vegas CC, Las Vegas, NV	72/7162
			Desert Inn CC, Las Vegas, NV	72/7111
			Spanish Trail G&CC, Las Vegas, NV	72/7088
1987	~Paul Azinger	271	Las Vegas CC, Las Vegas, NV	72/7162
			Desert Inn CC, Las Vegas, NV	72/7111
			Spanish Trail G&CC, Las Vegas, NV	72/7088
1988	~Gary Koch	274	Las Vegas CC, Las Vegas, NV	72/7162
			Desert Inn CC, Las Vegas, NV	72/7111
			Spanish Trail G&CC, Las Vegas, NV	72/7088
LAS VEGAS INVITATIONAL				
1989	*Scott Hoch	336	Las Vegas CC, Las Vegas, NV	72/7162
			Desert Inn CC, Las Vegas, NV	72/7111
			Spanish Trail G&CC, Las Vegas, NV	72/7088
1990	*Bob Tway	334	Las Vegas CC, Las Vegas, NV	72/7162
			Desert Inn CC, Las Vegas, NV	72/7111
1991	*Andrew Magee	329	Las Vegas CC, Las Vegas, NV	72/7162
			Desert Inn CC, Las Vegas, NV	72/7111
			Sunrise GC, Las Vegas, NV	72/6914
1992	John Cook	334	Las Vegas CC, Las Vegas, NV	72/7162
			Desert Inn CC, Las Vegas, NV	72/7111
			TPC at Summerlin, Las Vegas, NV	72/7243
1993	Davis Love III	331	Las Vegas CC, Las Vegas, NV	72/7162
			Desert Inn CC, Las Vegas, NV	72/7111
			TPC at Summerlin, Las Vegas, NV	72/7243

THE TOUR CHAMPIONSHIP

Year	Winner	Score	Location	Par/Yards
VANTAGE CHAMPIONSHIP				
1986	~Ben Crenshaw	196	Oak Hills CC, San Antonio, TX	70/6576
NABISCO CHAMPIONSHIPS OF GOLF				
1987	Tom Watson	268	Oak Hills CC, San Antonio, TX	70/6576
NABISCO GOLF CHAMPIONSHIPS				
1988	*Curtis Strange	279	Pebble Beach GL, Monterey Peninsula, CA	72/6815

KEY * = Playoff # = Amateur ~ = Rain-curtailed

Year	Winner	Score	Location	Par/Yards
NABISCO CHAMPIONSHIPS				
1989	*Tom Kite	276	Harbour Town GL, Hilton Head, SC	71/6657
1990	*Jodie Mudd	273	Champions GC, Houston, TX	71/7187
THE TOUR CHAMPIONSHIP				
1991	*Craig Stadler	279	Pinehurst No. 2, Pinehurst, NC	71/7005
1992	Paul Azinger	276	Pinehurst No. 2, Pinehurst, NC	71/7005
1993	Jim Gallagher, Jr.	277	The Olympic Club, San Francisco, CA	71/6812

LINCOLN-MERCURY KAPALUA INTERNATIONAL

Year	Winner	Score	Location	Par/Yards
KAPALUA INTERNATIONAL				
1983	Greg Norman	268	Bay Course, Kapalua GC, Kapalua, Maui, HI	71/6731
1984	Sandy Lyle	266	Bay Course, Kapalua GC, Kapalua, Maui, HI	71/6731
ISUZU KAPALUA INTERNATIONAL				
1985	Mark O'Meara	275	Bay Course, Kapalua GC, Kapalua, Maui, HI	72/6731
1986	Andy Bean	278	Bay Course, Kapalua GC, Kapalua, Maui, HI	72/6731
1987	Andy Bean	267	Bay Course, Kapalua GC, Kapalua, Maui, HI	72/6731
1988	Bob Gilder	266	Bay Course, Kapalua GC, Kapalua, Maui, HI	72/6731
1989	*Peter Jacobsen	270	Bay Course, Kapalua GC, Kapalua, Maui, HI	72/6731
1990	David Peoples	264	Bay Course, Kapalua GC, Kapalua, Maui, HI	71/6731
PING KAPALUA INTERNATIONAL				
1991	*Mike Hulbert	276	Plantation Course, Kapalua GC, Kapalua, Maui, HI	73/7263
LINCOLN-MERCURY KAPALUA INTERNATIONAL				
1992	Davis Love III	275	Plantation Course, Kapalua GC, Kapalua, Maui, HI	73/7263
			Bay Course, Kapalua GC, Kapalua, Maui, HI	71/6731
1993	Fred Couples	274	Plantation Course, Kapalua GC, Kapalua, Maui, HI	73/7263
			Bay Course, Kapalua GC, Kapalua, Maui, HI	71/6731

FRANKLIN FUNDS SHARK SHOOTOUT

Year	Winner	Score	Location	Par/Yards
RMCC INVITATIONAL				
1989	Curtis Strange/ Mark O'Meara	190	Sherwood CC Thousand Oaks, CA	72/7025
1990	Ray Floyd/ Fred Couples	182	Sherwood CC Thousand Oaks, CA	72/7025
SHARK SHOOTOUT BENEFITING RMCC				
1991	Tom Purtzer/ Lanny Wadkins	189	Sherwood CC Thousand Oaks, CA	72/7025
FRANKLIN FUNDS SHARK SHOOT OUT				
1992	Davis Love III/ Tom Kite	191	Sherwood CC Thousand Oaks, CA	72/7025
1993	Steve Elkington Ray Floyd	188	Sherwood CC Thousand Oaks, CA	72/7025

SKINS GAME

Year	Winner	Winnings	Location	Par/Yards
1983	Gary Player	$170,000	Desert Highlands CC, Scottsdale, AZ	72/7100
1984	Jack Nicklaus	$240,000	Desert Highlands CC, Scottsdale, AZ	72/7100
1985	Fuzzy Zoeller	$255,000	Bear Creek CC, Murietta, CA	72/7024
1986	Fuzzy Zoeller	$370,000	TPC at PGA West, La Quinta, CA	72/7271
1987	Lee Trevino	$310,000	TPC at PGA West, La Quinta, CA	72/7271
1988	Ray Floyd	$290,000	TPC at PGA West, La Quinta, CA	72/7271
1989	Curtis Strange	$265,000	TPC at PGA West, La Quinta, CA	72/7271
1990	Curtis Strange	$225,000	TPC at PGA West, La Quinta, CA	72/7271
1991	Payne Stewart	$260,000	TPC at PGA West, La Quinta, CA	72/7271
1992	Payne Stewart	$220,000	Bighorn GC, Palm Desert, CA	72/6848
1993	Payne Stewart	$280,000	Bighorn GC, Palm Desert, CA	72/6848

KEY * = Playoff # = Amateur ~ = Rain-curtailed

JCPENNEY CLASSIC

HAIG & HAIG SCOTCH FOURSOME

Year	Winner	Score	Location	Par/Yards
1960	*Jim Turnesa		Pinecrest Lake Club, Avon Park, FL	72/6449
	Gloria Armstrong	+139	Harder Hall, Sebring, FL	72/6300
1961	Dave Ragan		Pinecrest Lake Club, Avon Park, FL	72/6449
	Mickey Wright	272	Harder Hall, Sebring, FL	72/6300
1962	Mason Rudolph		Pinecrest Lake Club, Avon Park, FL	72/6449
	Kathy Whitworth	272	Harder Hall, Sebring, FL	72/6300
1963	Dave Ragan		Pinecrest Lake Club, Avon Park, FL	72/6449
	Mickey Wright	273	Harder Hall, Sebring, FL	72/6300
1964	Sam Snead		Pinecrest Lake Club, Avon Park, FL	72/6449
	Shirley Englehorn	272	Harder Hall, Sebring, FL	72/6300
1965	Gardner Dickinson			
	Ruth Jessen	281	La Costa CC, Encinitas, CA	72/6607
1966	Jack Rule			
	Sandra Spuzich	276	La Costa CC, Encinitas, CA	72/6607

PEPSI-COLA MIXED TEAM

Year	Winner	Score	Location	Par/Yards
1976	Chi Chi Rodriguez			
	JoAnn Washam	275	Doral CC, Miami, FL	72/6939
1977	Jerry Pate			
	Hollis Stacy	270	Bardmoor CC, Largo, FL	M-72/6957, W-72/6464

JC PENNEY CLASSIC

Year	Winner	Score	Location	Par/Yards
1978	*Lon Hinkle			
	Pat Bradley	267	Bardmoor CC, Largo, FL	M-72/6957, W-72/6464
1979	Dave Eichelberger			
	Murle Breer	268	Bardmoor CC, Largo, FL	M-72/6957, W-72/6464
1980	Curtis Strange			
	Nancy Lopez	268	Bardmoor CC, Largo, FL	M-72/6957, W-72/6464
1981	Tom Kite			
	Beth Daniel	270	Bardmoor CC, Largo, FL	M-72/6957, W-72/6464
1982	John Mahaffey			
	JoAnne Carner	268	Bardmoor CC, Largo, FL	M-72/6957, W-72/6464
1983	Fred Couples			
	Jan Stephenson	264	Bardmoor CC, Largo, FL	M-72/6957, W-72/6464
1984	Mike Donald			
	Vicki Alvarez	270	Bardmoor CC, Largo, FL	M-72/6957, W-72/6464
1985	Larry Rinker			
	Laurie Rinker	267	Bardmoor CC, Largo, FL	M-72/6957, W-72/6464
1986	Tom Purtzer			
	Juli Inkster	267	Bardmoor CC, Largo, FL	M-72/6957, W-72/6464
1987	Steve Jones			
	Jane Crafter	268	Bardmoor CC, Largo, FL	M-72/6957, W-72/6464
1988	John Huston			
	Amy Benz	269	Bardmoor CC, Largo, FL	M-72/6957, W-72/6464
1989	*Bill Glasson			
	Pat Bradley	267	Bardmoor CC, Largo, FL	M-72/6957, W-72/6464
1990	Davis Love III			
	Beth Daniel	266	Innisbrook Resort, Tarpon Springs, FL	M-71/7031, W-71/6400
1991	*Billy Andrade			
	Kris Tschetter	266	Innisbrook Resort, Tarpon Springs, FL	M-71/7031, W-71/6400
1992	Dan Forsman			
	Dottie Mochrie	264	Innisbrook Resort, Tarpon Springs, FL	M-71/7031, W-71/6400
1993	Mike Springer			
	Melissa McNamara	265	Innisbrook Resort, Tarpon Springs, FL	M-71/7031, W-71/6400

KEY * = Playoff # = Amateur ~ = Rain-curtailed

THE PLAYERS CHAMPIONSHIP

Tournament Players Club at Sawgrass, Ponte Vedra, FL

YEAR	WINNER	SCORE	RUNNERUP	PLAYED AT
1974	Jack Nicklaus	272	J. C. Snead	Atlanta CC, Atlanta, GA
1975	Al Geiberger	270	Dave Stockton	Colonial CC, Fort Worth, TX
1976	Jack Nicklaus	269	J. C. Snead	Inverrary G&CC, Lauderhill, FL
1977	Mark Hayes	289	Mike McCullough	Sawgrass, Ponte Vedra, FL
1978	Jack Nicklaus	289	Lou Graham	Sawgrass, Ponte Vedra, FL
1979	Lanny Wadkins	283	Tom Watson	Sawgrass, Ponte Vedra, FL
1980	Lee Trevino	278	Ben Crenshaw	Sawgrass, Ponte Vedra, FL
1981	Ray Floyd*	285	Barry Jaeckel	Sawgrass, Ponte Vedra, FL
			Curtis Strange	
	*(Won playoff with par on first extra hole)			
1982	Jerry Pate	280	Scott Simpson	TPC at Sawgrass, Ponte Vedra, FL
			Brad Bryant	
1983	Hal Sutton	283	Bob Eastwood	TPC at Sawgrass, Ponte Vedra, FL
1984	Fred Couples	277	Lee Trevino	TPC at Sawgrass, Ponte Vedra, FL
1985	Calvin Peete	274	D. A. Weibring	TPC at Sawgrass, Ponte Vedra, FL
1986	John Mahaffey	275	Larry Mize	TPC at Sawgrass, Ponte Vedra, FL
1987	Sandy Lyle*	274	Jeff Sluman	TPC at Sawgrass, Ponte Vedra, FL
	*(Won playoff with par on third extra hole)			
1988	Mark McCumber	273	Mike Reid	TPC at Sawgrass, Ponte Vedra, FL
1989	Tom Kite	279	Chip Beck	TPC at Sawgrass, Ponte Vedra, FL
1990	Jodie Mudd	278	Mark Calcavecchia	TPC at Sawgrass, Ponte Vedra, FL
1991	Steve Elkington	276	Fuzzy Zoeller	TPC at Sawgrass, Ponte Vedra, FL
1992	Davis Love III	273	4 Tied at 277	TPC at Sawgrass, Ponte Vedra, FL
1993	Nick Price	270	Bernhard Langer	TPC at Sawgrass, Ponte Vedra, FL

Eligibility Requirements for the 1994 PLAYERS Championship

The starting field for the 1994 PLAYERS Championship shall consist of the following players:

1) The top 125 PGA TOUR members from Final 1993 Official Money List.
2) All winners of PGA TOUR events awarding official money and official victory status in the preceding 12 months concluding with the Nestle Invitational.
3) Designated players.
4) Any foreign player meeting the requirements of a designated player, whether or not he is a PGA TOUR member.
5) Winners in the last 10 calendar years of THE PLAYERS Championship, Masters, U.S. Open, PGA Championship and NEC World Series of Golf.
6) British Open winners since 1990.
7) Six players, not otherwise eligible, designated by THE PLAYERS Championship Committee as "special selections."
8) To complete a field of 144 players, those players in order, not otherwise eligible, from the 1994 Official Money List, as of the completion of the Nestle Invitational.

Nick Price's win in THE PLAYERS Championship was his first of four victories in 1993.

THE TOUR CHAMPIONSHIP

Each year the top-30 PGA TOUR members on the money list compete at the season-ending TOUR Championship.

YEAR	WINNER	SCORE	RUNNERUP	PLAYED AT
1986	Ben Crenshaw	196~	Payne Stewart	Oak Hills CC, San Antonio, TX
1987	Tom Watson	268	Chip Beck	Oak Hills CC, San Antonio, TX
1988	Curtis Strange*	279	Tom Kite	Pebble Beach GL, Pebble Beach, CA
	*(won playoff with birdie on second extra hole)			
1989	Tom Kite*	276	Payne Stewart	Harbour Town GL, Hilton Head, SC
	*(won playoff with par on second extra hole)			
1990	Jodie Mudd*	273	Billy Mayfair	Champions GC, Houston, TX
	*(won playoff with birdie on first extra hole)			
1991	Craig Stadler*	279	Russ Cochran	Pinehurst Resort & CC, Pinehurst, NC
	*(won playoff with birdie on second extra hole)			
1992	Paul Azinger	276	Corey Pavin	Pinehurst Resort & CC, Pinehurst, NC
			Lee Janzen	
1993	Jim Gallagher, Jr.	277	Greg Norman	The Olympic Club, San Francisco, CA
			David Frost	
			John Huston	
			Scott Simpson	

~= Rain shortened   *= Playoff

Jim Gallagher, Jr., set The Olympic Club course record with his opening round 8-under-par 63.

NEC WORLD SERIES OF GOLF

Firestone Country Club, South Course, Akron, OH

From 1962 through 1975, the World Series of Golf was played as a four-man, 36-hole exhibition. All monies won in the tournament were unofficial. The winners in those years (with winning totals in parentheses):

1962—Jack Nicklaus (135)
1963—Jack Nicklaus (140)
1964—Tony Lema (138)
1965—Gary Player (139)
1966—Gene Littler (143)

1967—Jack Nicklaus (144)
1968—Gary Player (143)
1969—Orville Moody (141)
1970—Jack Nicklaus (136)
1971—Charles Coody (141)

1972—Gary Player (142)
1973—Tom Weiskopf (137)
1974—Lee Trevino (139)
1975—Tom Watson (140)

Fulton Allem's final round 8-under-par 62 earned him a five-stroke victory

YEAR	WINNER	SCORE	RUNNERUP
1976	Jack Nicklaus	275	Hale Irwin
1977	Lanny Wadkins	267	Hale Irwin
			Tom Weiskopf
1978	Gil Morgan*	278	Hubert Green
	*(Won playoff with par on first extra hole)		
1979	Lon Hinkle	272	Bill Rogers
			Larry Nelson
			Lee Trevino
1980	Tom Watson	270	Raymond Floyd
1981	Bill Rogers	275	Tom Kite
1982	Craig Stadler*	278	Raymond Floyd
	*(Won playoff with par on fourth extra hole)		
1983	Nick Price	270	Jack Nicklaus
1984	Denis Watson	271	Bruce Lietzke
1985	Roger Maltbie	268	Denis Watson
1986	Dan Pohl	277	Lanny Wadkins
1987	Curtis Strange	275	Fulton Allem
1988	Mike Reid*	275	Tom Watson
	*(Won playoff with par on first extra hole)		
1989	David Frost*	276	Ben Crenshaw
	*(Won playoff with par on second extra hole)		
1990	Jose M. Olazabal	262	Lanny Wadkins
1991	Tom Purtzer*	279	Jim Gallagher Jr.
			Davis Love III
	*(Won playoff with par on second extra hole)		
1992	Craig Stadler	273	Corey Pavin
1993	Fulton Allem	270	Nick Price, Jim Gallagher, Jr., Craig Stadler

Eligibility Requirements for the 1994 NEC World Series of Golf

1) The defending champion, Fulton Allem
2) Winner, 1994 PLAYERS Championship
3) Winner, 1994 PGA Championship
4) Winner, 1994 Masters Tournament
5) Winner, 1994 United States Open
6) Winner, 1994 British Open
7) Winner, 1993 PGA National Club Pro Championship
8) All winners of PGA TOUR co-sponsored events since the preceding year's WSOG.
9) Winners of the following overseas events:

PGA European Tour
a. Volvo European PGA Championship
b. Johnnie Walker World Championship
c. Scottish Open
d. Dunhill British Masters
e. Trophee Lancome
f. Volvo Masters
g. Mercedes German Masters
h. Toyota World Match Play
i. Carroll's Irish Open
j. GA European Open

PGA Tour of Japan
a. Visa Taiheyo Club Masters
b. Dunlop Phoenix
c. Bridgestone Open
d. Chunichi Crowns
e. Japan Open
f. ANA Sapporo Open
g. Casio World Open
h. ABC Lark Cup
i. Asahi Beer Golf Digest Open
j. Japan PGA Championship
k. Japan Series of Golf

Australasian PGA Tour
a. Pyramid Australian Masters
b. Australian Open
c. Greg Norman's Holden Classic
d. Ford Australian PGA Championship

South African Tour
a. Sun City $1,000,000 Challenge
b. FNB Players Championship
c. Lexington PGA Championship
d. South African Open

Asian Tour
a. Hong Kong Open

10) Individual winner, 1993 World Cup

THE MASTERS TOURNAMENT

Augusta National Golf Club, Augusta, Georgia

YEAR	WINNER	SCORE	RUNNERUP
1934	Horton Smith	284	Craig Wood
1935	*Gene Sarazen (144)	282	Craig Wood (149)
1936	Horton Smith	285	Harry Cooper
1937	Byron Nelson	283	Ralph Guldahl
1938	Henry Picard	285	Ralph Guldahl, Harry Cooper
1939	Ralph Guldahl	279	Sam Snead
1940	Jimmy Demaret	280	Lloyd Mangrum
1941	Craig Wood	280	Byron Nelson
1942	*Byron Nelson (69)	280	Ben Hogan (70)
1943	No Tournament—World War II		
1944	No Tournament—World War II		
1945	No Tournament—World War II		
1946	Herman Keiser	282	Ben Hogan
1947	Jimmy Demaret	281	Byron Nelson, Frank Stranahan
1948	Claude Harmon	279	Cary Middlecoff
1949	Sam Snead	282	Johnny Bulla, Lloyd Mangrum
1950	Jimmy Demaret	283	Jim Ferrier
1951	Ben Hogan	280	Skee Riegel
1952	Sam Snead	286	Jack Burke, Jr.
1953	Ben Hogan	274	Ed Oliver, Jr.
1954	*Sam Snead (70)	289	Ben Hogan (71)
1955	Cary Middlecoff	279	Ben Hogan
1956	Jack Burke, Jr.	289	Ken Venturi
1957	Doug Ford	282	Sam Snead
1958	Arnold Palmer	284	Doug Ford, Fred Hawkins
1959	Art Wall, Jr.	284	Cary Middlecoff
1960	Arnold Palmer	282	Ken Venturi
1961	Gary Player	280	Charles R. Coe, Arnold Palmer
1962	*Arnold Palmer (68)	280	Gary Player (71), Dow Finsterwald (77)
1963	Jack Nicklaus	286	Tony Lema
1964	Arnold Palmer	276	Dave Marr, Jack Nicklaus
1965	Jack Nicklaus	271	Arnold Palmer, Gary Player
1966	*Jack Nicklaus (70)	288	Tommy Jacobs (72), Gay Brewer, Jr. (78)
1967	Gay Brewer, Jr.	280	Bobby Nichols
1968	Bob Goalby	277	Roberto DeVicenzo
1969	George Archer	281	Billy Casper, George Knudson, Tom Weiskopf
1970	*Billy Casper (69)	279	Gene Littler (74)
1971	Charles Coody	279	Johnny Miller, Jack Nicklaus
1972	Jack Nicklaus	286	Bruce Crampton, Bobby Mitchell, Tom Weiskopf
1973	Tommy Aaron	283	J. C. Snead
1974	Gary Player	278	Tom Weiskopf, Dave Stockton
1975	Jack Nicklaus	276	Johnny Miller, Tom Weiskopf
1976	Ray Floyd	271	Ben Crenshaw
1977	Tom Watson	276	Jack Nicklaus
1978	Gary Player	277	Hubert Green, Rod Funseth, Tom Watson
1979	*Fuzzy Zoeller	280	Ed Sneed, Tom Watson
1980	Seve Ballesteros	275	Gibby Gilbert, Jack Newton
1981	Tom Watson	280	Johnny Miller, Jack Nicklaus
1982	*Craig Stadler	284	Dan Pohl
1983	Seve Ballesteros	280	Ben Crenshaw, Tom Kite
1984	Ben Crenshaw	277	Tom Watson
1985	Bernhard Langer	282	Curtis Strange, Seve Ballesteros, Ray Floyd
1986	Jack Nicklaus	279	Greg Norman, Tom Kite
1987	*Larry Mize	285	Seve Ballesteros, Greg Norman
1988	Sandy Lyle	281	Mark Calcavecchia
1989	*Nick Faldo	283	Scott Hoch
1990	*Nick Faldo	278	Ray Floyd
1991	Ian Woosnam	277	Jose Maria Olazabal
1992	Fred Couples	275	Ray Floyd
1993	Bernhard Langer	277	Chip Beck

* WINNER IN PLAYOFF.

FIGURES IN PARENTHESES INDICATE SCORES.

UNITED STATES OPEN CHAMPIONSHIP

YEAR WINNER	SCORE	RUNNERUP	PLAYED AT
1895 Horace Rawlins	173-36 Holes	Willie Dunn	Newport GC, Newport, RI
1896 James Foulis	152-36 Holes	Horace Rawlins	Shinnecock Hills GC, SouthHampton, NY
1897 Joe Lloyd	162-36 Holes	Willie Anderson	Chicago GC, Wheaton, IL
1898 Fred Herd	328-72 Holes	Alex Smith	Myopia Hunt Club, Hamilton, MA
1899 Willie Smith	315	George Low	Baltimore CC, Baltimore, MD
		Val Fitzjohn	
		W. H. Way	
1900 Harry Vardon	313	J. H. Taylor	Chicago GC, Wheaton, IL
1901 *Willie Anderson (85)	331	Alex Smith (86)	Myopia Hunt Club, Hamilton, MA
1902 Laurie Auchterlonie	307	Stewart Gardner	Garden City GC, Garden City, LI, NY
1903 *Willie Anderson (82)	307	David Brown (84)	Baltusrol GC, Short Hills, NY
1904 Willie Anderson	303	Gil Nicholls	Glen View Club, Golf, IL
1905 Willie Anderson	314	Alex Smith	Myopia Hunt Club, Hamilton, MA
1906 Alex Smith	295	Willie Smith	Onwentsia Club Lake Forest, IL
1907 Alex Ross	302	Gil Nicholls	Philadelphia Cricket Club, Chestnut Hill,PA
1908 *Fred McLeod (77)	322	Willie Smith (83)	Myopia Hunt Club, Hamilton, MA
1909 George Sargent	290	Tom McNamara	Englewood GC Englewood, NJ
1910 *Alex Smith (71)	298	John McDermott (75)	Philadelphia Cricket Club, Chestnut Hill, PA
		Macdonald Smith (77)	
1911 *John McDermott (80)	307	Mike Brady (82)	Chicago GC, Wheaton, IL.
		George Simpson (85)	
1912 John McDermott	294	Tom McNamara	CC of Buffalo, Buffalo, NY
1913 *Francis Ouimet (72)	304	Harry Vardon (77)	The Country Club, Brookline, MA
		Edward Ray (78)	
1914 Walter Hagen	290	Charles Evans, Jr.	Midlothian CC, Blue Island, IL
1915 Jerome Travers	297	Tom McNamara	Baltusrol GC, Short Hills, NJ
1916 Charles Evans, Jr.	286	Jock Hutchison	Minikahda Club, Minneapolis, MN
1917—1918 No Championships Played—World War I			
1919 *Walter Hagen (77)	301	Mike Brady (78)	Brae Burn CC, West Newton, MA
1920 Edward Ray	295	Harry Vardon	Inverness CC, Toledo, OH
		Jack Burke	
		Leo Diegel	
		Jock Hutchison	
1921 James M. Barnes	289	Walter Hagen	Columbia CC, Chevy Chase, MD
		Fred McLeod	
1922 Gene Sarazen	288	John L. Black	Skokie CC, Glencoe, IL.
		Robert T. Jones, Jr.	
1923 *Robert. T. Jones, Jr. (76)	296	Bobby Cruickshank(78)	Inwood CC, Inwood, LI, NY
1924 Cyril Walker	297	Robert T. Jones, Jr.	Oakland Hills CC, Birmingham, MI
1925 *W. MacFarlane (147)	291	R. T. Jones, Jr. (148)	Worcester CC, Worcester, MA
1926 Robert T. Jones, Jr.	293	Joe Turnesa	Scioto CC, Columbus, OH
1927 *Tommy Armour (76)	301	Harry Cooper (79)	Oakmont CC, Oakmont, PA
1928 *Johnny Farrell (143)	294	R. T. Jones, Jr. (144)	Olympia Fields CC, Matteson, IL
1929 *Robert.T. Jones, Jr. (141)	294	Al Espinosa (164)	Winged Foot GC, Marmaroneck, NY
1930 Robert T. Jones, Jr.	287	Macdonald Smith	Interlachen CC, Hopkins, MN
1931 *Billy Burke (149-148)	292	George Von Elm (149-149)	Inverness Club, Toledo, OH
1932 Gene Sarazen	286	Phil Perkins	Fresh Meadows CC, Flushing, NY
		Bobby Cruickshank	
1933 Johnny Goodman	287	Ralph Guldahl	North Shore CC, Glenview, IL
1934 Olin Dutra	293	Gene Sarazen	Merion Cricket Club, Ardmore, PA
1935 Sam Parks, Jr.	299	Jimmy Thompson	Oakmont CC, Oakmont, PA
1936 Tony Manero	282	Harry Cooper	Baltusrol GC, Springfield, NJ
1937 Ralph Guldahl	281	Sam Snead	Oakland Hills CC, Birmingham, MI
1938 Ralph Guldahl	284	Dick Metz	Cherry Hills CC, Denver, CO
1939 *Byron Nelson (68-70)	284	Craig Wood (68-73)	Philadelphia CC, Philadelphia, PA
		Denny Shute (76)	
1940 *Lawson Little (70)	287	Gene Sarazen (73)	Canterbury GC, Cleveland, OH

* WINNER IN PLAYOFF

FIGURES IN PARENTHESES INDICATE SCORES

YEAR	WINNER	SCORE	RUNNERUP	PLAYED AT
1941	Craig Wood	284	Denny Shute	Colonial Club, Fort Worth, TX
1942—1945	No Championships Played—World War II			
1946	*Lloyd Mangrum (72-72)	284	Vic Ghezzi (72-73)	Canterbury GC, Cleveland, OH
			Byron Nelson (72-73)	
1947	*Lew Worsham (69)	282	Sam Snead (70)	St. Louis CC, Clayton, MO
1948	Ben Hogan	276	Jimmy Demaret	Riviera CC, Los Angeles, CA
1949	Cary Middlecoff	286	Sam Snead	Medinah CC, Medinah, IL
			Clayton Heafner	
1950	*Ben Hogan (69)	287	Lloyd Mangrum (73)	Merion Golf Club, Ardmore, PA
			George Fazio (75)	
1951	Ben Hogan	287	Clayton Heafner	Oakland Hills CC, Birmingham, MI
1952	Julius Boros	281	Ed Oliver	Northwood CC, Dallas, TX
1953	Ben Hogan	283	Sam Snead	Oakmont CC, Oakmont, PA
1954	Ed Furgol	284	Gene Littler	Baltusrol GC, Springfield, NJ
1955	*Jack Fleck (69)	287	Ben Hogan (72)	Olympic Club, San Francisco, CA
1956	Cary Middlecoff	281	Ben Hogan	Oak Hill CC, Rochester, NY
			Julius Boros	
1957	*Dick Mayer (72)	282	Cary Middlecoff (79)	Inverness Club, Toledo, OH
1958	Tommy Bolt	283	Gary Player	Southern Hills CC, Tulsa, OK
1959	Billy Casper	282	Bob Rosburg	Winged Foot GC, Mamaroneck, NY
1960	Arnold Palmer	280	Jack Nicklaus	Cherry Hills CC, Denver, CO
1961	Gene Littler	281	Bob Goalby	Oakland Hills CC, Birmingham, MI
			Doug Sanders	
1962	*Jack Nicklaus (71)	283	Arnold Palmer (74)	Oakmont CC, Oakmont PA
1963	*Julius Boros (70)	293	Jacky Cupit (73)	The Country Club, Brookline, MA
			Arnold Palmer (76)	
1964	Ken Venturi	278	Tommy Jacobs	Congressional CC, Washington, DC
1965	*Gary Player (71)	282	Kel Nagle (74)	Bellerive CC, St Louis, MO
1966	*Billy Casper (69)	278	Arnold Palmer (73)	Olympic Club, San Francisco, CA
1967	Jack Nicklaus	275	Arnold Palmer	Baltusrol GC, Springfield, NJ
1968	Lee Trevino	275	Jack Nicklaus	Oak Hill CC, Rochester NY
1969	Orville Moody	281	Deane Beman	Champions GC, Houston, TX
			Al Geiberger	
			Bob Rosburg	
1970	Tony Jacklin	281	Dave Hill	Hazeltine GC, Chaska, MN
1971	*Lee Trevino (68)	280	Jack Nicklaus (71)	Merion Golf Club, Ardmore, PA
1972	Jack Nicklaus	290	Bruce Crampton	Pebble Beach GL, Pebble Beach, CA
1973	Johnny Miller	279	John Schlee	Oakmont CC, Oakmont, PA
1974	Hale Irwin	287	Forrest Fezler	Winged Foot GC, Mamaroneck, NY
1975	*Lou Graham (71)	287	John Mahaffey (73)	Medinah CC, Medinah, IL.
1976	Jerry Pate	277	Tom Weiskopf	Atlanta Athletic Club, Duluth, GA
			Al Geiberger	
1977	Hubert Green	278	Lou Graham	Southern Hills CC, Tulsa, OK
1978	Andy North	285	Dave Stockton	Cherry Hills CC, Denver, CO
			J. C. Snead	
1979	Hale Irwin	284	Gary Player	Inverness Club, Toledo, OH
			Jerry Pate	
1980	Jack Nicklaus	272	Isao Aoki	Baltusrol GC, Springfield NJ
1981	David Graham	273	George Burns	Merion GC, Ardmore, PA
			Bill Rogers	
1982	Tom Watson	282	Jack Nicklaus	Pebble Beach GL, Pebble Beach, CA
1983	Larry Nelson	280	Tom Watson	Oakmont CC, Oakmont, PA
1984	*Fuzzy Zoeller (67)	276	Greg Norman (75)	Winged Foot GC, Mamaroneck, NY
1985	Andy North	279	Dave Barr	Oakland Hills CC, Birmingham, MI
			T.C. Chen	
			Denis Watson	
1986	Ray Floyd	279	Lanny Wadkins	Shinnecock Hills GC, Southampton, NY
			Chip Beck	
1987	Scott Simpson	277	Tom Watson	Olympic Club Lake Course, San Francisco,CA
1988	*Curtis Strange (71)	278	Nick Faldo (75)	The Country Club, Brookline, MA
1989	Curtis Strange	278	Chip Beck	Oak Hill CC, Rochester, NY
			Mark McCumber	
			Ian Woosnam	

* WINNER IN PLAYOFF

FIGURES IN PARENTHESES INDICATE SCORES

YEAR	WINNER	SCORE	RUNNERUP	PLAYED AT
1990	*Hale Irwin (74)+3	280	Mike Donald (74)+4	Medinah CC, Medinah, IL
1991	*Payne Stewart (75)	282	Scott Simpson (77)	Hazeltine National GC, Chaska, MN
1992	Tom Kite	285	Jeff Sluman	Pebble Beach GL, Pebble Beach, CA
1993	Lee Janzen	272	Payne Stewart	Baltusrol GC, Springfield, NJ

THE BRITISH OPEN

1860	Willie Park	174	Tom Morris, Sr.	Prestwick, Scotland
	(The First Event Was Open Only To Professional Golfers)			
1861	Tom Morris, Sr.,	163	Willie Park	Prestwick, Scotland
	(The Second Annual Open Was Open To Amateurs Also)			
1862	Tom Morris, Sr.	163	Willie Park	Prestwick, Scotland
1863	Willie Park	168	Tom Morris Sr.	Prestwick, Scotland
1864	Tom Morris, Sr.	160	Andrew Strath	Prestwick, Scotland
1865	Andrew Strath	162	Willie Park	Prestwick, Scotland
1866	Willie Park	169	David Park	Prestwick, Scotland
1867	Tom Morris, Sr.	170	Willie Park	Prestwick, Scotland
1868	Tom Morris, Jr.	154	Tom Morris, Sr.	Prestwick, Scotland
1869	Tom Morris, Jr.	157	Tom Morris, Sr.	Prestwick, Scotland
1870	Tom Morris, Jr.	149	David Strath	Prestwick, Scotland
			Bob Kirk	
1871	No Championship Played			
1872	Tom Morris, Jr.	166	David Strath	Prestwick, Scotland
1873	Tom Kidd	179	Jamie Anderson	St. Andrews, Scotland
1874	Mungo Park	159	No Record	Musselburgh, Scotland
1875	Willie Park	166	Bob Martin	Prestwick, Scotland
1876	Bob Martin	176	David Strath	St. Andrews, Scotland
			(Tied, But Refused Playoff)	
1877	Jamie Anderson	160	R. Pringle	Musselburgh, Scotland
1878	Jamie Anderson	157	Robert Kirk	Prestwick, Scotland
1879	Jamie Anderson	169	A. Kirkaldy	St. Andrews, Scotland
			J. Allan	
1880	Robert Ferguson	162	No Record	Musselburgh, Scotland
1881	Robert Ferguson	170	Jamie Anderson	Prestwick, Scotland
1882	Robert Ferguson	171	Willie Fernie	St. Andrews, Scotland
1883	*Willie Fernie	159	Robert Ferguson	Musselburgh, Scotland
1884	Jack Simpson	160	D. Rolland	Prestwick, Scotland
			Willie Fernie	
1885	Bob Martin	171	Archie Simpson	St. Andrews, Scotland
1886	David Brown	157	Willie Campbell	Musselburgh, Scotland
1887	Willie Park, Jr.	161	Bob Martin	Prestwick, Scotland
1888	Jack Burns	171	B. Sayers	St. Andrews, Scotland
			D. Anderson	
1889	*Willie Park, Jr.	155 (158)	Andrew Kirkaldy (163)	Musselburgh, Scotland
1890	John Ball	164	Willie Fernie	Prestwick, Scotland
1891	Hugh Kirkaldy	166	Andrew Kirkaldy	St. Andrews, Scotland
			Willie Fernie	
	(Championship Extended From 36 to 72 Holes)			
1892	Harold H. Hilton	305	John Ball	Muirfield, Scotland
			H. Kirkaldy	
1893	William Auchterlonie	322	John E. Laidlay	Prestwick, Scotland
1894	John H. Taylor	326	Douglas Rolland	Royal St. George's, England
1895	John H. Taylor	322	Alexander Herd	St. Andrews, Scotland
1896	*Harry Vardon	316 (157)	John H. Taylor (161)	Muirfield, Scotland
1897	Harold H. Hilton	314	James Braid	Hoylake, England
1898	Harry Vardon	307	Willie Park, Jr.	Prestwick, Scotland
1899	Harry Vardon	310	Jack White	Royal St. George's, England
1900	John H. Taylor	309	Harry Vardon	St Andrews, Scotland

* WINNER IN PLAYOFF   FIGURES IN PARENTHESES INDICATE SCORES

THE BRITISH OPEN (CONT'D.)

YEAR WINNER	SCORE	RUNNERUP	PLAYED AT
1901 James Braid	309	Harry Vardon	Muirfield, Scotland
1902 Alexander Herd	307	Harry Vardon	Hoylake, England
1903 Harry Vardon	300	Tom Vardon	Prestwick, Scotland
1904 Jack White	296	John H. Taylor	Royal St. George's, England
1905 James Braid	318	John H. Taylor	St. Andrews, Scotland
		Rolland Jones	
1906 James Braid	300	John H. Taylor	Muirfield, Scotland
1907 Arnaud Massy	312	John H. Taylor	Hoylake, England
1908 James Braid	291	Tom Ball	Prestwick, Scotland
1909 John H. Taylor	295	James Braid	Deal, England
		Tom Ball	
1910 James Braid	299	Alexander Herd	St. Andrews, Scotland
1911 Harry Vardon	303	Arnaud Massy	Royal St. George's, England
1912 Edward (Ted) Ray	295	Harry Vardon	Muirfield, Scotland
1913 John H. Taylor	304	Edward Ray	Hoylake, England
1914 Harry Vardon	306	John H. Taylor	Prestwick, Scotland
1915—1919 No Championships Played			
1920 George Duncan	303	Alexander Herd	Deal, England
1921 *Jock Hutchison	296 (150)	Roger Wethered (159)	St Andrews, Scotland
1922 Walter Hagen	300	George Duncan	Royal St. George's, England
		James M. Barnes	
1923 Arthur G. Havers	295	Walter Hagen	Troon, Scotland
1924 Walter Hagen	301	Ernest Whitcombe	Hoylake, England
1925 James M. Barnes	300	Archie Compston	Prestwick, Scotland
		Ted Ray	
1926 Robert T. Jones, Jr.	291	Al Watrous	Royal Lytham, England
1927 Robert T. Jones, Jr.	285	Aubrey Boomer	St. Andrews, Scotland
1928 Walter Hagen	292	Gene Sarazen	Royal St. George's, England
1929 Walter Hagen	292	Johnny Farrell	Muirfield, Scotland
1930 Robert T. Jones, Jr.	291	Macdonald Smith	Hoylake, England
		Leo Diegel	
1931 Tommy D. Armour	296	J. Jurado	Carnoustie, Scotland
1932 Gene Sarazen	283	Macdonald Smith	Prince's, England
1933 *Denny Shute (149)	292	Craig Wood (154)	St. Andrews, Scotland
1934 Henry Cotton	283	S. F. Brews	Royal St. George's, England
1935 Alfred Perry	283	Alfred Padgham	Muirfield, Scotland
1936 Alfred Padgham	287	J. Adams	Hoylake, England
1937 Henry Cotton	290	R. A. Whitcombe	Carnoustie, Scotland
1938 R. A. Whitcombe	295	James Adams	Royal St. George's, England
1939 Richard Burton	290	Johnny Bulla	St. Andrews, Scotland
1940—1945 No Championships Played			
1946 Sam Snead	290	Bobby Locke	St. Andrews, Scotland
		Johnny Bulla	
1947 Fred Daly	293	R. W. Horne	Hoylake, England
		Frank Stranahan	
1948 Henry Cotton	294	Fred Daly	Muirfield, Scotland
1949 *Bobby Locke	283(135)	Harry Bradshaw (147)	Royal St. George's, England
1950 Bobby Locke	279	Roberto DeVicenzo	Troon, Scotland
1951 Max Faulkner	285	A. Cerda	Portrush, Ireland
1952 Bobby Locke	287	Peter Thomson	Royal Lytham, England
1953 Ben Hogan	282	Frank Stranahan	Carnoustie, Scotland
		D. J. Rees	
		Peter Thomson	
		A. Cerda	
1954 Peter Thomson	283	S. S. Scott	Royal Birkdale, England
		Dai Rees	
		Bobby Locke	
1955 Peter Thomson	281	John Fallon	St. Andrews, Scotland
1956 Peter Thomson	286	Flory Van Donck	Hoylake, England
1957 Bobby Locke	279	Peter Thomson	St Andrews, Scotland

YEAR	WINNER	SCORE	RUNNERUP	PLAYED AT
1958	*Peter Thomson	278(139)	Dave Thomas (143)	Royal Lytham, England
1959	Gary Player	284	Fred Bullock	Muirfield, Scotland
			Flory Van Donck	
1960	Kel Nagle	278	Arnold Palmer	St. Andrews, Scotland
1961	Arnold Palmer	284	Dai Rees	Royal Birkdale, England
1962	Arnold Palmer	276	Kel Nagle	Troon, Scotland
1963	*Bob Charles	277(140)	Phil Rodgers (148)	Royal Lytham, England
1964	Tony Lema	279	Jack Nicklaus	St. Andrews, Scotland
1965	Peter Thomson	285	Brian Huggett	Southport, England
			Christy O'Connor	
1966	Jack Nicklaus	282	Doug Sanders	Muirfield, Scotland
			Dave Thomas	
1967	Roberto DeVicenzo	278	Jack Nicklaus	Hoylake, England
1968	Gary Player	289	Jack Nicklaus	Carnoustie, Scotland
			Bob Charles	
1969	Tony Jacklin	280	Bob Charles	Royal Lytham, England
1970	*Jack Nicklaus	283 (72)	Doug Sanders (73)	St. Andrews, Scotland
1971	Lee Trevino	278	Lu Liang Huan	Royal Birkdale, England
1972	Lee Trevino	278	Jack Nicklaus	Muirfield, Scotland
1973	Tom Weiskopf	276	Johnny Miller	Troon, Scotland
1974	Gary Player	282	Peter Oosterhuis	Royal Lytham, England
1975	*Tom Watson	279 (71)	Jack Newton (72)	Carnoustie, Scotland
1976	Johnny Miller	279	Jack Nicklaus	Royal Birkdale, England
			S. Ballesteros	
1977	Tom Watson	268	Jack Nicklaus	Turnberry, Scotland
1978	Jack Nicklaus	281	Ben Crenshaw	St. Andrews, Scotland
			Tom Kite	
			Ray Floyd	
			Simon Owen	
1979	Seve Ballesteros	283	Ben Crenshaw	Royal Lytham, England
			Jack Nicklaus	
1980	Tom Watson	271	Lee Trevino	Muirfield, Scotland
1981	Bill Rogers	276	Bernhard Langer	Royal St George's, England
1982	Tom Watson	284	Nick Price	Royal Troon, Scotland
			Peter Oosterhuis	
1983	Tom Watson	275	Andy Bean	Royal Birkdale, England
1984	Seve Ballesteros	276	Tom Watson	St. Andrews, Scotland
			Bernhard Langer	
1985	Sandy Lyle	282	Payne Stewart	Royal St. George's, England
1986	Greg Norman	280	Gordon Brand	Turnberry GL, Scotland
1987	Nick Faldo	279	Paul Azinger	Muirfield, Gullane, Scotland
			Rodger Davis	
1988	Seve Ballesteros	273	Nick Price	Royal Lytham and St. Annes, St. Annes-On-The-Sea, England
1989	*Mark Calcavecchia	275	Wayne Grady	Royal Troon GC, Troon, Scotland
			Greg Norman	
1990	Nick Faldo	270	Payne Stewart	St. Andrews, Scotland
			Mark McNulty	
1991	Ian Baker-Finch	272	Mike Harwood	Royal Birkdale, England
1992	Nick Faldo	272	John Cook	Muirfield, Gullane, Scotland
1993	Greg Norman	267	Nick Faldo	Royal St. George's, England

PGA CHAMPIONSHIP

YEAR	WINNER	SCORE	RUNNERUP	PLAYED AT
1916	James M. Barnes	1 up	Jock Hutchison	Siwanoy CC, Bronxville, NY

1917—1918 No Championships Played—World War I

* WINNER IN PLAYOFF

FIGURES IN PARENTHESES INDICATE SCORES

YEAR	WINNER	SCORE	RUNNERUP	PLAYED AT
1919	James M. Barnes	6 & 5	Fred McLeod	Engineers CC, LI, NY
1920	Jock Hutchison	1 up	J. Douglas Edgar	Flossmoor CC, Flossmoor, IL
1921	Walter Hagen	3 & 2	James M. Barnes	Inwood CC, Far Rockaway, NY
1922	Gene Sarazen	4 & 3	Emmet French	Oakmont CC, Oakmont, PA
1923	Gene Sarazen	1 up (38)	Walter Hagen	Pelham CC, Pelham N Y
1924	Walter Hagen	2 up	James M. Barnes	French Lick CC, French Lick, IN
1925	Walter Hagen	6 & 5	William Mehlhorn	Olympia Fields, Olympia Fields, IL
1926	Walter Hagen	5 & 3	Leo Diegel	Salisbury GC, Westbury, LI, NY
1927	Walter Hagen	1 up	Joe Turnesa	Cedar Crest C C, Dallas TX
1928	Leo Diegel	6 & 5	Al Espinosa	Five Farms CC Baltimore, MD
1929	Leo Diegel	6 & 4	Johnny Farrell	Hillcrest CC Los Angeles, CA
1930	Tommy Armour	1 up	Gene Sarazen	Fresh Meadow CC, Flushing, NY
1931	Tom Creavy	2 & 1	Denny Shute	Wannamoisett CC Rumford, RI
1932	Olin Dutra	4 & 3	Frank Walsh	Keller GC, St. Paul MN
1933	Gene Sarazen	5 & 4	Willie Goggin	Blue Mound CC, Milwaukee, WI
1934	Paul Runyan	1 up (38)	Craig Wood	Park CC, Williamsville NY
1935	Johnny Revolta	5 & 4	Tommy Armour	Twin Hills CC, Oklahoma City, OK
1936	Denny Shute	3 & 2	Jimmy Thomson	Pinehurst CC, Pinehurst NC
1937	Denny Shute	1 up (37)	Harold McSpaden	Pittsburgh Field Club, Aspinwall, PA
1938	Paul Runyan	8 & 7	Sam Snead	Shawnee CC, Shawnee-on-Delaware,
1939	Henry Picard	1 up (37)	Byron Nelson	Pomonok CC, Flushing LI, NY
1940	Byron Nelson	1 up	Sam Snead	Hershey CC, Hershey, PA
1941	Vic Ghezzi	1 up (38)	Byron Nelson	Cherry Hills CC Denver CO
1942	Sam Snead	2 & 1	Jim Turnesa	Seaview CC, Atlantic City, NJ
1943—No Championship Played—World War II				
1944	Bob Hamilton	1 up	Byron Nelson	Manito G & CC, Spokane WA
1945	Byron Nelson	4 & 3	Sam Byrd	Morraine CC, Dayton, OH
1946	Ben Hogan	6 & 4	Ed Oliver	Portland GC, Portland, OR
1947	Jim Ferrier	2 & 1	Chick Harbert	Plum Hollow CC, Detroit, MI
1948	Ben Hogan	7 & 6	Mike Turnesa	Norwood Hills CC St. Louis MO
1949	Sam Snead	3 & 2	Johnny Palmer	Hermitage CC, Richmond, VA
1950	Chandler Harper	4 & 3	Henry Williams, Jr.	Scioto CC, Columbus, OH
1951	Sam Snead	7 & 6	Walter Burkemo	Oakmont CC Oakmont PA
1952	Jim Turnesa	1 up	Chick Harbert	Big Spring CC, Louisvillie, KY
1953	Walter Burkemo	2 & 1	Felice Torza	Birmingham CC, Birmingham, MI
1954	Chick Harbert	4 & 3	Walter Burkemo	Keller GC, St. Paul, MN
1955	Doug Ford	4 & 3	Cary Middlecoff	Meadowbrook CC Detroit MI
1956	Jack Burke	3 & 2	Ted Kroll	Blue Hill CC, Boston, MA
1957	Lionel Hebert	2 & 1	Dow Finsterwald	Miami Valley CC, Dayton, OH
1958	Dow Finsterwald	276	Billy Casper	Llanerch CC, Havertown, PA
1959	Bob Rosburg	277	Jerry Barber Doug Sanders	Minneapolis GC, St. Louis Park, MN
1960	Jay Hebert	281	Jim Ferrier	Firestone CC, Akron, OH
1961	*Jerry Barber (67)	277	Don January (68)	Olympia Fields CC, Olympia Fields, IL
1962	Gary Player	278	Bob Goalby	Aronomink GC, Newtown Square, PA
1963	Jack Nicklaus	279	Dave Ragan, Jr.	Dallas Athletic Club, Dallas, TX
1964	Bobby Nichols	271	Jack Nicklaus Arnold Palmer	Columbus CC, Columbus, OH
1965	Dave Marr	280	Billy Casper Jack Nicklaus	Laurel Valley CC, Ligonier, PA
1966	Al Geiberger	280	Dudley Wysong	Firestone CC Akron OH
1967	*Don January (69)	281	Don Massengale (71)	Columbine CC, Littleton, CO
1968	Julius Boros	281	Bob Charles Arnold Palmer	Pecan Valley CC, San Antonio, TX
1969	Ray Floyd	276	Gary Player	NCR CC, Dayton, OH
1970	Dave Stockton	279	Arnold Palmer Bob Murphy	Southern Hills CC, Tulsa, OK
1971	Jack Nicklaus	281	Billy Casper	PGA National GC, Palm Beach Gardens, FL
1972	Gary Player	281	Tommy Aaron Jim Jamieson	Oakland Hills CC, Birmingham, MI

* WINNER IN PLAYOFF

FIGURES IN PARENTHESES INDICATE SCORES

PGA CHAMPIONSHIP (CONT'D.)

YEAR	WINNER	SCORE	RUNNERUP	PLAYED AT
1973	Jack Nicklaus	277	Bruce Crampton	Canterbury GC, Cleveland, OH
1974	Lee Trevino	276	Jack Nicklaus	Tanglewood GC, Winston-Salem, NC
1975	Jack Nicklaus	276	Bruce Crampton	Firestone CC, Akron OH
1976	Dave Stockton	281	Ray Floyd	Congressional CC, Bethesda, MD
			Don January	
1977	*Lanny Wadkins	282	Gene Littler	Pebble Beach GL, Pebble Beach, CA
1978	*John Mahaffey	276	Jerry Pate	Oakmont CC, Oakmont, PA
			Tom Watson	
1979	*David Graham	272	Ben Crenshaw	Oakland Hills CC, Birmingham, MI
1980	Jack Nicklaus	274	Andy Bean	Oak Hill CC, Rochester NY
1981	Larry Nelson	273	Fuzzy Zoeller	Atlanta Athletic Club, Duluth, GA
1982	Raymond Floyd	272	Lanny Wadkins	Southern Hills CC, Tulsa, OK
1983	Hal Sutton	274	Jack Nicklaus	Riviera CC, Pacific Palisades, CA
1984	Lee Trevino	273	Gary Player	Shoal Creek, Birmingham, AL
			Lanny Wadkins	
1985	Hubert Green	278	Lee Trevino	Cherry Hills CC, Denver CO
1986	Bob Tway	276	Greg Norman	Inverness Club, Toledo OH
1987	*Larry Nelson	287	Lanny Wadkins	PGA National, Palm Beach Gardens, FL
1988	Jeff Sluman	272	Paul Azinger	Oak Tree GC, Edmond, OK
1989	Payne Stewart	276	Mike Reid	Kemper Lakes GC, Hawthorn Woods, IL
1990	Wayne Grady	282	Fred Couples	Shoal Creek, Birmingham, AL
1991	John Daly	276	Bruce Lietzke	Crooked Stick GC, Carmel, IN
1992	Nick Price	278	John Cook	Bellerive CC, St. Louis, MO
			Jim Gallagher, Jr.	
			Gene Sauers	
			Nick Faldo	
1993	*Paul Azinger	272	Greg Norman	Inverness Club, Toledo, OH

* WINNER IN PLAYOFF

FIGURES IN PARENTHESES INDICATE SCORES

RYDER CUP MATCHES

The Ryder Cup Matches developed from a match played between representatives of the American and British Professional Golfers' Association in England in 1926. That unofficial match, incidentally, was won by the British 13 1/2 to 1 1/2.

Following this highly successful exhibition, Samuel A. Ryder, a wealthy British seed merchant, offered to donate a solid gold trophy bearing his name to be competed for in a series of matches between professionals of the two nations.

From the start of the series through the 1959 Ryder Cup matches, the competition was comprised of four foursome matches one day and eight singles matches the other day, each at 36 holes.

In 1961, the format was changed to provide for four 18-hole foursomes the morning of the first day and four more that afternoon, then for eight 18-hole singles the morning of the second day and eight more that afternoon. As in the past, one point was at stake in each match, so the total number of points was doubled.

In 1963, for the first time, a day of four-ball matches augmented the program to add new interest to the overall competition. This brought the total number of points to 32.

In 1977, the format was altered once again. This time there were five foursomes on the opening day, five four-ball matches on the second day, and ten singles matches on the final day. This reduced the total number of points to 20.

For 1979, eligibility for the Great Britain-Ireland side was expanded to include all British PGA/European TPD members who are residents of European nations.

The 1995 Ryder Cup Matches will be played September 21-24, 1995, at Oak Hill CC, Rochester, NY

Year	Played at	Date	Result			
1927	Worcester Country Club, Worcester, MA	June 3-4	U.S.	9 1/2	Britain	2 1/2
1929	Moortown, England	May 26-27	Britain	7	U.S.	5
1931	Scioto Country Club, Columbus, OH	June 26-27	U.S.	9	Britain	3
1933	Southport & Ainsdale Courses, England	June 26-27	Britain	6 1/2	U.S.	5 1/2
1935	Ridgewood Country Club, Ridgewood, NJ	Sept. 28-29	U S.	9	Britain	3
1937	Southport & Ainsdale Courses, England	June 29-30	U.S.	8	Britain	4
	Ryder Cup Matches not held during World War II years.					
1947	Portland Golf Club, Portland, OR	Nov. 1-2	U.S.	11	Britain	1
1949	Ganton Golf Course, Scarborough, England	Sept 16-17	U.S.	7	Britain	5
1951	Pinehurst Country Club, Pinehurst, NC	Nov. 2-4	U.S.	9 1/2	Britain	2 1/2
1953	Wentworth, England	Oct. 2-3	U.S.	6 1/2	Britain	5 1/2
1955	Thunderbird Ranch and CC, Palm Springs, CA	Nov. 5-6	U.S.	8	Britain	4
1957	Lindrick Golf Club, Yorkshire, England	Oct. 4-5	Britain	7 1/2	U.S	4 1/2
1959	Eldorado Country Club, Palm Desert, CA	Nov. 6-7	U.S.	8 1/2	Britain	3 1/2
1961	Royal Lytham and St. Anne's Golf Club, St. Anne's-On-The-Sea, England	Oct. 13-14	U.S.	14 1/2	Britain	9 1/2
1963	East Lake Country Club, Atlanta, GA	Oct. 11-13	U.S.	23	Britain	9
1965	Royal Birkdale Golf Club, Southport, England	Oct. 7-9	U.S.	19 1/2	Britain	12 1/2
1967	Champions Golf Club, Houston, TX	Oct. 20-22	U.S.	23 1/2	Britain	8 1/2
1969	Royal Birkdale Golf Club, Southport, England	Sept. 18-20	U.S.	16-Tie	Britain	16
1971	Old Warson Country Club, St. Louis, MO	Sept. 16-18	U S.	18 1/2	Britain	13 1/2
1973	Muirfield, Scotland	Sept. 20-22	U.S.	19	Britain	13
1975	Laurel Valley Golf Club, Ligonier, PA	Sept. 19-21	U.S.	21	Britain	11
1977	Royal Lytham and St. Anne's Golf Club, St. Anne's-On-The-Sea, England	Sept. 15-17	U.S	12 1/2	Britain	7 1/2
1979	Greenbrier, White Sulphur Springs, WV	Sept. 13-15	U.S.	17	Europe	11
1981	Walton Heath Golf Club, Surrey, England	Sept. 18-20	U.S.	18 1/2	Europe	9 1/2
1983	PGA National GC, Palm Beach Gardens, FL	Oct. 14-16	U.S.	14 1/2	Europe	13 1/2
1985	The Belfry Golf Club Sutton, Coldfield, England	Sept. 13-15	Europe	16 1/2	U.S.	11 1/2
1987	Muirfield Village Golf Club, Dublin, OH	Sept. 24-27	Europe	15	U.S.	13
1989	The Belfry Golf Club, Sutton Coldfield, England	Sept. 22-24	U.S.	14-Tie	Europe	14
1991	The Ocean Course, Kiawah Island, SC	Sept. 26-29	U.S.	14 1/2	Europe	13 1/2
1993	The Belfry Golf Club, Sutton Coldfield, England	Sept. 24-26	U.S.	15	Europe	13

RECAPITULATION: 30 Events, U.S. 23 wins—Europe 5 wins—Ties 2.

THE RYDER CUP

The 1995 U.S. Ryder Cup Team will be selected by way of Ryder Cup points earned from the beginning of 1994 through the 1995 PGA Championship. The top ten point-getters qualify for the 12-man team. Then the U.S. Captain will select the final two players to complete the team.

Points are awarded to the first ten positions in each PGA TOUR event on the following basis with points being weighted towards the 1995 season:

PGA Championship, U.S. Open, Masters Tournament and the British Open (1994/1995): 1st-225/300; 2nd-135/180; 3rd-120/160; 4th-105/140; 5th-90/120; 6th-75/100; 7th-60/80; 8th-45/60; 9th-30/40; 10th-15/20.

All other PGA TOUR events (1994/1995): 1st-75/150; 2nd-45/90; 3rd-40/80; 4th-35/70; 5th-30/60; 6th-25/50; 7th-2040; 8th-15/30; 9th-10/20; 10th-5/10.

If a player who is ineligible finishes in one of those positions, no points are awarded for that position. In order to be eligible, a player must be a U.S. citizen and a member of the PGA of America.

1993 MATCH RESULTS

FIRST DAY

Foursomes--United States 2, Europe 2

Lanny Wadkins/Corey Pavin (U.S.) def. Sam Torrance/Mark James, 4&3
Ian Woosnam/Bernhard Langer (Europe) def. Payne Stewart/Paul Azinger, 7&5
Tom Kite/Davis Love III (U.S.) def. Seve Ballesteros/Jose Maria Olazabal, 2&1
Nick Faldo/Colin Montgomerie (Europe) def. Raymond Floyd/Fred Couples, 4&3

Four-Ball--Europe 2 1/2, United States 1 1/2

Woosnam/Peter Baker (Europe) def. Jim Gallagher, Jr./Lee Janzen, 1 up
Wadkins/Pavin (U.S.) def. Langer/Barry Lane, 4&2
Azinger/Couples (U.S.) halved with Faldo/Montgomerie
Ballesteros/Olazabal (Europe) def. Kite/Love, 4&3

Totals: Europe 4 1/2, United States 3 1/2

SECOND DAY

Foursomes--Europe 3, United States 1

Faldo/Montgomerie (Europe) def. Wadkins/Pavin, 3&2
Woosnam/Langer (Europe) def. Azinger/Couples, 2&1
Floyd/Stewart (U.S.) def. Baker/Lane, 3&2
Ballesteros/Olazabal (Europe) def. Kite/Love, 2&1

Totals: Europe 7 1/2, United States 4 1/2

Four-Ball--United States 3, Europe 1

John Cook/Chip Beck (U.S.) def. Faldo/Montgomerie, 2 up
Pavin/Gallagher (U.S.) def. James/Constantino Rocca, 5&4
Woosnam/Baker (Europe) def. Azinger/Couples, 6&5
Floyd/Stewart (U.S.) def. Olazabal/Joakim Haeggman, 2&1

Totals: Europe 8 1/2, United States 7 1/2

THIRD DAY

Singles--United States 7 1/2, Europe 4 1/2

Couples (U.S.) halved with Woosnam
Beck (U.S.) def. Lane, 1 up
Montgomerie (Europe) def. Janzen, 1 up
Baker (Europe) def. Pavin, 2 up
Haeggman (Europe) def. Cook, 1 up
Wadkins (U.S) halved with Torrance
(Match not played by agreement. Torrance forced to withdraw due to injury. Each player awarded one-half point)
Stewart (U.S.) def. James, 3&2
Love (U.S.) def. Rocca, 1 up
Gallagher (U.S.) def. Ballesteros, 3&2
Floyd (U.S.) def. Olazabal, 2 up
Kite (U.S.) def. Langer, 5&3
Azinger (U.S.) halved with Faldo.

Totals: United States 15, Europe 13

WINNERS OF MAJOR U.S. AMATEUR EVENTS

NCAA CHAMPIONS (SINCE 1949)

Year	Winner
1949	Harvie Ward, North Carolina
1950	Fred Wampler, Purdue
1951	Tom Nieporte, Ohio State
1952	Jim Vickers, Oklahoma
1953	Earl Moeller, Oklahoma State
1954	Hillman Robbins, Memphis State
1955	Joe Campbell, Purdue
1956	Rick Jones, Ohio State
1957	Rex Baxter Jr. Houston
1958	Phil Rodgers, Houston
1959	Dick Crawford, Houston
1960	Dick Crawford, Houston
1961	Jack Nicklaus, Ohio State
1962	Kermit Zarley, Houston
1963	R.H. Sikes, Arkansas
1964	Terry Small, San Jose State
1965	Marty Fleckman, Houston
1966	Bob Murphy, Florida
1967	Hale Irwin, Colorado
1968	Grier Jones, Oklahoma State
1969	Bob Clark, Los Angeles State
1970	John Mahaffey, Houston
1971	Ben Crenshaw, Texas
1972	Ben Crenshaw, Texas
	Tom Kite, Texas
1973	Ben Crenshaw, Texas
1974	Curtis Strange, Wake Forest
1975	Jay Haas, Wake Forest
1976	Scott Simpson, USC
1977	Scott Simpson, USC
1978	David Edwards, Oklahoma State
1979	Gary Hallberg, Wake Forest
1980	Jay Don Blake, Utah State
1981	Ron Commans, USC
1982	Billy Ray Brown, Houston
1983	Jim Carter, Arizona State
1984	John Inman, North Carolina
1985	Clark Burroughs, Ohio State
1986	Scott Verplank, Oklahoma State
1987	Brian Watts, Oklahoma State
1988	E.J. Pfister, Oklahoma State
1989	Phil Mickelson, Arizona State
1990	Phil Mickelson, Arizona State
1991	Warren Schutte, Nevada-Las Vegas
1992	Phil Mickelson, Arizona State
1993	Todd Demsey, Arizona State

U.S. AMATEUR CHAMPIONS (SINCE 1949)

Year	Match Play
1949	Charles R. Coe
1950	Sam Urzetta
1951	Billy Maxwell
1952	Jack Westland
1953	Gene A. Littler
1954	Arnold Palmer
1955	E. Harvie Ward, Jr.
1956	E. Harvie Ward, Jr.
1957	Hillman Robbins, Jr.
1958	Charles R. Coe
1959	Jack W. Nicklaus
1960	Deane R. Beman
1961	Jack W. Nicklaus
1962	Labron E. Harris Jr.
1963	Deane R. Beman
1964	William C. Campbell

Year	Stroke Play	
1965	Robert J. Murphy	291
1966	Gary Cowan	285
1967	Robert B. Dickson	285
1968	Bruce Fleisher	284
1969	Steven N. Melnyk	286
1970	Lanny Wadkins	*279
1971	Gary Cowan	280
1972	Vinny Giles	285

Year	Match Play
1973	Craig Stadler
1974	Jerry Pate
1975	Fred Ridley
1976	Bill Sander
1977	John Fought
1978	John Cook
1979	Mark O'Meara
1980	Hal Sutton
1981	Nathaniel Crosby
1982	Jay Sigel
1983	Jay Sigel
1984	Scott Verplank
1985	Sam Randolph
1986	Buddy Alexander
1987	Bill Mayfair
1988	Eric Meeks
1989	Chris Patton
1990	Phil Mickelson
1991	Mitch Voges
1992	Justin Leonard
1993	John Harris

U.S. PUBLIC LINKS CHAMPIONS (SINCE 1949)

Year	Match Play
1949	Kenneth J. Towns
1950	Stanley Bielat
1951	Dave Stanley
1952	Omer L. Bogan
1953	Ted Richards, Jr.
1954	Gene Andrews
1955	Sam D. Kocsis
1956	James H. Buxbaum
1957	Don Essig, III
1958	Daniel D. Sikes, Jr.
1959	William A Wright
1960	Verne Callison
1961	Richard H. Sikes
1962	Richard H. Sikes
1963	Robert Lunn
1964	William McDonald
1965	Arne Dokka
1966	Lamont Kaser

Year	Stroke Play	
1967	Verne Callison	287
1968	Gene Towry	292
1969	J. M. Jackson	292
1970	Robert Risch	293
1971	Fred Haney	290
1972	Bob Allard	285
1973	Stan Stopa	294
1974	Chas. Barenaba	290

Year	Match Play
1975	Randy Barenaba
1976	Eddie Mudd
1977	Jerry Vidovic
1978	Dean Prince
1979	Dennis Walsh
1980	Jodie Mudd
1981	Jodie Mudd
1982	Billy Tuten
1983	Billy Tuten
1984	Bill Malley
1985	Jim Sorenson
1986	Bill Mayfair
1987	Kevin Johnson
1988	Ralph Howe
1989	Tim Hobby
1990	Mike Combs
1991	David Berganio, Jr.
1992	Warren Schutte
1993	David Berganio, Jr.

1993 PGA TOUR AWARDS

David Frost won the Canadian Open and
Hardee's Golf Classic in consecutive weeks.

1993 PGA TOUR
PLAYER of the Year

TOURNAMENT HIGHLIGHTS:

- Won 1993 PLAYERS Championship
- Won 1993 Canon Greater Hartford Open
- Won 1993 Sprint Western Open
- Won 1993 Federal Express St. Jude Classic

- Earned PGA TOUR single season record $1,478,557

- Won at Hartford, Chicago and Memphis in consecutive starts

- Won Vardon Trophy with 69.11 scoring average

NICK PRICE

PGA TOUR PLAYER OF THE YEAR	
1990	Wayne Levi
1991	Fred Couples
1992	Fred Couples
1993	Nick Price

1993 PGA TOUR
ROOKIE of the Year

TOURNAMENT HIGHLIGHTS:

- Won Buick Classic in a playoff over Mark Wiebe

- Finished as runner-up to Ben Crenshaw at the Nestle Invitational

- Posted six top-10 finishes on the year

- Established PGA TOUR record for earnings by a rookie — $657,831

VIJAY SINGH

PGA TOUR ROOKIE OF THE YEAR	
1990	Robert Gamez
1991	John Daly
1992	Mark Carnevale
1993	Vijay Singh

Arnold Palmer Award

Awarded each year to the PGA TOUR's leading money winner.

1981	Tom Kite	$ 375,699	1988	Curtis Strange	$1,147,644
1982	Craig Stadler	$ 446,462	1989	Tom Kite	$1,395,278
1983	Hal Sutton	$ 426,668	1990	Greg Norman	$1,165,477
1984	Tom Watson	$ 476,260	1991	Corey Pavin	$ 979,430
1985	Curtis Strange	$ 542,321	1992	Fred Couples	$1,344,188
1986	Greg Norman	$ 653,296	1993	Nick Price	$1,478,557
1987	Curtis Strange	$ 925,941			

Card Walker Award

The Card Walker Award is given annually by the PGA TOUR to the person or group who has made significant contributions to the support of Junior Golf.

1981	Mrs. Lou Smith
1982	Frank Emmet
1983	Jack Nicklaus
1984	Sally Carroll
1985	Don Padgett, Sr.
1986	Chi Chi Rodriguez
1987	James S. Kemper
1988	William V. Powers
1989	Selina Johnson
1990	Tucson Conquistadores
1991	American Junior Golf Association
1992	Bill Dickey
1993	Western Golf Association
1994	Fred Engh

PGA TOUR Charity of the Year Award

The PGA TOUR Charity of the Year Award was started in 1987. Charities are nominated by the American Golf Sponsors and voted on by the Tournament Policy Board.

1987	Egleston Hospital for Children	BellSouth Classic
1988	Siskin Memorial Foundation	Chattanooga Classic
1989	Bobby Benson Foundation	United Airlines Hawaiian
1990	Salesmanship Club	GTE Byron Nelson Classic
1991	Arrowhead Ranch for Boys	Hardee's Golf Classic
1992	United Health Services System	B.C. Open
1993	Chinquapin School	Shell Houston Open

Other Awards Won by PGA TOUR Golfers

Sporting News Man of the Year

1971	Lee Trevino

Sports Illustrated Sportsman of the Year

1960	Arnold Palmer
1964	Ken Venturi
1971	Lee Trevino
1978	Jack Nicklaus

Associated Press Male Athlete of the Year

1932	Gene Sarazen
1944	Byron Nelson
1945	Byron Nelson
1953	Ben Hogan
1971	Lee Trevino

VARDON TROPHY

The Vardon Trophy is awarded each year by the PGA of America to the PGA TOUR player who posts the season's best scoring average. The system was amended in 1988 to allow all TOUR members to compete for the prestigious award provided they have played in 60 rounds. The new system also uses an "adjusted" score for purposes of computing the scoring average. The adjusted score is computed based upon the average score of the field at each tournament. As a result, a player's adjusted score may be higher or lower than his actual score. For example, a player shoots 70 each day at a tournament while the field average was 73. His 280 total would then be adjusted to 268 since he actually played 12 shots better than the field did during the tournament. The Vardon Trophy is a bronze-colored plaque measuring 39" by 27".

Year	Winner	Average	Year	Winner	Average
1937	Harry Cooper	*500	1967	Arnold Palmer	70.18
1938	Sam Snead	520	1968	Billy Casper	69.82
1939	Byron Nelson	473	1969	Dave Hill	70.34
1940	Ben Hogan	423	1970	Lee Trevino	70.64
1941	Ben Hogan	494	1971	Lee Trevino	70.27
1942-			1972	Lee Trevino	70.89
1946	No Award-World War II		1973	Bruce Crampton	70.57
1947	Jimmy Demaret	69.90	1974	Lee Trevino	70.53
1948	Ben Hogan	69.30	1975	Bruce Crampton	70.51
1949	Sam Snead	69.37	1976	Don January	70.56
1950	Sam Snead	69.23	1977	Tom Watson	70.32
1951	Lloyd Mangrum	70.05	1978	Tom Watson	70.16
1952	Jack Burke	70.54	1979	Tom Watson	70.27
1953	Lloyd Mangrum	70.22	1980	Lee Trevino	69.73
1954	E. J. Harrison	70.41	1981	Tom Kite	69.80
1955	Sam Snead	69.86	1982	Tom Kite	70.21
1956	Cary Middlecoff	70.35	1983	Raymond Floyd	70.61
1957	Dow Finsterwald	70.30	1984	Calvin Peete	70.56
1958	Bob Rosburg	70.11	1985	Don Pooley	70.36
1959	Art Wall	70.35	1986	Scott Hoch	70.08
1960	Billy Casper	69.95	1987	Dan Pohl	70.25
1961	Arnold Palmer	69.85	1988	Chip Beck	69.46
1962	Arnold Palmer	70.27	1989	Greg Norman	69.49
1963	Billy Casper	70.58	1990	Greg Norman	69.10
1964	Arnold Palmer	70.01	1991	Fred Couples	69.59
1965	Billy Casper	70.85	1992	Fred Couples	69.38
1966	Billy Casper	70.27	1993	Nick Price	69.11

*Point system used, 1937—'41.

PGA PLAYER OF THE YEAR AWARD

1948—Ben Hogan
1949—Sam Snead
1950—Ben Hogan
1951—Ben Hogan
1952—Julius Boros
1953—Ben Hogan
1954—Ed Furgol
1955—Doug Ford
1956—Jack Burke
1957—Dick Mayer
1958—Dow Finsterwald
1959—Art Wall
1960—Arnold Palmer
1961—Jerry Barber
1962—Arnold Palmer
1963—Julius Boros

1964—Ken Venturi
1965—Dave Marr
1966—Billy Casper
1967—Jack Nicklaus
1968—Not Awarded
1969—Orville Moody
1970—Billy Casper
1971—Lee Trevino
1972—Jack Nicklaus
1973—Jack Nicklaus
1974—Johnny Miller
1975—Jack Nicklaus
1976—Jack Nicklaus
1977—Tom Watson
1978—Tom Watson

1979—Tom Watson
1980—Tom Watson
1981—Bill Rogers
1982—Tom Watson
1983—Hal Sutton
1984—Tom Watson
1985—Lanny Wadkins
1986—Bob Tway
1987—Paul Azinger
1988—Curtis Strange
1989—Tom Kite
1990—Nick Faldo
1991—Corey Pavin
1992—Fred Couples
1993—Nick Price

Each year the PGA of America honors the TOUR's leading player by presenting him with the PGA Player of the Year Award.

The award now is made on the basis of playing record for the year. Points are awarded on the following basis: 30 points to winner of Masters, U.S. Open, British Open, PGA Championship. 20 points to winner of THE PLAYERS Championship, NEC World Series of Golf. 10 points to winners of all other co-sponsored or approved events. Points also awarded to top 10 on the year's money list and top 10 on year's scoring average list (20 for first, 18 for second, 16 for third, etc. down to 2 for 10th).

PGA HALL OF FAME
Palm Beach Gardens, Florida

1940	Willie Anderson, Tommy Armour, Jim Barnes, Chick Evans, Walter Hagen, Bobby Jones, John McDermott, Francis Ouimet, Gene Sarazen, Alex Smith, Jerry Travers, Walter Travis.
1953	Ben Hogan, Byron Nelson, Sam Snead,
1954	Macdonald Smith
1955	Leo Diegel
1956	Craig Wood
1957	Denny Shute
1958	Horton Smith
1959	Harry Cooper, Jock Hutchison, Sr., Paul Runyan
1960	Mike Brady, Jimmy Demaret, Fred McLeod
1961	Johnny Farrell, Lawson Little, Henry Picard
1962	Dutch Harrison, Olin Dutra
1963	Ralph Guldahl, Johnny Revolta
1964	Lloyd Mangrum, Ed Dudley
1965	Vic Ghezzi
1966	Billy Burke
1967	Bobby Cruickshank
1968	Chick Harbert
1969	Chandler Harper
1974	Julius Boros, Cary Middlecoff
1975	Jack Burke, Jr., Doug Ford
1976	Babe Zaharias
1978	Patty Berg
1979	Roberto DeVicenzo
1980	Arnold Palmer
1982	Gene Littler, Billy Casper

PGA WORLD GOLF HALL OF FAME
Pinehurst, North Carolina

1974	Patty Berg, Walter Hagen, Ben Hogan, Robert T. Jones, Byron Nelson, Jack Nicklaus, Francis Ouimet, Arnold Palmer, Gary Player, Gene Sarazen, Sam Snead, Harry Vardon, Babe Zaharias
1975	Willie Anderson, Fred Corcoran, Joseph C. Dey, Chick Evans, Tom Morris, Jr., John H. Taylor, Glenna C. Vare, Joyce Wethered
1976	Tommy Armour, James Braid, Tom Morris Sr., Jerome Travers, Mickey Wright
1977	Bobby Locke, John Ball, Herb Graffis, Donald Ross
1978	Billy Casper, Harold Hilton, Dorothy Campbell, Herd Howe, Bing Crosby, Clifford Roberts
1979	Louise Suggs, Walter Travis
1980	Lawson Little, Henry Cotton
1981	Lee Trevino, Ralph Guldahl
1982	Julius Boros, Kathy Whitworth
1983	Bob Hope, Jimmy Demaret
1985	JoAnne Carner
1986	Cary Middlecoff
1987	Robert Trent Jones, Betsy Rawls
1988	Tom Watson, Peter Thomson, Bob Harlow
1989	Raymond Floyd, Nancy Lopez, Roberto De Vicenzo, Jim Barnes
1990	William C. Campbell, Paul Runyan, Gene Littler, Horton Smith
1992	Hale Irwin, Chi Chi Rodriguez, Richard Tufts, Harry Cooper

NOTE: Selected by the Golf Writers Association of America

Payne Stewart earned $982,875 on
the strength of 12 top-10 finishes

PGA TOUR MARKETING PARTNERS

ANHEUSER-BUSCH

One of golf's most enduring corporate supporters, Anheuser-Busch, is now one of the PGA TOUR's leading sponsors. The Michelob family of beers and the PGA TOUR have signed an agreement which crowns Michelob's association with the game, which now spans more than 30 years. As part of the partnership, O'Doul's, Anheuser-Busch's industry leading non-alcoholic beverage, will be the offical non-alcoholic beer of the PGA TOUR and Senior PGA TOUR.

Through the years, Michelob, which is brewed by Anheuser-Busch, has sponsored thousands of local golf tournaments, a host of touring pros and a long list of professional tournaments.

Primary features of the new Michelob/PGA TOUR relationship include presenting sponsor rights for THE TOUR Championship, media-driven national sweepstakes, extensive participation in ESPN's TOUR coverage and heavy involvement on both TOURs with a unique interactive display called the "PGA TOUR 19th Hole."

In addition, O'Doul's TOUR program includes network television advertising, national point-of-sale promotions and tournament sampling opportunities.

BUICK

Buick Motor Division is a long-time marketing partner of the PGA TOUR. The relationship between the TOUR and Buick over the last 30 years has led to sponsorship of PGA TOUR tournaments across the country.

It all began with the Buick Open, now the PGA TOUR event with the longest continuing sponsorship. The tournament is played in Flint, Mich., Buick's "hometown." Each year, countless Buick employees use their vacation time to volunteer at the event, which they consider their own.

contd.

Buick's partnership with the PGA TOUR now includes the sponsorship of four tournaments: the Buick Open (Flint, Mich.); Buick Southern Open (Callaway Gardens, Ga.); the Buick Invitational of California (San Diego, Calif.); and the Buick Classic (Rye, N.Y.).

To enhance fan's awareness of Buick's tournaments, the company has set up a nationwide sweepstakes that encourages fans to test drive and register to win a Buick. The company has said its golf-related promotions are the most successful it has ever run.

COCA-COLA

For the third year, Coca-Cola will sponsor the Coca-Cola Scoreboards on the PGA TOUR. Coca-Cola, in partnership with IBM, has updated the scoreboards, making them more informative and easier to read.

Coca-Cola has provided the capital for the operation of the scoreboards, which display Coca-Cola's corporate logo. The boards provide current scores, weather advisories, statistical data and other vital information.

Coca-Cola's relationship with the TOUR also can be seen on the local level. As part of the local package, the soft-drink giant sponsors Coca-Cola Clinics at nearly every tournament site. These events attract fans of all ages and feature PGA TOUR members, who demonstrate fundamentals and increase interest in the sport.

DELTA

Delta Air Lines is the "official airline of the PGA TOUR." Delta promotes air travel to golf destinations and keeps its Frequent Fliers abreast of PGA TOUR activities. News of the PGA TOUR appears in Delta's SKY Magazine, and all Delta timetables feature schedules from the PGA TOUR and Senior PGA TOUR. TOUR members and staff receive special airfares.

IBM

In one of the most appropriate sports collaborations ever, IBM entered into an agreement with the PGA TOUR to develop the IBM Scoring System. This is an agreement which benefits everyone, from the players to the television viewers to the spectators at each PGA TOUR event.

The IBM Scoring System is so fast that scoring updates are seen just seconds after a player completes a hole. Players and galleries on the course know where the field stands at all times. Remote computers keep fans informed at other locations such as hospitality areas, host hotels, etc.

In addition to the information available on the scoreboards, IBM sets up "fan information centers" around the course. These multi-media setups allow fans to receive a wealth of timely information at the touch of a key at an IBM PC.

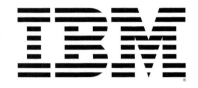

MERRILL LYNCH

Merrill Lynch sponsors the popular Merrill Lynch Shoot-Outs at PGA TOUR, Senior PGA TOUR and Nike Tour events. The 10-man, nine-hole elimination competitions culminate at year-end finals. The Shoot-Outs are crowd pleasers wherever they are played. ABC will televise the Shoot-Out Final for the PGA TOUR from the Mid-Ocean Club, Tucker's Town, Bermuda. The Senior PGA TOUR Shoot-Out final, to be played at Manele Bay, Lanai, Hawaii, will air on ESPN. Information on the 1993 PGA TOUR Final can be found on page 365.

PGA TOUR MARKETING PARTNERS *continued*

EASTMAN KODAK

In its capacity as the "official film, photographic paper and processing company of the PGA TOUR," the company furnishes the PGA TOUR with film supplies for its photographers and on-site promotions staff.

NATIONAL INTERRENT

National InterRent is the "official car rental company of the PGA TOUR" and offers excellent rental rates to PGA TOUR members and staff. National also supplies the courtesy cars for THE PLAYERS Championship. The company publicizes its relationship with the TOUR in its Emerald Club Newsletter for frequent renters.

ROYAL CARIBBEAN CRUISE LINE

Royal Caribbean is the "official cruise line of the PGA TOUR." The company offers special Golf Ahoy! cruises along with special cruise rates for PGA TOUR members. In 1994, for the fifth consecutive year, the Royal Caribbean Classic will be played on Key Biscayne, FL., as part of the Senior PGA TOUR.

To acknowledge the dedication of thousands of volunteers throughout the year, Royal Caribbean will sponsor the "Volunteer of the Year" program on the PGA TOUR and Senior PGA TOUR in 1994. Four times a year, a volunteer from each TOUR will be selected to receive a complementary cruise for two from Royal Caribbean.

♔Royal Caribbean Cruise Line

Official PGA TOUR Golf Destinations

CATALONIA, SPAIN

Catalonia, Spain, the newest PGA TOUR golf travel destination, received widespread publicity as host of the 1992 Summer Olympic Games. Soon, it may be equally well known as a golf destination.

The courses in Catalonia are as diverse as the scenery. Seaside and mountain courses can be found at Costa Brava, north of Barcelona. To the South is the Mediterranean Sea, which is visible from nearly every course in the area. Finally, a course in the Pyranees, two hours to the east, lets you play golf in the morning and, in the spring and fall, ski in the afternoon...or vice versa.

Catalunya

BRITISH COLUMBIA

British Columbia offers a wide variety of spectacularly beautiful golf travel opportunities.

Coastal Victoria and Vancouver courses allow play nearly year-round thanks to warm currents offshore. The central region gets the most sunshine of any part of the province, with plenty of golf available from April to October. The eastern mountains, meanwhile, offer some of the most spectacular and ruggedly beautiful golf in the world.

Super, Natural British Columbia

CANADA

Publications

BUSINESS WEEK

Once again in 1993, <u>Business Week</u> will publish two special supplements which deal exclusively with the PGA TOUR. In the spring, "The 1994 Senior TOUR Journal" will be published. "The Business of the PGA TOUR" will be published in mid-year.

GOLF MAGAZINE

<u>Golf Magazine</u> covers events on the PGA TOUR in <u>TOUR Magazine</u>. This insert appears in the magazine's January issue and as a handout at most PGA TOUR events. <u>Golf Magazine</u> also produces a supplement which is distributed at NIKE TOUR events.

PGA TOUR PARTNERS

The PGA TOUR Partners program gives its members the chance to look inside the PGA TOUR, with its players, tournaments and charities. The program was established in 1991 to help the fan get closer to the PGA TOUR. For an annual membership fee of $38, the Partner receives many benefits including the Official Media Guide, an annual subscription to ON TOUR Magazine, a free ticket to a PGA TOUR event and the opportunity to compete in the Partners Team Competition game.

ON TOUR is a monthly publication which goes behind the scenes of the TOUR. It features players, golf tips, stories on the PGA TOUR players and their celebrity friends, a calendar of events and much more.

The PGA TOUR Partners Golf Classics allow the Partner to travel to some of the most exciting places in the world and play in a PGA TOUR-style tournament on some of the finest resort courses. This is an excellent opportunity for the Partner to play the courses the pros play for a great value.

The Partners Team competition is another privilege of the program. The Partner picks four players to represent his team throughout the year. The players' money winnings added together determine your standing against the other partners. The competition gives you a chance to win a number of exciting prizes, with the grand prize an all-expenses paid trip to THE TOUR Championship, including a spot in the Pro-Am.

Besides drafting a four-man team, each Partner picks a charity for his team to represent. The top 42 winners of the competition will win charity dollars for their chosen tournaments. Last year, the grand prize winner chose the NEC World Series of Golf as his designated charity, and the tournament received $100,000 of the $1 million charity fund.

The program is administered by the PGA TOUR Marketing Department under

the direction of Tom Wade, Vice President, Consumer Marketing. Patti Veale is the Program Manager.

The PGA TOUR Partners Program is an innovative program designed for fan enhancement, while supporting charities throughout the country.

For information about becoming a PGA TOUR Partner, call: 1-800-545-9920.

Tom Wade
Vice President
Consumer Marketing

Patti Veale
Program
Manager

MERRILL LYNCH SHOOT-OUT SERIES

A ten-man competition covering nine holes of play, the Merrill Lynch Shoot-Out Series, now in its eighth season, will be held at 19 different PGA TOUR events in 1994 with the weekly winners collecting $5,000 from the $15,100 purse.

What is a Shoot-Out? The format is easy to understand and a pleasure to watch. Ten players begin. On each hole, the player with the highest score is dropped from the field. If there is a tie, those players participate in a sudden-death playoff where a pitch shot, a chip or a long putt is executed to eliminate the player farthest from the hole.

Weekly Shoot-Outs: The 1994 Merrill Lynch Shoot-Out Series Competitions will be held on Tuesday of tournament week. The field for each Shoot-Out consists of that tournament's defending champion, the six leading money winners entered into that tournament and three sponsor selections.

Shoot-Out Championship: The field for the final competition consists of the top three money winners on the 1994 PGA TOUR Official Money List and seven sponsor selections. Ten players will vie for $500,000 in prize money, with $130,000 going to the winner. Davis Love III won the title in 1993 at The Experience at Koele on the island of Lanai, Hawaii. The 1994 Merrill Lynch Shoot-Out Championship will be held September 26-27 at the Mid Ocean Club in Tucker's Town, Bermuda.

1993 MERRILL LYNCH SHOOT-OUT WINNERS

AT&T Pebble Beach National Pro-Am	Jeff Sluman
Bob Hope Chrysler Classic	Keith Clearwater
Nissan Los Angeles Open	rained out
THE PLAYERS Championship	John Daly
Freeport-McMoRan Classic	Donnie Hammond
MCI Heritage Classic	Rick Fehr
Kmart Greater Greensboro Open	John Daly (2)
Shell Houston Open	Rick Fehr (2)
BellSouth Golf Classic	Nick Price
GTE Byron Nelson Golf Classic	Nick Price (2)
Kemper Open	Brett Ogle
Federal Express St. Jude Classic	Jeff Maggert
NEC World Series of Golf	David Frost
Greater Milwaukee Open	Richard Zokol
Hardee's Golf Classic	rained out
B.C. Open	Brett Ogle/Rick Fehr/ Mike Hulbert
Walt Disney World/Oldsmobile Classic	Chip Beck
Las Vegas Invitational	Vijay Singh

1994 MERRILL LYNCH SHOOT-OUT SCHEDULE

AT&T Pebble Beach National Pro-Am	Feb.	1
Nissan Los Angeles Open	Feb.	8
Bob Hope Chrysler Classic	Feb.	15
THE PLAYERS Championship	Mar.	22
Freeport-McMoRan Classic	Mar.	29
MCI Heritage Classic	Apr.	12
Kmart Greater Greensboro Open	Apr.	19
Shell Houston Open	Apr.	26
BellSouth Classic	May	3
GTE Byron Nelson Classic	May	10
Kemper Open	May	31
Motorola Western Open	June	28
Federal Express St. Jude Classic	July	26
NEC World Series of Golf	Aug.	23
Greater Milwaukee Open	Aug.	30
Hardee's Golf Classic	Sept.	13
B.C. Open	Sept.	20
Walt Disney World/Oldsmobile Classic	Oct.	4
Las Vegas Invitational	Oct.	18

CHAMPIONSHIP WINNERS

1987	Fuzzy Zoeller
1988	David Frost
1989	Chip Beck
1990	John Mahaffey
1991	Davis Love III
1992	Chip Beck
1993	Davis Love III

1994 CHAMPIONSHIP PRIZE MONEY BREAKDOWN

1st	$130,000
2nd	80,000
3rd	55,000
4th	40,000
5th	35,000
6th	34,000
7th	33,000
8th	32,000
9th	31,000
10th	30,000

WEEKLY PRIZE MONEY BREAKDOWN

1st	$5,000
2nd	3,000
3rd	1,500
4th	1,100
5th	1,000
6th	900
7th	800
8th	700
9th	600
10th	500

CENTINELA FITNESS CENTER

The "Official Hospital of the PGA TOUR" since 1984, Centinela Hospital Medical Center in Inglewood, CA, again will sponsor the Centinela Hospital Fitness Center (CHFC) on TOUR in 1994.

One of the most popular innovations on the circuit, the CHFC is a mobile gymnasium that includes state-of-the-art exercise equipment, television, stereo, three treatment tables, various physical therapy modalities, and a full line of vitamins.

Staffed by qualified physical therapists, the CHFC travels to the vast majority of TOUR events across the country providing both rehabilitative and preventative care.

Through its first nine years on the TOUR, the Centinela Hospital Fitness Center has attracted the interest of virtually every player with at least 80 percent using the mobile unit on a regular basis. Housed in a 45-foot long trailer (expandable to 24' wide when parked), the Centinela Hospital Fitness Center enables TOUR pros to maintain peak levels of performance at absolutely no cost to the individual player.

According to Dr. Frank Jobe, Medical Director of the PGA TOUR and team physician to the Los Angeles Dodgers, "Centinela Hospital Medical Center provides each player with a personal physical conditioning program based on that individual's current level of conditioning." Dr. Jobe is assisted by Dr. Lewis Yocum, his associate and orthopedic consultant to the California Angels.

The CHFC has made its impact with many players finding the center and available technicians an invaluable aid to their success on the TOUR. In fact, many players have commented that they would have been unable to compete in some tournaments without the facility.

"If they had this setup several years ago," Fuzzy Zoeller said, "It might have saved me from having back surgery."

"If it wasn't for Centinela Hospital's Fitness Center," said Curtis Strange, "I wouldn't be here."

Centinela Hospital's Biomechanics Laboratory has done research and testing on professional golfers' swings and, based on the results, developed scientific exercise programs which are available through books and videotapes. These programs, designed by Dr. Jobe and Dr. Yocum, have helped countless golfers stretch their potential while minimizing their risk of injury. For more information, contact Centinela Hospital.

Advil (a product of Whitehall Labs) supports the Centinela Hospital Fitness Van by providing some of the leading pain-relievers available on the market today. As is the case with the other sponsors of this facility, Advil will also be exploring new ways of providing better healthcare products for golfers.

The products contributed by each sponsor of the Centinela Hospital Fitness Van have helped make the facility such a success that a similar Fitness Van was introduced on the Senior TOUR in late 1986.

The Centinela Hospital Fitness Center will again be on the PGA TOUR in 1994

PGA TOUR AND AGS DONATE RECORD $22.8 MILLION TO CHARITY IN 1993

PGA TOUR events raised a record charitable contribution of $22,752,137 in 1993.

The $22.8 million generated by TOUR events last year tops the $22.2 million contributed in 1992 and boosts the overall contribution from PGA TOUR events to more than $230 million since 1938.

"Each of our 45 tournament organizations have collectively made this record contribution possible," said American Golf Sponsors President Eric Fredericksen. "It is a tribute to the dedicated efforts of our tournament volunteers and local sponsors who support the TOUR weekly."

The final figure of $22.8 million includes $20.8 million from the tournaments and a combined $2 million from the PGA TOUR's Team Charity and PGA TOUR Partners Team Charity Competitions.

"We are very proud of our players, tournament sponsors and tournament volunteers who make this type of announcement a yearly pleasure," said PGA TOUR Commissioner Deane R. Beman. "We are very excited about establishing another one-season record."

Since the formation of the AGS in 1977, record contributions have been made in 16 of the 17 years. In the decade of the 90s alone, some $84.7 million has been raised for more than 900 charities represented by PGA TOUR events across the United States and Canada.

In September 1992 the TOUR and the AGS were proud to announced that they had surpassed the $200 million mark in charitable contributions.

A Brief History of TOUR Charitable Contributions

1938	First Contribution	$ 10,000	(Palm Beach Invitational)
1950	Contributions reach	$ 1,000,000	
1960	Contributions reach	$ 5,000,000	
1976	TOUR reaches	$10,000,000	
1977	AGS formed	$ 3,300,000	for year
1978		$ 4,300,000	"
1979	$20 million overall	$ 4,400,000	"
1980		$ 4,500,000	"
1981	$30 million overall	$ 6,800,000	"
1982		$ 7,200,000	"
1983		$ 7,800,000	"
1984	$50 million overall	$ 9,400,000	"
1985		$11,300,000	"
1986		$16,100,000	"
1987	$100 million overall	$17,600,000	"
1988	$125 million overall	$18,390,000	"
1989	$145 million overall	$19,779,000	"
1990	$165 million overall	$20,191,000	"
1991	$185 million overall	$19,534,000	"
1992	$200 million overall	$22,223,055	"
1993	$230 million overall	$22,752,137	"

CHARITY is the leading winner on the PGA TOUR

SONY RANKING

Originally formulated in 1986, and approved by the PGA TOUR's Tournament Policy Board since 1990, the Sony Ranking is a computerized system which provides a reference source to the relative performances of the world's leading professional golfers.

The Sony Ranking is issued every Monday, following the completion of the previous week's tournaments from around the world. The official events from all the world's golf tours are taken into account. Points are awarded according to the players' finishing positions and the number and ranking of the players in the respective tournament fields.

The Masters Tournament, United States Open, British Open, PGA Championship and THE PLAYERS Championship are rated separately to reflect the higher quality of the events and the stronger fields participating.

The Sony Ranking is based on a three-year "rolling" period weighted in favor of the more recent results. Points accumulated in the most recent 52-week period are multiplied by four, points earned over the previous 52-week period are doubled and points from the first 52-week period are simply added to the total.

Each player is then ranked according to his average points per tournament, which is determined by dividing his total number of points by the number of tournaments he has played over that three-year period. There is a minimum requirement of 20 tournaments for each 52-week period.

For example, if a player were in 32 tournaments in the most recent 52 weeks, 15 tournaments in the previous 52 weeks, and eight tournaments in the first 52 weeks, his divisor would be 72 (32 plus 20 plus 20). A player who was in 32 tournaments in each of the three 52-week periods would have a divisor of 96 (32 plus 32 plus 32).

The winners of the Masters, U.S. Open, British Open and PGA Championship are awarded 50 points (x4) and the winner of THE PLAYERS Championship is awarded 40 points (x4), which also is the most points possible to be earned from winning any other tournament in the world. The winner of a tournament with a strong field probably would receive approximately 25-30 points (x4).

Minimum points for the winners of official tour events have been set at six points for Asia and South Africa, eight points for Australia/New Zealand and Japan, and 10 points for Europe and the PGA TOUR. In addition, the PGA Championship in Europe has a minimum of 32 points (x4) for the winner, and the Open Championships of Australia and Japan have a minimum of 16 points (x4) for the winner.

Points are reduced proportionally for tournaments curtailed for 36 or 54 holes because of inclement weather or other reasons.

The Sony Ranking Advisory Committee, and an international panel which includes a representative from the PGA TOUR, meets periodically to review and monitor the Sony Ranking system in order to recommend refinements or modifications for the consideration of the Championship Committee of the Royal and Ancient Golf Club of St. Andrews, the sanctioning body of the Sony Ranking.

The Sony Ranking is available each week at PGA TOUR sites. The top 20 as of Dec. 5, 1993, follows.

POS.	PLAYER	AVERAGE	POS.	PLAYER	AVERAGE
1.	Nick Faldo	21.51	11.	David Frost	9.51
2.	Greg Norman	19.45	12.	Jumbo Ozaki	9.28
3.	Bernhard Langer	17.11	13.	Payne Stewart	9.25
4.	Nick Price	15.89	14.	Jose Maria Olazabal	8.91
5.	Paul Azinger	14.87	15.	Colin Montgomerie	8.80
6.	Fred Couples	14.81	16.	Vijay Singh	8.59
7.	Ian Woosnam	11.69	17.	Mark McNulty	8.34
8.	Tom Kite	10.39	18.	John Cook	8.15
9.	Davis Love III	9.91	19.	Steve Elkington	7.47
10.	Corey Pavin	9.64	20.	Lee Janzen	6.71

1994 PGA TOUR CHARITY TEAM COMPETITION DRAFT

1. DEPOSIT GUARANTY GOLF CLASSIC
1. Jim Gallagher, Jr.
2. Wayne Levi
3. Mike Springer
4. Robert Wrenn

2. MERCEDES CHAMPIONSHIPS
1. Fred Couples
2. Mike Hulbert
3. Bob Tway
4. Larry Nelson

3. MOTOROLA WESTERN OPEN
1. Greg Norman
2. Brian Claar
3. Morris Hatalsky
4. Chris DiMarco

4. BOB HOPE CHRYSLER CLASSIC
1. Paul Azinger
2. Russ Cochran
3. Kirk Triplett
4. Jesper Parnevik

5. MEMORIAL TOURNAMENT
1. Payne Stewart
2. Sean Murphy
3. Kenny Perry
4. Hal Sutton

6. BUICK SOUTHERN OPEN
1. Davis Love III
2. John Inman
3. Steve Lowery
4. Scott Gump

7. THE TOUR CHAMPIONSHIP
1. Nick Price
2. Michael Allen
3. John Flannery
4. Jeff Woodland

8. NEC WORLD SERIES OF GOLF
1. David Frost
2. John Daly
3. Ken Green
4. Bobby Clampett

9. THE INTERNATIONAL
1. Lee Janzen
2. Jay Don Blake
3. Ted Schulz
4. Ray Floyd

10. KMART GREATER GREENSBORO OPEN
1. Tom Kite
2. Greg Twiggs
3. Jay Delsing
4. Mike Smith

11. BELL CANADIAN OPEN
1. Steve Elkington
2. Bruce Lietzke
3. Dillard Pruitt
4. Robin Freeman

12. PHOENIX OPEN
1. Phil Mickelson
2. Howard Twitty
3. Tom Purtzer
4. Dave B. Stockton

13. ANHEUSER-BUSCH GOLF CLASSIC
1. Curtis Strange
2. Roger Maltbie
3. Gene Sauers
4. Mark Carnevale

14. LAS VEGAS INVITATIONAL
1. Rocco Mediate
2. Dave Rummells
3. Bob May
4. Guy Boros

16. KEMPER OPEN
1. Vijay Singh
2. Fred Funk
3. David Peoples
4. Steve Lamontagne

17. SOUTHWESTERN BELL COLONIAL
1. Corey Pavin
2. D.A. Weibring
3. Russell Beiersdorf
4. Clark Dennis

18. CANON GREATER HARTFORD OPEN
1. John Cook
2. Donnie Hammond
3. Tom Watson
4. Brian Henninger

19. DORAL-RYDER OPEN
1. Fulton Allem
2. Lanny Wadkins
3. Bruce Fleisher
4. Denis Watson

20. TEXAS OPEN
1. Jeff Maggert
2. Mike Standly
3. David Ogrin
4. Ed Fiori

21. GREATER MILWAUKEE OPEN
1. Mark Calcavecchia
2. Bob Lohr
3. Joe Ozaki
4. Skip Kendall

22. BUICK INVITATIONAL OF CALIFORNIA
1. Chip Beck
2. Greg Kraft
3. Ted Tryba
4. Tim Simpson

23. BUICK OPEN
1. Tom Lehman
2. Ben Crenshaw
3. Brian Kamm
4. Dan Pohl

24. LINCOLN-MERCURY KAPALUA INTERNATIONAL
1. Scott Simpson
2. Hale Irwin
3. David Feherty
4. Andy Bean

25. NESTLE INVITATIONAL
1. Nolan Henke
2. Duffy Waldorf
3. Ed Dougherty
4. John Mahaffey

26. AT&T PEBBLE BEACH NATIONAL PRO-AM
1. Larry Mize
2. Bill Glasson
3. Doug Martin
4. Larry Rinker

27. NORTHERN TELECOM OPEN
1. Jim McGovern
2. Andrew Magee
3. Ronnie Black
4. Larry Silveira

28. BUICK CLASSIC
1. John Huston
2. Mark Wiebe
3. Ed Humenik
4. Olin Browne

29. JCPENNEY CLASSIC
1. Billy Mayfair
2. Robert Gamez
3. Tom Sieckmann
4. David Toms

30. FREEPORT-McMoRan CLASSIC
1. Rick Fehr
2. Kelly Gibson
3. Phil Blackmar
4. Tommy Moore

31. WALT DISNEY WORLD/ OLDSMOBILE CLASSIC
1. Dan Forsman
2. Mark McCumber
3. Brad Bryant
4. Lennie Clements

32. NEW ENGLAND CLASSIC
1. Brad Faxon
2. Peter Jacobsen
3. Don Pooley
4. P.H. Horgan III

33. NISSAN LOS ANGELES OPEN
1. Bob Estes
2. Billy Ray Brown
3. Brandel Chamblee
4. Joel Edwards

34. THE PLAYERS CHAMPIONSHIP
1. Jay Haas
2. Fuzzy Zoeller
3. John Adams
4. Ty Armstrong

35. B.C. OPEN
1. Mark O'Meara
2. Jeff Sluman
3. Jodie Mudd
4. Glen Day

36. FEDERAL EXPRESS ST. JUDE CLASSIC
1. Craig Parry
2. Ian Baker-Finch
3. Curt Byrum
4. John Morse

37. MCI HERITAGE CLASSIC
1. Grant Waite
2. Steve Pate
3. Dick Mast
4. Doug Tewell

38. GTE BYRON NELSON CLASSIC
1. David Edwards
2. Loren Roberts
3. Trevor Dodds
4. Stan Utley

39. UNITED AIRLINES HAWAIIAN OPEN
1. Craig Stadler
2. Scott Hoch
3. Neal Lancaster
4. Bob Gilder

40. HONDA CLASSIC
1. Gil Morgan
2. Brett Ogle
3. Richard Zokol
4. Gary Hallberg

41. HARDEE'S GOLF CLASSIC
1. Blaine McCallister
2. Joey Sindelar
3. Willie Wood
4. Steve Stricker

42. BELLSOUTH CLASSIC
1. Billy Andrade
2. Keith Clearwater
3. Michael Bradley
4. Dave Barr

43. SHELL HOUSTON OPEN
1. Mark Brooks
2. Dudley Hart
3. Marco Dawson
4. Bill Britton

FINAL 1993 PGA TOUR CHARITY TEAM COMPETITION STANDINGS

	TOURNAMENT NAME	TOURNAMENT TOTAL	TOURNAMENT BONUS
1.	SHELL HOUSTON OPEN	2,096,639	$100,000
2.	BELLSOUTH CLASSIC	1,946,963	75,000
3.	HARDEE'S GOLF CLASSIC	1,862,892	50,000
4.	HONDA CLASSIC	1,802,065	40,000
5.	UNITED AIRLINES HAWAIIAN OPEN	1,758,360	35,000
6.	GTE BYRON NELSON GOLF CLASSIC	1,582,236	30,800
7.	MCI HERITAGE GOLF CLASSIC	1,535,178	28,000
8.	FEDERAL EXPRESS ST. JUDE CLASSIC	1,487,855	27,000
9.	B.C. OPEN	1,466,099	26,000
10.	THE PLAYERS CHAMPIONSHIP	1,458,015	25,000
11.	NORTHERN TELECOM OPEN	1,430,767	17,600
12.	BUICK CLASSIC	1,276,755	17,600
13.	LAS VEGAS INVITATIONAL	1,259,282	17,600
14.	WALT DISNEY WORLD/OLDSMOBILE GOLF CL	1,205,025	17,600
15.	CANON GREATER HARTFORD OPEN	1,174,787	17,600
16.	ANHEUSER-BUSCH GOLF CLASSIC	1,146,972	17,600
17.	THE INTERNATIONAL	1,146,809	17,600
18.	DEPOSIT GUARANTY GOLF CLASSIC	1,135,134	17,600
19.	JCPENNEY CLASSIC	1,121,117	17,600
20.	FREEPORT-MCMORAN CLASSIC	1,091,486	17,600
21.	BOB HOPE CHRYSLER CLASSIC	1,074,608	17,600
22.	MEMORIAL TOURNAMENT	1,054,373	17,600
23.	GREATER MILWAUKEE OPEN	1,049,072	17,600
24.	NEC WORLD SERIES OF GOLF	1,031,857	17,600
25.	LINCOLN MERCURY KAPALUA INTERNATIONAL	990,748	17,600
26.	TOUR CHAMPIONSHIP	988,906	17,600
27.	PHOENIX OPEN	963,548	17,600
28.	KMART GREATER GREENSBORO OPEN	952,642	17,600
29.	AT&T PEBBLE BEACH NATIONAL PRO-AM	943,665	17,600
30.	THE NEW ENGLAND CLASSIC	940,243	17,600
31.	INFINITI TOURNAMENT OF CHAMPIONS	921,288	17,600
32.	BUICK OPEN	891,908	17,600
33.	SPRINT WESTERN OPEN	840,709	17,600
34.	DORAL-RYDER OPEN	834,265	17,600
35.	SOUTHWESTERN BELL COLONIAL	693,879	17,600
36.	THE NESTLE INVITATIONAL	690,397	17,600
37.	KEMPER OPEN	660,087	17,600
38.	NISSAN LOS ANGELES OPEN	606,127	17,600
39.	BUICK SOUTHERN OPEN	587,705	17,600
40.	BUICK INVITATIONAL OF CALIFORNIA	544,992	17,600
41.	H-E-B TEXAS OPEN	510,620	17,600
42.	CANADIAN OPEN	469,580	17,600
		Total	$1,000,000

CUMULATIVE TEAM CHARITY COMPETITION

TEAM	1986	1987	1988	1989	1990	1991	1992	1993	TOTAL
Mercedes Championships	$1,562.50	$300,000.00	$7,500.00	$500,000.00	$12,000.00	$8,500.00	$120,000.00	$17,600.00	$967,162.50
MCI Heritage Classic	1,562.50	5,555.56	250,000.00	10,500.00	90,000.00	500,000.00	10,000.00	28,000.00	867,618.06
Walt Disney World/Oldsmobile Classic	500,000.00	130,000.00	11,500.00	90,000.00	9,250.00	70,000.00	10,000.00	17,600.00	838,350.00
Shell Houston Open	11,500.00	5,555.55	500,000.00	27,000.00	24,000.00	28,000.00	10,000.00	100,000.00	706,055.55
Las Vegas Invitational	26,000.00	500,000.00	21,000.00	17,000.00	21,000.00	50,000.00	10,000.00	17,600.00	662,600.00
Phoenix Open	14,000.00	5,555.55	27,000.00	8,500.00	500,000.00	24,000.00	10,000.00	17,600.00	606,655.55
JCPenney Classic	120,000.00	13,000.00	150,000.00	10,000.00	25,000.00	9,750.00	180,000.00	17,600.00	525,350.00
Honda Classic	16,000.00	38,000.00	5,500.00	12,500.00	250,000.00	150,000.00	10,000.00	40,000.00	522,000.00
The International	18,000.00	60,000.00	9,000.00	250,000.00	40,000.00	80,000.00	10,000.00	17,600.00	484,600.00
Hardee's Golf Classic	1,562.50	50,000.00	80,000.00	19,000.00	11,500.00	250,000.00	10,000.00	50,000.00	472,062.50
B.C. Open	20,000.00	70,000.00	60,000.00	125,000.00	14,000.00	27,000.00	75,000.00	26,000.00	417,000.00
United Airlines Hawaiian Open	1,562.50	200,000.00	9,500.00	50,000.00	10,500.00	9,000.00	100,000.00	35,000.00	415,563.50
THE PLAYERS Championship	300,000.00	5,555.56	24,000.00	7,000.00	28,000.00	15,000.00	10,000.00	25,000.00	414,555.56
Buick Open	1,562.50	100,000.00	125,000.00	7,500.00	125,000.00	11,000.00	10,000.00	17,600.00	397,662.50
Freeport-McMoRan Classic	32,000.00	5,555.55	23,000.00	40,000.00	150,000.00	19,000.00	30,000.00	17,600.00	317,155.55
Greater Milwaukee Open	1,562.50	20,500.00	20,000.00	80,000.00	30,000.00	125,000.00	10,000.00	17,600.00	304,662.50
Deposit Guaranty Golf Classic	60,000.00	5,555.55	10,000.00	150,000.00	8,500.00	13,000.00	40,000.00	17,600.00	304,655.55
Southwestern Bell Colonial	1,562.50	80,000.00	50,000.00	13,500.00	13,500.00	100,000.00	10,000.00	17,600.00	286,162.50
Buick Southern Open	200,000.00	5,555.56	7,000.00	20,000.00	11,000.00	12,000.00	10,000.00	17,600.00	283,155.56
Buick Invitational of California	40,000.00	90,000.00	10,500.00	9,000.00	10,000.00	30,000.00	60,000.00	17,600.00	267,100.00
New England Classic	80,000.00	33,000.00	15,500.00	60,000.00	20,000.00	26,000.00	10,000.00	17,600.00	262,100.00
Kmart Greater Greensboro Open	140,000.00	5,555.56	5,000.00	28,000.00	9,500.00	21,000.00	35,000.00	17,600.00	261,655.55
Sazale Classic	100,000.00	12,000.00	8,500.00	8,000.00	100,000.00	16,000.00	------------	------------	244,500.00
Nissan Los Angeles Open	35,000.00	5,555.55	90,000.00	30,000.00	16,000.00	40,000.00	10,000.00	17,600.00	244,155.55
BellSouth Classic	1,562.50	10,000.00	12,500.00	22,000.00	19,000.00	90,000.00	10,000.00	75,000.00	237,062.50
Bob Hope Chrysler Classic	1,562.50	5,555.55	11,000.00	100,000.00	17,000.00	60,000.00	10,000.00	17,600.00	222,718.05
Canon Greater Hartford Open	22,000.00	5,555.55	6,000.00	70,000.00	60,000.00	25,000.00	10,000.00	17,600.00	216,155.55
Buick Classic	50,000.00	18,000.00	18,000.00	13,000.00	70,000.00	11,500.00	10,000.00	17,600.00	208,100.00
Kemper Open	24,000.00	5,555.55	100,000.00	12,000.00	15,000.00	17,000.00	10,000.00	17,600.00	201,155.55
AT&T Pebble Beach National Pro-Am	1,562.50	5,555.56	70,000.00	15,000.00	22,000.00	22,000.00	10,000.00	17,600.00	163,718.06
Lincoln-Mercury Kapalua International	------------	5,555.56	25,000.00	11,000.00	80,000.00	12,500.00	10,000.00	17,600.00	161,655.56
Chattanooga Classic	12,500.00	43,000.00	28,000.00	24,000.00	12,500.00	9,500.00	25,000.00	------------	154,500.00
Texas Open	------------	------------	13,000.00	25,000.00	27,000.00	14,000.00	45,000.00	17,600.00	141,600.00
Northern Telecom Open	29,000.00	15,000.00	12,000.00	26,000.00	13,000.00	10,500.00	10,000.00	17,600.00	133,100.00
Federal Express St. Jude Classic	10,000.00	25,500.00	13,500.00	23,000.00	9,750.00	10,000.00	10,000.00	27,000.00	128,750.00
NEC World Series of Golf	1,562.50	5,555.56	17,000.00	6,000.00	50,000.00	20,000.00	10,000.00	17,600.00	127,718.06
Motorola Western Open	1,562.50	16,000.00	29,000.00	9,500.00	23,000.00	18,000.00	10,000.00	17,600.00	124,662.50
GTE Byron Nelson Golf Classic	1,562.50	5,555.56	30,000.00	21,000.00	9,000.00	9,250.00	10,000.00	30,000.00	116,368.06
Pensacola Open	70,000.00	23,000.00	14,000.00	6,500.00	------------	------------	------------	------------	113,500.00
Bell Canadian Open	------------	11,000.00	22,000.00	11,500.00	18,000.00	23,000.00	10,000.00	17,600.00	113,100.00
Gatlin Brothers Southwest Classic	45,000.00	28,000.00	26,000.00	------------	------------	------------	------------	------------	99,000.00
TOUR Championship	1,562.50	5,555.56	6,500.00	18,000.00	26,000.00	13,500.00	10,000.00	17,600.00	98,718.06
Nestle Invitational	------------	------------	------------	------------	------------	------------	------------	17,600.00	17,600.00
Memorial Tournament	------------	------------	------------	------------	------------	------------	------------	17,600.00	17,600.00
Doral-Ryder Open	------------	------------	------------	------------	------------	------------	------------	17,600.00	17,600.00
Anheuser-Busch Golf Classic	------------	------------	------------	------------	------------	------------	------------	17,600.00	17,600.00

TOURNAMENT PLAYERS CLUBS

An original concept of the PGA TOUR, Tournament Players Clubs have gone from a dream to a network that now encompasses 19 courses in 12 states and, with the addition of International TPC, two countries.

It was the TOUR's view that the spectator had been left out in golf course design throughout the years. When it came time for the PGA TOUR to build its own course, the opportunity presented itself to design a course that not only challenged the players but also allowed spectators to see the action as never before.

It's called "Stadium Golf"-- and once you've viewed a tournament on a Stadium Golf Course, you'll understand why the network has grown in such a short period of time.

Spectator mounds abound that afford fans unrestricted views whether on tee shots, fairway shots or on the greens. In fact, the 18th hole at the original TPC at Sawgrass can accommodate crowds of some 30,000 people--all with a clear view of the action. You won't see any periscopes at an event on a Players Club course.

The network began in 1980 with the club at Sawgrass, where it annually hosts THE PLAYERS Championship, and quickly grew into the present number of 19. All TPCs are designed to host PGA TOUR or Senior PGA TOUR events, and to date the clubs have been designed by some of the top architects in the business--Pete Dye, Arnold Palmer, Arthur Hills, Jay Morrish, Bob Cupp, the Von Hagge/Devlin team and Jack Nicklaus, to name just a few.

In addition, one of the things that adds a bit of spice to all TPCs is that a PGA TOUR player (or, in some cases, two) is assigned to serve as consultant to the designer. To date, Ed Sneed, Tom Weiskopf, Fuzzy Zoeller, Hubert Green, Craig Stadler, Ben Crenshaw, Al Geiberger and Chi Chi Rodriguez have been among those lending their expertise to the TPC Network.

In reality a nationwide country club, a membership at one TPC affords the member a chance to play at any of the other clubs across the country and an opportunity to view the greatest players in the world in action on his own course once a year.

Since the Tournament Players Club at Sawgrass opened, the TPC Network has now truly become "the best set of clubs in America."

U.S. TPC Network

Club	Architect	Consultant	Host
1. **TPC at Sawgrass** Ponte Vedra, FL	Pete Dye	--	THE PLAYERS Championship
2. **TPC at Eagle Trace** Coral Springs, FL	Arthur Hills	--	--
3. **TPC at River Highlands** Cromwell, CT	Pete Dye/ Robert Weed	Howard Twitty/ Roger Maltbie	Canon Greater Hartford Open
4. **TPC at Prestancia** Sarasota, FL	Ron Garl	Mike Souchak	Chrysler Cup
5. **TPC at Avenel** Potomac, MD	Ed Ault	Ed Sneed Associates	Kemper Open
6. **TPC of Scottsdale** Scottsdale, AZ	Jay Morrish/ Tom Weiskopf	Jim Colbert/ Howard Twitty	Phoenix Open
7. **TPC at Piper Glen** Charlotte, NC	Arnold Palmer	--	PaineWebber Invitational
8. **TPC at Southwind** Memphis, TN	Ron Prichard	Hubert Green/ Fuzzy Zoeller	Federal Express St. Jude Classic
9. **TPC of Michigan** Dearborn, MI	Jack Nicklaus	--	FORD Senior PLAYERS Championship
10. **TPC of Tampa Bay** Tampa, FL	Robert Weed	Chi Chi Rodriguez	GTE Suncoast Classic
11. **TPC at Summerlin** Las Vegas, NV	Robert Weed	Fuzzy Zoeller	Las Vegas Invitational

Tournament Players Courses (Licensed Facilities)

1. **TPC at The Woodlands** The Woodlands, TX	Von Hagge/ Devlin	--	Shell Houston Open
2. **TPC at Las Colinas** Irving, TX	Jay Morrish	Ben Crenshaw/ Byron Nelson	GTE Byron Nelson Classic
3. **TPC at PGA West** La Quinta, CA	Pete Dye	--	--

Future TPCs-(Announced, Planned and Under Construction)

TPC at Snoqualmie Ridge King County, WA	Robert Weed	Don January/ Peter Jacobsen	TBA
TPC at Ka'upulehu Kona, HI	Jack Nicklaus	--	TBA
TPC of San Diego (North) (South)	Robert Weed Rees Jones	Johnny Miller Mark O'Meara	TBA --

International TPC

ITPC of Batoh
Tochigi Prefecture, Japan
ITPC of Mito
Ibaraki Prefecture, Japan

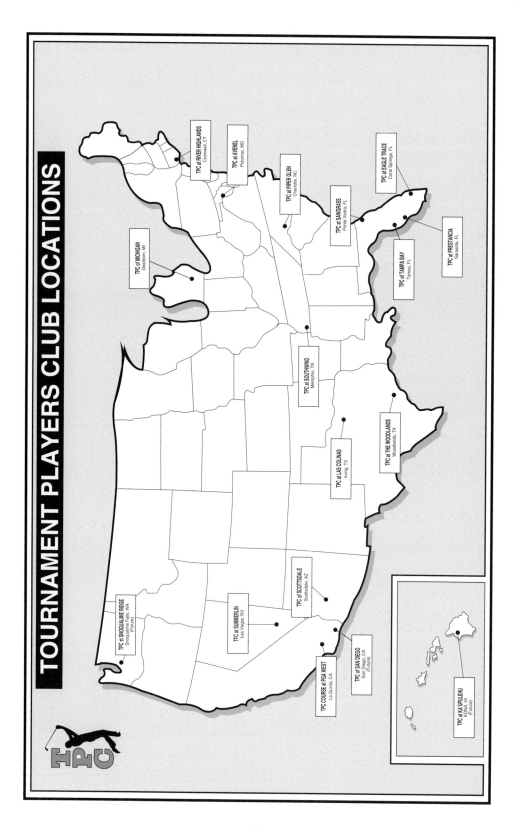

TOURNAMENT PLAYERS CLUB LOCATIONS

TPC of RIVER HIGHLANDS
Cromwell, CT

TPC at AVENEL
Potomac, MD

TPC at PIPER GLEN
Charlotte, NC

TPC at EAGLE TRACE
Coral Springs, FL

TPC at SAWGRASS
Ponte Vedra, FL

TPC at PRESTANCIA
Sarasota, FL

TPC of MICHIGAN
Dearborn, MI

TPC of TAMPA BAY
Tampa, FL

TPC at SOUTHWIND
Memphis, TN

TPC at THE WOODLANDS
Woodlands, TX

TPC at LAS COLINAS
Irving, TX

TPC of SCOTTSDALE
Scottsdale, AZ

TPC at SNOQUALMIE RIDGE
Snoqualmie Falls, WA
(Future)

TPC at SUMMERLIN
Las Vegas, NV

TPC COURSE at PGA WEST
La Quinta, CA

TPC of SAN DIEGO
San Diego, CA
(Future)

TPC at KA'UPULEHU
KONA, HI
(Future)

PGA TOUR PRODUCTIONS

PGA TOUR Productions is the television and video production company of the PGA TOUR.

Most fans know PGA TOUR Productions by its award-winning "Inside the PGA TOUR" and "Inside the Senior PGA TOUR" programs which are broadcast each week on ESPN. This year "Inside the PGA TOUR" is celebrating its 10th anniversary.

Productions is a diverse company delivering a wide range of services and talents to an international clientele. Their film capacity has expanded to include production of the TOUR's PSA campaign, as well as commercials and travel pieces. Additional programming includes made for TV events such as the Merrill Lynch Shoot-Out and United Van Lines Aces Championship, as well as tournament and pro-am highlight programs, corporate promotional and sales videos and home videos.

PGA TOUR Productions also serves its worldwide clientele by producing, in conjunction with the networks, international live telecasts of PGA TOUR events.

Along with the latest in television and communication technology, PGA TOUR Productions houses the world's most extensive library of golf footage. In the near future, PGA TOUR Productions will move its headquarters to the World Golf Village complex that will be located in St. Johns County, FL.

The PGA TOUR Productions van covers TOUR events across the country.

WORLD GOLF VILLAGE

Florida's First Coast, home of the PGA TOUR since 1979, soon will be home to the World Golf Village, expected to be operational by 1995.

Situated in St. Johns County near St. Augustine and south of Jacksonville, the World Golf Village will offer year-round golf and resort facilities, not to mention three Halls of Fame. The World Golf Village's International Golf Museum and Hall of Fame will feature Halls for the PGA TOUR, the Daytona Beach-based LPGA, and the PGA of America, headquartered in Palm Beach Gardens, FL. The latter's World Golf Hall of Fame and artifacts will move from Pinehurst, NC to the World Golf Village.

In addition, there will be many other exhibits about the game and participation by other major golf groups: the United States Golf Association, Royal & Ancient Golf Club of St. Andrews, Augusta National Golf Club, the National Golf Foundation, and the Golf Writers Association of America, among others.

Ruffin Beckwith, Acting Executive Director of the World Golf Village and Chairman of the Advisory Board overseeing the World Golf Village project, has said: "I don't know of any other sport that can claim a project of this magnitude that all organizations within the sport support.

"It's a credit to (PGA TOUR) Commissioner (Deane) Beman's vision and a project of tremendous impact for St. Johns County and Northeast Florida."

Along with the Halls of Fame, the complex, situated along busy I-95, also will feature the national headquarters for PGA TOUR Productions, a four-star resort hotel, 36 holes of golf, and a golf academy. The PGA TOUR Hall of Fame will be designed with two goals in mind: (1) to honor the people involved in helping make the TOUR what it has become and (2) to provide an enriching and entertaining collection of exhibits for visitors.

The 6,300-acre development also will include 7,200 residential units, along with over six million square feet of office, commercial and industrial facilities. The complex, situated as it will be in the heart of Northeast Florida, will be convenient to major Florida metropolitan areas and provide a unique tourism and business destination.

INTERNATIONAL GOLF MUSEUM AND HALL OF FAME

MEDIA REGULATIONS

THE GENERAL REGULATIONS

The following regulations are to be followed by *all* members of the Media:

1. *An ARMBAND is necessary* to walk inside the galley ropes. Stay within an arm's length of the ropes, so as to blend into the gallery and appear to be part of the gallery at all times.
2. Players are not to be distracted during play. DO NOT interview players or ask them to pose for photographs during their round.
3. DO NOT interview players or ask them to pose for photographs during their practice sessions prior to their round except by prior arrangement with the player.
4. If an interview is to be conducted in the practice areas, either the range or the putting green, it must be done by PRIOR ARRANGEMENT WITH THE PLAYER and up against the ropes and NOT in the middle of the areas where it could be distracting to other players.
5. DO NOT disturb players at their 18th green and/or scoring tent until after they have checked, signed and returned their scorecards.

WORKING PRESS REGULATIONS

To avoid embarrassment to you and distraction to the contestants:

1. Do not walk or stand in playing areas.
2. Follow directions of marshals and other officials.
3. Do not interview during play. The leading players each day—and others requested—will be interviewed following their rounds in the Media Room interview area.

TAPE RECORDER REGULATIONS

1. All tape recorder work should be done in the proximity of the Media Room and/or Clubhouse.
2. Tape recorders are *NOT* permitted in the locker room.
3. Tape recorders are *NOT* permitted within the playing area of the golf course unless written permission has been granted from the PGA TOUR and/or the tournament sponsor.

RAIN DELAY GUIDELINES

1. During rain delay situations, NO ONE other than players and essential staff will be permitted in the locker room. This means the Media is not permitted in the locker room in such situations. However, whenever possible, arrangements will be made to provide players for interviews during such situations.
2. Fully accredited members of the news media WILL BE WELCOMED into the locker room at all other times to carry out their assigned duties. (Note: Cameras and tape recorders are NOT permitted.)

This Tournament is essentially for the players and spectators. Fair play requires that there be no noise or distractions. The interests of all others must be subordinated to the player's interests. The result of any one shot could decide the Tournament.

Only ACCREDITED PHOTOGRAPHERS for RECOGNIZED NEWS MEDIA will be permitted to take pictures during the Tournament. Photo assistants may be issued a credential, but not photo arm bands for access inside the ropes. Photography will be restricted to news use. Commercial and personal photography is prohibited (except that spectators may take pictures on practice days and during a Pro-Am). Free lance photographers shooting on speculation will NOT BE ACCREDITED.

The following regulations apply to accredited news and television photographers and videotape cameramen as a condition of the privilege of taking pictures:

PHOTOGRAPHY REGULATIONS

GENERAL—ALL PHOTOGRAPHERS

- Photography will be restricted to NEWS use only. COMMERCIAL and PERSONAL photography is prohibited (except that spectators may take pictures on practice days and during a pro-am). Freelance photographers shooting on speculation WILL NOT BE ACCEDITED.
- A photographer must not ask a player to pose or in any way verbally distract a player during a round.
- If a player or an official requests that no photographs be taken in a certain situation, the request must be honored immediately, without discussion.
- A camera must not be pointed at a player about to make a stroke in any manner which might tend to disturb him or distract his attention.
- At the 9th and the 18th greens, photographers must not approach, delay or distract a player until he has checked, signed and returned his scorecard to the proper official. Under the Rules of Golf, a player turning in an incorrect scorecard in stroke play may be disqualified.
- Cameras are not permitted in the locker room.
- Use of golf carts or other means of transportation on the course during tournament play is prohibited.

STILL PHOTOGRAPHERS

- Only still photographers to whom armbands have been issued will be permitted inside gallery ropes. They must station themselves immediately inside such ropes, and not more than an ARM'S LENGTH FROM THE ROPES, so as to blend into the gallery and appear to be part of the gallery. They must not take conspicuous positions in the open. Any photographer who violates this regulation will forfeit the right to working inside the ropes and possibly to work at the tournament.
- Close-up action shots are prohibited.
- All pictures must be taken at appreciable distances, as far from the players as possible and from angles which are not acute to the line of play.
- When working at a green, photographers must not position themselves directly in a player's putting line.
- Pictures, even from a distance, may not be made until the player has completed his stroke. The photographer must not release his camera shutter until the shot is made.

TELEVISION/VIDEOTAPE CAMERAMEN

- Television and videotape filming may be done from inside the gallery ropes, or from areas approved by the PGA TOUR. All camera personnel who have been issued PHOTO armbands will be permitted inside the gallery lines but this does not include other members of the crew. Camera personnel must station themselves immediately inside the gallery lines, not more than an arm's length from those lines, so as to blend into the gallery. They must not take conspicuous positions in the open.
- The only EXCEPTIONS to the above regulation concern workers from the presenting network, or PGA TOUR Productions who have greater liberties in filming the event. Only these two groups will be allowed to move freely inside the ropes.
- Filming may be done from the locations described above during a player's stroke, provided modern equipment that produces a minimum of noise is used.
- Post-round interviews must be filmed far enough away from the arena of play to eliminate the possibility of distraction to those competing.

Difficulties will be avoided if photographers are fair and will treat players as they themselves would wish to be treated in similar circumstances.

The cooperation of all photographers will be appreciated.

PRIZE MONEY DISTRIBUTION CHARTS

POSITION	$700,000 PRIZE	$900,000 PRIZE	$1,000,000 PRIZE	$1,100,000 PRIZE	$1,200,000 PRIZE
1	$126,000	$162,000	$180,000	$198,000	$216,000
2	75,600	97,200	108,000	118,800	129,600
3	47,600	61,200	68,000	74,800	81,600
4	33,600	43,200	48,000	52,800	57,600
5	28,000	36,000	40,000	44,000	48,000
6	25,200	32,400	36,000	39,600	43,200
7	23,450	30,150	33,500	36,850	40,200
8	21,700	27,900	31,000	34,100	37,200
9	20,300	26,100	29,000	31,900	34,800
10	18,900	24,300	27,000	29,700	32,400
11	17,500	22,500	25,000	27,500	30,000
12	16,100	20,700	23,000	25,300	27,600
13	14,700	18,900	21,000	23,100	25,200
14	13,300	17,100	19,000	20,900	22,800
15	12,600	16,200	18,000	19,800	21,600
16	11,900	15,300	17,000	18,700	20,400
17	11,200	14,400	16,000	17,600	19,200
18	10,500	13,500	15,000	16,500	18,000
19	9,800	12,600	14,000	15,400	16,800
20	9,100	11,700	13,000	14,300	15,600
21	8,400	10,800	12,000	13,200	14,400
22	7,840	10,080	11,200	12,320	13,440
23	7,280	9,360	10,400	11,440	12,480
24	6,720	8,640	9,600	10,560	11,520
25	6,160	7,920	8,800	9,680	10,560
26	5,600	7,200	8,000	8,800	9,600
27	5,390	6,930	7,700	8,470	9,240
28	5,180	6,660	7,400	8,140	8,880
29	4,970	6,390	7,100	7,810	8,520
30	4,760	6,120	6,800	7,480	8,160
31	4,550	5,850	6,500	7,150	7,800
32	4,340	5,580	6,200	6,820	7,440
33	4,130	5,310	5,900	6,490	7,080
34	3,955	5,085	5,650	6,215	6,780
35	3,780	4,860	5,400	5,940	6,480
36	3,605	4,635	5,150	5,665	6,180
37	3,430	4,410	4,900	5,390	5,880
38	3,290	4,230	4,700	5,170	5,640
39	3,150	4,050	4,500	4,950	5,400
40	3,010	3,870	4,300	4,730	5,160
41	2,870	3,690	4,100	4,510	4,920
42	2,730	3,510	3,900	4,290	4,680
43	2,590	3,330	3,700	4,070	4,440
44	2,450	3,150	3,500	3,850	4,200
45	2,310	2,970	3,300	3,630	3,960
46	2,170	2,790	3,100	3,410	3,720
47	2,030	2,610	2,900	3,190	3,480
48	1,918	2,466	2,740	3,014	3,288
49	1,820	2,340	2,600	2,816	3,120
50	1,764	2,268	2,520	2,772	3,024
51	1,722	2,214	2,460	2,706	2,952
52	1,680	2,160	2,400	2,640	2,880
53	1,652	2,124	2,360	2,596	2,832
54	1,624	2,088	2,320	2,552	2,784
55	1,610	2,070	2,300	2,530	2,760
56	1,596	2,052	2,280	2,508	2,736
57	1,582	2,034	2,260	2,486	2,712
58	1,568	2,016	2,240	2,464	2,688
59	1,554	1,998	2,220	2,442	2,664
60	1,540	1,980	2,200	2,420	2,640
61	1,526	1,962	2,180	2,398	2,616
62	1,512	1,944	2,160	2,376	2,592
63	1,498	1,926	2,140	2,354	2,568
64	1,484	1,908	2,120	2,332	2,544
65	1,470	1,890	2,100	2,310	2,520
66	1,456	1,872	2,080	2,288	2,495
67	1,442	1,854	2,060	2,266	2,472
68	1,428	1,836	2,040	2,244	2,448
69	1,414	1,818	2,020	2,222	2,424
70	1,400	1,800	2,000	2,200	2,400

PRIZE MONEY DISTRIBUTION CHARTS

$1,250,000 POSITION	PRIZE	$1,300,000 POSITION	PRIZE	$1,400,000 POSITION	PRIZE	$1,500,000 POSITION	PRIZE	$2,500,000 POSITION	PRIZE
1	$225,000	1	$234,000	1	$252,000	1	$270,000	1	$450,000
2	35,000	2	140,400	2	151,200	2	162,000	2	270,000
3	85,000	3	88,400	3	95,200	3	102,000	3	170,000
4	60,000	4	62,400	4	67,200	4	72,000	4	120,000
5	50,000	5	52,000	5	56,000	5	60,000	5	100,000
6	45,000	6	46,800	6	50,400	6	54,000	6	90,000
7	41,875	7	43,550	7	46,900	7	50,250	7	83,750
8	38,750	8	40,300	8	43,400	8	46,500	8	77,500
9	36,250	9	37,700	9	40,600	9	43,500	9	72,500
10	33,750	10	35,100	10	37,800	10	40,500	10	67,500
11	31,250	11	32,500	11	35,000	11	37,500	11	62,500
12	28,750	12	29,900	12	32,200	12	34,500	12	57,500
13	26,250	13	27,300	13	29,400	13	31,500	13	52,500
14	23,750	14	24,700	14	26,600	14	28,500	14	47,500
15	22,500	15	23,400	15	25,200	15	27,000	15	45,000
16	21,250	16	22,100	16	23,800	16	25,500	16	42,500
17	20,000	17	20,800	17	22,400	17	24,000	17	40,000
18	18,750	18	19,500	18	21,000	18	22,500	18	37,500
19	17,500	19	18,200	19	19,600	19	21,000	19	35,000
20	16,250	20	16,900	20	18,200	20	19,500	20	32,500
21	15,000	21	15,600	21	16,800	21	18,000	21	30,000
22	14,000	22	14,560	22	15,680	22	16,800	22	28,000
23	13,000	23	13,520	23	14,560	23	15,600	23	26,000
24	12,000	24	12,480	24	13,440	24	14,400	24	24,000
25	11,000	25	11,440	25	12,320	25	13,200	25	22,000
26	10,000	26	10,400	26	11,200	26	12,000	26	20,000
27	9,625	27	10,010	27	10,785	27	11,550	27	19,250
28	9,250	28	9,620	28	10,360	28	11,100	28	18,500
29	8,875	29	9,230	29	9,940	29	10,650	29	17,750
30	8,500	30	8,840	30	9,520	30	10,200	30	17,000
31	8,125	31	8,450	31	9,100	31	9,750	31	16,250
32	7,750	32	8,060	32	8,680	32	9,300	32	15,500
33	7,375	33	7,670	33	8,260	33	8,850	33	14,750
34	7,065	34	7,345	34	7,910	34	8,475	34	14,125
35	6,750	35	7,020	35	7,560	35	8,100	35	13,500
36	6,435	36	6,695	36	7,210	36	7,725	36	12,875
37	6,125	37	6,370	37	6,860	37	7,350	37	12,250
38	5,875	38	6,110	38	6,580	38	7,050	38	11,750
39	5,625	39	5,850	39	6,300	39	6,750	39	11,250
40	5,375	40	5,590	40	6,020	40	6,450	40	10,750
41	5,125	41	5,330	41	5,740	41	6,150	41	10,250
42	4,875	42	5,070	42	5,460	42	5,850	42	9,750
43	4,625	43	4,810	43	5,180	43	5,550	43	9,250
44	4,375	44	4,550	44	4,900	44	5,250	44	8,750
45	4,125	45	4,290	45	4,620	45	4,950	45	8,250
46	3,875	46	4,030	46	4,340	46	4,650	46	7,750
47	3,625	47	3,770	47	4,060	47	4,350	47	7,250
48	3,425	48	3,562	48	3,836	48	4,110	48	6,850
49	3,250	49	3,380	49	3,640	49	3,900	49	6,500
50	3,150	50	3,276	50	3,528	50	3,780	50	6,300
51	3,075	51	3,198	51	3,444	51	3,690	51	6,150
52	3,000	52	3,120	52	3,360	52	3,600	52	6,000
53	2,950	53	3,068	53	3,304	53	3,540	53	5,900
54	2,900	54	3,016	54	3,248	54	3,480	54	5,800
55	2,875	55	2,990	55	3,220	55	3,450	55	5,750
56	2,850	56	2,964	56	3,192	56	3,420	56	5,700
57	2,825	57	2,938	57	3,164	57	3,390	57	5,650
58	2,800	58	2,912	58	3,136	58	3,360	58	5,600
59	2,775	59	2,886	59	3,108	59	3,330	59	5,550
60	2,750	60	2,860	60	3,080	60	3,300	60	5,500
61	2,725	61	2,834	61	3,052	61	3,270	61	5,450
62	2,700	62	2,808	62	3,024	62	3,240	62	5,400
63	2,675	63	2,782	63	2,996	63	3,210	63	5,350
64	2,650	64	2,756	64	2,968	64	3,180	64	5,300
65	2,625	65	2,730	65	2,940	65	3,150	65	5,250
66	2,600	66	2,704	66	2,912	66	3,120	66	5,200
67	2,575	67	2,678	67	2,884	67	3,090	67	5,150
68	2,550	68	2,652	68	2,856	68	3,060	68	5,100
69	2,525	69	2,626	69	2,828	69	3,030	69	5,050
70	2,500	70	2,600	70	2,800	70	3,000	70	5,000

COMPLETE SCHEDULES

1994	PGA TOUR	SENIOR PGA TOUR
Jan. 6-9	Mercedes Championships	Mercedes Championships
13-16	United Airlines Hawaiian Open	Open
20-23	Northern Telecom Open	Open
27-30	Phoenix Open	Senior Skins Game#
Feb. 3-6	AT&T Pebble Beach National Pro-Am	Royal Caribbean Classic
7-8		Senior Slam of Golf#
10-13	Nissan Los Angeles Open	GTE Suncoast Classic
17-20	Bob Hope Chrysler Classic	The IntelliNet Challenge
24-27	Buick Invitational of California	Chrysler Cup#
March 3-6	Doral Ryder Open	GTE West Classic
10-13	Honda Classic	Vantage at the Dominion
17-20	Nestle Invitational	TBA
24-27	THE PLAYERS Championship	Doug Sanders Celebrity Classic/ (AmEx
Apr. 31-3	Freeport-McMoRan Classic	Grandslam)*
7-10	The Masters*	The Tradition
14-17	MCI Heritage Classic	Open
21-24	Kmart Greater Greensboro Open	PGA Seniors Championship
28-**May** 1	Shell Houston Open	Muratec Reunion Pro-Am
5-8	BellSouth Classic	Las Vegas Senior Classic
12-15	GTE Byron Nelson Classic	Liberty Mutual Legends of Golf#
19-22	Memorial Tournament	PaineWebber Invitational
26-29	Southwestern Bell Colonial	Cadillac NFL Golf Classic
June 2-5	Kemper Open	Bell Atlantic Classic
9-12	Buick Classic	Bruno's Memorial Classic
16-19	U.S. Open*	Nationwide Championship
23-26	Canon Greater Hartford Open	(Name TBA)
30-**July** 3	Motorola Western Open	FORD SENIOR PLAYERS Championship
7-10	Anheuser-Busch Golf Classic	U.S. Senior Open
14-17	Deposit Guaranty Classic / British Open*	Kroger Senior Classic
21-24	New England Classic	Ameritech Senior Open
28-31	Federal Express St. Jude Classic	Southwestern Bell Classic
Aug. 4-7	Buick Open	Northville Long Island Classic
11-14	PGA Championship*	Bank of Boston Senior Golf Classic
18-21	The International	First of America Classic
25-28	NEC World Series of Golf	Burnet Senior Classic
Sept. 1-4	Greater Milwaukee Open	Franklin Quest Championship
8-11	Bell Canadian Open	GTE Northwest Classic
15-18	Hardee's Golf Classic	Quicksilver Classic
22-25	B.C. Open	Bank One Classic
29-**Oct.** 2	Buick Southern Open	GTE North Classic
6-9	Walt Disney World Oldsmobile Classic	Vantage Championship
13-16	Texas Open	The Transamerica
19-23	Las Vegas Invitational	Raley's Senior Gold Rush
27-30	THE TOUR Championship	Ralphs Senior Classic
Nov. 3-6	Lincoln-Mercury Kapalua International #	Kaanapali Classic
10-13	World Cup of Golf#	Open
17-20	Franklin Funds Shark Shoot-Out#	Senior TOUR Championship
26-27	The Skins Game#	Du Pont Cup Japan vs. U.S. Matches#
Dec. 1-4	JCPenney Classic#	Open
9-12	Diners Club Matches#	Diners Club Matches#

* non-PGA TOUR co-sponsored events
# Unofficial victory and money

NOTES

NOTES